KINGDOM
in the
WEST
The Mormons and the American Frontier

Will Bagley, series editor

VOLUME 9

Annie Clark before her marriage
to Joseph Marion Tanner. Her memoir,
A Mormon Mother, is a classic account
of life under the Principle.
Obert C. Tanner Collection, Marriott Library.

Doing the Works of Abraham

Mormon Polygamy
Its origin, practice, and demise

Edited by
B. Carmon Hardy

THE ARTHUR H. CLARK COMPANY
Norman, Oklahoma
2007

Library of Congress Catalog Card Number 2006027640
ISBN 978-0-87062-344-8 (trade edition)
ISBN 978-0-87062-352-3 (collector's edition)
ISBN 978-0-87062-274-8 (entire series)

Library of Congress Cataloging-in-Publication Data

The works of Abraham : Mormon polygamy : its origin, practice, and demise /
edited by B. Carmon Hardy.
     p. cm. — (Kingdom in the west : the Mormons and the American fron-
tier ; v. 9)
  Includes bibliographical references and index.
  ISBN 0-87062-344-3 (trade hardcover : alk. paper) — ISBN 0-87062-352-4 (limited ed. hardcover : alk. paper)
  1. Polygamy—Religious aspects—Mormon Church. 2. Book of Abraham. 3.
Church of Jesus Christ of Latter-day Saints—Doctrines. 4. Mormon
Church—Doctrines. I. Hardy, B. Carmon. II. Title. III. Series.

BX8641.W77 2006
261.8'3584230882893—DC22

                                            2006027640

The paper in this book meets the guidelines for permanence and
durability of the Committee on Production Guidelines for Book
Longevity of the Council on Library Resources. ∞

For Kamillia M. Hardy, my wife, and our children—Melody, Cristine, David, Amelia, and Robin. Their interest in the subject arises from roots that, like my own, run deeply into the Mormon past. I am enormously grateful for the support, love, and patience they displayed while enduring the seemingly endless labor required by "Dad's book."

GO YE, THEREFORE, and do the works of Abraham; enter ye into my law and ye shall be saved.

But if ye enter not into my law ye cannot receive the promise of my Father, which he made unto Abraham.

God commanded Abraham, and Sarah gave Hagar to Abraham to wife. And why did she do it? Because this was the law; and from Hagar sprang many people.

D&C 132:32–34.

THEN IF WE ARE HIS CHILDREN will we not do the works of faithful Abraham? . . . Are we Abraham's seed, or are we bastards and not sons. That is the question.

"Lecture. By Elder Orson Hyde," 6 Oct. 1854,"
Des. News [Weekly], 19 Oct. 1854, 4:32 [1/2].

SALT LAKE IS ON THE HIGH ROAD between San Francisco and Chicago, neither of which cities is celebrated for the purity of its morals. Whether this facility of intercourse will result in the Mormons . . . taking only one wife at a time, or in the San Franciscans and Chicagans becoming saints and polygamists, who shall say?

Thérèse Yelverton, *Teresina in America* (1875), 2:48–49.

CONTENTS

ILLUSTRATIONS

FOREWORD

No issue in the history of the Church of Jesus Christ of Latter-day Saints, today abbreviated as the LDS church and whose followers are popularly known as Mormons, has attracted more attention than celestial marriage, the "doctrine of the plurality of wives," better known as polygamy. From its contentious and secretive beginnings in the 1830s to its public proclamation in 1852, through almost four decades of bitter conflict to the renunciation of the practice in 1890, this belief helped define a new religious identity and unify the Mormon people, just as it scandalized their neighbors and handed their enemies the most effective weapon they wielded in their battle against Mormon theocracy.

It was not mere happenstance that the practice became infamous as the second "relic of barbarism," the phrase the Republicans used to characterize the Mormon marriage system in their first party platform. The belief of the nineteenth-century Saints, as they liked to be known then and still prefer to be called, that God's law trumped the laws of a mere republic fueled their resolute determination to protect what they saw as a constitutional right. This long struggle still resonates in American religious law, and throughout the West thousands of families continue to practice the Principle of plurality of wives, once known as celestial marriage.

No one can come of age in Mormon Country without appreciating the double-edged legacy of polygamy. Latter-day Saints are both proud and embarrassed that their pioneer ancestors conducted the longest campaign of civil disobedience in American history. Like nothing else, the doctrine gave our much-married progenitors a compelling, distinctive theology, and it established our reputation as a "peculiar people," a badge Mormons still wear with pride. But its odd and unconventional nature discomforts the faithful who do not like to be reminded that the doctrine remains a central element of Mormonism's revolutionary theology and devoutly wish the world would forget about this abandoned practice.

Like many native Utahns, my own polygamous roots run deep. Two of my great-great-grandfathers served prison sentences for illegal cohabitation in the Utah Territorial Penitentiary, and George Brown Bailey was a repeat offender. According to family lore, federal judge Charles S. Zane severely chastised Bailey when he reappeared before his bench and sentenced him to a second six-month term. When Grandpa showed up for a third time, Zane asked the defendant why he looked familiar. Bailey explained this was his third trial for cohabiting illegally, and Zane knew a hopeless case when he saw one: he allegedly dismissed the charges with a curt "Get the hell out of my courtroom."

Although I grew up in East Mill Creek, the Salt Lake City neighborhood that gave birth to the modern fundamentalist polygamous movement, the doctrine and practice seemed like a distant historical artifact, and I had no idea that the identical bungalows that electrical genius Nathaniel Baldwin had built along Evergreen Avenue housed his multiple wives. I certainly felt no living family connection to polygamy—until I asked two of my great-aunts about it at my grandfather's ninetieth birthday in 1982. I was astonished at their impassioned response, especially Aunt Bea's. She spoke at length about the pain and suffering Grandfather Bailey had inflicted on our grandmother. "Polygamy," she said in anger and disgust, "was just a way for old men to marry young girls."

Such passions run deep in the Great Basin, and the long-abandoned practice hangs around the neck of the modern LDS church like the ancient mariner's albatross—and no matter how mightily the church's public relations representatives try, there is no prying that particular bird loose. Besides the enduring public identification of Mormonism with polygamy, the revelation that codified the doctrine is still found in the official canon of LDS scriptures, and the LDS church still quietly seals devout widowers to additional wives. Since World War I, the religion may have done its best to stop the practice, but it refuses to forsake the doctrine or abandon the revelation with its baffling references to "many wives and concubines" and instructions on how to avoid adultery and be justified while espousing ten virgins.

The media has not lost its appetite for the topic, and there appears to be an inexhaustible supply of news stories about polygamy. Reports of abused and enslaved multiple wives, "Lost Boys" cast out from mysterious compounds, concrete polygamous temples rising out of West Texas dust, and under-aged girls marrying doddering patriarchs in the Great Western Outback make the problem hopeless for those trying to rescue Mormonism's image from its ancient stereotype. The central place of the doctrine in a host of popular novels, movies, and HBO soap operas makes their job no easier—and such publicity makes the anonymity that many law-abiding "Joseph Smith Mormons" seek by their quiet practice of the doctrine much more difficult to achieve. Understanding why thousands, and perhaps tens of thousands, of modern Americans remain as passionately attached to "the principle and doctrine of their having many wives" as were their pioneer ancestors is a daunting task—and there is simply no way to acquire such an understanding of the modern phenomenon without comprehending the origins, practice, and history of the "new and an everlasting covenant" the Lord revealed to Joseph Smith in July 1843.

Polygamy's story is filled with examples of the strangely powerful bond that both men and women formed with the Principle and the spiritual manifestations that created such passionate attachments. "The spirit told me," Bishop Samuel Woolley recalled, "that that revelation was of God and that no man could or would receive a fulness of Celestial Glory except he obeyed that law and had more than one living wife at the same time"—and a descendant reported that this particular spirit was an angel dressed in a suit of black broadcloth.

Especially moving is the stout defense that Emmeline Wells, Martha Hughes Cannon, and Annie Clark Tanner made of the doctrine, even as they suffered mightily from its practice. Men who entered plurality seldom found any of the sensual delights of Mohammedan heaven, and almost one thousand Latter-day Saint men served time in the penitentiary as "prisoners for conscience sake." None of this would make sense unless one knows that the Mormon people kept this new and everlasting covenant because they believed that if they did not, they would not attain the highest realms of eternal glory.

Many nineteenth-century comments on Mormonism still ring true: Samuel Bowles's observation that "Mormon religion is an excellent institution for maintaining masculine authority in the family" remains as correct today as it was when he wrote it in 1866, and Kate Field would still find that "Babies unseen [are] present to the ear" at LDS services. At the same time, the "poor, ungainly and pathetically 'homely' creatures" Mark Twain claimed he saw in Salt Lake are far outnumbered by their many attractive descendants who grace today's metropolis. These echoes rebound off the ironic attempts of the modern LDS church to distance itself from the doctrine of plurality by vilifying those who continue the practice, using the same tactics their religion's enemies exploited in the 1880s. Such Houdini-like efforts to escape the practice's historical and doctrinal significance and divert the eyes of modern believers from the subject will inevitably fail.

I may be the only working historian of Mormonism who agrees with Robert N. Baskin. According to George Alfred "Dirty Jim" Townsend (one of nineteenth-century Mormonism's journalistic hired guns), Baskin said before Judge James McKean "that if Joseph Smith had been a eunuch he would never have received the revelation on polygamy." In contrast to such hardboiled realism, apologetic Mormon historians try to paper-over or even justify Joseph Smith's sexual conquests, while others attempt to soften polygamy's image, often misrepresenting how the system actually worked and its signal importance in LDS theology. For example, some historians argue that holding church offices in the 1880s did not require participation in the Principle, ignoring the letters in which leaders such as John Taylor made that policy unambiguous.

No scholar has contributed more to our understanding of Mormon polygamy than B. Carmon Hardy. His seminal work, *Solemn Covenant: The Mormon Polygamous Passage*, is widely acknowledged as one of the essential studies of the subject, and he brings a depth of understanding to this problematic religious tradition that few can match. *Doing the Works of Abraham* represents decades of delving into polygamy's documentary wellsprings and reflects his deep understanding of the subject, his balanced and sensitive perspective, and the devotion to precision and accuracy that has always characterized Professor Hardy's scholarship. Using essential and representative sources, he tells this amazing story with a refreshing honesty, letting the people and facts speak for themselves. He has taken to heart the principle that young Mormons learn in a popular hymn: "Do what is right; let the consequence follow."

Carmon Hardy has ranged far and wide to assemble the most revealing sources on the Mormon practice of plural marriage, searching libraries and archives, historic newspapers and magazines, oral histories, the collections of the Daughters of Utah Pioneers, legal records, and the letters, diaries, and printed and unpublished discourses of early Mormon leaders. His meticulous scholarship, his mastery of the subject, and his appreciation of the human anguish behind so much of this story are everywhere apparent in this work.

Doing the Works of Abraham encompasses sources that speak to the origins, theology, practice, problems, and the joys and evils of polygamy in the American West. It provides a sourcebook, a comprehensive survey of the existing literature, and the considered wisdom of a distinguished scholar who has devoted much of his career to the study of this singular institution. Like any good history, the book resurrects haunting voices from the dust of the past. Striking firsthand accounts provide a personal view of the Principle from those who practiced it and forfeited so much for it, and the counter perspective of those who reviled the practice and ultimately defeated it. We see the passionate conviction that animated both plurality's defenders and its enemies and hear remarkable voices: it is impossible not to share Isaac Nash's sense of pride and pain when he told a judge weighing his sentence that he and people like him had built this country—"helped to build bridges, kill snakes and fight the Indians."

A compassionate reader will acquire a deeper appreciation of the sacrifices the devout made to practice their religion and a keener insight into the indignation of those who considered the doctrine a social evil equal to slavery. It may help the thousands of Americans who owe their very existence to their ancestor's practice of the Principle develop a more sympathetic perspective on the sacrifices their ancestors made for their faith. Such an understanding may prove useful should the Supreme Court reconsider whether polygamy is an offence against society simply because it is "exclusively a feature of the life of Asiatic and of African people," or if it is instead a sacred practice of many ancient and modern religions, including Islam, one of the world's three great faiths.

WILL BAGLEY
May 2006

EDITORIAL PROCEDURES

Despite a broad and continuing stream of publications devoted to Mormon polygamy, few attempts have been made to assemble an extensive collection of sources on the subject.[1] At the same time, there is an imposing abundance of writings by and about polygamists during the years of its formal acceptance by Mormonism. The number of texts is so great that, as this author-editor soon realized, every chapter and theme in the book could easily be enlarged into a separate volume of its own. So much published research on Mormon plurality continues to appear that it challenges an interested scholar to provide even a generalized sense of its direction.

I am keenly aware that other historians would have selected different themes and documents than appear in this volume and would sometimes have given different emphases to those that I have chosen. My primary objective throughout has been to present as full and balanced a portrait of nineteenth-century polygamous Mormonism as possible, so the reader will encounter frequent passages of exploration and suggestion of my own. I also found it regretfully necessary to abbreviate many texts, such as the 1843 revelation, due to limitations on the size of this volume.

The work is broadly organized chronologically, first focusing on Joseph Smith and the introduction of polygamy. It concludes with examinations of the 1890 Manifesto and its consequences. Within its chronological framework, the book is broken into sections devoted to related themes. To present these topics as clearly as possible I use sources both well known and obscure, published and unpublished. Always, the criterion has been to choose mate-

---

[1] Best known is the four-volume gathering, [Fulton and Allred], *Most Holy Principle*. This and compilations such as Alter's documentary chapters on the subject in *Utah*, 1:395–439, contain material chiefly selected to support polygamy and/or defend the church. Such compilations, while helpful, fall short of the scope of inquiry and balance expected in historical scholarship.

rials that present as accurate an image of the time, people, and place as possible. Since the book is primarily concerned with nineteenth-century Mormonism, and because the subsequent, century-long drama of polygamous fundamentalism has acquired a distinct history of its own, this fascinating denouement is confined to a few pages at the end of the work.

While I am generally partial to primary materials and early editions, whenever I found that a manuscript source has been reliably transcribed and printed, I employ the more accessible, published edition rather than the original work. Scott G. Kenney's superb typescript of Wilford Woodruff's journals is an instance. Karl and Katharine Larson's presentation of the diaries of Charles Lowell Walker is also illustrative. And passages from B. H. Roberts's published edition of the manuscript histories of the church are yet another. Mormon sermons appearing in the *Deseret News* are generally cited from the *News*, although the *Journal of Discourses* and other printings of them are used as well. I have also sought to reference multiple secondary investigations of the many issues addressed. While this results in extensive notation, it fulfills the historian's obligation to provide a consensual basis for his statements as well as pointing interested readers to related studies. Biographical data, such as dates and other relevant information, are given when appropriate. Always, the object has been to assemble a useful resource for readers casual and scholarly alike.

When dealing with the Latter-day Saints, this work uses the term "polygamy." Though technically incorrect, with few exceptions, "polygamy" was the overwhelming choice of Saints and Gentiles alike. ("Gentiles," the mildly pejorative name Mormons applied to non-believers, including Jews, is another precarious but serviceable word used in this book.) "Polygyny" is used to describe non-Mormon peoples practicing a plurality of wives, as when citing the work of anthropologists and, of course, when appearing in quotations from the materials of scholars and others. "Plurality," "plural marriage," and "patriarchal marriage" are also usages appropriated from nineteenth-century Mormon idiom. Another term, "the Principle," refers to the same practice but is capitalized to distinguish it from the more ordinary use of the word.

I have occasionally added punctuation to make the documents more readable, but spelling, grammar, and capitalization are left unchanged in documents unless meaning is affected. In those instances brackets [ ] set off phrases used to clarify the author's intent. For the same reason [*sic*] is sparingly employed. Words inserted both above and below the line are contained in angle brackets: < >. Strikethroughs are shown as they appear in the original texts. Underlined words appear in italic, but double and triple underlines are shown as in the original. References in my footnotes are by author, abbreviated title, and page. The *Millennial Star, Woman's Exponent, Contributor, Ensign*, and other official church-related publications, however, are provided with full citations. This applies to Reorganized Church of Jesus Christ of Latter Day Saints (RLDS), fundamentalist, and other factional printings, including the *Anti-Polygamy Standard*. Court cases do not appear in the bibliography but are fully cited in footnotes. Consistent with the documentary nature of the volume, quotations consisting of fewer than six or seven lines are sometimes set in block form.

Newspaper articles are not in the bibliography but are fully cited in the footnotes. Wherever possible such references include not only date, volume, and number, but provide page and column divided by a solidus. When papers did not use page numbers, as with the *Deseret News* during certain years, I place my own page count and column number inside brackets at the end of the citation. For example: *Des. Eve. News*, 17 Feb. 1882, 15:76 [2/3]. To avoid confusion with later daily printings of the *Deseret News*, the earlier weekly edition of the paper is cited as *Des. News* [Weekly].

Documents collected in a work of this kind are often inherently rhetorical, describing the world in ways more personally construed than actual. While I try to balance this tendency with selections that provide contrasting perspectives, as well as relevant comment in both text and footnotes, it is always important to keep the intentionality of diaries, sermons, and journalistic essays in mind. Finally, I am fully aware there was more to nineteenth-century Mormonism than polygamy—significant as it was—but the purpose of this volume is to illuminate *that* subject, one which made this dynamic young religion so controversial and compelling, both then and now.

ABBREVIATIONS

AZU   University of Arizona Library, Tucson, Arizona.

CCL-A   Community of Christ Library-Archives, Independence, Missouri.

CSmH   Henry E. Huntington Library, San Marino, California.

CU-B   Hubert Howe Bancroft Library, University of California, Berkeley, California.

Clark, ed., *Messages*   Clark, James R., ed. *Messages of the First Presidency of The Church of Jesus Christ of Latter-Day Saints 1833–1964.* 6 vols. S.L.C: Bookcraft, Inc., 1965–1975.

Comp.   *Compilation of the Messages and Papers of the Presidents.* 20 vols. James D. Richardson, comp. N.Y: Bureau of National Literature, Inc., 1897–1911.

D&C   *Doctrine and Covenants of the Church of Jesus Christ of Latter-Day Saints.* S.L.C: Church of Jesus Christ of Latter-day Saints, 1982 edn. unless otherwise indicated.

Des. News [Weekly]   *Deseret News,* published weekly, 1850–1898.

Des. Semi-Weekly News   *Deseret Semi-Weekly News,* 1865–1920.

Des. Eve. News   *Deseret Evening News,* 1867–1920.

Des. News   *Deseret News,* 1920–1952.

Dialogue   *Dialogue: A Journal of Mormon Thought.*

FMC   Papers of the Austin and Alta Fife Mormon Collection, MSS 211, Archives and Special Collections, Milton R. Merrill Library, Utah State University, Logan, Utah.

JH   Journal History. A daily scrapbook of Mormon history consisting of journals, letters, and newspaper articles by Andrew Jenson. LDS Archives.

JMH   *Journal of Mormon History.*

Journal of Discourses   *Journal of Discourses by Brigham Young, President of the Church of Jesus Christ of Latter-day Saints, His Two Counsellors, the Twelve Apostles, and others . . . ,* 26 vols. Liverpool: Franklin D. Richards et al., 1855–1886.

LAHA Leonard J. Arrington Historical Archives, MSS 1, Archives and Special Collections, Milton R. Merrill Library, Utah State University, Logan, Utah.

Lib. of Cong. Library of Congress.

LDS Church of Jesus Christ of Latter-day Saints.

LDS Archives Archives and Library, Church of Jesus Christ of Latter-day Saints, S.L.C., Utah.

Mil. Star *Latter-day Saints' Millennial Star*, 1840–1970.

OHP LDS Polygamy Oral History Project, Charles Redd Center for Western Studies, Brigham Young University, Provo, Utah.

Proceedings U.S. Congress, Senate, *Proceedings before the Committee on Privileges and Elections of the United States Senate in the Matter of the Protests against the Right of Hon. Reed Smoot, a Senator from the State of Utah, to Hold His Seat.* 4 vols. Senate Doc. 486 (59-1) 1906, Serial 2932–35.

RG48, N.A. Record Group 48, Interior Department Territorial Papers, Utah 1850–1902, M428, film, roll 4, National Archives.

RLDS Reorganized Church of Jesus Christ of Latter Day Saints (Community of Christ).

Roberts, *Comprehensive History* Brigham H. Roberts, *Comprehensive History of the Church of Jesus Christ of Latter-day Saints, Century 1.* 6 vols. S.L.C: Deseret News Press, 1930.

Roberts, ed., *History of the Church* Brigham H. Roberts, ed. *History of the Church of Jesus Christ of Latter-day Saints. Period 2. Apostolic Interregnum. From the Manuscript History of Brigham Young and Other Original Documents,* vol. 7. S.L.C: Deseret News, 1932.

RSI Report of the Secretary of the Interior. *Multi-volume compilation of messages and documents communicated to the two houses of Congress by the Secretary of the Interior annually, containing reports by territorial governors and, from 1882 through 1896, reports of the "Utah Commission."*

Smith Jr., *History of the Church* Smith, Joseph, Jr. *History of the Church of Jesus Christ of Latter-day Saints. Period 1. History of Joseph Smith, the Prophet, by Himself.* Edited by Brigham H. Roberts. 6 vols. S.L.C: Deseret Book, 1973. 2nd edn. rev.

Sunstone *Sunstone: Mormon Experience, Scholarship, Issues, and Art* [Periodical], S.L.C., Utah.

Uhi Utah State Historical Society, S.L.C., Utah.

UHQ *Utah Historical Quarterly.*

ULA Milton R. Merrill Library, Utah State University, Logan, Utah.

UPB Harold B. Lee Library, Brigham Young University, Provo, Utah.

UU J. Willard Marriott Library, University of Utah, S.L.C., Utah.

Acknowledgments

All scholars know that their intellectual debts extend far beyond sight. Mine are so great that I hesitate to identify those remembered because of the many that are not. Much of what went into this volume was acquired from individuals who assisted me with other projects, in conversation, and in ways often quite beyond their knowing. I am grateful in this regard to Leonard J. Arrington, Kent Fielding, Richard Holzapfel, Klaus Hansen, Victor W. Jorgensen, Leo Lyman, Ronald Walker, and David J. Whittaker. Lavina Fielding Anderson, Kathryn Daynes, Kenneth Driggs, Dan Erickson, H. Michael Marquardt, William P. MacKinnon, Michael Quinn, Greg Thompson, and George D. Smith, laborers in the same or neighboring vineyards, all started me down new and fruitful rows more than once.

The Library-Archives of the Historical Department, Church of Jesus Christ of Latter-day Saints (cited as LDS Archives), is the depository where most of the sources used in this book are located. Of those associated with that facility, no one was more helpful than Ronald G. Watt, Senior Archivist. The breadth of his knowledge concerning the archives' resources is exceeded only by the solicitous manner with which he made them available to me. I will always be indebted to him. W. Randall Dixon, Bill Slaughter, James Kimball, Linda Haslam, and other staff members were also of service and politely helped me over decades of work.

Ron Romig and Barbara Bernauer at the Library and Archives of the Community of Christ in Independence, Missouri, were generous with holdings at their facility. Stan Larson, Curator of Manuscripts at Special Collections in the Marriott Library of the University of Utah, helped me with several essential manuscripts, as have the staffs of Special Collections of the Merrill Library at Utah State University; the Utah State Historical Society; Arizona State Historical Society; L. Tom Perry Special Collections Division of the Lee

Library at Brigham Young University; the Bancroft Library at the University of California, Berkeley; and Peter J. Blodgett at the Henry E. Huntington Library in San Marino, California. Tom Alexander and Jessie Embry of the Charles Redd Center for Western Studies at Brigham Young University kindly permitted me to use materials from their large collection of interviews with polygamous family members. Professor Arthur Hansen and Mrs. Cathy Frazee at the Center for Oral and Public History at California State University, Fullerton, provided assistance with transcripts and documents in their possession. And, owing to the indefatigable efforts of the interlibrary-loan division of the Pollak Library, California State University, Fullerton, I was able to obtain many items immensely important for completion of the book.

I am grateful to my former graduate assistant Sharon Kay Evanshine, now a college instructor in her own right, for providing helpful editorial suggestions that improved the book. Her husband, Bob, generously resolved several computer problems encountered while preparing the manuscript. Colleagues and friends Charles Frazee, William Haddad, Jackson Putnam, Seymour Scheinberg, Wendy Scheinberg, Gary Shumway, Marianne T. Watson, Anne Wilde, Ogden Kraut, and Ardis Parshall provided thoughtful conversation and various materials over many years. And my wife, Kamillia M. Hardy, has repeatedly enriched me with insight into the Mormon polygamous experience through countless discussions. Both this book and I are greatly in her debt.

Lowell "Ben" C. Bennion, Todd Compton, and Michael Homer deserve special mention. They read the manuscript of this work from beginning to end and made helpful suggestions for its improvement. Their familiarity with and interest in the subject specially qualified them to critique the volume and I will always be grateful to them for their comments.

Lastly, I must thank Will Bagley, general editor of the KINGDOM IN THE WEST series, for his extraordinary patience with the long process required to assemble this work. His impressive breadth of knowledge about Mormon and Western American history has been invaluable. Ariane Smith, with her keen eye for detail and knowledge of editorial procedure, made essential contributions to the book's finished form and appearance. And Bob Clark, publisher of the series, also gave the manuscript a thorough review, with numerous suggestions for its improvement. Their help and recommendations have immensely affected the final version of this volume.

INTRODUCTION

Most who investigate Mormon polygamy soon discover that, with all that made it astonishing, it was but a late chapter in an already thick and ancient volume. Not only is polygyny still the most widely approved form of marriage throughout the world, as nineteenth-century Mormon defenders were fond of saying, but spirited controversy surrounded the practice in both Europe and America long before Joseph Smith introduced the doctrine.[1] The polygynous examples of biblical patriarchs and its practice among peoples located outside Europe invited intense debate from canonical scholars before monogamy was galvanized on Catholic Christianity at the Council of Trent.[2]

Advocacy for the idea was heard repeatedly during and after the time of the Reformation. The Münster Anabaptists, permission given by Luther and Melanchthon to Philip of Hesse, Milton's approval of the idea, and the 1650 Nürnberg ordinance allowing men to marry multiple wives to restore population lost during the Thirty Years' War are but a few instances of support for the arrangement, Protestant and Catholic alike.[3]

---

[1] On polygyny's widespread acceptance as a "preferred" marital arrangement, see Murdock, "World Ethnographic Sample," 686, table 2; and *idem*, Social Structure, 27–28. A survey focusing on socio-biological explanations concluded that not only is the human species "mildly polygynous" but that a "majority" of human societies permit the practice. Daly and Wilson, *Sex, Evolution and Behavior*, 69, 266, 310, 328. For Mormon comment on widespread approval for "polygamy," see Pratt, "Notes Concerning Marriage," *Mil. Star*, 36:41 (13 Oct. 1874), 644–47; "Lecture By Elder Orson Hyde," 6 Oct. 1854, *Des. News* [Weekly], 19 Oct. 1854, 4:32 [1/5]; and Thatcher, *Poligimia mormona*, 13.

[2] The condemnation of anyone advocating the lawfulness of polygamy is found in sess. 24, can. 2, 11 Nov. 1563, and can be read in Schroeder, *Canons and Decrees*, 181. Also see Esmein, *Mariage en droit canonique*, 2:154, 269–73. Brundage, *Law, Sex, and Christian Society*, 477–79, discusses medieval controversies, including Aquinas's concession that it was allowed under certain circumstances.

[3] For Luther's and the Landgrave of Hesse's acceptance of the practice and other examples, see all of Rockwell, *Doppelehe*; Westermarck, *History of Human Marriage*, 3:51; Cairncross, *After Polygamy Was Made a Sin*, 1–93; and Smith, "Strange Bedfellows," 41–45. For Mormon appropriation of Milton on behalf of the cause, see Tanner, "Making a Mormon of Milton," 191–206; and Whittaker, "Early Mormon Polygamy Defenses," 60.

Beginning in the 1600s, natural-law advocates vigorously debated the practice, prompting an outpouring of books and pamphlets on the subject until well into the eighteenth century.[4] Enlightenment thinkers, including Montesquieu, Pufendorf, and Paley, addressed the subject.[5] One scholar said support for plural marriage in eighteenth-century Europe reached such proportions that it became a cause célèbre.[6] Another described it as "a doctrine daily defended in conversation and often in print by a great variety of plausible arguments."[7]

Polygyny's best-known English champion was Martin Madan in his three-volume *Thelypthora*, first published in 1780. Madan brought together justifications employed for centuries, arguments that were also later used by the Saints: scriptural precedent; plurality's effectiveness for restoring patriarchal authority in the home; and its alleged tendency to eliminate adultery and prostitution. Others arose to defend the practice but none proved so formidable nor were so often assimilated into Mormon discourse as Madan. One later Mormon apostle urged that those reluctant to enter polygamy read Madan, for, he said, "no mortal man can overturn the arguments of the author."[8] With so much attention to the subject it was only natural that discussion about it would be carried to American shores where, as in Europe, it was evinced as much by those writing to oppose as those who embraced it.[9]

Living with multiple spouses was common in many American Indian tribes. Those who resided among or near them often copied their ways. The Duke of Württemberg, who visited the frontier in the 1820s, remarked that when residing among Indians almost everyone of "whatever color, class, or sta-

---

[4] Erle, *Ehe im Naturrecht*, 259. Also see "Erunt Tres Aut Quattuor In Carne Una," 71–91; "Zur Genese Theologisch-Juristischer Kontroversen (de polygamia)," 374–406; and Vogel, "Political Philosophers and the Trouble with Polygamy," 229–51.

[5] Montesquieu, *Spirit of Laws*, 16, 1–15; Pufendorf, *Of the Law of Nature and Nations*, 6.1.16; Paley, *Principles of Moral and Political Philosophy*, 1:319–25; and all of Prémontval, *Monogamie*.

[6] Cairncross, *After Polygamy Was Made a Sin*, 141. This may have been but a dimension of the general irregularity afflicting marriage in places like England during the eighteenth century. Brown, "Rise and Fall of the Fleet Marriages," 117–36.

[7] [Delany], *Reflections upon Polygamy*, 1; and Towers, *Polygamy Unscriptural*, 5.

[8] John Henry Smith to Joseph Smith III, Salt Lake City, 21 April 1886, Subject Folder Collection, CCL-A. Also see Veritas, "Plural Marriage," *Mil. Star*, 36:38 (22 Sept. 1874), 593–97; and "A Strong Defense of Plural Marriage," *Des. Eve. News*, 20 April 1882, 15:127 [2/1–2].

[9] See, for example, Miner, *Dr. Miner's Defense*; toleration for the practice among non-Christian peoples by Baptist missionaries as described by Brown, *History of Missions*, 2:196–97; the arguments by Benajah McCall as described in Cross, *Burned-over District*, 37; its advantages as set forth in "Enquirer," *Cleveland Liberalist* 1 (4 Feb. 1837), 164/2–3; and commentaries in Dwight, *Hebrew Wife*, and Shelford, *Critical Treatise*.

tion" was promiscuous, living with and bearing children by native women.[10] It was to be expected then that some, like William Hepworth Dixon, an English white supremacist, saw parallels between life among American aboriginals and Mormons, and believed the Saints' plurality had an entirely native inspiration: "a growth of the soil, older than the advent of Brigham Young, older than the revelation of Joseph Smith . . . derived . . . and adopted . . . from the Indian lodge."[11]

The natural alliance of patriarchy with a plurality of wives also drew on influences current in the early republic. The period of Mormonism's founder was host to a blur of assumptions concerning gender relations, attitudes at once liberal and conservative. The young nation's democratic passions were frequently qualified by what Susan Juster called "the imbrication of sexual and racial anxieties."[12] Female independence was sometimes as much resented as the abolitionist critique of black slavery. Those who, like Sarah Grimké, saw male dominance as wrong defied what many, including Mormons, considered the order of nature itself.[13] Catherine Brekus found that even in the "feminine sphere" of religion, after an initial period of increasing female evangelism, women met with a wave of criticism in the 1820s and 1830s for the forwardness of their sex.[14]

It was an issue that provoked responses in Europe as well as the United States, and many reacted by simply asserting male preeminence more defiantly than before.[15] Arthur Schopenhauer, using descriptions employed on

[10] Württemberg, *Travels*, 198. Also see the description of "an American polygamist" and his three Indian wives in Hamilton, *Men and Manners in America*, 340. Spanish priests often found Indian polygyny too pervasive to uproot. Esquivel Obregón, *Apuntes*, 2:583–87. Many early nineteenth-century observers commented on relaxed sexual morality among Indians. See James, *Account of an Expedition*, 15:11–17; Brown, *History of Missions*, 2:503; McCulloch Jr., *Researches*, 165; Flint, *History and Geography*, 1:122; and Catlin, *Letters and Notes*, 1:118–19.

[11] Dixon, *White Conquest*, 1:183–84.

[12] Juster, "Spirit and the Flesh," 353. This important essay recognizes reactive themes qualifying the democratic impulses said to be so extensive in American antebellum religion. Hatch, *Democratization of American Christianity*.

[13] Grimké, *Letters on the Equality of the Sexes*, 3, 11, 122 passim. The Jeremiads that such sentiments provoked are illustrated in J. F. Stearns's *Discourse on Female Influence* (1837), in Furness, *Genteel Female*, 215. The determination of early nineteenth-century reformers, including Mormons, to secure patriarchal authority in the face of female revolt is a major theme in Kern, *Ordered Love*.

[14] Brekus, "'Let Your Women Keep Silence in the Churches,'" 2:308–53.

[15] For accounts of this matter in Europe during the nineteenth century, see Gay, *Education of the Senses*, 424–25; Perrot, *From the Fires of Revolution to the Great War*, 4:173–76 passim. In the U.S., see all of Grossberg, *Governing the Hearth*; and Mintz and Kellogg, *Domestic Revolutions*, 45–55 passim. The case of the Mormons is explored in Hardy, "Lords of Creation," 119–52.

both sides of the Atlantic, said women were no more than "big children all their life long," needing male direction.[16] Monogamy accounted for "that discord in married life which is so frequent, and almost the normal state," he said, because it pampered female self-will. This made the marriage of one man to several women preferable and, he believed, was one of the attractions accounting for Mormonism's many converts.[17] Latter-day Saint apologists for plural marriage spoke in a similar voice, displaying almost an obsession with patriarchal order.

Neither can we discount the hot winds of revivalism that swept the American frontier in the first decades of the nineteenth century, touching every religious reformer of the day. Evangelists of the time commonly spoke of imminent terrestrial doom to be followed by an equally transforming era of millennial grace. The promise that old things were to be supplanted by a new, heavenly order led some to believe that traditional matrimony could not escape the fire.

Few of those claiming inspiration from heaven were more relevant for Mormonism than Perfectionist advocates of spiritual marriage. Contending that holy relationships entirely spiritual in nature would replace carnal love and that legal fictions of this world must yield to the more enduring contractions of heaven, Perfectionists said that when souls were sympathetically mated their unions lasted forever. William Hepworth Dixon, who devoted two volumes to the phenomenon in its varied forms, remarked on the temporal coincidence of movements embracing these ideas in East Prussia, England, and frontier America.[18] While there are important differences, the similarity between polygamous Mormonism and Perfectionist thought is striking—including the sometime use by Mormons themselves of the term "spiritual wives."[19]

There were also the residual effects of the Revolution and Enlightenment skepticism. Tocqueville remarked on the tendency in young democracies to deprecate old forms, and America's early national period was one of ideolog-

---

[16] *Essays of Arthur Schopenhauer,* 435. For an American who employed almost identical language to that of Schopenhauer, not only in his declarations of female incapacity but as a non-Mormon champion of their polygamy, see Howard, *Plea for Polygamy.*

[17] *Essays of Arthur Schopenhauer,* 439, 444.

[18] Dixon, *Spiritual Wives.*

[19] Helen Mar Whitney, *Plural Marriage,* 15; and Emily Dow Partridge, as quoted by Compton, *In Sacred Loneliness,* 407. Perfectionist religion is most extensively treated in Warfield, *Perfectionism.* See also Flew, *Idea of Perfection in Christian Theology.* For a discussion of the Perfectionist religious milieu of early Mormonism, see Hansen, *Mormonism and the American Experience,* 59–62.

ical challenge.[20] The New World seemed especially inviting to social theorists, and the mixture of frontier freedom with utopian musing was an infectious draft. "There are no people, probably, in the world," pronounced the *Cincinnati Literary Gazette* in 1825, "who are so ready to make experiments respecting social relations and domestic arrangements, as those of the western country,— none who are so little fettered by established habits, or who are less disposed to consider hereditary prejudices as heir-looms which cannot be parted with."[21] Both Robert Dale Owen and Charles Fourier, who were widely imitated, sought greater freedom in sexual relations, Fourier specifically saying that polygynous alliances were an inevitable feature of human behavior.[22]

Whether such Utopian departures sought the suffocation of all sexual impulse, as with the Rappites and Ann Lee's Shaker followers, or ran to the permissive indulgences of Frances Wright at Nashoba, the times were ablaze with rumors of marital reconfiguration.[23] The Cochranites of Maine, for example, who engaged in a variety of connubial arrangements and whose representatives carried their inspirations throughout New England, were thought by one historian of the region to have influenced the Mormons.[24] Those calling for a sexual reformation, however, never captured support from a majority of Americans.[25] But as Taylor Stoehr said, the advocates of change spoke with powerful and eloquent voices.[26] It is entirely consistent with what we

---

[20] Tocqueville, *Democracy in America*, 2:325–27.

[21] This by one "Z," discussing prospects for Robert Owen's American Utopian communities in 1825. "Review," 193. As late as the 1870s, a non-Mormon was quoted to say of the Saints: "as to a man having as many wives as he can get, why, so long as they fancy it, it's all fair play; and where you can get a divorce for twenty dollars, why it stands as a natural consequence, that it is all up with monogamy. You see . . . we are a new country, and we can't be cramped with all these old world notions." Yelverton, *Teresina in America*, 2:37.

[22] Beecher and Bienvenu, *Utopian Vision of Charles Fourier*, 333. Also see Jones, "Free Love and Communal Households," 9:93–102.

[23] For Rapp's religious attachment to celibacy, see Arndt, *George Rapp's Harmony Society*, 416–48. For the Shakers and their sexual restrictions, see Stein, *Shaker Experience in America*, 34–37, 50, 95–96, 159. Regarding Frances Wright, see Morris, *Fanny Wright: Rebel in America*, 141–47 passim.

[24] For Jacob Cochran and the alleged influence of his ideas on Brigham Young, see Ridlon Sr., *Saco Valley Settlements*, 269–85. There is also Emmons, *Philosophy of Popular Superstitions*, 92–94. Two recent writers who, like Ridlon, contend that early Mormons borrowed polygamy from the Cochranites are Price and Price, *Joseph Smith Fought Polygamy*, 1:1–39.

[25] These experiments tended to follow a course like that of Robert Matthews, an astonishing rogue who once visited with Joseph Smith. Most of Matthews's followers became disillusioned because, as one put it, "there is too much changing of wives here. I have a nice little woman, and I should not much like to lose her." Johnson and Wilentz, *Kingdom of Matthias*, 132. For Smith's encounter with Matthews, see Smith Jr., *History of the Church*, 9 Nov. 1835, 2:304–7.

[26] Stoehr, *Free Love in America*, 3. The literature on sexual reform in nineteenth-century America is enormous. Traditional treatments of the early period include Muncy, *Sex and Marriage in Utopian Communities*; Walters, *American Reformers*; and, for the later nineteenth century, Sears, *Sex Radicals*.

know of human nature to assume that the ears of early Mormons were no more closed to ultraist peals of this kind than others—and the prophet Joseph Smith seemed always to possess a special genius for refracting the vast affluence of opinions that coursed his age.

Finally, any reconnaissance of possible sources for Mormon polygamous advocacy must not ignore recollections of the church's own followers. Most believers, both before and after the Principle was publicly acknowledged, construed Mormon plurality as entirely divine. It would be as partial to disregard this as to ignore its context. Efforts to fully understand historical events must give respectful attention to the claims of actors involved. Recitations of historical precedent, frontier libertarianism, patriarchal defensiveness, and acknowledgement of polygamy's kinship to other sexual experiments of the time would be incomplete without the testimonies of Mormon believers themselves.

The caution William James gave a century ago remains compelling. Not only are supposedly objective methods of analysis the products of time and place, but the "enchantment" of religious transport "is not rationally or logically deducible from anything else." It is a category of experience having unique qualities of its own.[27] While historians are always obliged to challenge collective memory, they must also respect it as an additional lens for exploring the past. We cannot, if we are to comprehend the Mormon polygamous phenomenon, disregard the fact that when formally dictating his own most extensive statement on plural marriage, Smith commenced with the imprimatur "Verily, thus saith the Lord unto you my servant Joseph." Our survey properly begins then with statements and recollections by participants themselves.

---

[27] James, *Varieties of Religious Experience*, 47, 55–56, 72–77.

Chapter 1

"Go Ye, Therefore, and Do the Works of Abraham"
Mormon Polygamous Beginnings

No one knows when Joseph Smith first decided that polygamous marriage was appropriate for his own time, but there is extensive evidence that both the belief and practice began among the Mormons well before the 1843 revelation commanding it. Brigham Young said the prophet became convinced of its propriety when translating *The Book of Mormon*.[1] There are problems with accepting Young's statement, especially since *The Book of Mormon* condemns polygamy as a "wicked practice" that was "abominable before me, saith the Lord."[2] Moreover, in an 1831 revelation the prophet clearly declared God's intent was that "Thou shalt love thy wife with all thy heart, and shalt cleave unto her and none else."[3] If Young's memory was accurate, however, it would date the origins of the doctrine to between the spring of 1829 and early 1830 when *The Book of Mormon* was published. The Bible, a volume familiar to

---

[1] According to Charles Lowell Walker, who recorded Young's remarks in 1872, Joseph Smith and Oliver Cowdery had a revelation at that time "that the order of Patriarchal Marriag and the Sealing was right." Larson and Larson, eds., *Diary of Charles Lowell Walker*, 26 July 1872, 1:349. For problems with Young's statement and difficulties with contentions that the prophet's interest in the subject occurred while translating *The Pearl of Great Price*, see Bachman, "Study," 61–68; the same author's "New Light," 22n10; and Van Wagoner, *Mormon Polygamy*, 11–12.

[2] See Jacob 1:15, 2:23–35, 3:5; Mosiah 11:2; Ether 10:5. To defend against the charge of ignoring these strictures, Mormons commonly pointed to Jacob 2:30: "For if I will, saith the Lord of Hosts, raise up seed unto me, I will command my people; otherwise they shall hearken unto these things." Writing in the early 1850s, Benjamin Ferris said the church, seizing on the exception, had "rushed through this gap like a flock of goats." Ferris, *Utah and the Mormons*, 234.

[3] *D&C* 42:22, 9 Feb. 1831. Two months later another revelation said men should "have one wife, and they twain shall be one flesh." *D&C* 49:16, Mar. 1831. And in the 1835 edition of the *Doctrine and Covenants*, the marriage ceremony required that couples pledge to keep themselves "wholly for each other, and from all others, during your lives." *D&C* (1835), 101:251–52.

Joseph Smith Jr. (1805–1844), founder of
the Church of Jesus Christ of Latter-day
Saints, author by revelation in 1843 of the
doctrine of polygamous marriage, and
husband to more than thirty plural wives.
Unless otherwise noted, illustrations are courtesy of
LDS *Church Archives, Salt Lake City, Utah.*

Smith from his youth, provides a more likely source of inspiration, for the
examples of polygynous Old Testament patriarchs confronted the young
prophet when he began to revise the scriptures between 1830 and 1833.[4]

"TAKE UNTO YOU WIVES OF
THE LAMANITES AND NEPHITES":
AN EARLY REVELATION ON POLYGAMY?

Whatever the difficulties in identifying the precise years when the young
prophet embraced the idea, later church leaders were undoubtedly correct in
saying that it occurred in the early 1830s.[5] An early revelation allegedly given
in Missouri told Mormon Elders to marry among the Indians, a directive

---

[4] Joseph B. Noble, who solemnized Smith's first Nauvoo polygamous marriage, said the prophet told
him the Principle was revealed to his mind when translating the Bible. "Plural Marriage," *Mil. Star* 45:29, 16
July 1883, 454.

[5] Lyman Johnson, an early apostle, told Orson Pratt that the prophet had said in 1831 that plurality was
a divine principle. "Report of Elders Orson Pratt and Joseph F. Smith," *Mil. Star* 40:50, 16 Dec. 1878, 788.
Also see Roberts, *Outlines of Ecclesiastical History,* 431; Roberts, *Comprehensive History,* 5:95–96; and Smith Jr.,
History of the Church, 5:xxx–xxxi.

subsequently interpreted as condoning plural relationships. *The Book of Mormon* claimed to be a record of pre-Columbian peoples in the Americas, and the scripture's stated purpose was to tell the Lamanites, the American Indians who were their surviving descendants, "what great things the Lord hath done for their fathers . . . that they might know the covenants of the Lord."[6] It was natural that Joseph Smith would attempt to convert Indians, and in the autumn of 1830 he sent messengers with copies of the volume to the western part of Missouri and "into the wilderness among the Lamanites."[7] Joseph Smith, William Wines Phelps, and others followed the initial company of missionaries to the frontier.[8] When Phelps recorded his memory of the event in a letter to Brigham Young in 1861, he emphasized that his recollection constituted *"The Substance"* of what the prophet said thirty years earlier. While one must view the document cautiously, if Phelps was correct this disclosure may constitute Mormonism's earliest formal approval of plural marriage.[9]

The justification given for marrying American Indian women—that it would produce more "delightsome" offspring with a lighter complexion—was also significant. Not only did this agree with *Book of Mormon* references to the native race as degenerate and unattractive, but it anticipated the eugenic arguments later used to justify polygamy.[10] The revelation's reference to female descendants of "the Lamanites and Nephites" as more "virtuous" than contemporary Gentile women is surprising, given the common perception dating from the colonial period that Indian women were afflicted with considerable "frailty . . . betwixt the garters and the girdle."[11] An explanation

---

[6] *The Book of Mormon*, title page.

[7] *D&C* 32:2, Oct. 1830.

[8] For background, see Ellsworth, "History of Mormon Missions," 74–88; Jennings, "First Mormon Mission to the Indians," 288–99; and Walker, "Seeking the 'Remnant,'" 1–33.

[9] Ezra Booth, who accompanied the Mormons to Missouri, told of the revelation. He became disaffected and wrote a series of published letters describing the experience. He did not mention polygamy but linked marriage to Indian women with the need for Mormons to obtain "residence in the Indian territory, independent of the [Indian] agent," who opposed them. Booth, "Mormonism—Nos. VIII–IX," *Ohio Star*, 2:49, 8 Dec. 1831 [1/1–4].

[10] See *The Book of Mormon*, II Nephi, 30:6–7. Joseph Smith was not the first to suggest changing Indian complexions through intermarriage. William H. Crawford had proposed it less than a decade earlier—and it was received with no more enthusiasm than Mormons gave it. Thomas Cooper's *Strictures*, 6, charged that it required young white men to "prostitute" themselves by marrying "dirty, draggle-tailed, blanketed, half human squaws." On later Mormon reluctance to "bleach" the Indians by marrying them, see Stenhouse, *Rocky Mountain Saints*, 658–59.

[11] Lawson, *History of Carolina*, 89. On the relaxed morality of Indian women, see McCulloch, *Researches*, 165; and Württemberg, *Travels*, 198. For varying estimates of American Indian character, especially during Joseph Smith's time, see Vogel, *Indian Origins*, 53–69.

for this apparent contradiction may be found in Smith's use of the term "virtuous." In his day, it did not refer singly to sexual purity but connoted character generally, including obedience to moral duty.[12] It may, then, have reflected concerns with growing forwardness by females, a matter later emphasized in Udney Hay Jacob's *Peace Maker*.

JOSEPH SMITH'S 17 JULY 1831 REVELATION,
IN WILLIAM WINES PHELPS TO BRIGHAM YOUNG,
12 AUG. 1861, REVELATIONS COLLECTION, LDS ARCHIVES.[13]

President B. Young I have the pleasure of sending you <u>*The Substance*</u> of a revelation by Joseph Smith Junr. Given over the boundary, west of Jackson Co. Missouri, on Sunday morning July 17, 1831, when Seven Elders, Viz: Joseph Smith Jun.[,] Oliver Cowdery, W.W. Phelps, Martin Harris, Joseph Coe, Ziba Peterson and Joshua Lewiz [Lewis] united their hearts in prayer, in a private place, to inquire of the Lord who should <preach> the first sermon to the remnant of the Lamanites and Nephites, and the people of that section, that should assemble that day, in the Indian Country, to hear the gospel and the revelations according to *The Book of Mormon*.

Among the company there being neither pen, Ink, or paper, Joseph remarked that the Lord could preserve his words, as he had ever done, till the time appointed, and proceeded:—

1 Verily, verily, saith the Lord, your Redeemer, even Jesus Christ, the light and the life of the world, ye cannot discern with your natural eyes, the design and the purpose of your Lord and your God, in bringing <you> thus far into <the> wilderness for a trial of your faith,—and to be especial witnesses, to bear testimony of this land, upon which the Zion of God shall be built up in the last days, when it is redeemed.

2 Verily, inasmuch as ye are united in calling upon my name to know my will concerning who shall preach to the inhabitants that shall assemble this day to learn what new doctrine you have to teach them, you have

---

[12] "Virtue," in Noah Webster, *American Dictionary*, 2:108. This may have been what George A. Smith meant when he later said: "After the remnants of Israel shall be gathered in, not many generations shall pass away before they shall become a white and delightsome people . . . wickedness and corruption have degraded them to their present condition, but according to the education they have had, the code of morals they have learned, they are more moral and virtuous than many of the white men in the world." Sermon, 6 April 1856, *Journal of Discourses*, 3:287.

[13] This document is not found in the LDS church's official canon of revelations. It is known from two manuscript copies prepared by William Wines Phelps (1792–1872), who was present when it was given on 17 July 1831 and recalled the event in this letter to Brigham Young. For other reproductions, see Collier, *Unpublished Revelations*, 57–58; and Marquardt, *Joseph Smith Revelations*, 374–76. For Professor Bradley's contention that Phelps's recollection "is at best a questionable source," see her "Out of the Closet," 310.

done wisely,—for so did the ancient prophets, even Enoch, and Abraham, and others. . .

4 Verily I say unto you, that the wisdom of man in his fallen state, knoweth not the purposes and the privileges of my Holy priesthood, but ye shall know, when ye receive a fullness by reason of the anointing: For it is my will, that in time, ye should take unto you wives of the Lamanites and Nephites, that their posterity may become white, delightsome and just; for even now their females are more Virtuous than the Gentiles . . . even so: Amen.

Reported by WWP.

About three years after this [was] given, I asked brother Joseph privately, how "We" that were mentioned in the revelation, could take "Wives" from the natives, as we were all married men? He replied instantly, "In the same manner that Abraham took Hagar and Keturah; and Jacob took Rachel, Bilhah and Zilpah, *by revelation*: the saints of the Lord are always directed by *revelation*.["]

Respectfully I have the faith to be, as ever,

Aug. 12, 1861   W. W. Phelps

"Eternal Union of the Sexes":
Marital Joy in Heaven

The exciting years following Mormonism's birth produced several concepts and teachings friendly to plural marriage. Joseph Smith told his followers in 1831 that the "High priesthood" gave its bearers power to seal or save the Saints in heaven.[14] While this did not yet include joining couples in eternal marriages, in Kirtland during the mid-1830s men and women were united in monogamous unions by priesthood authority, sometimes with and sometimes without civil approval.[15] "Sealing" women to men, men to men, and families to families was an important ingredient in the prophet's thinking about eternal relationships and continued to evolve almost until the time he was

---

[14] Cannon and Cook, *Far West Record*, 20–21 (25 Oct. 1831); and *D&C* 68:12, Nov. 1831. This is most fully discussed in Buerger, "'Fulness of the Priesthood,'" 10–44; and history of the "sealing" authority provided in Cook, *Nauvoo Marriages*, x–xiv.

[15] Smith Jr., *History of the Church*, 20 Jan. 1836, 2:377; Parkin, "Nature and Cause," 174–77; Bachman, "New Light," 29–31; and Quinn, *Mormon Hierarchy*, 1:624. But cf. Bradshaw, "Joseph Smith's Performance of Marriages," 23–69. A Mormon apostle later said in Salt Lake City that parents who married without Latter-day Saint authority left their children "bastardized" in the hereafter. Orson Pratt, 7 Oct. 1874, *Journal of Discourses*, 17:225–29.

killed.[16] Closely related to "sealing" was the prophet's vision of a heaven of graduated glories described in a revelation of 1832. That revelation did not, however, refer to marriage in the hereafter.[17] But by 1835 the prophet was discussing sexual and procreational opportunities in heaven with some of his followers.

To describe heaven as a place where marriage and family relations continue as they are on earth was not unique to Mormons. The visions of Emanuel Swedenborg set forth similar ideas, and these perspectives agreed with Romantic imagery that increasingly portrayed the next life in familiar, anthropocentric terms.[18] Joseph Grafton Hovey, who was baptized a Mormon in 1839, remembered that his father, a "Close Communion Baptist," often prayed that parents and children "might be Bound up in the same bundle of eternal Life."[19] It was an ancient hope that Mormons transformed into an integral part of their theology. In the words of Fawn Brodie, "Converts reared on a diet of harps and angels found this heaven exciting."[20]

Parley Parker Pratt (1807–1857) was one of the most important thinkers in the early LDS church. Ordained an apostle in 1835, he composed hymns, wrote pamphlets and books, and went on numerous missions in the U.S. and abroad, and his devotion to Joseph Smith's teachings on polygamy would eventually cost him his life. With the assistance of John Taylor, Parley Parker Pratt Jr. posthumously edited and published his father's autobiography in 1874, including this passage written in 1850, referring to conversations with Joseph Smith in late 1839 and early 1840. Autobiographies are retrospective, so it is always possible that later memories are fused with earlier ones, but in Pratt's case, the writings of William W. Phelps confirm that the Mormon prophet was commenting on the marriage relation in heaven as much as five years before the incident Pratt here describes.[21]

---

[16] After the prophet's death the inclination to enlarge one's kingdom by splicing other men and their families into one's own led to a kind of "game of kingdoms," as Apostle Amasa Lyman put it. See George Q. Cannon, in A. H. Cannon Journals, 5 April 1894, UPB, 18:68. For the history of LDS adoption rites, see Irving, "Law of Adoption," 291–314; Buerger, "'Fullness of the Priesthood;'" and Cooper, *Promises Made to the Fathers*, 168–99. For the use of "sealed" and "sealing" as terms connoting plural contractions during the Nauvoo period, see *Reorganized Church vs. Church of Christ*, 399, 406, 470, 475–76.

[17] *D&C* 76:50–113, 16 Feb. 1832.

[18] "Marriage," in Warren, *Compendium*, 440–79; and, "Love in the Heavenly Realm" in McDannell and Lang, *Heaven*, 228–75.

[19] Hovey, Reminiscences and Journals, 1845–1856, LDS Archives, 1:2.

[20] Brodie, *No Man Knows My History*, 300.

[21] William Wines Phelps, "Letter No. 8," *Latter Day Saints' Messenger and Advocate* 1 (June 1835), 130; and Van Orden, "Writing to Zion," 563–64. Also see Bishop, "Eternal Marriage," 77–88.

PARLEY P. PRATT [JR.], ED., *AUTOBIOGRAPHY*
OF *PARLEY PARKER PRATT* (1874), 259–60.

In Philadelphia I had the happiness of once more meeting with President Smith, and of spending several days with him and others, and with the Saints in that city and vicinity.

During these interviews he taught me many great and glorious principles concerning God and the heavenly order of eternity. It was at this time that I received from him the first idea of eternal family organization, and the eternal union of the sexes in those inexpressibly endearing relationships which none but the highly intellectual, the refined and pure in heart, know how to prize, and which are at the very foundation of everything worthy to be called happiness.

Till then I had learned to esteem kindred affections and sympathies as appertaining solely to this transitory state, as something from which the heart must be entirely weaned, in order to be fitted for its heavenly state.

It was Joseph Smith who taught me how to prize the endearing relationships of father and mother, husband and wife; of brother and sister, son and daughter.

It was from him that I learned that the wife of my bosom might be secured to me for time and all eternity; and that the refined sympathies and affections which endeared us to each other emanated from the fountain of divine eternal love. It was from him that I learned that we might cultivate these affections, and grow and increase in the same to all eternity; while the result of our endless union would be an offspring as numerous as the stars of heaven, or the sands of the sea shore.[22]

It was from him that I learned the true dignity and destiny of a son of God, clothed with an eternal priesthood, as the patriarch and sovereign of his countless offspring. It was from him that I learned that the highest dignity of womanhood was, to stand as a queen and priestess to her husband, and to reign for ever and ever as the queen mother of her numerous and still increasing offspring.

I had loved before, but I knew not why. But now I loved—with a pureness—and intensity of elevated, exalted feeling, which would lift my soul from the transitory things of this groveling sphere and expand it as the ocean. I felt that God was my heavenly Father indeed; that Jesus was my brother, and that the wife of my bosom was an immortal, eternal companion; a kind ministering angel, given to me as a comfort, and a crown of glory for ever and ever. In short, I could now love with the spirit and with the understanding also.

Yet, at that time, my dearly beloved brother, Joseph Smith, had barely touched a single key; had merely lifted a corner of the veil and given me a single glance into eternity.

---

[22] Marriage inspired all social joys and affections, Pratt later argued, and that to repress natural affection was not true religion. Pratt, *Appeal to the Inhabitants of the State of New York*, 37–38.

"And You Are the Woman":
The Prophet's Polygamous Alliances

Many factors influenced the emergence of the Mormon polygamous family. Most scholars find the notion that the prophet's sexual ardor inspired his interest in taking additional wives to be too simplistic.[23] As noted, the Mormon prophet's mind encompassed eugenic plans to make American Indians "white and delightsome," as well as Romantic visions of the hereafter. Smith was also inclined to extend his hierarchical authority through dynastic alliances and to give his most faithful followers successively greater crowns: endowments bequeathing wives, families, powers, and kingdoms both here and in the hereafter.[24] Anti-pluralist responses to uncertainties of the day undoubtedly played a part as well.[25] Polygamous marriage and its "sealing" ceremonies, secrecy, and promises of special rewards can be seen as attempts to secure the Saints against both the general commotion of their age and threats from their enemies. Explanations of Smith's polygamy are both numerous and intertwined with the broader issue of his religious persona.[26] To fully explain the prophet's inspirations, especially regarding polygamy, will long remain a nearly impossible task. "The possibilities," in one historian's words, "are almost endless, and one can only speculate about motives."[27]

While admitting the dense nature of the question, without surrendering to an over-reductive explanation, it is difficult to ignore the lively sexual dynamics of early Mormonism, which affected leaders and followers alike. While the evidence for this is extensive, one need look no further than the censure provided in Mormon scripture itself. The 1835 edition of the *Doctrine and Covenants* acknowledged that "Inasmuch as this church of Christ has been

---

[23] For an excellent overview of the issue, see Compton, "Fawn Brodie on Joseph Smith's Plural Wives and Polygamy," 154–64.

[24] White Jr., "Ideology of the Family," 300–1; and Daynes, "Family Ties," 63–75. Regarding ritualistic rewards for faithfulness and their relation to polygamy, see Quinn, "Latter-day Saint Prayer Circles," 84–96; *Mormon Hierarchy*, 1:491–519; Buerger, "'Fulness of the Priesthood,'" 10–24; all of Bergera, "Earliest Eternal Sealings"; and the secret orders and quorums that, as Todd Compton indicates, often intersected with polygamy, granting distinction to the most faithful. See his comments in Anderson and Bergera, *Joseph Smith's Quorum of the Anointed*, ix–xi and xiii–xxx.

[25] A sample of the extensive literature dealing with this theme is DePillis, "Quest for Religious Authority," 68–88; Pollock, "In Search of Security"; Wood, "Evangelical America and Early Mormonism," 358–86; Spencer, "Anxious Saints," 43–53; and Hill, *Quest for Refuge*.

[26] For example, see Foster, "Sex and Prophetic Power"; and the perceptive review of Fawn Brodie's psycho-biographical interpretations in Cohen, "No Man Knows My Psychology," 55–78.

[27] Conkin, *American Originals*, 195. Jan Shipps, referring to Smith's claims and revelations generally, appropriately called the problem "The Prophet Puzzle."

reproached with the crime of fornication, and polygamy: we declare that we believe, that one man should have one wife; and one woman, but one husband."[28] One of the things hastening disintegration of the community at Kirtland, Benjamin F. Johnson said, was that rumors of celestial marriage so seized some that they ran to free love.[29] The Mormon reputation was such that on the way to Missouri in 1837 church members were asked "daily and hourly by all classes of people," among other things, if they believed in having multiple wives.[30] And the prophet, in a letter from Liberty Jail in December 1838, rebuked followers "whose eyes are full of adultery and cannot cease from sin."[31]

Some who later described themselves as overcome with loathing when first told of plural marriage on other occasions stated that they had been led by the spirit to anticipate such a teaching. Brigham Young, Heber C. Kimball, and Lorenzo Snow all said that before the prophet told them about the Principle, the spirit had already given them "an intimation" of the doctrine.[32] John Taylor, whether serious or in jest, wrote his wife Leonora in 1841 that he and returning English missionaries might follow the example of the ancient Israelites and take additional wives as consorts.[33] Mary Elizabeth Rollins Lightner recalled that, though married to another before the prophet invited her to become his secret wife, she thought herself a sinner because she had already dreamed of it for years. Brigham Young said that the prophet told the Quorum of Twelve Apostles they would have more difficulty with temptations associated with women than anything else.[34] The milieu of early Mormonism was crossed with sexual implications at many levels.

---

[28] *D&C* (1835), Appendix, Sec. 101:251. This section was added to the 1835 printing of the *D&C* and approved by a conference of Saints on 17 Aug. 1835 in Kirtland, Ohio. Marquardt, "John Whitmer and the Revelations of Joseph Smith," 39–49.

[29] Johnson, *My Life's Review*, 88.

[30] *Elders Journal* 1 (Nov. 1837), 28; and B. H. Roberts in Smith Jr., *History of the Church*, 5:xxx.

[31] Jessee, *Personal Writings of Joseph Smith*, 381. On the frequency of adultery cases in the early years, see the recollections of Heber C. Kimball, 11 Jan. 1857, *Journal of Discourses*, 4:170–71; George A. Smith, 10 Jan. 1858, ibid., 7:114 ; and idem, 15 Nov. 1864, ibid., 11:10.

[32] This is how Eliza R. Snow described her brother Lorenzo's preconception of polygamy in her *Biography and Family Record of Lorenzo Snow*, 68–69. For similar statements by Young and Kimball, respectively, see Brigham Young, 23 June 1874, *Journal of Discourses*, 18:241, and Whitney, "Scenes in Nauvoo," *Woman's Exponent* 10:9 (1 Oct. 1881), 66. Their claims of repugnance when first told of plural marriage are in "Provo Conference . . . July 14, 1855," *Des. News* [Weekly], 14 Nov. 1855, 5:36 [282/2]; and Whitney, "Scenes and Incidents in Nauvoo," *Woman's Exponent* 10:10 (15 Oct. 1881), 74.

[33] John Taylor to Leonora Cannon Taylor, 13 Feb. 1841, Taylor Family Papers, Special Collections, UU. For Taylor's statement of astonishment and dislike when first told of the Principle, see "Discourse," *Des. Eve. News*, 15 April 1882, 15:123, 2/1.

[34] Brigham Young, 25 April 1860, *Journal of Discourses*, 8:55.

The identity of all of Joseph Smith's female partners has never been established. There is little question, however, that he commenced forming unions of one kind or another with women other than his wife Emma at least as early as 1835.[35] Problems associated with the practice, as indicated, contributed to difficulties afflicting the Saints at Kirtland. In Nauvoo, the number of Smith's relationships mounted rapidly. The best estimates place them at more than thirty.[36] During the same period, thirty or so of his disciples also took plural companions of their own.[37] Involvements of this kind required that the parties act in great secrecy.[38] To even approach women with such proposals was fraught with peril, which is undoubtedly why they sometimes required special revelations from heaven.[39] When the prophet proposed to her as a sixteen-year-old in 1842, Lucy Walker recalled, he told her that he had "been commanded of God to take another wife, and you are the woman."[40] Intermediaries were employed as well as claims of promises predating life on earth.[41]

The imposing authority of Smith as a prophet of God also influenced those to whom he gave attention. Eliza Maria Partridge told how while she and her sister Emily were lodging at the Smith residence, Joseph "taught to us the plan of celestial marriage, and asked us to enter into that order with him. This was truly a great trial to me, but I had the most implicit confidence in him as a prophet of the Lord, and could not but believe his words,

---

[35] Rather than the "dirty, nasty, filthy affair" described by Oliver Cowdery, some believe Smith's relationship with Fanny Alger could have been his first plural marriage. See Assistant Church Historian Andrew Jenson's count of the prophet's wives, where Alger is placed near the beginning of his list of twenty-seven women: Jenson, "Plural Marriage," 233. Compton dates the relationship to 1833. See his "Fanny Alger," 174–207; and *In Sacred Loneliness*, 25–42. Cowdery's charge is found in his letter to Warren Cowdery, 21 Jan. 1838, Cowdery Letterbook, CSmH.

[36] Compton, *In Sacred Loneliness*, 1–2, 4–6, 10–11; and the same author's "Trajectory of Plurality," 1–38. For other estimates, see Jenson, "Plural Marriage," 233–34; Brodie, *No Man Knows My History*, 457–88; Ivins, "Notes on Mormon Polygamy," 232–33; Bachman, "Study," 104–16; and Quinn, *Mormon Hierarchy*, 2:179–81.

[37] Smith, "Nauvoo Roots of Mormon Polygamy," 1–72; and, Bergera, "Identifying the Earliest Mormon Polygamists," 1–74.

[38] The prophet was always concerned about confidentiality. Mary Elizabeth Lightner said after Smith proposed, he asked her if she would be a "traitor" by telling of his advances. She answered she would tell no one that she "had such talk from a mortal man." Lightner, "Address," UPB, 3. Also see Ebenezer Robinson to Dear Madam, 7 July 1888, Miscellaneous Collection, fd. III, CCL-A.

[39] See, for example, the revelation Joseph Smith produced to win the hand of seventeen-year-old Sarah Ann Whitney, whom he married on 27 July 1842, in Marquardt, *Joseph Smith Revelations*, 315–16, no. 166. Also see references and discussion in Whitney, "Newell K. Whitney," *Contributor* 6:4 (Jan. 1885), 131; and Compton, *In Sacred Loneliness*, 719n4.

[40] Walker's statement is in Littlefield, *Reminiscences*, 46. For more, see Compton, *In Sacred Loneliness*, 463–66.

[41] For example, see the prophet's role in a plural marriage sought by Apostle Orson Hyde: Mrs. Mary Ann Hyde, Autobiography, 20 Aug. 1880, CU-B, 3. For claims of pre-mortal alliances, see Compton, *In Sacred Loneliness*, 19–21.

and as a matter of course accept the privilege of being sealed to him as a wife for time and all eternity."[42]

The following manuscript accounts are retrospective and must be read with that in mind. They not only reveal the way Smith introduced the Principle to both men and women in Nauvoo, but they also provide a sense of the vibrant emotions accompanying Mormon polygamy in its earliest years.

Benjamin Franklin Johnson (1818–1905), a close friend of the prophet at Kirtland and Nauvoo, followed Brigham Young to Utah, where he led an adventurous life, performing many services for the church. He was a spirited champion of "celestial marriage," taking seven wives and leaving, at the time of his death in 1905, hundreds of descendents. More than half a century after the events he described, Johnson answered questions relating to early polygamy asked of him by George Francis Gibbs, an assistant to the LDS church's First Presidency.[43]

BENJAMIN FRANKLIN JOHNSON TO GEORGE F[RANCIS] GIBBS,
1903, BENJAMIN FRANKLIN JOHNSON PAPERS,
1852–1911, LDS ARCHIVES, 25–37.

[And now To your Question] "How Early did <the Prophet> Joseph Practice Poligamy?"—I hardly know how *wisely* to Reply—For the *Truth* at times may be better withheld. But as what I am writing is to be published only under Strict *Scrutiny* of the *wisest*, I will Say That the Revilation to the Church at Nauvoo July 12*th* 1843 on the eternity of the Marriage Covenant and Law of plural Marriage was not the first Rivilation of that Law Received & Practiced by the Prophet—In *1835* at Kirtland I learned from my Sisters Husband Lyman R Shirman,[44] who was *close* to the Prophet and Received it from him, "That the ancient order of plural marriage was again to be practiced by the Church[."] This at the time did not impress my mind deeply. Altho there then lived with his Family a Neighbors daughter Fanny Alger. A varry nice & Comly young woman about my own age. Towards <whoom> not only Myself but every one Seemed *partial* for <the> ameability of her character and <it> was whispered eaven <then> that Joseph *Loved her*. After this there

---

[42] Partridge, ed., *Eliza Maria Partridge Journal*, 9–10.

[43] See Johnson's funeral eulogy at the close of his *My Life's Review*, 388. This letter, written on lined paper in Johnson's hand, resembles an earlier affidavit he prepared to help refute RLDS assertions that Joseph Smith neither proposed nor practiced polygamy. "Benjamin F. Johnson's Testimony," 221–22. Accompanying Johnson's letter in the church archives is Charles S. Sellers's 1911 commentary, along with a corrected copy of the 1903 letter. This slightly altered version appears to be the basis for the account in Johnson's posthumously published *My Life's Review*, 94–97. There is also a film of Sellers's corrected version in the Mormon collection at CSmH; and two typewritten copies of the letter in the Stanley Ivins Collection, boxes 8 and 9, Uhi. For more, see Sellers, "Last Witness," 544–47; and LeBaron, "Benjamin Franklin Johnson in Nauvoo," 175–94.

[44] Lyman Royal Sherman married Johnson's older sister, Delcena, on 16 Jan. 1829.

was Some trouble with Jarid Carter,[45] and through Bro Shirman I learned that "As he had built himself a new house he now wanted another wife" which Joseph would not permit and then there was Some trouble with Oliver Cowdery. And *whisper* Said it was Relating to a girl then living in his Family. And I was afterwords told by Warren Parish[46] That He himself & Oliver Cowdery did know that Joseph had Fanny Alger as a wife for They were *Spied upon* & found together. And I Can now See that as at Nauvoo So at Kirtland That the Suspician or Knowledge of the Prophets Plural Relation was one of the Causes of Apostacy & disruption <at *Kirtland*> altho at the time there was little Said publicky upon the Subject. . . And now in visiting My Sister. The widow of Lyman R. Shirman who died a Martyr to <the> Conditions of Far West, I found with her a former acquaintance Sister Louisa Beeman[47] and I Saw from apearances that <they> ware both in his Care and that he provided for there Comfort. And as I was held closely to buisness And my home At Ramus was 20 miles distant I Saw but little of them untill after the Prophet in early Spring <of 43> had come to Ramus to teach Me Plural Marriage and to ask my other Sisters to be his wifes an acount of which I have heretofore given by Sworn Statement.[48] But will here Repeat as it occurred—It was Sunday morning April 3*d* or 4*th* 1843 that the prophet was at my home in Ramus and after breakfast he . . . proceeded at once to open to me the Subject of plural & Eternal marriage. And he Said That Years ago in Kirtland the Lord had Revealed <to him> the ancient Order of Plural marriage and the necesity for its practice and did command him <then> to take another wife and that among his first thoughts was to Come to my Mother for Some of her daughters. And as he was again Required of the Lord to take more wives he had Come now to ask <me> for my Sister Almera.[49] His words astonished me and almost *took* my *breath*. I Sat for a time amazed and finally almost Ready to burst with Emotion I looked him Straight in the Face & Said "Brother Joseph This is Something I did not Expext & I do not understand it. You know whether it is Right. I do not. I want to do <just> as you tell me and I will try. But if I ever Should know that you do this to Dishonor & debauch my Sister I will kill you as Shure as the Lord Lives. And while his Eye did not move from mine He Said with a Smile and in a Soft tone "But Benjamin you will never

---

[45] The early church both praised and censured Jared Carter. See entries under his name in the index to Smith Jr., *History of the Church*, 55.

[46] Warren Parrish was one of those who, with Oliver Cowdery, attacked the character of the prophet in Kirtland and Missouri. Smith Jr., *History of the Church*, 3:16, 11 April 1838; and Parkin, "The Nature and Cause," 163–74.

[47] Louisa Beaman was married to Joseph Smith as a plural wife in 1841 and, after the prophet's death, to Brigham Young in 1844. See Joseph B. Noble, "Plural Marriage," *Mil. Star* 45:29 (16 July 1883), 454–55; and Compton, *In Sacred Loneliness*, 55–70.

[48] This was, as cited above, "Benjamin F. Johnson's Testimony," 221–22.

[49] Almera Johnson confirmed her marriage to the prophet as a plural wife in Almera W. Johnson affidavit, Aug. 1883, Joseph F. Smith Affidavits [on celestial marriage], 1869–1915, fd. 1, LDS Archives.

know that. But you will know the principle is true & will greatly Rejoice in what it will bring to you." But How I asked. Can I teach my Sister what I mySelf do not understand or *Show* her what I do not mySelf See? "But you will See & underStand it" <he Said> and when you open your mouth to talk to your Sister light will come to you & your mouth will be full & your toung loose. "And I will today preach a Sermon <to you> that no one but you will understand." Both of these promices ware more than fulfilled—The text for his Sermon was Our use of the "*One, Five, & Ten* talents." And as God had now Commanded Plural marriage and as Exaltation & dominion of the Saints depended upon the number of there Righteous posterity. From him ~~him~~ who was found but with the one Talent It would be taken & given to him that had *Ten.* . . And I now bear an Earnest Testimony That his other prediction was more than fulfilled. For when with great hesitation and Stamering I called my Sister . . . and Stood before her Shaking with fear. Just So Soon as I found powr to *open* my *mouth* it was filled for the Light of the Lord Shone upon my understanding and the Subject that had Seemed So dark, now apeared of all Subjects pertaining to our Gospel the most lucid & plain. And So both my Sister & mySelf ware converted togather. And never <again> did I need evidence or argument to Sustain that high & Holy principle.

And within a few days of this period my Sister acompanied me to Nauvoo where at our Sister Delcenas we Soon met the prophet with his *Bro* Hyrum and *Wm* Clayton as his private *Sec* who always acompanied him—Brother Hyram at once took me in hand aparently in fear I was not fully Converted and this was the manner of his talk to me—"Now Benjamin you must not be afraid of this new doctrine for it is all Right. You Know Brother Hyram don't get Carried away by worldly things, and he faught this principle untill the Lord Showed him it was true. . ." This was the manner of *Bro* Hyrams teaching to me. Which I then did not need as I was *fully Converted*—Meanwhile the Prophet with Louisa B<eeman> and my Sister Delcena had it agreeably aranged with Sister Almara and after a little instruction, She Stood by the Prophets Side & was Sealed to him as a wife by Brother Clayton. After which the Prophet asked me to take my Sister to ocupy Room No 10 in his Mansion home dureing her Stay in the City. But as I could not long be absent from my home & Buisness We Soon Returned to Ramus. Whare on <the> 15*th* of May Some three weeks later the Prophet again Came and at my house ocupied the Same Room & Bed with my Sister that the month previous he had ocupied with the Daughter of the Late Bishop Patridge[50] as his wife and at this time he Sealed to me <my> First wife for Eternity. And gave to me my first Plural wife. Mary Ann Hale an ophan girl—Raised by my Mother Then living with us—Who is Still with me. . .

---

[50] Edward Partridge (1793–1840) was ordained as the first bishop of the LDS church in 1831. After his death and the remarriage of his wife Lydia, their daughters Eliza Maria and Emily Dow lived in the prophet's home with his wife Emma. Both became his plural wives in Mar. 1843. After Smith's death, Emily was sealed to Brigham Young and Eliza to Amasa Lyman. Compton, *In Sacred Loneliness,* 396–456.

Emma Hale Smith Bidamon (1804–1879), shown here in her later years, was the wife of Mormon prophet Joseph Smith Jr. and a resolute enemy of polygamy. Refusing to follow the Saints west to the Rocky Mountains, she nurtured the conviction in her son, Joseph Smith III, founder of the Reorganized Church of Jesus Christ of Latter Day Saints, that her husband had neither taught nor practiced the plurality doctrine.

On learning from the prophit That eaven in Kirtland "the Lord had Required him to take plural wives and that he had then thought to ask for Some of my Sisters"—The past with its conditions & influences began more fully to unfold to my mind the causes That <must> at least in part have led to the great Apostacy & disruption in Kirtland.

Joseph Smith chose several of his plural wives from women already married.[51] Among them was Mary Elizabeth Rollins Lightner (1818–1913).[52]

MARY ELIZABETH ROLLINS LIGHTNER, AUTOBIOGRAPHY,
SUSA YOUNG GATES COLLECTION, UHI, 18–22, 24–25.

Brother Joseph, and Brother Brigham, came to see me, and invited me to go the next day to his Office in the Brick Store. I was surpris<ed> at this, he asked me if I was afraid to go? I replied, why should I be afraid of a Prophet

---

[51] Bachman, "Study," 124–36; and Van Wagoner, "Mormon Polyandry in Nauvoo," 67–83.

[52] Todd Compton pointed me to Lightner's handwritten autobiography. His overview of Lightner's life and relationship with her husband, Adam, is the best available. For this and related sources on Lightner, see Compton, *In Sacred Loneliness*, 205–27, 686.

of God? He said Bro'Young would come for me. That night I dreamed I was married to him. And occupied an upper Room, in a New House, in the Morning, we were Called to Breakfast, and I wondered what Emma would say to me for I was afraid of her, but Joseph took me by the hand and led me down Stairs, at the foot of wich, Stood Emma smiling at us and conducted us to the Breakfast Room. I awoke then, and did not know what to think of my dream. But on going to the office next day, I received the interpretation for what was my astonishment, When Joseph made Known to me that God had Commanded him in July 1834 to take me for a Wife, but he had not dared to make it known to me, for when he received the Revelation; I was in Missouri and when he did see me, I was married. But he was again commanded, to fulfil the first revelation; or Suffer condemnation—for I was created for him before the foundation of the Earth was laid. I said if the Lord told You such a thing, why dont he come and tell Me? Furthermore, I never would consent to be sealed to him, unless I had a witness for myself. He told me a Great many things concerning the Order, and the Blessings pertaining to it &c. I felt that he and I <were> both wrong for I had dreamed for Years that I belonged to him; and had besought the Lord to take away such thoughts from my heart—No human being can tell my feelings on this occasion.[53] My faith in him, as Prophet almost failed me. I could not sleep, and scarsely Eat. Next day Bro Young came to see me, and said after we left the Office, Joseph told him that an angel appeared to him, and told him that the Lord was well pleased with him; and that I should have a Witness that what he told me was true. I marveled at this—but made it a Subject of prayer, night and day. One night in February I felt impressed to pray as Moses did, in the Battle of Israel, with the Amelekites by holding up my hands towards heaven, I also covered my head with a White Cloth, and I prayed with all <my> soul, that if the doctrine was true, to give me a witness of the same. One night I retired to Bed, but not to sleep; for my mind was troubled so sleep fled from me. My Aunt Gilbert was sleeping with me at the time, When a great light appeared in the Room thinking the Kindling wood was on fire, that was spread on the hearth; I rose up in Bed to look, when lo, a Personage stood in front of the Bed looking at me. Its clothes were whiter than anything I had ever seen, I could look at its Person, but when I saw its face so bright, and more beautiful than any Earthly <being> Could be, and those eyes pearcing me through, and through, I could not endure it, it seemed as if I must die with fear, I fell back in Bed and Covered up my head so as not to see it, I pushed Aunt very hard to have her look up and see it too; but I could not wake her and I could not speak. I thought if she were awake, I would not feel so afraid. As it is, I can never forget that face, it seems to be ever before me. A few days after this Joseph asked

---

[53] In her 1905 address on the subject, Lightner said she felt she was a sinner for such thoughts, but Smith relieved her anxieties in the matter. Lightner, "Address," UPB, 3.

me if I had received a witness Yet? I said no, he said you soon will have; for the Angel expresly told me you should Have—then I told him what I had seen, for I fully realized what I had lost by my cowardice. . . After receiving other Testimonies, I felt I could no longer disbelieve, and in the month of March 1841 Brigham Young Sealed us for time, and all Eternity. . .

[Some time later, after the assassination of Joseph and his brother Hyrum] the Temple was ready for giving the Endowmen<ts>. I with Others, received the Ordinances of that House with its Blessings—I was also sealed to B Young as [as an earthly, temporal] proxy for Joseph—Our persecutions at that time were very hard to bear and we were again obliged to leave our Homes, but we had no means to go with the Church, in fact, we could hardly get enough to eat. But Mr L[ightner], sold some land for W.W Phelps and got money Enough to take us Deck passage to Galena [Illinois]. Brigham asked me if I would go [west] with the Saints, I told him I wanted to, he said that was right. A few days after this conversation, Mr Burk came in and said B Young and family were Crossing the River on the ice, I went out to see if it was true. It was— I felt stuned, the thought came to me that Poligamy was of the Devil—and Brigham knew it, or he would have cut off his right hand before he would have left me, for he Said he would give anything to have seen what I had— And if it had not have taken place I should have denied the faith, there, and then. I wept myself sick, and felt to give up, and go among the Gentiles in fact I felt as though I was like one in an open Boat at Sea, without Compass or Rudder—So when spring opened we went aboard the War Eagle bound for Galena, just before we started, B Young sent word back from Winter Quarters, for me to come on; and the Lord would bless me.

Helen Mar Kimball (1828–1896), the oldest living daughter of Heber Chase and Vilate Murray Kimball, was but fourteen years of age when sealed to Joseph Smith in the spring of 1843. Smith had not dictated his revelation on the subject, but a few of his disciples already had entered the Principle, including Helen's father.[54] In this 1881 reminiscence, Helen recalled the poignant feelings the occasion brought, both for herself and her mother.

HELEN MAR KIMBALL WHITNEY, AUTOBIOGRAPHY,
30 MAR. 1881, LDS ARCHIVES.

Salt Lake City, March 30th 1881
. . . Years passed away and we were living in the City of Nauvoo. Just previous to my father's starting upon his last mission but one, to the Eastern States, he taught me the principle of Celestial marriage, & having a great desire to be connected with the Prophet, Joseph, he offered me to him; this I after-

---

[54] Bergera, "The Earliest Eternal Sealings," 49–50.

Helen Mar Kimball Whitney (1828–1896) was married at fourteen years of age to the Mormon prophet Joseph Smith, as one of his many plural wives. After Smith's death she married Horace Kimball Whitney, who also became a pluralist. Despite personal sorrows associated with the practice, she wrote forcefully in its defense.

wards learned from the Prophet's own mouth. My father had but one Ewe Lamb, but willingly laid her upon the alter: how cruel this seamed to the mother whose heartstrings were already stretched untill they were ready to snap asunder, for he had taken Sarah Noon to wife & she thought she had made sufficient sacrafise, but the Lord required more. I will pass over the temptations which I had during the twenty four hours after my father introduced to me this principle & asked me if I would be sealed to Joseph, who came next morning & with my parents I heard him teach & explain the principle of Celestial marrage—after which he said to me, "If you will take this step, it will ensure your eternal salvation and exaltation & that of your father's household & all of your kindred.["] This promise was so great that I willingly gave myself to purchase so glorious a reward. None but God & his angels could see my mother's bleeding heart—when Joseph asked her if she was willing, she replied "If Helen is willing I have nothing more to say." She had witnessed the sufferings of others, who were older & who better understood the step they were taking, & to see her child, who had scarcely seen her fifteenth summer, following in the same thorny path, in her mind she saw the misery which was as sure to come as the sun was to rise and set; but it was all hidden from me.[55]

---

[55] This account, written for her children, is in Holzapfel and Holzapfel, eds., *A Woman's View*, 482, 486. Editors Jeni and Richard Holzapfel helped me locate the original manuscript.

"So As To Keep It Hid": Polygamy and Secrecy

The prophet and others used mistruths to hide plural marriage, establishing a precedent that was followed in later decades.[56] Other subterfuges were also used, such as a pretended marriage between one of Smith's wives and another man that was performed to mask her connection with the prophet.[57] He also married the Partridge sisters a second time to hide an earlier connection with them unknown to his wife Emma.[58] The puzzling absence of offspring from his plural unions, a lively question that later fueled quarrels between Latter-day Saints in Utah and the Reorganized Church in Missouri, helped obscure Joseph's activities at the time.[59] Regarding the problem that pregnancy created for pluralists generally, there was Ebenezer Robinson's recollection that when Hyrum Smith urged him to enter the Principle, Robinson (1816–1891) was told how the difficulty could be disposed.[60]

Ebenezer Robinson to Jason Briggs, 28 Jan. 1880,
Pleasanton, Iowa, Ebenezer Robinson Collection, lds Archives.

Jason W. Briggs, Dear Bother,[61]

Yours of the 11th inst. is before me, in which you introduce a subject which is not pleasant to dwell upon; but it is not wise for us as individuals, or as a

---

[56] Mormons later argued that false pretense concerning polygamy was required in Nauvoo to save them from persecution. See "Lecture," *Des. News* [Weekly], 19 Oct. 1854, 4:32, 1/4. See also examples in Bachman, "Study," 189–203; Hardy, "Lying for the Lord," *Solemn Covenant*, 363–88; and the thoughtful article by Booth, "Rhetoric of Hypocrisy," 119–33.

[57] Joseph Kingsbury pretended to marry Sarah Ann Whitney on 29 April 1843, but Smith had secretly married her on 27 July 1842. In addition to History of Joseph Corroden Kingsbury, lds Archives, 2, see Marquardt, *Strange Marriages of Sarah Ann Whitney*.

[58] Compton, *In Sacred Loneliness*, 409.

[59] When rlds authorities pointed to this as proof that Joseph Smith could not have taken plural wives, Lucy Walker blamed the "hazardous . . . harassed and hounded" life he lived. Littlefield, *Reminiscences*, 50. The prophet's defenders added that the problem was due to the difficulty of making "connections" with his wives at the right times of the month. See George Albert Smith to Glen Cargyle, 4 Oct. 1949, Subject Folder Collection, ccl-a. Regarding Josephine Rosetta Lyon Fisher, the best-known candidate as Smith's polygamous offspring, see her handwritten statement, 24 Feb. 1915, Joseph F. Smith Affidavits [on celestial marriage], 1869–1915, fd. 1, lds Archives. The question has generated a long shelf of comment. For two examples, see Harold H. Jenson to C. J. Hunt, 20 April 1946; and G. T. Harrison to rlds First Presidency, 16 May 1949, both in fd. 41, P 22, Subject Folder Collection, ccl-a; and Compton, "Fawn Brodie on Joseph Smith's Plural Wives," 164–73.

[60] Robinson first made a statement when Joseph Smith III and others insisted the church's founder did not espouse plurality. Affidavit, 29 Dec. 1873, Robinson Collection, lds Archives. Six years later, replying to claims that he had repudiated his affidavit, Robinson emphatically reaffirmed its contents. Robinson to E. L. Kelley, Esq., 24 Nov. 1879, lds Archives.

[61] After Joseph Smith's death, Jason Briggs (1821–1899) first supported Brigham Young and then, successively, James J. Strang, William Smith, and Joseph Smith III.

people, to ignore the truths of the past, but to look the history of the past squarely in the face, so that we may be the better prepared to shun the errors and emulate the good.

You ask me *ten* questions which you number in order:

"1st Where and at what time do you date the introduction of polygamy in the church?"

Answer—The doctrine of "spiritual wives" was talked ~~freely~~, *privately* in the church in Nauvoo, in 1841. This I always considered polygamy. . .

"4th "How did Hyrum Smith teach you to practice polygamy so as to keep it hid?"

Answer—He instructed me <in Nov. or Dec. 1843,> to make a selection of some young woman, and he would seal her to me, and I should take her home, and if she should have an offspring give out word that she had a husband, an Elder, who had gone on a foreign mission.

"5th Was there a place appointed in Iowa, 12 or 18 miles from Nauvoo to send female victims to hid[e] polygamous births?"

Answer—We were told that there was a place, a few miles out of Nauvoo, in Illinois, where females were sent for that purpose. . .

"6th "Did you understand from Hyrum Smith in 1843 that polygamy & spiritual wifery was identical?["]

Answer—I did. . .

"10th & last "Do you believe that any kind of deception or falsehood can promote truth or is in any sense justifiable?"

Answer—I do not.

Respectfully & Truly, Yours
E. Robinson

"BENNETT MADE ME DO IT!": SCANDAL ERUPTS

Despite efforts to hide plural marriage, public debate on the subject erupted in 1842. This went beyond concern over occasional lapses by missionaries and others that occur in every religious organization.[62] Dr. John C. Bennett (1804–1867), an opportunist of questionable credentials but one given high ecclesiastical honor by the prophet, was found taking liberties with Nauvoo's wives and daughters. The news was especially unsettling because the Lord had supposedly told Joseph Smith in 1841 that He had accepted and approved Bennett's work, and if continued would "crown him with blessings and great glory."[63] In response to Bennett's charges that he was not alone, Mormon lead-

---

[62] As a Mormon instance, see problems described in the Diary of Joseph Fielding, bk. 4, 3 Sept. 1841, LDS Archives, 76–77.   [63] *D&C* 124:17, 19 Jan. 1841.

ers published explicit denials that they practiced polygamy and excommunicated him.[64] As a parting blow, however, Bennett wrote scurrilous accounts
of Smith's alleged sexual adventures in letters to the *Sangamo Journal*, a Whig
newspaper in Springfield, Illinois.[65] These were subsequently gathered into a
book in which Bennett embroidered his original statements yet further. The
book claimed, for example, that the church president organized Nauvoo women
into secret, lodge-like orders where unrestrained sexual indulgence was practiced, an erroneous but likely reference to the Female Relief Society, where
most of its officers had secretly become plural wives of the prophet.[66]

"FURTHER MORMON DEVELOPMENTS!! 2ND LETTER FROM GEN. BENNETT,"
SANGAMO JOURNAL, 15 JULY 1842, 10:47, 2/3–5.

John C. Bennett, To the Editor of the Journal . . . 2 July 1842.
    . . . Joe Smith stated to me at an early day in the history of that city [Nau-
voo], that he intended to make that amiable and accomplished lady [Mrs.
Sarah M. Pratt] one of his *spiritual wives,* for the Lord had given her to him,
and he requested me to assist him in consummating his hellish purposes, but
I told him that I would not do it—that she had been much neglected and
abused by the church during the absence of her husband [Apostle Orson Pratt]
in Europe, and that if the Lord had given her to him he must attend to it
himself. I will do it, said he, for there is no harm in it if her husband should
never find out . . . accordingly in a few days. . . We then proceeded to the
house where Mrs. Pratt resided, and Joe commenced [to?] discourse as follows: "Sister Pratt, the Lord has given you to me as one of my spiritual wives.
I have the blessings of Jacob granted me, as he granted holy men of old, and
I have long looked upon you with favor, and hope you will not deny me." She
replied: "I care not for the blessings of Jacob, and I believe in no such revelations, neither will I consent under any circumstances. I have one good husband and that is enough for me." Joe could not come it! He then went off to
see Miss ———. . . Three times afterward he tried to convince Mrs. Pratt

---

[64] *Times and Seasons* 3:23, 1 Oct. 1842, 939–40. How Bennett could have deceived Mormon leaders, who
admitted they received early notice of his character, is puzzling. See Smith Jr., *History of the Church,* 5:35–36.
"Bennett was probably the greatest scamp in the western country," Gov. Thomas Ford wrote, and in Ohio,
Indiana, and Illinois "he was every where accounted the same debauched, unprincipled and profligate character." Ford, *History of Illinois,* 263. For more on Bennett's sordid career, see Bachman, "Study," 218–33, 249–57;
and Smith, *Saintly Scoundrel.*

[65] These were: "Astounding Mormon Disclosures! Letter from Gen. Bennett," *Sangamo Journal,* 8 July
1842, 10:46 [2/4–6]; "Further Mormon Developments!! 2nd Letter from Gen. Bennett," ibid., 15 July 1842,
10:47 [2/3–5]; in the same issue, "Gen. Bennett's third Letter," ibid.; and, finally, "Gen. Bennett's 4th Letter," ibid., 22 July 1842, 10:48 [2/3–4].

[66] Bennett, *History of the Saints,* 220–25 passim. Regarding Smith's relationship with the Relief Society,
see Newell and Avery, *Mormon Enigma,* 108–9, 114–15.

of the propriety of his doctrine, and she at last told him: "Joseph, if you ever attempt anything of the kind with me again, I will tell Mr. Pratt on his return home. I will certainly do it." Joe replied, "Sister Pratt, I hope you will not expose me. Will you agree *not* to do so?" "If," said she, "you will never insult me again, I will not expose you unless strong circumstances require it." "Well, sister Pratt," says Joe, "as you have refused me, it becomes sin, unless *sacrifice* is offered;" and turning to me he said, "General, if you are my friend I wish you to procure a lamb and have it slain, and sprinkle the door posts and the gate with its blood, and take the kidneys and the entrails and offer them upon an altar of twelve stones that have not been touched with a hammer, as a burnt offering, and it will save me and my priesthood.[67] Will you do it?" I will, I replied . . . and Joe said, "all is now safe—the destroying angel will pass over, without harming any of us." Times passed on in apparent friendship until Joe grossly insulted Mrs. Pratt again, after her husband had returned home, by approaching and kissing her. This highly offended her, and she told Mr. Pratt, who was much enraged and went and told Joe never to offer an insult of the like again.—Joe replied, "I did not desire to kiss her, Bennett made me do it!" Joe, you can't come it! Mrs. Pratt is far above your foul and polluted breath, your calumny and detraction. I now appeal to Mrs. Pratt if this is not true to the very letter. Just speak out boldly.[68]

"GREAT HAIL STONES OF TRUTH": DEFENDING THE PRINCIPLE

The Bennett affair was only the most conspicuous indicator of moral disquietude in Nauvoo. From 1842 until the exodus west, Mormon society was never free from the tar of sexual scandal. And alleged unsavory behavior extended beyond the activities of a knave like Bennett. "Adulterors fornicators & evil persons," Wilford Woodruff wrote, "crept into our midst."[69] Telling of

---

[67] Despite his exaggerations, Bennett is not entirely without credibility. As a young treasure hunter, Joseph Smith allegedly used animal sacrifice to increase his success. Vogel, *Joseph Smith*, 73, 89. And, two years previous to the Bennett episode, the prophet stated that burned offerings would be restored under the direction of the priesthood. Smith Jr., *History of the Church*, 4:210–12. For a derisive, contemporary response to Bennett's claims concerning animal sacrifice, see "Bennett As He Is," *Wasp* 1:15, 23 July 1842, 58.

[68] Forty years later, Sarah Pratt's recollections of the prophet's attentions said nothing about animal sacrifice but were basically the same as those recited by Bennett. See Workings of Mormonism related by Mrs. Orson Pratt, 1884, LDS Archives. When in 1842 Mrs. Pratt told her husband about the prophet's advances, a rupture occurred between the two men, resulting in Orson Pratt's excommunication. He was eventually restored to the apostleship and, ironically, became Mormonism's best-known champion of the Principle, a husband to at least seven wives and sire of forty-five children. See Van Wagoner, "Sarah M. Pratt," 69–72.

[69] Kenney, ed., *Wilford Woodruff's Journal*, 27 May 1842, 2:177.

"seducing efforts" and "carnal connexion," respected Saints like Orson Spencer leveled charges against men and women alike for "unchaste and unvirtuous conduct."[70] Church leaders were rumored to be proposing liaisons with women other than their wives.[71] And some, pointing to the authorities, used their example to justify a more relaxed ethic, as illustrated in the declaration by one that "such illicit conduct was practiced by the Heads of the Church & that the time would come when men would have more wives than one, & he wished that time would come."[72]

Concern arose over prostitution in Nauvoo and its suburbs.[73] When the Female Relief Society enlarged its purposes to include moral surveillance, the prophet told members to temper their vigilance and spare the community greater scandal.[74] Admitting that there was "a great noise in the City" concerning his reputation and that some were insisting that with so much smoke there must be fire, Smith did not deny the allegations, only saying that if such things were so then the discredited John C. Bennett's stories were true as well. He pleaded that church members stop "devouring" themselves with gossip and incrimination.[75] With candor, Smith confessed to human weakness: "I am," he said, "subject to like passions as other men, like the prophets of olden time."[76]

Joseph Smith clearly grew impatient with deceit and showed signs of fully opening the Principle to all his followers.[77] In a sermon given only days after dictating the revelation on plural marriage, he spoke of eternal family life, "but on account of the unbelief of the people," he said, "I cannot reveal the fullness of these things at present."[78] This may be why he sometimes tested

[70] Smith Jr., *History of the Church*, 24 May 1842, 5:18; ibid., 27 June 1842, 5:21; Orson Spencer affidavits, 29 Aug. and 4 Sept. 1842, Nauvoo Stake High Council Court Papers, fd. 1, LDS Archives; and the hearings reviewed by Bergera in "'Illicit Intercourse,' Plural Marriage, and the Nauvoo Stake High Council," 59–90.

[71] See, for example, accusations surrounding Brigham Young and Martha Brotherton. Van Wagoner, *Mormon Polygamy*, 20.

[72] Spencer affidavit, 29 Aug. 1842, Nauvoo Stake High Council Court Papers, fd. 1, LDS Archives.

[73] Smith Jr., *History of the Church*, 14 May 1842, 5:8; testimony given in *Reorganized Church vs. The Church of Christ*, 190–93; and Bergera, "'Illicit Intercourse,'" 66.

[74] Smith Jr., *History of the Church*, 30 Mar. 1842, 4:570; ibid., 26 May 1842, 5:19–21; ibid., 31 Aug. 1842, 5:140; ibid., 15 Oct. 1843, 6:58; and Newell and Avery, *Mormon Enigma*, 106–18.

[75] Church Historian's Office History of the Church, reel 4:1675, 21 Feb. 1843, LDS Archives.

[76] Ibid., reel 4:1680, 23 July 1843; and ibid., reel 4:1555, 21 May 1843, both in LDS Archives.

[77] History of Joseph Lee Robinson, 9, LDS Archives; and George A. Smith, 18 Mar. 1855, *Journal of Discourses*, 2:217.

[78] Church Historian's Office History of the Church, reel 4:1675, 16 July 1843, LDS Archives.

his closest associates, asking them to give him their wives.[79] And it may have been partly responsible for the publication of Udney Hay Jacob's thirty-seven-page pamphlet, consisting of two chapters of a promised forthcoming book. Extensively edited here, Jacob (1781–1860) wrote it even before he joined the church. Addressed to the general citizenry of the nation, it was printed on Joseph Smith's press in Nauvoo and circulated in the autumn of 1842. John D. Lee later said that church authorities persuaded Jacob to issue the pamphlet as a "feeler among the people, to pave the way for celestial marriage."[80]

Lee may have overstated the work's connection with Mormon leaders. The best explanation for the treatise, simply linking its inspiration to defense of the Saints against criticism, appears in Jacob's own 1851 statement to Brigham Young: "that pamphlet was not written for this people but for the citizens of the United States who professed to believe the Bible. At the same time it was an apology for this people who were accused by them of Polygamy."[81] If this was the work's intent, it did not succeed, coming as it did on the heels of the Bennett episode and similar disturbances. While Joseph Smith publicly repudiated the essay, as Lawrence Foster observed, the prophet only "mildly dissociated himself" from it.[82] In addition to a scriptural defense of polygamy and integral to its justification for the practice, the work pleaded for a restoration of firm patriarchal authority in the home, an argument repeated many times by Mormons in decades to come.[83] Indeed, some contend that the anomie created by plural marriages, especially those involving women already espoused to others, naturally cultivated female reliance on patriarchal authority.[84]

---

[79] Smith's motives here, as with much that he did, are unlikely ever to be understood completely. A later Mormon spokesman said it was primarily to test other men's devotion to their priesthood leaders that Smith sometimes asked for their wives. See "Discourse By Jedediah M. Grant," 19 Feb. 1854, *Des. News* [Weekly], 8 June 1854, 4:15 [1/6]. For further commentary on "tests," see Van Wagoner, *Mormon Polygamy*, 41–49; Cook, "William Law," 65n; and Bergera, "Church and Plural Marriage," 12, 14.

[80] Lee, *Mormonism Unveiled*, 146.

[81] Jacob to Brigham Young, 5 Mar. 1851, Miscellaneous Collection, ccl-a.

[82] Foster, "Little-known Defense," 24.

[83] Cooper, *Promises Made to the Fathers*, 132–99. As late as 1895 Joseph F. Smith cited the pamphlet as authority on divorce and fornication. A. H. Cannon Journals, 10 Oct. 1895, upb, 19:172. The similarity of its arguments to other Mormon statements led some to say it was the work of Joseph Smith himself. In the mid-twentieth century fundamentalist advocates of polygamy printed excerpts as "The Little-Known Discourse of Joseph Smith." See Godfrey, "New Look," 49–53. Lawrence Foster, however, convincingly demonstrated that Jacob was the author. He was baptized into the church in 1843, given his endowments in the Nauvoo temple in 1846, and went west to Salt Lake City, where he died in 1860. Foster, "Little-known Defense," 21–34.

[84] Bradley and Woodward, "Plurality, Patriarchy, and the Priestess," 84–118.

CHAPTER XVIII.

ON THE LAW OF MARRIAGE

. . . Adam was enslaved by the woman, not by the serpent in the first instance, as we are taught by the word; Adam was not deceived, but the woman being deceived was in the transgression. She gave unto the man and he did eat. Therefore said Paul, I suffer not a woman to teach *or to usurp authority over the man, but to be in subjection.* Her law and government over a man we are thus taught by the Holy Spirit is an usurpation of power. But Adam was enslaved by the woman, and so are we. . . Hence we have lost the original dignity, nobleness, and excellency of the masculine mind; and have . . . become effeminate . . . but the alienation of the mind or affections from her husband constitutes fornication in a married woman . . . when a woman apostatizes in spirit from her husband, she then commits fornication against the spiritual law of marriage. . . A right understanding of this matter, and a correct law properly executed, would restore this nation to peace and order; and man to his true dignity, authority and government of the earthly creation. . . Gentlemen, the ladies laugh at your pretended authority. They, many of them hiss, at the idea of your being the lords of the creation. . . But God has positively required this of them. . . Even as Sarah of old that excellent woman, having now no parallel on Earth. And under existing circumstances our wives can never become the daughters of Sarah in the spirit. . . *These are great hail stones of truth that cannot be resisted.* . . Children begotten and born of an alienated woman, are born of fornication in the spirit or mind. This is a great injury to the minds of such children. It injures their intellectual powers, and disposition of mind. . . It is evident that minds or souls are propagated by natural generation as well as bodies. No marvel that wise men are so rare in Christendom. . . But if the husband commit fornication, shall not the wife be entitled to a bill against him? Impossible. . . Where did you ever read in the law of God, or in the holy book, such a false idea?. . . How can property put away its owner? . . .

In ancient times under the law of God, the permission of a plurality of wives had a direct tendency to prevent the possibility of fornication in the wife. For the . . . law of divorcement, and all the law on the subject, sustained the lawful and independent power of the husband over the wife; and his dignity of character was thereby supported. The interest, the hopes, the prospects of the wife, were all turned in the opposite direction by the law; where indeed her mind always should be. Her main object was to win, and retain the affections of her husband. And there was no means more successful for this purpose, than to bear him many children. . . And the wife was perfectly passive,

submissive and non-resisting towards her husband. The existence of fornication in a married woman, that distructive evil, even to her posterity, was then
hardly possible. . .

CHAPTER XIX.
SEVERAL IMPORTANT LAWS OF GOD

. . . But suppose a man (that has already a wife) entice a maid; how then
could he marry her? If a man entice a maid that is not betrothed, and lie with
her, he shall surely endow her to be his wife. Ex. 22:16. There is no condition
that can justify him in refusing to marry her. . . There is no positive law of
God against a man's marrying Leah and Rachel both. So long as he is a good
and faithful husband, he is justified by the law of Christ his lawful head. But
one objects, that it is written, they twain, (not they three) shall be one flesh.
From this he infers that the law of God forbids him to marry more than one
wife. Yet you allow a man to marry another wife if his first wife be dead; which
would constitute three, one flesh, as much so, as if both wives were alive at
the same time. But the fact is, two females cannot become one flesh.—When
Jacob married Leah, they twain became one flesh; of this compound Rachel
formed no part. And when Jacob married Rachel, they twain became one flesh;
of this compound Leah constituted no part, any more than if she had been
dead, when Jacob married Rachel. It is still no more than twain that became
one flesh. And it is evident that none other could be the result, had Jacob
married as many wives as King David; a man after God's own heart, or even
as King Solomon. . . But if you my countrymen refuse voluntarially to restore
the law of God, to your own glory and honor; the Son of Man may compel
you to do it; to your everlasting loss: . . . For the *marriage* bed is shorter than
that a man can stretch himself on it; and the covering is narrower than that
he can wrap himself in it.

"A NEW AND AN EVERLASTING COVENANT": THE 1843 REVELATION

Inasmuch as some of the most intense opposition to plural marriage originated inside the church, including from the prophet's own wife, Hyrum Smith
suggested that Joseph reduce God's revelation to paper, thinking divine command would convince her and other doubters.[85] The prophet consented and
William Clayton (1814–1879), his assistant, recorded the message. Years later,
when the prophet's son and others alleged that the practice was an invention

---

[85] For difficulties in Nauvoo after the Bennett affair, see Godfrey, "Causes of Mormon–Non-Mormon Conflict," 95–132; Bachman, "Study," 218–60; and Newell and Avery, *Mormon Enigma*, 95–182.

of Brigham Young, church leaders in Utah gathered material to refute the claim.[86] One of the most important pieces of evidence obtained was Clayton's notarized statement describing the dictation of the revelation and identifying some of the women the prophet took as his plural wives.[87]

[WILLIAM CLAYTON], "CELESTIAL MARRIAGE:
HOW AND WHEN THE REVELATION WAS GIVEN,"
DES. EVE. NEWS, 20 MAY 1886, 19:151, 2/2–3.

Inasmuch as it may be interesting to future generations of the members of the Church of Jesus Christ of Latter-day Saints to learn something of the first teachings of the principle of plural marriage by President Joseph Smith, the Prophet, Seer, Revelator and Translator of said Church, I will give a short relation of facts which occurred within my personal knowledge, and also matters related to me by President Joseph Smith. . .

During this period the Prophet Joseph frequently visited my house in my company, and became well acquainted with my wife Ruth, to whom I had been married five years. One day in the month of February, 1843 . . . the Prophet invited me to walk with him. During our walk, he said he had learned that there was a sister back in England, to whom I was very much attached. I replied, there was, but nothing further than an attachment, such as a brother and sister in the Church might rightfully entertain for each other. He then said, "Why don't you send for her?" I replied, "In the first place, I have no authority to send for her, and if I had, I have not the means to pay expenses." To this he answered, "I give you authority to send for her, and I will furnish you the means," which he did. This was the first time the Prophet Joseph talked with me on the subject of plural marriage. He informed me that the doctrine and principle was right in the sight of our Heavenly Father and that it was a doctrine which pertained to Celestial order and glory. After giving me lengthy instructions and information concerning the doctrine of celestial or plural marriage, he concluded his remarks by the words, "It is your privilege to have all the wives you want." After this introduction, our conversations on the subject of plural marriage were very frequent, and he appeared to take particular pains to inform and instruct me in respect to the principle. He also informed

---

[86] Joseph F. Smith Affidavits [on celestial marriage], 1869–1915, 4 fds., LDS Archives. Ebenezer Robinson chastised Joseph Smith III for denying that his father had introduced the practice: "Having a perfect personal knowledge of these facts, together with many others not here stated, a denial of them sounds to me like a *great lie*. I am sorry it is so. But we cannot undo the past." Robinson to Smith [III], Jan. 1888, Miscellaneous Collection, fd. III, CCL-A.

[87] This statement closely resembles an earlier letter Clayton wrote in 1871. See Clayton to Madison M. Scott, 11 Nov. 1871, LDS Archives. Clayton prepared the statement reproduced here in 1874. It was enclosed with a Joseph F. Smith 15 May 1886 letter to the *Deseret News*. The original 1874 document is in Joseph F. Smith Affidavits [on celestial marriage], 1869–1915, fd. 1, LDS Archives. It was republished as "Celestial Marriage," *Woman's Exponent* 15:1 (1 June 1886), 1–2, and again as Clayton, "William Clayton's Testimony," 224–26.

me that he had other wives living besides the first wife Emma, and in partic-ular, gave me to understand that Eliza R. Snow, Louisa Beman, Desdamona C. Fullmer and others, were his lawful wives in the sight of Heaven. . .

On the 1st day of May, 1843, I officiated in the office of an Elder by Mar-rying Lucy Walker to the Prophet Joseph Smith, at his own residence.

During this period the Prophet Joseph took several other wives. . .

On the morning of the 12th of July, 1843, Joseph and Hyrum Smith came into the office in the upper story of the "brick store," on the bank of the Mis-sissippi river. They were talking on the subject of plural marriage. Hyrum said to Joseph, "If you will write the revelation on Celestial Marriage, I will take and read it to Emma, and I believe I can convince her of its truth, and you will hereafter have peace." Joseph smiled and remarked, "You do not know Emma as well as I do." Hyrum repeated his opinion and further remarked, "The doc-trine is so plain, I can convince any reasonable man or woman of its truth, purity and heavenly origin," or words to their effect. Joseph then said, "well, I will write the revelation and we will see." He then requested me to get paper and prepare to write. Hyrum very urgently requested Joseph to write the rev-elation by means of the Urim and Thummim, but Joseph, in reply said he did not need to, for he knew the revelation perfectly from beginning to end.[88]

Joseph and Hyrum then sat down, and Joseph commenced to dictate the revelation on Celestial Marriage, and I wrote it, sentence by sentence, as he dictated. After the whole was written, Joseph asked me to read it through, slowly and carefully, which I did and he pronounced it correct. He then remarked that there was much more that he could write, on the same subject, but what was written was sufficient for the present.

Hyrum then took the Revelation to read to Emma. Joseph remained with me in the office until Hyrum returned. When he came back Joseph asked how he had succeeded. Hyrum replied that he had never received a more severe talk-ing to in his life, that Emma was very bitter and full of resentment and anger.

Joseph quietly remarked, "I told you, you did not know Emma as well as I did." Joseph then put the Revelation in his pocket, and they both left the office.

The Revelation was read to several of the authorities during the day. Towards evening Bishop Newel K. Whitney asked Joseph if he had any objections to his taking a copy of the Revelation; Joseph replied that he had not, and hand-ed it to him. It was carefully copied the following day by Joseph C. Kings-bury. Two or three days after the Revelation was written Joseph related to me and several others that Emma had so teased and urgently entreated him for the privilege of destroying it, that he became so weary of her teasing, and to

---

[88] An instrument used for translating ancient records and communicating with deity. Mentioned in the Bible (Exodus 28:30 and Numbers 27:18–21), it also was used by Joseph Smith and referred to in his writ-ings. "Urim and Thummim," Ludlow, *Encyclopedia of Mormonism*, 4:1499–1500.

get rid of her annoyance, he told her she might destroy it and she had done so, but he had consented to her wish in this matter to pacify her, realizing that he knew the Revelation perfectly, and could re-write it at any time if necessary.[89]

The copy made by Joseph C. Kingsbury is a true and correct copy of the original in every respect. The copy was carefully preserved by Bishop Whitney, and but few knew of its existence until the temporary location of the Camp of Israel at Winter Quarters, on the Missouri River, in 1846.

After the Revelation on celestial marriage was written Joseph continued his instructions, privately, on the doctrine, to myself and others, and during the last year of his life we were scarcely ever together, alone, but he was talking on the subject, and explaining that doctrine and principles connected with it. He appeared to enjoy great liberty and freedom in his teachings, and also to find great relief in having a few to whom he could unbosom his feelings on that great and glorious subject.

From him, I learned that the doctrine of plural and celestial marriage is the most holy and important doctrine ever revealed to man on the earth, and without obedience to that principle no man can ever attain to the fulness of exaltation in celestial glory.

(Signed) William Clayton.
Salt Lake City, February 16th, 1874.

Clayton's recollection puts the 1843 revelation in context. The prophet had unquestionably entertained justifications for the Principle for some time, and he incorporated earlier teachings, such as those relating to the sealing power and the nature of life in heaven, in the 1843 document. As William Clayton indicated, the prophet said he already "knew the revelation perfectly from beginning to end." But rather than the teleological unfolding that some impose on the doctrine's formal appearance, its issuance appears to be quite pragmatic.[90] Joseph F. Smith, a nephew, admitted years later that it took the form it did because of problems with the church founder's wife.[91] It seems most likely that the 1843 writing was a summation of Smith's thought over many years, includ-

---

[89] For Emma's alleged destruction of the original copy of the revelation, see Newell and Avery, *Mormon Enigma*, 153–54; and Quinn, *Mormon Hierarchy*, 1:147.

[90] For descriptions of the 1843 revelation as a logical sequel to earlier Mormon doctrines, see Roberts in Smith Jr., *History of the Church*, 5:xxix–xxxii; Dorius, "Marriage and Family," 155–68; and Godfrey, "Plural Marriage," 927–29. Bachman said that the 1843 document was a union of two revelations, one the prophet received perhaps as early as 1831, and that of July 1843. Bachman, "Study," 58–59.

[91] "Discourse Delivered By Elder Jos. F. Smith," 7 July 1878, *Des. News* [Weekly], 11 Sept. 1878, 27:32, 498/4. Grant Ivins told Mary Bennion Powell that his father, stake president and later Apostle Anthony W. Ivins, told him that, regarding the prophet's issuance of the doctrine, "He had to have a revelation, my boy, he had to!" Powell to Stewart, CSmH, 183.

ing recitations to friends,[92] expositions to prospective wives, and conflicted conversations with his wife Emma—but at last formally dictated only because of crisis. In the end, however, whatever explanations historians retrospectively impose on the document, we must in fairness to Smith accept the dictation as his most complete, putatively inspired justification for the Principle.

As William Clayton noted, the Saints carried but one copy of the revelation west. Willard Richards probably copied it again after the pioneers reached Winter Quarters.[93] Eventually other reproductions were made and circulated by members and non-members of the church. It was not included in the *Doctrine and Covenants*, however, until 1876, thirty-three years after the prophet's original dictation. That printing omitted the 1835 section affirming the Mormon commitment to monogamy. An analysis by Robert Woodford of the versified, 1876 printing shows that while alterations of punctuation and spelling occurred, there has been a remarkable fidelity to the earliest extant texts.[94] The following is an edited copy of the Kingsbury transcription.[95]

THE 1843 REVELATION, REVELATIONS COLLECTION,
REEL 2, LDS ARCHIVES.

Nauvoo, July 10th, 1843

Verily thus saith the Lord, unto you, my Servant Joseph, that inasmuch as you have enquired of my hand to know and understand wherein! [*sic*] I the Lord justified my Servants, Abraham Isaac and Jacob; as also, Moses, David and Solomon, my Servants, as touching the principle and doctrin of their having many Wives and Concubines: Behold! And Lo, I am the Lord thy God, and will answer thee as touching this matter: Therefore prepare thy heart to receive and obey the instructions which I am about to give unto you, for all

---

[92] For example, see the prophet's "instructions" given two months before the revelation of 12 July 1843, in *D&C* 131:1–4, 16–17 May 1843.

[93] Helen Mar Whitney, "Scenes and Incidents at Winter Quarters," *Woman's Exponent*, 14:4 (15 July 1885), 30–31; and Woodford, "Historical Development," 3:1738.

[94] Woodford, "Historical Development," 1:4.

[95] This is taken from Joseph Kingsbury's transcription, but a second copy, probably the one Willard Richards made at Winter Quarters, is in the same folder. The last page of Kingsbury's script is in an unidentified hand, perhaps that of Richards, who may also have inserted new punctuation marks and darkened faded ones in the manuscript. The original editor inserted paragraphing marks that are shown here as π, but the script also included spaces that may have indicated paragraph breaks. These are inserted as they appear in the hand-written document. I have attempted to retain all insertions and marks in the Kingsbury copy. Other accounts of how and when the copying was done are William Clayton to Madison M. Scott, 11 Nov. 1871, LDS Archives; Kingsbury, "Joseph C. Kingsbury's Testimony," 226; and Kingsbury's recollections in *Reorganized Church vs. Church of Christ*, 333–43. Bachman made a carefully referenced study of the provenance of the Kingsbury copy in his "The Authorship," 32–36. Willard Richards, in his copy, corrected the date to 12 July 1843, a date William Clayton confirmed in his affidavit. Marquardt printed the entire revelation, taken from the same source, in his *Joseph Smith Revelations*, 323–28, no. 169.

those, who have this law revealed unto them, must obey the Same; for behold! I reveal unto you a new and an everlasting Covenant, and if ye abide not that Covenant, then are ye damned; for no one Can reject this Covenant, and be permitted to enter into my glory; . . . and as pertaining to the new and everlasting Covenant, it was instituted for the fulness of my glory; and he that receiveth a fulness thereof, must and shall abide the law, or he shall be damned, saith the Lord God. And verily I say unto you, that the Conditions of this law are these: all Covenants, Contracts, bonds; obligations, oaths, vows, performances, Connexions, associations or expectations that are not made and entered into and Sealed by the Holy Spirit of promise of him who is anointed both as well for time and for all eternity, and that too most holy, by Revelation and Commandment, through the medium of mine anointed whom I have appointed on the earth to hold this power, and I have appointed unto my servant Joseph to hold this power in the last days, and there is never but one on the earth at a time on whom this power and the keys of this priesthood is confered . . . for all Contracts that are not made unto this end, have an end when men are dead. . . π Therefore, if a man marry him a Wife, in the World, and he marry her not by me, nor by <my> Word; and he Covenant with her so long as he is in the World, and She with him, their Covenant and marriage is not of force when they are dead, and when they are out of the World; therefore, they are not bound by any law when they are out of the World; therefore, when they are out of the World, they neither marry nor are given in marriage, but are appointed angels in heaven, which angels are ministering servants to minister for those, who are Worthy of a far more, and an exceeding, and an eternal weight of glory; for these angels did not abide my law, therefore they cannot be enlarged, but remain separately and Single without exaltation in their Saved Condition to all eternity, and from henceforth are not Gods, but are angels of God for ever and ever. . . π And again, verily I say unto you, if a man marry a wife by my Word, which is my law, and by the new and everlasting Covenant, and it is Sealed unto them by the Holy Spirit of promise, by him who is anointed, unto Whom I have appointed this power, and the keys of this priesthood, and it shall be said unto them ye Shall come forth in the first resurrection; and if it be after the first resurrection, in the next resurrection, and shall inherit thrones, kingdoms, principalities, and powers, dominions, all heights and depths, then Shall it be written in the Lamb's book of life, that he shall Commit no murder, whereby to shed innocent blood; and if ye abide in my Covenant and Commit no murder whereby to Shed innocent blood, it shall be done unto them in all things whatsoever my Servant hath put upon them in time and through all Eternity; and shall be of full force when they are out of the World, and they shall pass by the angels and the Gods which are set there, to their exaltation and glory in all things, as hath been sealed upon their heads, which glory shall be a fulness, and a continuation of the seeds forever and ever. π Then shall they be Gods, because they have no end, therefore shall they be from everlasting to everlasting, because they continue, then shall they be above all, because all things are subject unto them. Then shall they be Gods. Because they have all power, and the angels are subject unto them... π This is eternal lives, to <know> the only Wise and true God, and Jesus Christ Whom he hath Sent. I am He. Receive ye, therefore, my law... π Verily, verily I Say unto you, if <a> man marry a Wife according to my Word, and they are Sealed by the Holy Spirit of promise, according to mine appointment, and he or She Shall Commit any sin or transgression of the new and everlasting Covenant whatever, and all manner of blasphemies, and if they Commit no murder, wherein they Shed innocent blood, yet they Shall Come forth in the first resurrection, and enter into their exaltation; but they Shall be destroyed in in the flesh, and Shall be delivered unto the buffetings of Satan unto the day of redemption, Saith the Lord God.   π The blasphemy against the Holy Ghost, Which Shall not be forgiven in the world, nor out of the world, is in that ye Commit murder, Wherein ye shed innocent blood, and assent unto my death, after ye have received my new and everlasting Covenant, Saith the Lord God; and he that abideth not this law, Can in no Wise enter into my glory, but Shall be damned, Saith the Lord.[96]   π I am the Lord thy God, and Will give unto thee the Law of my Holy priesthood, as was ordained by me and my Father before the World Was, Abraham received all things, Whatsoever he received, by Revelation and Commandment, by my word, Saith the Lord, and hath entered into his exaltation, and Sitteth upon his throne. π Abraham received promises Concerning his Seed, and of the fruit of his loines, from Whose loins ye are, viz; my Servant Joseph, Which Were to Continue So long as they were in the World; and as touching Abraham and his Seed, out of the World, they Should Continue, both in the World and out of the World Should they Continue as innumerable as the Stars; or if ye were to Count the Sand upon the Sea Shore, ye Could not number them.   This promise is yours also, because ye are of Abraham, and the promise Was made unto Abraham, and by this law are the Continuation of the works of my Father Where in he gloryfieth himself. Go ye, therefore, and do the Works of Abraham; enter ye into my law, and ye Shall be Saved. But if ye enter not into my law, ye Cannot receive the promises of my Father; Which he made unto Abraham.[97]   π God Commanded Abraham, and Sarah gave Hagar to Abraham to wife And Why did She do it? Because this Was the law, and from Hagar Sprang many people. This Therefore, Was

---

[96] The concern with shedding innocent blood found in this revelation may be related to the later doctrine of blood atonement. There is a considerable bibliography on the subject, but one can begin with statements by Joseph Smith, in Smith Jr., *History of the Church*, 5:296, 4 Mar. 1843, and Brigham Young, 8 Feb. 1857, *Journal of Discourses*, 4:219.

[97] The prominence of Abraham in Mormon thought, especially in the nineteenth century, is one of many parallels with Islam. See, for instance, the remarks of Peters, *Monotheists*, 102–3. For more on the special role given Abraham by Mormons, with the complexities brought by that relationship, see Mauss, *All Abraham's Children*.

fulfilling among other things the promises. Was Abraham, therefore, under condemnation? Verily, I say unto you, *Nay*, for I the Lord commanded it. Abraham Was commanded to offer his Son Isaac; nevertheless, it was written thou Shalt not kill; Abraham however, did not refuse, and it was accounted unto him for righteousness.   π Abraham received Concubines, and they bare him children, and it Was accounted unto him for righteousness, because they Were given unto him, and he abode in my law: as Isaac also, and Jacob did none other things, than that which they were Commanded; and because they did none other things than that Which they were Commanded, they have entered into their exaltation according to the promises, and Sit upon thrones; and are not angels, but are Gods.   David also received many Wives and Concubines, as d̶ also Solomon, and Moses my Servant; as also many others of my Servants from the beginning of Creation until this time; and in nothing did they Sin, Save in those things Which they received not of me. π David's Wives and Concubines Were given unto him, of me, by the hand of Nathan my Servant, and others of the prophets Who had the keys of this power, and in none of these things did he Sin against me, Save in the case of Uriah and his Wife, and therefore, he hath fallen from his exaltation, and received his portion; and he Shall not inherit them out of the World; for I gave them unto another, saith the Lord.   π I am the Lord, thy God, and I gave unto thee, my Servant Joseph, an appointment, and restore all things; Ask What ye Will and it Shall be given unto you, according to my Word; and as ye have asked concerning adultery, Verily, Verily I Say unto you, if a man receiveth a Wife in the new and Everlasting Covenant, and if She be With another man, and I have not appointed unto her by the holy anointing, She hath Committed adultery, and Shall be destroyed. If She be not in the new and Everlasting Covenant, and she be With another man, She has Committed adultery; and if her husband be with another Woman, and he was under a vow, he hath broken his vow, and hath committed adultery; and if She hath not Committed adultery, but <is> innocent, and hath not broken her Vow, and She knoweth it, and I reveal it unto you, my Servant Joseph, then Shall you have power by the power of my Holy priesthood to take her, and give her unto him that hath not Committed adultery, but hath been faithful; for he Shall be made ruler over many; for I have Conferred upon you the Keys and power of the priesthood, wherein I restore all things, and make known unto you all things in due time.[98]   π And Verily, Verily I say unto you, that Whatsoever you Seal on Earth Shall be Sealed in heaven, and Whatsoever you bind on earth in my name, and by my Word, Saith the Lord, it Shall be eternally bound in the heavens; and W̶h̶o̶s̶o̶e̶v̶e̶r̶ Whosesoever Sins you remit on earth, Shall be remitted eternally in the heavens; and Whosesoever Sins you retain on earth, Shall be retained in heaven.   And again,

---

[98] Raising the issue of adultery here seems to confirm Joseph Lee Robinson's statement that the prophet said he was concerned that he would be penalized in the next life for adultery. Smith said the Lord told him he had not committed adultery, Robinson reported. See History of Joseph Lee Robinson, LDS Archives.

Verily I Say Whomsoever you bless, I will bless; and Whomsoever you Curse, I will Curse, Saith the Lord, for I the Lord am thy God. . .   π Verily I say unto you, a Commandment I give unto mine handmaid, Emma Smith, your Wife, Whom I have given unto you, that She Stay herself and partake not of that Which I commanded you to offer unto her.[99] For I did it, saith the Lord, to prove you all, as I did Abraham; and that I might require an offering at your hand by Covenant and Sacrifice: and let my handmaid, Emma Smith, receive all those that have been given unto my Servant Joseph, and who are virtuous and pure before me; and those who are not pure, <and have said they ware pure>, Shall be destroyed, saith the Lord God. . .   and I Command mine handmaid, Emma Smith, to abide and Cleave unto my Servant Joseph; and to none else;[100] But if She will not abide this Commandment, She Shall be destroyed, Saith the Lord; for I am the Lord thy God, and Will destroy her, if She abide not in my law; but if She Will not abide this Commandment, then Shall my Servant, Joseph, do all things for her, even as he hath Said, and I Will bless him, and multiply him, and give unto him an hundred fold in this World of ~~fathers and~~ fathers and mothers, brothers and Sisters, houses and lands, Wives and Children, and crowns of eternal life in the eternal Worlds.   And again, Verily I Say, ~~unto you~~ let mine handmaid forgive my Servant Joseph his trespasses, and then Shall She be forgiven her trespasses, Wherein She hath trespaseth against me, and the Lord thy God Will bless her, and multiply her, and make her heart to rejoice. . . [*A different hand completed the transcription from this point.*]   & again, as pertaining to the Law of the priesthood; <I>f any man espouse a virgin, & desire to espouse another, & the first give her consent, & if he espouse the Second, & they are virgins, and have vowed to no other man, then is he justified; he cannot commit adultery, for they are given unto him; for he Cannot commit adulterty with that, that belongeth unto him, & to none else; & if he have ten virgins given <unto> him by ~~this~~ this Law, he cannot Commit adultery, for they belong to him, & they are given unto him, therefore <is he justified>. But if one, or either of the ten virgins, after She is espoused, Shall be with another man, She has Committed adultery, & Shall be destroyed; for they are given unto him to multiply & replenish the earth, according to my Commandment, & to fulfill the promise Which Was given by my father before the foundation of the world, & for their exaltation in the eternal Worlds, that they may ~~have~~ <bear> the Souls of men, for herein is the Work of my father Continued, that he may be Glorified.   π And again, Verily, Verily I Say unto you, if any man have a Wife Who holds the keys of this power, & he teaches unto her the Law of my priesthood as pertaining to these things, then Shall She believe

---

[99] Belief that the prophet contemplated a "spiritual swop" of wives with William Law, based on Joseph Jackson's statement in his exaggerated *Narrative*, 20–21, should be viewed with caution. The best review of the matter remains Newell and Avery, *Mormon Enigma*, 176–77.

[100] In the heat of disagreement, Smith's wife Emma threatened that "if he would indulge himself she would too." See Clayton's journal for 23 June 1843, Smith, ed., *Intimate Chronicle*, 108.

& administer unto him, or She Shall be distroyed, Saith the Lord your God; for I Will distroy her; for I Will magnify my name, upon all those who receive & abide in my law. Therefore, it Shall be lawful in me, if She receive not this law, for him to receive all things, Whatsoever I the lord, his God, Will give unto him, because She did not believe & administer unto him according to my Word; & She then becomes the transgresser, & he is exempt from the law of Sarah, Who administered unto Abraham according to the law, When I Commanded Abraham to take Hagar to Wife. And now, as pertaing [*sic*] to this law, Verily, Verily I Say unto you, I Will reveal more unto you hereafter; therefore, let this suffice for the present. Behold I am Alpha & Omega: <u>Amen</u>.

"An Endless Exaltation": Response to the 1843 Revelation

As noted, Hyrum Smith's hope that a revelation on plurality would subdue opposition from the prophet's wife met with disappointment. Emma was not alone in her reaction. Another Mormon female, listening to Hyrum Smith read the document, told him to stop and said: "'I am full up to here,' drawing her hand across her throat."[101] William Law, a counselor to Joseph Smith in the First Presidency, and three members of the Nauvoo High Council also rejected the revelation.[102] The general ratio of church members who believed the doctrine to those who did not, however, is uncertain.[103] Some who initially struggled with it were eventually converted. An example is Joseph Holbrook (1806–1885), who remembered late in life that, after troubling over the subject while cutting hay one day outside Nauvoo in the summer of 1845, he received a vision in which he saw the grand consequences of plural marriage.

JOSEPH HOLBROOK, LIFE OF JOSEPH HOLBROOK,
WRITTEN BY HIS OWN HAND (CA. 1871), LDS ARCHIVES, 82–83.

I continued to make hay on the prairie during the hay season which was ten miles from Nauvoo. While I was mowing one forenoon in the month of Aug. alone I <had> been much of the time a meditating upon the principle of the doctrine of having more wives than one which I could not so well understand

---

[101] Woolley, "S. A. Woolley's Testimony," 231. Charlotte Haven, a non-member residing in Nauvoo, remembered that as word of the revelation ran through the community, citizens huddled to "whisper what they dare not speak aloud." Haven, "Girl's Letters," 635–36.

[102] See affidavit of Thomas Grover, in L. O. Littlefield to Joseph F. Smith, 7 June 1883, Smith, Incoming Correspondence, 1855–1918, box 12, fd. 16, LDS Archives; and affidavits of David Fullmer and Austin Cowles in Smith, *Blood Atonement*, 79 and 85, respectively.

[103] It gives no sense of the number who accepted the doctrine, but George A. Smith said years later that between one and two hundred Nauvoo residents knew of the revelation. Smith, 13 Aug. 1871, *Journal of Discourses*, 14:213.

but still I believed that it was true because the revelation of God had so declared it by our prophet Joseph Smith when all at once a sensation came over me that I could see worlds upon worlds and systems upon systems and endless eternity of them that no man could number for thousands of solar systems like unto the one that our world forms a part seemed to pass before me in quick succession and I marveled at the power by which all those systems moved in so much harmony for there were systems upon systems moving in their orbits as harmonius as our earth with other planets move in their orbits around the grand center of our system and as space was endless so were the creations of God Endless in point of time or duration and all this is brought about by the revelation I have awarded to my servant Joseph Smith and there is an endless exaltation to man if he will so receive it. Amen and Amen. When I came to myself I was standing . . . with the hule of my scythe on the ground which I had been a mowing as <though> nothing had happened. From this time to <the> present time has been no doubts with regard to those who embrace the New and everlasting covenant which I pray that I may enjoy with all my children from generation to generation.[104]

"Their Unholy Designs":
Opposition Outside the Church

Neighbors of the Saints were especially critical of them, and none were more scathing than Thomas C. Sharp, editor of the *Warsaw Signal*.[105] Using both prose and verse, Sharp attacked the Saints at every opportunity, commonly printing several articles about them in the same issue.[106] Proudly displaying its bitterness, Sharp's paper became a standing anti-Mormon broadside.

[Thomas Sharp], "Why Oppose The Mormons?"
Warsaw Signal and Agricultural, Literary and Commercial Register,
25 April 1844, New Series, 1:11, whole no. 128, 2/2–3.

It is a fact, that can be substantiated by the most unimpeachable testimony, that the discontented spirits in Nauvoo, dare not speak or write one word against the Prophet without risking their lives. And even those who have left the Church will hint at iniquities, which they dare not proclaim. . .

It can be proven that some of Smith's principal supporters, and confidential friends, are among the basest seducers, and violators of female virtue—

---

[104] See also Holbrook and Holbrook, eds., *History of Joseph Holbrook*, 33; and Holbrook's edited journal, Holbrook, ed., "Life of Joseph Holbrook," 1:169–216.

[105] For more on Sharp, see Bergera, "Buckeye's Laments," 350–51; and Oaks and Hill, *Carthage Conspiracy*, 56–58 passim.

[106] An example is the oft-reprinted "Buckeye's Lamentation for Want of More Wives," most fully explicated by Bergera in his "Buckeye's Laments."

that Smith himself has aided these villains to accomplish their unholy designs; and unscrupulously avered that he acted from the impulse of Heaven's dictation, while endeavoring to rob virtuous females of their chastity. . .

It can be proven, that Smith and his coadjutors have propagated the doctrine that a man may have spiritual wives—thus by a cunning stroke of priestcraft, throwing wide open the door for every species of licentiousness, that can disgrace or degrade a community.

It can be proven, that many of the leaders in Nauvoo, have "spiritual wives," by which means, females have been so debased, as unblushingly to boast of their connection with Mormon Elders, and with pride point to the fathers of their illigitimate offspring. . .

These are only a part of the flagrant outrages on decency, morality, and the rights of other citizens, committed by the Holy brotherhood at Nauvoo. And now . . . with these facts staring you in the face, can you blame us for opposition to this unholy clan . . . ?

"To Explode the Vicious Principles": Dissent Mounts

During the last two years of his life, Joseph Smith seemed especially absorbed with plural marriage. His secretary, William Clayton, in his 1874 affidavit, remembered that they were seldom together when the prophet did not talk to him about it. Referring to exhilarations that surely included his marital alliances, Smith himself said, "Excitement has almost become the essence of my life. When that dies away, I feel almost lost."[107] Controversy and indiscretion arose to harass the prophet from every side in the spring of 1844. Talk of immoral activity involving both men and women, exceeding even the scandal of the Bennett affair, threatened to overturn the church. Allegations of seduction were traded, indictments charging adultery sworn, and remembered offenses rehearsed again and again. Missionaries carried abroad reports that the leaders were both preaching and practicing the "spiritual wife doctrine." The prophet himself was often at the center of these accounts, his accusers joining descriptions of sexual misdeeds with claims that he was guilty of fraud and abuse of his authority.[108]

---

[107] Smith Jr., *History of the Church*, 14 May 1843, 5:389.

[108] These matters are documented in Smith Jr., *History of the Church*, 6:331–415. Also see the conference talk by Hyrum Smith in Church Historian's History of the Church, reel 4, 8 April 1844, LDS Archives; the case of the mercurial George J. Adams in Smith Jr., *History of the Church*, 11 Feb. 1843, 5:271; and "Notice to the Churches Abroad," *Times and Seasons* 6:7, 15 April 1845, 878. Adams rivaled John C. Bennett in his capacity for scandal and deceit. Aman, "Prophet in Zion," 477–500.

Despite the agitation, Smith remained committed to the doctrine, as an encounter between the prophet and William Law in early 1844 illustrated. Law served as a counselor to the church president but became convinced with others that Smith was a "fallen prophet." Law was excommunicated and, as spring progressed, organized a reformed church of his own.[109] But before Law's defection reached this extreme, he confronted his leader, put his arms about the prophet's neck, and tearfully pleaded with him to renounce plurality. Smith, also crying, answered that he could not, that the Almighty had commanded it, and he had no choice but to obey.[110]

After being excommunicated, some of the detractors founded the *Nauvoo Expositor* to publicize their grievances. One observer remembered that it was sold on the main street of Nauvoo for a nickel and "every one who could raise 5 Cts. bought a copy."[111] Charges included excessive concentrations of political, economic, and judicial power. But more menacing for a religious leader than all else were statements alleging immoral behavior. As it had at Kirtland, sexual irregularity combined with other resentments to threaten the church.[112]

Nauvoo Expositor 1:1, 7 June 1844 [1/6 to 2/1–4].

PREAMBLE . . .
We are earnestly seeking to explode the vicious principles of Joseph Smith, and those who practice the same abominations and whoredoms; which we verily know are not accordant and consonant with the principles of Jesus Christ and the Apostles; and for that purpose, and with that end in view, with an eye single to the glory of God, we have dared to gird on the armor, and with God at our head, we most solemnly and sincerely declare that the sword of truth shall not depart from the thigh, nor the buckler from the arm, until we can enjoy those glorious privileges which nature's God and our country's laws have gurantied to us—freedom of speech, the liberty of the press, and the right to worship God as seemeth us good. . .
Many of us have sought a reformation in the church, without a public exposition of the enormities of crimes practiced by its leaders, thinking that if

---

[109] For these developments, see Smith Jr., *History of the Church*, 13 April 1844, 6:333; ibid., 18 April 1844, 6:341; and ibid., 26 April 1844, ff., 6:344–45.

[110] As told in Van Wagoner, *Mormon Polygamy*, 66; and Cook, "William Law," 66.

[111] John Rigdon Affidavit, 28 July 1905, Joseph F. Smith Affidavits [on celestial marriage], 1869–1915, fd. 3, LDS Archives.

[112] For contemporary criticism of the prophet concerning polygamy and his attempts to conceal it, the best account is Bergera's "Buckeye's Laments." Also see Van Wagoner, *Sidney Rigdon*, 369–76. Regarding the claim of William Marks and others that plural marriage so threatened the church with upheaval that, in the months before his death, Joseph Smith considered ending it, see Newell and Avery, *Mormon Enigma*, 179–80; and Quinn, *Mormon Hierarchy*, 1:146–48.

they would hearken to counsel, and show fruit meet for repentance, it would be as acceptable with God, as though they were exposed to public gaze . . . but our petitions were treated with contempt; and in many cases the petitioners spurned from their presence, and particularly by Joseph, who would state that if he had sinned, and was guilty of the charges we would charge him with, he would not make acknowledgment, but would rather be damned, for it would detract from his dignity, and would consequently ruin and prove the overthrow of the Church. We would ask him on the other hand, if the overthrow of the Church was not inevitable; to which he often replied, that we would all go to Hell together, and convert it into a heaven, by thrusting the Devil out; and says he, Hell is by no means the place this world of fools suppose it to be, but on the contrary, it is quite an agreeable place. . .

It is absurd for men to assert that all is well, while wicked and corrupt men are seeking our destruction, by a perversion of sacred things; for all is not well, while whordoms and all manner of abominations are practiced under the cloak of religion. . .

It is a notorious fact, that many females . . . on their arrival . . . are visited by some of the Strikers, for we know not what else to call them, and are requested to hold on and be faithful, for there are great blessings awaiting the righteous; and that God has great mysteries in store for those who love the Lord, and cling to brother Joseph, They are also notofied that brother Joseph will see them soon, and reveal the mysteries of Heaven to their full understanding, which seldom fails to inspire them with new confidence in the Prophet. . . They are visited again, and what is the result? They are requested to meet brother Joseph, or some of the Twelve, at some insulated point, or at some particularly described place on the bank of the Mississippi, or at some room, which wears upon its front—*Positively No Admittance.* The harmless, inoffensive, and unsuspecting creatures, are so devoted to the Prophet, and the cause of Jesus Christ, that they do not dream of the deep-laid and fatal scheme which prostrates happiness, and renders death itself desirable; but they meet him, expecting to receive through him a blessing, and learn the will of the Lord concerning them, and what awaits the faithful follower of Joseph, the Apostle and Prophet of God, when in the stead thereof, they are told, after having been sworn in one of the most solemn manners, to never divulge what is revealed to them, with a penalty of death attached, that God Almighty has revealed it to him, that she should be his (Joseph's) Spiritual wife; for it was right anciently, and God will tolerate it again; but we must keep those pleasures and blessings from the world, for until their is a change in the government, we will endanger ourselves by practicing it—but we can enjoy the blessings of Jacob, David, and others. . . She is thunder-struck, faints, recovers, and refuses. The Prophet damns her if she rejects. She thinks of the great sacrifice, and of the many thousand miles she has traveled over sea and land, that she might save her soul from pending ruin, and replies, God's will be done, and not mine. The Prophet and his devotees in this way are gratified.

"The Thing Which Put Them into the Power of Their Enemies": The Death of the Prophet and His Brother

With Joseph Smith presiding, the city council condemned the *Nauvoo Expositor* as a nuisance and ordered it destroyed.[113] Charged with riot and destruction of property, within three weeks the Mormon leader was jailed outside Nauvoo and he and his brother Hyrum were assassinated by a crazed mob. It was a tragic demise for one of America's greatest religious figures. While their deaths were due to more than plural marriage, there was compelling reason for Sidney Rigdon's charge that it was chiefly this that brought the prophet and his brother to their ends.[114]

> We are well aware that the leaders of this people, introduced many corruptions among them, and was the thing which gave their enemies power over them, had they not have become basely corrupt, no enemy would have had power over them. They introduced a base system of polygamy, worse by far than that of the heathen; this system of corruption brought a train of evils with it, which has terminated in their entire ruin. After this system was introduced, being in opposition to the laws of the land, they had to put the truth at defiance to conceal it, and in order to do it, perjury was often practiced. This system was introduced by the Smiths some time before their death, and was the thing which put them into the power of their enemies, and was the immediate cause of their death.[115]

More poignant was the angry declaration by the prophet's widow: "it was secret things that had cost Joseph and Hyrum their lives."[116]

The Principle Established

Mormons often repeat the story that an angel with a drawn sword confronted the prophet when he hesitated to commence plural marriage, threatening

---

[113] See the relevant documents of May and June 1844, in Smith Jr., *History of the Church*, 6:432–52; and Oaks, "Suppression of the Nauvoo Expositor," 862–902.

[114] Sidney Rigdon (1793–1876), a follower of Alexander Campbell, was an important early convert who served as first counselor to Joseph Smith for many years. He was a rival of Brigham Young in the succession crisis following the death of the prophet. The best account of Rigdon's views regarding polygamy, as well as his contest with Brigham Young and the apostles, is Van Wagoner, *Sidney Rigdon*, 330–87.

[115] Sidney Rigdon to Mr. Editor, in "Communications," *Messenger and Advocate* 2:6, Whole No. 20 (June 1846), 474–75.

[116] Emma Smith in conversation with William Clayton, 15 Aug. 1844, in Smith, ed., *Intimate Chronicle*, 144. William Law also saw Smith's murder as God's response to "Cries of [offended] innocence and virtue." Law to Issac Hill, 20 July 1844, LDS Archives.

destruction if he did not proceed.[117] If Smith acted because he believed heaven had so warned, his end was doubly tragic, for obedience to the command hastened his death. The contradictions attending his life were as visible to Joseph Smith, however, as to others. George A. Smith, his cousin and supporter, quoted the prophet to say in the spring of 1844 that no one knew his history or understood his heart and that, except that he had experienced it, even he could not have believed all that befell him.[118]

Smith's death did not end the practice of plural marriage. After moving west the Saints granted it high regard, both teaching and practicing the precept on a scale greater than ever before. And because of it, in part, Mormonism emerged as perhaps the most distinctive religious movement in American history.

---

[117] Lightner said the prophet told her the angel spoke to him three times between 1834 and 1842 and threatened to slay him on the third appearance. Lightner, "Address," 2–3, UPB. The story is told in "History of Joseph Lee Robinson," LDS Archives, 26–27; and Lorenzo Snow, "Reminiscences of the Prophet Joseph Smith," *Des. Eve. News*, 23 Dec. 1899, 36:29, 17/3.

[118] As quoted by George A. Smith to Joseph Smith III, 9 Oct. 1869, Historian's Office Letterpress Copy Books, LDS Archives. I am indebted to George D. Smith for alerting me to this letter.

Chapter 2

"Let the Monogamic Law Sink to Rise No More"
Mormons Tell the World about Polygamy

With Mormon removal west came a sense of emancipation. Caleb Green, a non-Mormon employed by Abraham O. Smoot to clerk for him while crossing the plains in 1856, described the experience:

. . . one feels as though there was a cutting loose from business, and the regular routine of every day life, that he has sufficient elbow room that he neither jostles or is jostled by any one, he experiences all the buoyancy of youth when liberated from the school room. His feelings and ideas expand in view of the boundless plains spread before, behind and around him.[1]

The consciousness of liberation must have been especially keen for Mormons who in Nauvoo had so often found it necessary to conceal their most controversial beliefs. This included the practice of polygamy and was undoubtedly what Lorenzo Snow was referring to when he said, "we felt as tho' we could [now] breath more freely and speak one with annother upon those things where in God had made us free with less carefulness than we had hitherto done."[2] Not only did the pace of plural marriages quicken but, overtaken by their liberty, some fell to consorting with "squaws of loose character," drinking whiskey, and behaving in ways that drew down the wrath of Brigham Young.[3] Nelson Wheeler Whipple, a member of the Springville

---

[1] Green, A Visit to the Great Salt Lake, Caleb Green Collection, Mo. Hist. Soc., 15.

[2] Beecher, ed., "Iowa Journal of Lorenzo Snow," 265. Mary Isabella Horne described the sense of release on the plains as a "splendid time," for they were at last "free from their persecutors, free as the air to speak and do as they pleased." Horne, Migration and Settlement of the Latter Day Saints, Salt Lake City, 1884, CU-B, 25.

[3] Jonathan Layne, Life Sketch, LDS Archives, 9; and Kenney, ed., Wilford Woodruff's Journal, 29 May 1847, 3:187.

Brigham Young (1801–1877) married many wives, led the church west after Joseph Smith's death, and publicly acknowledged the doctrine of patriarchal marriage in 1852. Young was president of the church during the greater part of Mormonism's nineteenth-century experience with plural marriage.

Branch Presidency near Garden Grove, Iowa, told of a mulatto named McCarry who adapted the doctrine of plural marriage and started his own religious organization, recruiting followers from among the migrating Mormons. McCarry persuaded several already-married Latter-day Saint females, including one "upwards of 60 years of age," to be sealed to him by his own authority. Each woman was required to go to bed with him three times, whereupon they were considered "seald to the fullist extent." When these activities were found out, excommunications followed and the "Nigger prophet" disappeared "on a fast trot."[4]

After arriving in the Great Basin, church leaders continued to deny to the outside world that they had anything to do with polygamy.[5] To further obscure the matter, Utah's territorial legislature enacted neither a marriage law nor

[4] Whipple, Autobiography and Journal, Nov. 1847, LDS Archives, 71–73. I am indebted to Ms. Barbara Gustaveson, who brought my attention to this journal.

[5] Taylor, *Three Nights' Public Discussion*, 8; and *Three Letters to the New York Herald, from J. M. Grant*, 44–45. Attempting to explain why Mormons denied the practice, one Elder simply said, "neither the body of the Saints nor Christendom were prepared for it. There is a time for all things. God does not reveal to His Church all knowledge at once." Jaques, "Polygamy, Is It Consistent with the Bible," *Mil. Star*, 15:11 (12 Mar. 1853), 165.

strictures criminalizing polygamy for the better part of half a century.[6] When non-Mormon federal officials discovered the truth about plural marriage, they raised alarm concerning it. Caught in their mistruths, church leaders decided to meet the issue directly and sent Jedediah Grant east to reply to their critics. Even before publicly acknowledging polygamy but eager for the encounter, Grant told Brigham Young: "Polygamy is the bone in the throat. It causes a grate deal of coughing and sneezing wind etc. But I shall give it to them as I would feed a hemlock tree to a jackass."[7]

"THIS GREAT, SUBLIME, BEAUTIFUL, AND GLORIOUS DOCTRINE": THE 1852 ANNOUNCEMENT

On the second day of a church conference in late August 1852, where more than one hundred missionaries were called to evangelize for Mormonism, Latter-day Saint leaders publicly proclaimed the doctrine of plurality. One scholar described the event as "the most courageous act of spiritual defiance in all American history."[8] While it is true that most who were church members in the Rocky Mountain West, and many who resided elsewhere, had been aware of plural marriage for years, it remains a marker in the experience of nineteenth-century Mormonism. Except for the 1842 Udney Hay Jacob pamphlet, it constituted the most extensive public treatment so far given the subject.[9] More than an acknowledgment, it was a doctrinal dissertation. The address related plural marriage to Mormon teachings about the soul's existence before life on earth and to a multiplicity of worlds needing to be peopled by human offspring. Most significantly, it raised an anthem of advocacy from the faithful themselves.

---

[6] For Utah's first marriage regulation, codified in 1888, see Chapter Eight. When attempts were made to turn an 1852 territorial law prohibiting "lewd and lascivious cohabitation" against polygamists, George A. Smith pointed out that authors of the law could never have intended it to be used to convict pluralists inasmuch as the territorial legislature at the time "were unanimously believers in, and four-fifths of them practical observers of, the law of celestial marriage." *Rise, Progress and Travels of the Church*, 69–70.

[7] Grant to Brigham Young, 10 Mar. 1852, in Sessions, *Mormon Thunder*, 98–99. Also see Whittaker, "Bone in the Throat," 293–314.

[8] Bloom, *American Religion*, 108.

[9] Joseph Smith's 1843 revelation had not yet been made public. Despite their general reticence, the Saints had publicly defended the doctrine before the 1852 conference sermon. See, for example, Capt. James Brown's 1847 speech in Ruxton, *Life in the Far West*, 285; George Brimhall's memory of the revelation being read in southern Utah in early January 1852 as told in his *Workers of Utah*, 19; and Parley P. Pratt's one-page polemic printed six weeks before his brother Orson's address in "Mormonism!" "Plurality of Wives!"

Brigham Young chose Apostle Orson Pratt, whom Jules Remy described as Mormonism's "philosopher and show-speaker," to deliver the proclamation on 29 August 1852 to a crowded audience in the old tabernacle, where the Assembly Hall on Temple Square now stands.[10] Pratt's remarks were so extended that they filled a special number of the *Deseret News*. They were also published the next year as a supplement to the *Millennial Star*, in volume one of the *Journal of Discourses*, and, somewhat abbreviated, in Burton's *City of the Saints*.[11]

In announcing the supplement's availability in the British Isles, the editor of the *Millennial Star* said the document contained "one of the most important Revelations . . . unto man in this last dispensation. None seem to penetrate so deep, or be so well calculated to shake to its very centre the social structure which has been reared, and vainly nurtured by this professedly wise and Christian generation."[12] The forty-eight-page *Deseret News* printing was advertised as costing fifty cents and "fast going." It was described as filled with "solid matter, sufficient for a book of 200 pages in popular style" and, as mentioned, contained the first printed copy of the "great REVELATION" on plural marriage.[13]

Brigham Young, who followed Pratt with an afternoon address, provided the event with its coda. Polygamy, he said, "will sail over, and ride triumphantly above all the prejudice and priestcraft of the day; it will be fostered and believed in by the more intelligent portions of the world, as one of the best doctrines ever proclaimed to any people."[14]

Deseret News, Extra, Containing A Revelation
on Celestial Marriage, 14–22.

Prayer by elder Ezra T. Benson, and singing. Professor Orson Pratt then said:

. . . It is well known . . . to the congregation before me, that the Latter Day Saints have embraced the doctrine of a plurality of wives, as a part of their religious faith. It is not, as many have supposed, a doctrine embraced by them to gratify the carnal lusts and feelings of man; that is not the object of the doctrine.

---

[10] Remy, *Journey to Great-Salt-Lake City,* 2:112. Edward W. Tullidge later referred to Orson Pratt as "the Paul of Mormondom." See his *Life of Brigham Young,* 404.

[11] Burton, *City of the Saints,* 422–28.

[12] "Revelation on Marriage, &c.," *Mil. Star* 15:1 (1 Jan. 1853), 25–26.

[13] *Deseret News Extra,* 18 Sept. 1852, 2:23 [3/1]. For other copies, see Pratt, "Revelation on the Patriarchal Order of Matrimony, or Plurality of Wives," *Seer* 1:1 (Jan. 1853), 7–11; and Woodford, "Historical Development," 3:1738–41.

[14] *Deseret News Extra,* 18 Sept. 1852, 25.

We shall endeavour to set forth before this enlightened assembly some of the causes why the Almighty has revealed such a doctrine, and why it is considered a part and portion of our religious faith. And I believe that they will not, under our present form of government, (I mean the government of the United States,) try us for treason for believing and practising our religious notions and ideas. I think, if I am not mistaken, that the constitution gives the privilege to all the inhabitants of this country, of the free exercise of their religious notions, and the freedom of their faith, and the practice of it. Then, if . . . the Latter-day Saints have actually embraced, as a part and portion of their religion, the doctrine of a plurality of wives, it is constitutional. And should there ever be laws enacted by this government to restrict them from the free exercise of this part of their religion, such laws must be unconstitutional. . .

The Lord ordained marriage between male and female as a law through which spirits should come here and take tabernacles, and enter into the second state of existence. The Lord himself solemnized the first marriage pertaining to this globe. . . I do not say pertaining to mortality; for when the first marriage was celebrated, no mortality was there. The first marriage that we have any account of, was between two immortal beings, old father Adam and old mother Eve; they were immortal beings; death had no dominion— no power over them. . . This marriage was celebrated between two immortal beings; for how long? until death? No. That was entirely out of the question; there could have been no such thing in the ceremony. . .

What is the object of this union?—is the next question. We are told the object of it, it is clearly expressed, for, says the Lord unto the male and female, I command you to multiply and replenish the earth. And inasmuch as we have proved that the marriage ordinance was eternal in its nature, previous to the fall, if we are restored back to what was lost by the fall, we are restored for the purpose of carrying out the commandment given before the fall, namely, to multiply and replenish the earth . . . consequently, when male and female are restored from the fall, by virtue of the everlasting and eternal covenant of marriage, they will continue to increase and multiply to all ages of eternity, to raise up beings after their own order, and in their own likeness and image, germs of intelligence, that are destined, in their times and seasons to become not only sons of God, but Gods themselves.

This accounts for the many worlds we heard Elder Grant speaking about, yesterday afternoon. The peopling of worlds, or an endless increase, even of one family, would require an endless increase of worlds, and if one family were to be united in the eternal covenant of marriage, to fulfil that great commandment to multiply his species and propagate them, and if there be no end to the increase of his posterity, it would call for an endless increase of new worlds. And if one family calls for this, what would innumerable millions of families call for? They would call for as many worlds as have already been discovered by the telescope, yea, the number must be multiplied to infinity in order that there may be room for the inheritance of the sons and daughters of the Gods...

We read that those who do the works of Abraham, are to be blessed with the blessings of Abraham. Have you not, in the ordinances of this last dispensation, had the blessings of Abraham pronounced upon your heads? . . . Why not look upon Abraham's blessings as your own, for the Lord blessed him with a promise of seed as numerous as the sand upon the sea-shore; so will you be blessed, or else you will not inherit the blessings of Abraham.

How did Abraham manage to get a foundation laid for this mighty kingdom? Was he to accomplish it all through one wife? No. Sarah gave a certain woman to him whose name was Hagar, and by her a seed was to be raised up unto him. Is this all? No. We read of his wife Keturah, and also of a plurality of wives and concubines—which he had—from whom he raised up many sons. Here, then, was a foundation laid, for the fulfillment of the great and grand promise, concerning the multiplicity of his seed. It would have been rather a slow process, if Abraham had been confined to one wife, like some of those narrow, contracted nations of modern Christianity.

I think there is only about one-fifth of the population of the globe, that believe in the one-wife system, the other four-fifths believe in the doctrine of a plurality of wives. They have had it handed down from time immemorial, and are not half so narrow and contracted in their minds, as some of the nations of Europe and America, who have done away with the promises, and deprived themselves of the blessings of Abraham, Isaac and Jacob . . . they are so penurious, and so narrow contracted, in their feelings, that they take every possible care not to have their families large; they do not know what is in the future, nor what blessings they are depriving themselves of, because of the traditions of their fathers; they do not know that a man's posterity, in the eternal worlds, are to constitute his glory, his kingdom, and dominion.

Again, let us look at Sarah's peculiar position in regard to Abraham. She understood the whole matter; she knew that unless seed was raised up to Abraham, that he would come short of his glory; and she understood the promise of the Lord, and longed for Abraham to have seed. And when she saw that she was old, and fearing that she should not have the privilege of raising up seed, she gave to Abraham, Hagar. Would Gentile Christendom do such things now-a-days? O no, they would consider it enough to send a man to an endless hell of fire and brimstone. Why?—Because tradition has instilled this in their minds as a dreadful, awful thing.

It matters not to them how corrupt they are in female prostitution, if they are lawfully married to only one wife, but it would be considered an awful thing by them to raise up a posterity from more than one wife; this would be wrong indeed—but to go into a brothel, and there debauch themselves in the lowest haunts of degradation all the days of their lives, they consider only a trifling thing; nay, they can even license such institutions in Christian nations, and it all passes off very well. . .

But again, there is another reason why this plurality should exist among the Latter-day Saints. . . I have already told you that the spirits of men and women, all had a previous existence, thousands of years ago, in the heavens, in the presence of God; and I have already told you that among them are many spirits that are more noble, more intelligent than others, that were called the great and mighty ones, reserved until the dispensation of the fulness of times, to come forth upon the face of the earth, through a noble parentage. . . The Lord has not kept them in store for five or six thousand years past, and kept them waiting for their bodies all this time, to send them among the Hottentots, the African negroes, the idolatrous Hindoos, or any other of the fallen nations that dwell upon the face of this earth. They are not kept in reserve in order to come forth to receive such a degraded parentage upon the earth; no, the Lord is not such a being; His justice, goodness, and mercy will be magnified towards those who were chosen before they were born, and they long to come, and they will come among the Saints of the living God; this would be their highest pleasure and joy, to know that they could have the privilege of being born to such noble parentage. . .

But, says one, how have you obtained this information? By new revelation. When was it given, and to whom? It was given to the Prophet, Seer, and Revelator, Joseph Smith, on the 12th day of July, 1843; only about eleven months before he was martyred for the testimony of Jesus. . .

Now, let us enquire, what will become of those individuals who have this law taught unto them in plainness, if they reject it? (A voice in the stand, they will be damned.) I will tell you, they will be damned, saith the Lord God Almighty, in the revelation He has given. Why? Because where much is given, much is required; where there is great knowledge unfolded for the exaltation, glory, and happiness of the sons and daughters of God, if they close up their hearts, if they reject the testimony of his word and will, not give heed to the principles he has ordained for their good, they are worthy of damnation, and the Lord has said they shall be damned. This was the word of the Lord to his servant Joseph the prophet himself. With all the knowledge and light he had, he must comply with it, or, says the Lord unto him, you shall be damned; and the same is true in regard to all those who reject these things. . .

We can only touch here and there upon this great subject, we can only offer a few words with regard to this great, sublime, beautiful, and glorious doctrine. . .

But while I talk, the vision of my mind is opened; the subject spreads forth and branches out like the branches of a thrifty tree; and as for the glory of God, how great it is. I feel to say hallelujah to his great name; for he reigns in the heavens, and he will exalt his people to sit with him upon thrones of power to reign for ever and ever. . .

"DARING THEM TO DO THEIR WORST": MORMON STALWARTS TAKE THE FIELD

For many believers who had not gathered to the Rocky Mountains, notably those in Great Britain, news of the doctrine came as a shock. Thomas B. Stenhouse, a Mormon in England, said at the time it "fell like a thunderbolt . . . and fearfully shattered the mission."[15] Hundreds left the church because of it. Stephen Forsdick, a British convert, recalled:

> In December 1852 at a General Conference in London a Revelation was read purporting to have been given by Joseph Smith, authorizing a man to have more than one wife and stating, that in this way only could a man inherit the Celestial Kingdom. This was the first time poligamy had ever been openly preached in England. The man who read it commented on it and said "No doubt many would be offended and deny the Faith." He was right, many did, himself among the number.[16]

Even among the Saints in Utah there was disillusionment, leading some into open dissent and apostasy.[17] And others, remaining faithful to the church, believed the public declaration on polygamy unwise. This included Utah's territorial delegate to Congress, John M. Bernhisel (1799–1881),[18] who expressed to Brigham Young his fears, concerns that were soon realized during congressional debates on public lands.[19]

JOHN M. BERNHISEL TO PRESIDENT BRIGHAM YOUNG, 8 NOV. 1852, BOX 60, FD. 13, REEL 70, BRIGHAM YOUNG COLLECTION, LDS ARCHIVES.

Dear Brother,

. . . The publication of the work mentioned in your last . . . will create a tremendous sensation, not only throughout the United States, but throughout all Christendom. To our friends at Washington they will prove a bitter pill, for they hoped that this subject would not be again agitated. Among others they will revive former prejudices and hostile feelings; and will be regarded by some members of Congress, and perhaps of the co-ordinate branches of the Government, as throwing down the glove, and daring them to do their

---

[15] Stenhouse, *Rocky Mountain Saints*, 200. Also see Foster, *Penny Tracts*, 149–53, 215.

[16] Forsdick, Autobiography, LDS Archives, 9.

[17] See the cases of James and George Dove in Holzapfel, "The Flight of the Doves," 199–200.

[18] John Milton Bernhisel (1799–1881) represented Utah in Congress from 1851 to 1859, and again from 1861 to 1863. Regarding Bernhisel and the announcement of polygamy, see Barrett, "John M. Bernhisel," 103–7.

[19] My thanks to William P. MacKinnon for bringing this letter to my attention.

worst. The prospect at present is, that I shall have the battles of the last session to fight over again, which will be anything but an agreeable task. I entertained strong hopes that we should be able to procure some appropriations, at least one for a penitentiary, and perhaps another for Indian depredations, at the ensuing session, but I apprehend that these publications will arouse such a feeling among the members of both branches of the National Legislature as to prevent us most effectually from obtaining a single dollar. They will also undoubtedly be strongly urged by our enemies upon the incoming administration, whether Whig or Democratic, as a reason for your removal from office, but with what success remains to be seen. And there is one set of scamps, to wit, Brocchus, Brandebury and Harris, with their co-adjutators, who will hail with pure and unmingled delight, these publications as going to sustain one of the most important and offensive charges in their villainous report, and they will take not little credit to themselves for having "smoked us out."[20] The public mind is exceedingly sensitive on this subject, and to all human appearances it seems at present utterly impossible that one in ten thousand will be convinced that the "Doctrine" is at all consistent with chastity, or even common morality, must [sic] less that it is a pure and righteous one. But as the publication of the works referred to may after all be for the best, I do not write complainingly, though I know and dread the scenes through which I shall have to pass the coming winter, and I could fervently pray in the language of our blessed Savior, that this cup might pass from me.

Despite Bernhisel's concerns, church authorities launched a crusade to defend the Principle. Writing and preaching followed like a freshet too long dammed from its course. The *Überfluss* saw William Clayton, the revelation's scribe, go to England "to preach the gospel and sustain the Revelation on Celestial Marriage."[21] Others were sent elsewhere to do the same thing: Erastus Snow with the *St. Louis Luminary*; George Q. Cannon and his *Western Standard* in San Francisco; John Taylor with the *Mormon* in New York City; and the pamphlet works of Richard Ballantyne in India, Jesse Haven in South Africa, and Benjamin F. Johnson in Hawaii.[22] Sermons and editorials supporting the practice were regularly printed in Mormonism's official voice, the *Deseret News*. Yet others were printed in the *Millennial Star*.

It was a bold strategy, one that condemned traditional Christian marriage while exalting the virtues of Mormonism's own. And none championed the Principle more vigorously than Orson Pratt. Appointed to preside over mis-

---

[20] For more on the "Runaway Officials," see Brocchus to Hon. Daniel Webster, 30 April 1852, in Chapter Six.   [21] Smith, ed., *Intimate Chronicle*, 28 Aug. 1852, 415.

[22] The best examination of these publications remains Whittaker, "Early Mormon Pamphleteering," 333–53.

sionary work in the U.S. and the British provinces of North America, Pratt was specifically instructed to defend plural marriage. This was done in public lectures as well as through his publication, the *Seer*, printed in Washington, D.C., and Baltimore.[23]

The *Seer*'s first issue printed Joseph Smith's revelation as "Celestial Marriage: A Revelation On The Patriarchal Order Of Matrimony, Or Plurality Of Wives."[24] Pratt then proceeded to discuss the subject in a long essay that was continued in subsequent issues. Most of this commentary enlarged on themes treated in his 1852 conference address but, as this selection illustrates, the *Seer* was more defiant in tone than the 1852 sermon. Pratt invited critics to engage the Saints in argument and prove them wrong if they could. Pratt also printed a copy of the ceremony that church authorities used to seal women to their husbands, a disclosure that drew criticism from Brigham Young.[25] This was exceptional, however, and nineteenth-century apologists used Pratt's defenses more frequently than all other writings on polygamy combined.

ORSON PRATT, "CELESTIAL MARRIAGE," *SEER* 1:1 (JAN. 1853), 11–13;
1:3 (MAR. 1853), 41–42; 1:4 (APRIL 1853), 58–60;
1:5 (MAY 1853), 75–80.

When a man who has a wife, teaches her the law of God, as revealed to the ancient patriarchs, and as manifested by new revelation, and she refuses to give her consent for him to marry another according to that law, then, it becomes necessary, for her to state before the President the reasons why she withholds her consent; if her reasons are sufficient and justifiable and the husband is found in the fault, or in transgression, then, he is not permitted to take any step in regard to obtaining another. But if the wife can show no good reason why she refuses to comply with the law which was given unto Sarah of old, then it is lawful for her husband, if permitted by revelation through the prophet, to be married to others without her consent, and he will be justified, and she will be condemned, because she did not give them unto him, as Sarah gave Hagar to Abraham, and as Rachel and Leah gave Bilhah and Zilpah to their husband, Jacob. . .

Jealousy is an evil with which the saints in Utah are but seldom troubled: it is an evil that is not countenanced by either male or female; and should any indulge such a passion, they would bring a disgrace and reproach upon themselves which they could not easily wipe away. And indeed, it is very rare, that

---

[23] John M. Bernhisel informed Brigham Young that in the nation's capital Pratt attracted only small audiences to his lectures on polygamy but large amounts of hostility. Bernhisel to Young, 5 Feb. 1853, Brigham Young Collection, LDS Archives.   [24] *Seer* 1:1 (Jan. 1853), 7–11.

[25] "Celestial Marriage," *Seer* 1:2 (Feb. 1853), 31–32; and Whittaker, "Early Mormon Pamphleteering," 335–36.

there are any causes for jealousy; for the citizens of that Territory think more of their virtue than they do of their lives. They know, that if they have any connections out of the marriage covenant, they not only forfeit their lives by the law of God, but they forfeit their salvation also. With such views resting upon the minds of both old and young, the people have the greatest of confidence in each other's integrity: they can entrust their wives and daughters, without any distrust, to the protection and care of their neighbors. . .

When nation rises against nation, and kingdom against kingdom, and the sword devours from one end of the earth to the other, as the prophets have predicted should be the case in the last days, many millions of fathers and brothers will fall upon the battle field, while mothers, and daughters, and widows will be left to mourn the loss. What will become of these females? Answer, the gospel will be preached to many of them, and they will flee out from among the nations, and be gathered with the Saints to Zion. Under these circumstances, the number of females will far exceed the number of males. How are the overplus females to obtain husbands for eternity? We will answer this question in the words of Isaiah, "In that day seven women shall take hold of one man, saying, We will eat our own bread, and wear our own apparel: only let us be called by thy name to take away our reproach." (Isaiah 4:1) . . .

Can a woman have more than one husband at the same time? No: Such a principle was never sanctioned by scripture. The object of marriage is to multiply the species, according to the command of God. A woman with one husband can fulfil this command, with greater facilities, than if she had a plurality; indeed, this would, in all probability, frustrate the great design of marriage, and prevent her from raising up a family. As a plurality of husbands, would not facilitate the increase of posterity, such a principle never was tolerated in scripture. But a plurality of wives would be the means of greatly increasing a family, and of thus fulfilling the command, not only to a far greater extent on the part of the husband, but also on the part of the females who otherwise might have been under the necessity of remaining single forever. . .

We should be pleased to have some of the wise theologians of our day bring forward even one passage from either the Old or New Testament to prove that the plurality of wives is an evil. Let them produce some passage, if they can, to show that such a practice was sinful either under the Patriarchal, Mosaic, or Christian dispensations. Let them show that the practice was not continued under the Christian dispensation. Where and when did our Saviour ever condemn it? Where and when did any of his Apostles ever condemn it? Here, then, ye ministers of Christendom, are some grave questions for you to settle. . . No sooner was it sounded abroad through the columns of the Seer that the Saints in Utah believed in and practiced the plurality of wives, than the whole army of editors and ministers throughout Christendom formed themselves in battle array; the thunder of their artillery is heard reverberating from nation to nation. . . But in this holy war where is the editor or minister that can brandish the sword of truth against that which he condemns? Where is the theological Golia[t]h of modern Christendom that can stand before the sling stones of truth as they are hurled by the power of Israel's God into the midst of the enemy's camp? Denunciations are not arguments—curses and vile reproaches will not convince the judgment nor enlighten mankind—Editors and ministers will find some wise men yet left on the earth who are not afraid of the Bible nor of Bible truths: . . .

God had declared himself to be the God of Abraham, the God of Isaac, and the God of Jacob, and had promised to bless the children of their numerous wives and multiply them like the dust of the earth. And Christ too, the greatest enemy which the Devil had, was so well pleased with this divine institution that he chose to come into the world through the lineage of a long list of Jewish and patriarchal Polygamists. . . Thus that order of plurality by which the twelve tribes of Israel were founded, and from which the Messiah, according to the flesh, came; that order which multiplied the chosen seed as the stars of Heaven, and in which all nations should be blessed; . . . that holy divine order has been overturned and abolished by human enactments and by human authority. Let Apostate Christendom blush at her sacrilegious deeds! let her be ashamed of her narrow contracted bigoted laws!

"Practiced It Himself": Jesus Was a Pluralist

In addition to the ancient patriarchs and modern revelation, Mormons summoned support from other well-known historical personalities who condoned polygamy.[26] Most important as approving precedents were God the Father and Jesus, personages that Heber C. Kimball once assured church members reproduced "upon the same principle as we produce one another."[27] At the end of the century, at a special meeting in the Salt Lake Temple, both President Lorenzo Snow and his counselor, George Q. Cannon, told men gathered there that some were the descendants of Jesus.[28] Buoyed by certainty that they were the special friends of God, the Saints fearlessly declared His secrets.

---

[26] As only a few instances, see Pratt, "Christian Polygamy in the Sixteenth Century," *Seer* 1:12 (Dec. 1853), 177–79; "'Daily Mail' and Plural Marriage," *Mil. Star* 38:7 (14 Feb. 1876), 105; and "John Milton on Plural Marriage," ibid., 38:11 (13 Mar. 1876), 161–65.

[27] "Remarks By Pres. H.C. Kimball . . . Nov. 29, 1857," *Des. News* [Weekly], 9 Dec. 1857, 7:40, 315/1. For other statements contending that God and Jesus were pluralists, see Orson Pratt, "Celestial Marriage," *Seer* 1:10 (Oct. 1853), 158–60; the same author at ibid., 1:11 (Nov. 1853), 172; and "Lecture By Elder Orson Hyde," 6 Oct. 1854, *Des. News* [Weekly], 19 Oct. 1854, 4:32 [1/2–4].

[28] A. O. Woodruff Journals, 2 July 1899, Abraham Owen Woodruff Collection, box 1, fd. 2, UPB, 91–92. Heber C. Kimball was remembered to say that he was "a direct descendant of the Savior of the world." See A. H. Cannon Journals, 5 April 1894, UPB, 18:69–70.

BENJAMIN F. JOHNSON, *WHY THE LATTER DAY SAINTS*
MARRY A PLURALITY OF WIVES . . . (1854), 13–15.

And were we called upon, we should feel abundantly able to show, not only that our Saviour honored this doctrine of polygamy, by being born into the world through . . . [a polygamous] lineage, but that He adopted and practiced it himself in a marriage with Mary, Martha and Mary Magdalene, which is not only shown by the predictions of the Prophets, but by His general demeanor and intercourse with them, whose affections for Him were in every way demonstrated by kindness, solicitude and attention; and such being His love for Mary and Martha that He sympathized in the death of their brother, and wept with them over his tomb, manifesting such especial regard for the sister of Martha that she became known as "the Mary whom Jesus loved;"[29] His marriage to whom, no doubt, occurred at Canaan of Galilee, where His mother, who officiated, called upon Him to furnish wine for the guests which was so miraculously produced by the changing of water into wine—His wives following Him whithersoever He went—being the last at the Cross and the first at the Sepulchre—unto whom he also first appeared after His resurrection from the dead.

Whosoever should doubt that our Saviour was to marry, let them turn to the 45th Psalm, where David, speaking of a personage whom he calls God, says that "kings' daughters shall be among his honorable women," which if properly rendered from the original, would read "honorable wives," while the "queen of Heaven should stand upon his right hand clothed with gold of Ophir," who is comforted with the assurance that the King shall greatly desire her beauty—bidding her, as he is lord, to worship him; and to show that this was to be literal, Paul quotes the sixth and seventh verses of the 45th Psalm in Hebrews, 1:8–9, showing distinctly that this personage who was called God—who was to have a *queen* in Heaven, with kings' daughters for his honorable wives, was none other than the Son of God himself.

Do you marvel . . . at this, while marriage appears so necessary to the future glory, as well as to the present happiness of man;—does it not appear evident from Scripture and reason that such relations existed in the eternal worlds before this earth was formed from the elements which existed, and that through those conjugal relations, the spirits of men were begotten and born unto Him "who is our Father in Heaven?" If not, who were all the "Sons of God who shouted for joy," and the "Morning *stars* that sang together," when the foundations of the earth were laid? (Job, 38:7.) If Jesus is the "Son of God," "our elder brother," and we are really his brother as is so plainly set forth in the Scriptures, then *reason* and *analogy* would teach us that there must be a mother also, as well as a father in heaven—did not Jesus say that He did nothing but what He saw His Father do—then must not His Father have passed

---

[29] John 11:5.

through a similar probation to secure a tabernacle, and contracted those conjugal relationships through which Jesus, with all of His younger brethren, the sons of God were begotten in the spirit world? To whom was the Father conversing when He said—"Let *us* make man in *our own* image, *male* and *female?*" With whom would a father converse upon the welfare of his children, if not with their mother?

"The Biggest Whoremasters on Earth": Apostate, Hypocritical Christianity

Unsparing indictments of Christian morality blended with Mormonism's claim that contemporary Christianity had departed from ancient teachings and that Joseph Smith had a special mandate to restore them. A theory first heard in the 1850s, colorfully rehearsed by Brigham Young, said that monogamy resulted from a scarcity of women among "the founders of the Roman empire," whom he characterized as "wandering brigands." Rome imposed this innovation "wherever her sway was acknowledged," Young said. "Thus this monogamic order of marriage, so esteemed by modern Christians as a holy sacrament and divine institution, is nothing but a system established by a set of robbers."[30] By adopting Roman monogamy, it was said, the early Christians apostatized from the older, divinely approved practice of polygamy among the Jews. The result was prostitution and moral rot. Abortion, adultery, and divorce or, as one Mormon called it, "a bastard and periodical kind of polygamy," became epidemic.[31]

Paired with the charge of hypocrisy was suspicion concerning the moral character of anyone outside the Mormon fold. Millenarianism, with its portrayal of increasing wickedness in the last days, belief that polygamy alone could check lustful behavior, and the effects of geographic isolation contributed to the attitude. Suspicion that most non-Mormons were ethically wanting characterized the Latter-day Saint outlook for decades. Horace Greeley, reflecting on his visit with Brigham Young and the Saints in 1859, noted:

> Another feature of President Young's remarks on this topic [polygamy] strikes me on revision. He assumed as undeniable that outside of the Mormon church,

---

[30] "Remarks By President Brigham Young," *Des. News* [Weekly], 6 Aug. 1862, 12:6, 41/4. Others repeated this theory, as in Richards and Little, *Compendium of the Doctrines of the Gospel*, 124. George Q. Cannon also indicted the Greeks on 6 April 1879, *Journal of Discourses*, 20:200–1.

[31] "Deceivers and Being Deceived," *Des. Eve. News*, 28 Feb. 1881, 14:81 [2/1]; and the equally harsh language in "Polygamy vs. Monogamy," *Mormon* 1:42 (8 Dec. 1855) [2/3].

married men usually keep mistresses—that incontinence is the general rule, and continence the rare exception. This assumption was habitual with the Mormons who, at various times, discussed with me the subject of polygamy.[32]

Mormons repeatedly emphasized that celibacy and monogamy were the consequence of Christian apostasy and major reasons for society's ills. Plurality, on the other hand, offered mankind a heaven-approved alternative.

"Monogamy, Polygamy, and Christianity,"
Mil. Star 15:32 (6 Aug. 1853), 513–17.

Protestant Christians . . . have derived their strict monogamic system from the Roman Catholic Church. Protestant Christians agree to call this Church Antichrist, the great whore who sitteth upon many waters, the mother of harlots and abominations of the earth, and a variety of other not very chaste or beautiful titles. And the Protestants affirm stoutly that the Roman Catholic Church richly deserves these titles. Well, let us believe the affirmations of the Protestants concerning their venerable mother, lady Rome. Let us take for granted all that the numerous and motley daughters of this ancient lady say of her. Let us believe that the Roman Church is indeed the great whore, the mother of harlots and abominations of the earth. What then? We are led to notice three things. First—The Romish Church is lewd. Second—The daughters of the Church of Rome are lewd. Third—The principal abominations upon the face of the earth are the practices introduced by the Church of Rome, and persevered in by herself and daughters. Let us briefly consider these charges separately, and see how far they can be substantiated. . .

The Lord ordained marriage for all who were worthy, and the Apostle Paul said marriage was honourable in all. Incidental to certain exigencies, the same Apostle gave counsel that those who married did well, but those who did not marry did better; and also that it was well for Bishops and Deacons to have one wife each. The Roman Church, with all the blindness characteristic of those who follow the letter, and miss the spirit, has founded arbitrary laws upon the basis of Paul's incidental and local counsel. Her priests are forbidden to marry at all, and no one within the pale of her influence is permitted to marry more than one wife. Rome has thus strained this counsel of Paul, until she acts in direct opposition to other of his teaching. . . Rome has institutions where young women are encouraged to take vows of perpetual celibacy, with the idea that a thorough conquest over, or rather an extermination of, sexual desire is peculiarly pleasing to God. This is a pitiable delusion. . .

In consequence. . . Licentiousness prevails among all nations. Adultery is so common as to be scarcely considered a punishable crime. Hundreds and thousands of women, prevented by law from becoming the wives of good

---

[32] Greeley, *Overland Journey*, 218n.

men whom they love, and obeying the impulses God has endowed them with, either throw themselves into the arms of those men they love, (though such men be previously married,) or become the wives of wicked, brutal men who, by their actions, evince that they have not the shadow of a right to the control of a woman's affections or person, or of a posterity. In the first case, infamy is the result; in the second, moral prostitution; . . . Thus . . . does Rome manifest . . . that the spirit which actuates her is a spirit of gross lewdness. . .

Second—The daughters of the Church of Rome are lewd. By the harlots—the daughters of the Church of Rome, may be understood all those societies whose pedigree can be traced up to her, and all those who adopt those of her principles and practices which foster lewdness. The whole Protestant world, according to their own showing, come under condemnation here, for as Rome enforced the one-wife system upon the Christian world, the Protestants, to prove their lineage to Rome, have followed in her track, and have continued the law of monogamy to this day. None of the Protestant societies have shown themselves pure and godly enough to condemn that law, though they could find no Scripture to support it. Luther and Melanchthon allowed polygamy, but they counselled against it, though, strange to say, Luther confessed that he could not see that it came in opposition to Holy Scripture. And some amongst the divers hosts of Protestants will not even advocate monogamy, but, with their venerable mother, recommend the adoption of perpetual celibacy. And thus do the whole body of the Protestants, while professing otherwise, proclaim their true lewd character and lineage, and consequently among Protestant nations we find licentiousness prevails to an alarming extent. . .

Third—The principal abominations upon the face of the earth are the practices introduced by the Church of Rome, and persevered in by herself and her harlot daughters. Had the question of monogamy or polygamy been left open, and allowed to work according to the law of God, the tributaries and streams of lewdness would have been checked and dried up long before this time. The startling figures on prostitution would not have found their way among the statistical tables of the nations. But this would not have suited the mother of harlots, nor her daughters—it would have ill comported with their genius. . . And so full is the earth, of the consequent abominations, that the Almighty has declared that all mankind have gone astray. . . And, according to the prediction of His Apostle John, the Lord has commissioned His servants to trumpet forth the command to the pure among all nations— "Come out of her, my people that ye be not partakers of her sins, and that ye receive not of her plagues. . ." It is of no use to disguise the fact that things have come to this pass—men must either take sides with the mother of harlots, and with her monogamy, and celibacy, and prostitution, or take sides with the Almighty, and with His holy law of polygamy, and sexual purity. Eventually none can stand neutral—all must take one side or the other.

Heber Chase Kimball (1801–1868) was an apostle and counselor to Brigham Young, a husband to many plural wives, and a plain-spoken advocate of the Principle.

Europe and the United States, church spokesmen declared, were equally besmirched. Utah alone escaped the malady. And when it came to unsparing language, no one was more direct than Brigham Young's counselor, Heber C. Kimball.

"Remarks By Pres. Heber C. Kimball," 26 July 1857,
Des. News [Weekly], 12 Aug. 1857, 7:23, 179/3–4.

We do not believe in whoredoms here; we do not admit of any such thing as women to whore it, or of men to come here to do any such thing. We have none of this. [Voice: "That is civilization."]

Yes, such as they have in New York at the Five Points there. Some of you have, perhaps, been there, and in Philadelphia, and in every other city in the United States. . .

Christians—those poor, miserable priests . . . some of them are the biggest whoremasters there are on the earth, and at the same time preaching righteousness to the children of men. . .

Plurality of wives—I have a good many wives. How much would you give to know how many? If I were to tell you, you would not believe it. . . Suffice it to say I have a good many wives and lots of young mustards that are growing and they are a kind of fruitful seed. . .

The priests of the day in the whole world keep women, just the same as the gentlemen of the legislatures do. The great men of the earth keep from two to three, and perhaps half-a-dozen private women. They are not acknowledged openly, but are kept merely to gratify their lusts; and if they get in the family way, they call for the doctors, and also upon females who practise under the garb of mid-wives, to kill the children, and thus they are depopulating their own species. . .

I have been taught it, and my wife was taught it in our young days, when she got in the family way, to send for a doctor and get rid of the child, so as to live with me to gratify lust. It is God's truth, and I know the person that did it. This is depopulating the human species; and the curse of God will come upon that man, and upon that woman, and upon those cursed doctors. There is scarcely one of them that is free from the sin. It is just as common as it is for wheat to grow. . .

I have had altogether about fifty children; and one hundred years won't pass away before my posterity will out-number the present inhabitants of the State of New York, because I do not destroy my offspring. I am doing the works of Abraham.

Statements such as this were not confined to the pulpit.[33] They were also privately recited by lay followers.

LUKE WILLIAM GALLUP TO DEAR AUNT,
2 JULY 1869, LDS ARCHIVES.

Our Country is dying. She is bleeding   old age is coming upon her. . . What they or any people sow they will have to reap . . . the States don't like . . . [polygamy] & we do. The States love houses of ill fame & love to make & have prostitutes & the Southerners the Negro wenches, & we don't. Look at European Cities (one third illegitimate pop.) in some instances. Dare any one set up a house of ill fame in Utah. No. If the[y] did it would be considered one of the greatest nuisances & would be very apt to fall down, or sure to meet with some extirminating accident. . .

The Bible proves poligamy from beginning to end & not a word against it. The principle is as old as the hills & practiced by nearly all the heathen nations who have never left it off & taken to Monogamy as the more enlightened nations have done   The new . . . principle [of monogamy] was adopted several hundred years after Christ by some Roman soldiery at a time when they took some prisoners (Ladies) & they had not enough for one apiece & so they made a law that a man should not have but one wife—a new invention & contrary to scripture.   The Subject of Poligamy is broad & wide. . .
     You can read it.[34]

---

[33] See, for example, "N," "Expressions from the People," *Des. Eve. News*, 26 Feb. 1886, 19:80 [4/3–4].

[34] For more of the same, charmingly expressed in an earlier letter, see Gallup to Milinda, Reminiscence and Diary, 24 Jan. 1868, LDS Archives, 318–20. An American convert to Mormonism who settled in Springville, Utah, Luke William Gallup (1822–1891) eventually drifted away from the church after an unhappy experience with plural marriage. Lowell "Ben" Bennion brought Gallup to my attention many years ago.

"Stalwart Sons and
Fair and Robust Daughters":
The Regenerative Powers of Mormon Polygamy

An important feature of Mormon polygamy was the assumed biological improvements it was believed to bring. Numbers of observers in Europe and America feared the race was dwindling in strength and size, and many attributed the loss of vigor not only to an inadequate diet but to failure to follow correct rules governing reproduction.[35] The Saints said their marriage system would produce greater health, a more powerful constitution, and restoration of the longevity of the ancients.

Mormon commentary in the late nineteenth century is rich with self-congratulation on the health-giving effects of plurality. Mary Jane Mount Tanner told Hubert Howe Bancroft in 1880 that polygamy was "given for the regeneration of mankind. There are no healthier, or better developed children than those born in polygamy."[36] Eliza Roxcy Snow, plural wife to both Joseph Smith and Brigham Young, said that the practice not only increased personal purity and character but was "also instrumental in producing a more perfect type of manhood mentally and physically, as well as in restoring human life to its former longevity."[37] George Q. Cannon asserted that "the children of our system are brighter, stronger, healthier every way than those of the monogamic system."[38] After a generation of trial in the 1880s, one contributor to the *Deseret News* asked how anyone could doubt such claims "when we daily meet boys," the product of polygamous unions, "weighing over 200 pounds and their parents perhaps not over 150."[39]

Central to the Mormon argument was the conviction that polygamy better accommodated the disparate sexual needs of men and women. Plural marriage removed the "unnatural restraint" imposed on males by the "one-wife system" with its temptation for men to engage in sexual activity apart from

[35] See the antebellum ultraist, Fowler, *Marriage*, 10–11, 12; "Have Americans Degenerated?" [New York] *Daily Graphic*, 21 Nov. 1873, 3:225, 139/2; and the Frenchman, Benedict Morel, as discussed in Haller, *Eugenics*, 14–17.

[36] Tanner to Bancroft, 29 Oct. 1880, cu-b, 5–6. Also see her comments to her aunt, in Tanner to Mary Bessac Hunt, 16 July 1882, Provo, Utah, in Tanner, *A Fragment*, 188.

[37] Snow, "Sketch of My Life," 17.

[38] Cannon to journalists, JH, 20 Mar. 1882, 3.

[39] William R. May, "Mormon Polygamy from a Philosophical Standpoint," *Des. Eve. News*, 15 Feb. 1881, 14:71 [2/3]. Catherine Bates, a British visitor of the 1880s, said one of "the strong arguments" yet employed by the Saints in behalf of plurality was "that a fine healthy race can be produced by this means alone." Bates, *Year in the Great Republic*, 2:225, 228.

reproduction.[40] The corrupting presence of lust, explained Mormon defenders, was what led to sexual excess, depleting the energies of monogamous married partners and imprinting a lascivious nature on their offspring. Beyond this, Mormon plural marriage provided better opportunities for males to achieve spermatic continence by confining sexual congress to encounters intending only reproduction.[41] Apostle Amasa Lyman described the Mormon system as "the great necessity of the age, because it is a means that God has introduced to check the physical corruption and decline of our race. . . [It will permit man] to live until he attain[s] to the age of a tree."[42] By faithfully adhering to the Principle, Mormon patriarchs said they would produce a rejuvenated race of athletes, scholars, and priests.[43]

The following selections, assaulting monogamous marriage while contending for the health-giving effects of plurality, are taken from the writings and sermons of two men who were editors of the *Deseret News*, apostles, and at one time or another counselors to presidents of the church: Charles W. Penrose (1832–1925) and Albert Carrington (1813–1889).

CHARLES W. PENROSE, "PHYSICAL REGENERATION," MIL. STAR, 29:32 (10 AUG. 1867), 497–99.

It is a fact which must be patent to all, that the present generation of men are much more feeble, undersized, and shorter lived, than their ancestors of a few generations ago. Armor preserved in old castles and museums, worn by the men-at-arms of former times, would weigh down our common soldiers and gay volunteers to the ground, and would fit the majority of them about as well as a sentry-box. The army recruiting standard reduced now to 5 ft. 5 in., will show the difficulty of obtaining men of stature sufficient to come up to the former idea of a soldier. Stand for a few minutes in a position to overlook either of the public thoroughfares of our large towns, and see how

[40] John Taylor, in "Polygamy vs. Monogamy," *Mormon*, 1:42 (8 Dec. 1853) [2/3]; Remy in *Journey to Great-Salt-Lake City*, 1:103 and 2:109n; George Q. Cannon, 9 Oct. 1869, *Journal of Discourses*, 13:206; Joseph Birch, "Is Polygamy 'Unnatural'?" *Mil. Star*, 36:3 (20 Jan. 1874), 33–35; and ibid. 36:4 (27 Jan. 1874), 49–51. A common nineteenth-century argument for prostitution was that it saved wives and daughters from male rapacity. See Lecky, *History of European Morals*, 2:299–300. Mary Bennion Powell said the more "passionate" nature of men was still evoked as a justification for polygamy in early twentieth-century Mormon homes. Powell to Stewart, 29 Jan. 1952, CSmH, 56–57. The entire subject is most extensively treated in the chapter, "Blessings of the Abrahamic Household," in Hardy, *Solemn Covenant*, 84–126; and Hardy and Erickson, "'Regeneration—Now and Evermore!'" 40–61.

[41] For discussion of theories prevalent in the nineteenth century concerning the dangers of excessive retention and/or loss of semen, see MacDonald, "The Frightful Consequences," 423–33; and Stolberg, "Self-pollution," 37–61.

[42] "Remarks by Amasa M. Lyman," *Des. News* [Weekly], 19 April 1866, 15:20, 154/1–2.

[43] Bertrand, *Mémoires d'un Mormon*, 208.

few of the genus homo you can discover who are blest with a full-developed physical organization. The great majority are small of stature, slight of limb, and look like boys turned old suddenly.

The age promised to man by his Maker after the flood, was a hundred and twenty years. The general term of his life in the days of King David, was three-score years and ten; but it is now reduced to an average of less than half the period stated by the Psalmist, and continues to grow smaller by degrees and alarmingly less as each generation passes from this brief existence. . .

The children now growing up to receive the cares and responsibilities of life, are generally speaking puny, spindly, and easily prostrated, their constitutions being so feeble that they become an easy prey to the many new diseases which are evolved in the gradual process of the general physical decay. . .

The cause of this physical degeneracy lies in the spirit of lasciviousness which increases in power with each successive generation, and in the absence of proper regulations for the marital relations of the sexes, and for the pro-creation of healthy and vigorous offspring. What nation, community, or soci-ety are taking this important subject into consideration, and giving it that attention which it deserves? We answer, the people who are called "Mormons" are the only people on the earth who are truly alive to the tremendous con-sequences involved in this question. While all the world is going down grad-ually to decay and death, this despised people, ridiculed and slandered, and considered to be outside of the pale of civilization, are engaged, in their lofty mountain retreat, in commencing the great work of physical regeneration. Hav-ing forsaken the world's path, they have begun to travel on the road that leads to the increase of life and the attainment of true happiness. To this mission they have been called by that Almighty God who is the Father of our spirits, the former of our bodies, and the Creator of the universe. . .

In building up a new and a holy nation, that shall serve the Lord and gov-ern the world by his power, the Lord has commenced at the foundation of all kingdoms, that is, family organization. . . He is gathering them together, and teaching . . . the principles of personal and family government, eminent-ly prominent among which is the law of chastity. His people are learning how to purge themselves from the old leaven of lasciviousness, which has wrought so much destruction in the world, and to govern themselves by principles of self-control and purity, that they may not bequeath to their posterity the same impulses towards unrestrained indulgence which mankind have inherited from their forefathers, and which has come down to them like an ever-swelling stream, increasing with every succeeding generation.

By the laws which pertain to the order of celestial marriage—called by the world polygamy—while provision is made for every virtuous woman to become an honored wife and happy mother, the relations of the sexes are hedged about with such natural and wholesome restrictions, that self-control becomes a duty and a joy, and the effects thereof are plainly manifest in a more vigorous, healthy, and well developed offspring. This is not mere theory made to put on paper, like many of the schemes and vagaries of the would-be sages of modern times, but these principles are being worked out practically in the Vales of Utah, under the direction of the Almighty, by the Latter-day Saints. And as results are the best proofs of the efficacy of principles, we point with joy and pride to the stalwart sons and fair and robust daughters of Zion. The mountain boys of Utah, powerful and well developed, able to wield the axe or hold the plough, to build up cities, bear weapons of defence, or preach the Gospel to the world, are the first fruits of the Lord's great work of regeneration.

ALBERT CARRINGTON, "PLURALITY OF WIVES—
PHYSIOLOGICALLY AND SOCIALLY," *DES. NEWS* [WEEKLY],
29 MAR. 1866, 15:17, 132/1–4; REPRINTED IN
MIL. STAR 28:22 (2 JUNE 1866), 340–41.

. . . in our last article on plurality of wives, [we] showed a widespread condition of social and moral degradation existing in Christendom, far beneath that of even the semi-barbarous oriental nations. The result is, an equally widespread enfeeblement of the race physiologically, an increase of diseases that prey upon the human system, a shortening of the already brief span of life, and a decrease of strength, vitality and soundness of physiological structure. So prevalent is the crime there alluded to [prostitution] that but comparatively few families entirely escape the poison of the evil in some degree. It has become fashionable to speak of the sensual misdeeds of young men as sowing their wild oats, and they are looked upon as a matter of course. The blood—the life of the system—becomes contaminated and vitiated, which makes itself manifest in various forms, not only in the actual transgressor, but in succeeding generations, the children bearing in part the penalty of the parent's guilt. . . There is, however, another thing, well known to exist, yet beyond the reach of all human enactments, which has its influence, and a weighty one, in deteriorating the human race physically. The intercourse of the sexes is not confined, in married life, to the perpetuating of the species. Long after that end has been attained the same communion is continued, robbing the future mother of that vigor which should nourish her embryotic offspring, and giving intensified sensual desires to that offspring when it comes to fill the measure of its creation. We do not care to pursue this part of the subject farther. It is so well known and universally admitted, that argument on it is needless.

An evil is here discovered which philanthropic physiologists deplore but cannot reach. It is not love, but lust. That it has grown and is growing, facts, patent to the world, declare. Preventives against increasing families are privately and publicly advertised. That they find a large sale is evident, or those furnishing them would not increase in number and add column to column of advertisements in widely circulated and influential newspapers. As a stronger proof of the ruling power of lust, the prevalency of abortions may be fairly adduced; not simply where erring frailty would seek to cover shame, but where there is no motive for concealment, only the desire to enjoy lustful communion without the responsibilities of parental care. . .

Apart from the higher condition of morality found in Utah, plurality of wives, as practiced here, produces a higher condition of physiological existence. Continence, from conception until the term of gestation ceases, gives to the dawning generation stronger and healthier organizations, purer desires, and a higher condition of physical and mental excellence. This is a scientific truth so well known, that the man who would dispute it would be looked upon with contempt by every one versed in physiological science.

We do not introduce these to prove our right to practice plurality of wives, but simply to show that when the Creator of man sanctioned, approved and commanded the principle, He gave to humanity one which if wisely used would be a means of increasing their power and strength, and of prolonging their existence on the earth. And that the very evils charged upon plurality of wives are reversed, its tendency and results being the direct opposite. . .

To-day the most stalwart and physically powerful men known are not found in Christian monogamic nations, but in polygamic Asia. To support this a host of reliable authorities could be produced had we space. And this where plurality of wives is merely regulated by caprice, desire or circumstances, not by the Divine command. The physiological arguments employed against plurality of wives turn around and cut the hands which used them. . .

We know the world, its hollowness and misery. We have lived in it, and have seen the bitter cup drained by thousands. And we know that in slandered and maligned Utah, with her plurality of wives, there is more real happiness than in all the rest of Christendom.

Belinda Marden Pratt (1820–1894), a plural wife of Apostle Parley P. Pratt, spoke from personal experience with polygamy. Her letter to her older sister, Mrs. Lydia Kimball of Nashua, New Hampshire, became one of the the Saints' most widely circulated pamphlets. Its importance arose from the attention it gave to the physiological advantages that polygamy brought to women. Pratt also addressed the issue of whether females should be permitted a plurality of husbands and the importance of patriarchal government in the home. It was an obvious boon to the Mormon cause to hear such words from a woman, the gender so frequently pitied as degraded by plurality. Not only did the LDS church publish the letter as a tract, but Richard Burton reprinted it in his *City of the Saints* and Jules Remy used it as the basis for a contrived dialogue on polygamy in his work.[44]

---

[44] Burton, *City of the Saints*, 483–93; and, Remy, *Journey to Great-Salt-Lake City*, 2:96–109.

[BELINDA PRATT], *DEFENCE OF POLYGAMY,*
BY A LADY OF UTAH (1854), 1–2, 4–7, 10–11.

Dear Sister: . . .

It seems my dear sister, that we are no nearer together in our religious views than formerly.

Why is this? . . .

Do we not all wish in our very hearts to be sincere with ourselves, and to be honest and frank with each other?

If so, you will bear with me patiently, while I give a few of my reasons for embracing, and holding sacred that particular point in the doctrine of the Church of the Saints, to which you, my dear sister, together with a large majority of Christendom so decidedly object.

I mean, a "plurality of wives." . . .

What then appears to be the great object of the marriage relations? I answer: the multiplying of our species—the rearing and training of children.

To accomplish this object, natural law would dictate, that a husband should remain apart from his wife at certain seasons, which, in the very constitution of the female are untimely. Or in other words, indulgence should not be merely for pleasure, or wanton desires, but mainly for the purpose of procreation.

The morality of nature would teach a mother, that, during nature's process in the formation and growth of embryo man, her heart should be pure, her thoughts and affections chaste, her mind calm, her passions without excitement; while her body should be invigorated with every exercise conducive to health and vigor; but by no means subjected to anything calculated to disturb, irritate, weary, or exhaust any of its functions.

And while a kind husband should nourish, sustain, and comfort the wife of his bosom by every kindness and attention consistent with her situation, and with his most tender affection; still he should refrain from all those untimely associations which are forbidden in the great constitutional laws of female nature; which laws we see carried out in almost the entire animal economy. Human animals excepted. . .

Dear sister, in your thoughtlessness, you inquire, "Why not a plurality of husbands as well as a plurality of wives?"

To which I reply:

1st, God has never commanded or sanctioned a plurality of husbands.

2nd, *"Man is the head of the woman,"* and no woman can serve two lords.

3rd, Such an order of things would work death and not life:—or, in plainer language, it would multiply disease instead of children.

In fact, the experiment of a plurality of husbands, or rather of one woman for many men, is in active operation, and has been for centuries in all the principal towns and cities of *"Christendom!"*

It is the genius of *"Christian institutions,"* falsely so called. It is the result of *"Mystery Babylon, the great whore of all the earth."* Or in other words, it is the result of making void the holy ordinances of God in relation to matrimony, and introducing the laws of Rome, in which the clergy and nuns are forbidden to marry, and other members only permitted to have one wife. . .

I again repeat, that nature has constituted the female differently from the male; and for a different purpose.

The strength of the female constitution is designed to flow in a stream of *life*, to nourish and sustain the embryo, to bring it forth, and to nurse it on her bosom.

When nature is not in operation within her in these particulars, and for these heavenly ends, it has wisely provided relief at regular periods, in order that her system may be kept pure, and healthy, without exhausting the fountain of life . . . till mature age, and approaching change of worlds would render it necessary for her to cease to be fruitful, and give her to rest awhile, and enjoy a tranquil life in the midst of that family circle, endeared to her by so many ties. . .

Not so with man. He has no such draw back upon his strength. It is his to move in a wider sphere. If God shall count him worthy of an hundred fold in this life, of wives and children, and houses and lands and kindreds, he may even aspire to Patriarchal sovereignty, to empire; to be the prince or head of a tribe, or tribes; and like Abraham of old, be able to send forth for the defence of his country, hundreds and thousands of his own warriors, born in his own house. . .

In the Patriarchal order of family government, the wife is bound to the law of her husband. She honors him, *"calls him lord,"* even as Sarah obeyed and honored Abraham. She lives for him, and to increase his glory, his greatness, his kingdom, or family.—Her affections are centered in her God, her husband, and her children.

The children are also under his government worlds without end. *"While life or thought, or being lasts, or immortality endures,"* they are bound to obey him as their father and king. . .

You enquire why . . . [a Mormon missionary], when at your house, denied that the Church of this age held to the doctrine of plurality. I answer, that he might have been ignorant of the fact, as our belief on this point was not published till 1852. And had he known it he had no right to reveal the same until the full time had arrived.

God kindly withheld this doctrine for a time, because of the ignorance and prejudice of the nations of Mystic Babylon, that peradventure he might save some of them. . .

Dear sister, do not let your prejudices and traditions keep you from believing the Bible; nor the pride, shame, or love of the world keep you from your seat in the kingdom of heaven, among the royal family of polygamists. Write often and freely.

With sentiments of the deepest affection and kindred feeling, I remain, dear sister, your affectionate sister,

Belinda Marden Pratt

"Reform Must Begin in the Marriage Bed": Plurality as a Socio-Political Imperative

One commentator, describing how Mormonism bundled the things of this world and the next together, said it promised followers "a bushel of potatoes, an extra wife, and a promise of life everlasting."[45] All things social and political were believed to benefit from the practice of plural marriage. It is not surprising then that plurality was recommended for its supposed helpfulness in caring for an assumed surplus of unmarried women.[46] It was an argument that comported with the expectation of apocalyptic upheaval and the widowing of thousands of females as Isaiah, whose prophecies the Mormons fondly remembered, foretold.[47] Difficulty arose, however, when census takers found that Utah, like the United States at large, counted more men than women.[48] Prior to the 1852 announcement Jedediah M. Grant used the census to prove that Mormons did *not* practice polygamy, saying that inasmuch as there were six men for every five women in the territory, "every wife must have more husbands than every husband has wives."[49]

Defenders also said, however, that by the time young people in Utah were of marriageable age the male population had declined, leaving women in the majority—a claim that may have been true in some communities, especially when non-Mormon soldiers, miners, and merchants were removed from the count.[50] Mormons also qualified census figures by arguing there were

---

[45] "Mahomet of the West," 237.

[46] As only two examples, see "Disparity of Sex," *Des. News* [Weekly], 5 Oct. 1854 [2/5]; and "Too Many Girls," *Mil. Star* 36:33 (13 Aug. 1874), 519.

[47] "And in that day seven women shall take hold of one man, saying, We will eat our own bread, and wear our own apparel; only let us be called by thy name, to take away our reproach." Isaiah 4:1.

[48] As one investigator indicated, every census in the nineteenth-century United States displayed an excess of males to females, especially in the American West. Potter, "Growth of Population in America," 636. Church authorities later admitted the greater proportion of males to females: George Q. Cannon, "Religious Service," *Des. News*. [Weekly], 28 July 1882, 31:22, 364/2; and Charles W. Penrose, in *Proceedings*, 2:261. The general parity of number between the sexes, often used to counter arguments for polygyny, seems to characterize even societies where the practice has existed for centuries. Binet, *Marriage en Afrique noire*, 85–89; and Clignet, *Many Wives, Many Powers*, 25.

[49] *Three Letters to the New York Herald*, 44. It is likely that Thomas Kane, rather than Grant, penned this pamphlet in response to charges made by the "run away judges." To privately persuade Kane of the need for polygamy, Grant took an opposite tack. He said Joseph Smith approached the Lord concerning polygamy because in Mormon society there were three females for every two males. Grant to Brigham Young, 30 Dec. 1851, in Sessions, *Mormon Thunder*, 92.

[50] See "Discourse on Celestial Marriage, delivered by Elder Orson Pratt," 7 Oct. 1869, *Des. News* [Weekly], 20 Oct. 1869, 18:37, 440/3–4; "Matrimony and the Census," *Des. News Weekly*, 27 April 1881, 30:13, 198/3–4; and "Superfluous Women," ibid., 14 April 1883, 16:121, 2/3–4. Daynes provides an analysis of the sex ratio, relevant variables including immigration, and their effect on Utah's nineteenth-century Mormon marriage market in *More Wives than One*, 110–15.

fewer *deserving* men than the number of worthy women.[51] Even without qualifications, however, the declaration that there were more women than men
throughout the land and that polygamy offered a way to provide all with homes
and families was heard for years.[52]

In 1870 John Hanson Beadle hyperbolized on the popularity of Mormon
sermons memorializing Joseph Smith's prediction of the Civil War and the
expectation of an accompanying flood of widows into the territory. He said
there was no quicker way to provoke a Saint to anger than to speak of peace
and calm outside Utah. "And my best [Mormon] friends," he said, "were
ready to knock me down at the statement that there were still more men than
women in the United States."[53]

Even without the sexual restrictions enjoined on Mormon believers, plurality's accommodation of male libidinous need and the promise of marriage that it offered to unwed females recommended the practice as a way of
ridding society of prostitution and disease.[54] Echoing Islamic interpreters
of the Quran and Martin Madan in his *Thelypthora*, both of which said plural marriage was God's remedy for ills associated with unattached females,
Latter-day Saints urged that the Principle would benefit all.[55] As George Q.
Cannon explained:

> We are solving the problem that is before the world to-day, over which they
> are pretending to rack their brains. I mean the 'social Problem.' We close the
> door on one side, and say that whoredoms, seductions and adulteries must
> not be committed amongst us . . . at the same time we open the door in the
> other direction and make plural marriage honorable.[56]

---

[51] Orson Pratt, "Celestial Marriage," *Seer* 1:7 (July 1853), 107; A[mos] M[ilton] Musser, "Polygamy," *Mil. Star* 39:26 (25 June 1877), 407; and again, Daynes, *More Wives than One*, 113–14.

[52] For example, see Mary F., "Patriarchal Order of Marriage," *Woman's Exponent* 10:16 (15 Jan. 1882), 121.

[53] Beadle, *Life in Utah*, 307–8. One scholar described Beadle as "a master of caricature . . . [engaging in] deliberate exaggeration." Arrington, *Kate Field and J. H. Beadle*, 12. For Joseph Smith's prediction of the Civil War, see *D&C* 87:1, 25 Dec. 1832; and ibid. 130:12, 2 April 1843.

[54] Prostitution was alleged to be directly proportional to the number of unmarried women in society. One Mormon defender told a journalist, "there were no single women in Utah, and that, with universal polygamy, there would be no single women anywhere." H.V.R., "City of the Saints," *Cincinnati Commercial*, 12 Mar. 1872, 32:192, Supplement, 9/4–5. Also see Alexander Robbins, "Baptism and Plurality of Wives," *Mil. Star*, 17:41 (13 Oct. 1855), 643; "Only Remedy," ibid., 29:38 (21 Sept. 1867), 593–94; and Brigham Young as quoted in Kenney, ed., *Wilford Woodruff's Journal*, 10 July 1870, 6:564.

[55] "What the World Owes to Polygamic Nations," *Mil. Star* 36:47 (24 Nov. 1874), 737–39; and Brigham Young's statement that plural marriage would "work out the moral salvation of the world." 9 Aug. 1868, *Journal of Discourses*, 12:261. For Islamic arguments in support of polygyny, see Ali, *Holy Qur'an*, 187n535. Martin Madan's pleas for plurality as an antidote for the swarms of English spinsters and prostitutes appears in *Thelypthora*, 1:6–7; 2:246–49, 256–57 passim.

[56] Cannon, 15 Aug. 1869, *Journal of Discourses*, 14:58; and again, 6 May 1883, ibid., 24:144–45.

The benefits of plural family life for marginalized women and its supposed tendency to diminish prostitution and disease were, however, but incidental consequences of a larger theo-political role that Mormons envisioned for the doctrine. In the early years of public commendation of the practice, church spokesmen argued for a thorough incorporation of the Principle into government policy. States and nations, they said, must raise their entire superstructure on the foundation of the Abrahamic, polygamous household. Orson Spencer called on congresses and parliaments to reverse their support for monogamy and replace it with vigorous legislative approval for plural marriage.[57]

The following extract is from one of several letters Spencer wrote to his friend, the Rev. William Crowel. The letter was then published by the church as a special sixteen-page tract.

ORSON SPENCER, *PATRIARCHAL ORDER, OR PLURALITY OF WIVES!* (1853), 1–3, 7–8, 12, 14.

Domestic compact is the first order of all social organization, and must even antecede all civil government, and contribute much to the genius and character of the same. It is the basis, upon which every superstructure of society must be reared. . . If the intercourse of the sexes is not regulated in wisdom and purity, the result will be that every consequent branch and order of society will be vitiated thereby. . .

Here let me say, that the family order which God established with Abraham and the Patriarchs, was the order observed among celestial beings, in the celestial world. And this family order is not only one at which God sits as the Head, and the first pattern in the series of matrimonial examples; but it is of perpetual duration, both in and beyond this world. . . When God sets up any portion of his kingdom upon the earth, it is patterned after his own order in the Heavens. When he gives to men a pattern of family organization on the earth, that pattern will be just like his own family organization in the heavens. The family of Abraham was a transcript of a celestial pattern. . .

The Almighty, dear sir, actually visited this husband of two wives, and went into a discussion of his family and domestic concerns. . . What did he say about his family matters? Did he say, Abraham; beware of a carnal mind! beware of the lust for woman! Did he say the first word of the kind? No, sir; I repeat it, no, sir; he said no such thing. Well, tell us plainly what he did say? Why, read it for yourself upon your knees, if your heart is not otherwise humble enough to receive this doctrine. He virtually said this to Abraham,—Abra-

---

[57] Well educated and a former Baptist minister, Orson Spencer (1802–1855) joined the Mormons in 1841. He went west in 1846, was appointed chancellor of the University of Deseret in 1850, sat in the territorial legislature, and died in St. Louis while on a mission in 1855.

ham, I find no fault with your taking two wives, but on the other hand, I bless you for it, and I bless you in doing it, and I bless them in becoming your wives, above all other women upon the earth. I bless you and your wife Sarah with the strength and joy of your youth; you shall have a son. You shall not only have a son, but you shall have even nations of sons and daughters. Your wife Hagar also shall be greatly blessed among women for what she has done kings and potentates, and even nations shall be among her offspring. Mine angel shall wait upon her, and instruct and comfort her, and see her wants supplied. And Sarah, seeing she had faith while herself was barren, to give Hagar to you to wife, shall herself even yet have a son, notwithstanding her age. And your posterity shall be as the dust of the earth for number and multitude, and as the sands upon the sea-shore. . .

Do not startle, sir, if I should tell you that monogamy, or the one wife system, adopted throughout Christendom, is a very defective system. It does not answer the demands of society, and it is altogether inferior to the Patriarchal system of polygamy, as introduced by God himself. Debauchery and whoredoms are preeminently practised among Christian nations. . . Heathen nations previous to their intercourse with Christian nations have been comparatively free from these abominable lusts. . .

Remember, sir, that the covenant made with Abraham, was everlasting, and it also embraced all the righteous seed of like faith, not only through and during the Apostolic age, but in all ages of the world. . . Now go forth from one side of Christendom to the other, from East to West, and from North to South, and tell me in what corner of Christendom, Abraham, or any like him, could dwell in peace with his wives and concubines? Or Elkanah and his wives? Or David, with his own wives, and the wives of King Saul, which God gave him? . . . The laws of Christian nations are an unmistakable answer to these serious questions. These laws would inflict heavy penalties of distress and infamy upon such men. And these laws too are the laws of Christian nations. The Turk and the Heathen have never cast the first vote to enact these laws. . .

If I had the voice of a trumpet and the engine of superhuman power, I would penetrate the ears of all Christendom with a sense of this awful, defiling, desolating sin! I would at once call the attention of congress and parliament, and civil and ecclesiastic cabinets, to this one great foundation of society. . .

Abraham is the rock—the father of the faithful! and Sarah is the mother and pattern for all women! She was the bright pattern of conjugal loyalty and faith for females, wives, and mothers, of all ages. . . Daughters of Israel! Look unto Sarah; her that bare you. If you suffer with her, you shall reign with her. Hear it! You shall be heirs of the same promise! . . .

And women . . . that knowingly undervalue this "promise" and Patriarchal order, do most alarmingly manifest symptoms of being without natural affection, and destitute of the faith and righteousness of holy women of old, and insensible to the blessing of becoming mothers of nations, and wearing the coronet of Sarah, Rachael, Hannah, Elizabeth, and Mary. They have forgotten the natural use of women, as revealed from heaven, and become despisers of thrones, and dominions, and principalities, and powers. . .

The grand design of God in bringing the spirits of men and women to occupy bodies upon this earth was, in order to establish a system of perfect Patriarchal government, according to the pattern of the family of Heaven.[58]

After arriving in the Great Basin, Apostle Parley P. Pratt helped write a constitution for the provisional state of Deseret, sat in the territorial legislature of Utah, and, in the winter of 1855–56, as chaplain of that body presented this address to members of the legislative council. Urging Utah's territorial legislature to enshrine polygamy and a strict moral code in its laws, Pratt warned that it was departure from such practices that led to the decline of societies elsewhere. If Utah were to escape the "rock and quicksands" on which other governments foundered, they must craft legislation to help citizens be faithful to the domestic arrangements of father Abraham.[59]

"MARRIAGE AND MORALS IN UTAH,"
DES. NEWS [WEEKLY], 16 JAN. 1856, 5:45, 356–57.
*An Address Written by Elder Parley P. Pratt, Read
in Joint Session by Mr. Thos. Bullock, chief Clerk of the House,
in Representatives Hall, Fillmore, Dec. 31, 1855. The Assembly Tendered
the Author their Thanks by a Unanimous Vote. And by a Like Vote,
Ordered the Address to Be Published in the Deseret News.*

Mr. President and Gentlemen:—

The All-wise Creator, the God of nature, has implanted in the human heart certain affections, which, under proper culture and direction, give rise to family ties: hence the necessity and importance of the moral and social relations and the institutions for their proper direction and government.

'Tis nature's universal law, and the just and great commandment with blessing: that each and every species should multiply and fill the measure of its creation. Hence the growth of families,—the germs of nations:—and hence,

---

[58] The imperative of the husband's rule is what accounted for the phrase "patriarchal order of marriage." Plurality and male dominance in the home were inseparable in Mormonism's vision of the ideal domestic arrangement. The patriarchal family was expected eventually to become the foundation for an eternal political structure. As one Saint put it, the liberties granted Americans by the nation's fathers, combined with Mormon family life, would lead to "A Patriarchal Commonwealth." Elder Wesley Wandell, "Extracts from an Oration Delivered at the Pajaro on the Fourth of July, 1857," *Western Standard*, 2:19 (17 July 1857), [1/5].

[59] The lecture was published in pamphlet form as Pratt, *Marriage and Morals in Utah*.

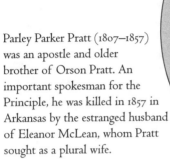

Parley Parker Pratt (1807–1857) was an apostle and older brother of Orson Pratt. An important spokesman for the Principle, he was killed in 1857 in Arkansas by the estranged husband of Eleanor McLean, whom Pratt sought as a plural wife.

as we before observed, the necessity of laws founded in wisdom, to guard, as it were, the fountain and issues of life.

In short—moral and social affections and institutions are the very foundation of all government, whether of family, church or state. If these are perverted, or founded in error, the whole superstructure is radically wrong, and will contain within itself the seeds of its own decay and dissolution. . .

I beseech, therefore, honorable gentlemen to hear me patiently. Abraham, the friend of God, lived in Asia upwards of four hundred years before the law of Moses was written on tables of stone, or thundered from Mount Sinai.

To this man God gave laws, commandments, statutes, and judgments in an everlasting covenant. . .

In connection with this covenant we have reason to believe that God would reveal laws, statutes, and institutions which would be productive of the greatest possible increase of a wise, healthy, and virtuous posterity.

In the precedents recorded of Abraham and his posterity two principles are conspicuous as being subservient to the carrying out of those ends: viz:—

First:—A plurality of wives:—

Second:—An entire prohibition of all sexual intercourse except upon the principle of marriage:—a breach of which was considered a capital offence, punishable with death. God provided Abraham with Sarah, Hagar, Keturah, and several other wives not named. By this means he became the father of many nations and his seed was multiplied exceedingly.

God also gave to Jacob, Abraham's grandson, four wives:—viz: Leah, Rachel, Bilhah, and Zilpah; by which means he became the father of twelve tribes. . .

Now after Abraham had obtained all these wives, and had raised up children by them, the Lord bears testimony in the 26th chapter of Genesis, verse 5th, saying:—"Abraham obeyed my voice and kept my charge, my commandments, my statutes, and my laws."[60]

Here then, we have demonstration that a man living four hundred years before the law of Moses was given, had statutes, commandments, and laws given him of God; and that he kept them.

These laws evidently included polygamy or plurality of wives, from the fact that he had them as a means of carrying out the promise of exceeding multiplicity. Here then, the matter is set for ever at rest, that polygamy is included in the ordinance of marriage, and in the everlasting covenant and laws of God; and that, under proper regulations, it is an institution holy, just, virtuous, pure, and, in the estimation of God, abundantly calculated to bless, preserve, and multiply a nation.

Hence the laws of some of our States, which recognize polygamy as a crime, are at once both unscriptural, and unconstitutional, as well as immoral. Common law in England, and in the United States, recognizes the Bible as the very foundation of all moral and criminal jurisprudence: and the Constitution of the United States, and of each State guarantees the liberty of, at least an enlightened conscience, founded on the moral law of God as found in that Holy Book. Hence, should an individual, or a community, in all good faith regulate their marriages by the laws of God as given to Abraham, no State law can harm them while the civil courts are bound to abide that holy and sacred guarantee of the Constitution: viz: "Liberty of conscience." . . .

It is true Jesus Christ and his Apostles, so far as their writings have come to us, have not dwelt on practical plurality in their own age, for the best of all reasons. Judea was then a Roman province, under Roman laws, which were opposed to polygamy. On this account the Jews had greatly degenerated; they had corrupted their way, and perverted the pure institutions of their more virtuous fathers. . .

But, one thing is certain—Jesus Christ and his Apostles always approved of Abraham, Isaac and Jacob and the holy prophets of old;—bore testimony of their virtue and faithfulness, and represented them as honorable fathers of the faithful, and members of rulers in the kingdom of God.

Jesus said, on one occasion to the Jews:—"If ye were Abraham's seed ye would do the works of Abraham." . . .

Paul and the apostles exhorted the saints to be like Abraham the father of the faithful, whose children they were through the gospel; and if children then heirs to the same covenants of promise. . .

---

[60] Pratt subsequently joined scriptural arguments used in his address with a copy of the Rev. David O. Allen's comments pleading for Protestant toleration of polygamy in India: Pratt, *Scriptural Evidences in Support of Polygamy*. Allen's book appeared in 1856 under the title *India, Ancient and Modern*.

Men, brethren and fathers:—In this review we have proved:—

First:—An everlasting covenant made with Abraham, in which all nations should be blessed:

Secondly:—That one main feature of this covenant pertained to the exceeding great multiplicity of our species, and to the organization, perpetuity and growth of families, nations and kingdoms:—

Thirdly:—That God, being the best judge of the means of multiplying, appointed a plurality of wives, for good and holy men, as a principal means of multiplying their seed, and forbade, on pain of death, all sexual intercourse, except that sanctioned by the holy laws of marriage:—

Fourthly:—That the covenant and laws pertaining to marriage and virtue, or the moral and social relations of the sexes, as held by Abraham, Isaac, and Jacob were never altered or disannulled either by Moses or the prophets, Jesus Christ or the Apostles; consequently that this covenant, and the laws, penalties, and promises thereunto pertaining, are, or by right ought to be, still of force.

Fifthly:—That all nations were to be blessed in these covenants and institutions; and that the gentiles were to become fellow heirs of the same by the gospel; through which they became the seed of Abraham:—

And, sixthly:—That to transgress these holy laws, change this ordinance, or break this everlasting covenant, would, according to Isaiah the prophet, "defile the very earth, under the inhabitants thereof." We next enquire:—What power has been guilty of such innovations? "Who has transgressed the laws—changed the ordinance,—broken the everlasting covenant?"

This we charge home upon Rome. She is the "fourth beast" of Daniel's vision:—"She ruled the earth as with a rod of iron:"—"She made war with the saints and overcame them:"—She changed the laws and institutions of both Jews and Christians:—by her sorceries were all nations deceived:—She, in short, is "Mystery, Babylon the Great,—the mother of harlots and abominations of the earth:"—She licensed whoredoms; but forbade to marry; allowing to none of her citizens but one wife, and to many of them, viz., the clergy, none at all.

Every, so called, Christian nation, including even Protestant England and the American States, has retained, at least, this one trait of her superstitions and abominations. They have either permitted or licensed whoredoms; and strictly prohibited a plurality of wives. They have punished lightly, or not at all, that which was, under all dispensations, by the law of God considered a capital offence—a crime unto death: and have made a crime, and annexed a heavy penalty to that which, according to the Bible, was never recognized as a crime at all, either by God, Jesus Christ, the Holy Ghost, angels, prophets, or apostles. Yea,—fellow citizens, the laws of some of our States, I am ashamed to tell it, would recognize as illegitimate the children of Abraham and Jacob; would take from them their wives; thus tearing asunder what God hath joined together; and would doom those holy patriarchs, themselves, to hard labor and solitary confinement within the walls of prison for years; and then suffer their wives and children to be prostituted with impunity:—and then, as if to crown the climax of inconsistency, such an order of things, taken together, would be called "Virtue," and such institutions be dignified by the name of "Christianity." Such institutions have filled "Christendom" with whoredoms, her cities with abominations, and the world with disease and rottenness: till the words of Isaiah have been fulfilled:—"The earth is defiled under the inhabitants thereof." . . .

What, then, shall the righteous do?

We reply:—Restore the law of God,—the new and everlasting covenant. Let every good citizen of both sexes marry at a proper age:—bless them, and say:—"Be fruitful and multiply." Make death the penalty for fornication and adultery: thus throwing a shield around our families and sacred domestic institutions. Let the monogamic law, restricting a man to one wife, with all its attendant train of whoredoms, intrigues, seductions, wretched and lonely single life, hatred, envy, jealousy, infanticide, illegitimacy, disease and death, like the millstone cast into the depths of the sea—sink with Great Babylon to rise no more. Let every man and woman be virtuous, pure, holy—filling the measure of their creation. And let us go to, and fill these mountains; the States, North and South America; the earth; and an endless succession of worlds with a holy, virtuous, and highly intellectual seed:—whose hearts shall delight in the law of God. . .

Most scholars have long believed that the eugenics movement began in 1883 with Charles Darwin's cousin, Sir Francis Galton, but George Q. Cannon (1827–1901), one of Utah's most influential nineteenth-century leaders, espoused many of the same ideas twenty-six years earlier. Building on its saving temporal gifts, Cannon argued that polygamy should be implemented through a careful management of all sexual relationships by the state. As editor and publisher of the *Western Standard* in San Francisco in the mid-1850s, Cannon was Mormonism's foremost spokesman on the Pacific Coast. He eventually represented Utah Territory in Congress and became a member of the LDS church's First Presidency.[61]

GEORGE Q. CANNON, "IMPROVEMENT OF OUR SPECIES,"
WESTERN STANDARD 2:22, 7 AUG. 1857 [2/4–6].

The physical nature of man is animal. The laws of generation, development, sustenance and health which apply to the lower orders of animals apply also to him. The causes which produce disease and degeneracy in them effect

---

[61] Ekins, ed., *Defending Zion*. For other religious advocates of the eugenics movement in the U.S., see all of Rosen, *Preaching Eugenics*.

the same results in him. Experience has long since taught mankind the necessity of observing certain natural laws in the propagation of animals, or the stock will degenerate and finally become extinct. But strange to say, in regard to the human animal, these laws, except in certain particulars, are more or less disregarded in these latter times. The inevitable consequence is, the race is degenerating, new diseases are introduced, while effeminacy and barrenness are on the increase: and worse than all, this evil condition of the body has its effect upon the mind. Children may no longer be compared to healthy plants growing upon good soil; but rather to the productions of the hot-house where vegetation is forced into premature and artificial growth and untimely ripeness... Doubtless it is and ought to be the duty of legislators and conservators of our race, to introduce such regulations and laws, and enforce them, as are best calculated to develop our physical nature. A well formed, healthy, vigorous race should be the end sought. This kept in view, it need not be difficult to know the means necessary to accomplish it. The ancient Spartans acted upon this policy, and the happy result was the production of a nation of the noblest men and women the world ever saw. No diseased and effeminate person was permitted to marry and curse the world with a tainted offspring. The children of the entire republic belonged to the Government, which appointed competent persons to superintend their physical and mental training, and when the fit time arrived they married them as they saw fit, keeping constantly in view the improvement of the race. It was early and constantly impressed upon the minds of the youth, that it was a duty which they owed to the nation to preserve the fountain of life pure within themselves and so to transmit it to their offspring. Those were days of wise thoughts and noble deeds; and Pagan though they were, they were incomparably more virtuous than is modern Christendom.

The rational principle of man is spiritual. Yet so intimately is that spirituality connected with his physical nature, that the full exercise of the one depends materially upon the perfect development of the other. A mal-formed man will have a mal-formed mind. A well developed intellectual brain will produce a philosophic mind. This is a truth that will bear investigation; and shews that our mental nature is a superstructure built upon the foundation of our physical structure. It also shows the utter folly of attempting to improve the moral condition of the world while its physical remains unimproved. Church going, reform associations, sabbath schools, etc., are mere palliatives not curatives. Notwithstanding these expedients, the moral sense of the people is being more and more blunted continually. This state of things must continue, until moralists and legislators find out that a true and effectual reform must begin in the marriage bed. Licence to marry should not come from the priest but from the physician. It will be when the law forbids the unhealthy to beget children—when it compels every healthy man to marry—when a

refusal to this will debar him from holding office—from voting—from sue-
ing at courts at law—from making contracts—from following any learned
profession—when it suffers no healthy girl to remain single after she becomes
of proper age—when no whore shall be permitted to live—when illicit intercourse shall be punished with death, that we shall witness any improvement
in the morals of the age. It is true, such a course would come in contact with
the ridiculous sentimentality of the age, and heaven knows, if that could be
overturned and rooted out it would be a substantial blessing. . .

This is precisely what the Saints in the valleys of the mountains are endeavoring to accomplish. Joseph Smith had penetration enough to know, that so
long as the bodies of men are weak, degenerate, and tainted with impurities
inherited from their fathers for a thousand generations, it is impossible to accomplish with them any great moral improvement, or indoctrinate them with many
divine truths. Therefore, being divinely aided, he introduced a system which
commenced precisely where the Christian dispensation began—"Behold, thou
shalt conceive in thy womb, and bring forth a son, and shalt call his name Jesus."
Luke, 1:21. He taught that none but healthy men should marry—that a man
should know his wife for the purpose of procreation and for that only—that
he should keep himself apart from her during the carrying and nursing periods—that it is lawful and right, God commanding, for a man to have more
than one wife—that adultery should be punishable with death—that whoredom should not be tolerated under any consideration—and that by observing these rules and the general laws of health, their posterity would become
healthy and vigorous, and the prophecy of Isaiah which says, As the age of a
tree, so shall the age of my people be, will be fulfilled. This theory is reduced
to practice in Utah Territory; and it is remarked by immigrants passing through
Salt Lake City, that the proportion of children is unusually great, and they are
uncommonly robust and healthy. Who cannot see that the mental vigor of those
children will be in proportion to their physical perfection? and that a generation is rising in the American interior, who will make their mark upon the history of their times? This is what the Gentiles with the priests at their head call
"Mormon abomination," and other hard names: but the question arises,
Which is the better? the Mormon, or the Christian practice in relation to this
matter? There is not a whore in Utah, neither is there a single female but what
can find a husband and a home if she so desires: whereas in Christian cities
harlots are numbered by the thousand. The genius of Christian monogamy is
to encourage prostitution; because it forbids plural marriages, yet compels no
man to marry, and thus debars thousands of females from gratifying the
strongest instincts of their nature, which are comprehended in the sacred names
of "wife" and "mother." Marriage is more general in the United States than
in any other part of Christendom: yet even here there are thousands of men
that refuse to marry. . . The result is, the country is cursed with that most dread-

ful of all curses, prostitution. . . Human nature must be taken as it is. Legalize polygamy, abolish whoredom by the strong arm of the law, and punish adultery with death, and numberless evils both physical and moral would disappear from the land. Wives who are now sickly and wretched, and who are giving to the world children filled with evil passions fastened upon them by the inordinate indulgence of their begetters, would become healthy and strong, and their offspring would grow up free from many evils which now taint them. Then when the people have laid the foundation for a healthy generation, their efforts at moral and spiritual improvement may result in success. But as long as monogamy is the law, bastardy, whoredom, and degeneracy will exist; and also their concomitants, irreligion, intemperance, licentiousness and vice of every kind and degree.

Builders of a New Civilization

In announcing the doctrine of polygamy the Saints publicly imprinted their religion with its most distinctive signature. They were unreserved in declaring the advantages that would follow a restoration of the Abrahamic plural household. Their vision combined a plurality of wives with male dominance and a disciplined, reproductively purposed sexuality, what one defender called "regulated and restricted plural marriage."[62] They justified the practice on the basis of modern revelation, scripture, and, as they understood it, natural law. They viewed non-Mormon monogamists as hypocritically conducting "their sexual intercourse by lustful feelings" instead of "the pure and holy feeling of procreation."[63] The prophet's 1843 declaration on plural wives and concubines, like the flowering rod of Aaron, wondrously branched after the Saints moved west, acquiring implications for Christology, historical interpretation, domestic order, personal health, and civil government. Mormons were so energetic in proclaiming its merits that they produced one of the larger bodies of apologetic material supporting polygynous marriage in world literature. And in doing so they spoke in ways contemporary Mormons would hesitate to own.

But to their minds, the Saints were laying the foundations of a new civilization, about to "revolutionize the whole earth."[64] Orson Hyde caught their

---

[62] "Way of the World," *Des. Eve. News*, 2 Sept. 1879, 12:237 [2/2].

[63] "Reply to the 'Christian Herald' on the Plurality of Wives," *Zion's Watchman* 1:4–5 (12 Nov. 1853), 31.

[64] Brigham Young, 19 June 1853, *Journal of Discourses*, 1:190.

enthusiasm: "[Polygamy] is the cord that shall revolutionize the whole world, and it will make the United States tremble from the very head to the foot; it is like leaven hid in three measures of meal until the whole is leavened. There is such a tide of irresistible arguments, that, like the grand Mississippi, it bears on its bold current everything that dares to oppose its course."[65]

Hannah T. King, who proudly embraced the gospel "*in its fullness*," found that joining the Saints in the Rocky Mountains was like "literally passing from one World to another!"[66] A spokesman of the same generation, also believing that a portentous change had occurred, told how "In the coming day—which, thank God, is now dawning upon humanity, and the early beams of which are shining upon the Saints in Utah—the old patriarchal institutions will be the prevailing fashion."[67]

---

[65] "Lecture By Elder Orson Hyde," *Des. News* [Weekly], 19 Oct. 1854, 4:32 [1/5].

[66] Hannah Tapfield King (1807–1886) was an English convert who, with her non-Mormon husband, came to Utah in 1853. For this quote, see her "Brief Memoir," cu-b.

[67] Charles W. Penrose, "Marriage," *Mil. Star* 30:22 (30 May 1868), 340.

Chapter 3

"The Root of the Matter"
Mormons Talk to
Themselves about Polygamy

If plural marriage startled non-Mormons, it was also fraught with challenge for many within the church. Orson Pratt's 1852 sermon was more than an acknowledgement. It was also a treatise intended to enlighten the faithful. While attempts to explain the doctrine to believers continued as long as the practice survived, the two decades or so following the 1852 announcement witnessed an especially large number of such commentaries. The daunting nature of the task faced by Mormon pluralists was illustrated in the comment of a Mormon mother that the Saints needed to "so live that when our children grow up they may feel that Plural Marriage is far superior to the one wife system, and that they may not have the prejudices to overcome that we have had through tradition, and that our children may be reconciled to it as the children of Jacob were."[1] To assist them church leaders regularly published sermons in the *Deseret News*, other church organs, and, beginning in 1855, in the *Journal of Discourses*.

Such lectures combined advice to the faithful with rehearsals of the justifying arguments given to Gentiles.

"No Exaltation Without It":
Importance of the Doctrine

Later claims that polygamy was never a central tenet of Mormonism, or that it was not essential for the highest reward in heaven, ignore a large body of

---

[1] Lizzie Leaker, "Patriarchal Marriage," *Woman's Exponent*, 6:2 (15 June 1877), 11. For more in the same vein, see Apostle Amasa M. Lyman, "Remarks," 5 April 1866, *Des. News* [Weekly], 15:20, 155/3; and Orson Pratt, 11 Aug. 1867, *Journal of Discourses*, 12:92.

teachings to the contrary. The subject was frequently addressed in religious meetings where church members were told to live in a manner worthy of entering the new order. Those who turned away from it were reproached. Polygamy, some said, was as important as baptism. Its practice was described as a necessary prerequisite for the Second Coming of Christ. And those who lived the Principle as instructed were told they could expect more domestic happiness than if they remained in monogamy. As one Mormon female put it:

> Plural marriage is the platform on which is built Endless Kingdoms and lives and no other or all combined principles revealed can be substituted as a compensation. It is only our want of knowledge, that we do not hail it as our greatest gift.[2]

When the national government began its campaign to eliminate polygamy from Mormon society and some church members sought to escape its practice, leaders spoke forcefully on its behalf. Daniel H. Wells (1814–1891), a counselor to President Brigham Young, stated in open court what the consequences were for refusing to live the Principle.

> [Counselor Wells testified that] It was a doctrine of the church that when male members came to a thorough understanding of the revelation on the principle of plural or celestial marriage, and other circumstances being favorable, if they failed to obey it they would be under condemnation, and would be *clipped in their glory* in the world to come. The circumstances that would excuse a person would be physical incapacity and the like. The revelation says that they to whom this revelation shall come and who can and will not obey it shall be damned. The doctrine was enjoined upon all male members of the Church whose circumstances were favorable to their taking a plurality of wives.[3]

Despite such statements, members continually raised the question. It was not a precept for the inhabitants of heaven only, church authorities repeatedly reminded them, but a doctrine to be lived in the present life.[4] Men who

---

[2] Esther Romania Bunnell Penrose, Memoir, LDS Archives, 6–7. For a few of many other statements supporting this view, see "Provo Conference. Remarks By Prest. Brigham Young," *Des. News* [Weekly], 14 Nov. 1855, 5:36, 282/2; "Plurality of Wives," ibid., 8 Mar. 1866, 15:14, 108/1; Geo. A. Smith, "The Opposers of Celestial Marriage," ibid., 27 Oct. 1869, 13:38, 452/3; "Discourse By Apostle George Teasdale," ibid., 6 Feb. 1884, 33:3, 35/1; the memory of Clawson Y. Cannon Sr. interview, OHP, 40; and the signed petition of Mormon women declaring that without plural marriage, "man cannot hereafter attain to a fullness of exaltation." See "Petition of 22,626 Women of Utah," House Misc. Doc. 42 (44-1), 1876, Serial 1698, 2.

[3] "The Reynolds Trial," *Des. News* [Weekly], 15 Dec. 1875, 24:46, 732/1.

[4] For a few of many examples, see George Q. Cannon, "Discourse on Celestial Marriage," *Des. News* [Weekly], 3 Nov. 1869, 13:39, 457/1; Orson Hyde, 3 Nov. 1878, *Journal of Discourses*, 20:99; reproof for failing to fully live the Principle in Graffam, ed., *Salt Lake School of the Prophets Minute Book*, 3 Oct. 1883, 12 Oct. 1883, 37, 48; the 1882 revelation to President John Taylor, as it related to Seymour B. Young, in Clark, ed., *Messages*, 2:348, 13 Oct. 1882; and the memory of Annie Clark Tanner, *Mormon Mother*, 62.

hesitated, especially leaders, were told they were failing to abide requirements imposed by God and it was best if they resigned their priesthood callings. George Q. Cannon said he "did not feel like holding up his hand to sustain anyone as a presiding officer over any portion of the people who had not entered into the Patriarchal order of Marriage."[5] Neither did living monogamously with a succession of women satisfy the requirement. Except for those who could not practice the Principle due to circumstances beyond their control, Cannon stated they "must have more than one wife at a time in order to obey that Law."[6] Joseph F. Smith (1838–1918), an apostle, counselor to three church presidents, and a church president himself, spoke forcefully on the subject:

"DISCOURSE DELIVERED BY ELDER JOS. F. SMITH,"
7 JULY 1878, DES. NEWS [WEEKLY], 11 SEPT. 1878, 27:32, 498/1–5.

There is a great deal said about our plural marriage by the outside world, and sometimes it is referred to by the Latter-day Saints at home. I fancy sometimes that not only is the world without knowledge in relation to this principle, but many of those who profess to be latter-day Saints are far from possessing a correct understanding of it. . .

Some people have supposed that the doctrine of plural marriage was a sort of superfluity, or non-essential to the salvation or exaltation of mankind. In other words, some of the Saints have said, and believe, that a man with one wife, sealed to him by the authority of the Priesthood for time and eternity, will receive an exaltation as great and glorious, if he is faithful, as he possibly could with more than one. I want here to enter my solemn protest against this idea, for I know it is false. . . The marriage of one woman to a man for time and eternity by the sealing power, according to the law of God, is a fulfillment of the celestial law of marriage in part—and is good so far as it goes—and so far as a man abides these conditions of the law, he will receive his reward therefore, and this reward, or blessing, he could not obtain on any other grounds or conditions. But this is only the beginning of the law, not the whole of it. Therefore, whoever has imagined that he could obtain the fullness of the blessings pertaining to this celestial law, by complying with only a portion of its conditions, has deceived himself. He cannot do it. . .

It need scarcely be said that the Prophet [Joseph Smith] found no one any more willing to lead out in this matter in righteousness than he was himself. Many could see it—nearly all to whom he revealed it believed it, and received

[5] Larson and Larson, eds., *Diary of Charles Lowell Walker*, 26 April 1884, 2:629; and statements by Joseph F. Smith and George Q. Cannon in the April 1884 general priesthood meeting as quoted in Journals of Thomas Memmott, April 1884, reel 3, LDS Archives, 102–3.

[6] Kenney, ed., *Wilford Woodruff's Journal*, 9 Mar. 1884, 8:235. Those contending that monogamous marriage to a succession of women met the requirement for reaching the highest kingdom in the hereafter, Joseph F. Smith said, were guilty of uttering "a damned lie." As quoted in Journals of Thomas Memmott, April 1884, reel 3, LDS Archives, 102.

the witness of the Holy Spirit that it was of God; but none excelled, or even matched the courage of the Prophet himself.

If, then, this principle was of such great importance that the Prophet himself was threatened with destruction, and the best men in the Church with being excluded from the favor of the Almighty, if they did not enter into and establish the practice of it upon the earth, it is useless to tell me that there is no blessing attached to obedience to the law, or that a man with only one wife can obtain as great a reward, glory or kingdom as he can with more than one, being equally faithful.

Patriarchal marriage involves conditions, responsibilities and obligations which do not exist in monogamy, and there are blessings attached to the faithful observance of that law, if viewed only upon natural principles, which must so far exceed those of monogamy as the conditions responsibilities and power of increase are greater. . .

The benefits derived from the righteous observance of this order of marriage do not accrue solely to the husband, but are shared equally by the wives; not only is this true upon the grounds of obedience to a divine law, but upon physiological and scientific principles. In the latter view, the wives are even more benefited, if possible, than the husband physically. But, indeed, the benefits naturally accruing to both sexes, and particularly to their offspring, in time, say nothing of eternity, are immensely greater in the righteous practice of patriarchal marriage than in monogamy, even admitting the eternity of the monogamic marriage covenant. . .

It is a glorious privilege to be permitted to go into a Temple of God to be united as man and wife in the bonds of holy wedlock for time and all eternity by the Authority of the Holy Priesthood, which is the power of God, for they who are thus joined together "no man can put asunder," for God hath joined them. It is an additional privilege for that same man and wife to re-enter the Temple of God to receive another wife in like manner if they are worthy. But if he remain faithful with only the one wife, observing the conditions of so much of the law as pertains to the eternity of the marriage covenant, he will receive his reward, but the benefits, blessings and power appertaining to the second or more faithful and fuller observance of the law, he never will receive, for he cannot. . . I understand the law of celestial marriage to mean that every man in this Church, who has the ability to obey and practice it in righteousness and will not, shall be damned, I say I understand it to mean this and nothing less, and I testify in the name of Jesus that it does mean that.

Simply stated, as members in St. George, Utah, were instructed: "it was the duty of the Elders of Israel to take more wives, and . . . there was no exaltation without it."[7]

---

[7] Charles Smith Journals, fd. 1, item 3, 26 April 1884, UPB, 172.

"LIKE SO MUCH HONEY":
POLYGAMY IN SONG AND STORY

Music also promoted the polygamous message. During the Mormon Reformation of the 1850s, members were instructed not only to keep their households clean, pay tithing, and support their leaders, but to enter the Principle. This verse appeared as part of a ballad sung to the tune of "Rosa May" in the 17th Ward School House in Salt Lake City, on 15 October 1856:

> Now, sisters, list to what I say,—
> With trials this world is rife,
> You can't expect to miss them all,
> Help husband get a wife!
> Now, this advice I freely give,
> If exalted you would be,
> Remember that your husband must
> Be blessed with more than thee.
> Then, O, let us say,
> God bless the wife that strives
> And aids her husband all she can
> T'obtain a dozen wives.[8]

Women were always a crucial audience when discussing polygamy. This fictional account appeared in the *Millennial Star*, a publication in Great Britain, where many Mormons responded to "the New Revelation" with shock. The article is notable for its candor in treating issues like jealousy and female sexual need—as in the Dickensian anecdote about sister "Hugall." Use of colloquy to explore a subject of this kind was a common journalistic device at the time.

"NELLY AND ABBY: A FAMILIAR CONVERSATION
BETWEEN TWO COUSINS, ON MARRIAGE,"
MIL. STAR 15:15–16 (9 AND 16 APRIL 1853), 225–29, 241–44.

Nelly.—Dear cousin Abby, I have been very anxious indeed to see you ever since I heard of the New Revelation. I know that nothing has ever come up yet in this Church, (unless it is now) that could stumble you. But I think now, when your John comes to get two or three more wives, you will feel as keenly as any of us; for I know that he has always been your idol; and to see him bestowing his affections upon others, as he has heretofore so exclusively done upon you; now, as sure as your name is Abby—but I won't say what you may

---

[8] "The Reformation," *Des. News* [Weekly], 26 Nov. 1856, 6:38, 302/1.

do, because you can always command your feelings; but I really believe, that if my husband should provoke me in that way, he might get a salutation from the candle-stick or broom-stick, sooner than I would ever kiss him again! . . .

Abby.—Well, cousin Nelly . . . I am . . . sorry to see your mind fluttered with the New Revelation! It is true, that I have never stumbled at any of the doctrines of this Church, because they all seem so pure and so well calculated to bless and unite all who will observe them in sincerity. . . Now, cousin Nelly, to be plain, I do not know what right you have even to call George your husband, or that I have to call John my husband. What the Lord has not bound upon earth cannot be bound in heaven. I would not like to displease the only authority that can legally unite me to the man that I dearly love. Before I dare to set up an exclusive claim to John, who is to be Prince Regent, and heir apparent to several thrones and principalities, I would like to have my own marriage ratified and sealed. . . Now if God is appointing His sons on the earth to fill thrones and occupy many principalities, and my husband means to be as worthy to fill thrones as others, then I will be content to share with him one throne, and rejoice at the same time to see others share with him other thrones, while my capacity will not allow me to share any more than my own. I know also, Nelly, that I appreciate a kind, intelligent, noble husband, that is ordained and anointed like unto Abraham, to be King over innumerable myriads of the human family, so highly, that I shall not make myself a widow or servant throughout all eternity by opposing what God has clearly revealed by all His Prophets, since the world began. The consequences of my opposing the Patriarchal Order of Marriage would be the loss of my husband for all eternity. . .

Nelly.—Let me interrupt you a moment, cousin Abby, before I forget the point that I wish to call up. Do you mean to say that a female cannot have any husband for the next world or for all the eternities to come, unless she is agreeable to the same law of marriage by which Sarah and Rachel were governed?

Abby.—Yes, cousin, I understand it in this light. The promise of God, to multiply Abraham, was made to all who should have the like faith, or to all who should have true faith in Jesus Christ, in whatever period of the world they might live. . . The order of plurality of wives is an everlasting and ceaseless order, designed to exalt the choicest men and women to the most superlative excellence, dominion, and glory. But I perceive the idea that is running in your mind, Nelly. You want to know if you cannot enjoy the society of your dear George as a husband in the eternal world, without allowing other females to share him with you?

Nelly.—Yes, cousin, that is just what I want to know; you have expressed my idea better than I could myself, because the idea of not having my husband in all eternity is dreadful; I know that I could never submit to it! Never see my husband again while eternity wastes away! Darling George, bless him;

I can hardly endure his absence for a month! . . . But why cannot I be married to him for eternity, and have him alone to myself?

Abby.—I have thought very seriously of this question, cousin, as well as you; and what at first appeared to me as desirable to a wife, I must confess now seems to wear a different aspect. If your George and you should be alone by the side of such a king as Abraham or Solomon, with all his queens and their numerous servants and waiting maids in courtly livery, would he not look like a mere rushlight by the side of such suns, or rather would he be seen at all! I should almost fear that your George would be taken for a servant, and you for a waiting maid; or if they should, in the galaxy and splendour of 144,000 such suns as Solomon, happen to see you and your George with a king's coronet upon his head, they might think him short of wedding garments, or that the selfishness of his wife had stinted his growth to such an insignificant, crabtree size! . . . The motive which would lead you to retain your husband exclusively to yourself, would contribute to make you comparatively unfruitful, and also vitiate the mental and bodily faculties of your offspring, and sow the seeds of death and mortality in their systems. I have come to the conclusion, Nelly, that the one-wife system not only degenerates the human family, both physically and intellectually, but it is entirely incompatible with philosophical notions of immortality; it is a lure to temptation, and has always proved a curse to a people. Hence I see the wisdom of God in not tolerating any such system among the celestial worthies who are to be kings and queens unto God for ever.

Nelly.—What's physically and intellectually?

Abby.—Why, their bodies are not so well formed for health and long life, nor do their minds possess much sense.

Nelly.—But what temptation is there in the one-wife system, more than in the other?

Abby.—Why, even the beasts leave each other alone when there is a prospect of increase. When God reveals the Patriarchal system of plurality to any people, He reveals it for their good, and for the blessing of both men and women; it is quite as great a blessing to the latter as to the former. And if they cannot abide that order, it shows conclusively that they cannot abide the purest and greatest blessings of eternity. . . When Jacob had many wives, he loved each of them more than he could have done any one of them that he might have had alone without the others. And his wives loved him and each other in the same ratio, and the tide and current of union and love among the whole family were stronger than they otherwise could be. . . One simple and irresistible reason is, that God has determined to bestow His greatest blessings upon the liberal order, and only very stinted favours upon the narrow, contracted order which you seem to desire. . .

Nelly.—You do beat all to prove your points! I wouldn't like to have George hear your arguments, for I know that he would swallow them down like so much honey. . . When I first heard of this New Revelation, I thought it was a cunning plan laid to make men and women conduct worse among themselves than they now do, if possible, and I snatched it out of George's hand and threw it into the fire; for I have seen so much abomination of this kind, that I didn't want my George to get in such a way as most married men do. I believe there is not another place in England as bad as this. Tell about a hundred thousand common ladies in London! My scratch; it is more difficult to tell who ain't bad here, than it is to tell who is profligate. . .

Abby.—My dear cousin Nelly, I am very happy to see that you are so well apprised of that awful profligacy and sexual pollution that exist in this place; although the same complaint exists in all other places; for the whole earth is defiled. I hope you are sufficiently sensible that the Lord, by this New Revelation, is determined to save a chosen few, whose garments shall not be defiled, and who will keep themselves unspotted from the world. These few He will make rulers over the rest. . .

Nelly.—O, George is too poor to think of taking anybody besides me.

Abby.—It is true he cannot take any other in this land, nor even contract with another, but he is not poorer than Jacob was when a wandering stranger from his father's house; Jacob had nothing but his staff in hand, and at that time the Lord visited him and promised him a very great family; and soon after, we see him with many wives and children, and sufficient property to support them all, and something to give away to his brother besides. He that increases the family will increase the substance that is required in order to support them.

Nelly.—But I shouldn't like for him to get other women and young girls, that he would like better than me.

Abby.—As to that, I suppose that young persons are not always as foxy rivals as older ones, but have access to the fulness of the same fountain of grace that they have. . .

Nelly.—Well, if George does take any others, I should like to have him take my sister Ann, for her disposition is so obliging and mild. . .

Abby.— . . . If you wish to honour your George, by giving him the delights of the sons of men, after the manner of holy women of old, don't be in haste, but let the will of the Lord be manifest from a proper source, else you may do more injury to George than good. . .

Nelly.— . . .Well . . . Do you know what offended sister Hugall the other night?

Abby.— . . . It appears that she and Elder Gamey had some conversation on this subject of marriage, in a little circle of brethren and sisters; and you know her thoughtless manner of speaking, according to the impulse of the moment. . .

Nelly.—What did she say? I heard that it made the sisters blush and turn away their faces, and the men put their pocket-handkerchiefs to their mouths, and looked around for the spit-box. But, what did she say?

Abby.—Why she simply said that she required a husband wholly to her-self, and she would tell Brigham Young so if he were there.

Nelly.—Did Elder Gamey say anything?

Abby.—No; nor did any one speak any more. It was silent as heaven for several minutes; each one seemed to think—and hang their heads, daring nei-ther to laugh nor to speak. At length Sister Hugall, not having where to hide her face, got up and shot out at the door, and went home without so much as putting a handkerchief on her head.

"Go to Work and Reckon It Up": Family Empire

In addition to its high priority, leaders gave forceful expression to what they believed God intended to accomplish with the Principle. And few of heav-en's purposes rivaled the injunction to multiply. Joseph Smith said that acquire-ments in this life would survive death and advantage men and women in the next.[9] The 1843 revelation promised the prophet that his plural marriages would "bless him and multiply him and give him an hundred-fold in this world, of fathers and mothers, brothers and sisters, houses and lands, wives and chil-dren, and crowns of eternal lives in the eternal worlds"[10] Not to be outdone, Brigham Young told George Q. Cannon that he could inform those curious about Young's household that he intended to have "wives and children by the million, and glory, and riches, and power, and dominion, and kingdom after kingdom."[11] Mormon sermons on plurality were freighted with talk of plen-itude and growth.

During periods like the Mormon Reformation in the 1850s, when pres-sure to enter polygamy was intense, the rush to take additional wives was so great that, in some localities, the supply of eligible women was nearly exhaust-ed.[12] A female member wrote her friend in 1857 that the leaders insisted that "the brethren here . . . take more wives, whether they want to or not. . . Indeed this is the greatest time for marrying I ever knew, even 'Al' Huntingdon has

---

[9] D&C 130:18–19, 2 April 1843. Benjamin F. Johnson remembered being taught that "Dominion & Powr in the great Future would be commensurate with the no of Wives childin & Friends that we inheret here and that our great mission to earth was to Organize a Neculi of Heaven to take with us. To the increace of which there would be no end." Benjamin Franklin Johnson to George F. Gibbs, 1903, Benjamin Franklin Johnson Papers, LDS Archives, 35.

[10] D&C 132:55, 12 April 1843.

[11] Brigham Young, 9 Sept. 1860, Journal of Discourses, 8:178–79.

[12] For studies of the subject, see Larson, "Mormon Reformation," 45–63; Peterson, "Mormon Refor-mation of 1856–1857," 59–87; and Bigler, Forgotten Kingdom, 121–37.

taken two girls at once, and . . . Uncle Daniel took four at once."[13] One observer said he knew of an instance where as many as eight wives were added to a man's household.[14] Queues of men formed outside President Young's office asking for the privilege.[15] The flood so overwhelmed the president that he delegated the responsibility, telling a subordinate to say "*yes*" to everyone recommended by their bishop.[16] Such haste sometimes led to unwise alliances. In the words of Peter Madsen in 1857: "Now we had lots of preaching and council but some of <it> vent little to far to be from the highest authority; some of this was about plural marriage. I was obeydient but not wise I married a girl, but she did it more of fright than of love, for that reason it could not last long only about 9 months then she was divorced."[17]

By marrying and multiplying, the faithful were promised they would not only aggrandize their heavenly estates but open portals to millions of spirits waiting to obtain "tabernacles" of flesh of their own. One church publication purported to show how the mathematics of plural marriage assured that a polygamist with forty wives, who each had ten children, at age 78 would number his descendants in the millions. By contrast, a poor monogamist of the same age, having parented the same number of children with one partner, could count his progeny at only 152.[18] The importance of offspring was stressed constantly, and women who had large families, whether monogamous or polygamous, were singled out for recognition.[19]

To marry additional wives on grounds that it would augment offspring more quickly than monogamy contradicted philosophers as well as observations by some who visited the Saints.[20] Because of reduced coital frequency

---

[13] Ellen Spencer Clawson to Ellen Pratt McGary, 15 Feb. 1857, in Ellsworth, ed., *Dear Ellen*, 38.

[14] Nelson Wheeler Whipple, Autobiography and Journal, Winter 1856–57, LDS Archives, 116.

[15] Wilford Woodruff, in Kenney, ed., *Wilford Woodruff's Journal*, 2 Feb. 1857, 5:14.

[16] Minutes of the President's Office, 13 and 22 Jan. 1857, box 14, fd. 2, Leonard J. Arrington Papers, LAHA, 1–2.

[17] Madsen, Autobiography, LDS Archives, 28. Ellen Spencer Clawson said that the emphasis church authorities gave the Principle made it such that "girls don't think of refusing, but take the first one that asks them." Clawson to Ellen Pratt McGary, 28 Feb. 1857, Ellsworth, ed., *Dear Ellen*, 39.

[18] "Varieties," *Mil. Star*, 19:24 (13 June 1857), 384; and ibid., 19:27 (4 July 1857), 432. Polygamous wife Annie Clark Tanner remembered that before the Manifesto of 1890 it was "taught that the purpose of increasing one's family, by marrying several wives, was to have a numerous posterity. It was taught that the larger the family, the greater would be the Kingdom over which the father in the Celestial order of Marriage would rule and reign in Eternity." Tanner, *Mormon Mother*, 221.

[19] For prizes given to especially fecund mothers, see Kenney, ed., *Wilford Woodruff's Journal*, 11 June 1878, 7:418–19.

[20] See, for example, Paley in his *Principles of Moral and Political Philosophy*, 1:320–21; Remy, *Journey to Great-Salt-Lake City*, 2:149–50; and Benjamin Ferris in Chapter Five, below.

as the number of wives increased, as well as truncated fertility completion for younger wives who were widowed, studies of polygynous societies generally find patterns of depressed fertility where many women marry a single husband.[21] For this reason one might question whether Mormon plural wives brought as many souls to Zion as they would have if all had remained monogamous.[22] Recent investigations of particular communities, however, indicate that Mormon polygamous wives, sometimes averaging nine and ten children each, equaled or exceeded the number brought to the homes of their one-wifed neighbors.[23] Moreover, as Kathryn Daynes has shown, polygamy allowed many who would otherwise have been left unmarried to become mothers, thereby further swelling the census.[24] Obtaining an accurate image of the Saints' reproductive habits is complicated, however, and a full account of this aspect of Mormon polygamy has yet to be written.[25]

Whatever the case with plural wives, the number of children a polygamous male could produce with all his partners was prodigious. George Q. Cannon found it required a converted schoolhouse to feed all his families at once.[26] At his death in 1905, Benjamin F. Johnson had an estimated 800 descendants.[27] The story that Brigham Young had so many children that he sometimes failed to recognize them in the street was a tale told of so many pluralists that it became a genre of LDS folklore.[28] Whether monogamous or plural, first wife or fifth, church members living in the Mormon commonwealth generally did all they could to enlarge the kingdom. By the 1880s, church spokesmen exult-

---

[21] Muhsam, "Fertility of Polygamous Marriages," 3–16; Clignet, *Many Wives, Many Powers,* 28–31; Kunz and Smith, "Polygyny and Fertility," 97–103; the same authors' "Polygyny and Fertility in Nineteenth-Century America," 467, 479–80; and Altman and Ginat, *Polygamous Families,* 83–84, 472–73.

[22] So suggested Ivins in his "Notes on Mormon Polygamy," 236–37. Also see Kunz, "One Wife or Several?" 59.

[23] See Logue's findings in his study of polygamy in St. George, Utah, in *Sermon in the Desert,* 76–80; and for Cedar City, see Bennion, "Polygamy's Contribution." Bean and Mineau, "Polygyny-Fertility Hypothesis," discuss the limitations of traditional studies. Perhaps the Mormons were like the Temne of Sierra Leone, where a decline in live births occurred only with the fourth and subsequent polygynous wives. Daly and Wilson, *Sex, Evolution, and Behavior,* 93–95.

[24] See both chapters, "The Marriage Market" and "Women Who Became Plural Wives," in Daynes, *More Wives than One,* 91–127.

[25] The research that Professors "Ben" Bennion and Kathryn Daynes are now conducting will teach us much on this and other questions related to Mormon polygamous life.

[26] Evans and Cannon, *Cannon Family Historical Treasury,* 329–31. An English observer in the early 1870s said of Mormon polygamous households, "There was a perfect swarm of children; I never could count to the end of the number." Yelverton, *Teresina in America,* 2:40.

[27] Johnson, *My Life's Review,* 388.

[28] Examples of the story, as told about several men, are found in FMC I, box 1, fd. 2, 77, 86; fd. 5, 372; fd. 6, 510; fd. 7, 384.

ed in the fact that one in three of Utah Territory's residents were under the age of eight.[29] Saint and Gentile alike commented on the great "flocks" of sun-bleached children seen on Zion's hills and in its valleys.[30]

In the colorful language for which he was known, Heber C. Kimball probably expressed the Saints' concern with fecundity better than anyone.

"REMARKS BY PREST. HEBER C. KIMBALL,"
8 FEB. 1857, *DES. NEWS* [WEEKLY], 25 FEB. 1857, 6:51, 405/1–2.

How long do you suppose it will take a little man like me, though I feel perfectly able to thrash any six common wicked men . . . to get into the celestial kingdom of God with my whole posterity, in case there should be no obstruction? How long do you suppose it will be before my posterity increases to over a million? A hundred years will not pass away before I will become millions myself. You may go to work and reckon it up, and twenty-five years will not pass away before brother Brigham and I will number more than this whole Territory. Now, if that number proceeds from us, I tell you our roots are fruitful. Take away every cause of death to those roots and nourish them and cherish them, and they will increase and you cannot help yourselves. In twenty-five or thirty years we will have a larger number in our two families than there now is in this whole Territory, which numbers more than seventy-five thousand. If twenty-five years will produce this amount of people, how much will be the increase in one hundred years? We could not number them, or if we did sum up the amount to any given time, they are still on the increase.

But some of you are taking a course to spend your lives for nought, while brother Brigham and I are becoming like Abraham, Isaac, and Jacob, and the Prophets. Why do you not be profitable to yourselves, and put out your lives to usury? Do you understand me?

"COPY HIS MIND AND SPIRIT": PATRIARCHAL DOMINION

While centralization of male authority in the home was an important theme when defending plural marriage to outsiders, Mormon leaders gave it even greater emphasis when talking to their followers. As Udney Jacob and Belinda Pratt wrote, polygamy naturally tends to subject women to their husbands.[31]

---

[29] L. John Nuttall Diary, 8 Dec. 1878, UPB, 1:220; Orson Pratt, 20 June 1880, *Journal of Discourses*, 21:277; Erastus Snow, 24 June 1883, ibid., 24:165.

[30] Burton, *City of the Saints*, 221; and Bowles, *Our New West*, 248. Charles Bliss, "Weak Point," 783, said, "Utah is full of children, and, in many communities children of school age comprise half the population."

[31] See all of Hardy, "Lords of Creation." One is reminded of a Muslim fragment in Moroccan folklore: "Debase a woman by bringing in [the house] another one." Quoted in Mernissi, *Beyond the Veil*, 48.

"Discourse By President Brigham Young," 21 Sept. 1856,
Des. News [Weekly], 1 Oct. 1856, 6:30, 235/4, 236/1.

. . . let the father be the head of the family, the master of his own household; and let him treat them [wives] as an angel would treat them; and let the
wives and the children say amen to what he says, and be subject to his dictates,
instead of their dictating the man, instead of their trying to govern him. . .[32]

But the first wife will say, "It is hard, for I have lived with my husband
twenty years, or thirty, and have raised a family of children for him, and it is
a great trial to me for him to have more women;" then I say it is time that
you gave him up to other women who will bear children. If my wife had borne
me all the children that she ever would bare [sic], the celestial law would teach
me to take young women that would have children. . .

It is the duty of every righteous man and woman to prepare tabernacles
for all the spirits they can; hence if my women leave, I will go and search up
others who will abide the celestial law, and let all I now have go where they
please. . .

True there is a curse upon the woman that is not upon the man, namely,
that "her whole affections shall be towards her husband," and what is the next?
"He shall rule over you."

Jedediah M. Grant (1816–1856) emphatically condemned women who insisted on their own ways or sought to leave a good man for a more pleasing companion.

"Discourse By Jedediah M. Grant," 26 Oct. 1856,
Des. News [Weekly], 5 Nov. 1856, 6:35, 275/2–3.

That woman who offends her husband, if he has on him the power of the
Priesthood and does right, I would not give a groat for all the blessings she
will get from the Holy Ghost. You may as well baptize a dog, or a skunk, as
such a woman, until she makes reconciliation with that man of God whom
she has offended. . .

A man is a president to his family. If the Church has a head, which is Christ,
then is the man the head of his family. Some men are not the heads of their
families, but their wives walk on them, their daughters walk on them, and
their sons walk on them, and they are as the soles of their shoes. . .

I want the women to understand, when they have a good husband, one
that does his duty, that he is president over them, and that they have made
covenants to abide the law of that husband. Talk about women leaving their
husbands! I would be far from taking a woman that would leave a good man.

---

[32] A remark Young made to Mormon Battalion veterans and their wives illustrates something of his
attitude: "Great God! . . . [female] council & wisdom . . . don't weigh as much with me as the weight of a
Fly Tird." Reported in Cleland and Brooks, eds., Mormon Chronicle: The Diaries of John D. Lee, 11 Mar. 1848, 1:7.

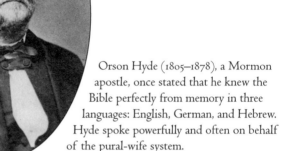

Orson Hyde (1805–1878), a Mormon apostle, once stated that he knew the Bible perfectly from memory in three languages: English, German, and Hebrew. Hyde spoke powerfully and often on behalf of the pural-wife system.

A woman that wants to climb up to Jesus Christ, and pass by the authorities between her and him, is a stink in my nostrils. I have large nostrils, and I often talk about smelling, for my olfactory nerves are very sensitive. I want women to know their places and do their duty; but there is a low, stinking pride in a woman, that wants to leave a good husband to go to another. What does it matter where you are, if you do your duty? Being in one man's family or the other man's family is not going to save you, but doing your duty before your God is what will save you.

Heaven placed men in "the first rank," said Orson Hyde. They should be addressed and respected for their priority.[33] However many wives a man had, Hyde contended, he could love them all and peace would reign in his family if women would pattern their thoughts and feelings on those of their husband.

"Discourse By Elder Orson Hyde," 4 Oct. 1857,
Des. News [Weekly], 14 Oct. 1857, 7:32, 251/2.

Can a man really love more than one wife at the same time? . . .

If a man have forty wives, and they all receive his mind and spirit, and are thus one in him, he can as easily love them all (because they are one) as a

---

[33] "Sermon by Elder Orson Hyde," *Des. News* [Weekly], 18 Mar., 1857, 7:2, 10/3.

father can love a half score of children who copy his mind and spirit. But if a woman rebel in her feelings against a good man and yield to the temptations of the devil, she may know that her husband may pity, but cannot love her, because she has ceased to be one with him and to partake of his mind and spirit.

If, therefore your husband be a good man, and you copy his mind and his spirit, he cannot help loving you, though he have forty other wives in the same situation.

"They Have Not Sense Enough": The Inferiority of Women

Associated with patriarchal authority was the assumption that women possessed lesser capacities than men. A long history reaching back at least as far as Aristotle and Saint Paul provided precedent for the idea, and Mormon leaders addressed the subject emphatically.[34] As Charles W. Penrose put it: "man as a sex, by reason of greater physical and mental strength, is placed by nature above woman in the scale of being."[35] William Hepworth Dixon, who took special interest in the Mormons, interviewed Brigham Young on the subject, and said that Young told him, "Women . . . will be more easily saved than men. They have not sense enough to go far wrong. Men have more knowledge and more power; therefore they can go more quickly and more certainly to hell."[36] It was an assumption naturally reinforced by plurality's gender configuration: a single male figure at the center of his kingdom with wives and children radiating from him in worshipful dependence.

In no case, the Saints were told, should wives aspire to inspiration or author-

[34] Aristotle, *Politics*, 1.12.42–43; 13.23–24; and Paul's remarks in 1 Corinthians, 11:7–9; 14:34–35; Ephesians 5:22–24; and 1 Timothy 2:12. Also see Horowitz, "Aristotle and Woman," 183–213; Charles, "Precedents for Mormon Women from Scriptures," 37–63; and Hardy, "Lords of Creation," 120–121.

[35] Penrose, "Family Government," *Mil. Star* 30:20 (16 May 1868), 307. Penrose's language resembled that found in the *Quran* 2.228, 282; and 4.11, 34. Before the anti-polygamy crusade led church leaders to strike a more friendly pose toward women's political capacities, Mormon males sometimes expressed disgust for "the unwomanly shriekers for woman's rights," who seek "that which is not appointed to . . . [females] by the Almighty nor adapted to their natural capacities." "Relative Position of the Sexes," *Mil. Star* 40:28 (15 July 1878), 433–34. For other illustrations, see Neff, "Attitudes toward Women's Rights and Roles in Utah Territory," 6–10.

[36] "The Mormon creed," observed Dixon, "appears to be that woman is not worth damnation." *New America*, 241. "I doubt," said Brigham Young, ". . . that there is a female in all the regions of hell." Sermon, 21 Oct. 1860, *Journal of Discourses*, 8:222. This despite James Brown's reported claim that the reason he took plural wives was "to pass unfortunate females into heaven. . . yes, to prevent 'em going to roaring flames and damnation that I does it." Ruxton, *Life in the Far West*, 285.

ity equal to that of husbands and male leaders of the church.[37] In an 1861 sermon Brigham Young spoke further concerning women, the curse of Eve, and the need for wives to yield to the requirement of plural marriage.

A Few Words of Docterine, Given by President Brigham Young in the Tabernacle in Great Salt Lake City Oct. 8th 1861. Reported by G. D. Watt. Leonard J. Arrington Papers, Box 14, Fd. 4, laha.

A few remarks on woman. She is the glory of the man, but she is not at the head in all the creations of God. Pertaing [*sic*] to his children on this earth she is not accountable for the sins that are in the world. God requires obedience from man, he ~~the~~ <is> Lord of creation, and at his hands the sin of the world will be required. Could the female portion of the human family fully understand this, they would see that they are objects of tender mercy, and greatly blessed. This no doubt <on a casual veiw> appears to my sisters a glorious docterine for them; ~~on a mere casual veiw of it~~, and some might be tempted in their ignorance to take unwarrantable liberties, corrupt themselves with sin, and then ~~to justify themselves, say~~ take shelter under the docterine that man alone is culpable for the sins they committ. There are, however, ~~exceptions to this aparently general rule~~ restrictions placed upon woman. I will quote a passage of scripture to illustrate this. "And the man that commiteth adultery with another man's wife, even he that commiteth adultery with his neighbors wife, the adulterer and the Adulteress shall surely be put to death."[38] ~~It would be well also to read the fifth chapter of Numbers. (See Num. 5th Ch.)~~ When the crime was <thus> atoned for ~~by death~~ then was she free, and prepared to receive in full the blessings she otherwise would have received ~~if she~~ had <she> not committed sin. ~~For all personal~~ <Woman ~~She~~ must atone for> sins committed by ~~woman under the action~~ <the volition> of her own choice, . . . but she will never become an angel to the devil, and sin so far as to place herself beyond the reach of mercy. ~~They~~ <She> will ~~suffer for their sins, and~~ suffer all that ~~they~~ <she> ~~have~~<s> strength to suffer according to the venality of ~~their~~ <her> sins. The woman is the glory of the man; what is the Glory of the woman? It is her virginity until she gives it into the hands ~~of~~ <of the man that will be> her Lord and master to all eternity. ~~Woman~~ <She> in many instances trifles with ~~their~~ <her> virtue and ~~they~~ will be damned for so doing, if it were not for more than five minutes. ~~It may be said that women are not to blame. Many~~

[37] "Remarks By Prest. Heber C. Kimball." 8 Feb. 1857, *Des. News* [Weekly], 25 Feb. 1857, 6:51, 405/2–3. Later that year Kimball said women held the priesthood only through their husbands and were to be led by the male head of the family. If he could not lead his own wives and were not a good man, Kimball said, he should be made a "eunuch" so as to "stop my propagation." "Remarks By President Heber C. Kimball," 12 July 1857, ibid., 22 July 1857, 7:20, 156/2–4.

[38] Leviticus 20:10.

~~are not to blame, they do nothing they should be blamed for. But~~, When a
woman <can> ~~says~~ <truly> to her husband who magnifies his preisthood "I
am as pure as you," she ought to remember that she is the glory of that Lord.
Is it her glory to have illicit intercourse with a gentile and then be sealed to a
good Elder and faithful servant of God? No. She will be damned for it, and
suffer the pangs of hell. It is her duty to let wickedness alone. Our sisters are
very tenacious with regard to a mans having more than one wife. Says the wife
"Husband I am capable of making your dinner, I can make your bed, I can
attend to your fisical wants, you do not need another woman in this house."
Do you not know that that is a curse placed upon woman? Why <so>? that
she may not become an angel to the devil. <It is> ~~The docterine of poligamy
is~~ the order of heaven she should suffer in the flesh. ~~Now will you rise up sisters, and say you~~ Will <You say you will> not suffer in the flesh, <that> you
will not be cursed; ~~but~~ <that> you will have the fullest satisfaction of this
<life> and let the next life take care of itself, "and now Mr husband if you
do not make a heaven for me I will leave you." You have a curse upon you that
the male portion of the human family have not got; their curse is to toil for a
subsistance for themselves and wives and children, to obtain from the ground
by the sweat of their brow, bread and fruit etc. "And unto Adam he said, Because
thou hast hearkened unto the voice of thy wife, and hast eaten of the tree of
which I commanded thee, saying, Thou shalt not eat of it: cursed is the ground
for thy sake; in sorrow shalt thou eat of it all the days of thy life; Thorns <also>
and thistles shall it bring forth to thee; and thou shalt eat the herb of the field:
In the sweat of thy face shalt thou eat bread,["] etc. Now notice the curse that
is placed upon the woman. "Unto the woman he said, I will greatly multiply
thy sorrow and thy conception; in sorrow thou shalt bring forth children. And
thy desire shall be to thy husband, and he shall rule over thee."[39] Yes your disire
shall be for your husband, your souls will long for him, and it ~~will be~~ <is>
one of the hardest things you can think of to consent ~~for~~ that your husband
should take another wife.[40] And when you bring forth it shall be in extreme
pain; Were it not for this curse woman would not have suffered pain in child
bearing. ~~Woman~~ <She> has taken the lead in committing sin, and she will fill
her days with sorrow, she shall disire this, and that and the other, and ~~your~~
<her> disposition, and affections, and ~~your~~ <her> whole ~~passions~~ <being>
shall be afflicted as much as the man, but his afflictions ~~is~~ <are> of another
kind.

Comparative female abundance, as construed by Mormons, combined with
their likely majority in heaven, further leveraged male importance. Heber C.

---

[39] Genesis 3:16–19.

[40] Young's linkage of the curse of Eve to female obligation to submit to polygamy is at odds with what
he said elsewhere. See, for example, his 14 July 1855 sermon, *Journal of Discourses*, 3:264–68.

Kimball said that if all his female companions left him, it mattered not. Upon arriving in heaven, he said, the prophet Joseph would provide: "Never mind . . . here are thousands, have all you want."[41] Women were most pleasing when displaying submission to righteous male authority. As a popular guidebook of the time put it, the female gift for spiritual influence was most effectively achieved through quietness, domesticity, and obedience to the superior sex. It was by meek example that women acquired moral power.[42] With Mormons, the few worthy men were called to marry the surplus of pious, yielding women and then, with households in tow, usher all to the mansions of the Almighty.[43]

The tendency that the male/female ratio in polygamous marriages had to fractionate women's importance could also lead to sequestered, chattel-like images of "the weaker sex." Inspiration for such thought dated to the early years of the church. William Phelps, for example, said that sermons of the prophet Joseph Smith led him to consider asking women in his family to wear veils.[44] Brigham Young allegedly said he left the care of his children to their mothers in the same way bulls pay no attention to calves.[45] Heber C. Kimball in the early 1850s remarked that he intended to place his wives with the rest of his property into the keeping of the church.[46] And a few years later in what became the most oft-quoted language on the subject, Kim-

---

[41] "Remarks By President Heber C. Kimball," 1 Feb. 1857, *Des. News* [Weekly], 11 Feb. 1857, 6:49, 388/2; and idem, *Journal of Discourses*, 12 July 1857, ibid., 5:28–29.

[42] Sanford, *Woman in Her Social and Domestic Character*, 57, 71 passim. Sanford's advice, like so much didactic literature on women, was borrowed from scripture, in this case 1 Peter 3:1–6. Mormons based much of their polygamous thought on the now-suspect belief in male-female "spheres," rooted in presumed natural differences. The topic's bibliography is vast, but see Kraditor, *Up from the Pedestal*; Welter, "Cult of True Womanhood"; Cott, "Passionlessness," 162–82; Degler, *At Odds*, 26–51; and, looking chiefly at Europe, Perrot, "Roles and Characters," 167–96. The ambiguous position of Victorian women, as described by two social historians, applies to Mormon females: "The Victorian woman was more spiritual than man, yet less intellectual, closer to the divine, yet prisoner of her most animal characteristics, more moral than man, yet less in control of her very morality." Rosenberg and Rosenberg, "Female Animal," 338.

[43] Eliza R. Snow made this point to the Young Ladies Retrenchment Association. Since only a few young men were worthy, she said, women must go to them in "groups" to be saved. Joseph Smith knew that "there were more good women than men on earth," she said, and that proved "the wisdom of plurality. Girls," she urged, "marry good, noble men. I don't care if they are old men if they are men of God." "Synopsis," *Woman's Exponent* 3:23 (1 May 1875), 178–79. Despite her disgust for male hauteur, Lucinda L. Dalton asked: "since there are vastly more good women than men on the earth, who will dare decide that it would not be better . . . to allow two or more of these good women to marry one good man." Dalton, Autobiography, CU-B, 8–9.

[44] William Wines Phelps to his wife Sally, 16 Sept. 1835, in Van Orden, "Writing to Zion: The William W. Phelps Letters," 563–66.

[45] Beadle, *Life in Utah*, 362.

[46] As reported in Kenney, ed., *Wilford Woodruff's Journal*, 6 May 1854, 4:270.

ball said no one had any more right to take his wives and daughters from him than they did his horses and cows.

HEBER C. KIMBALL, IN SAMUEL BOWLES, "SUPPLEMENTARY PAPERS,"
ACROSS THE CONTINENT (1866), 397–98.

Ladies and gentlemen, good morning. I am going to talk to you by revelation. I never study my sermons, and when I get up to speak, I never know what I am going to say only as it is revealed to me from on high; then all I say is true; could it help but be so, when God communicates to you through me? The Gentiles are our enemies; they are damned forever; they are thieves and murderers, and if they don't like what I say they can go to hell, damn them! They want to come here in large numbers and decoy our women. I have introduced some Gentiles to my wives, but I will not do it again, because, if I do, I will have to take them to my houses and introduce them to Mrs. Kimball at one house, and to Mrs. Kimball at another house, and so on; and they will say Mrs. Kimball such, and Mrs. Kimball such, and so on, are w___. They are taking some of our fairest daughters from us now in Salt Lake City, damn them. If I catch any of them running after my wives I will send them to hell! And ladies you must not keep their company, you sin if you do, and you will be damned and go to hell. What do you think of such people? They hunt after our fairest and prettiest women, and it is a lamentable fact that they would rather go with them damned scoundrels than stay with us.[47] If Brother Brigham comes to me, and says he wants one of my daughters, he has a right to take her, and I have the exclusive right to give her to who I please, and she has no right to refuse; if she does, she will be damned forever, and ever, because she belongs to me.[48] She is part of my flesh, and no one has a right to take her unless I say so, any more than he has a right to take one of my horses or cows.[49]

---

[47] Mormon relations with itinerant Gentiles were often cordial, but exceptions occurred, as in 1854 when Maj. Edward J. Steptoe's soldiers began courting Mormon women, married and unmarried alike. Church leaders took alarm, fearing their wives and daughters would run away. See Sylvester Mowry to Edward J. Bicknall, 17 Sept. 1854, in Mulder and Mortensen, eds., *Among the Mormons*, 274. This led Orson Hyde to condemn "loose" women who took up with "those cursed scrape-graces that are passing through here to California." "Lecture," *Des. News* [Weekly], 19 Oct. 1854, 4:32 [1/6]. Bowles said soldiers at Camp Douglas were currying the interests of Mormon women when he was there in 1865. About twenty-five were carried off as wives to California, he said, and fifty more were in the camp seeking refuge "from unhappy homes and fractional husbands." Bowles, *Across the Continent*, 116.

[48] As a possible instance, see the case of Eudora Lovina Young, the twenty-five-year-old daughter of Brigham Young, given by the church leader as a present to seventy-one-year-old Wilford Woodruff. Alexander, *Things in Heaven and Earth*, 230.

[49] Kimball's remarks were referred to on countless occasions. Two widely broadcast examples are Hingston, *Artemus Ward (His Travels)*, xxv; and Ann Eliza Young, *Wife No. 19*, 292. Such language offended even church members. In the early twentieth century, Mary Bennion Powell was shocked by a polygamous uncle who, when asked if it were true that each of his two wives had a dozen children, answered yes, that both his "sows had a litter of twelve." Powell to Dr. George R. Stewart, 26 Jan.–25 Feb. 1952, CSmH, 164.

"When the Proper Intercourse Takes Place": Restoration of the Strength and Longevity of the Ancients

As noted, Mormon leaders insisted that impregnation was the only proper purpose for sexual congress and departure from the rule was both sinful and a threat to health.[50] Decadence resulting from craven surrender to sexual pleasure so dominated humankind, the Saints taught, that longevity had dwindled until the race was approaching extinction. It was of the highest priority, then, to reverse the decline. This is why, as one apostle put it, they should work most on getting "the body improved . . . that the spirit may live and dwell in a pure tabernacle. When this is done, we can go and cultivate the spirit as much as is needful."[51] Plural marriage, if properly lived, Heber C. Kimball said, promised to renew its practitioners.

> I would not be afraid to promise a man who is sixty years of age, if he will take the counsel of br. Brigham and his brethren, that he will renew his age. I have noticed that a man who has but one wife, and is inclined to that doctrine, soon begins to wither and dry up, while a man who goes into plurality looks fresh, young, and sprightly.[52] Why is this? Because God loves that man, and because he honours His work and word. Some of you may not believe this, but I not only believe it but I also know it. For a man of God to be confined to one woman is small business; for it is as much as we can do now to keep up under the burdens we have to carry; and I do not know what we should do if we had only one wife apiece.[53]

The challenge lay in finding a way to procreate without succumbing to carnal appetite. Mormon belief drew on those streams of Christian thought that, as Elaine Pagels shows, acquired a distinctly ascetic turn in the early centuries of our era. Appropriating scripture in new ways, especially the story of Adam and Eve, many early church fathers looked upon sexual lust as the

---

[50] The Mormon polygamous ideal, said John Gunnison, imposed "the severest chastity . . . upon one sex, and rigid continence on the other during gestation and nursing of children." Gunnison, *Mormons or Latter-Day Saints*, 69.

[51] "Remarks By Amasa M. Lyman," 5 April 1866, *Des. News* [Weekly], 15:20, 155/3.

[52] A few months later, speaking on the need to multiply provisions, Kimball again challenged men's sexual capacities: "I could even take a great many men and hang them up on a pole, and they will dry in a week, because there is little or no juice in them; and the less juice there is in them the less time it takes them to dry up, upon natural principles. If a cow gives only a gill of milk, do you not know that you can dry her quicker than when she gives a pailful?" "Remarks By President Heber C. Kimball," 12 July 1857, *Des. News* [Weekly], 22 July 1857, 7:20, 157/1.

[53] "Discourse By President Heber C. Kimball," 6 April 1857, *Des. News* [Weekly], 22 April 1857, 7:7, 52/2–3.

preeminent manifestation of original sin.[54] Like countless others in the Judeo-Christian tradition, Mormons embraced the divine command to reproduce while, at the same time, feeling discomfort with the sensuous pleasures attending it. Echoing Augustine, they concluded sexual union might proceed so long as one shut out the lascivious imagination it aroused. It was lust, not the coital act, which brought moral decadence and physical decline.[55] But the saving formula required extraordinary restraint and ever-vigilant sexual awareness.

Leaders spoke often to the issue with frequent attestations of personal triumph over physical pleasure. Brigham Young claimed he commenced the practice of polygamy and continued it with an eye single to the siring of noble children. He would rather die, he said, than allow "passion" to enter the relations he had with his wives.[56] And George Q. Cannon once commented that, if God required it, he could be as celibate as a monk.[57] During the years when Mormon polygamy was urged upon the church's membership, few subjects received greater or more frequent emphasis than warnings against permitting physical desire to influence sexual union under any circumstance. "We do not believe it is right to do so either in plural or single marriage or outside of it," said Charles W. Penrose.[58]

Whatever the reality in practice, one cannot read Mormon sermons and writings during the years of polygamy's ascendance in the church without encountering frequent exhortations in behalf of restrained, if not abstemious, sexual behavior. For these reasons a well-known biographer of Brigham Young referred to their system as "Puritan Polygamy."[59] One defender in the 1880s, boasting of the Saints' rigor, said he doubted that a Mormon husband with four or five wives indulged himself sexually in twenty years as much as most non-Mormon monogamists did in two.[60]

---

[54] Pagels, *Adam, Eve, and the Serpent*, esp. 57–97. Lecky, *History of European Morals*, 2:298, expressed the same interpretation of early Christianity more than a century earlier.

[55] Augustine's *City of God*, 14:23–26. None, so far as this researcher knows, went so far as Sir Thomas Browne, who, while approving polygyny, said he would be content to procreate like the trees, without any "conjunction" whatsoever. *Religio Medici*, pt. 2, sec. 9.

[56] Brigham Young, 7 April 1861, *Journal of Discourses*, 9:36; and his earlier warnings in "Provo Conference. Remarks By Prest. Brigham Young," *Des. News* [Weekly], 14 Nov. 1855, 5:36, 282/1–2.

[57] "Discourse by President George Q. Cannon," *Des. Eve. News*, 28 Oct. 1882, 15:288 [1/4].

[58] Charles W. Penrose, 26 July 1884, *Journal of Discourses*, 25:227. For more examples, see "Reply to the 'Christian Herald' on the Plurality of Wives," *Zion's Watchman* 1:4–5 (12 Nov. 1853), 31; "'Mormonism' Not Sensual," *Mil. Star* 39:49 (3 Dec. 1877), 789–90; and a polygamous child's comments on her parents in Winnie Haynie Mortensen interview, 26 Jan. 1980, OHP, 19–20.   [59] Werner, *Brigham Young*, 280–320.

[60] "N," "Expressions from the People," *Des. Eve. News*, 26 Feb. 1886, 19:80, 4/4.

Here, as with other subjects, early Mormonism overflowed with conflicting themes. If the Saints were warned to beware of sexual delight, it was in the same way they viewed a lovely meadow containing sinks of poison. It was largely an admonition to take care. Mormons were not sexual abolitionists. They permitted sexual pleasure more than some of their contemporaries who carried fear of it to extremes, and it is unlikely that nineteenth-century Mormons were much different than men and women of today in accommodating nature's impulses.

Parley P. Pratt expressed something of this in his characterization of a critic of polygamy as one whose perceptions were "blunted by Roman superstitions and Puritan littleness," or Brigham Young's remark that "Some say we have spiritual wives but I think God has made us all natural & I think we should be Natural."[61] As Rosabeth Moss Kanter commented, religious communities often display opposing tendencies, favoring at once both severity and indulgence.[62] So it is that while displaying a proclivity for the ascetic, Mormons also praised the virile and fecund.

Mormonism's predominant *rhetorical* disposition, it seems to this scholar, most resembled Thomas Hooker's call for "selfe-denial and selfe-tryall."[63] Mormon sexual attitudes shifted with their relocation to the American West. If not dramatically so, and perhaps only reflecting a growing Victorian temper, late-nineteenth-century Latter-day Saints displayed greater anxiety about such matters than during their earlier midwestern period.[64] It was a change that maintained a presence in LDS counsels long after the abandonment of plural marriage.[65] Not only was sexual intercourse to be indulged only for reproduc-

---

[61] Kenney, ed., *Wilford Woodruff's Journal*, Dec. 1851, 4:85. Pratt's remark is found in Pratt, *Autobiography of Parley P. Pratt*, 384. Another Saint argued that the church's teachings were at war with the "Puritanical spirit." John V. Hood, "New Heaven and the New Earth," *Mil. Star* 26:47 (19 Nov. 1864), 740.

[62] Kanter, *Commitment and Community*, 221–22.

[63] Hooker, *Christians Two Chief Lessons*. Allegations charging Mormons with moral abandonment were grossly exaggerated. The late-nineteenth-century church, thoroughly Victorian in attitude, was almost obsessed with avoiding sexual sin. See, for example, the admonitions of leaders in Joseph H. Richards Diary, 5 April 1886, Mormons and Mormonism in Arizona, 1873–1888 Collection, fd. 11, AZU; John W. Young's advice to his sons, in Young to "My Dear Sons," 1 Mar. 1886, John Willard Young Letterbooks, UHi; Apostle John Henry Smith's condemnation of waltzing because it arose from immoral influences at a Stake Quarterly Priesthood meeting, 18 May 1901, General Minutes, Colonia Juarez Mexico Stake, bk. E, 1901–1906, LDS Archives, 14; and Apostle John W. Taylor's strictures on sexual intercourse with pregnant wives, in ibid., 125, 12 Mar. 1904. For growing reticence and repression of sexuality in American society generally during the late nineteenth century, see Rosenberg, "Sexuality, Class and Role," 131–53.

[64] An excellent review of reasons accounting for this change is in the too-often-overlooked study by Grover-Swank, "Sex, Sickness and Statehood," 28–48.

[65] Answering an inquiry about polygamy, LeGrand Richards, who later became presiding bishop of the church and an apostle, said that most monogamous couples, if the truth were known, displeased God in their sexual relations. "And why [do] . . . they not find favor? Because they are not the result of holy desires." Richards to Mary S. Gilstrap, 22 Nov. 1935, Subject Folder Collection, CCL-A.

tion but it was sometimes referred to as almost inherently corrupting. Wilford Woodruff told those attending the 1883 School of the Prophets to come in a spirit of prayer and fasting, with clean bodies and garments, having abstained from sexual intercourse with their wives.[66] The attitude revealed itself in other ways equally ancient. According to Brigham Young, husbands should not have sex with their wives several days before obtaining their endowments, and women should remain away from the temple for a week after their menses.[67]

The contention that a single man needed to marry a plurality of women to reach the highest kingdom in heaven may have been historically singular, but Mormons were hardly alone in clothing sexual behavior with Lenten restraint. Undoubtedly, as with men and women wherever such views were held, anxiety must often have afflicted the conscience, and they were matters on which Latter-day Saints needed frequent counsel.[68]

Orson Hyde delivered this discourse on bridling sexual passion before a body of church members, male and female, at the schoolhouse in Springville, Utah Territory, at the height of the Mormon Reformation. Philip M. Wentwood, official recorder for the event, transcribed it, and then Luke William Gallup, who was also present, copied it in his diary. The apostle's sermon is one of the most remarkable in all Mormon literature.

ORSON HYDE, IN LUKE WILLIAM GALLUP,
REMINISCENCES AND DIARY, 11 FEB. 1857, LDS ARCHIVES, 193–95.

I find a great spirit in men for getting more wives, & I have heard that in this place, there is not a girl knee high to a toad (using a strong figure) that is not engaged. I do not know, that you have outstript the mark. If you have gone into this, with the sanction of your Bishop, or the First Presidency, all is right; but if not, it is not right. . . I hear that they have gone in couples, triples, quadruples, & even sexruples, to Salt Lake City; & the President may think I am raising the very Devil here. . .

The *Reformation* is not over yet. We now design going to the root of the matter. Let me ask you the question, Why is it, that our lives, are not as long as the Fathers that have gone before us? They could live to Eight or Nine hun-

---

[66] Graffam, ed., *Salt Lake School of the Prophets Minute Book*, 23 Dec. 1883, 63.

[67] JH, 31 Jan. 1868, 1. It is unclear to what degree nineteenth-century Mormons consciously imitated the Israelites, as prescribed in Exodus 19:15; Lev. 12:2–5; 15:18–27; and 1 Sam. 21:4–5. Judeo-Christian nervousness about menstruants and ejaculants endured a long time. See Cohen, "Menstruants and the Sacred in Judaism and Christianity," 273–99.

[68] Not only were guilt and shame common in Mormon polygamy, Kimball Young observed, but the emphasis placed on hypocritical, lustful behavior by monogamous Gentiles was a projection of struggles within themselves. *Isn't One Wife Enough?* 291–92. The statement was made early on that God forbade polygamous practice in the past only when it was abused. "Polygamy," *Mil. Star* 15:11 (12 Mar. 1853), 168–69. For more, see Hardy, "Self Blame and the Manifesto," 43–57.

dred years. Shall I tell you the reason, will you give me the privilege, to tell you the reason? (Yes) Well then I'll show the reason of this. Every thing in creation has its proper uses & qualifications. . . So also man has been endowed with certain qualifications, which, if not perverted would enable him to live long on the Earth, but if taken away or perverted the man goes down to death. . . Now, when the proper intercourse which is necessary for the propagation of our species takes place between a man & a woman, & no more than that—the ballance of his power of muscle [illegible word] goes to strengthen other parts of his system, & thus gives him power over disease & enables him to prolong his life. But when the contrary is the case the man becomes prostrated, by this over indulgence, & having given his strength to women, he becomes prostrated, & is rendered liable to disease—not only this but the man who is given to great indulgence in this habit becomes weak in mind, & debilitated in intellect & his mind is feeble. . . How often do we see cripples born into the world. And why is it, that some are born Idiots? It is because the laws of nature have been interferred with; & they were not let alone, in their Mothers womb. These laws have been violated again, & again; & because of this, many children have scarcely opened their eyes upon the world when they gasp & die.

The laws of Nature have been violated, by their fathers & mothers, & from one generation to another, diseases have been generated in the children, by their parents, & by their degeneracy; & now instead of raising up a *healthy progeny* & a *noble race*, we raise a puny set, a race of helpless, scrubby children. Is this acting as wise stewards and keeping the command of God to be fruitful, & replenish the earth. We see many persons, who are naturally addicted to lying, Stealing & drinking liquors to excess. Who is the cause of this? The sin was begotten in them by their parents. I will venture to say, that in a Majority of cases, out of one hundred times, one has gone to propagate our species & ninety nine to the gratification of our baser passion. The Bible says that "he that soweth to the flesh shall of the flesh, reap corruption." And is not this indeed sowing to the flesh when ninety nine parts of our intercourse has been to gratify our debased passions. Now do we suppose that God is going to send angels to us while we are so low & debased in our feelings & sensual in our minds. Will he fight our battles while we are in this state? . . .

We find that the Ancients took a wife & went in unto her, & she conceived, & then they let her alone. Their children were begotten in faith & purity, & their faith was transmitted to their children & they grew up to reverence their Parents. Now what is the reason that men cannot govern their families? As long as you give your strength unto women you never will do it. It is this practice that brings jealousies into your wives, and grieves the spirit of God; & the spirit of lust reigns in the family, & that spirit begets hatred & not love.[69] It begets insub-

---

[69] A Mormon female writer made the same point, saying that if plural marriages were conducted properly with the elimination of lust, jealousy would disappear. Polygamy so lived was thus "a refining Element," purifying its practitioners for the celestial kingdom. Esther Romania Bunnell Penrose, Memoir (1881), LDS Archives, 6.

ordination in the wife to her husband, & in the children to their parents. Now suppose a pair to have no intercourse save what is necessary for the propagation of their species; just as you plant the seeds of your gardens, even as squash seeds. You wouldnt plant even a squash seed in the *Fall.* It is true that goats it is said will have sexual intercourse within fifteen minutes of the moment when the kid is born. Monkeys also, as some writers affirm are as debased in their practices, but most of the lower animals, may give us a lesson. And it is considered a trial for men to be as temperate as the beasts, unless they may be goats & monkeys.[70] I say suppose a family, where there is no intercourse of this kind, only with the prospect of having children born,—*That family can be governed.* . .

Now in the midst of this Reformation we no doubt tho't we were sailing into the ports of eternal glory. We now see there is still need of reform, and that, not only in our outward conduct . . . but in our secret acts, in the private intercourse of men & women; there is a great need of repentance &c.

I call upon you to repent of these secret sins, for they are a kind of murder. And, if I stifle, & crush the infant germ of my offspring by my unholy indulgence, it is pretty nearly murder. In such a case the Spirit returns to the God that gave it & there makes its complaint that it has been wronged in its mission, & disappointed in its intention. . .[71]

I warn you my brethren & Sisters, I warn you of these practices. I love women, but I find that, there is a love above the love of women. I say unto you do right, & may the spirit and blessing of God be with you from this time forth when you act in obedience to his commandments, for Jesus Sake—Amen.

Not only did Brigham Young reinforce the need for sexual discipline in plural marriage, he said it was the only way to raise up "a royal Priesthood."

I am now almost daily sealing young girls to men of age and experience; love your duties, sisters. Are you sealed to a good man? ["]Yes, to a man of God." It is for you to bear fruit and bring forth, to the praise of God, the spirits that are born in yonder heavens and are to take tabernacles on the earth. You have the privilege of forming tabernacles for those spirits, instead of their being brought into this wicked world, that God may have a royal Priesthood— a royal people—on the earth. That is what plurality of wives is for, and not to gratify lustful desires. Sisters, do you wish to make yourselves happy? Then

---

[70] Mormon views here agree with those of other polygynous societies where the taboo on post-partum sexual intercourse is generally more insistent and of longer duration than among monogamous peoples. Daly and Wilson, *Sex, Evolution, and Behavior,* 289.

[71] Heber C. Kimball, 27 Dec. 1857, *Journal of Discourses,* 6:187, endorsed Hyde's belief in the old theory that sperm contained living beings, homunculi, and that all were present in the body of Adam. Martin Madan said that the human species was "wholly in the loins of their first parent." *Thelypthora,* 3:246. Wesley Grindle, a non-Mormon, also said in 1857 that every drop of semen was "the habitation of living beings." *New Medical Revelations,* 45. For fears surrounding the loss of semen, especially in the nineteenth century, see Neuman, "Priests of the Body," 25–32; and Hare, "Masturbatory Insanity," 2–25.

what is your duty? It is for you to bear children, in the name of the Lord, that are full of faith and the power of God. To receive, conceive, bear, and bring forth in the name of Israel's God, that you may have the honour of being the mothers of great and good men—of kings, princes, and potentates, that shall yet live on the earth and govern and control the nations. Do you look forward to that? or are you tormenting yourselves by thinking that your husbands do not love you? I would not care whether they loved a particle or not: but I would cry out, like one of old, in the joy of my heart, "I have got a man from the Lord," "Hallelujah, I am a mother, I have borne an image of God!" . . . The man that enters into this order by the prompting of passion, and not with a view to honor God and carry out his purposes, the curse of God will rest upon him, and that which he seems to have will be taken from him and given to those that act according to principle. Remember it.[72]

To engage in sexual relations after a wife had conceived or with a barren companion, Heber C. Kimball said, was adulterous and threatened both parents and children with physical decline.[73]

"DISCOURSE BY PREST. HEBER C. KIMBALL," 23 JAN. 1857,
DES. NEWS [WEEKLY], 25 MAR. 1857, 7:3, 19/2.

Many who have but one wife, and several of those who have more than one, take a course to excite a spirit of adultery; and what is much worse, they often take that course at the most improper and unwise times, and thereby seriously injure their offspring. If husbands and wives will pursue a righteous course in this matter, their children will be much less subject to lustful desires. . . For this purpose God has instituted the plurality of wives.

How I would like to talk to you in the plainest way that the Spirit dictates to me, but the delicacies and wickedness of the corrupt and ungodly cannot bear it. . .

Some of you are living in adultery, or in the spirit of adultery. And some have wives that do not bear children. Why don't you let them alone? Why don't you take a course to regenerate, and not to degenerate?

Pointing to other polygynous societies as well as to the health and virtue of citizens in their own territory, George Q. Cannon praised Mormon polygamists for offering the world an alternative to decadent, monogamous Christianity. By displacing lust with purity in sexual relations, plurality promised

---

[72] "Remarks By President Brigham Young," 7 April 1861, *Des. News* [Weekly], 29 May 1861, 11:3, 97/4, and 98/1–2.

[73] Apostle John Henry Smith also told an audience in the Salt Lake Tabernacle that married men and women who indulged themselves "for any other passion than to beget children, really committed adultery." A. H. Cannon Journals, 8 Sept. 1890, UPB, 13:85.

to lift the curse of Eve and eliminate jealousy in the righteous home. He encouraged church members to endure, faithfully modeling their households on that of Abraham, the "friend of God."

"Discourse on Celestial Marriage,
Delivered by Elder George Q. Cannon,"
8 Oct. 1869, *Des. News* [Weekly], 3 Nov. 1869,
13:39, 457/1, 458/2–4, 459/1–4.

We have heard, during Conference, a great many precious instructions, and in none have I been more interested than in those which have been given to the Saints concerning that much mooted doctrine called Patriarchal or Celestial Marriage. I am interested in this doctrine, because I see salvation, temporal and spiritual, embodied therein... It is gratifying to know ... that we are not the first of God's people unto whom this principle has been revealed; it is gratifying to know ... that we are only following in the footsteps of those who have preceded us in the work of God, and that we, to-day, are only carrying out the principle which God's people observed, in obedience to revelation from Him, thousands of years ago. It is gratifying to know that we are suffering persecution, that we are threatened with fines and imprisonment for the practice of precisely the same principle which Abraham, the "Friend of God," practiced in his life and taught to his children after him...

The history of the world goes to prove that the practice of this principle, even by nations ignorant of the Gospel, has resulted in greater good to them than the practice of monogamy or the one-wife system in the so-called Christian nations. To-day, Christendom holds itself and its institution aloft as a pattern for all men to follow. If you travel throughout the United States and through the nations of Europe in which Christianity prevails, and talk with the people about their institutions, they will boast of them as being the most permanent, indestructible and progressive of any institutions existing upon the earth; yet it is a fact well known to historians, that the Christian nations of Europe are the youngest nations on the globe. Where are the nations that have existed from time immemorial? They are not to be found in Christian monogamic Europe, but in Asia, among the polygamic races—China, Japan, Hindostan and the various races of that vast continent. Those nations, from the most remote times, practiced plural marriage handed down to them by their forefathers. Although they are looked upon by the nations of Europe as semi-civilized, you will not find among them woman prostituted, debased and degraded as she is through Christendom...

Thus far I have referred only to the necessity and benefit of this principle being practiced in a moral point of view. I have said nothing about the physiological side of the question. This is one, if not the strongest, source of argument in its favor... We are all, both men and women, physiologists enough to know that the procreative powers of man endure much longer than those of woman. Granting, as some assert, that an equal number of the sexes exist, what would this lead to? Man must practice that which is vile and low or submit to a system of repression; because if he be married to a woman who is physically incapable, he must either do himself violence or what is far worse, he must have recourse to the dreadful and damning practice of having illegal connection with women, or become altogether like the beasts. . .

I know [plural marriage] . . . is true on the principle that I know that baptism, the laying of hands, the gathering, and everything connected with the Gospel is true. If there were no books in existence, if the revelation itself were blotted out, and there was nothing written in its favor, extant among men, still I could bear testimony for myself that I know this is a principle which, if practiced in purity and virtue, as it should be, will result in the exaltation and benefit of the human family; and that it will exalt woman until she is redeemed from the effects of the Fall, and from that curse pronounced upon her in the beginning. I believe the correct practice of this principle will redeem woman from the effects of that curse—namely, "Thy desire shall be to thy husband, and he shall rule over thee." All the evils connected with jealousy have their origin in this. . .

There are many points connected with the question, physiologically, that might be dwelt upon with great advantage. . . There are no brighter children to be found in the world than those born in this Territory. Under the system of Patriarchal Marriage, the offspring, besides being equally as bright and brighter intellectually, are much more healthy and strong. . . To you who are married. . . You all know that many women are sent to the grave prematurely through the evils they have to endure from their husbands during pregnancy and lactation, and that their children often sustain irremediable injury.

The question of how, in a specific way, men and women should proceed with the procreative act so as to avoid sin undoubtedly concerned many Mormon believers. Building on the doctrine of acquired characteristics as well as Mormon teachings, Hannah Tapfield King (1807–1886) made suggestions as to how couples should approach their sexual encounters.

HANNAH TAPFIELD KING, "PROCREATION,"
WOMAN'S EXPONENT 14:7 (1 SEPT. 1885), 51.

What a wonderful and mysterious work is Procreation! how little, if at all, understood by the world or even by a large majority of the Latter-day Saints. It is shocking to think and know, how it is performed in what is called the world! without one thought of preparation; or the mighty results of such communion. One party perhaps, charged with nothing but coarse animal passion, even if not inflamed by stimuli, which is often the case, while the other, it may be, is refined, delicate, and elevated in her very nature. As a wife, pure and holy, and desiring worthily to fulfill her marital covenants, but without any previous drawing out of her love, or endearments or the slightest reflection of the end and purpose of such an association, she is seized as the victim, or receptacle of mere animal passion? Imagine the constant repetition of such a course, can love hold out, and endure such a semblance of ravishment, and prostitution? harsh words these, but no other would rightly portray the acts, tho' a wedded wife, she feels outraged, and how many bitter tears fall as an accompaniment. She cannot but feel she is degraded. No wonder if her cry at such a moment is that she may be released from such a tie; or supposing not quite so bad a case, yet where the mind and the system has had no previous preparation, where is the joy, the love, the extacy [sic] that should attend the procreation of an immortal being. Will a passive endurance, or animal love alone produce a tabernacle worthy of an immortal being, which should be one partaking of the elements of which eternity is composed, and which ought to inspire its conception? . . .

Would it not be worthy therefore to study how we may prepare ourselves to procreate beings the elements of whom shall be life, strength and unfading beauty, not disease, distortion, decay, and death. To obtain the former, we must be filled with life-giving principles at the moment of conception of that being, then it will be an honor to the great Father of "the spirits of all flesh," as also to its earthly parentage, and a blessing temporally and eternally to the individual being . . . beings meditating such communion should draw out by the best affections each possess by kind and elevating association for they are equal in this wondrous act. . . The Duetto should endeavor to elevate their individual nature and character and so act and react on each other; agreeable reading or conversation, beautiful soul thrilling music and even agreeable food; all these and much more are essentials.

There is a language without sound, which the loving soul intuitively comprehends. Should the mind of either be harassed it should be soothed by gentle sympathy till calm, and peace is restored to the whole organization; omit nothing that will strengthen, purify, refine and elevate both mind and body; give the body especial and refining attention, for it is to transmit a temple for an immortal being. Then when thus molded and prepared, and a sweet and heavenly mood produced, let hands be joined in holy love and confidence, and kneeling together in holy prayer, implore the sanctifying, purifying influence of the Spirit of God to be infused into each system, that the act may be pure and holy, that a tabernacle may be organized in which a noble spirit may "enter in and dwell there;" that when in days to come it may enter upon its earthly career, in the rich abundance of maturity, all shall be constrained to say "behold one who was born in Zion, whom the Lord hath blest." To be an agent, a co-partner in such a heavenly enterprise who would shrink from suffering. Volumes might be written upon this marvelous, mysterious subject, but I pray even this hint may cause deeper thoughts to arise in the pure bosom, that yearns to know the way of truth and holiness. . .

Hannah T. King S.L.C., Aug. 1885.

"WASH & DRESS THEM UP": INTERMARRIAGE WITH NATIVE AMERICANS

Mormon leaders did not forget that an early revelation of Joseph Smith told missionaries to take plural wives from among the Indian tribes, that they might be civilized and their complexions whitened. They revived the injunction upon their removal west as yet another dimension of polygamy's eugenic promise. As Brigham Young said in his first speech after arriving in Salt Lake Valley in 1847:

> He intended to have evry hole & corner from the Bay of Francisco to Hudson bay known to us And that our people would be connected with every tribe of Indians throughout America & that our people would yet take their squaws wash & dress them up teach them our language & learn them to labour & learn them the gospel of there forefathers & raise up children by them & teach the Children & not many generations Hence they will become A white & delightsome people & in no other way will it be done & that the time was nigh at hand when the gospel must go to that people to[o].[74]

Despite Young's contention that intermarriage alone could transform the native race, Mormon Elders were loath to answer the call.[75] Some who did soon soured on the enterprise, one saying of the Shoshones at Fort Supply that he "wouldn't give his horse to save all the d—d Indians from hell."[76] And as James S. Brown remembered when negotiating with the same tribe near Fort Bridger in the mid-1850s, the Indians themselves questioned whether Mormons would take much interest in their daughters. Predictably perhaps, Brown said that Shoshone insistence that, to be fair, their tribesmen should be permitted to choose wives from among Mormon women, also deterred the missionaries.[77]

---

[74] Kenney, ed., *Wilford Woodruff's Journal*, 28 July 1847, 3:240–41. Thomas Bullock summarized the same remarks in his journal. Bagley, ed., *Pioneer Camp of the Saints*, 243–44.

[75] See Brigham Young's comments in Kenney, ed., *Wilford Woodruff's Journal*, 18 Nov. 1858, 5:240.

[76] John Pulsipher, in Brooks, "John Pulsipher," 359.

[77] James Stephens Brown (1828–1902) is renowned in Mormon pioneer history, and his missions, service, and adventures were all extraordinary. His journals and account books begin after this published recollection of his encounter with the Shoshone.

. . . the only objection that was raised to our proposition was when we suggested that some of us might want to take some of the young Indian women for wives. One old and wise counselor said, "No, for we have not got daughters enough for our own men, and we cannot afford to give our daughters to the white man, but we are willing to give him an Indian girl for a white girl. I cannot see why a white man wants an Indian girl. They are dirty, ugly, stubborn and cross, and it is a strange idea for white men to want such wives. But I can see why an Indian wants a white woman." Then the old man drew a graphic picture of the contrast he was making, and we gave up that point without pursuing our suit farther. Chief Washakie, however, said the white men might look around, and if any one of us found a girl that would go with him, it would be all right, but the Indians must have the same privilege among the white men. With this the council ended.[78]

In the face of many obstacles, a few Mormon Elders valiantly sought marital alliances to redeem the Lamanites, "civilizing and teaching them to work, trying to raise them up from their low, filthy condition, and be self sustaining."[79] Hosea Stout (1810–1889), another of the giant figures of nineteenth-century Mormonism, described how even in the case Brown recalled, notwithstanding the reservations of Washakie and his councilmen, a Mormon stalwart attempted a marriage with one of the tribe's women.

JUANITA BROOKS, ED., *ON THE MORMON FRONTIER:*
THE DIARY OF HOSEA STOUT, 2:516–17.

Tuesday 9 May 1854.
Elder [Orson] Hyde held a meeting in the evening. In the discourse he recommended the marrying of squaws in the most positive and strong terms and particularly the immediately taking Mary an old haggard mummy looking one who had been here all winter   He was very eloquent on the occasion all of which was generally understood to be squinting at M. M. Sanders[80] who already seemed to have some inklings that way and was well pleased with

---

[78] Brown, *Life of a Pioneer* (1900), 318. Washakie was the famous leader of the Northern Shoshones. Wakara, the powerful Ute leader with whom the Saints fought a war, proposed to a young Mormon female in Manti, causing a serious dilemma. The way the difficulty was resolved became legend among Mormons. See FMC I, 119, 120, box 1, fd. 3. Daynes provides an excellent retelling, *More Wives than One*, 43–44.

[79] Autobiography of William Adams, LDS Archives, 22. Juanita Brooks recalled that when her grandfather took a Southern Paiute as a plural wife he felt embarrassed and was called a "squaw man." FMC I, 545, box 1, fd. 7. Attempts to graft Indian daughters onto the Mormon tree were also made at Fort Limhi in Oregon Territory between 1855 and 1858, but doubts on both sides meant few if any such alliances were consummated. See the colorful account in Bigler, *Fort Limhi,* 147–49, 161–73. Also see Nash, "The Salmon River Mission of 1855," 22–31; Ellsworth, "History of Mormon Missions," 304–13; and Law, "Mormon Indian Missions—1855," 84–92.

[80] Moses Martin Sanders Sr. (1803–1878) was already married to two and possibly three women: Amanda Armstrong Faucett (md. 1826), Mary Jane Sparks Sanderson (md. 1847), and Anna Stout (md. 1852).

fair opportunity thus to safely commit himself so he readily bit at the bait and the courtship commenced immediately after meeting by interpreters for he could not talk with her   She wanted time to consider he being a stranger & she dont like him much any how. The affair created an unusual amount of fun & jokes among the *disinterested*

Wednesday 10 May 1854.

About noon to day the proxied courtship between Sanders & Mary the Shoshoni (the flower of the desert as Elder Hyde called her) was brought to close and they both were launched into a State of matrimony by Elder Hyde who acted the Parson   The cerimony being performed over by the interpreter James Bullock our joy now was full & the fun loving corps enjoyed the time to the best possible advantage. . .

Friday 12 May 1854.

Some six wagons started to Green River ferry to day having to face a Severe snow squall on the road and camped half mile below [Fort] Bridger   Sanders came with us to Bridger to purchase some goods for "Flower of the desert," which however we afterwards learned she would not accept and even refused to have any thing to do with him   The Matrimonial alliance thus entered into has proved a signal failure

Despite such results, desultory efforts at miscegenation continued. Missionaries to the Navajo in the late 1880s asked President John Taylor for permission to wed Indian women.[81] Still, Latter-day Saint intermarriage, along with establishment of schools and farms on Indian lands, met with very limited success in altering either the complexion or culture of native western peoples.[82] William McIntosh expressed the judgment of many Saints: "sometimes when I look at them and think of the darkness which they linger in and the degraded State in which they live I think that by A natural process it will take Along while to bring them to a knowledge of the Gospel and [make them] A white and A delightsome People."[83]

---

[81] L. C. Burnham and E. A. Tietjen to President John Taylor, 6 Jan. 1887, Taylor Family Papers, box 4-B, fd. 9, Special Collections, UU. For preaching on the subject in the 1870s, see Andrew Jackson Allen, Record, 18 Mar. 1873, Uhi, 82; and ibid., 8 April 1875, 105.

[82] Though more than a half-century old, the long article by Juanita Brooks remains, in my estimate, the best overview yet written: "Indian Relations on the Mormon Frontier," 1–48. For a more approving estimate of LDS work among the Indians, especially the Shoshone, see Coates, "Mormons and Social Change among the Shoshoni," 3–11; and the historiographical account of Jones, "Saints or Sinners?" 19–46. For church efforts to improve the "Lamanites" in the twentieth century by means other than marriage, see Mauss, *All Abraham's Children*, 74–113.

[83] Diary of William McIntosh, 15 July 1860, UPB, 62. Also see the comments of Brigham Young and George A. Smith in JH, 8 May 1853, 1, and ibid., 17 Oct. 1861, 5, respectively; as well as the discouraged admission by Orson Hyde, 6 April 1875, *Journal of Discourses*, 17:354.

THE MILLENNIUM IN VIEW

The emphasis given plural marriage, combined with the relative geographic isolation of the church, makes the thirty or so years after their arrival in the Great Basin the most revealing in Mormon polygamous history. At the same time, the energy that leaders gave their solicitations may have distorted the character of the practice. Visitors commonly discovered that the stables of women they expected to see kept by Mormon patriarchs were almost nowhere to be found. The majority of Mormon men who engaged in plurality, like those in most polygynous societies, had only two wives, with sharply decreasing numbers taking three, four, five, and more.[84] The fifty or so wives of Brigham Young, the more than forty of Heber C. Kimball, who once boasted he had enough wives to "whip the United States," and the nineteen of John D. Lee were rare exceptions.[85] Beyond this, the proportion that entered plural life quite steadily diminished, especially after 1860, suggesting that declining numbers of Saints found the practice attractive.[86]

Nevertheless, researchers suggest that, while varying from area to area and year to year, the number living in polygamous families was greater than previously believed and may have averaged between 15 and 30 percent of all Mormon households.[87] Plurality was a dominating social force in some communities. A study of marriage patterns in nineteenth-century St. George, Utah, for example, found that "Excluding those families where the husband was probably ineligible for polygamy because of his inactivity in the church, over a third

[84] For Mormons, see Ivins, "Notes on Mormon Polygamy," 233; Pace, "Wives of Nineteenth-Century Mormon Bishops," 53–54; and Embry, *Mormon Polygamous Families*, 34. For a similar pattern among Muslims, see Chamie, "Polygyny among Arabs," 57. And with polygynous peoples generally, there is Altman and Ginat, *Polygamous Families*, 241.

[85] On Lee's marriages, see Cleland and Brooks, eds., *A Mormon Chronicle*, 1:xxii–xxiii. Regarding Kimball's remark, he said his wives would not need to fight American soldiers because they would defeat themselves. Heber C. Kimball, 20 Sept. 1857, *Journal of Discourses*, 5:250. Identifying the exact number of wives married to Brigham Young is difficult. See Arrington, *Brigham Young*, 420–21; and Johnson, "Determining and Defining 'Wife': The Brigham Young Households," 57–70.

[86] For the quantitative pattern of Mormon plural marriages in the community of Manti, Utah, see Table 3 and Figure 3, in Daynes, *More Wives than One*, 101–2.

[87] Bennion, "Incidence of Mormon Polygamy in 1880," 27–42. Other investigations providing varying figures, but all greater than traditional church estimates, are: Ivins, "Notes on Mormon Polygamy," 230–32; Smith and Kunz, "Polygyny and Fertility in Nineteenth-Century America," 468–71; May, "People on the Mormon Frontier," 172; Logue, *Sermon in the Desert*, 44–71; Altman and Ginat, *Polygamous Families*, 460–61; and Daynes, *More Wives than One*, 100–1. For the even higher incidence of polygamy among church leaders, see Pace, "Wives of Nineteenth-Century Mormon Bishops," 49–57; and the long discussion in Quinn, *Mormon Hierarchy*, 2:178–97.

of all husbands' time, nearly three-quarters of all woman-years, and well over half of all child-years were spent in polygamy before 1880."[88] And, as Lowell Bennion found in his study of the northern Utah community of Brigham City, because the extended families of so many monogamists included pluralists, the Principle touched a majority of those living there in one way or another. He suggests the likelihood that, except for gender and demographic limitations, the number of plural unions might have been even higher.[89] Still, counting only those living beneath the roofs of polygamous households, there is reason to assume that, over the decades of its approval by the church, the total number of men, women, and children in polygamous homes amounted to many thousands of people, constituting perhaps the largest formally prescribed departure from monogamous marriage, excepting religious celibacy, in either European or American Christian society for centuries.[90]

For Mormons of the time, plural marriage was a teaching of more than spiritual and eugenic importance. It was an undertaking related to God's own timetable. Surveying Salt Lake Valley after his arrival in 1847 and filled with a vision of his people's future, Brigham Young spoke of Mormon intermarriage with the Indians, of plurality, "& how our descendants may live to the age of a tree & be visited & hold communion with the Angels; & bring in the Millenium."[91] More than thirty years later, captive to the same reverie, Romania Pratt said if church members would only enter the Principle and practice it as their leaders taught, "the millennium would . . . come."[92]

---

[88] Logue, "A Time of Marriage," 25.

[89] Bennion, Morrell, and Carter, *Polygamy in Lorenzo Snow's Brigham City*, 26.

[90] As the forces seeking to destroy polygamy gained strength, to refute Mormon claims that anti-polygamy legislation would render 50,000 women and their children homeless, the *Salt Lake Tribune* contended that the number was greatly inflated. "More Lies from the Hens," *Salt Lake Tribune*, 16 Jan. 1879, 6:73 [1/6]; "Washington," ibid., 23 Jan. 1879, 16:79 [4/2]; and esp. "Address to Congress," ibid., 9 Feb. 1879, 16:94 [2/2]. The *Tribune* said the actual number was closer to 10,000. Even this figure, however, if extrapolated to the entire period of formally endorsed polygamy among the Saints, would be considerable.

[91] As quoted in Bagley, ed., *Pioneer Camp of the Saints*, 28 July 1847, 243–44.

[92] "Extract from Dr. R. B. Pratt's Lecture," *Woman's Exponent* 10:2 (15 June 1881), 16.

Chapter 4

"Her Comfort Must Be Wholly in Her Children"
Polygamy at Home

As seen in the last chapter, in addition to declaring their domestic innovation to the world, LDS leaders made great efforts to assist church
members to better understand the practice. Private attitudes, however, are often difficult to discern. The Saints were thoroughly Victorian in
outlook, displaying a characteristic circumspection about their private lives.
There was also Mormonism's always-defensive posture, reinforced by bitter
campaigns levied against its best-known doctrine. Beyond this, the exalted
reputation that plural marriage held in their society meant women, who by
definition constituted the majority of adults in polygamous families, hesitated to discuss the arrangement.[1] As Jane Snyder Richards indicated in her
interview with Mrs. Bancroft provided below, wives were counseled not to
speak of domestic difficulties even to trusted Mormon neighbors.

Mormon awareness that their marriage doctrine was an object of interest to outsiders undoubtedly accounted for attestations by both male and
female Saints that their homes were happier than those found in monogamy.
In the words of one Elder, "no better time have I had in thirty years of married life than when I had three wives given me of God, and occupying one
habitation."[2] It is true that these were chiefly the expressions of men, especially those whose ecclesiastical responsibilities colored their remarks, but

---

[1] See Dushku and Eaton-Galsby, "Augusta J. Crocheron," 491–92.

[2] Henry W. Naisbitt, 8 Mar. 1885, *Journal of Discourses*, 26:124. As late as the mid-twentieth century, a high
church authority yet said that polygamous households experienced more happiness than monogamous ones.
See Widtsoe, "Evidences and Reconciliations: Why Did The Church Practice Plural Marriage in Earlier
Days," *Improvement Era* 46:3 (Mar. 1943), 191.

much the same can be said of women.[3] Still, with all that was done to bright-
ly clothe the Principle, records exist that are filled with honest descriptions
of polygamous practice.

"Not Half as Much a Slave": Public Comment By Women

The following two interviews do more than reveal Latter-day Saint determination to present plural marriage in its best light. Surprisingly free in expression, they introduce this chapter because of the generality of their remarks,
providing candid, public reflections on the practice by individuals who lived
it. The first is an 1880 handwritten transcript of remarks by Jane Snyder
Richards (1823–1913) made to Mrs. Matilda Coley Griffing Bancroft.[4]
Richards married Franklin Dewey Richards (1821–1899) in 1842, the first of
the apostle's many spouses. The interviewer's third-person voice throughout
the account notwithstanding, it offers a personal description by one involved
with polygamy from the time it was introduced in Nauvoo through the time
of the Saints' residence in Utah late in the century.

Mrs. F[ranklin] D[ewey] Richards, Inner Facts of Social Life in Utah, Interview with Mrs. Matilda Coley Griffing Bancroft, San Francisco, Calif., 1880, cu-b.

Mrs [Jane Snyder] Richards in private conversation with me, related the
following in regard to her personal experience. A few months previous to her
marriage [18 Dec. 1842] the idea of more than one wife was <generally> spoken of, tho' the practice of polygamy was of later growth. It was ~~as~~ repugnant to her ideas of virtue and it was not until she saw Joseph Smith in a
vision, who told her in time all would be explained, that she was satisfied to
abide by Mormon teachings whatever they were. About eight months after
her marriage, Elder [Franklin Dewey] Richards told her he felt he should like
to have another wife. It was crushing at first, but she said that as he was an

---

[3] See, for example: Isabella Thwaites, "A Woman's View of Woman's Mission," *Mil. Star* 30:35 (29 Aug.
1868), 551–52; E. McKay's letter in the "Women's Voice" column, *Woman's Exponent*, 1:20 (15 Mar. 1873), 154;
"Still Agreeable," ibid., 2:13 (1 Dec. 1873), 101; and, somewhat later, Gates, "Family Life Among the Mormons," 342–49.

[4] For reference to the interview, see Bancroft, *Literary Industries*, 640; and Ellsworth, "Hubert Howe Bancroft," 109–10. For Mrs. Richards's life, see Cannon, "Jane Snyder Richards," 173–98; and the older work of
her grandson, West, *Life of Franklin D. Richards*, 258–68.

Because of its importance, and as an example to others, church leaders were especially urged to enter the Principle. Here Mormon bishop Ira Eldredge (1810–1866) is shown with his three wives about 1864. The women, in Mormon homespun, are from left to right: Nancy Black, married in 1833; Hannah Mariah Savage, espoused in 1852; and Helvig Marie Andersen, sealed to Eldredge in 1861.

elder and if it was necessary to her salvation that she should let another share her pleasures, she would do so even if it was necessary for her to do the other thing. He wanted to know what that was, and if she thought she could not be happy in such a relation he would not enter into it. She said if she found they could not live without quarrelling she should leave him. At last <two or three years later> he told her that in three or four days he should bring such a one home as his wife. It was a surprise to her that he should select as he did; she knew the young woman [Elizabeth McFate][5] very well; she was amiable and all lived happily together. But on their journeyings toward Utah, this wife died of consumption. . .

When the subject of polygamy was first talked of between Mr Richards and herself, she used to say that she could yield herself to everything but the

<hr />

[5] Elizabeth McFate, born in 1825, married Franklin D. Richards on 31 Jan. 1846.

children; but that she should feel like wringing the neck of any other child than hers that should call him papa. . .

When the first child was born in ~~polg~~ polygamy, she thinks it was fortunate perhaps that her husband was in England. She had lost a daughter, Wealthy, and her heart yearned for another little girl. When she found this child was a ~~b~~ girl, her heart failed her. But she said she soon recovered herself and dressed the baby and took care of it a great deal. . . For these children she has always felt an interest, though it is not at all the same feeling she has for her own flesh and blood. If his ~~childre~~ and hers were drowning and but one could be saved, she should save her own. In reply to the question, she thought her husband would be in a dilemma, and would have to take the first that came along. . .

One little incident of home life illustrates considerable. Mr Richards had returned to his wives after a Mission in England, bringing with [him] shawls and other presents. These he displayed to his family asking them to take their choice. Of course Mrs Richards should have her first choice as a right; but she was always accustomed to yielding that privilege and as in this case she said "no girls, you care more about these things than I do; take your choice and I will be satisfied with what is left." Although she saw at once which she would have selected. Something in the intimation, unconsciously given that she yielded to their selfishness aroused their anger and all refused the selection. She went to her room and cried. Her husband came in and with his mannature was dull enough not to percieve the true cause and told her she never cared for any presents he brought her. Then she begged he never again would bring them all presents alike, but get a variety and himself make the selection and give to each what was his own choice; then each would be satisfied. Afterwards they all met together in the room and she said "Now girls, I have suggested this, which I am sure you will approve, and now he will distribute these according to his own discretion." She had previously suggested that . . . none of them would take any pleasure in wearing what each of the rest of the dozen or half dozen had a counterpart of.

Previous to ~~a~~ Mr Richards taking a plural wife. . . He told her that he would not marry if he did not think she would love his wives as much as he himself, which, she says to me, shows his love was not lustful; that he married simply because his religion demanded it.

Mr Richards in talking of these early days, and in reply to my questions as to how he reasoned about it when the matter was first considered as a personal obligation was a little evasive but at last told me, that at first it was a bitter pill but "the Lord required it, and we had to look for the explanation and reason afterward." . . .

It was about a month before her ~~marriage~~ baby's birth, polygamy was first talked of between her husband and herself; as she told him he talked of it to make a crooked road straight; but he did not enter into it for two or three years afterwards—she thinks he deferred it on account of the <long> sickness of Elizabeth's mother; and though she isn't certain about it she thinks her husband thought as she was so delicate Elizabeth would take care of her while he was away. So Elizabeth came into their family ~~t~~ while Mrs Richards was very miserable from a miscarriage, and obliged to have a hired girl. Elizabeth says as she entered the house. "I don't know how we are going to get along, but I will try and not make you miserable, Mrs Richards". I replied, "dont call me Mrs Richards; ~~I am Jane~~ call me Jane. I wont quarrel whatever happens". Elizabeth at once undertook the work of the house and said we didn't need a hired girl, and ~~I~~ <Mrs Richards> directed as before; she was but seventeen and very pretty. She had the upper story and I <Mrs Richards> the lower. If she was washing ~~I~~ <Mrs Richards> would do the cooking and so they got on nicely together.

Elizabeth was very considerate as this little instance shows. Mrs Richards was suffering from severe pain in her face, and Elizabeth asked Mr R. if she shouldn't take "our Wealthy", his little daughter up stairs that night so she shouldn't disturb her mother who was sleeping. In the night Mrs Richards awoke and her husband <who> had remained in the next room for fear of wakening her came to her. She asked him to go up stairs and see if Wealthy was warmly enough covered. The next morning Elizabeth says "I took Wealthy last <night> for I didn't want you to feel I should want ~~hi~~ Franklin to stay with me when you were suffering so much." Mrs R. had said that Wealthy slept with Elizabeth the night before; whether that implied a taking turns I couldn't tell. . .

[Mr. Richards] seems remarkably considerate and kind and speaks of her [Jane S. Richards] with gratitude and pride, and that he wanted her ~~I~~ to enjoy this little visit to California for she has suffered so much affliction and so many hardships that he wants whatever she can enjoy in life now to be hers. This was the way he first talked of his wife to Mr <Bancroft> ~~Richards~~ as they first met; and his attentions and kind consideration of her are very marked. She is certainly very devoted to him, and I am imagining this trip and the one that they have just returned from East, as a sort of honeymoon in middle-life. . .

She says Mr Richards had just written a letter when she enquired of him if he was writing to one of their children; "no," he said, "it was to one of his wives", and asked if she should like to read it. Altho' her face was turned he saw her smiling as she read and he asked if she was laughing at him; that his wife was sick and he thought that it would comfort her, don't you? And that he hadn't for years written such an affectionate letter to anyone. ~~I~~ Mrs Richards said that showed he wasn't afraid of exciting any jealousy or ill-will on her part or he wouldn't have shown her such a letter. I should not think such things would be calculated ~~in ere~~ [to] increase ones peace of mind. . .

In speaking of his marriages while his circumstances were so straightened he said that in ~~re~~ raising that objection when Brigham Young was suggesting another marriage, the President said: "when you had but one wife the Lord provided, though even then you could not see the way, why then will he not provide for you now?" I could not but think as he spoke, of the narration of hardship I had just listened to from the one wife so illy provided for; yet she never complained of her lot being hard, though <the> severe sicknesses ~~was~~ she endured, the care of delicate children, the earning of their livelihood by braiding straw hats and keeping boarders, ~~edu~~ teaching them to read and sewing for them, ~~all this~~ all combined to make a hard lot harder; and it seems as though it needed some divine grace to prevent her repining ~~that~~ at the wisdom of dividing her little heritage with another. But she says that when Mr Richards would ask her how she felt about that, she would reply "if I am able to divide your time with other wives, when your [*sic*] are away nine weeks in ten, I can dispense with the money; that is the last and least of my troubles". She says that in the first fifteen years of her married life he was away ~~ten~~ on missions ten years. In fact he was away so much she learned to live comfortably without him, as she would tell him to tease him sometimes; and even now he is away two thirds of the time as she is the only wife in Ogden, so that she often forgets <when> he is home, and has even sat down at meals forgetting to call him. She says she always feels very badly about it when it happens, but that he was more necessary to her in her earlier life. And yet she is a very devoted wife and he is remarkably attentive to her. To see them together I should never imagine either had a thought but what the other shared. . .

Mrs John Taylor was considerably older than Mrs Richards and advised her in a motherly way in regard to how she should live in polygamy. She asked her how she was getting along; "not very well, I guess", was Mrs Richards reply, "why what do people say about it"? "I never have heard a thing", replied Mrs Taylor "and I think you have too much pride and grit to let any of your domestic trials be known to the world". And Mrs Richards most certainly has. Mrs Taylor told her that everything would grow right and easy as time went on, and accepting the situation with a religious spirit, she would be happy. Shortly after this, at a dinner Mrs Taylor sat at one end of the table and Mrs Richards at the other; and something was said about trials, when Mrs Taylor spoke up, "Mrs Richards thinks everything has its trials, even polygamy". Mrs Richards said she was dreadfully annoyed by that, although it was said as a joke.

A neighbor once called to talk with Mrs Richards about what she should do a if her husband took another wife. Mrs Richards told her "there wasn't as much trouble in reality as there was in sweating about it beforehand".[6] Later the man married and again the wife came to Mrs Richards for counsel. Mrs Richards told her that she was making a mistake at the outset; she must not

---

[6] Another plural wife, who probably met its trials as successfully as anyone, made a different comment. Women contemplating a plural marriage, she said, "will learn more in one week of practice than in years of theory." Musser, *Early Autobiography and Diary of Ellis Reynolds Shipp*, 8 Feb. 1874, 153–54.

make a confidant of anybody. As long as she had lived in polygamy she had never spoken to any one of her troubles or allowed that she had any trials. "If you proceed in this way your husband will soon begin to feel that I am acquainted ~~will be~~ with all your difficulties, and will hate me for it, and soon will begin to despise you in consequence". The result of ~~t~~this advice was that the woman ceased her complaints and years after thanked Mrs Richards for ~~what~~ her wise counsel. She apparently lived happily in polygamy. . .

She said that in a woman's accepting the position of a plural wife, she knew she must submit to some such privations and if she felt inclined to complain she would remember she entered that state voluntarily and that would act as a sort of curb.

On the whole it seems to me that they considered it wholly as a religious duty and schooled themselves to bear its discomforts as a sort of religious penance; and that it was a matter of pride to make everybody believe they lived happily and to persuade themselves and others that it was not a trial; and that a long life of such discipline makes the trial lighter. Mrs Richards remarked that her face is wrinkled and care worn, but that polygamy has been the least of her troubles, [though] people would attribute her looks to that.

Martha Hughes Cannon (1857–1932), best remembered as the first woman in the United States to be elected a state senator, was the fourth wife of Angus Cannon, a prominent Salt Lake City Mormon. As a physician, she devoted much of her adult life to public-health measures. She also gave considerable energy to avoiding law-enforcement officers seeking to imprison her husband for violating laws prohibiting polygamy. Dr. Cannon's ideas concerning birth control, polygamy in the millennium, and other questions contrast interestingly with those of her church at the time. She championed plurality for what she saw as its emancipating effects on women. As scholars have discovered, however, privately she suffered keenly from the strains of marital isolation and other difficulties the Principle brought.[7]

ANNIE LAURIE, "FIRST SENATOR AMONG WOMEN
[MARTHA HUGHES CANNON]," *SAN FRANCISCO EXAMINER*,
63:131 (9 NOV. 1896), 1/1–2, 2/5.

"I believe in polygamy. My father and mother were Mormons and I am a Mormon. Of course the law of the United States says 'No,' and we must obey. But that does not alter one's belief in the right of the thing. A plural wife is not half as much a slave as a single wife. If her husband has four wives she

---

[7] White, "Martha H. Cannon," 391–94. There is also Lieber and Sillito, eds., *Letters from Exile*. For more on her husband, Angus M. Cannon, see Chapter Seven.

has three weeks of freedom every single month. She and her children order their lives and do not have to wait and be ready for husband when the fourth week comes around. She's glad to see him, and she does not mind getting three meals a day for him and making the children stop breathing to give him a chance to read. A plural wife has more time to herself and more independence every way than a single one.

"But then, of course, that is not the reason I believe in it. I believe in it because I think it is right. Jealousy, unhappiness? Not half as much of it among plural wives as there is among single wives. Plural wives look upon marriage as a sacred duty and not as a means of self-seeking vanity. I've heard sentimentalists say that polygamy destroys poetry and takes all the sentiment out of life. Nonsense. A man loves all his wives. He is not in love with just one of them. . .

"Europe? Oh, yes, I went there when I was under-ground. Oh, I forgot, you're a gentile. Well, when the anti-polygamy law came into force we plural wives went, as we called it, under-ground. We went away and waited for things to blow over. I took my children to Europe and then to California. . .

"Motherhood is a great thing, a glorious thing, and it ought to be a successful thing. It will be when it is regulated. Some day there will be a law compelling people to have no more than a certain amount of children and the mothers of the land can live as they ought to live, free, happy, healthy lives. That's one thing about us Mormons. You know we never did let a man marry till he showed conclusively that he could take good care of his wife and family. We never raise paupers. . .

"Our great teacher, Brigham Young, understood all these [things]. He said, I heard him say it with these ears of mine, 'The day shall come when men and women shall walk together side by side in the temple.' That day is dawning now. Electricity will soon do away with much of the domestic drudgery. Women are growing wise and men are growing gentle. I think the millennium is coming sooner than we dare to hope."

"In the millennium," I [Annie Laurie] said, "will there be polygamy?"

"No," said Mrs. Cannon, "we won't need it then. Each will then find his affinity and be happy."

"Spooning Aunt Nellie": Courting Plural Wives

A conspicuous feature of the Mormon marriage system, especially after the Nauvoo period, was the forwardness that both men and women suitors displayed searching for partners. One of the institution's acclaimed advantages was that it permitted unmarried females to wed already married men, pro-

viding these women with greater freedom of choice than existed in monogamous societies and sparing less-sought-for women the prospect of a barren old age. In the words of one likely spinster whose husband, home, and
offspring were the gifts of plurality, "it was the consummation of all my
earthly wishes."[8]

Nevertheless, men seeking additional women in the face of a first wife's
opposition, even with the church's permission, could bring intense anguish.[9]
And husbands who courted others in their first wife's presence sometimes
inflicted never-forgotten pain.

CLARENCE ALLEN, ORAL INTERVIEW BY JAMES COMISH,
15 FEB. 1980, COVE, UTAH, OHP, 22.

Clarence Allen: All I know is, Mother says that she remembers her being
in bed over there in the back bedroom. We had a big front porch on that house
at that time; it was a beautiful moon light night. She says she can remember
she knew that Dad was out spooning Aunt Nellie out on this porch.

FA [Florence, the daughter-in-law]: She told me that she looked out and
she could see them in the moon light. He was holding Nellie in his arms and
kissing her. She [Betsy, the first wife] said, "Oh, I just cried and cried." She
cried until her milk dried up. She was nursing the baby. It was just kind of a
heartbreak to her to see that. She said, "I cried until my milk dried up because
I was so broken hearted over it." Later they both came and told her that they
were in love and were going to get married. So she said, "What could I do
about it?"[10]

New plural wives were usually aware of the feelings their entry into the
marriage brought, as Eliza Avery Clark (1882–1953) expressed in this note to
her suitor, Abraham Owen Woodruff (1872–1904). Abraham, a son of President Wilford Woodruff, married Helen May Winters as his first wife on 30
May 1896. He was called to be an apostle at conference that fall. Miss Clark
was engaged to another young man when Woodruff visited her Wyoming com-

---

[8] Martha Spence Heywood, as quoted in Brooks, ed., *Not by Bread Alone*, 77. Also see Elizabeth Oakes
Smith, "Should Women Propose?" *Mil. Star* 30:19 (9 May 1868), 289–93.

[9] Benjamin F. Johnson, a close friend of Joseph Smith, said that if first wives were like Sarah of old, it
would be unnecessary to obtain their permission to take additional wives. If, however, a wife opposed her
husband after being taught the Principle, Johnson said the consequences described in the 1843 revelation
(*D&C* 132:64–65) applied: she was a "transgressor" and would be "destroyed." Johnson to George F. Gibbs,
1903, Johnson Papers, box 2, fd. 1, LDS Archives.

[10] Clarence and FA [Florence] Allen are the son and daughter-in-law of Betsy and James Carson Allen
(1868–1935) of Cache Valley, Utah. James married Betsy Lowe, the older of two sisters, on 1 Mar. 1883, and
wed "Nellie" Lowe, the younger sister with whom he was seen "spooning," on 11 Sept. 1884.

munity and expressed his interest in her. Since Woodruff was already married, the anticipated alliance would be a post-Manifesto plural marriage, one of hundreds secretly approved by church authorities, so their courtship was conducted surreptitiously. Such couples sometimes destroyed their romantic communications, used aliases, and, as in this letter, left them unsigned.

[Eliza Avery Clark] to Abraham Owen Woodruff,
25 Oct. 1900, box 3, fd. 11,
Abraham Owen Woodruff Collection, upb.

Dear Bro. Woodruff:— . . .

A happier hour of my life was never spent than was during the conversation that we had. It filled me with joy and gladness that has not departed from me, and I thank God that I am so highly favored for I feel that I am. I feel more and more inclined toward you and have more affection and a higher respect for you than have I ever had for any other. I am satisfied with my lot as yet and think I always shall be. I am also thankful to her who gave her consent and sacrificed that she all ready has for my sake and for principle's sake, for it must have been contrary to the natural feelings, which we all have. I do not worry about the financial part of it and think you need not. I will try to be a help meet, any how you know I have not been raised in great luxuries and don't expect them. . .

I humbly ask God's blessings upon us in all. From one True and Sincere,—[11]

"The Grandest Step of My Whole Life": Male Courtship of Plural Wives

Though constrained from courting women already married, men still enjoyed considerable liberty in the search.[12] The openness with which Mormon males could advertise themselves in the hunt for wives is recalled in the legend of Chris L. Christensen, which Juanita Brooks recorded from stories told her by Dr. Joseph Walker. This document, amounting perhaps to no more than third-or-fourth-hand hearsay, describes a search for a plural wife in "Dixie," Utah's southern region. Christian Lyngaa [Lingo] Christensen (1855–1940)

---

[11] Apostle Matthias F. Cowley married Woodruff and Clark in January 1901. For more, see Hardy, *Solemn Covenant*, 208–9, and Appendix II, no. 213.

[12] Regarding pursuit of women already married, there were exceptions, as in the case of Joseph Smith and, more fatefully, that of Parley P. Pratt with the separated but yet-married Eleanor McLean. Pratt, "Eleanor McLean and the Murder of Parley P. Pratt," 225–26.

served many missions to assist in building the St. George Temple, helped settlers along the Little Colorado River, and proselyted the Indians. He married his first wife, Ann Elizabeth Thompson, on 5 April 1874. Severina Jensen
became his wife on 24 April 1879.

> Juanita Brooks, "Hint to Young Men in Search of Wives,"
> *uhq* 29:3 (July 1961), 299–300.
>
> The Cotton Factory at Washington was the scene of romances and heart-
> breaks and thrills. At the peak of its production it employed a personnel of
> twenty-seven people, sixteen of whom were women and young girls. Since
> their hours were long and their week a full six days, they had little opportu-
> nity for recreation that would bring them into contact with eligible men, and
> any courtship was a matter of group knowledge and interest.
>
> One of the most colorful courtships was that of C. L. Christensen, who
> was coming to Dixie for the first time. Though he had other business, he also
> had been charged by his first wife to bring back a second, in order that he
> might be eligible for a higher church position.
>
> He arrived at the factory just at noon, as the girls were coming out of doors
> to eat their lunch, buxom, healthy girls eager to get out into the spring air.
> Quickly he formulated a plan. Mounting a large rock near the place where
> the girls had spread out their food, he took off his hat—conscious, perhaps,
> that his six-foot-two height, curly blond hair, and fine set of teeth made him
> not hard to look at—and called out in the manner of a Mormon mission-
> ary at a street meeting:
>
> "Give me your attention, please! I am Chris Christensen of San Pete Coun-
> ty, commonly called Chris Lingo. I have come to Dixie on business and will
> be here only a short time. One of my hopes is that I may be able to find for
> myself a second wife, that I may please my first and fulfill the celestial law.
> Look me over, girls, and if any of you would like to get better acquainted, I'd
> be very glad to visit with you after dinner."
>
> The girls giggled and whispered and dared each other, until finally a group
> of a half-dozen or more went to talk with him. He found his wife Serenie
> [Severina] there, married her and took her back with him. They later moved
> to San Juan County, where the story of the courtship is legend.[13]

Looking to reassure themselves, Mormon swains sometimes asked for
omens in the search.[14] Some said they were led by revelation, and at least one
aspiring Abraham enlisted supernatural help from a "peep stone."

---

[13] Christensen's diary mentions many trips to St. George but says nothing of the wife-hunting episode
Brooks described. See Christensen, Reminiscences and Diary, lds Archives.

[14] See Goodson, "Plural Wives," 94–95.

Luella Parkinson Cowley, "Parkinson Romance,"
in "Pioneer Courtships," 14–15,
Daughters of Utah Pioneers Historical Pamphlet.
Kate B. Carter, Comp., May 1940.

Samuel R. Parkinson and his wife Ar[a]bella lived in Kaysville, Davis County.[15] In 1855 he lost his team of mules. After hunting for them for two days, without success, he went to see a man who had a peep stone.[16] Father described his mules and the man looked into a large glass ball and saw the mules lying down under a tree, about four miles away. He then asked father if he would like to look and see if he could see them, as there were few people who could see anything in a peep stone. But to father's great surprise he could see his mules. Father then turned to his wife and said: "Is there anything you would like me to inquire about?" She answered: "Ask to see your other wife, if there is one for you." At that time there was a great deal said about men taking other wives, so father asked to see his other wife. Immediately he saw two young girls, dressed just alike, and they stood arm in arm. He called his wife to come and look, and to her surprise she saw the two girls. She described them many times to others. Going home father asked his wife: "If you ever see those two girls will you consent for me to marry them?" And she answered: "Yes, but never until then."

Five years passed and they were called as pioneers to Franklin, Idaho, and Thomas Smart, whose home was in Provo, was called to go there about the same time. These two men started a grist mill and a saw mill. Because of their business associations, they visited each other's families.

In the summer of 1865 President Young was coming to visit Franklin and elaborate preparations were being made for his visit. The day finally arrived and my father being in the Bishopric, sat on the stand at the meeting that was held in President Young's honor. While the opening song was being sung, two girls, dressed alike and walking arm in arm, came in. They had on new hats, the first imported hats worn in Franklin. Father recognized them as the girls of the peep stone. Even though he knew them well, as they were the daughters of his friend, Pioneer Smart, he had never thought of them before in this way. At the close of the meeting he took his wife where they would meet them face to face. When she saw the girls, she, too, recognized them. Father said: "Who did those girls remind you of?" She reluctantly answered that they were the girls she had seen in the peep stone.

In less than a year father married the oldest and a year later, he married the other. He never told either of them his experience until after he had mar-

---

[15] Samuel Rose Parkinson (1831–1919) married Arabella Ann Chandler in 1852.

[16] Magical stones are a part of Mormon history. One early critic said Joseph Smith's "seer stone" was "the acorn of the Mormon oak." Tucker, *Origin, Rise and Progress of Mormonism,* 26.

ried them both. They lived in one house until there were seventeen children and when father built another house a block away and moved my mother there, it was hard to separate.[17]

Charles Ramsden Bailey (1839–1901) was an English convert who settled at Maughan's Fort, or Wellsville, Utah. His reminiscence told not only how dreams and special blessings entered the thinking of Mormon men looking for wives but provides us with an instance of two women being sealed to one husband on the same day. Before these marriages occurred, Bailey was involved in a brief, unhappy monogamous relationship, excluded from the excerpt below.[18]

AUTOBIOGRAPHY OF CHARLES R. BAILEY, FD. 1, ULA, 38–46.

[After he divorced his first wife in 1860, Bailey says]: I Returned home feeling Much better than when I went away on my way home   Stopd with friends at Willard and they was glad I had got Rid of her, And When I got into Wellsville . . . Presedend Peter Maughan Met me and Said . . . I am glad Said he you have got Rid of her She would have done you no good.[19] Now Said he be faithful And I will promise you when you Marrey again you will Marrey two good faithful Latterday Saints And Shall be Blessed with a large famely of Children   this made me feel curious but I thanked him Kindley for [h]is Interest he took in me and for his Blessing and Promise   now this was in the Spring of 1860 and it took three and half years to Bring it about, however I went along Minding my own buisness and did not pay any atention to anyone for nerley two years. . . But in order to make my Jurnel More Complete I Must here Relate A dream I had [in 1861] on the Weeber River in Coleville. . . Sleeping in the waggon And I dremt that [I]was about to Marrey again And I was going to Marrey two wifes   one I had Seen and was aquainted with but I Could not Place her And the other I had not yet Seen And I awoke. . . And I went to Sleep And drempt Same dream again And then the third time however I thought it Strange Myself that I Should dream the Same thing three times in Succession as I was not verey much in favour

---

[17] Samuel wed Charlotte H. Smart as a plural wife on 8 Dec. 1866, a marriage that brought ten children. Less than two months later, on 4 Feb. 1867, he married Charlotte's sister, Mariah. They had thirteen children. As residents of Franklin, Idaho, the family endured the trials of the anti-polygamy crusade, and Samuel eventually spent time in the Idaho penitentiary in Boise, Idaho. These events are described, without reference to the "peep stone," in Parkinson, Life Sketch of Samuel Rose Parkinson, Uhi.

[18] Born in England, his given name was Charles Ramsden. After converting to the LDS church he added the name of Bailey, perhaps from disrespect for an abusive father. Long and Long, Charles Ramsden Bailey, 3.

[19] Wellsville, Bailey's home, is eight miles southwest of Logan, Utah. It was originally called Maughan's Fort, after Peter Maughan, the ecclesiastical leader Bailey often refers to in this account. It was later renamed after Daniel H. Wells, a counselor to Brigham Young.

of that Princple for I had lived with famelies in Plurel Marrige And Could see it was Somthing for Merraid women to do to live it but the Matter Confrunted And I went along thinking about it and the Promise Mad by Peter Maughan And Somtimes wondered Could there be any thing [in] it And thought I would leave it in the hands of God. . .

[Serving as a volunteer, Bailey went east to Florence, Nebraska, to assist migrating Saints on their way to the Salt Lake Valley.][20] for Nerley one Month bye and bye the Emegrants Came up the River two or three thousand And there was lots of fine looking girls as one Could wish to See And of Course the young men was Making Selections out of them however this did not Enter My mind so I made no Selection at all[21]   after a while we got our loads of People. . . And I think I had a Choice load And we got along niceley all the way. . . however after being on the road a few days A verey nice girl told Bro John Owens[22] that She had took to me more than any one in the Company and asked him all about me and he told her And Encouraged her in her venture And he told me all about her and what she had said. . . the next day after dinner while waiting for the Cattle she wanted to walk out of Camp And Chatt a litle I didnt Care about going but Bro Owens Says go on so we went along and I Soon found out her Mind but did not give her any Answer then as the Cattle Came in I told her I would See her again. . . so in about two days I told her I wanted to See her and after Prayers we walked along to our places And I asked her if She had not fallen in love with me And she frankley admited She had   I told her She Should not have done so. . . then I Said I was promised to one at home thinking that would Change her Mind but She Answered are you not a latterday Saint   Said I yes then She Said well you Can Marrey her And then Me afterwards   then My dream Came to me as fresh as when I dreamd it And it remaind so all the way to Salt Lake but as we will see later on it was not the time And She was not the one. . . but I hold that the Lord had laid out the plann And I had to wait [H]is time   however the Reason of [this] Narrative is to Show to my Sons & daughters that there was as Much Inspiration about My Entering into Plurel Marrige as there was in one being

---

[20] For accounts of church projects to transport migrants to the Salt Lake Valley, see Arrington, *Great Basin Kingdom*, 105–11; and Hulmston, "Mormon Immigration in the 1860s," 32–48.

[21] On reaching the Salt Lake Valley, Caleb Green, a Gentile, commented on the interest Mormon men displayed toward new female immigrants: "Filled with the idea of enhancing their glory in the future world Grey headed old men <with wrinkled faces>, who ought to be thinking of God and their graves, pester the young girls in the arriving trains, ~~they use the prophets name in order to frighten their victims into marrying them~~ using the terrors of Brigham's name and threatening the penalty of excommunication and consequent perdition, in order to induce them to marry them." Caleb Green Journal, 1862, Missouri Hist. Soc., 40. The prospect inspired even Brigham Young: "If the companies are composed solely of young females, they may come by tens of thousands, if they like, for I have never yet seen anything in this market that can equal the hand-cart girls." Sermon of 1 Feb. 1857, *Journal of Discourses*, 4:206.

[22] This was most likely Evan Richards Owen (1832–1906) of Wellsville, Utah.

born into this world at the time and place or in being Baptized into the Church
And that the Lord brought it about in [H]is own way and at that Perticuler
time and as to who those wifes Should be because that Man of God Bro Peter
Maughan spoke by the spirit of the Lord at the time he Made the promise in
1860. . . the Spring of 1863 Came along all right and another Call for Men and
teams. . . I was Calld at the head of the list to take Charge of Wellsville[,]
Mendon[,] Hyrum[,] & Paredice teams 20 in Number this Season[23] . . . in latter part of June we arived at florance[24] . . . one Morning I woke And Said to
Joseph Kay[25] My bed Mate I Said let us go down to town to day what for I
dont Know but I feel I must go. . . And [we] went down to florance 5 Miles
there   as Soon as we got to the Store Bro Cluff[26] who had Charge of the
Scandinaviea Saints Asked us if we was from the Cash valley Company   yes
we are   Can you take Some folks that is Campt out here as they want to go
in that Company   I Said yes And told Jos Kay to go after them and I Said to
Joseph Il bet you my Girl is there   do you think so he Said so he went and I
went into the Store in a Short time I See him Coming he waved [h]is whip
and hat then I knew She was there. . . they Remaind in Jos Kays waggon all
the way And was Close bye all the time. . . after a hard Jurney we arived in Salt
lake City And fanialey got unloaded now I did not no wether Johannah & her
Mother[27] was going to Stop in the City or going to Cash [Valley] with me as
I let them have their own way about it And there had been so many friends to
See them and took them buggey riding while we was unloading but the time
Came to Move north for feed and I went And Asked Johannah & Mother what
they was going to do go with me or Stop in the City And the answer was we
are going with you   all right I Said so we Started and three days brought us
to Wellsville [written at top of page: Arived Sep 27] then trouble Comenced
if I dare Call it Such for as I had forgot to State that I had a girl at home that
I had Kept Company with for one year & half And of Course Medlers would
Medle And try to Mak trouble however I Kept Coole And did all I Could to
Keep things level And after every body that wanted to Say so much then I
Comenced in real Ernest And Said what I had to Say   I remember the first
night I took Susannah[28] home from Singing Practice. . . A voice Said to me
Charles is going [to marry] Both them girles. . . And I now began to See my
dream Coming to pass about the 20t of October I went over to Presedent Peter
Maughan And took the girls with me And asked him for A Recomend to go

---

[23] Bailey refers to the Cache Valley Company of the William Preston church train in 1863. Mendon,
Hyrum, and Paradise, small Cache Valley communities, are all located within ten miles of Logan, Utah.

[24] Florence, Nebraska, was a gathering place from which, with the assistance of church wagon trains,
arriving converts made their way to the Salt Lake Valley in the 1860s.

[25] Joseph Chatterly Kay (1844–1891), also of Wellsville.

[26] Probably William Wallace Cluff (1832–1915) of Provo, Utah.

[27] Johannah Adamson (1844–1914) and her mother, Johannah Hurtig.

[28] Susannah Hawkins (1847–1936).

to the Endowment house And take these two girls for wifes   Yes Said he Cheer-
fuley And then he Said did I not Promise this to you   I answered you did   he
Said I felt in My verey bones And thank God it is Come to Pass go on you
have my blessing And in spite of all the oposision and Peculier Circumstances
that took Place from the time I had the dream was fullfilled[29] . . . And I May
Say that it was the Grandest Step of My whole life And while it Brought its
Many Cares And as Some would Call triels yet I never felt it as Such   while
Maney things Might have been Avoided had we Known better but we had to
Pass through the Experiance to find out who we were but by Proving true and
faithful to the End the Promise is Sure no Matter who May Say to the Con-
traria   Now I have Narrated My Cortship And Marrige to Show to My fame-
leys that I was not the Instegater of this Matter for I was not fully converted
to that Princple from what I had Seen and herd but I was brought to See it in
a Marvolous way And was brought to beleive it and to obay it and Can Say of
A Surety that I Know it be true as Much so as Baptisem for the Remission of
Sins And I Say if Plurel Marrige or Celestial Marrige is not true then Mor-
monasim is all a [word illegible] And the day will Come that the world will
beleive it to be true   well thank God I had the Courage to Embrace it in My
youth And found how to go hand in hand with Me Notwithstanding we have
lots of Oposision but through the blessing of God we are doing as well as we
Can. . . And are as prospourous as those that have onley the one [wife]. . . we
made good Money on the Rail Rods   in the winter [1868–69] I made four
trips out to the Promenterey with Lumber and Potatoes and did prety well   it
was during this winter I took it on myself to take Another wife And I mad
the Choice of Hannah Jones as the one to be my wife So I made atempt and
after a time Succeeded   there was Maney obstacles Came in My way but I
fanealey over came them And during the winter Paid my Adresses to her And
took her to theatres and dances And in the Spring of 1869 Married her.[30]

"I WRESTLED WITH MY HEAVENLY FATHER":
ACCEPTING THE PRINCIPLE

The process by which women came to accept plurality was almost always
difficult. It commonly involved initial rejection of the doctrine, depression,
and confusion, followed by some form of spiritual witness as a response to
prayer. It was a pattern visible from the time plurality was introduced in the
1840s, as Lucy Walker's account reveals. After the prophet first proposed to

---

[29] Both Johannah Adamson and Susannah Hawkins married Bailey on 7 Nov. 1863.

[30] Bailey's account, orthographically and grammatically revised, can be read in *Our Pioneer Heritage*, 5:171–79;
and again, in ibid., 17:284–88. Bailey actually married Hannah Jones (1853–1923) on 4 April 1870.

her in late 1842, Lucy said she felt as if struck by a "thunderbolt." On the urging of the prophet she prayed for guidance as to what to do. But only "gross darkness" followed. Finally, after torturing over the matter for some time, she was persuaded. Following an intense night of prayer, her soul was filled with peace and joy.[31]

For most women, belief that the Principle was divinely inspired was essential. Whatever economic benefits may have accrued to the widowed and bereft, women consenting to polygamy were influenced most by religious conviction, however acquired. Helen Mar Whitney recalled how Mary Ellen Harris stressed the importance of her belief in the divinity of the practice.

> Sister Mary Ellen Harris . . . is one of my father's [Heber C. Kimball's] . . . widows . . . [and] She has testified to me that she was sealed in that Temple [Nauvoo] to my father and that she chose him because he was a man of God, though her heart was grieved that she should cause Sister Vilate Kimball [Kimball's first wife] one pang, but she felt that if she did not take this step her own glory would be clipt. . . There were over twenty women sealed to my father in that Temple for the same conscientious reasons expressed by Sister Mary Ellen . . . five of them . . . as. . . [widows] of the Prophet Joseph. These women were actuated by the one principle, salvation and exaltation in our Father's Kingdom. . . All [these women] had refused offers from single men, and no earthly inducements were held out to them to enter the plural order.[32]

Difficulty was generally most acute for first wives. Phebe Whittemore Carter (1807–1885), first wife of church president Wilford Woodruff, provides an example.

> When the principle of polygamy was first taught I thought it the most wicked thing I ever heard of; consequently I ~~supp~~ opposed it to the best of my ability, until I became sick and wretched. As soon, however, as I became convinced that it originated as a revelation from God through Joseph, and knowing him to be a prophet, I wrestled with my Heavenly Father in fervent prayers, to be guided aright at that all important moment of my life. The answer came. Peace was given my mind. I knew it was the will of God; and from that time to the present I have sought to faithfully honor the patriarchal law.[33]

---

[31] Littlefield, *Reminiscences*, 46–48. Compton, *In Sacred Loneliness*, 463–66, provides a longer account.

[32] Whitney, "Scenes in Nauvoo, and Incidents from H. C. Kimball's Journal," *Woman's Exponent* 12:10 (5 Oct. 1883), 74. For more on the plural marriages of Heber C. Kimball, see Kimball, *Heber C. Kimball: Mormon Patriarch and Pioneer*, 227–44; and Kimball's remarks at Vilate's funeral, in Kenney, ed., *Wilford Woodruff's Journal*, 26 Oct. 1868, 6:435.

[33] Phebe W. Carter Woodruff, Autobiographical Sketch, 9 Dec. 1880, CU-B, 5.

The rapid increase of plural marriages after the prophet's death and the move west were especially difficult for first wives. Writing from Winter Quarters to her missionary husband in England, Mary Haskin Parker Richards told him, "there is no such thing as happiness known here where a man has more than one &C it realy seems to me that this is a day in which Woman is destined to misery."[34] Remembering the journey west and her first years in the Salt Lake Valley, Helen Mar Whitney was deeply troubled, especially on behalf of her mother, Vilate Kimball. "I had, in hours of temptation, when seeing the trials of my mother, felt to rebel," she wrote. "I hated polygamy in my heart."[35] Spiritual reassurance alone assuaged the pain. Even then, reminders of the Principle's high importance were needed, as Helen told her husband, Horace Kimball Whitney, in an 1869 letter.

> [Summarizing a church address that William Clayton delivered the previous Sunday, she said] his subject was polygamy, showing why it was so necessary, & the great loss of those that did not practice it; proving it by scripture, that what seemed to be theirs would be taken and given to another. that men with only one wife would be nothing but angels in the next world. it was very interesting; & I confess I understood things that night that I never did before, & saw not only the necessity but the beauty of polygamy our trials here look so small, when I look at the great glory that is in store for the few that will hold out faithfull to the end.[36]

"The Agony and the Exaltation": Repression of Romantic Love

Nineteenth-century Mormons were susceptible to the same emotions as men and women elsewhere. Both sexes admitted that attractions such as the appearance of an ankle, the shape of another's head, or an individual's speaking voice enticed them into the plural order.[37] But because romantic feelings interfered with the selflessness needed for stable plural relationships, church leaders urged that such passions be put aside.[38] The result was often the cool

---

[34] Ward, ed., *Winter Quarters*, 78. Also see Beecher, "Women in Winter Quarters," 11–19.

[35] Helen Mar Whitney, in Crocheron, *Representative Women of Deseret*, 111–13.

[36] Whitney to Horace K. Whitney, 17 Dec. 1869, Whitney Family Papers, box 1, fd. 1, ULA.

[37] See, for example, Macfarlane, *Yours Sincerely, John M. Macfarlane*, 90; Sevey, "Alfred Baker," 21; and Archie L. Jenkins interview, OHP, 16.

[38] Brigham Young, 28 Aug. 1852, *Journal of Discourses*, 6:276; idem, 15 June 1856, ibid., 3:360–61; Charles C. Rich, 11 Nov. 1877, ibid., 19:167; and George Q. Cannon, 31 Oct. 1880, ibid., 22:126. Also see Lynn, "Courtship and Romance in Utah Territory," 211–23.

domestic atmosphere that many visitors to Mormon communities observed. In the words of one outsider, the restrained mood in Latter-day Saint homes made Utah "the Massachusetts of the West."[39] It was undoubtedly an unremitting struggle, but religion so suffused Mormon thinking about the Principle that, as Sarah Comstock said when discussing what she saw of the repression of affection among them, "the agony and the exaltation became one."[40]

Once the step was taken, challenges came on rapidly and, for some, plagued them for years. Testimonies to this effect are numerous. Mary J. Morrison, after telling the story of Miriam, who was smitten with leprosy for criticizing Moses' marriage to "the Ethiopian woman," disclosed what must have been a common suspicion: "I wonder," she said, "how many cases of leprosy there would be at present, if every [Mormon] woman was stricken with it that speaks against Celestial Marriage."[41] The remark of another wife, inadvertent in its candor, further revealed how widespread unhappiness was. Grateful for the harmony between herself and sister wives, she resolved that her husband "may never have to admit the humiliating truth as many good faithful elders do, that there is no peace, no love, no union in his home."[42] It was, Mary Isabella Horne indicated, loss of "oneness" between husband and wife that hurt most. Even with the boasted independence polygamy brought to women, Horne said she still deeply missed the closeness monogamy alone permits.[43] As another plural wife told Julius Birge when he asked if she truly favored the arrangement: "'Yes,' she replied slowly, and then added 'but it is because it is God's will. I would prefer to have a whole husband.'"[44]

Certainty that God decreed the Principle for their eternal benefit was not

[39] Cobb, "Mrs. Stearns and Mormonism," 524. Mormon courtship, no less than life after marriage, required careful discipline of the emotions. One study described polygamous courtship among the Saints as "mechanical, businesslike, hurried, and brief." See Altman and Ginat, *Polygamous Families*, 118. Nels Anderson saw frontier life as an explanation for such behavior. *Desert Saints*, 403–4. For the circumstances confronting western women generally, see Faragher, *Women and Men on the Overland Trail*, 147–48, 158, 180.

[40] Comstock, "Mormon Woman," 17. Also see Gallichan, *Women under Polygamy*, 304–5. The loneliness and isolation that plural wives endured is the primary theme of Compton, *In Sacred Loneliness*; and Katz, "Sisters in Salvation." There is a parallel with some North African Islamic peoples where, for the same purpose, sexual and emotional restraint is urged in the name of moral superiority. See Abu-Lughod, *Veiled Sentiments*, 332–33.

[41] "Celestial Marriage," *Woman's Exponent* 10:17 (1 Feb. 1882), 135. The story of Miriam and Moses' marriage to the Ethiopian woman is in Numbers 12:1, 10.

[42] Musser, *Early Autobiography and Diary of Ellis Reynolds Shipp*, 160.

[43] Horne, "Migration and Settlement of the Latter Day Saints," CU-B, 34–35.

[44] Birge, *Awakening of the Desert*, 346. Mormon female attitudes were probably similar to those Chamie found among Muslims. There, he said, most preferred being the only wife but would rather live in plurality than remain single. Chamie, "Polygyny among Arabs," 66.

always enough, and some women found it necessary to develop additional strategies for accommodating polygamy's trials. Sarah Ann Sutton Cooke related Vilate Kimball's advice to another polygamous wife on how to deal with her sorrows.

> Mrs Heber C. Kimball was a noble woman and was pointed out as an example to other wives to follow. One woman asked <Mrs Kimball> ~~her~~, after her first year of polygamy when she had striven <in vain> to yield herself to the situation that it might be for her husband's exaltation, what should she do? She had been married many years and had encouraged him to take another wife thinking she could stand the test; she said many a time she would go into the cellar and pray in ~~an~~ agony asking if it was really's [sic] God's will that polygamy exist. Mrs Kimball told her that ~~for~~ she, too, had suffered as she did until she had learned, as the women must learn, that her comfort must be wholly in her children; that she must lay aside wholly ~~added~~ <all> interest or thought in what her husband was doing when he way [sic] away from her; ~~and~~ she said she was pleased to see him when he came in as she was pleased to see any friend, "and thus she counseled me," says she to Mrs. Cooke, "to simply be indifferent to my husband if I would be happy."[45]

Where harmony proved impossible, most held on and made whatever adjustments were required. A common arrangement was to establish separate households for additional wives, as described by Jane Blood.

> JANE WILKIE HOOPER BLOOD, DIARIES, LDS ARCHIVES.
>
> Nov. 18 [1872] William married Sarah Jane Colemere. This was the greatest trial I ever passed thro. I gave my concent and was determined to stand it if it killed me. He brought her to live in my house. I gave her my bedroom and did all I could to be just with her in everything. She was sulky and a hard person to have sit in the home and be waited on all the time but I did it. She had a son born . . . then we waited on both. . .
>
> April 18 [1873] I could not endure it longer to live with Sarah because I would not do or say any thing cross to her and she was too trying to live with. Wm. rented a home for her two blocks north and moved her there.[46]

---

[45] Sarah A. Cooke left Mormonism after becoming disillusioned with polygamy and the leadership of Brigham Young. See Scott, "Sarah Ann Sutton Cooke," 1–27; and idem, "The Widow and the Lion of the Lord," 189–212. Sarah A. Cooke, Theatrical and Social Affairs in Utah, S.L.C., 1884, CU-B, 5–6.

[46] For an abridged edition of this diary, see Hill, ed., *Jane Wilkie Hooper Blood*. Jane Wilkie Hooper (1845–1898) married William Blood (1839–1917) on 9 September 1861. As indicated in her diary, William married Sarah Jane Colemere (1854–1935) eleven years later. His sons Henry and William visited their father while he was serving a prison term for illegal cohabitation in 1888, and Henry served as Utah's governor from 1933 to 1941. William's diary, perfunctory throughout, is completely silent on tensions between his wives. Blood, Diaries, LDS Archives. For a summary of evidence indicating that a majority of nineteenth-century polygamous wives had private lodging of their own, see Altman and Ginat, *Polygamous Families*, 189–90.

"Not in Want of Me": Patriarchy and Polygamy

The matter of religiously approved male dominance confronted all Mormon women. Emphasis on patriarchal authority, present from the beginning in Mormon plurality, became increasingly conspicuous after the Saints relocated in the West.[47] Lucinda Lee Dalton deeply believed in the church but delayed marriage because she saw so much about her that "was disagreeable and humiliating to women." She bemoaned the "foggy superstition about man's being created first and *consequently* best, noblest, and supreme-*est*."[48] One plural wife said her husband's manner was so towering that it was only in the year before he died that she found the courage to stand up to him.[49]

Clara Maria Rogers reminded her husband that "While it was ordained that man should be at the head it does not say that woman should be at the foot."[50] Combined with jealousy and compromised exclusivity, plurality fractionated wives' opinions, adding further to the sense of distance from their husbands.[51] Even such a strong-minded member of the Mormon female elite as Emmeline Blanche Woodward Wells (1828–1921) felt marginalized as a plural wife.[52]

Emmeline B. Wells Journals, 1844–1891,
L. Tom Perry Special Collections, upb.

2:8, 4 Sept. 1874: I was up at the house but my husband was not to be seen, O how I want to see him, how long the time seems, and how weary I grow

---

[47] On the Nauvoo period, see Bradley and Woodward, "Plurality, Patriarchy, and the Priestess." For the entire Mormon plural experience and its growing intensity in the West, see Hardy, "Lords of Creation."

[48] Dalton, Autobiography, cu-b, 15, 18. Dalton said she married when she found a man "who did not think that <merely> because he is male he stands a whole flight of stairs higher in creation than a woman." Ibid., 18. For Dalton's life, see Anderson, "Lucinda L. Dalton," 139–71. Intertwined with Mormon patriarchal life were statements that suffering endured by women in polygamy helped atone for Eve's role in the fall of man. Rockwood, "Redemption of Eve," 3–36.

[49] As described in Hulett Jr., "Social Role and Personal Security in Mormon Polygamy," 546.

[50] Andrew S. Rogers, Autobiographical Sketch, azu, 191.

[51] At the same time, as Martha Hughes Cannon contended in her interview, polygamous wives often enjoyed greater independence from their husband's control than in monogamy. The irony of such independence, in the face of the submissiveness preached by church leaders, has been remarked on for decades: Hulett, "Social Role and Personal Security," 546; Bushman, *Mormon Sisters*, xix; Burgess-Olson, "In Her Own Words," 58; and Iversen, "Feminist Implications of Mormon Polygyny," 511–13. For discussion of female independence and matrilineal tendencies in other polygynous societies, see Binet, *Marriage en afrique noire*, 106–7; and Clignet and Sween, "For a Revisionist Theory of Human Polygyny," 445–65.

[52] Emmeline B. Wells (1828–1921), an activist for women's rights, president of the Women's Relief Society, and editor of the *Woman's Exponent*, was a plural wife of Daniel Hanmer Wells (1814–1891) of the First Presidency. For more on Wells's experience, contrasting her private sentiments with her public statements, see Eaton-Gadsby and Dushku, "Emmeline B. Wells," 466–67; and Madsen, "Mormon Woman in Victorian America," 57–60, 88–92.

for one sight of his beloved face one touch of his dear hand; O how I love him and he feels it not nor realizes all the prangs [*sic*] and tortures he has made me suffer. . .

2:11, 13 Sept. 1874: . . . this evening I fully expected my husband here but was again disappointed if he only knew how much good it would do me and what pleasure and happiness it brings to my subsequent days he would not be so chary of his attentions, I suppose it is rather an exertion in him to come, he is not in want of me for a companion or in any sense, he does not need me at all, there are plenty ready and willing to administer to every wish caprice or whim of his, indeed they anticipate them, they are near him always, while I am shut out of his life, and out of sight out of mind, it is impossible for me to make myself useful to him in any way while I am held at such a distance

"With Fortitude and Faith": Triumph in the Principle

For those believing that plural marriage was the family pattern of heaven and that adherence to its requirements would bless them, extraordinary efforts came easier. Mary Jane Redd (1858–1945), for example, found that blessings and encouragement from others lightened the task. She married Alma Platte Spilsbury (1850–1920), a widower, in the St. George Temple in 1880. Three years later he took Margaret Jane Klingensmith (1863–1936) as a plural wife. After moving both families to the Salt River Valley of Arizona, he fled to Mexico to avoid arrest. Taking "Janey," the younger wife, with him, he left Mary Jane behind with the promise he would send for her within a year—a promise he kept. But it was a difficult separation for Mary Jane, who remembered the ordeal and retold it years later to her daughter, Nelle Spilsbury Hatch. Nelle said her mother's memory was extraordinary, even in old age, and that she copied her mother's recollections "as they fell from her lips in almost the exact words with which she told them."[53]

NELLE SPILSBURY HATCH, *MOTHER JANE'S STORY* (1964), 102–5.
Just a year ago, Alma had ridden off with Janey [to avoid anti-polygamy prosecution] to join the fleeing fugitives who were finding . . . security in Mexico. I had told them goodbye feeling brave and hopeful. My sixth baby, little black-eyed Ruby, was but a few weeks old. But all of us were well and in spite of much to do to get ready to follow him, I was sure we could do it, that the

---

[53] Hatch, Preface, *Mother Jane's Story.*

year would pass quickly, and before we knew it we would all be together again. I had looked forward as hopefully as either of them to the move into a foreign land, and had cooperated dutifully in the plan that left me behind to get ready to join them when they had prepared a place for us all. And for the first few months, my chin was high with optimism, my heart and soul were at peace and I was reconciled to the future fate was shaping for me.

But . . . as the days passed, finding me up with the break of day and still going when nightfall came, and falling into my bed too weary to enjoy the few hours of sleep allotted me, I began to wear. As my body tired, my high spirits lowered and soon I began to give way to misgivings and doubts. . .

And once the demon of doubt entered my tired mind, I knew little more of peace. I forgot that I had agreed with my husband that this sacrifice was necessary, and lost that unselfish desire to work with him and help him succeed in the step he had taken. Before I knew it, I was in the grip of another demon, that of self pity. From then on I was miserable indeed, most miserable of all when, with fresh courage in the morning I would show a little fight and make another desperate attempt to regain my faith and courage, and would lose it all as my body tired and my worries mounted. Try as I would, I could feel like nothing but the neglected wife, the sap who was left to work her life out so that others might enjoy their life together.

I had counted on letters from Alma to keep me bolstered, and on his hopeful forecast of the future to keep me fortified. But they came so seldom and were so short that they brought little comfort. The first one told of Janey's confinement, of Carmelita's birth in Colonia Dublan, April 27, 1891, where Alma had located her until she was able to be with him again. The second told me he had been given Church cattle to care for and that he had a ranch all ready for me to move onto as soon as he could find time to come for me. None of the few letters which followed passed on to me the assurance that they needed me, the assurance I was so desperately in need of. Or that they would be happier when I was with them again.

And so the blackness deepened. I was ripe for destruction. . .

Needless to say, I was ready . . . when [Patriarch George Brimhall came.] With the first impact of his hands on my head, my whole being was shaken. His first words spoke to my soul. They seemed to speak to God and bring Him nearer to me than He had been for months. My worries fell from me like a useless cape dropped to the floor. And, even though the blessings he said were in store for me might easily be called anything but blessings, he filled me so full of courage to meet them that I shall always give him credit for the high hope that entered my soul, for the feeling that "come what may," I was prepared to face it with fortitude and faith. . .

. . . these blessings . . . brought a return of . . . spiritual uplift . . . and filled me with desires to measure up to my plural marriage responsibilities. . .

I made 10 quilts. As I worked, I supervised the piecing of another quilt by Katie Pearl and Sarah Ann [daughters]. They were just little tots of eight and ten years of age, but working by my side and copying my ways, they did very well. . .

I peeled and dried 100 pounds of peaches. I picked and dried 100 pounds of grapes. I made a five-gallon can of grape jelly and I sealed a five-gallon can of honey. I made fig preserves, twelve cans of it. I stored up a supply of dishes—bought plates, platters, tureens, glasses, cups and saucers . . . and packed them, ready to move.

I bought cloth and trimming for the little girls' dresses, all they would need for a year, and determined to get as many made as possible, and take the rest with me to finish as I could. But my kind-hearted neighbors made a finished job possible. Walking in one morning, dragging a sewing machine and armed with scissors, needles and thimbles, they put into action the "Bee" they had planned. When they were through that night, there were thirty-five finished articles, buttonholes and all. About all I had done was cook the big chicken dinner and try to show my love and appreciation for my friends and neighbors.

And all this, and more, I was able to get done—because of the blessing.

In addition to prayer and blessings, as Hannah Hood Hill Romney (1842–1928) discovered, sheer hard work helped her bear the sorrows of a polygamous wife. Born in Canada, she crossed the plains barefoot as a girl with her family and married Miles Park Romney (1843–1904) as his first wife on 10 May 1862. Two days after the marriage Miles was sent on a mission to England. Returning to Salt Lake in 1865, he was called within the year to enter the Principle.[54]

HANNAH HOOD HILL ROMNEY, AUTOBIOGRAPHY, CSmH.

In that same year [1866] Heber C. Kimball told my husband to take another wife. The next week President Young met him and said, "Brother Miles I want you to take another wife." He felt as if he must obey counsel so in due time he married his second wife. I felt that was more than I could endure to have him divide his time and affections from me. I used to walk the floor and shed tears of sorrow. If anything will make a woman's heart ache it is for her husband to take another wife, but I put my trust in my Heavenly Father and prayed and plead[ed] with him to give me strength to bear this great trial, and to give me a knowledge of the truth of that principle that I might be able to bear so great a trial that had come to me, that I might be a support to my husband. So long as I had given my consent for him to enter into this prin-

---

[54] For most, but not all, of Romney's diary, see "Hannah Hood Hill Romney," *Our Pioneer Heritage*, 5:262–84.

ciple I felt it was my duty to sustain him in it and constantly plead with the Lord. I was able to live in the principle of polygamy and give my husband many wives.

In September [1866] my baby took sick and died. I thought that was more than I could bear. But we cannot stay the hand of death for it comes to all, so I lived and trusted in the Lord for comfort. I felt that I could not bear the loss of my baby. A week after my baby died President Young sent for my husband and his wives to come and have their second anointings. I found putting my trust in the Lord that our trials are made easier and our burdens lighter. . .

Carrie, Brother Romney's other wife, was always jealous of him [Hannah's first-born son], on account of his name being Miles, as her first child was called William, named after her father. Carrie, was quite a pretty woman but had a temper. She was very jealous of me.[55] She wanted all of my husband's attention. When she couldn't get it there was always a fuss in the house. He being a just man didn't give way to her tantrums. We lived that kind of a life until her second baby was born, a girl. I took care of her and her children and did all that I could to keep peace in the family, but she was not satisfied. She finally went to President Brigham Young and advised him to send her to her parents in Salt Lake which he did. Before she left our home Brother Romney told her she would be sorry for the course she was taking, that she would marry some low down gentile and die an awful death, which she did. . .

In September, 1873, my husband [traveled from St. George] . . . to Salt Lake to take another wife, Catherine Cottam, of a good family, a girl of good principle and a good Latter Day Saint.[56] He took my oldest daughter with him. . . While they were gone to Salt Lake I had part of my house finished, plastered, painted, and papered. I sewed carpet rags and carried my warp and rags five blocks to the weavers to have it woven. After it was done I went after dark and carried it home. When I got home I was exhausted. I could not rest all night I was so tired. The next morning I got up, washed and dressed my little children and gave them breakfast, then sewed my carpet, tacked it on the floor, cleaned furniture, pictures and curtains and arranged them to suit my taste, as I was very particular about my home and took great pains in having everything in "apple pie" order. I worked hard all day and part of the night. I had a room finished for Catherine with new carpet and furniture all ready for her. I cannot explain how I suffered in my feelings while I was doing all this hard work, but I felt that I would do my duty if my heart did ache. I had such a hard time with his other wife that I feared I would have the same kind of trial again, but when I came to live with Sister Catherine it was quite different. She was considerate of my feelings and good to the children. She helped in the house and did not expect all my husband's attention. When he came home he appreciated what I had done. He admired the home arrangements

[55] Caroline Lambourne (1846–1879) married Romney on 23 Mar. 1867.
[56] Catherine Jane Cottam (1855–1918) married Romney on 15 Sept. 1873.

and was surprised that I had accomplished so much in such a short time. His appreciation of my work partly took away the heart ache. At the time I was doing all this work, and with heart aches and worries, many nights I could cry myself to sleep. I was in a delicate condition and when my baby came it was born dead. It was a great sorrow to me as I reproached myself. I felt I had caused it by doing so much hard work. I wonder if the Lord will forgive me for such an act. Sister Catherine waited on me and did all she could. My husband did all he could to comfort me. I preferred to have Catherine live with me as I felt I could not have the father of my children away from our fire side at nights in another home. My health was very poor all the next year. . .

We worked [in the St. George Temple] . . . until we were called to go to St. Johns, Arizona. He took other wives.[57] We lived and raised our children in the same house. I felt I could not endure my husband to have another home where I could not be so would rather have the wives come to my home rather than have him away from home, but only those who have lived that principle . . . can realize how I felt.[58]

"Never a Cross Word": Support and Community Among Women in Polygamy

In a society that placed as much importance on progeny as did Mormonism, childless marriages were a great sadness. If the difficulty arose from a wife's inability to conceive, plurality offered a way to circumvent the problem. The Principle provides remarkable instances of altruism in this regard. The two plural wives of John Ulrich Stucki both gave their first-born children to Stucki's barren first wife. Cora May Hatch, at ten months of age, was given as a Christmas present to a first wife who had recently lost a child of her own.[59]

The plural system brought other gifts as well. To assist widows and neglected females, Mormon men sometimes invited them into their households where they could be cared for with a variety of understandings about their marital status.[60] The Saints were told that, as in ancient Israel, men were expect-

[57] Miles Romney married at least two other women of record: Annie Marie Woodbury (1858–1930) in 1877, and Emily Henrietta Eyring Snow (1870–1947) in 1897.

[58] Lucy Walker Kimball also thought having her husband's other wives under her own roof was a better arrangement—but for a different reason. "I can truthfully state," she said, ". . . that there is less room for jealousy where wives live under the same roof. They become interested in each other's welfare; they love each other's children." Littlefield, *Reminiscences*, 50.

[59] Hatch and Johnson, "Charles William Merrell," 483. For the Stucki cases, see Ezra Spori Stucki, Address in Paris, Idaho, Aug. 1954, LDS Archives.

[60] For discussion of various marital arrangements in nineteenth-century Mormon homes, see Daynes, *More Wives than One*, 76–82.

The family of Jonathan Heaton (1857–1930). The well-constructed, neatly roofed home and formal, Victorian attire were typical of the majority of Mormon polygamous families by the late nineteenth century. Heaton married his first wife, Clarrissa Amy Hoyt, standing immediately to Jonathan's right and holding a grandchild, in 1875. Lucy Elizabeth Carroll, on Jonathan's left, was married to Heaton as a plural wife in 1878. Taken in 1907 at their home in Moccasin Springs, Arizona, this photograph displays most of their twenty-six children and numbers of their grandchildren.

ed to marry the widows of their deceased brothers.[61] Partly out of regard for the command to multiply, however, polygamists generally married younger women. Consequently, husbands often predeceased their partners, leaving younger spouses behind as widows in turn. But these, research suggests, tended to remarry as well.[62]

Even when allowance is made for their excessively positive attitudes, the memories of children from polygamous households recorded by Jessie Embry and her staff indicate that plural marriage could provide broad emotional support, especially for young people; that plural wives often nursed and cared both for one another and for each other's children; and that they could become best friends.[63]

The tendency among pluralists to marry sisters resulted as much from desire for compatibility as from proximity, and scholars have often seen it as characteristic of many polygynous societies. As Richard Burton explained when comparing sororal polygamy among the Mormons with that of the Sioux and Dakota, "the tent is more quiet."[64] Beyond this, there are examples of first wives who sought the addition of other women to the family circle, sometimes against their husband's inclinations, that all might reach the highest level of glory in the next life.[65] Practical considerations could also play a part, as when Daniel Skousen's wife told him that since they needed a hired girl he might as well marry one and keep "'the money in the house.'"[66] The number of Mormon Sarahs who brought Hagars to their Lords, however, was never large.

Mary Eliza Tracy (1873–1949) married Byron Harvey Allred Sr. (1847–1912) as a plural wife on 21 November 1890. She was twenty-six years younger than

---

[61] "Discourse by Prest. Geo. Q. Cannon," *Des. Eve. News*, 13 Dec. 1884, 18:19 [1/5].

[62] See the findings of Daynes in the Mormon community of Manti. *More Wives than One*, 168. But cf. Pace, "Wives of Nineteenth-Century Mormon Bishops," 52–53; and Bean and Mineau, "Polygyny-Fertility Hypothesis," 77–78, 81. On widowhood and loneliness, see Beecher, Madsen, and Anderson, "Widowhood among the Mormons," 117–39; and Todd Compton's comments in Hatch and Compton, *Widow's Tale*, 20.

[63] As only a few examples, see these interviews from the Polygamy Oral History Program collection at BYU: Thora Harvey McConkie, 5; Elizabeth H. Packer, 5; Merle Gilbert Hyer and Estell Hyer Rire, 14; and Abraham L. Stout, 10–11.

[64] Burton, *City of the Saints*, 128. For more on sororal polygamy among the Mormons, see Larsen, "Childhood in a Mormon House," 484; Ivins, "Notes on Mormon Polygamy," 234; Burgess-Olson, "Family Structure," 87–90; and Embry, *Mormon Polygamous Families*, 141–42. For non-Mormon cultures, see Westermarck, *History of Human Marriage*, 3:94–97.

[65] See, for example, Whitney, *Through Memory's Halls*, 194–95; Ellice Marie Bentley LeBaron interview, LDS Archives, 4; William L. Wyatt interview, OHP, 10; and Alder, "History of Mary Theresa Thompson Call," 1.

[66] Asenath Skousen Walser interview, OHP, 23.

her husband and twenty-one years junior to his first wife, Phoebe Irene Cook (1852–1913). Allred's other plural wife was Alta Matilda Rolph (1855–1948). She wed Allred on 31 May 1875. Mary Allred's reminiscence not only provides an example of plural marriage where the women were remarkably compatible but also describes the difficulty plural wives sometimes encountered keeping their polygamous marriages secret from potential suitors.

Mary Eliza Tracy Allred,
Typewritten Dictation to Emily Black in 1937,
box 19, fd. 11, #5, Collection of Mormon
Biographies, lds Archives, 4–7.

Mrs. [Phoebe] Allred liked me. Both of her children were married. She wanted a companion. For twenty-five years, we lived together, she and I—from the time of my marriage until we were driven from Mexico. There was never a cross word between us. We loved each other more devotedly at the end of our companionship than at the beginning. . .

She was lovely. She liked me. Wanted me. We believed in polygamy. We decided among us, that Brother Allred would marry me. Polygamists were not safe in the United States. We went to Mexico. Brother Allred and I went alone at first. . .

The home Auntie [the first wife] and I made together [in Mexico] was a tent. We lived there for three years. Our furniture consisted of a stove, a table, a chair each, and two beds. We had no carpets, but we would sweep off the loose soil, keep the floor damp, and pat it down. It became hard. In this way, we kept it clean. We hung up pictures. The two of us lived in one tent for three years—happily.

Our next home was an adobe house with two bedrooms and one kitchen. . .

We were asked to keep our marriage quiet at first. I let people gather that I was a friend, a sister, or a visitor. A Mexican teacher boarded with us. He taught Spanish in a night school for the adults. . . The Mexican slept and had his meals in a tent beside our house. He attended day school among our own people. He fell in love with me. One night when Auntie [the first wife] and Brother Allred [their husband] were in church, and . . . [the children] had gone to bed, the Mexican seemed uneasy.

He wanted to talk all evening. He asked all kinds of questions. How did I come there? Why? I did not explain the situation. Did I think of marrying? How long was I going to stay? He wanted to know all the story of my life. Had I ever wanted to marry?

No.

Did I want to marry?

No.

Could I ever love him?

Never. It was the farthest thing from my mind.

What could he do to win my love?

Nothing.

He would give me a few days to think about it.

Brother Allred worried. The Mexicans had many friends. Mexicans liked white girls.

"It Was Their Duty": Male Life in the Principle

Women were not alone in finding polygamy difficult. Brigham Young's statement that he often heard stories of such bitterness about the practice that it was like "drinking a cup of wormwood" probably referred to male as well as female complaints.[67] As one polygamist was quoted to say, the happiest thing he could imagine would be to have all three of his wives come "downstairs . . . saying 'Good Morning' pleasantly to each other."[68] Rep. Justin S. Morrill, a determined enemy of the plural system, claimed it was a Mormon himself who suggested that if Gentiles really wanted to destroy plurality, they need only find a way to require that all who had more than one wife "shall be *compelled to live under the same roof with them!*"[69] This said, men generally found polygamy less emotionally bruising than their wives.

Charles Edmund Richardson (1858–1925) and his brother, Sullivan Calvin Richardson (1861–1950), born in Manti, Utah, were orphaned in their teens. After subscribing to one of Mormonism's communitarian economic efforts, they settled with other participants along the Little Colorado River in northern Arizona, where Charles eventually married three women. The crusade against polygamy in the United States drove him, like hundreds of others, to the Mormon colonies in Mexico where he took a fourth wife and became a lawyer. Together, he and his wives parented thirty-six children and from every appearance found it a happy and successful arrangement.[70] In this interview, Elva Richardson Shumway, a daughter by Charles's third wife, Caroline Rebecca Jacobson, tells of both her father and uncle.

---

[67] Brigham Young, 20 May 1860, *Journal of Discourses*, 8:63.

[68] Quoted in Hulett, "Social Role of The Mormon Polygamous Male," 282.

[69] "Speech of Hon. J. S. Morrill," 23 Feb. 1857, Appendix, 289.

[70] For Charles's ancestors, his life and those of his wives, see Johnson, Shumway, and Mangelson, *Charles Edmund Richardson: Man of Destiny*.

ELVA RICHARDSON SHUMWAY, INTERVIEWED BY LEONARD R. GROVER,
25 APRIL 1980, MESA, ARIZONA, OHP, 3–7, 9–11.

S[humway]: . . . Papa went on his mission around Albuquerque and Taos, and in northern Arizona and learned to speak Spanish. . .

When he came back, many of the young people had married and Sade [Sarah Louisa] Adams had grown up a little. It seemed like he was interested in her even though she was very young. Her parents, Brother and Sister Jerome Adams approved of him and they were kind of encouraging this to go on. So papa had to wait a little bit for Aunt Sade to grow up. She didn't grow up very much. I think that she was only fourteen or maybe fifteen when they were married in the St. George temple. . . one of the General Authorities [of the LDS church] came down to the stake conference that they held right there in Wilford [Arizona] and preached polygamy. He taught a lot about polygamy. He said it was a fine principle and it was their duty, if possible, to enter into this thing. This is why Uncle Sullie [Sullivan Calvin Richardson] left because he became converted and married into polygamy. . . Uncle Sullie felt that he should probably follow the teachings.

He had a special premonition, or something that helped him know. He said he had looked around and wondered whom he should approach for a plural wife. One of his friends said, "What about Teressa Leavitt? You've known her all through the United Order days, and she is a good young woman. Why don't you ask her?" Uncle Sullie wasn't too anxious. He hadn't thought of anyone else anyway in this light. He was very much in love with his wife, Irena Curtis, but he prayed that if it should be that he should marry Teressa Leavitt that he would see her that day. The Leavitt family apparently was over there around Heber. It wasn't very likely that he would see her because at this time that he was praying he was way up in the canyon and had to go a long way to get home. When he got down there and was unloading or unhitching or something, somebody said, "Well, is that all you have to do?" He looked up and it was this saucy Teressa Leavitt! So he felt that that was the answer. He had seen her as he had asked and that was what he should do. In the course of time, he proposed and they were married.

Then he was in polygamy. There was lots of persecution going on, so along with many of the others he then moved to Mexico before my father did.

G[rover]: Your father was still in monogamy at this time?

S: Yes, he was. He was going back and forth doing missionary work and likely never heard the sermon at all. Dear Aunt Sade, as sweet and young a person as she was, became converted by the sermon. She talked to Papa. She said that it was his duty to enter into polygamy and to take another wife. He didn't take that kindly to it. By then the headquarters of the stake were over in Snowflake and they usually held conference there. But this particular time I'm speaking of they held conference in Wilford. Heber at that time was just a branch of Wilford.

Mormon fathers were seldom photographed with only their daughters. Here we see Joseph F. Smith (1838–1918), president of the church from 1901 to 1918, posing with several of his sons in 1895. Portraits such as this illustrate the patriarchal ideal of nine-teenth-century Mormonism. *Used by permission, Utah State Historical Society, all rights reserved.*

In their going back and forth to Snowflake they became acquainted with people there. I don't know exactly how the acquaintance came about, but Sarah Rogers was a sweet little woman there who had heard Papa speak in church and had been impressed. In those days I guess they became what you call old maids rather young. I doubt that she was all that old though, because she was only two years older than my father. She was desirous of marriage and of hav-ing a family. The story is that she approached Papa and asked him if he would marry her. That was quite an unusual thing for a young woman to do. My father was rather floored about the whole thing. He said that he couldn't give her an answer at the time. So he went home and talked about it with Aunt Sade who reminded him of his duty. She said, "You know that you should be entering into this principle and you have no right to deprive that good woman of having a family. She hasn't had an opportunity for marriage thus far and you have an obligation to give it to her."

The story is that he paced the floor all night worrying and wrestling with it. He said, "I don't love her. I have no feeling and I wouldn't want to marry her without loving her." She said, "Sarah isn't asking that. I know that you would be fair with her and love would probably come."

So with that, he went in to Snowflake and talked to her and to her folks. It was decided. He told Aunt Sarah that he respected her although he didn't love her. If she still wished it under those circumstances he would marry her and would do his very best to be fair and to be a good husband. So they went to St. George along with some others and were married. I have been told that through the years whenever there was a choice to be made for anything, such as a cow, Papa would always say, "We'll give the best to Sarah."

When they came back they had to be very quiet because of persecution; the marriage was not widely known at the time. . .

It was about then [after moving his families to Mexico] that my mother, Rebecca Jacobson (Aunt Becky) entered the family picture.[71] She had known them earlier while her family was living in Heber. Papa had hired her to work for Aunt Sade in Wilford and he had proposed marriage to her then but she declined (and regretted it later). When the Jacobsons also moved to Mexico Mama again worked for Aunt Sade. . . Aunt Sade seemed sensitive to Mama's feelings. Papa had written Aunt Sade and said that he was quite interested in one of the Indian women. She was a very lovely fine woman. Aunt Sade wrote to him and said, "You can have all of the Indians that you want but if you would follow my advice, when you come home you would marry this sweet Rebecca Jacobson. She is a wonderful woman and very strong. She would make you a marvelous wife and I love her already. She is a wonderful friend to me, and she takes care of me. And I think that she has probably changed her mind." After Papa came back and started teaching school he gave Mama another chance, and this time she accepted readily.

They then drove to Colonia Juarez and were married by the proper author- ity on Mama's seventeenth birthday. This was in 1889. Aunt Sade was just beau- tiful. She has said that she was really jealous of my mother. She hadn't been jealous of Aunt Sarah although it was a hard thing the first time that she knew that Papa had gone away to spend the night. It hurt her up in Snowflake. When he married Mama, she said it was a great trial because she was jealous of Mama. She knew that Papa loved her, but she was a "big" woman; she swallowed it all. She even let Mama wear her dress to be married in because times were hard. Aunt Sade's house only had three rooms, but she fixed one bedroom up beautifully for Mama. Then the two of them had lots of fun as young girls. When Papa would go, they would put their ears down on the ground at night to listen if he was coming. When they would hear the wagon, they would play tricks on him and have lots of fun. Later he built a house for Mama. Then he moved Aunt Sarah down from Snowflake with her two-

---

[71] Caroline Rebecca Jacobson Richardson (1872–1945).

year-old son, Mark. Of course he had to provide another home. By then there
were the three separate homes that the families lived in, in Colonia Diaz. . .

G: . . . Tell me about your memories. What was your father's visiting schedule? Did he have a fixed visiting schedule?

S: Yes, but only when the families were in the same area. He took turns.
There was no way that he could always do so because sometimes his law business would take him as far down as Mexico City and often to Chihuahua City
and to El Paso or Ciudad Juarez. He had a very unpredictable schedule. He
would just be with the family that he was nearest. . . He would go and take
turns, one night with Aunt Sarah and one night with Mama. . .

G: Of your memories before the Exodus [from Mexico] . . . , how much
contact did you have with Aunt Sarah?

S: A lot. I would see her everyday. She would maybe do up her work and
then she would come down and be with Mama and the rest of us. Her house
was not far away and so it just seemed more like all one happy family. We
surely loved Aunt Sarah. . .

G: How did your father handle church attendance with the three families?
Would he go to church with all three or just with the two?

S: I think that he would go with the family that he happened to be stay-
ing with Saturday night. Come Sunday he would go with them to church.
Down in Mexico it was a familiar thing for everybody to have multiple families and it wasn't anything to see a man with one one time and another one
the next. It was harder when they came out of Mexico. . .

"Enough of Polygamy": Failure in the Principle

The women who, in addition to enduring the rigors of overland travel and
life on the frontier, had to welcome other females to their husband's bed,
should be counted the most heroic of their church's westering bands. In the
words of Edward W. Tullidge, "it was with them faith, not sight."[72] And with
so many difficulties, it is not surprising that hundreds of wives asked their
leaders to dissolve their marriages. Scholars calculate that divorce in polygamy
probably exceeded by several times that among monogamous church members.[73] One study found that in the nineteenth-century Mormon community of Manti more than a third of all polygamous husbands lost wives through
divorce.[74] While plurality unquestionably generated more divorces than
Mormon monogamy, thereby challenging its alleged superiority, to some

---

[72] Tullidge, *Women of Mormondom*, 331. For an exploration of Tullidge's views of Mormon women, see
Bushman, "Edward Tullidge," 15–26.   [73] Kunz, "One Wife or Several?" 68–69.

[74] Daynes, *More Wives than One*, 162–63. Also see Altman and Ginat, *Polygamous Families*, 469–70.

degree Mormon marital failure was but a mirror of life in the American West generally where, according to one authority, broken families in the late nineteenth century occurred more frequently than anywhere else in the world.[75]

Men and women asked to dissolve their plural marriages for a variety of reasons, including incompatibility.[76] Some of the problem likely arose from uncertainty as to what was and was not expected from partners in such relationships.[77] But whatever grievances were alleged, jealousy commonly accompanied petitioners' complaints. As Nelson Wheeler Whipple explained in 1879, describing the departure of one of his wives: "on the whole She would no doubt have made as good a Wife in Monogimy as a man need wish but in Poligimy She is to much inclind to tamper with the afaris of others which has together with jeliousy bin the gratest caus of all dificulty."[78] Some plural wives, especially those married to prominent churchmen, took pleasure in their circumstances, while others found the private compromises of polygamous life too much to bear. A plural partner of Apostle Abraham Cannon, for example, threatened to end her marriage, saying that the arrangement left her feeling disgraced and no better than a prostitute.[79]

Economic hardship also created problems. Even apart from divorce, plural wives sometimes sought material assistance from the church, as this letter shows.[80]

> BRIGHAM YOUNG TO BRO. BAMFORD, G.S.L. CITY, 6 SEPT. 1854,
> LETTERBOOK 1851–1855, BRIGHAM YOUNG PAPERS, LDS ARCHIVES.
> Bro. Bamford,
> Your wife has made application to me for support. It seems needless to me for you to have women sealed to you whom you cannot support. You must make provision for her unless you can show satisfactory reasons why you cannot, and not cause her to be thrown upon the resources of the Church.
> Your immideate attention to this subject is expected, and you will by so doing much oblige.
> Your friend and brother in the Gospel of Peace.
Brigham Young

---

[75] Riley, *Building and Breaking Families in the American West*, 113–44.

[76] For those married in monogamy, Utah had early provided liberal grounds, including mutual antagonism, as an acceptable basis for ending the marriage. "An Act in Relation to Bills of Divorce," 6 Mar. 1852, *Acts, Resolutions and Memorials . . . 1851*, 82–84.

[77] Campbell and Campbell, "Divorce among Mormon Polygamists," 4–23, proposed anomie or normlessness as a reason for divorce in polygamous households. Cf. Daynes, *More Wives than One*, 210.

[78] Nelson Wheeler Whipple, Autobiography and Journal, 1879, LDS Archives, 432.

[79] A. H. Cannon Journals, 8 July 1890, UPB, 11:216.

[80] Difficulty supporting families distant from each other must have afflicted many. See, for example, William Henry Solomon Diary, 8 Nov. 1873, AZU, 11.

Some men faltered simply from disillusionment with the system, as illustrated by the husband who refused either to live with or support a plural wife because, as his bishop said, he simply "had enough of polygamy."[81] Whatever the grounds, after hearing a grievance and concurring with the petition, Brigham Young sent a "schedule" to both husband and wife, requiring that it be signed and returned with ten dollars per divorce.[82] The parties then received a formal declaration of dissolution in the mail, sometimes containing words of admonishment. And just as women sometimes married a husband in pairs, they also left in pairs, as this letter from President Young's clerk reveals.

DAVID O. CALDER TO ELDER LORENZO SNOW,
23 AUG. 1858, LDS CHURCH LETTERBOOK 3, REEL 2,
NO. 351, BRIGHAM YOUNG COLLECTION, UU.

Dear Bro.

The President has granted Susan Mary and Nicholina Jepson a bill of divorce from their husband; and it is herewith enclosed for his signature: As soon as it is signed please return to this office. Before they can have their bill [of divorce] $20.00 must be paid.

Your Bro. In the Gospel
David O. Calder
Clerk

While liberally responding to most petitions, Brigham Young told the Saints that divorces were likely to have no efficacy in heaven.[83]

A FEW WORDS OF DOCTERINE, GIVEN BY PRESIDENT BRIGHAM YOUNG
IN THE TABERNACLE IN GREAT SALT LAKE CITY OCT. 8TH 1861, A.M.
REPORTED BY G. D. WATT. LEONARD J. ARRINGTON
PAPERS, BOX 14, FD. 4, LAHA.

I will give you a few words of docterine, upon which there has been much inquiry, and with regard to which considerable ignorance exists. . .

We are continually sealing women to men; and continually giveing divorses. I now inform every one of my sisters that when they come to get a divorce, paying me ten dollars for it, you may just as well tare off a peice of your shirt

---

[81] Bishop Stephen Walker to President John Taylor, 16 Feb. 1887, Taylor Family Papers, Letters, box 1-B, fd. 28, Special Collections, UU.

[82] See, as instances, letters in the Leonard J. Arrington Papers, 822–24, box 3, fd. 4; 94, 95, 118, box 3, fd. 5; and 742, 784, 838, box 4, fd. 3, LAHA.

[83] For more on divorce in Mormon polygamy, see Foster, "Polygamy and the Frontier," 284–85; Campbell and Campbell, "Mormon Family," 379–412; Madsen, "Beyond the Limits," 7–10ff; idem, "'At Their Peril,'" 425–43; and Daynes, More Wives than One, 141–70.

tail <and lay it by, and call it a divorce,> so far as any good that <peice of paper called a> divorce will do you. I express myself in this wise, not because I admire course figures of language, but, my object is to use language that will rivite the idea I wish to convey upon your memories. Can a woman be freed from a man to whome she is sealed? Yes. But ~~coming to me for~~ a bill of divorcement<~~from me~~> does not free her. There is no such law given by the God of heaven to the children of men. Moses gave a law to the children of Isreal as follows. "When a man hath taken a wife, and married her, and it come to pass that she find no favor in his eyes, because he hath found some uncleanness in her: then let him write her a bill of divorcement, and give it in here hand, and send her out of his house. And when she is departed out of his house, she may go and be another man's wife.["][84] Jesus, ~~by~~ in the Gospel by Math [Matthew]. says, "It hath been said, Whosoever shall put away his wife, let him give her a writing of divorcement: But I say unto you, that whosoever shall put away his wife, saving for the cause of fornication, causeth her to commit adu[l]tery: and whosoever shall marry her ~~that is~~ that is divorced, commiteth adultery.["][85] In the Gospel by Mark it is said. "And Jesus answered and said unto them, <(the pharrisees,)> for the hardness of your heart, he (Moses) wrote you this precept: (refering to the law on divorcement) But from the bigginning of the creation, God made them male and female. For this cause shall a man leave his father and mother, and cleave to his wife; And they twain shall be one flesh: so then they are no more twain, but one flesh. What therefore, God hath joined together, let not man put asunder."[86] I am suffered to give bills of divorcement unto you because of your blindness, ignorance, and hardness of heart; otherwise it would be a sin in me. How can a woman be <made> free from a man to whome she has been sealed for time and all eternity? There are two ways. All the Elders in Isreal will not magnify their preisthood that are now in the habit of taking women, not careing how they get them; they get them frequently by stealth. I will diverge a little here to comment on the way some get their wives. They will <actually> commit adultery for the sake of getting a woman sealed to them, but they will probably ~~be mistaken~~ find in the morning of the resurrection that they have not attained their end. Wives obtained in this way will be ~~taken from such~~ given to those who are more worthy. This I mean to apply to you Elders on my right and left, who forfiet ~~their~~ <your> covenants, and violate the regulations of his holy order of matrimony, which is to live Godly in Christ Jesus every hour of ~~their~~ <our> lives. To return to the thread of the subject before us. If a man magnifies his preisthood, observing faithfully his covanants to the end of his life, all the wives, and children sealed to him, all the blessings,

---

[84] Deuteronomy 24:1–2.

[85] Matthew 5:31–32.

[86] Mark 10:5–9.

and honers, promised to him in his ordinations and sealing blessings, are immutably and eternally fixed. No power can wrench them from his possession. ~~There is however, one provise~~ <that> ~~must be added here~~ You may inquire. In case a wife becomes dissatisfied with her husband, her affections ~~are~~ lost— <and> she becomes alianated from him, and wishes <to be the wife of> another can she not leave him? I know of no law in heaven or on earth by which she can be made free while her husband remains faithful and magnifies his preisthood before God, and he is not disposed to put her away, she having done nothing worthy of being put away. . . The faithful Elders have then proved themselves worthy of their wives, and are prepared to be crowned Gods, <to> be filled with all the attributes of Gods that dwell in eternity. Could <the> ~~those you who are~~ dissatisfied <~~ones~~> ones <see a> ~~have the~~ vision <even> of the future glorified state of your ~~men~~ <husbands> ~~that they now say they cannot bare~~, love for them would immediatly spring up within You, and <no> sercumstance could prevail upon <you> to forsake them. The second way in which a wife can be separated from her husband, while he continues to be faithful to his God and his priesthood, I have not revealed, except to ~~a~~ few persons in this Church; and a few have received it from Joseph the prophet as well as myself. ~~This other path a woman may take if she can get a divorce.~~ <do it in that ~~accordance~~ with the order of heaven,> If ~~she~~ <a woman> can find a man holding the keys of the preisthood ~~and~~ <holding with> higher ~~in~~ power and authority than her husband <~~holds~~>, and he is disposed to take her he can do so, otherwise she has got to remain where she is.[87] ~~This is the second way in which a woman can leave her husband to whome she has been sealed to for time and all eternity.~~ In either of these ways of separation, you can discover, there is no need for a bill of divorcement. To recapitulate. First If a man forfiets his covenants with a wife, or wives, becoming unfaithful to his God, <and> his preisthood, that wife or wives are free from him without a <bill of> a divorcement. Second. If a woman claimes protection at the hands of A man, possessing more power in the priesthood and higher keys, if he is disposed to <~~and has obtained the consent of her husband~~> rescue her <and has obtained the consent of her husband ~~to make he~~> ~~from and~~ to make her his wife he can do so without a bill of divorcement ~~by~~ <first asking the> ~~the free consent of her husband. Then a peice of blank paper will answer just as good a purpose for a bill of divorcement as~~

---

[87] The declaration that women might honorably leave their husbands for men of higher priesthood had momentous implications. It may have found its seed in Young's 1846 statement that, in the next life, a woman's love for her husband will "be according to his exhaltation and glory." Kenney, ed., *Wilford Woodruff's Journal*, 23 Dec. 1846, 3:104. Young said he and others learned this from Joseph Smith. Perhaps the best-known example was that of Zina Diantha Huntington Jacobs Smith Young, told in Bradley and Woodward, *4 Zinas*, 129–34; and Compton, *In Sacred Loneliness*, 71–113. Something similar to what Young set forth may occur in contemporary fundamentalist communities. See the discussion of "hypergamy" in Bennion, *Women of Principle*, 88–89.

~~the bills the sisters get from me.~~ If after she has left her husband, and is sealed to another, she shall again cohabit with him it is illicit intercourse, and extremely sinfull. ~~To enter fully into the numerous particulars, and the many circumstances~~. . . I do not wish any of the Elders to speculate upon what I have now advanced, but ponder these words in your hearts in silence. There may be only a few that can understand this item of docterine, and retain it in their memories as I have spoken it.

"Keep Your House As Becomes a Saint": Variation Within the Principle

Given the varieties of human response to any circumstance, it is likely there were countless differences in the ways individual men and women adapted to life in polygamy. One investigator found more variation in everyday plural practice than in monogamy.[88] At the same time, a study of monogamous and polygamous homes in Brigham City, Utah, found them often to be architecturally indistinguishable.[89] Moreover, to the minds of some the difficulties encountered were the same whether there was one wife or several. In the homely language of Orson Pratt, there were quarrels in monogamous and polygamous families alike, so it made no sense to do away with either simply "because they pull hair occasionally."[90] When domestic upheaval became too great, the leaders did what they could to impose peace, as this communication illustrates.

Brigham Young to Bro Thomas Hollis,
20 Oct. 1853, G.S.L. City, Letterbook 1851–1855,
Brigham Young Papers, lds Archives.

From what I learn, and observe myself, you do not conduct yourself, nor keep your house as becomes a Saint, and I wish you to reform in these particulars, and treat your wife kindly, and as a wife should be treated, and keep an orderly quiet house, unless you prefer to incur severer treatment than a brotherly hint.

Your Brother in the Gospel,
Brigham Young

[88] Burgess-Olson, "Family Structure," 136. Also see the varied interpersonal adjustments described in Young, "Variations in Personality Manifestations," 285–314.

[89] Bennion, Morrell, and Carter, *Polygamy in Lorenzo Snow's Brigham City*, 17–18.

[90] Orson Pratt, 11 Aug. 1867, *Journal of Discourses*, 12:91.

"The Martyr's Crown": Judging Mormon Polygamy

Any extensive reading of accounts dealing with the Saints' plurality leads one to recognize the similarity of nineteenth-century Mormon sensibilities to those of men and women today. For that reason, the emotional burdens of those living the Principle, especially women, seem undeniably wounding. At the same time, religious conviction clearly played an immense role in Latter-day Saint responses to plural marriage. The succinct conclusion of Samuel Bowles may have said it best: "Their religion is of course the great reason for polygamy; it is the excuse of the men; it is the reconciliation of the women."[91]

For most Mormons who subscribed to the polygamous way, questions of sacrifice and happiness were subsumed within a larger theological frame.[92] Eliza R. Snow's reported response to a Mormon wife who felt she might die when her husband entered polygamy shows the emollient of their faith: "What if you should?" Snow said. "What if it kills the body, then your's is the martyr's crown; such graves are strewn from Nauvoo to this place; it is a martyrdom that has its reward in heaven."[93] Determined to do as they were commanded, like the consecrated of any order, they bent both bodies and emotions to the task. That mortal failings sometimes intruded only increases our marvel at the attempt.

---

[91] Bowles, *Our New West*, 249.

[92] It is impossible to judge whether most men and women were "happy" in polygamy. Based on the large archive she and others compiled from interviews with the children of polygamous parents, Jessie Embry concluded that, if afflicted by more day-to-day difficulties than traditional unions, Mormon polygamous families were nevertheless more contented than usually described and are best understood as simply an adapted form of the Victorian monogamous home. Embry, *Mormon Polygamous Families*, 134–35, 192–94. This is close to the summary of Juanita Brooks: "I am sure there were many terrible things about polygamy, even under the best of conditions, but I am equally sure that it was not so bad as it has been painted." Brooks, "Close-Up of Polygamy," 307.

[93] As remembered by Cooke, Theatrical and Social Affairs in Utah, cu-b, 5.

Chapter 5

"They Practise . . . As a Virtue What Others Do Secretly As a Sin"

Non-Mormons Look at Polygamy

R elocation to the valley of the Great Salt Lake never completely insulated the Latter-day Saints from the rapidly expanding American republic. Some twenty-five thousand goldseekers tramped through Mormon communities on their way to California in 1849 and 1850, and thousands of other dreamers determined to start a new life in the West also passed that way.[1] Military and surveying expeditions came to Utah, and non-Mormon merchants and federal appointees lived there. With the extension of rails across the continent, as Edward Tullidge said, all could make their way to "the New Jerusalem of the West in luxurious palace cars."[2] And so they did. One historian of transport found that while Utah was slow to develop tourist resorts, Salt Lake City rapidly became the most popular of all side trips from the Union and Central Pacific lines.[3] As late as 1901, John Fiske said red Indians, buffaloes, and Mormons were still what foreigners most associated with America.[4] Of the thousands who trooped to the Mormon Zion, many left a record of their impressions. And nothing so captivated them as polygamy.

The Saints were part of the larger dramatic struggle between eastern institutions and the frontier. Polygamy, whether Mormon or Apache, was looked

[1] Madsen, *Gold Rush Sojourners in Great Salt Lake City*, 129; and "The Mormon 'Halfway House,'" in Unruh Jr., *Plains Across*, 302–37.

[2] Tullidge, *Life of Brigham Young*, 216.

[3] Fifer, *American Progress*, 285. Also see Pomeroy, *Pacific Slope*, 344. Michael W. Homer has assembled a remarkable collection of these accounts in his *On the Way to Somewhere Else: European Sojourners in the Mormon West, 1834–1930*. [4] Fiske, *American Political Ideas*, 17.

upon as crude and inferior. Utah's natural wonders reminded some of the Holy Land, which they juxtaposed to the blight of Mormon sexuality.[5] Others saw the gnarled, desolate features of the region as an appropriate setting for so alien a practice as polygamy. As one traveler put it, "the grim, tremendous cañons through which . . . [one's] overland stage rolls down to the City of the Saints are strangely fit avenues to an anomalous civilization."[6] At once salacious and disturbing, Mormon plural marriage was part of the enigma associated with America's vast western terrain.[7] At the same time, as Robert Athearn indicated, most who visited Utah praised the industry, cleanliness, and order of its people, especially in Salt Lake City.[8] After miles of bleak shantytowns, Latter-day Saint villages were an impressive achievement. Only polygamy detracted from the scene. And this, more than anything, drew the curious to Mormon doors.

"NOT A SPECIALLY SENSUAL PEOPLE": FIVE REMARKABLE OBSERVERS OF MORMON POLYGAMOUS LIFE

Many of the most impartial and instructive accounts concerning the Mormons appeared within the single decade between 1852 and 1861. One of the best of these was that of John Williams Gunnison (1812–1853), who accompanied the Stansbury Expedition to the Great Salt Lake in 1849.[9] Three years later he published what was probably the finest description of life among the Saints with the exception of that by Richard Burton nearly a decade later. Captain Gunnison led another expedition to Utah in 1853 to survey the central railroad route to the Pacific Ocean. Tragically, Pahvant Indians attacked the exploring party near the Sevier River in October 1853, killing Gunnison and seven of his men.[10]

JOHN WILLIAMS GUNNISON, THE MORMONS, OR, LATTER-DAY SAINTS (1852), 67–77.

[The Mormons have] constantly denied that it is a doctrine of theirs to have "*spiritual* wives." . . . That many have a large number of wives in Deserét,

---

[5] Hafen, "City of Saints, City of Sinners," 352–54.

[6] [Ludlow], "Among the Mormons," 479.

[7] Billington, *Land of Savagery, Land of Promise*, esp. 79–104, 152–53; and Goetzmann and Goetzmann, *West of the Imagination*, 100–205.

[8] Athearn, *Westward the Briton*, 34–37.

[9] Stansbury, *Expedition to the Valley of the Great Salt Lake of Utah*.

[10] Fielding, *Unsolicited Chronicler*, 145–67, provides a gripping account of the attack.

is perfectly manifest to any one residing long among them, and, indeed, the subject begins to be more openly discussed than formerly. . .

The revelation of Joseph on the subject of polygamy has probably never been printed, or publicly circulated. When he declared to the council the revelation, it was made known that he, like the saints of old, David, Solomon, and Jacob, and those He thought faithful, should be privileged to have as many wives as they could manage to take care of, to raise up a holy household for the service of the Lord. Immediately rumors were spread that the wives of many of the people were *re-married* to the leaders and high-priests, and subject to them, which they declared to be a slander; and maintain that the relation existing among them is a pure and holy one, and that their doctrine is, that every man shall have one wife, and every woman only one husband, as is laid down in the Book of Covenants by revelation.

Yet they affirm that this allows to the man a plurality, as the phrase is peculiarly worded;—the *only* applying to the female alone. They go so far as to say that our Savior had three wives, Mary and Martha and the other Mary whom Jesus loved. . .

Again, they teach that the use and foundation of matrimony is to raise up a peculiar, holy people for the Kingdom of God the Son, that at the Millennium they may be resurrected to reign with him, and the glory of the man will be in proportion to the size of his household of children, wives, and servants. . . It is to be a pure and holy state; the religious motives or a sense of duty, should alone guide; and that for sensual gratifications it is an abomination.

Infidelity and licentiousness are held up for abhorrence; and when the "plurality" law shall be promulgated, they will be punished by the decapitation of the offender and the severest chastity inculcated upon one sex, and rigid continence on the other during the gestation and nursing of children. Thus the time of weaning will again become a feast of joy, next to the celebration of the nuptial rite, and patriarchal times return.

Quoting the Scripture that "the man is not without the woman, nor the woman without the man," they affirm that it is the duty of every man to marry at least once, and that a woman cannot enter into the heavenly kingdoms without a husband to introduce her as belonging to himself.

And it has been said that some women, distrusting the title of their spouses to enter at all, have been desirous to take hold of the skirt of an apostle or high-priest with superior credentials; how far correct we are not sufficiently informed to state positively, and can only speak of such rumors as existing, and beg pardon for mentioning the scandal. . .

Thus guarded in the motive, and denounced as sin for [any] other consideration than divine, the practical working of the system, so far as now extended, has every appearance of decorum. The romantic notion of a single love is derided, and met by calling attention to the case of parental affection; where the father's good will is bestowed alike on each of his many children; and they pretend to see a more rational application of a generous soul in loving more than one wife, than in the bigotry of a partial adhesion. The Seer alone has the power, which he can use by delegation, of granting the privilege of increasing the number of wives: the rule of primitive ages is applied in the case, and the suitor must first have the consent of the parents, then consult the lady, and the Seer.

Every unmarried woman has a right to demand a man in marriage, if she is neglected, on the ground of the privilege of salvation; and the President who receives the petition must provide for her; and he has the authority to command any man he deems competent to support her, "to seal her" to himself in marriage; and the man so ordered must show just cause and impediment why it should not be done, if he dislikes the union; or else be considered contumacious and "in danger of the council." . . .

In some instances several wives occupy the same house and the same room, as their dwellings have generally only one apartment, but it is usual to board out the extra ones, who most frequently "pay their own way," by sewing, and other female employments. It is but fairness to add that they hold the time near at hand predicted by Isaiah, "when seven women shall take hold of the skirt of one man and say, We will eat our own bread, but let us be called by thy name:"—which gives the assurance that plurality is foretold and correctly practised by them.

It is only a little in anticipation of the time when "the battles of the Lord" are to begin, and then, as the women are far more pure than the men, the females will greatly outnumber the males, for the latter will be swept off by sword and pestilence, and the other reserved to increase the retinue of the saints; and many women will thus be compelled to choose the same man, in order to secure a temporal home and temporal salvation, as also to obtain eternal right to a terrestrial or celestial queenship.

It is further maintained that there is great disparity of numbers between the sexes, and that the predominance of the female is more than can be accounted for from war, the dangers of the sea and other perils, and therefore nature indicates the propriety of plurality, as "marriage is honorable to all;" but the decision of this question can safely be intrusted to the relative numbers of the sexes, as exhibited in our census returns.

They also assure us that this system is the preventive and cure for the awful licentiousness—the moral and physical degradation in the world: and they make it both a religious and a social custom, a point of personal honour for a man whose wife, daughter, or sister has been led astray, to kill the seducer; and considering this as "common Mountain law," based on the Mosaic code, a jury will acquit the murderer. . .[11]

---

[11] For the case of Howard Egan, who was acquitted by a Mormon jury after murdering James Monroe for seducing Egan's wife, see Cannon II, "'Rocky Mountain Common Law,'" 308–27.

That the wives find the relation often a lonesome and burdensome one, is certain; though usually the surface of society wears a smiling countenance, and to all who consent from a sense of duty or enthusiasm the yoke is easy.

The wife of the prophet Joseph rebelled against it, and declared if he persisted she would desert for another, but the only satisfaction she received was "that a prophet must obey the Lord." When such wives rebel, the proceedings are very summary, and public opinion sustains the cause against the woman. A very exemplary lady in the valley is looked upon as having broken her vows for deserting the "Sealed one" and marrying another, and therefore is not invited into social parties. . .

The cheerful, happy faces—the self-satisfied countenances—the cordial salutation of brother or sister on all occasions of address—the lively strains of music pouring forth from merry hearts in every domicil, as women and children sing their "songs of Zion," while plying the domestic tasks, give an impression of a happy society in the vales of Deserét.

The influence of their nomenclature of "brethren and sisters" is apparent in their actions, and creates the bond of affection among those who are more frequently thrown together. It is impressed on infantile minds by the constant repetition, and induces the feeling of family relationship. A little boy was asked the usual question, "whose son are you?" and he very naively replied, "I am brother Pack's son;" a small circumstance truly, but one that stamps the true mark of the Mormon society. The welfare of the order becomes therefore paramount to individual interest; and the union of hearts causes the hands to unite in all that pertains to the glory of the State; and hence we see growing up and prospering, the most enterprising people of the age.

William Chandless (1829–1896) made his way across the plains with the Saints as a common teamster in 1855. This gives his account special credibility, for it permitted him to study the Mormons at close range with a minimum of suspicion and to report with confidence on the common run of their members.[12]

WILLIAM CHANDLESS, *VISIT TO SALT LAKE* (1857), 190–94.

Probably few people have been more abused than the Mormons. Feelings and prejudices against them are very natural and very strong. By natural prejudices, I mean opinions that appear very natural deductions from admitted facts, but which when you come to actual observation, are found to be untrue, and are therefore prejudices.

The course of this narrative will best distinguish the real and imaginary effects of polygamy in Utah; polygamy, as it exists elsewhere, is no part of my subject; nor would it be safe to draw inferences from Eastern countries,

---

[12] For a study of this underappreciated observer, see Snow, "William Chandless," 116–36.

where the seclusion of women is a main element of the system, as to a country where it is not so. Apart from the deeper and more social deterioration polygamy must effect, it will, wherever it exists, be abused more or less for mere purposes of sensuality; nevertheless, where it is not regarded as illicit or opposed to religion, and is sanctioned by law and custom, the generality of men (I think) are scarcely more impelled by mere sensual feeling in taking a second or a third wife than others in a first marriage. Of the Mormons, thus much I can say from having mixed with them: first, the community at large—for about the few who maintain large harems I say nothing—believe the custom allowable and good. Secondly, as a matter of fact, they are not a specially sensual people; nor, from the nature of the country, as already described, could an indolent race avoid starving.

The institutions relating to marriage (regarded from their point of view) are judiciously planned, and tend to mitigate, in some degree, the external evils of the system; but the inequality of the sexes is a doctrine of their religious belief, as well as a rule of life. The husband is regarded as a patriarch, and his family is subject to him as its head: wives are bound to obey their husbands in all things, wrong or right. The husband's command is accounted their justification, both in this world and the next; he is said to be their "priest and king," they should not look beyond him: nay, the time is looked for when disobedient children shall be stoned with all the Mosaic rigour. Every-day life, however, modifies such extreme theories very much in practice. Solomon's heart, we know, was turned by his wives, and so are those of many less wise than he.

No man is allowed to marry more wives than he can show he is capable of supporting properly, and in the humblest class, at least a separate bedchamber for each wife is required. Men cannot obtain divorces, except for adultery; women for very trivial causes—disagreement with other wives, &c. Divorces of this kind are neither common nor yet exceedingly rare, and the divorced wives obtain new partners with as much ease as widows elsewhere in the world: they, too, have the care of their children, while their ex-husband must give a portion of his property for their support. Were men the subjects and women the objects of sensuality, or were the latter looked upon as mere concubines, even if the mother's love were not debased, children would stand a great chance of neglect and ill-treatment. Probably no people (speaking collectively) set a higher value upon their children than Mormons do; and (though women must in time become a scarce article) upon boys particularly: not certainly without a sort of Spartan feeling that their sons belong to their country and faith, to co-operate in the building up of the "church and kingdom." Polygamy, rightly or wrongly, is valued as a means of numerical increase.

The wretchedness of wives in Utah has been greatly exaggerated. It is true there can be no position more painful than that of a woman who has come to Salt Lake half ignorant of the existence of polygamy, and, perhaps, a Mormon only because her husband is so, when she finds him about to take another wife. Many actually do live in a continually vague fear of such an event, and, perhaps, by the favour of poverty after all escape it; those again who have been divorced, no doubt, have little love for this "peculiar institution," though from more external reasons. But one must look to the average, not to the exceptions; and if most first wives feel some disappointment at the presence of a rival, as we should say, but a sister as they are taught to consider each other, this—judging from actual observation—wears off: human nature is apt to suit itself to necessities, and many among their daily occupations have little time for repining, and find their life in the main pass happily enough; while to those, who have been Mormons from their birth or girlhood, polygamy seems not merely a law of the society but natural: they have never looked forward to being "sole wives." Certainly a man can love each of several wives, and they may all love him; if the affection in marriage is less than in monogamic countries, infidelity is not more frequent: most women, I know, would repel, as an insult, a proposition from another man quite as strongly as wives of any other country could do; though fidelity may be supported in some cases by a vague terror of "disappearing," and in more still by dread of the houseless, hopeless condition of a cast-off wife in Utah. . .

The degrees within which marriage is forbidden are narrow. Agreeably to patriarchal (that is ante-Mosaic) custom, two sisters may have the same husband; and such marriages are not uncommon: possibly, no idea of incest being entertained, they are among the happiest.

As editor of the *New-York Daily Tribune*, Horace Greeley (1811–1872) was known for high journalistic standards, enjoyed a national readership, and in 1872 ran unsuccessfully for the U.S. presidency. He memorialized his 1859 journey across the continent by stagecoach in a series of newspaper sketches later published in book form.[13] Greeley took pride in the fairness of his reports, referring to the trait in the description of Brigham Young provided here. The encounter has been described as "the first published verbatim journalistic interview with a famous person in American history."[14] It is also notable for Greeley's postscript to the exchange in which he drew attention to Mormon attitudes toward women, a subject of large importance during the nation's subsequent campaign against plural marriage. The interview occurred on 13 July 1859, a week before its publication. Wilford Woodruff, one of those present, took careful notes, reporting the discussion in greater detail than Gree-

---

[13] Greeley, *Overland Journey* (1860).
[14] Eliason, "Curious Gentiles," 166.

ley himself. Woodruff was unimpressed, saying: "I found Mr Greely A Singular looking man. He was middling well dressed white but bald Headed. His head vary dirty. Looked as though He had not washed his Head since He Came off the plains. He had quite a feminine soft green appearance. He asked many Question[s]."[15]

HORACE GREELEY, "OVERLAND JOURNEY. XXI.
TWO HOURS WITH BRIGHAM YOUNG,"
NEW-YORK DAILY TRIBUNE, 20 AUG. 1859, 19:5,718, 5/6–6/1–2.

My friend, Dr. Bernhisel, m.c., took me this afternoon, by appointment, to meet Brigham Young, President of the Mormon Church. . .[16] We were very cordially welcomed at the door by the president, who led us into the second-story parlor of the largest of his houses (he has three). . . After some unimportant conversation on general topics, I stated that I had come in quest of fuller knowledge respecting the doctrines and polity of the Mormon Church, and would like to ask some questions bearing directly on these, if there were no objections. President Young avowed his willingness to respond to all pertinent inquiries, the conversation proceeded substantially as follows: . . .

H.G.—With regard, then, to the grave question on which your doctrines and practices are avowedly at war with those of the Christian world—that of a plurality of wives—is the system of your church acceptable to the majority of its women?

B.Y.—They could not be more averse to it than I was when it was first revealed to us as the Divine will. I think they generally accept it, as I do, as the will of God.[17]

H.G.—How general is polygamy among you?

B.Y.—I could not say. Some of those present [heads of the Church] have each but one wife; others have more; each determines what is his individual duty.

H.G.—What is the largest number of wives belonging to any one man?

B.Y.—I have fifteen; I know no one who has more; but some of those sealed to me are old ladies whom I regard rather as mothers than wives, but whom I have taken home to cherish and support.

H.G.—Does not the Apostle Paul say that a bishop should be "the husband of one wife?"

---

[15] Kenney, ed., *Wilford Woodruff's Journal*, 13 July 1859, 5:359. For a longer transcript of the interview as it touched on issues other than polygamy, see Mulder and Mortensen, eds., *Among the Mormons*, 321–28.

[16] John Milton Bernhisel was Utah's territorial delegate to Congress, 1851–59 and 1861–63.

[17] At this point Wilford Woodruff indicated that Brigham Young asked Greeley how many wives he had. When Greeley answered, "Only one," Heber C. Kimball, one of those present, intruded with: "How many Misses do you keep?" Greeley replied, "Not any." Kenney, ed., *Wilford Woodruff's Journal*, 13 July 1859, 5:363. Mormons were convinced that sexual hypocrisy was rampant outside their faith. See Chapter Two.

Horace Greeley (1811–1872), by Napoleon Sarony. One of America's best-known journalists and publisher of the *New York Tribune*, Greeley traveled to Utah in 1859. He was especially concerned with what he believed were the repressive and confining effects that polygamy imposed on Mormon women. *Courtesy National Portrait Gallery, Smithsonian Institution.*

B.Y.—So we hold. We do not regard any but a married man as fitted for the office of bishop. But the Apostle does not forbid a bishop having more wives than one.

H.G.—Does not Christ say that he who puts away his wife, or marries one whom another has put away, commits adultery?

B.Y.—Yes; and I hold that no man should ever put away a wife except for adultery—not always even for that. Such is *my* individual view of the matter. I do not say that wives have never been put away in our Church, but that I do not approve of the practice. . .

[In a postscript, Greeley added that Young] spoke readily, not always with grammatical accuracy, but with no appearance of hesitation or reserve, and with no apparent desire to conceal anything, nor did he repel any of my questions as impertinent. He was very plainly dressed in thin summer clothing, and with no air of sanctimony or fanaticism. In appearance, he is a portly, frank, good-natured, rather thick-set man of fifty-five, seeming to enjoy life, and be in no particular hurry to get to heaven. His associates are plain men, evidently born and reared to a life of labor, and looking as little like crafty hypocrites or swindlers as any body of men I ever met. The absence of cant or snuffle from their manner was marked and general, yet, I think I may fairly say that their Mormonism has not impoverished them—that they were generally poor men when they embraced it, and are now in very comfortable circumstances—as men averaging three or four wives apiece certainly need to be. . . But I have a right to add here, because I said it to the assembled chiefs at the close of the above colloquy, that the degradation (or, if you please, the restriction) of Woman to the single office of child-bearing and its accessories, is an inevitable consequence of the system here paramount. I have not observed a sign in the streets, an advertisement in the journals, of this Mormon metropolis, whereby a woman proposes to do anything whatever. No Mormon has ever cited to me his wife's or any woman's opinion on any subject; no Mormon woman has been introduced or has spoken to me; and, though I have been asked to visit Mormons in their houses, no one has spoken of his wife (or wives) desiring to see me, or his desiring me to make her (or their) acquaintance, or voluntarily indicated the existence of such a being or beings. I will not attempt to report our talk on this subject, because, unlike what I have above given, it assumed somewhat the character of a disputation, and I could hardly give it impartially; but one remark made by President Young I think I can give accurately, and it may serve as a sample of all that was offered on that side. It was in these words, I think exactly: "If I did not consider myself competent to transact a certain business without taking my wife's or any woman's counsel with regard to it, I think I ought to let that business alone." The spirit with regard to Woman, of the entire Mormon, as of all other polygamic systems, is fairly displayed in this avowal. Let any such system become established and prevalent, and Woman will soon be confined to the harem, and her appearance in the street with unveiled face will be accounted immodest. I joyfully trust that the genius of the Nineteenth Century tends to a solution of the problem of Woman's sphere and destiny radically different from this.

French botanist Jules Remy (1826–1893) and the British Lord Julius Brenchley spent more than a month in Utah in late summer and early autumn 1855. Remy had a keen interest in comparative religion and introduced his two-volume account of the Mormons with a long essay on religious developments in the United States. Though he claimed to have based his comments on personal observation only, Remy read extensively from the works of others and borrowed liberally from some of them, notably Belinda Marden Pratt and John Hyde. Unlike most others of the time, however, he included in his volumes a bibliography of books on the Mormons as well as a copy of Joseph Smith's 1843 revelation. Remy's description is interesting because his private bias was so strongly formed against polygamy. He repeatedly affirmed that view but admitted that much about Mormon plural life did not conform to his expectations. These excerpts are taken from the 1861 English edition of the original French publication, *Voyage au Pays des Mormons*.

JULES REMY, *JOURNEY TO GREAT SALT LAKE CITY* (1861),
2:82–83, 96–97, 130–32, 136–42, 149–50, 156–60.

. . . who is there that was not startled when he heard that a sect, affecting to be Christian beyond all other sects, which had sprung up in broad day from amidst the civilization of the United States, and which draws its adherents from the most enlightened nations of Europe, was asserting in the name of natural law, of written law, of the Bible, and the Gospel, the lawfulness of a plurality of wives? Who would have thought such a pretension possible at an epoch of brilliant civilization, when all well-ordered societies regard polygamy as a barbarous and bestial thing, a crime to be punished by their laws? . . .

[W]hatever be the value of the objections which can be made to polygyny, it possesses a great influence over the Mormons; and such is the infatuation produced by it, that women, even the best educated,—women brought up in the principles of Christianity,—have suffered themselves to be seduced into it, and whether it be from impulse of feeling, or aberration of intellect, have become its sincere converts. I had the opportunity of conversing on this delicate subject with a woman who is considered extremely ladylike among the Mormons, and would be so esteemed everywhere. It is impossible to conceive with what earnestness of mind, with what an air of sincerity and conviction she defended the new doctrine and met the objections made to it, and what a modesty of manner and language she brought to the support of so bad a cause. . .

It is very difficult, to say nothing stronger, to conceive that a man can have a completely equal affection for all his wives; and, even when he distributes his attentions conscientiously among them all, it is hardly possible to understand how he should be without any preference whatever: hence jealousies and rival contests must arise; and, in fact, these are not absolutely unknown among the Mormons, in spite of the admirable resignation which the women profess. To obviate these evils, the husband restrains the natural warmth of his feelings, and confines himself to a chilly, formal dignity, prescribed by the exigencies of justice and peace, but which is hardly compatible with love. It is true that as the conjugal relations must, and do, as every one might anticipate, under these circumstances model themselves upon the example of the lower animals, polygamy makes very light of moral affection. Moreover, and in conformity with the same model, the husband being no longer bound to discharge the conjugal duty to the wife after she has conceived, his tenderness must necessarily be restricted to those of his wives who have yet shown no sign of pregnancy. . .

Marriage, it must be acknowledged, is among the Mormons in general, destitute of all that gives it a character of delicacy and purity among Christians, and imparts to it its essential charm. It has but one object, to multiply the family. It is an article of faith with them that in the world to which they will go on leaving this one, each man will reign over his children, who will constitute his kingdom; that the more children, the more the glory; and that if they have neither wives nor children upon earth, they will enjoy no glory whatever. . . how can a man, metamorphosed into a procreator, preserve anything of affection, and seek in the complicated relations which polygyny imposes on him, anything else than his animal gratification? Another necessary consequence is, that the faithful are unduly occupied with the task of getting as many wives as they can. . .

It is scarcely necessary for us to say, so self-evident is it, that the Mormons, though maintaining polygyny for the avowed purpose of having more children, do not attain this end in individual cases save at the expense of frustrating the general increase of the population. We do not deny that a man can have more children with ten women than with one only; for this would be to contradict all received evidence. But these ten women, are they likely to have more children by one husband in common than by a husband apiece? We have not a moment's hesitation in answering in the negative. There can be no doubt that the wives of Brigham Young, who have certainly borne him more children than he would have had by one woman only, would have had as many, if not more children, had each had a husband. It is quite certain, too, they each of them could have found this husband amongst the numerous bachelors of the Salt Lake. . . Brigham Young has scarcely more than thirty children living, and several of his wives are barren. Of all Joseph Smith's descendants there is but one surviving. . .

The invincible repugnance we have for the polygynic doctrine, the profound disgust we entertain for the practices to which it has given rise, and for those attributed to it with or without reason, must not prevent our saying that the Mormons appeared to us less licentious than we were naturally inclined to suppose. The careful minuteness with which we have set down everything that has come to our ears of a nature to disparage polygamy, should render our testimony all the less suspicious when we affirm that personally, during our stay at Utah, we saw scarcely anything which seemed to be at variance with the strictest morality. No question, polygyny is extensively practised by the Mormons, and we believe it to be a bad and horrible thing. Still, if we may trust exclusively to our own observation, we are in no position to condemn the practice, however ruthlessly we may persist in rejecting the theory. Love of truth compels us to say that we were, generally speaking, edified with all that we saw, and that as far as external appearances go, Utah is the most moral country in the world. All the males in it are usefully employed; we met neither sluggards, idlers, gamblers, nor drunkards. The polygamist-Saints, almost without exception, left upon us the impression of being good fathers and husbands. All that passed under our eyes was decorous, and we have a decided objection to supposing that we had to deal only with hypocrites. Besides, who are we to reconcile their industry, their love of work, their continual occupation, with the debauched habits that are ascribed to the Mormons? Experience has sufficiently proved that the industrious man is not thinking of what is evil. Polygyny—we cannot repeat it too often—is a detestable thing; but these men have embraced it in all sincerity, and we have had the opportunity of ascertaining that they observe it with chastity and propriety as a Divine command. . . We are satisfied that the Mormons are, in general, better than their system, and in our appreciation of them we must make a large allowance for fanaticism, and acknowledge that the majority of them are honest men, entitled to our esteem on more grounds than one, in spite of what is revolting and absurd in some of their superstitions.

If, on the other hand, we were called upon to furnish an estimate of the moral value of the Mormon women, we should not have the slightest hesitation in asserting that they are much superior to the reputation assigned to them, while at the same time we as little hesitate to say that they surpass in fanaticism anything we could possibly have conceived. In emphatically declaring that they are pious, modest, chaste, faithful, devoted, sincere, laborious, honest, honourable in all respects, it is satisfactory to find ourselves agreeing with every traveller who, like us, has spent some time on the borders of the Salt Lake. . . For our part, we affirm that after travelling for ten years over almost every part of the globe, it is still a question with us if there be any country in which the women are generally more virtuous, and more moral, than they are amongst the Mormons. . .

After having rendered the Mormon women this homage—most certainly a disinterested one—let us inquire if they find in their lot the happiness which they merit. I should with difficulty bring myself to assert that they are happy; I do not think so, even after severely scrutinizing my own impartiality for the purpose of discovering if my doubts on this matter be not attributable solely to a preconceived idea, to the idea that happiness in polygyny would be in manifest contradiction with one of the leading laws that regulate our affections. Still I am bound to acknowledge that the immense majority of female Saints say they are happy, and that many of them appear to be perfectly content.

Of the many visitors who wrote about the Saints, few brought a wider, more tolerant perspective to the experience than the English explorer Richard Francis Burton (1821–1890). Urbane, insightful, and an excellent stylist, Burton's account of polygamy and of Mormonism is one of the best of any age by an outsider. Though he spent only three weeks with them, his comments could not have been more thoughtful had he lived among them for decades. This memoir of his visit in late summer 1860 appeared the next year.

RICHARD F. BURTON, *CITY OF THE SAINTS* (1861), 476–83.

It will, I suppose, be necessary to supply a popular view of the "peculiar institution," at once the bane and blessing of Mormonism—plurality. I approach the subject with a feeling of despair, so conflicting are opinions concerning it, and so difficult is it to naturalise in Europe the customs of Asia, Africa, and America, or to reconcile the habits of the 19th century A.D. with those of 1900 B.C. . . .

There is a prevailing idea, especially in England, and even the educated are labouring under it, that the Mormons are Communists or Socialists of Plato's, Cicero's, Mr. Owen's and M. Cabet's school; that wives are in public, and that a woman can have as many husbands as the husband can have wives—in fact, to speak colloquially, that they "all pig together." The contrary is notably the case. . .

The marriage ceremony is performed in the temple, or, that being impossible, in Mr. Brigham Young's office, properly speaking by the Prophet, who can, however, depute any follower, as Mr. Heber Kimball, a simple apostle, or even an elder, to act for him. When mutual consent is given, the parties are pronounced man and wife, in the name of Jesus Christ, prayers follow, and there is a patriarchal feast of joy in the evening.

The first wife, as among polygamists generally, is *the* wife, and assumes the husband's name and title. Her "plurality"—partners are called sisters—such as sister Anne or sister Blanche—and are the aunts of her children. The first wife is married for time, the others are sealed for eternity.[18] Hence, according to the Mormons, arose the Gentile calumny concerning spiritual wifedom, which they distinctly deny. Girls rarely remain single past sixteen—in England the average marrying age is thirty—and they would be the pity of the community, if they were doomed to a waste of youth so unnatural.

Divorce is rarely obtained by the man who is ashamed to own that he cannot keep his house in order; some, such as the President, would grant it only in case of adultery; wives, however, are allowed to claim it for cruelty, desertion, or neglect. Of late years, Mormon women married to Gentiles are cut off from the society of the Saints, and without uncharitableness men suspect a sound previous reason. . .

The literalism with which the Mormons have interpreted Scripture has led them directly to polygamy. The texts promising to Abraham a progeny numerous as the stars above or the sands below, and that "in his seed (a polygamist) all the families of the earth shall be blessed," induce them, his descendants, to seek a similar blessing. The theory announcing that "the man is not without the woman, nor the woman without the man," is by them interpreted into an absolute command that both sexes should marry, and that a woman

---

[18] For one ordinarily careful with facts, Burton's impression here was erroneous. All of a Mormon's wives, including the first, could be, and generally were, sealed to him for eternity.

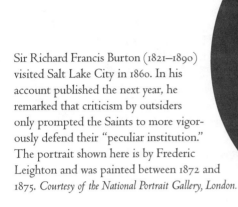

Sir Richard Francis Burton (1821–1890) visited Salt Lake City in 1860. In his account published the next year, he remarked that criticism by outsiders only prompted the Saints to more vigorously defend their "peculiar institution." The portrait shown here is by Frederic Leighton and was painted between 1872 and 1875. *Courtesy of the National Portrait Gallery, London.*

cannot enter the heavenly kingdom without a husband to introduce her. A virgin's end is annihilation or absorption, *nox est perpetua una dormienda*; and as baptism for the dead—an old rite, revived and founded upon the writings of St. Paul— . . . [and] vicarious marriage for the departed also enters into the Mormon scheme. Like certain British dissenters of the royal burgh of Dundee, who in our day petitioned parliament for permission to bigamise, the Mormons . . . in the Old dispensation . . . find the practice sanctioned in a family, ever the friends of God, and out of which the Redeemer sprang. Finally, they find throughout the nations of the earth, three polygamists in theory to one monogame.

The "chaste and plural marriage" being once legalised, finds a multitude of supporters. The anti-Mormons declare that it is at once fornication and adultery—a sin which absorbs all others. The Mormons point triumphantly to the austere morals of their community, their superior freedom from maladive influences, and the absence of that uncleanness and licentiousness which distinguish the cities of the civilised world. They boast that if it be an evil they have at least chosen the lesser evil, that they practise openly as a virtue what others do secretly as a sin—how full is society of these latent Mormons! . . . Like its sister institution Slavery, the birth and growth of a similar age, Polygamy acquires *vim* by abuse and detraction; the more turpitude is heaped upon it, the brighter and more glorious it appears to its votaries.

There are rules and regulations of Mormonism—I cannot say whether they date before or after the heavenly command to pluralise—which disprove the popular statement that such marriages are made to gratify licentiousness, and which render polygamy a positive necessity. All sensuality in the married state is strictly forbidden beyond the requisite for ensuring progeny,—the practice, in fact, of Adam and Abraham. During the gestation and nursing of children, the strictest continence on the part of the mother is required—rather for a hygienic than for a religious reason. The same custom is practised in part by the Jews, and in whole by some of the noblest tribes of savages; the splendid physical development of the Kaffir race in South Africa is attributed by some authors to a rule of continence like that of the Mormons, and to a lactation prolonged for two years. . . Spartan-like the Faith wants a race of warriors, and it adopts the best means to obtain them.

Besides religious and physiological, there are social motives for the plurality. As in the days of Abraham, the lands about New Jordan are broad and the people few. Of the three forms that unite the sexes, polygamy increases, whilst monogamy balances, and polyandry diminishes progeny. The former as Montesquieu acutely suggested, acts inversely to latter, by causing a preponderance of female over male births. . .[19]

At Gt. S. L. City there is a gloom, like that which the late Professor H. H. Wilson described as being cast by the invading Moslem over the innocent gaiety of the primitive Hindu. The choice egotism of the heart called Love, that is to say, the propensity elevated by sentiment, and not undirected by reason, subsides into a calm and unimpassioned domestic attachment: romance and reverence are transferred, with the true Mormon concentration, from Love and Liberty to Religion and the Church. The consent of the first wife to a rival is seldom refused, and a *ménage à trois*, in the Mormon sense of the phrase, is fatal to the development of that tender tie which must be confined to two. In its stead there is household comfort, affection, circumspect friendship, and domestic discipline. Womanhood is not petted and spoiled as in the Eastern States; the inevitable cyclical revolution, indeed, has rather placed her below par, where, however, I believe her to be happier than when set upon an uncomfortable and unnatural eminence. . .

For the attachment of the women of the Saints to the doctrine of plurality there are many reasons. The Mormon prophets have expended all their arts upon this end, well knowing that without the hearty co-operation of mothers and wives, sisters and daughters, no institution can live long. They have

---

[19] For Montesquieu's contention, see his 1748 work, *Spirit of Laws*, 16.4. Belief that polygyny increased female births was a common assumption well into the nineteenth century. See Grégoire, *L'Influence du christianisme sur la condition des femmes*, 15–16; Ryan, *Philosophy of Marriage*, 108; and Wright, *Marriage and Parentage*, 184. John Hyde, *Mormonism*, 74, claimed it occurred in Utah, as did Remy, *Journey to Great-Salt-Lake City*, 2:150, 171; and Greeley, *Overland Journey*, 242. Westermark refuted the myth in his *History of Human Marriage*, 2:150.

bribed them with promises of Paradise—they have subjugated them with threats of annihilation. With them once a Mormon always a Mormon. . . all the fervour of a new faith burns in their bosoms, with a heat which we can little appreciate, and the revelation of Mr. Joseph Smith is considered on this point as superior to the Christian as the latter is in others to the Mosaic Dispensation. Polygamy is a positive command from heaven: if the flesh is mortified by it *tant mieux*—"no Cross, no Crown;" "blessed are they that mourn." I have heard these words from the lips of a well-educated Mormon woman who, in the presence of a Gentile sister, urged her husband to take unto himself a second wife. The Mormon household has been described by its enemies as a hell of envy, hatred, and malice—a den of murder and suicide. The same has been said of the Moslem harem. Both, I believe, suffer from the assertions of prejudice or ignorance. . .

Another curious effect of fervent belief may be noticed in the married state. When a man has four or five wives with reasonable families by each, he is fixed for life: his interests, if not his affections, bind him irrevocably to his New Faith. But the bachelor, as well as the monogamic youth, is prone to backsliding. Apostasy is apparently so common that many of the new Saints form a mere floating population. He is proved by a mission before being permitted to marry, and even then women, dreading a possible renegade with the terrible consequences of a heavenless future to themselves, are shy of saying yes.

"Pathetically 'Homely' Creatures": Humorists, Cartoonists, and Novelists Take Aim

Humorists naturally found Mormon plurality an inviting target, and the subject attracted the frontier's most renowned wits, Charles Farrar Browne (1834–1867) and Samuel Langhorne Clemens (1835–1910), now famous as Artemus Ward and Mark Twain. Ward and Twain influenced each other considerably, especially in their views of polygamy.[20] Ward visited the Saints in 1864 and made the most of his visit, applying his gift for vocal caricature to an uproarious lecture, "Among the Mormons," which he gave repeatedly in both the United States and England.

E. P. Hingston, ed., *Artemus Ward*
(*His Travels*) *Among the Mormons* (1865), 76–78.

Are the Mormon women happy?
I give it up. I don't know. . . Apparently, the Mormon women are happy. . .

---

[20] Cracroft, "'Ten Wives Is All You Need,'" 197–211; and his "Gentle Blasphemer," esp. 137–40.

The Mormon girl is reared to believe that the plurality system (as it is delicately called here) is strictly right; and in linking her destiny with a man who has twelve wives, she undoubtedly considers she is doing her duty. She loves the man, probably, for I think it is not true, as so many writers have stated, that girls are forced to marry whomsoever "the Church" may dictate. . .

The Mormon woman is early taught that man, being created in the image of the Saviour, is far more godly than she can ever be, and that for her to seek to monopolize his affections is a species of rank sin. So she shares his affections with five or six or twenty other women, as the case may be. . .

I had a man pointed out to me who married an entire family. He had originally intended to marry Jane, but Jane did not want to leave her widowed mother. The other three sisters were not in the matrimonial market for the same reason; so this gallant man married the whole crowd, including the girl's grandmother, who had lost all her teeth, and had to be fed with a spoon. The family were in indigent circumstances, and they could not but congratulate themselves on securing a wealthy husband. It seemed to affect the grandmother deeply, for the first words she said on reaching her new home, were: "Now, thank God! I shall have my gruel reg'lar!"

Mark Twain completed *Roughing It* ten years after visiting Great Salt Lake City in 1861, using newspaper clippings, other writers, and his brother Orion's journal to reinforce his memory. He discussed subjects like *The Book of Mormon* and the Mountain Meadows Massacre, but Twain knew that polygamy would amuse readers most. Months before it appeared, he feared for the success of *Roughing It*, because western travelogues had become so "hackneyed."[21] Twain's concern was unfounded and, as with Ward's performances, the book enjoyed a popular reception. The best-remembered passage from Twain's comments on the Mormons is his opinion of their women.

Our stay in Salt Lake City amounted to only two days, and therefore we had no time to make the customary inquisition into the workings of polygamy and get up the usual statistics and deductions preparatory to calling the attention of the nation at large once more to the matter. I had the will to do it. With the gushing self-sufficiency of youth I was feverish to plunge in headlong and achieve a great reform here—until I saw the Mormon women. Then I was touched. My heart was wiser than my head. It warmed toward these poor, ungainly and pathetically "homely" creatures, and as I turned to hide the generous moisture in my eyes, I said, "No—the man that marries one of them has done an act of Christian charity which entitles him to the kindly applause of mankind, not their harsh censure—and the man that marries sixty

---

[21] See Harriet Elinor Smith's introduction to the 1993 edition of *Roughing It*, 797.

of them has done a deed of open-handed generosity so sublime that the nation should stand uncovered in his presence and worship in silence."[22]

In the wake of the success of Ward and Twain, an explosion of colored and illustrated journalism using caricature, sensational portrayal, and ridicule brought further attention to the Saints and their sexual behavior. Publications such as *Harper's Weekly, Leslie's Weekly, Lippincott's Monthly Magazine,* and *Puck* accommodated a growing prurient fascination with the Mormons.[23] Subscribers' appetites for such topics seemed insatiable, and editors obliged them. Playing to the same audience, scores of deprecatory novels poured from the imaginations of nineteenth-century writers. In the half-century after the formal unveiling of plural marriage, outsiders, most of whom never set foot in Utah, wrote at least one novel every year about the Mormons.[24]

As Karen Lynn observed, polygamy, the dominant theme of such books, was custom-made to please middle-class tastes. It allowed authors to denounce what was broadly accepted as immoral behavior, and it was easy to craft tales of murder, seduction, and pursuit around the church's priestly orders. Gothic temples and dark canyons provided sinister settings for the plots, and the triumph of virtuous heroines over Mormon pashas played to the aspirations of reform-minded women in the East.[25] Of course, as scholars have long observed, the success enjoyed by writers and illustrators when treating the topic probably told less of Mormon polygamy than it did of those so anxious to read about it.[26] More ominously, authors occasionally reported the stories as fact, and politicians cited them to justify suppression of alleged immorality in Utah.[27] Such narratives not only fed the attack on polygamy but, as historian Sarah Gordon argues, they transformed the anti-slavery impetus into a national, anti-polygamy crusade.[28]

---

[22] Twain, *Roughing It,* 117–18.

[23] The best survey remains Bunker and Bitton's *Mormon Graphic Image.*

[24] None, perhaps, was more popular than Maria Ward's *Female Life among the Mormons,* first published in 1855 and then in several foreign languages. It was reprinted almost annually for the rest of the century.

[25] Lynn, "Sensational Virtue," 101–11. Other treatments are Lambert, "Saints, Sinners and Scribes," 63–76; Arrington and Haupt, "Intolerable Zion: The Image of Mormonism," 243–60; Cracroft, "Distorting Polygamy for Fun and Profit," 272–88; McKay, "The Puissant Procreator," 15–17; Gordon, "War of Words," 747–64; and Givens, *Viper on the Hearth.*

[26] Tappan, "Mormon-Gentile Conflict," 416–17; Fryer, "American Eves in American Edens," 85–86; and Cannon, "Awesome Power of Sex," 62.

[27] See the examples provided in Givens, *Viper on the Hearth,* 117–19.

[28] Gordon, "'Our National Hearthstone': Anti-Polygamy Fiction," 295–350.

"THE YELLOW, SUNKEN, CADAVEROUS VISAGE": POLYGAMY AND PHYSIOLOGY

As early as the 1850s Mormons were described as both physically and mentally in decline—liabilities, it was believed, arising from their practice of polygamy. Women especially were represented as unattractive. Not only were they wretched to look at but, some said, they were mentally dull.[29] How else, asked a journalist, could one explain their acceptance of the plural system?[30] William Hepworth Dixon claimed Brigham Young and Orson Pratt agreed with the unflattering estimates of strangers. He quoted the two leaders to say that physical attraction had nothing to do with their own plural marriages. Dixon said the two men testified "with a laughing eye, that they would put their wives in evidence," many of them "being old, plain, uneducated, ill-mannered."[31] Beyond denigrating portrayals of the women, and more condemning of their doctrine, some saw Mormon polygamy as a threat to the species at large, an aberration entailing degenerate natures on all. Though Brigham Young told the Saints they were destined to become "the best-looking people there is on the earth," it would have required, in the minds of some, a major improvement over their appearance at the time.[32]

When President Buchanan sent an expeditionary force to Utah in 1857, Dr. Roberts Bartholow accompanied it as an assistant army surgeon. Dealing with everything from botany to zoology, his report to the surgeon general, reprinted in both medical and popular journals across the country, included an account of the Mormon people and what he perceived as the physiological effects of polygamy.[33] As a physician, his words carried special influence, and many criticisms made of the Mormons took rise from them.[34]

---

[29] See, for example: Trautmann, "Salt Lake City through a German's Eyes," 53; Bates, *Year in the Great Republic*, 2:225; and Oscar Wilde's remark that Mormon women were "very, very ugly." Wilde to Mrs. Bernard Beere, 17 April 1882, in Hart-Davis, *Letters of Oscar Wilde*, 110–11. [30] "Scenes in an American Harem," 649.

[31] Dixon added, however, that in his own observation numbers of plurals were "young, fresh, delicate, and charming." *New America*, 207.

[32] G. D. Watt, "Summary of Instructions Given by President Brigham Young," *Des. News* [Weekly], 9 Aug. 1865, 14:45, 354/1.

[33] Perhaps the most widely cited of these was the paper by Forshey and Cartwright, "Hereditary Descent," 206–16. "If the future of Mormondom were left to the offspring of polygamy, it would, indeed, be short lived," Bartholow wrote nearly a decade after his visit to Utah. "Lean and weak of body, depraved of mind, precocious manhood and womanhood are the characteristics of the new population—the results of polygamy." "Physiological Aspects of Mormonism,"197.

[34] The best overview of Bartholow's treatment of the Mormons and its impact is Bush Jr., "Peculiar People," 61–83. Bartholow was not the only medical observer of the Mormons who contended for the degenerating effects of polygamy. See Bush's account of Dr. Charles C. Furley in ibid., 68–69.

ROBERTS BARTHOLOW, "SANITARY REPORT—
UTAH TERRITORY (1860)," 283–304.

The Mormon, of all the human animals now walking this globe, is the most curious in every relation. It would be quite beyond the scope of this report to say anything of the political and religious aspects of Mormonism; but as a great social solecism, seriously affecting the physical stamina and mental health, it is full of interest to the medical philosopher. Isolated in the narrow valleys of Utah, and practising the rites of a religion grossly material, of which polygamy is the main element and cohesive force, the Mormon people have arrived at a physical and mental condition, in a few years of growth, such as densely-populated communities in the older parts of the world, hereditary victims of all the vices of civilization, have been ages in reaching. This condition is shown by the preponderance of female births, by the mortality in infantine life, by the large proportion of the albuminous and gelatinous types of constitution, and by the striking uniformity in facial expression and in physical conformation of the younger portion of the community. The "peculiar institution," is practically upheld by the older men, the elders, bishops, apostles, and prophets; and so eager is the search for young virgins, that notwithstanding the preponderance of the female population, a large percentage of the younger men remain unmarried. To sustain the system, girls are "sealed" at the earliest manifestations of puberty, and I am credibly informed, that means are not unfrequently made use of to hasten the period. The activity of the reproductive function, as a rule, is not diminished by polygamy; on the contrary, the women are remarkable for fecundity; but in the harems the proportion of children arriving at maturity, is much less than in the rural districts of our country. An illustration of this fact is afforded by the results in that chief of polygamists, Brigham Young's case. He has, at least, forty wives. A large number of children have been born to him, a majority of whom died in infancy, leaving twenty-four, according to the most reliable accounts. These forty women in monogamous society, married, would have borne, probably, one hundred and sixty children, two thirds of whom under hygienic circumstances equally favorable, would have been reared. In Brigham and his wives, we have presented the most favorable conditions for successful polygamy possible in Mormon society, yet, in this instance, the violation of a natural law, has been speedily evinced. One of the most deplorable effects of polygamy, is shown in the genital weakness of the boys and young men, the progeny of the "peculiar institution." The most observant Mormons, cannot hide from themselves the evidence of these sad effects. . . The sexual desires are stimulated to an unnatural degree at a very early age, and as female virtue is easy, opportunities are not wanting for their gratification. It is a curious fact, that Mormonism makes its impress upon the countenance. Whether owing to the practice of a purely sensual and material religion, to the premature development of the passions, or to isolation, there is, nevertheless, an expression of countenance and a style of feature, which may be styled the Mormon expression and style; an expression compounded of sensuality, cunning, suspicion, and a smirking self-conceit. The yellow, sunken, cadaverous visage; the greenish-colored eyes; the thick, protuberant lips; the low forehead; the light, yellowish hair; and the lank, angular person, constitute an appearance so characteristic of the new race, the production of polygamy, as to distinguish them at a glance. The older men and women, present all the physical peculiarities of the nationalities to which they belong; but these peculiarities are not propagated and continued in the new race; they are lost in the prevailing Mormon type.

If Mormonism received no additions from outside sources, these influences continuing, it is not difficult to foresee that it would eventually die out. The increase of population, independently of large annual accessions from abroad, has not been coequal with the increase in other portions of our country. The results of polygamy here are not to be compared, without some limitations, to the results of the same institution elsewhere: its decadence must follow more speedily. In eastern life, where it has been a recognized domestic institution for ages, women are prepared for its continuance, and do not feel degraded by their association with it. The women of this Territory, how fanatical and ignorant soever, recognize their wide departure from the normal standard in all Christian countries; and from the degradation of the mother follows that of the child, and physical degeneracy is not a remote consequence of moral depravity.

Alexander Badger, a St. Louis merchant or jobber who transported supplies to Fort Douglas, and Rev. John G. Fackler wrote descriptions that illustrate the increasingly popular image of polygamous Mormons as a maimed species. Both paint examples of the divided portrait that persisted for decades: a people seriously flawed by polygamy while, at the same time, capable of impressive husbandry, agriculture, and material creations.

ALEX [BADGER] TO DEAR MOTHER [MRS. ALEXANDER BADGER SR.], 11 JAN. 1863, SALT LAKE CITY, U.T. ARCHIVES, MO. HIST. SOC.

But about the Saints—I am certainly amongst a curious people—they are a riddle to me—and all other Gentiles and I suppose to themselves. There is quite a large City here in the valley—spread over a large space, and entitled to the name of "City of Suburbs or Magnificent Distances," as much so, as Washington City. . .[35] The people, are about the commonest looking set of beings I ever saw, *awful* homely—men and women—with scarcely an exception. There doesn't seem to be much intelligence among them, to look at them—they look as though they were made to *labor* and not to *think*—and

---

[35] A suburb of St. Louis.

you may be sure they do labor. Brigham does the thinking for them all—he directs, controls and owns everything. Most of the people are in a state of abject poverty—and they are kept so. So long as they are poor they cannot leave the valley, and Brigham can use them to effect all his purposes.

ALEX BADGER TO DEAR MOTHER, 10 MAY 1863,
CAMP DOUGLAS, U.T. ARCHIVES, MO. HIST. SOC.

I hope the Lord will deliver me from the land of Zion. Excuse my impiety—but if this is the valley where the Lord intends to Corral the saints, I would rather dwell with the lost sheep somewhere in the Mississippi valley or California.

I don't think I have ever given you a good description of this vally, and will endeavor now to give you some idea of the place. . . Grasshoppers, Crickets, ants, owls, Cyotes, Crow[,] badgers, (I am ashamed of the rascals) skunks and Mormons are the principal inhabitants. Milk and honey does not flow down the mountain sides as some have asserted. I have however, seen the women drive the cows down the mountain sides in the evening, which is the nearest approach to milk and honey I have seen. . . The Mormons have made the City and the land bordering the Jordan [River] to bloom and blossom as the rose. The City at present is very beautiful in appearance. On each side of the streets, locust and cottonwood trees are planted and are green and shady. Grass grows on each side of the gutters and gives to the streets a fresh appearance. Every house or family has a large garden—most of them full of peach and apple trees. The fragrance from the blooming peach trees is delightful. I often think though, that the city is like a whitened sepulcher—fair without, but within—full of rottenness and dead bones.

I am acquainted with a Mormon wo[m]an in town, who said to a friend of mine the other day, "that now her husband had gone east, she felt contented in mind for he was free from tem[p]tation and evil["]—that is, he was free from the temptation of taking a second wife. Poor woman, she has lived in an agony of fear while her husband was here, for fear he (whom she loves with all her heart) would take a second wife. Just think—she has lived with him for a number of years—has borne him seven children—and at this late day to have a rival share his love—to bad—Would you, could *any* woman of spirit bear it? And yet this is but one case of hundreds—some, *many*, much sadder.

A Methodist missionary, John G. Fackler and his wife left St. Joseph in May 1864, bound for Sacramento. His party reached the valley of the Great Salt Lake on 28 July 1864 and departed on 16 August 1864. While camping near Salt Lake and preparing for a desert crossing by way of the Humboldt route on 9 August, Fackler observed that "the valley has been made to bloom like a garden."

JOHN G. FACKLER, BRIEF NOTES OF TRAVILS
A CROSS [*sic*] THE PLAINS FROM ST. JOSEPH MO. TO
CALIFORNIA IN 1864, ARCHIVES, MO. HIST. SOC., 85–90.

Saturday August 13th [1864]
[Looking for grain to buy in preparation for their journey gave Fackler]
a good opportunity to see many of the Mormon women & judge concerning the question of their domestic happiness. We frequently found three &
four women in one small home. They seem without exception, to belong to
an ignorant class & all of them wear a sad & dejected look. The[y] work in
the most menial employments, and are certainly not far removed from the
condition of the slaves. The children—of whom there are very many—have
a dull, & in numerous instances, almost an idiotic expression of countenance.
We returned to camp more & more assured with the conviction, that Mormonism is rather a huge system of *moral corruption* voluntarily adopted, than
a *superstition*.

Sabbath August 14th [1864]
… Made about 22 miles & camped on Weber Creek not far from the Town
of Ogden, in a Mormon settlement. Pastured the stock on the meadow & in
the stubble field of a man, who extorted from us the sum of $25—above the
amount, we had agreed to pay him. Theft, fraud & rascality, appear to constitute the Creed & practice of these ~~serou~~ scoundrels. The valley of the Weber
thrives like a garden—The lands are irrigated.

"THE MOST STARTLING DROPPING OFF FROM MY EYES": TOLERANCE FOR THE MORMONS

The image of Mormon decadence, including stories of their physical appearance, was so entrenched that when visiting their settlements in the early 1870s,
Elizabeth Wood Kane felt compelled to contradict it, saying that, rather than
the figures described in so many travel accounts, Mormon female countenances were much the same as those of women elsewhere.[36] Theressa
Yelverton also found Mormon semblance different than she expected: "The

---

[36] Kane, *Twelve Mormon Homes*, 42. LDS women attending suffrage conventions in the East recalled that
outsiders were surprised to discover they were neither a tribe of Indians nor a people of "degraded" appearance. See Romania B. Pratt, "Woman's Suffrage Convention," *Woman's Exponent* 10:19 (1 Mar. 1882), 146; and
Ellen B. Ferguson, "New York Letter," ibid., 10:21 (1 April 1882), 165. George Q. Cannon, territorial congressional delegate, did all he could to dispel such impressions. Whenever possible he took visiting family
members to the White House to display their cheerful faces and healthy bodies. Cannon, "Mormon Issue
in Congress," 137, 170. A reporter said Utah's delegate walked about Washington sporting a perpetual smile.
"Washington," *Salt Lake Tribune*, 21 Jan. 1879, 16:17 [4/4].

most startling dropping off from my eyes of the cherished scales of prejudice occurred during my visit to the state of Utah!"[37]

More than surprise, James Bodell (1831–1892) was so impressed that he considered joining them. The son of poor English parents, Bodell enlisted in the military at age 16 and spent the rest of his life traveling throughout the empire. In and out of the army, he engaged in a variety of pursuits before commencing his reminiscences in 1881. For one whose education was meager, his recollections, as Keith Sinclair observed, are "extraordinarily accurate."[38] During a journey from New Zealand to England he crossed the United States, stopping briefly in Salt Lake City in 1883.

KEITH SINCLAIR, ED., *SOLDIER'S VIEW OF EMPIRE* (1883), 193–94.

After leaving the Tabernacle we inspected everything about the Mormon Church and other Buildings. Not far away from the Tabernacle there is a large Yard, Building on two Sides and several Barn like Buildings on opposite end and another Building near the Centre of Yard, this latter Building standing in front of us on our entrance into the yard a load of green feed on a cart going in and a jolly looking individual opening the gates. We went up to this Person and in a few minutes we were in conversation which continued for the next two hours. He became very communicative. He told us the Mormon Form of Worship was taken from the Bible and he said the load of green Grass you have seen delivered is part Payment due for *Tithes* from the Farmer who sent it. He said all Mormons have to pay 10 per cent of their earnings, a Farmer 10 per cent on his Produce a business man the same on his Profits and in this way the Mormons get the Capital to pay for the various Elders, Bishops and other Ministers connected with the Mormon Church. . .

When I asked him how any man could manage so many Wives he said easily enough. He said I have two and have been a Mormon 30 years and am 63 years old. Still I am thinking of taking a third Wife. I remarked I considered him too old, not a bit of it said the old chap it would be more of a Variety and would make things livelier at home. Why said he some of our Friends have 4 & 6 and look at our President (Taylor) he has 20 wives. Look over there said the old chap holding out his arm you see that Building with 10 Windows upstairs, them are 10 of the 20 Wives' Bedrooms and on other side of House there are 10 other Bedrooms but I remarked it could not be expected that one man could keep these 20 Women under subjection and keep peace at home. He said if a man has 10 wives and he takes another and any one of the 10 are dissatisfied the one dissatisfied can retire and become a Pensioner.

---

[37] Yelverton, *Teresina in America*, 2:35. Theressa Yelverton, Viscountess Avenmore, (1832?–1881) was a well-known traveler and author whose favorable comments on the Saints were repeated in "The Women of Utah," *Des. News* [Weekly], 11 Nov. 1874, 23:41, 642/1–2.

[38] Sinclair, *Soldier's View of Empire*, 10.

Those wives who are satisfied know it is no use grumbling afterwards. Still sometimes there is bickerings at Home.

He said do you know you Gentiles practise grievous Sin in what way you take unto yourself one wife. You lay with her, she proves to be in the Family way and still you lay and have connection with her and by this you are disobeying God's Laws. Read your Bible and I can prove it. All we Mormons do and practise in our Law is taken from the Bible. All you Gentiles sow your Seed on unfruitful Places, having to do with a woman when she is bearing a child is against the Laws of God. We Mormons never lie with a Woman after she is proved to be in child she is left alone for 18 months. The woman is not touched for 9 months after the child is born so as the Mother can give all her strength to her offspring. I certainly was non plussed here and there were some truth in his remarks.

It was a most interesting two hours conversation and I may say instructive also. I certainly felt inclined to become a Mormon and told him so.

"THEY MUST SOON GIVE WAY": WARNING VOICES

There were others, however, observers neither hostile toward nor persuaded by the Saints, who disapproved of Mormon polygamy and warned that they must change if they wished to remain in the republic. Journalist Samuel Bowles (1826–1878) accompanied Speaker of the House Schuyler Colfax on his tour of the American West in 1865 and returned with Colfax, now vice president under Grant, in 1869. Again, Bowles wrote about his experience, enlarging upon the descriptions of his earlier visit to Utah.[39] As editor of the Springfield, Massachusetts, *Republican*, one of the day's most influential newspapers, Bowles's comments were widely reprinted. This excerpt is taken from sketches Bowles assembled the year following his first journey.

[SAMUEL BOWLES], *ACROSS THE CONTINENT* (1866), 123–27, 130.

Down east, you know, many a husband calculates on stealing into heaven under the pious petticoats of his better wife; here the thing is reversed, and women go to heaven because their husbands take them along. The Mormon religion is an excellent institution for maintaining masculine authority in the family; and the greatness of a true Mormon is measured, indeed, by the number of wives he can keep in sweet and loving and especially obedient subjugation. Such a man can have as many wives as he wants. . .

---

[39] Bowles, *Our New West*, 202–70. Some experts believe Bowles was the man Emily Dickinson called "my closest earthly friend," while others speculate that the poet had an affair with the married publisher.

Samuel Bowles II (1826–1878), by Napoleon Sarony.
Bowles succeeded in making the Springfield, Massachusetts, *Republican* one of the most eminent newspapers
in the United States. In it he wrote often of his travels
to the American West. He believed the inherent
superiority of European and American monogamous
ideals would persuade Mormons to discontinue
their practice of plural marriage. *Courtesy National
Portrait Gallery, Smithsonian Institution.*

In many cases, the Mormon wives not only support themselves and their
children, but help support their husbands. Thus a clerk or other man, with similar limited income, who has yielded to the fascinations and desires of three or
four women, and married them all, makes his home with number one, perhaps,
and the rest live apart, each by herself, taking in sewing or washing, or engaging in other employment, to keep up her establishment and be no charge to her
husband. He comes around, once in a while, to make her a visit, and then she
sets out an extra table and spends all her accumulated earnings to make him as
comfortable and herself as charming as possible, so that her fraction of the
dear sainted man may be multiplied as much as possible. Thus the fellow, if he
is lazy and has turned his piety to the good account of getting smart wives,
may really board around continually, and live in clover, at no personal expense
but his own clothing. Is not this a divine institution, indeed! . . .

Handsome women and girls, in fact, are scarce among the Mormons of
Salt Lake,—the fewer "Gentiles" can show many more of them. Why is this?
. . . good-looking women being supposed to have more chances for matrimony than their plainer sisters, do they all insist upon having the whole of one
man, and leave the Mormon husbands to those whose choice is like Hob-
son's? The only polygamist, into whose family circle we were freely admitted,
had, however, found two very pretty women to divide him between them; and
I must confess they appeared to take their share of him quite resignedly, if

not amicably. They were English, and of nearly equal years; appeared together in the parlor and public with their husband, and dressed alike; but they had the same quiet, subdued, half-sad air that characterized all the Mormon women, young and old, that I saw in public or private. . .

Even without the interference of government, they must soon give way here, in their peculiar sway and their revolting institution, before the progress of population and the diversification of civilized industry that come along with it. Our bachelor stage-driver out of Salt Lake, who said he expected to have a revelation soon to take one of the extra wives of a Mormon saint, is a representative of the Coming Man. Let the Mormons look out for him.

William Hepworth Dixon (1821–1879) seemed always interested in the Latter-day Saints.[40] An English historian, journalist, and dedicated racist, Dixon wrote numerous books, travel accounts, and edited the London *Athenaeum*. He saw plurality as both impractical and a reversion to primitive ways. Believing the Saints had borrowed polygamy from American Indians, he was convinced that polygamous Mormonism, like the aboriginal race itself, must succumb to the irresistible tide of northern European civilization.[41] Dixon here reports a conversation on the subject with two LDS church authorities in the 1870s.

WILLIAM HEPWORTH DIXON, *WHITE CONQUEST*
(1876), 1:194–95, 198–206.

A railway train has done it all. . .

In other days plurality was a rage. You heard of nothing else. . . To have a plural household was a sign of perfect faith and walking in the highest light. To be a member of the Church, and yet refrain from sealing wife on wife, was a discredit to the priesthood; and an elder so remiss in duty was unable to get on. That rage in favour of plurality is past. Some leaders have renounced the practice, others have denounced the dogma, of polygamy. . .

'Well, in the city, you may note such cases,' says the Apostle [John Taylor], putting my case aside, with what appears to me a weary shrug. 'A Gentile influence has been creeping in, no doubt; and business people are the first to see things in a worldly light; but on the country farms and in the lonely sheep-runs you will find a pastoral people, eager to fulfil the law as it is given to us, and to enjoy the blessings offered by God to his obedient Saints.' . . .

No sooner was the railway built, the valley opened, and the stranger admitted, than a change of view set in. . .

---

[40] See, for example, Dixon's *New America*, 127–247; and his *Spiritual Wives*, 81, 287, 350.

[41] This was a view common in Europe as well as the United States. See Billington, "Native Americans: Doomed to Extermination," in *Land of Savagery*, 129–49.

'Do you wish me to infer,' I ask Apostle Taylor, 'that the rich and educated Mormons are giving up polygamy, and the poor and ignorant brethren are taking to it?'

'No,' he answers me with meek reproof, 'we should not like to put the matter so. Some worldly men are weary of obedience to the law; while others, pure in heart and true in faith, are ready to assume their cross.' . . .

'I gather, not from what you tell me only, but from every word I hear, and every man I see, that there is change of practice, if not change of doctrine,' I remark to President [Daniel] Wells and Apostle Taylor.

'That is your impression?' Asks the Apostle.

'Yes, my strong impression; I might say my strong conviction. Pardon me for saying that the point is very serious. If you mean to dwell in the United States, you must abate the practice, even if you retain the principle, of plural wives. Nature, Law, and Accident are all against your theories of domestic life. Nature puts the male and female on the earth in pairs; and thereby sets her fact against your theories. The Law of every Christian State declares that one man shall marry one woman, and no more. Accidents, which have left a surplus of females in Europe, have brought a surplus of males to America. In England, where in every thousand persons, five hundred and fourteen are females, four hundred and eighty-six males, you might pretend to find a physical basis for your theory. But in these States and territories, out of every thousand persons, five hundred and five are males, four hundred and ninety-five females. There are not enough women for every man to have one wife. Even in Utah you have fifteen hundred more men than women. In the face of such facts, your "celestial law" of polygamy will be hard to carry out. Man will find his mate, or die for her.'

"CATTLE ON TWO LEGS":
GENTILES AND TABERNACLE SERMONS

After its completion in 1870, tourists to Salt Lake City were as likely to visit the great tabernacle as visitors today. The only difference is that modern travelers go mostly to hear Mormonism's famous Tabernacle Choir. Nineteenth-century outsiders chiefly hoped to learn something about polygamy. Little is known of the Englishman John Mortimer Murphy except that he explored and wrote about western locations suited to game hunting.[42] Here he tells his experience with a polygamist in the tabernacle.

---

[42] For the scant information available on Murphy, see bibliographical notes in Athearn, *Westward the Briton*, 197; and Rapson, *Britons View America*, 244–45.

JOHN MORTIMER MURPHY, *RAMBLES IN*
NORTH-WESTERN AMERICA (1879), 238–40.

At 2 P.M. I went to hear Brigham Young preach, and vulgar as I thought
the assertions in the morning, I must say that those uttered by the Prophet,
Seer, and Revelator were much worse; they were, in fact, so shockingly inde-
cent that I wondered that any woman could listen to them. Some gentiles
could not, so they and their escorts left the building, and when the majority
had gone he applied the vilest epithets to them. The whole harangue was a
combination of blasphemy, scurrility, and the most vulgar indecency; yet not
a Mormon maiden, so far as I could see, blushed at this insulting chattering,
whilst those who bore wifely looks seemed as indifferent to the vile words as
the surrounding walls. Had the same iniquitous language been used in any
other civilized city the speaker would have been tried in a court of justice for
defamation of character, blasphemy, and indecency.[43] Several of the men
appeared to think it a most invincible assault on the gentiles, however, judging by their pleased smiles, and one little fellow who sat near me gave me a
poke in the ribs and said, "That's the way to give it on to 'em; nothink can
stand that. We'll drive 'em to — before we get through with 'em." As I did
not enter into any display of feeling over the matter, he eyed me closely, scanned
me from top to toe, then turned round and spoke to some men beside him,
and they in turn stared me full in the face.

When the services were over, the little fellow, who said he was a Yorkshire-
man, told me that . . . every word uttered among themselves was spread abroad
by the Salt Lake gentiles, and they were by this means creating a prejudice
against them all over the country.

"They tell a million lies a day of us," said he, with emphasis, "although
we are the best people in the world, and don't allow whisky-drinking or
immorality among us. We are the Lord's chosen people, and we will yet own
the whole world, and all your people will be our servants in the future life, if
any of you can get to heaven."

I thought this was the language of a fanatic, but when I learned that the
speaker had been a missionary to England for some years, and that the Prophet
had taught such doctrines, I ceased to wonder, and asked him in what portion of the Scriptures he found such statements. He replied that they had
been revealed to the Prophet, and that he had also been informed that Napoleon
I, General Grant, Queen Victoria, and the Emperor of Germany would be

---

[43] Many visitors commented on Brigham Young's profanity, and even members complained of his use
of "language so beastly and degraded." He admitted many found his vulgarity offensive, saying he had
"package after package of letters, yes, a wheelbarrow load of them," asking him "to be careful how you
speak." He was not repentant. Such complaints made him "feel just like rubbing their noses with them. If
I am not to have the privilege of speaking of Saint and sinner when I please," the prophet said, "tie up my
mouth and let me go to the grave, for my work would be done." Brigham Young, 6 Oct. 1855, *Journal of Dis-*
courses, 3:48–49. See also Ekins, ed., *Defending Zion*, 107–14.

his own servants if he wished to have them. He was getting interesting, so I asked him if he believed in polygamy, and he replied most positively that he did, as the highest purpose of man was to people the Lord's kingdom, and that men were only honoured and blessed according to the number of their wives and children. I asked him how many wives he had, and he replied "seven;" but the number of his children he could not state, as he had not counted them for two years. He had been a Mormon twenty-five years, and as he commenced with two wives he thought he might have nearly a score living. When I looked astonished at this statement, he said he was proud of his family; that he was not like a majority of the Americans, who looked upon children as a curse. He then quoted glibly the average number of children in the New England families, and proved to his own satisfaction that the descendants of the Puritans would soon be wiped off the face of the earth for their wickedness.

Mary Katherine Keemle [Kate] Field (1838–1896) was probably the best-known female journalist of her time. Broadly informed and strongly opinionated, she always reported matters in a humorous but provocative manner. Arriving in Salt Lake City in 1883 on her way to the Pacific Coast, she found life in Utah so interesting that she remained for several months. Mormon women, impressed with her independence, hoped their marital circumstance would earn from her a plea for national tolerance. They urged she be given a platform to instruct and entertain local audiences.[44] When Field's reports appeared in print, the sisters undoubtedly changed their views. As she stated in essays and lectures throughout the United States over the next few years, Mormon theocracy was a danger to the republic and more threatening than polygamy. But neither had she any love for the plural system. As this commentary shows, she felt only disgust for what she considered the supine acquiescence of church members to their leaders, whatever the subject. This passage comes from one of a series of articles Field wrote as a special correspondent for the *Boston Herald.*

"Kate Field in Utah," *Boston Herald,* 20 April 1884, 14/1–6.

Salt Lake City, U., April 8, 1884.
"Unless you've attended a Mormon conference, you can have little idea of the complete subjection of the people to their rulers," said a highly intelligent apostate to me some days ago. Twice in the year are the Saints convened for church purposes, on April 6 and Oct. 6. . . And so it came to pass that I have been a faithful attendant upon the spring conference of 1884. . .

[44] "Kate Field," *Woman's Exponent,* 12:11 (1 Nov. 1883), 84. For more on Field's career, including her anti-Mormon declamations, see Whiting, *Kate Field;* Moss, *Kate Field, Selected Letters;* and Arrington, *Kate Field and J. H. Beadle,* 1–11.

The first morning of the conference was not very well attended, and I had a choice of seats. I therefore endeavored to avoid the neighborhood of infants in arms. Impossible! Utah's best crop pervaded the tabernacle. Babies unseen were present to the ear, and I soon began to wonder which would be the more audible, the babies or the speakers. Mormon mothers are, as a rule, their own servants and nurses; consequently, if they go abroad, they must take their offspring

AND MAKE EVERYBODY

about them uncomfortable. It is hard for women to be deprived of their church and theatre going because of maternity, but which is more Christian: To seek pleasure at the expense of hundreds or thousands, or to sacrifice inclination to consideration for the feelings of others? . . .

[After President John Taylor opened the proceedings] . . . George Q. Cannon thanked the Lord in prayer for the beautiful weather, the mountains, the vales, the pure air . . . and for the peace which reigns among the Saints. Their congressional delegate was especially thankful for God's deliverances when he thought of all that is said and done by "enemies" and legislation to destroy the organization of the church. He asked for God's blessing upon his chosen people, especially upon the holy priesthood, and was followed by John Taylor, who played upon a harp of one string. The iteration and reiteration of Mormon harangues is a marvel to strangers. The phraseology and themes are so stereotyped that, after hearing a Saint once, I can give a very good guess as to what he will say the moment he rises to instruct the brethren. The venerable Taylor, despite his age, made himself heard over infant voices, and informed his people that they were "engaged in a great work." This statement has been ground into them for so many years as to have produced an egotism that has not its equal. Everything Mormon is superior to everything Gentile, because God rules here and Satan rules the rest of the world. President Taylor said this was "the dispensation of the fulness of times," and the Saints were indebted to the wisdom and guidance of God for the beginning and continuance of their work. . . After telling the Saints that their actions . . . would have a bearing upon nations, as well as individuals, in the future, "the mouthpiece of the Almighty" extended his arms toward the congregation and exclaimed with great energy: "God bless Israel! God bless those who love Israel! and may God's wrath and indignation be upon all enemies!" "Amen!" shouted Israel in chorus.

Apostle Teasdale's voice was frequently eclipsed by that of the pervading baby, but, unabashed, he declared that he belonged to the only true and progressive religious society on earth, and as proof of progress brought forth its alliance with Abraham. "Like Abraham of old we have obeyed the doctrines of the Lord, and we worship the true God, who has raised us up to edify him. He has restored the apostolic law; he has restored the priesthood, and given us the keys to eternal life, that we may work in his light and be prepared when he shall come." Reference to Abraham generally precedes the subject of polygamy, and very soon Apostle Teasdale touched upon marriage. There was monogamy and plural marriage, and he knew that there was more trouble in monogamous than in polygamic families. How did he know it? By the reports of the bishops' courts, where such cases are tried. Saints living in plural marriage live in love and happiness unanimously. Yes, Apostle Teasdale dared to make a statement, proof against which can be produced by every one who has investigated Mormonism. . .

At Sunday's conference, Zion was in gala dress. The sun still shone, and the streets bounding temple block were alive with country wagons. You'd have thought that an agricultural fair or circus had come to town. . .

THE WOMEN WERE

kind good-natured creatures, ignorant and unreasoning. Soon the first presidency, the apostles, the seventies and other high priests took their seats. . .

"Just look at them," said one woman. "How they can persecute such a set of men I don't know. All you've got to do is to gaze at them to know they are honest."

I gazed, and I did not see with that good soul's eyes. I noted more thick necks and sensual or cruel mouths than in any body of men I ever beheld elsewhere.

"When they're gone there will be plenty to fill their places," added an old woman with great satisfaction. "Was there ever a more eminent, noble man in the kingdom than President Taylor! . . ."

Looking down on that congregation, I understood why the church held its sway. There were thousands of human beings, ranging from infancy to extreme old age; there were bodies and no brains. All were clothed with bad taste, when there was an attempt at more than decent covering; all looked foreign, and not one pleasing face could I discern, apart from a few of the young Saints born in Zion. The vast majority were cattle on two legs—obedient, subservient cattle, not to be blamed for being themselves. They are the results of hundreds of years of European feudalism, and the United States government is called upon to solve the problem made possible by their ignorance!

Services opened with prayer by Joseph F. Smith, who invoked God's wrath and indignation on Zion's adversaries. He asked to be delivered from the machinations of the ungodly, to be kept out of the hands of "the enemy." . . .

"Don't Bro. Taylor look noble?" murmured a voice near me. . .

There followed an address from the "president" that was singularly barren of fire or ideas. . . The "president" talked about Elijah and Lucifer; about heroic measures to be used against the Saints, such as Cain used against Abel, and the devil used against the righteous. I heard again about the unconstitutionality of the laws, and how the world could not comprehend what the Saints are doing. . . I heard about obedience to the gospel, obedience to the laws of God. "It is him that has introduced this work!" said the ungrammatical revelator. . ." "No power can hurt us if we trust in God. All who believe in this, say Aye!"

As one man, those thousands shouted "Aye!"

"I bless you in the name of the holy priesthood. Amen!" were John Taylor's last words, and thus ended the 54th Mormon conference.

At the April conference of 1871, John Taylor . . . exclaimed: "They tell us that the government will send troops here to enforce the laws. Who the d— cares for their troops? As long as the United States lets us alone, we'll let them alone, but let them dare to lay so much as a finger on us, and we'll soon show them what we can do."

I ask thoughtful Americans to read this report, long as it is. It contains much food for reflection. I ask them to note the difference between John Taylor's language in 1871 and in 1884. He is the same man, but he realizes that 55,000,000 of people are beginning to listen to Mormon utterances. He reminds me of Falstaff. He is very bold when the enemy is out of sight. He will be the first to run away when the United States government "dares to lay its finger on him." He is so cowardly a Saint as not to live under the roof with even one of his many wives. A sister presides over the "Gardo house." And this is the man who, four years ago, after announcing that polygamy was divine, cried aloud: "I defy the United States; I will obey God!"

Fudge!   Kate Field

"AN OLIVER CROMWELL KIND OF MAN": CALL TO BATTLE

Novels, travel accounts, and lectures critical of Mormon plural marriage appeared with increasing frequency until an impatient government was forced to act. An example of the accumulating discontent, employing denigrating stereotypes, is William Proctor Hughey. Hughey resided in St. Louis and worked as a clerk for the Missouri Pacific Railway Company. He may have been related to temperance activist George Washington Hughey, a pastor of the Methodist Episcopal Church in St. Louis, but biographical information on Hughey is almost non-existent except for *Gould's St. Louis Directory* of 1885, which listed him as a resident. He traveled extensively in the West and wrote several letters to the president of the United States warning of dangers posed by the Saints.

Wm. Proctor Hughey to President Grover Cleveland,
5 April 1885, rg48, N.A.

Hon. Grover Cleveland President U.S.

Your Excellency—

The next war the United States will have will be with the Mormons. There is a disposition to ignore and pooh-pooh the matter which only proves a lamentable lack of information [and] general ignorance concerning it. During a five years residence on the Pacific Slope I made the people a study and my investigations satisfy me, that whenever the Government starts in with an honest square determination to stamp out polygamy, that war will commence. Heretofore and now permit me to say, no effort has been made to suppress it which the Mormons regarded as serious and earnest, and *unbuyable*. therefore no open war has resulted as yet. . .

The results of all efforts for its suppression have been to strengthen and diffuse Polygamy.—The various Commissions of superannuated Governors, senators and Judges have done little else than enjoy a junket at public cost to view the wonders of Nature in that wonderful region and sit down to banquets given them by the very men they were sent to investigate and punish.— These commissioners who went there without any well defined idea or notion about the evil they wished to eradicate—No man should be sent to Utah who has to make up his opinion after he gets there because the cunning of that people would inveigle and baffle the very elect. An Oliver Cromwell kind of man is the only one that will ever stamp out Mormon polygamy.

Whenever this government sets about this work in earnest then war will come, and it will not be done without war. Then our government will awake to the fact that it has a large job—which will require untold millions of money and an ocean of blood.—It will awake to the fact that thro apathy it has allowed a people to grow to powerful numbers right in the heart of our Western empire,—a peculiar people united in principles totally antagonistic and bitterly inimical to the spirit of our institutions, a people picked and recruited from the nations of the old world most noted for bigotry and obstinancy and whether openly belligerant or secretly opposing a stubborn foe to come. Among this people you can find more men whose eyebrows meet across the bridge of the nose and whose under lips protrude, than can be found any where else— comparatively.

The traditions they hold are as sacred to them as those of Israelites of old and they as firmly believe the martyrdom of their prophet Joe Smith is to be finally fearfully avenged upon this nation, as the Israelites did that they should return to the promised land. With such tenets held by such a race, argument is useless.—the only plan that will succeed is that which has been recommended to make "good Indians"—When that time comes those who seem to think the Mormons are all in Utah . . . will speedily find that every fertile valley in five of our western territories, embracing an empire half as large as Europe, has been silently and quietly colonized by these people and that a close fraternizing with all the wild Indians of the West has been sedulously accomplished. . . The very latest movement that has been allowed to be known is their treaty with the terrible unconquered and unconquerable Yaqui Indians of Mexico who have so successfully held their own for three hundred years against the Mexican power.[45] John Taylor and his coadjutators take a long look ahead, and see that thro' the land of the Yaqui they can reach the ocean and the time may come when such an outlet will be useful and profitable for the Saints.

SHAPING THE MORMON IMAGE

Just as Mormon sermons affected the Saints' own perception of polygamy and its promise, accounts by visitors, journalists, and fiction writers fed a growing hostility to the practice among outsiders. Increasingly, as decades passed, they described Mormons as on a degenerative path, their women as victims of servitude and emotional torture, and their leaders as religious counterfeits exploiting vapid belief.[46]

The examination of French, British, and American portrayals of Near Eastern culture in Edward Said's study of the evolution of "Orientalism" is relevant. Relying partly on fear and partly on the power of the exotic, such descriptions subordinated the similarities between the Levant and the West to evocations of the titillating and repulsive. In a similar way, non-Mormons increasingly expected the Saints to appear as travel books and novels described them, imposing on the Mormon a resemblance to the depraved Asiatic. To compare criticisms of Mormons with Western characterizations of people in the Near East and Asia is instructive not only because many described the

---

[45] Hughey was incorrect only in stating that a treaty was made between the two peoples. Beginning with Brigham Young and continuing for many years, Mormons seriously considered Yaqui lands in northern Mexico as a place of refuge for pluralists, but neither settlement on their lands nor a treaty with the tribe ever resulted. A full record of these attempts has yet to be written. For Mormon interest in and embassies to the tribe, see McClintock, *Mormon Settlement in Arizona*, 201–3; Brigham Young [Jr.], Journals, 16 Dec. 1884 ff., LDS Archives; Heber J. Grant Journal Books, vol. 7, 25 Nov. 1884 ff., LDS Archives; and the abortive efforts of Samuel Brannan in Bagley, ed., *Scoundrel's Tale: The Samuel Brannan Papers*, 367–77.

[46] Drawing on regional and gendered conceits, as Morin and Guelke have shown, public opinion cast Mormon women in the mold of exploited colonial inferiors. "Strategies of Representation, Relationship, and Resistance," 436–62.

Saints as non-Western, but because commentaries about the two groups followed a similar paradigm. Thoughtful discourse yielded to polemic, and that to arguments for assimilation.[47] The sympathetic Gunnisons, Burtons, Bowles, and Dixons gave way to the antagonistic Fields and Hugheys, and their exhortations led to the coercive excesses of the anti-polygamy crusade.

But before opposition to polygamy acquired irresistible energy, outsiders produced a surprising amount of keen observation in commentaries on Mormonism's peculiar institution. One scholar contends that the best of it actually pioneered the more objective, reportorial style associated with twentieth-century anthropology.[48] Anyone interested in Mormon polygamy, if they seek a fuller picture of its career, must return to the portraiture it evoked: the frank and insightful, the humorous and imaginative, the insolent and affronted. Alternately repelled and fascinated, these observers preserved for us the wonder of a race of modern Jacobs, with their Leahs and Rachels, multiplying for God in the American desert.

---

[47] Said, *Orientalism*, 96. Also see Daniel, *Islam and the West*.

[48] Eliason, "Curious Gentiles," 155–90.

This early cartoon from *Harper's Weekly*, 10 October 1857, shows that the stereotypic image of Mormon polygamous life emerged within a decade of the Mormon arrival in the Salt Lake Valley. The unidentified cartoonist probably never visited Utah. None of the figures resemble either Brigham Young or his wives, including the disapproving female farthest to the right.

Chapter 6

"THE JENTILES AR ON THE TRACK OF THE SAINTS"
A National Crusade Begins

Before the LDS church formally discontinued plural marriage, opposition to its practice fell into three periods. There were first the moral criticisms of the arrangement in Nauvoo that contributed to the prophet's death and the exodus of his followers to the Great Basin. After Mormon removal to the West, a new phase of anti-Mormon denunciations commenced and continued for thirty years. Though filled with bristling attacks on Mormon plurality, this, the longest stage of the contest, failed to suppress it.[1] The final struggle occurred in the decade of the 1880s, when the movement against polygamy acquired such strength that the Saints were compelled to put the practice away.

From the 1850s until well into the 1880s, Latter-day Saint defenses of the Principle made its presence more conspicuous than it otherwise would have been.[2] Neither did it help that, as with all socially variant groups, the Saints attracted non-Mormon eccentrics to their cause.[3] Mormons also invited suspicion by the secrecy with which they cloaked plural marriage ceremonies.

---

[1] There is an extensive body of work on federal concerns with the Mormons during this period, including polygamy. Most helpful are Dwyer, *Gentile Comes to Utah*; Hansen, *Quest for Empire*, 121–79; Poll, "Mormon Question Enters National Politics," 117–31; Lyman, *Political Deliverance*, 7–40; Bigler, *Forgotten Kingdom*, 281–339; and Gordon, *Mormon Question*, 1–145.

[2] As Richard Poll pointed out long ago, attacks on the Saints were largely proportional to the vigor with which they themselves carried the argument to the Gentiles, condemning monogamy while defending polygamy (see Chapter Two). Poll, "Mormon Question, 1850–1865," 25.

[3] Some defended Mormons by arguing that all Americans should be free enough to have "as many slaves as Abraham, and as many wives as Solomon." [Lea], *Bible View of Polygamy by Mizpah*, 1. Also see Ross and Colenso, *Dr. Ross and Bishop Colenso; or, The Truth Restored in Regard to Polygamy and Slavery . . .*; and Bitton's "George Francis Train and Brigham Young," 410–27.

And questions arose from the ease with which divorce occurred.[4] Whatever the justification, the vehemence displayed in attacking polygamy is startling.

Every argument ever raised against Mormon plural marriage can be found in speeches and essays of the first two decades after they arrived in the Rocky Mountains. At the base of every assault made on the institution was the same presumed error: its alleged immorality. Assertions that personal health would decline if monogamy were compromised, that plurality always brought with it a degradation of women, and that it invariably encouraged anti-republican tendencies were all explained as the results of sexual relationships inherently evil.[5] Its influence, it was said, coarsened men and women alike. One Victorian observer, illustrating the vulgarizing effect of polygamy, said he heard Mormon leaders use words like "legs," "bellies," and "nasty"—in mixed company![6] Most commentators were either indifferent to or ignorant of the restraints Mormon preachment imposed on sexual activity. Mormons were said to resemble Blacks and American Indians, not only because they were believed to intermarry with them, but from the deteriorating effects brought by sexual excess.[7] Unless resisted, the argument went, monogamy was imperiled and Mormon profligacy would spread like a wasting disease, robbing the nation of its strength.[8]

"PROMISCUOUS AS THE CATTLE IN THE FIELDS": ATTACKS COMMENCE

Less than half a decade elapsed after the Saints took refuge in the desert before charges began cascading upon them from the mouths and pens of federal

---

[4] Territorial governor George L. Woods commented that, among Mormons, divorce was easily procured "under the slightest pretense" and their marriage ceremonies were "said to be vulgar." Recollections of George L. Woods, in Biographical Sketches, Utah, cu-b, 63.

[5] Many believed that the American constitutional order and the nation's moral values shared a linked dependence on the Christian monogamous home. Mormonism's theocratic organization, it was argued, was bad enough. But when this was joined with patriarchal, polygamous marriage, the nation was doubly imperiled. "Mormons," Harper's, 257; and "Speech of Hon. J. S. Morrill," Appendix, 280, 285, 287–88.

[6] Mayhew, Religious, Social, and Political History, 424; and portrayals in "Celia Logan on Mormon Life—1," [New York] Daily Graphic, 28 Nov. 1873, 3:230, 181/1–5.

[7] So far as bracketing Mormons, Blacks, and Indians together as degenerate because of immoral behavior, one cannot improve upon Charles A. Cannon who, describing the popular judgment of that time, said: "the child of Mormon polygamy was simply a white Negro." Cannon, "Awesome Power of Sex," 79. Also see the portraits of Mormon "half-breeds" in Ward, Male Life Among the Mormons, 49, 88–98, 167–68; and the description of Mormons baptizing and raising blacks to apostleship, then sending them forth "in squads to capture squaws" in Mormoniad, 17–18, 41–42. For national concern during these same decades over polygynous and other sexual practices among non-Mormon Blacks and American Indians, see Cott, Public Vows, 25–26, 88–92, 120–23.

[8] Thompson, Mormonism, 8; and the anonymous Opinions Concerning the Bible Law of Marriage, 229. On the assumed superiority of monogamy, see Cott, Public Vows, 9–23.

appointees. When the government of the United States formally extended its authority to the territory of Utah, they named both Mormons and non-Mormons as territorial officials.[9] Most conspicuous among the former was Governor Brigham Young. Non-Mormon officers, unfortunately, were often men of questionable ability, sometimes amounting to no more than political "hacks."[10] Among the latter were Sec. of State Broughton D. Harris, chief justice of the territorial supreme court Lemuel G. Brandebury, and associate justice of the court Perry E. Brocchus. After arriving in Utah, these men soon were embroiled in conflict with church leaders over a variety of matters. Fearing for their safety, they fled the territory and ever after were referred to as the "runaway officials." The "runaways" of 1851 were but the first of several government men who quarreled with the Mormons and accused them of immoral conduct. Whatever their merits, non-Mormon judges and administrators made allegations that in time aroused a nation.[11]

In an 1851 document, Harris, Brandebury, and Brocchus stated that, in addition to their theocratic government, the Saints were seditionist, obscene, and polygamous. Even before their report was published in the nation's capital, accounts of its content appeared in eastern papers.[12] More directly, Perry Brocchus stated what he saw as the fearful consequences of Mormon marital habits in a public letter to Sec. of State Daniel Webster.

> There is every reason to believe that, when their importations of women from foreign lands shall have ceased, or shall have so greatly subsided as to fail to answer their demands, they will, in pursuance of their system of polygamy, take to their harems Indian squaws from the adjacent regions. The fanatical and seditious Mormon crossed on the wild and hostile Indian will make a terrible race of people who, growing up with feelings of imbittered hostility

---

[9] Utah's territorial government was formally organized under federal authority in "Act to Establish a Territorial Government for Utah," U.S., *Statutes at Large*, 9:51, 9 Sept. 1850, 453–58. For an account of the origins of Utah's territorial government, see all of Morgan, *State of Deseret*.

[10] See Poll, "Mormon Question, 1850–1865," 14–21; and Furniss, *Mormon Conflict*, 21–44.

[11] The initial conflict is described in Tullidge, *History of Salt Lake City*, 85–97; Barrett, "John W. Bernhisel," 94–103, 123; and Bigler, *Forgotten Kingdom*, 56–61. For subsequent problems involving Judges W. W. Drummond and George P. Stiles, see Drummond to Attorney General Jeremiah Black in "Resignation of Judge Drummond," 30 Mar. 1857, Utah Expedition, House Exec. Doc. 71 (35-1), 26 Feb. 1858, Serial 955, 212–14; and Stenhouse, *Rocky Mountain Saints*, 281–91. An important issue attending the conflict involved Mormon attempts to minimize the influence of common law. See "An Act Containing Provisions Applicable to the Laws of the Territory of Utah," 14 Jan. 1854, *Acts and Resolutions . . .* , 16, sec. 1; and Homer, "The Judiciary and the Common Law in Utah Territory," 97–108.

[12] The House report, dated 19 Dec. 1851, can be read in *Cong. Globe* (32-1), 9 Jan. 1852, Appendix, 84–93. For journalistic attention to the matter, see "Highly Important and Extraordinary Development of Mormonism," *New York Herald*, 5 Jan. 1852, 17:4 [2/4–5]; and "Territory of Utah," *New York Tribune*, 6 Jan. 1852, 11:3, 344, 6/1–4.

to the Government and people of the United States, will so pervade and infest those remote mountains and valleys, as to entirely exclude therefrom all other settlers, and to render emigration across the continent, from the western portion of our country, utterly impracticable, without the protection of a large and expensive military escort.[13]

Benjamin Ferris, another federal officer who went to Utah after departure of the "runaways," wrote a book-length account of the Mormons, including a scathing description of their home life. Ferris's writings contributed to a growing impression that Mormon polygamy threatened all Americans.

Benjamin G. Ferris, *Utah and the Mormons* (1854), 247–56, 258–61.

No nation of ancient or modern times, in which polygamy has existed as a part of its political or religious institutions, has exhibited a permanent degree of vigor or prosperity. It did not prevail, except in one or two extraordinary instances, among the Greeks, nor at all among the Romans until, for a period, during the corruptions of the Empire. The modern nations of Europe are free from this scourge. It belongs now to the indolent and opium-eating Turks and Asiatics, the miserable Africans, the North American savages, and the Latter-day Saints. It is the offspring of lust, and its legitimate results are soon manifest in the rapid degeneracy of races. . .

. . . About one fourth of the adult male population [among the Mormons] are polygamists, varying in the number of their wives from two up to fifty. . . Larger numbers would undoubtedly enter into it but for the scarcity of women and the want of means to support them. The census of 1851 disclosed the fact that there were 698 more males than females in the Territory. Subsequent emigrations have not probably much changed this proportion. For each man to have two wives would require twice as many females as males. Of course it follows that, where the chief bashaws have from ten to fifty in their harems, large numbers can not have even one.

The effect upon population is decidedly deleterious. The prophet Joseph had over forty wives at Nauvoo, and the rest of the priesthood had various numbers, corresponding to their standing and inclinations; and nearly all the children of these polygamous marriages died at that place; indeed, it is alleged by Mormons that not one was taken to Utah. Brigham Young has thirty children, of whom eight are by his first and second lawful wives; the remaining twenty-two are by his spirituals. He has about fifty wives, some of whom were widows of Joseph Smith, and are probably past the time of having children; but, supposing him to have thirty who are capable of having issue—which is

---

[13] Judge Perry Brocchus to Hon. Daniel Webster, 30 April 1852, *Letter of Judge Brocchus*, 26.

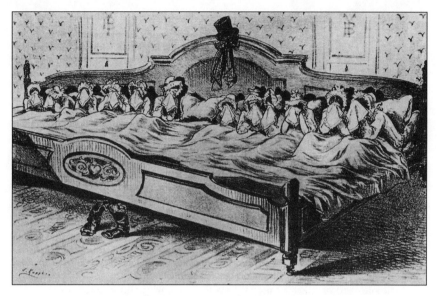

"In Memorium Brigham Young.
'And the Place Which Knew Him Once Shall Know Him No More.'"
Puck, 5 September 1877. Marking the recent death of Brigham Young,
readers were invited to imagine the sorrows of his bedroom.

below the true number—the twenty-two children would be less than one child
to a concubine. If each of these degraded females could have been the honored wife of one husband, the aggregate number of children, according to
the usual average of four in a family, would be one hundred and twenty, showing a loss in population of ninety-eight. . .

The argument . . . most relied on in support of the system is, that it tends
to good morals, by taking away the inducements to unlawful pleasures; that,
inasmuch as a man has as many wives as he pleases, he has no temptation to
wander in forbidden paths. They even go so far as to claim that it is the only
system of domestic polity by which purity can be preserved. In following out
this idea, they are industrious in gathering up and publishing in the Deseret
News the numerous cases of seduction, adultery, and elopement occurring
in the States, which find their way into the public prints, and are fond of contrasting the purity of morals in Utah in this respect with these irregularities,
and with the tolerated houses of ill fame in the great cities of the Old and
New World. . .

Their system of plurality has obliterated nearly all sense of decency, and would seem to be fast leading to an intercourse open and promiscuous as the cattle in the fields. A man living in common with a dozen dirty Arabs, whether he calls them wives or concubines, can not have a very nice sense of propriety. It is difficult to give a true account of the effects which have resulted from this cause, and, at the same time, preserve decency of language. . . The Saints are progressive. Three in one bed sleep warmer than two, when wood is scarce and a kingdom is to be built up. . . There are a number of cases in which a man has taken a widow and her daughter for wives at the same time. One has a widow and her two daughters. There are also instances of the niece being sealed to the uncle, and they excite no more attention than any ordinary case. How far the plague-spot is to spread in this direction remains to be seen. . .

. . . In a conversation with one of the missionaries (and withal, a man of more than ordinary shrewdness), I asked him what the effect of the system was upon the domestic relations. "Why," said he, "you must be aware that human nature among the first wives is opposed to it. When a man's wife gets a little old, and he takes a fancy to a young one, why, you know, the old one will feel jealous that she is to give way to the other; but it is the order of the Church, and she must submit to it." This was accompanied with a sly leer, such as would have done credit to a satyr.

Apostates' shafts have the capacity to more seriously wound because they can be so credibly placed. John Hyde Jr. (1833–1876) was born in England and baptized into the church at age 15. While serving as a missionary in the Channel Islands under Apostle John Taylor, Hyde had problems arising from misbehavior toward the opposite sex. Rumor of the doctrine of plural marriage led to improprieties by several men. "All of us," Hyde told Curtis E. Bolton, "have been pretty evenly splashed with the same mud."[14] Subsequently Hyde emigrated, crossed the plains, married, and worked as a schoolteacher in Salt Lake City until the mid-1850s. While on a mission to Hawaii, he became convinced that Mormonism was but religious folly. After lecturing on the subject in both California and the eastern states, he was excommunicated. He then published the book from which the comments below are taken.[15]

---

[14] John Hyde Jr. to Curtis E. Bolton, 24 Sept. 1852, recorded in the journal of James H. Hart and published in Hart, "John Hyde, Jr.," 310.

[15] For the excommunication of Hyde, see Heber C. Kimball, 11 Jan. 1857, *Journal of Discourses*, 4:165. Hyde was useful to others. Jules Remy, though convinced that Hyde was excessive in his criticism, borrowed liberally from him. Remy, *Journey to Great-Salt-Lake City*, 2:135. And for the legal consequences that followed Hyde's English petition for a divorce from his Utah wife, see Cannon II, "Strange Encounter," 73–83.

John Hyde, Jun., *Mormonism: Its Leaders and Designs*
(1857), 51–57, 62.

The Mormon polygamist has no HOME. Some have their wives lotted off by pairs in small disconnected houses, like a row of out-houses. Some have long low houses, and on taking a new wife build a new room on to them, so that their rooms look like rows of stalls in a cow-barn! Some have but one house and crowd them all together, outraging all decency, and not leaving even an affectation of convenience. Many often remain thus, until some petty strife about division of labor, children's quarrels, difference of taste, or jealousy of attention kindles a flame, only to be smothered by separation...

The Mormon polygamist ... has to maintain a constant guard over himself. Any husband might feel to kiss his wife gladly: to go round a table and kiss half a dozen, is no joke. It is so in every thing with him. With a dozen eyes to notice at what time he retires to rest, or arises on any one occasion, and half a dozen mouths to talk about it, he must be perfectly governed by rule. Every look, every word, every action has to be weighed, or else there is jealousy, vituperation, quarreling, bitterness... Warmth of feelings, tenderness of attachment, devotedness of attention to a woman, is there called, by that worst of Mormon epithets, "Gentilish." "Man must value his wife no more than any thing else he has got committed to him, and be ready to give her up at any time the Lord calls him," said Brigham one Sunday afternoon; and J. M. Grant followed the remark by saying, "If God, through his prophet, wants to give my women to any more worthy man than I am, there they are on the altar of sacrifice; he can have them, and do what he pleases with them!" ...[16]

They quote the animals as an argument in favor of polygamy, and adopt their instincts as models for practice. Marriage is stripped of every sentiment that makes it holy, innocent, and pure. With them it is nothing more than the means of obtaining families; and children are only desired as a means of increasing glory in the next world; for they believe that every man will reign over his children, who will constitute his "kingdom;" and, therefore, the more children, the more glory! ...

The utmost latitude of choice is permitted to the faithful, in their selection of wives. It is very common for one man to marry two sisters; Brigham advises, indeed, that they both be married on the same day, "for that will prevent any quarreling about who is first or second!" ... A Curtis E. Bolton is married to a woman and her daughter. A Captain Brown is married to a woman and two daughters and lives with them all. When their children's children are born it will be bewildering to trace out their exact degrees of relationship.

---

[16] While Hyde takes liberty with their sequence and language, he reports their remarks correctly: "Discourse By Jedediah M. Grant," 19 Feb. 1854, *Des. News* [Weekly], 8 June 1854, 4:15 [1/6]; and "Discourse By President Brigham Young," 15 June 1856, ibid., 16 July 1856, 6:19, 146/4, 147/1.

This may appear disgusting enough, and prove degradation enough. A G. D. Watt has excelled either of them. He brought from Scotland his half sister to Salt Lake City: took her to Brigham, and wished to be married to her for his second wife. Brigham objected, but Watt urged that Abraham took his half sister and "reckoned he had just as much right as Abraham." The point was knotty and difficult. If Abraham's example justified polygamy then it must equally justify this action. "God blessed Abraham although he did it," say the Mormons, "and ought to bless me if I do it too." The girl happened to be good-looking, though, and so, to cut this knot he could not untie, Brigham took her himself. So far so well. But she was not contented, or Brigham had reconsidered the matter, or from some cause, after a few weeks he told Watt that, after all, there was force in his argument, that it was just as lawful in him as in Abraham, and, accordingly, G. D. Watt accepted his half sister to wife from the arms of Brother Brigham! . . .[17]

. . . It is pretended that the consent of the first wife is obtained to such subsequent marriages. That consent is asked by the husband, and who knows not the thousand petty tyrannies that a husband can use toward his wife to extort or compel acquiescence? If the consent be given, she is willing to contribute to his glory, and the ceremony is performed. If she do not consent, women must not be an impediment either in doing one's duty, or obtaining one's salvation; so, therefore, the ceremony is performed just the same, whether she consent or no, whether she like the girl or no; for her husband to will it, is for the Lord to will it, and nothing is left to her but to bend and groan.

"This Creeping Leprosy": Polygamy and Public Lands

How the United States would dispose of its vast public domain led to recurring controversies throughout the nineteenth century. While debating the preemption and surveying of such lands in the early 1850s, a proviso was offered in Congress that forbade giving certificates of ownership to claimants having plural wives.[18] As Rep. Hiram Walbridge put it: "when we come to donate the fairest portion of this hemisphere, without money and without price, we have the right to prescribe the condition that no immoral and vicious prin-

---

[17] For a review of the Bolton, Watt, and other cases, see Embry, "Ultimate Taboos," 93–113.

[18] President Franklin Pierce's request that Congress extend benefits of the nation's land laws to New Mexico and Utah territories, "with such modifications as their peculiarities may require," is in Pierce's First Annual Message of 5 Dec. 1853, *Comp.*, 6:2749. On the question generally, see Gates, *History of Public Land Law.*

ciple of social order shall be introduced."[19] When asked if the amendment denying such lands to pluralists would disadvantage Utah's citizenry, territorial delegate John M. Bernhisel's answer elicited a mirthful response: "I will state that the proviso will work injury to a very considerable number of the inhabitants of the Territory of Utah. The more wives a man has, the more farms he needs to support them. [Laughter.]"[20]

Rep. Caleb Lyon of New York felt little humor when it came to Mormon polygamy. His colleagues enthusiastically received his address supporting such a restriction in federal land law, a sentiment accounting for Utah's exclusion from full enjoyment of federal land policies until 1869.[21]

CALEB LYON, *CONG. GLOBE* (33-1), 4 MAY 1854, 1100–1.

Mr. LYON. Mr. Chairman, this Territorial bill proposes to give, upon certain conditions, one hundred and sixty acres of land to every single man, and three hundred and twenty to every married man, *"provided further, that the benefits of this act shall not extend to any person who shall now, or at any time hereafter, be the husband of more than one wife."* Against the striking out of this proviso I most earnestly protest. . . I would appeal to the hearty patriotism of every member present, educated, as they have been, in the principles of the Pilgrim fathers, Cavaliers, and the Huguenots—the descendants of men who fled from profligate, libidinous, and licentious courts to enjoy a virtuous quiet in the unbroken wilderness of the West—if they are willing to see this Government disgrace itself by express or implied legislation, in any way sanctioning the practice of polygamy in this country. Its enormity as a crime has been made the subject of stringent statutes in every State in the Confederacy.[22] Is a premium to be paid, in fertile lands, for the debauching of our daughters and the deluding of our wives? Is this Congress so weak as basely to stoop to such a purpose, reversing all the cherished associations and instructions of our childhood? Is this black cancer sore, this creeping leprosy, to be encouraged?

When the people of Utah are placed on the same basis as the people of other Territories, is not that sufficient, is not that enough? Strike out the clause, and what will be its actual consequences? Individuals will go there whose senses are stronger than their sentiments, whose passions override their principles, and avail themselves of Government bounty, and, like Persians, Hindoos,

---

[19] *Cong. Globe* (33-1), 4 May 1854, Appendix, 593.

[20] Ibid. (33-1), 4 May 1854, 1092. For more on Bernhisel and the public-lands debate, see Barrett, "John M. Bernhisel," 126–28.

[21] Larson, "Land Contest in Early Utah," 309–25; and Wahlquist, "A Review of Mormon Settlement Literature," 4–21.

[22] Lyon's use of the term "Confederacy" does not refer to the Southern Confederacy of the Civil War. Prior to that crisis, the term was widely used to refer to the federal union.

and Musselmen, fill their houses with the blooming beauties of the North, and the witching women of the South, provided they have wealth or personal attractions to induce such a painful and horrid sacrifice . . . when polygamy is tacitly *respectableized* by an American Congress, it may not be so difficult to fill with sisters and daughters—those whom God destined for a nobler domestic sphere—an American Harem, a Mormon Seraglio.[23]

Let us look for a moment to those countries where polygamy exists—to the feeble and dismembered empire of the Sultan, at present under the protectorate of England and France. Women, according to the Koran, have no immortal souls;[24] women are sold as slaves; women are protected by high walls, guarded by eunuchs, the creatures of appetite, ministering to the most inflammable passions of our nature. The bitter unhappiness of Harem life is little understood—its degradation of woman, its brutalization of man. The innocent young creatures who seek Constantinople, and other cities of the Orient, look upon it as destiny; and bear their lot, prisoned by marble walls, amid the splendid misery of hanging gardens, sparkling fountains, radiant flowers, breathing perfumes, with sad and breaking hearts. And, sir, do you think things are different among the "Latter-Day Saints" in the Mormondom of Utah? No, sir; just as bad. Amid the jealousies of a plurality of wives the respect of parental authority is lost, the gentleness of fireside instruction and hearthstone memories is destroyed. Crime of the most revolting character ensues; infanticide follows as a matter of course as soon as the husband finds he is getting more children than he can support. Sir, human nature is just the same in every land. Do you think Abdul Medjid,[25] with three hundred and seventy wives, has been the father of only five children? It is impossible. [Applause and laughter.] The bodies of dead infants float on the sapphire tide of the Bosphorus, and the Light of many a harem, from the destruction of her offspring, has been lost among the dark shadows of the cypress of Scutari.[26] There is not a drug shop in an Oriental city but sell the means of destroying the new-born. And, being warned of these things, let us not fix this plaguespot upon the route to the golden gate of the Pacific, the western pathway of empire. Posterity, sir, will anathematize this kind of legislation to the latest years of the Republic. We all shall die, crumble to dust, our names be lost in

---

[23] During the debate Alexander Stephens of Georgia opposed federal discrimination against Mormon polygamy on grounds that the U.S. Constitution protected it. Rep. Gerritt Smith, an abolitionist and enemy of Mormon plurality, taunted the southerner by asking if his tolerance was so broad as to permit Black men to marry all the women they wanted, thereby reducing the number available to whites. *Cong. Globe* (33-1), 4 May 1854, Appendix, 1094.

[24] It is difficult to know where Representative Lyon derived this idea. Not only did Mormons never contend that women were without souls, but Islamic belief holds that men and women were alike created from the same source and partake of the same nature. See *Quran* 4.1; and 21.91, respectively.

[25] Abdülmecid I (1823–1861), an Ottoman sultan.

[26] This is Üsküdar, the ancient Chrysopolis, a suburb of Istanbul.

oblivion, but the principle we establish by implication, as the ghost of Hamlet's father, will evidence against us when we have passed away. Let us meet this subject, discourage it, condemn it, reject it. And, sir, it will be an honorable precedent, *not for a day, but for all time*. . .

One idea further, in continuation. Point me to a nation where polygamy is practiced, and I will point you to heathens and barbarians. It seriously affects the prosperity of States, it retards civilization, it uproots Christianity.[27] The Ottomans or Turks are the best specimens of this system; and although they import, and have for centuries, the most beautiful women from the mountains of Georgia and of the valleys of Circassia, those free and brainful countries, Tarta maidens from beyond the Caspian, and the Arabian girls from Yemen, yet, effeminacy and weakness, lack of intellectual strength, bodily energy, national decay, is its sad, unfailing result, while the Greeks, the Jews, and the Armenians have increased in numbers and enterprise under the iron heel of their merciless oppressors. . .

It has been doubted by gentlemen whether this clause is constitutional; yet, with the following words in relation to the powers of Congress, tender must be their scruples if they doubt it. Section third of the Constitution of the United States reads as follows:

"Congress shall have power to dispose of, and make all needful *rules* and *regulations* respecting, the Territories."

This is one of the necessary *regulations*—one of the wholesome *rules*. We are told by the Delegate from Utah [MR. BERNHISEL] that it is an "ecclesiastical establishment," a religious law, and over such many strict constitutional constructionists believe we have no control. The Thugs or stranglers of men, the Phansegars, the Buddhists, who worship Juggernaut, the Seftis, who perform every year human sacrifices, all have a right to practice their abominations under the territorial government of the United States, if once settled here.[28] They all have an equal claim to their "religious establishment," no matter how demoralizing or inhuman, over which it is said Congress has no right to interfere or control; but that we have power to prevent giving a bounty for its encouragement, I think I have fairly shown. If the many-wifed demoralizers get outnumbered by the virtuous single-wifed, a wise State government may yet be formed that will do honor and credit to the Union. Let us nip this evil in the bud, for the sake of morality, religion, and Christianity. . .

[27] The charge that Mormon polygamy was destructive to both Christianity and the American political system was heard again and again. Rep. Hiram Walbridge, for example, said: "Licentiousness has ever been the precursor of political enslavement." *Cong. Globe* (33-1), 4 May 1854, Appendix, 593. And Rep. John A. McClernand of Illinois later said polygamous family life was "a scarlet whore," a "reproach to . . . Christian civilization," and "an adjunct to political despotism." *Cong. Globe* (36-1), 3 Apr. 1860, 1514.

[28] Phansigar (not phansegar) refers to Hindoo thugs. Where Lyon says "Seftis," he undoubtedly refers to the Sufi.

Sir, this is a

> "Monster of so frightful mien
> As, to be hated, needs but to be seen;
> Yet, seen too oft, familiar with her face,
> We first endure, then *pity*, THEN EMBRACE."

By the blessed memory of those virtuous spirits who battled for LIBERTY not LICENTIOUSNESS it should be blotted out, as a stigma, a dishonor, a disgrace, from existence on the soil of NORTH AMERICA. [Sensation, and cries of "Good!" "Good!" "Well done!"]

"APPLY THE KNIFE":
POLYGAMY AND POPULAR SOVEREIGNTY

Quarrels over popular sovereignty also implicated the Saints. The freedom of local populations to introduce ownership of slaves among themselves logically required that the same license be extended to those eager for plural wifery.[29] Mormons openly argued that the democratic principle inherent in contentions for local control entitled them to practice both slavery and polygamy if they chose to do so.[30] For abolitionists and Republicans, however, compromises such as the Omnibus Bill of 1850 and the Kansas-Nebraska Act were betrayals of high principle.[31] To countenance either polygamy or slavery anywhere in the republic, said Hiram Walbridge, was to invite the wrath of God as when "He visited with fire and vengeance the cities of the plain."[32] Carrying their convictions into the 1856 presidential campaign, at a Republican Party parade in Indianapolis reputed to be the largest gathering ever held west of the Ohio River, someone representing Brigham Young, surrounded by six wives of black, white, and spotted complexions, waved a banner declaring: "Hurrah for the Kansas-Nebraska bill—it introduces Polygamy and Slavery."[33]

---

[29] See, for example, the comments of Sen. William Henry Seward in "The Presidential Contest," *New York Times*, 23 Oct. 1856, 6:1590, 2/3. On the relationship between Senator Douglas, primary advocate of the idea of "squatter sovereignty," Mormon polygamy, and politics in the early 1850s, see Poll, "Mormon Question, 1850–1865," 34–38; and the observations of Beveridge, *Abraham Lincoln*, 3:236–37.

[30] "Higher Law vs. Constitutional," *Mormon*, 1:39 (17 Nov.1855) [2/1].

[31] *Cong. Globe* (34-1), 28 June 1856, 681. Using the argument employed by Charles Sumner, Rep. Justin Morrill said slavery and polygamy must submit to the "higher laws" of heaven. Morrill, in ibid.; and Sumner's speech on repeal of the Fugitive Slave Act on 26 Aug. 1852, in *Charles Sumner: His Complete Works*, 3:361–66.

[32] *Cong. Globe* (33-1), 4 May 1854, Appendix, 593.

[33] "Immense Meeting in Indianapolis," *New York Times*, 21 July 1856, 5:1509, 2/2–3. For Mormon support of the Kansas-Nebraska legislation, allowing them to "settle the slave, and other vexed questions" locally, see "The Nebraska-Kansas Bill," *Des. News* [Weekly], 24 Aug. 1854, 4:24 [2/5].

Sen. Stephen Arnold Douglas (1813–1861), the best-remembered advocate of "popular sovereignty," sometimes acted as a friend to the Mormons, both during their residence in Nauvoo and after their arrival in the Great Basin. The Saints had good reason, therefore, to expect his continued support.[34] As criticism of the Mormons increased in the 1850s, Douglas, like others in the Democratic Party, found himself caught between the freedom his views granted to local peoples and the unpopularity of regional practices such as polygamy. Already criticized for permissiveness toward slavery, President Buchanan and Democrats such as Douglas hoped a strong stand on Mormonism would redeem their political image. It was within this context that Senator Douglas addressed the matter, along with other subjects, in a speech given in Springfield, Illinois, in 1857. It is significant that Abraham Lincoln was in the audience when Douglas made his remarks and, in replying to them two weeks later, agreed with what the "Little Giant" said about the Mormons, only emphasizing the inconsistency of Douglas's philosophy of "popular sovereignty" with his willingness to authorize federal intervention in Utah.[35]

"REMARKS OF HON. STEPHEN A. DOUGLAS,
DELIVERED IN THE STATE HOUSE AT SPRINGFIELD, ILLINOIS,
ON THE 12TH JUNE, 1857," DAILY MISSOURI REPUBLICAN
35:142, 18 JUNE 1857 [2/3–6].

When the authentic evidence shall arrive, if it shall establish the facts that are believed to exist, it will become the duty of Congress to apply the knife and cut out this loathsome, disgusting ulcer. [Applause.] No temporizing policy— no half-way measures will then answer. It has been supposed by those who have not thought deeply upon the subject that an act of Congress prohibiting murder, robbery, polygamy and other crimes, with appropriate penalties for those offenses, would afford adequate remedies for all the enormities complained of. Suppose such a law to be on the statute book, and I believe they have a criminal code, providing the usual punishment for the entire catalogue of crimes, according to the usages of all civilized and Christian countries, with the exception of polygamy, which is practised under the sanction of the Mormon church, but is neither prohibited nor authorized by the laws of the Territory.

---

[34] A good, if dated, account of the relationship between Douglas and the Mormons in Illinois is available in Johnson, Stephen A. Douglas, 57–61. A more critical study that described Douglas's policies toward the Mormons as politically opportunistic, both early and late, is Willis, Stephen A. Douglas, 53–69.

[35] Johnson, Stephen A. Douglas, 567–68, 573–74. Mormons themselves judged Douglas severely. Heber C. Kimball in a tabernacle sermon referred to him as "that little nasty snot-nose." Kimball, 8 Nov. 1857, Journal of Discourses, 6:38. His reputation among the Saints gained little in succeeding decades, earning from some nothing less than the condign punishment of God. See Roberts, Comprehensive History, 2:187.

Suppose, I repeat, that Congress should pass a law prescribing a criminal code, and punishing polygamy among other offenses, what effect would it have—what good would it do? Would you call on twenty-three grand jury-men, with twenty-three wives each, to find a bill of indictment against a poor miserable wretch for having two wives? [Cheers and laughter.] Would you rely upon twelve petit jurors, with twelve wives each, to convict the same loath-some wretch for having two wives? [Continued applause.] Would you expect a grand jury composed of twenty-three "Danites," to find a bill of indict-ment against a brother "Danite" for having murdered a Gentile, as they call all American citizens under their direction? . . . No. If there is any truth in the reports we receive from Utah, Congress may pass what laws it chooses; but you can never rely upon the local tribunals and juries to punish crimes commited by Mormons in that Territory. Some other and more effectual rem-edy must be devised and applied. In my opinion, the first step should be the absolute and unconditional repeal of the organic act—blotting the territori-al government out of existence—upon the ground that they are alien ene-mies and outlaws, denying their allegiance and defying the authority of the United States. [Immense applause.]

The territorial government once abolished, the country would revert to its primitive condition prior to the act of 1850, "under the sole and exclusive jurisdiction of the United States," and should be placed under the operation of the act of Congress of the 30th of April, 1790 . . . "providing for the pun-ishment of crimes against the United States within any fort, arsenal, dock-yard, magazine, or ANY OTHER PLACE OR DISTRICT OF COUNTRY, UNDER THE SOLE AND EXCLUSIVE *jurisdiction of the United States.*"[36] All offenses against the provisions of these acts are required by law to be tried and punished by the United States courts in the States or Territories where the offenders shall be "FIRST APPREHENDED OR BROUGHT FOR TRIAL." Thus it will be seen that under the plan proposed Brigham Young and his confederates could be "appre-hended and brought for trial" to Iowa or Missouri, California or Oregon, or to any other adjacent State or Territory, where a fair trial could be had, and justice administered impartially—where the witnesses could be protected and the judgment of the court could be carried into execution, without violence or intimidation. I do not propose to introduce any new principles into our jurisprudence, nor to change the modes of proceeding or the rules of prac-tice in our courts. I only propose to place the . . . Territory of Utah under the operation of the same laws and rules of proceeding, that Kansas, Nebras-ka, Minnesota and our other territories were placed before they became organ-ized Territories. . .

I have thus presented plainly and frankly my views of the Utah question—

---

[36] Douglas refers to "An Act for the Punishment of Certain Crimes against the United States," U.S., *Statutes at Large*, 1:9, 30 April 1790, 112.

the evils and the remedy—upon the facts as they have reached us, and are supposed to be substantially correct. If official reports and authentic information shall change or modify these facts, I shall be ready to conform my action to the real facts as they shall be found to exist. I have no such pride of opinion as will induce me to persevere in an error one moment after my judgment is convinced. If, therefore, a better plan can be devised—one more consistent with justice and sound policy, or more effective as a remedy for acknowledged evils, I shall take great pleasure in adopting it, in lieu of the one I have presented to you to-nite. . .

[The speaker closed amid immense applause and three hearty cheers were given for DOUGLAS, and repeated.]

"To Punish and Prevent the Practice of Polygamy": The Federal Government Acts

After raising the issue of plural marriage in connection with public lands and slavery, congressmen followed with proposed legislation to punish Mormonism's alleged wickedness.[37] Anti-polygamous sentiment acquired such importance with Republicans that they joined its destruction with the crusade against slavery in their first national platform of 1856:

> *Resolved:* That the Constitution confers upon Congress sovereign powers over the Territories of the United States for their government; and that in the exercise of this power, it is both the right and the imperative duty of Congress to prohibit in the Territories those twin relics of barbarism—Polygamy, and Slavery.[38]

During the campaign to elect John C. Frémont to the presidency, Republicans spoke often on the paired, immoral nature of the "relics": one politician warning that slavery and polygamy introduced into American life "the Turkish slave bazaar, and the Turkish harem," inviting them to "live in love together under the sanction of our laws."[39]

Following the debates closely, the Saints found condemnation of their marriage practices hypocritical and unconnected to land policy or any other proper concern of government. They said Congress ought not to busy itself with

---

[37] See Ohio representative Edward Ball's speeches in *Cong. Globe* (34-1), 14 April 1856, 895; and Vermont representative Justin Morrill in ibid. (34-1), 26 June 1856, 1491, 1501.

[38] "Republican Platform of 1856," Johnson and Porter, *National Party Platforms, 1840–1972,* 27. For the origin of the "twin relics" phrase, see Wills, " 'Twin Relics of Barbarism,'" 40–44.

[39] Rep. John U. Pettit of Indiana, in *Cong. Globe* (34-1), 2 Aug. 1856, Appendix, 1283.

Justin Smith Morrill (1810–1898), influential
United States senator from Vermont, in 1862
authored the first federal law passed by Congress prohibiting polygamy in the territories.
Considered liberal in other regards, Morrill did
all her could to rid the nation of what he and
fellow Republicans called a "relic of barbarism."
Courtesy of Vermont Historical Society.

their marital philosophy any more than with what a man ate for breakfast.[40]
Moreover, Brigham Young declared, if Congress sought to incarcerate all who
were polygamists they would need to roof over a space extending from the
Rocky Mountains to the Sierras of California.[41] Indifferent to Mormon objections, congressional committees on the territories and the judiciary, the two
forums in which polygamy was most debated, moved ahead with the matter.

Though Republicans lost their presidential bid to Democrats in 1856, and
problems in Kansas swamped federal lawmakers, both public prints and politicians would not let go the issue of Mormonism. Democrats, anxious to shift
the nation's attention away from slavery, seized on the Mormon question as

---

[40] This language was borrowed from an article in *Nichol's Journal*, a New York City periodical, and reprinted as "Polygamy in Utah," *Des. News* [Weekly], 5 Oct. 1854, 4:30 [2/4–5]. Also see "Discourse of Elder
Orson Pratt," 7 Oct. 1874, ibid., 6 Jan. 1875, 23:49, 773/5. This was, of course, at odds with earlier insistence by Parley P. Pratt, George Q. Cannon, and others that family structure and morality were and ought
to be of preeminent concern to government. Mormon responses to federal efforts to suppress polygamy
were identical to those made by advocates of free love. E. H. Heywood, for example, asked: "Why should
priests and magistrates supervise the sexual organs of citizens any more than the brain and stomach?" Heywood, *Cupid's Yokes*, 21.

[41] Brigham Young, 31 Aug. 1856, *Journal of Discourses*, 4:38–40.

a way to purchase moral ground with the electorate. Uncertain of their course, as one historian put it, the Buchanan administration "groped its way to the conclusion" that the Mormon people were in a state of disorder and dispatched an army in 1857 to assert federal control of the territory.[42] The Utah Expedition succeeded in replacing Brigham Young with a non-Mormon governor, Alfred Cumming, but the military campaign was a fiasco. And the church not only continued to exercise large influence over affairs in Utah but polygamy flourished. For all their rhetoric, the enemies of plural marriage came to the end of the 1850s with no more to show for their struggle against the peculiar institution of Utah than that in the South.

Undaunted, in 1860 the House Judiciary Committee's chairman, Thomas Amos Rogers Nelson (1812–1873) of Tennessee, reported Vermont's Rep. Justin Smith Morrill's anti-polygamy bill and recommended it for passage. Making the case for its acceptance, Nelson venomously condemned the "execrable heresy" of polygamy.

> "Polygamy in the Territorities [sic] of the United States,"
> House Report 83 (36-1), 14 Mar. 1860, Serial 1067, 1–5.
>
> Whatever differences of opinion may exist as to whether marriage is a civil or canonical contract, the whole civilized world regard the marriage of one man to one woman as being alone authorized by the law of God, and that while the relation of husband and wife exists, neither can be lawfully married to another person. . . Our ancestors brought with them to this country a sacred regard for the precepts of the Bible, and polygamy never having been tolerated in the colonies, was not recognized or permitted by the laws of any State of the confederacy, at the time of the adoption of the federal Constitution. In every State of the Union it is still treated as a crime, and in most, if not all of them, punished as a felony. . . No argument is deemed necessary to prove that an act should be regarded as criminal which is so treated by the universal concurrence of the Christian and civilized world. Marriage is the foundation of civil society. . . Barbarians may disown it, but enlightened nations everywhere respect and encourage it.
>
> While such is the estimate placed upon the marital relation in our own and other countries, the moral sense of our own people, as well as of every refined and intelligent community upon the habitable earth, has been shocked by the open and defiant license which, under the name of religion and a latitudinous interpretation of our Constitution, has been given to this crime in

---

[42] Furniss, *Mormon Conflict*, 95. For President Buchanan's justifications, see his first annual message of 8 Dec. 1857, in *Comp.*, 6:2985–87.

one of our Territories. While persons have been excluded from society and are expiating as felons, in every penitentiary of the Union, the offence of polygamy, the citizens of Utah . . . laugh to scorn the sacredness of the Bible and the majesty of our laws, and, claiming the largest liberty, under the exemptions from religious tests and the establishment of religion, deride an institution which was honored by the presence of our Savior as a farce, and stigmatize its observance as worse than a solemn mockery. It would, perhaps, require no elaborate statement to demonstrate that the framers of the Constitution, when they provided that "no religious test should ever be required as a qualification to any office or public trust under the United States," had in view the Test Oaths which were required by statute in the reign of Charles II,[43] and that when they declared "Congress shall make no law respecting the establishment of religion or the free exercise thereof," they did not mean to dignify with the name of religion a tribe of Latter Day Saints disgracing that hallowed name, and wickedly imposing upon the credulity of mankind . . . surely they never intended that the wild vagaries of the Hindoo or the ridiculous mummeries of the Hottentot should be ennobled by so honored and sacred a name. Be this as it may, the question recurs, has Congress no power to prohibit a practice which is a disgrace to our country and a libel upon our institutions? . . .[44]

The committee . . . cannot abstain from declaring it as their solemn conviction whether it be necessary, in order to reform one of the most glaring abuses of the present century, to redivide the Territory of Utah, or bring its citizens to a faithful observance of the Constitution and laws of the United States, by the employment, if need be, to its utmost extent, of our military power; the most prompt and energetic measures are demanded to show our abhorrence of a vile superstition, which is antagonistic alike to the laws of God and man, and disgraceful to the spirit of the age in which we live.

The committee therefore report the bill as submitted to them, and respectfully recommend its passage.

Despite Nelson's speech and approval of the measure in the House, the 1860 bill died in the Senate. It was owing to a further attempt by Representative Morrill that the bill finally passed Congress and was signed by President Lincoln in 1862. Generally liberal in his views, Morrill once boasted, "nothing American is alien to me."[45] This notwithstanding, he was unalterably opposed to Mormon plurality. One biographer speculated that the anti-polygamy animus

---

[43] *Statutes of the Realm*, 25 Charles II, c.2 (1673); and ibid., 30 Charles II, st.2. c.1 (1678).

[44] Rep. Justin Morrill, author of the bill under consideration, extensively explored the question of Congress' authority to pass laws criminalizing polygamy in the territories at the time such regulations were first attempted. See his remarks in *Cong. Globe* (34-1), 26 June 1856, 1491. For more on this issue, see Sears, "Punishing the Saints," 601–6.   [45] *Cong. Globe* (34-1), 28 June 1856, Appendix, 679.

that he and his colleagues George Franklin Edmunds, Luke Potter Poland, and
Judge James B. McKean exhibited might have arisen from their desire to excul-
pate the reputation of Vermont. They, like Joseph Smith, Brigham Young, and
Heber C. Kimball, were all natives of the Green Mountain State.[46]

U.S., STATUTES AT LARGE, CHAP. 126, 12:126,

2 JULY 1862, 501–2.

*An Act to punish and prevent the Practice of Polygamy in the Territories of the United
States and other Places, and disapproving and annulling certain Acts of the Legislative Assembly of the Territory of Utah.*

*Be it enacted by the Senate and House of Representatives of the United States of America
in Congress assembled,* That every person having a husband or wife living, who
shall marry any other person, whether married or single, in a Territory of the
United States, or other place over which the United States have exclusive jurisdiction, shall, except in the cases specified in the proviso to this section, be
adjudged guilty of bigamy, and, upon conviction thereof, shall be punished
by a fine not exceeding five hundred dollars, and by imprisonment for a term
not exceeding five years: *Provided, nevertheless,* That this section shall not extend
to any person by reason of any former marriage whose husband or wife by
such marriage shall have been absent for five successive years without being
known to such person within that time to be living; nor to any person by reason of any former marriage which shall have been dissolved by the decree of
a competent court; nor to any person by reason of any former marriage which
shall have been annulled or pronounced void by the sentence or decree of a
competent court on the ground of the nullity of the marriage contract.

SEC. 2. *And be it further enacted,* That the following ordinance of the provisional government of the State of Deseret, so called, namely: "An ordinance
incorporating the Church of Jesus Christ of Latter Day Saints," passed February eight, in the year eighteen hundred and fifty-one, and adopted, reen-
acted, and made valid by the governor and legislative assembly of the Territory of Utah by an act passed January nineteen, in the year eighteen hundred
and fifty-five, entitled "An act in relation to the compilation and revision of
the laws and resolutions in force in Utah Territory, their publication, and dis-
tribution," and all other acts and parts of acts heretofore passed by the said
legislative assembly of the Territory of Utah, which establish, support, maintain, shield, or countenance polygamy, be, and the same hereby are, disapproved
and annulled: *Provided,* That this act shall be so limited and construed as not
to affect or interfere with the right of property legally acquired under the
ordinance heretofore mentioned, nor with the right "to worship God accord-

---

[46] Parker, *Life and Public Services of Justin Smith Morrill,* 83. Werner commenced his biography of Brigham
Young by telling of the chagrin that citizens of Whitingham, Vermont, felt concerning their most famous
son. *Brigham Young,* 3–4.

ing to the dictates of conscience," but only to annul all acts and laws which establish, maintain, protect, or countenance the practice of polygamy, evasively called spiritual marriage, however disguised by legal or ecclesiastical solemnities, sacraments, ceremonies, consecrations, or other contrivances.

SEC. 3. *And be it further enacted,* That it shall not be lawful for any corporation or association for religious or charitable purposes to acquire or hold real estate in any Territory of the United States during the existence of the territorial government of a greater value than fifty thousand dollars; and all real estate acquired or held by any such corporation or association contrary to the provisions of this act shall be forfeited and escheat to the United States: *Provided,* That existing vested rights in real estate shall not be impaired by the provisions of this section.

APPROVED, JULY 2, 1862.[47]

"INCESTUOUS CONNECTIONS AND THE CRIME OF BIGAMY": A MILITARY OFFICER COMPLAINS

The secession crisis necessarily absorbed Lincoln and the Republicans more than the aberrations of a religious sect in the Far West.[48] Beyond this, because of the Morrill Act's language, it did not reach the private ceremonies the Saints used to contract plural unions. The dearth of accessible marriage records, combined with Mormon control of territorial courts, prevented a single conviction under the statute for more than a decade. But anti-polygamy sentiment had acquired such momentum that it would not die. Col. P. E. Connor, for example, sent numerous missives to other officers while stationed at Great Salt Lake City complaining of Mormon wickedness.[49] Connor stated that if the Civil War was God's punishment for some great sin, it was for allowing the Mormons and their polygamy to continue within the nation's borders. During his tenure at Camp Douglas, Connor's descriptions helped form the attitudes of General Grant and others toward the Saints.[50]

---

[47] Formal announcement of Lincoln's signing of the act is found in *Cong. Globe* (37-2), 3 July 1862, 3088.

[48] There were, to be sure, concerns over Mormon loyalty and related issues. See all of Long, *Saints and the Union.*

[49] A native of Ireland, Patrick Edward Connor (1820–1891) emigrated to the U.S. where, after serving in the army during the War with Mexico, he worked in construction in California. He was called to lead the state's Third Volunteer Regiment in 1862 and sent to Utah to protect the overland route to the Pacific. He began sending critical accounts of life in Utah to his superiors, describing the Mormons as "a community of traitors, murderers, fanatics and whores." Connor to Drum, 14 Sept. 1862, *War of the Rebellion,* 50: pt. 2, 119. Brigham D. Madsen provides a biographical portrait of Connor in his *Glory Hunter.*

[50] Long, *Saints and the Union,* 263–64, 268–76 passim.

Col. P[atrick] Edw[ard] Connor to
Lieut. Col. R[ichard] C. Drum, 19 Feb. 1863,
War of the Rebellion, Series 1, 50: pt. 2, 318.

Colonel: I desire respectfully, to call the attention of the general commanding to the state of affairs existing in this Territory, and to matter[s] which, in
my opinion, should receive the immediate attention of the Government. I can
only allude briefly to the frequent and flagrant violations of the law and the
audacious interference with its operations. The law for the prohibition of
polygamy is daily violated under the very eyes of the Federal courts by citizens and members of the Mormon Church, who are composed chiefly of the
very lowest class of foreigners and aliens. Naturally opposed to our laws, they
do not hesitate at violating them, and are willing tools in the hands of their
leaders, hesitating at the commission of no crime. . .[51] Not the least respect is
paid to the marriage relation; instances of incestuous connections and the crime
of bigamy are not only tolerated but encouraged by the Mormon creed, which
is inimical to the U.S. laws, winks at murder, pillage and rapine, and is the very
embodiment of hypocrisy; mocks at God and insults the nation . . . and if the
crimes and designs of this people were known and understood by the people
of the United States . . . it would cause such a burst of indignation as would
result in the utter annihilation of this whole people, and if the present rebellion is a punishment for any national sin, I believe it is for permitting this unholy,
blasphemous, and unnatural institution to exist almost in the heart of the nation,
ignoring its horrid crimes and allowing it to extend its ramifications into every
grade of society in defiance of laws human and divine. To relate the revolting
crimes and the numerous outrages which are daily perpetrated by Brigham and
his church were superfluous. Suffice it to say, then, if the social and political
attitude of this people is such as I believe it is, the sooner we are rid of the
evil, and the nation of the stigma, the better it will be for us. . .

Very respectfully, your obedient servant,
P. Edw. Connor,
Colonel Third Infantry California Volunteers, Commanding.

"Asiatic Effeminancy": Reconstruction and Utah

The stacking of arms at Appomattox was hardly complete before bills designed
to bring morality to Utah began crossing the desks of congressmen again.
All sought to amend the ineffectual Morrill Act and all failed to survive con-

[51] As territorial governor Stephen S. Harding did the year before, Connor is alluding to the Morrill
Act and the Mormon failure to observe it. See "Governor's Message to the Territorial Legislature of Utah,"
Senate Misc. Doc. 37 (37-2), 28 Feb. 1863, Serial 1150, 6–7.

gressional debate—largely due to their severity and the effectiveness of Apostle George Q. Cannon's lobbying efforts.[52] Measures introduced by Sens. Benjamin F. Wade and Aaron H. Cragin, for example, denied Mormon authorities the right to perform marriage ceremonies and abolished trial by jury in cases arising under the anti-bigamy law of 1862.[53] Rep. James M. Ashley proposed taking huge swaths of ground from Utah's possession and awarding them to surrounding states. Ashley was unapologetic in explaining that his purpose was "to blot out the territory."[54] The bill failed not only because it was considered extreme, but from belief that the removal of Mormons to new jurisdictions would only see them, hydra-headed, reassert their influence elsewhere.[55]

But strong anti-polygamy biases, combined with the Republican, Reconstructionist temper, assured that efforts to suppress polygamy would continue. The most threatening of such attempts was the bill assembled by Rep. Shelby M. Cullom of Illinois in early 1870. Its thirty-four sections, seeking to dispose of the polygamy problem once and for all, proposed a massive overhaul of the territory.[56] The measure passed the House and for a time looked as though it would become law. Defending the provision's extreme nature, Cullom told fellow congressmen that plural marriage, "Instead of being a holy principle, receiving the sanction of Heaven . . . is an institution founded in the lustful and unbridled passions of men, devised by Satan himself to . . . authorize whoredom."[57]

Insouciant until this time, Mormons took alarm. Andrew Jackson Allen, a Latter-day Saint living in Draper, Utah, exclaimed: "the Jentiles ar on the

---

[52] A chart listing all federal anti-polygamy legislation, most of which failed, is provided as Appendix J in Poll's "Twin Relic: A Study of Mormon Polygamy," 393–94.

[53] Sen. Benjamin Wade introduced his bill on 12 July 1866. *Cong. Globe* (39-1), 3750. For Sen. Aaron Cragin's proposed law, see *Cong. Globe* (40-2), 13 Dec. 1867, 162. Commentary is available in Roberts, *Comprehensive History*, 5:225–27; and Larson, *"Americanization" of Utah*, 64–65.

[54] Ashley's description of the bill is in *Cong. Globe* (40-3), 14 Jan. 1869, 363–64. A history of Utah's diminishing boundaries is provided by MacKinnon, "'Like Splitting a Man Up His Backbone'. . . ," 100–24.

[55] "Utah," *New York Times*, 27 Jan. 1869, 18:5412, 5/3.

[56] The measure gave greater authority to marshals and district attorneys to arrest and indict polygamists. It provided that a lawful wife could testify against her husband; criminalized "concubinage" or privately solemnized domestic relations; prohibited polygamist aliens from becoming citizens; denied polygamists the right to vote or preempt land; repealed all congressional and territorial laws relating to the government of Utah; and authorized the use of U.S. troops when federal marshals were resisted in their duties.

[57] *Cong. Globe* (41-2), 17 Feb. 1870, 1373. A lengthy compilation of testimony, state laws prohibiting bigamy, and other materials in support of Cullom's proposal is provided in "Execution of the Laws in Utah," Report 21 (41-2), 3 Feb. 1870, Serial 1436, pts. 1–2.

track of the saints. Congress are trying to make a law to put down poligemy."[58] Mass meetings of Mormon men and women assembled objecting to the proposed enactment.[59] And these, along with a territorial law enfranchising females in 1870, left many astonished to learn that Latter-day Saint women were as devoted to the Principle and took as much effrontery at attempts to destroy it as their men.[60] Most outsiders, however, believed that women's suffrage in Utah was but a Mormon maneuver to secure patriarchal theocracy. An eastern reporter's description of a Utah election in 1870 was typical of Gentile skepticism.

> The polls were open from sunrise until sunset... The Gentiles made no demonstration on election day, but the Mormons had several bands of music marching about town from morning until evening, and a number of wagons running all day conveying women to and from the polls. Indeed, the principal feature of the whole election was the novelty of women voting. Some men walked with their women and brought them into the polling places like so many cattle. Women in Utah are often treated more like cattle than ladies. Heber C. Kimball, who, before his death, was next in authority to Brigham Young, used to call his women his "herd of cows."[61] Other men brought their women in wagons, some of the women bringing their babies with them. Polygamy was thus publicly paraded through the streets of this city and the settlements... Many of the women and many of the men whom I saw vote did not seem to comprehend what they were doing; they simply put into the ballot box the ticket that was handed them.[62]

Neither was it possible to forget plurality's threatening physiological consequences. The widely read American physician, Dr. George Napheys, renewed Roberts Bartholow's predictions from the 1850s (see Chapter Five) two decades later.[63]

[58] Record of Andrew Jackson Allen, 1 Mar. 1870, 75, Uhi.

[59] "Great Indignation Meeting of the Ladies of Salt Lake City, to Protest against the Passage of Cullom's Bill," Des. Eve. News, 14 Jan. 1870, 3:44 [2/1–5]; continued under same title in ibid., 15 Jan. 1870, 3:45 [2/1–4]. Also see "Memorial," Senate Misc. Doc. 112 (41-2), 12 Apr. 1870, Serial 1408.

[60] Utah's territorial law granting women the vote is "An Act Conferring upon Women the Elective Franchise," 12 Feb. 1870, Acts, Resolutions, and Memorials (1870), 8. One popular magazine declared: "Utah is the land of marvels. She gives us first, polygamy, which seems to be an outrage against 'woman's rights,' and then offers to the nation a 'Female Suffrage Bill,' ... Was there ever a greater anomaly known in the history of society?" "William H. Hooper, the Utah Delegate and Female Suffrage Advocate," 328–29.

[61] For Heber C. Kimball's famous comparison of his wives and daughters to "cows," see Chapter Three.

[62] "Utah," New York Herald, 14 Aug. 1870, 35:226, 11/1–2.

[63] Dr. George Henry Napheys (1842–1876) published widely on women's health. I am indebted to Mrs. Melody G. Robertson of San Diego, California, for bringing this document to my attention.

GEORGE H. NAPHEYS, *THE PHYSICAL LIFE OF WOMAN* (1876), 64.

What has been said of divorce applies with tenfold force to the custom of a woman living as wife to several men, or of a man as husband to several women. We should not speak of these customs, but that we know both exist in America, not among the notoriously wicked, but among those who claim to be the peculiarly good—the very elect of God. They prevail, not as lustful excesses, but as religious observances.

It is worth while to say that such practices lead to physical degradation. The woman who acknowledges more than one husband is generally sterile; the man who has several wives has usually a weakly offspring, principally males. Nature attempts to check polygamy by reducing the number of females, and failing in this, by enervating the whole stock. The Mormons of Utah would soon sink into a state of Asiatic effeminancy were they left to themselves.

"ALREADY IN THE DEATH-GASP": PLEAS FOR MODERATION

Edward Tullidge was convinced that protest meetings by Mormon women were central to the defeat of Cullom's legislation.[64] But neither such gatherings nor the spectacle of women forming lines outside polling booths moved congressmen so much as politics within their own chambers. As Gustive O. Larson indicated, it was a concerted effort including railroad interests that hobbled the measure, keeping it off the floor of the Senate and eventually allowing it to expire.[65] And William H. Hooper's eloquent address as a territorial delegate tallied more resistance to Cullom's proposed statute than all other Mormon speeches, with their printed remonstrances and long lists of Mormon names, put together. Pointing to the cleanliness and order of Utah's villages, Hooper asked that Congress judge the tree of Mormonism by its fruit. "A community given up to lust," he said, "does not build factories and fill the land with thrifty farms." Like Orson Pratt, he invited those who disagreed with the Saints on polygamy to reveal to them their error, whether in scripture or social consequence. In any case, he insisted, "it is the field for the missionary and not for the jurist or soldier."[66]

---

[64] Tullidge, *Life of Brigham Young*, 390.   [65] Larson, *"Americanization" of Utah*, 65–72.

[66] The entire address is "Polygamy in Utah. Speech of Hon. W. H. Hooper, of Utah, In the House of Representatives, March 22 and 23, 1870," *Cong. Globe* (41-2), Appendix, 173–79. William Henry Hooper (1813–1882), who served as Utah's territorial delegate to Congress during the years 1859–1861 and 1865–1873, enjoyed a reputation for geniality and eloquence. His oration against the Cullom Bill was so popular that several thousand copies, along with a memorial by women in Utah, were printed and distributed to the public. *Utah Bill.*

There were others who considered Cullom's bill draconian and said so. Some of what accounted for their views was belief that patience could better solve the problem than coercion. It was generally assumed that monogamous family life was the product of social evolution and would continue to grow in its persuasion. Its choice as a preferred system of marriage was the result of historical experience. "Modern society reposes upon the monogamian family," Lewis Henry Morgan explained. "The whole previous experience of mankind culminated and crystallized in this pre-eminent institution."[67] Polygamy, as a less evolved practice, would inevitably yield, such observers said, to the transforming effect of civilization.[68] A group of merchants and intellectuals seeking to liberalize Mormonism from within supported these sentiments. Referred to as the New Movement, these Latter-day Saints sought to persuade national leaders that their own efforts in Utah were transforming the church and that all that was needed was time and contact with the outside world.[69]

Even before the Cullom Bill was proposed, William Hepworth Dixon contended that polygamy would die a natural death from the effects of education. In the account below, he tells of a conversation with politicians, lawyers, and journalists in Philadelphia shortly after the Civil War. The "English traveller" to whom he refers is undoubtedly himself.[70]

WILLIAM HEPWORTH DIXON, *NEW AMERICA* (1867), 241–47.

THE REPUBLICAN PLATFORM.

"We mean to put the business of the Mormons through," says a New England politician; "we have done a bigger job than that in the South; and we shall now fix up things in Salt Lake City."

"Do you mean by force?" asks an English traveller.

"Well, that is one of our planks. The Republican Platform pledges us to crush those Saints."

This conversation, passing across the hospitable board of a renowned publicist in Philadelphia, draws towards itself from all sides the criticism of a

---

[67] Morgan, *Ancient Society*, 512. Also see Lecky, *History of European Morals*, 2:294–95; and "'Evolution of Marriage,'" *Boston Herald*, 26 Feb. 1884 [1/4–5].

[68] For example, see Cannon, "Leopold Bierwirth's Impressions of Brigham Young and the Mormons," 148; "Undermining Mormonism," *Cincinnati Commercial*, 14 Mar. 1872, 32:194, 4/3; and "Anti-Polygamy Bill," *New York Herald*, 24 Mar. 1870, 35:83, 7/2.

[69] Some members of the Movement outlined steps by which polygamous marriages could be humanely dissolved. Godbe, *Polygamy*, 8–13. The best study is Walker, *Wayward Saints*, 212–31.

[70] Mulder and Mortensen, eds., *Among the Mormons*, 364–68, provides a more complete reproduction of this essay.

distinguished company of lawyers and politicians; most of them members of Congress; all of them soldiers of the Republican phalanx.

"Do you hold," says the English guest,—"you as a writer and thinker,—your party as the representatives of American thought and might,—that in a country where speech is free and tolerance wide, it would be *right* to employ force against ideas,—to throw horse and foot into a dogmatic quarrel,—to set about promoting morality with bayonets and bowie-knives?"

"It is one of our planks," says a young member of Congress, "to put down those Mormons, who, besides, being infidels, are also Conservatives and Copperheads."[71]

"Young is certainly a Democrat," adds an Able Editor from Massachusetts, himself a traveller in the Mormon land;[72] "we have no right to burn his block on account of his politics; nor, indeed, on account of his religion; we have no power to meddle with any man's faith; but we have made a law against plurality of wives, and we have the power to make our laws respected everywhere in this Republic!"

"By force?"

"By force, if we are driven by disloyal citizens to the use of force."

"You mean, then, that in any case you will use force—passively, if they submit; actively, if they resist?"

"That's our notion," replies our candid host. "The government must crush them. . ."

"You hold it right, then, to combat such an evil as polygamy with shot and shell?"

"We have freed four million Negroes with shot and shell," replies a sober Pennsylvanian judge.

"Pardon me, is that a full statement of the case? That you have crushed a movement of secession by means of military force is true; but is it not also true that, five or six years ago, every one acknowledged that slavery was a legal and moral question, which, while peace and order reigned in the slave-states, ought not to be treated otherwise than on legal and moral grounds?"

"Yes, that is so. We had no right over the Negroes until their masters went into rebellion. I admit that the declaration of war gave us our only standing."

. . .

"When New England," adds a representative from Ohio, with a laugh, "goes mad on any point, you will find that she contrives in this Republic to have her way." . . .

"But will Harvard and Cambridge support an attack by military power on religious bodies because they have adopted the model of Abraham and David?

---

[71] The charge of Utah's indifference to the outcome of the Civil War and suspicions of Mormon disloyalty were issues involved in the affair of Gov. Stephen S. Harding and his removal. Roberts, *Comprehensive History*, 5:19–20; and all of Long, *Saints and the Union*.

[72] Samuel Bowles, editor of the Massachusetts *Springfield Republican*.

You have in those western plains and mountains a hundred tribes of red-men who practise polygamy; would you think it right for your missionary society to withdraw from among them the teacher and his Bible, and for General Grant to send out in their stead the soldier and his sword? You have in those western territories a hundred thousand yellow men who also practise polygamy; would you hold it just to sink their ships, to burn their ranches, to drive them from your soil, with sword and fire?"

"Their case is different to that of the Saints," rejoins the Able Editor; "these red-skins and yellow-skins are savages; one race may die out, the other may go back to Asia; but Young and Kimball are our own people knowing the law and the Gospel; and whatever they may do with the Gospel, they must obey the law." . . .

"We must put them down," cries the young member of Congress.

"Have you not tried that policy of putting them down twice already? You found them twelve thousand strong at Independence, in Missouri; not liking their tenets (though they had no polygamy among them then), you crushed and scattered them into thirty thousand at Nauvoo; where you again took arms against religious passion, slew their Prophet, plundered their city, drove them into the desert, and generally dispersed and destroyed them into one hundred and twenty-seven thousand in Deseret! You know that some such law of growth through persecution has been detected in every land and in every church. It is a proverb." . . .

"But we can hardly leave these pluralists alone."

"Why not—so far at least as regards bayonets and bowie-knives? Have you no faith in the power of truth? Have you no confidence in being right? Nay, are you sure that you have nothing to learn from them? Have not the men who thrive where nobody else can live, given ample evidence that, even though their doctrines may be strange and their morals false, the principles on which they till the soil and raise their crops, are singularly sound?"

"I admit," says the Able Editor, "they are good farmers."

"Good is a poor term, to express the marvel they have wrought. In Illinois, they changed a swamp into a garden. In Utah, they have made the desert green with pastures and tawny with maize and corn. Of what is Brigham Young most fond? Of his harem, his temple, his theatre, his office, his wealth? He may pride himself on these things in their measure; but the fact of his life which he dwelt upon most, and with the noblest enthusiasm, is the raising of a crop of ninety-three and a half bushels of wheat from one single acre of land. The Saints have grown rich with a celerity that seems magical even in the United States. Beginning life at the lowest stage, recruited only from among the poor, spoiled of their goods and driven from their farms, compelled to expend millions of dollars in a perilous exodus, and finally located on a soil from which the red-skin and the bison had all but retired in despair, they have yet contrived to exist, to extend their operations, to increase their stores. The hills and valleys round Salt Lake are everywhere smiling with wheat and rye. A city has been built; great roads have been made; mills have been erected; canals have been dug; forests have been felled. A depot has been formed in the wilderness from which the miners from Montana and Nevada can be fed. A chain of communication from St. Louis to San Francisco has been laid. Are the Republican majority prepared to undo the progress of twenty years in order to curb an obnoxious doctrine?" . . .

"Then you see no way of crushing them?"

"Crushing them! No; none. I see no way of dealing with any moral and religious question except by moral means employed in a religious spirit. Why not put your trust in truth, in logic, in history? Why not open good roads to Salt Lake? Why not encourage railway communication; and bring the practical intellect and noble feeling of New England to bear upon the household of many wives? Why not meet their sermons by sermons; try their science by science; encounter their books with books? . . . It will be for you a trial of strength; but the weapons will be legitimate and the conclusions will be blessed. Can you not trust the right side and the just cause, to come out victoriously from such a struggle?" . . .

"And now pass the wine."

Annoyed by congressional inaction, President Grant urged a stern response to "anarchy" in Utah in his annual message of 1873.[73] But an anonymous article published in the New York *Daily Graphic* counseled forbearance and trust in the effects of civilization.

"Meddling With The Mormons," [New York] *Daily Graphic*, 9 Dec. 1873, 3:239, 250/2–3.

One of the recommendations of the President in his message looks to an interference with Mormonism on the part of Congress. His suggestions are designed to run a ploughshare through the greensward of Mormondom and turn polygamy under the sod forever. A strong party in Congress favor measures of direct interference for the suppression of polygamy in Utah. It is thought that such measures will hasten the downfall of a disgraceful custom, be popular in the country, and cover its advocates with honor, especially in the eyes of religious people. Brigham Young is neither venerable nor interesting, and a war upon him and his peculiar institution might be as popular in the country as the Crusades were in Europe a half-dozen centuries ago. Who knows that the Home against the harem might not prove as pow-

---

[73] Ulysses S. Grant, "Fifth Annual Message," 1 Dec. 1873, *Comp.*, 9:4204. For Congress' failure in 1873 to pass the anti-Mormon measure proposed by Sen. Frederick Theodore Frelinghuysen of New Jersey, see the interesting account in Bitton, *George Q. Cannon*, 178–80.

erful a rallying call in the nineteenth century as the Cross against Crescent was in the twelfth!

It is easy to excite popular prejudice against polygamy. But statesmen do not dabble in sensations. The fact that a particular policy falls in with vulgar prejudice, and will be popular with the ignorant and passion-moved masses, may stimulate demagogues to advocate it, and there are always men enough of this species in public life to seize upon such measures in order to gain a cheap notoriety and political elevation. There is no question that a raid on polygamy would be popular in certain quarters, and that political adventurers might make capital from its advocacy. But would it be wise? . . . Is it not one of the customs that can safely be left to the intelligence and moral sentiment of the community in which it exists, and the laws of economic and social welfare?

Such questions admit of only one answer. An unprovoked warfare on Mormonism would wear the aspect of persecution, and excite a sympathy more dangerous than the ism it is waged to suppress.[74] It was the persecution in Ohio and Missouri that built Nauvoo, and it was the destruction of Nauvoo that settled Utah. There is no denying the fact that Brigham Young has converted a desert into a garden, and built up flourishing and populous cities in what was a barren and inhospitable wilderness. He led a fanaticism. . . But his institution is an anomaly and an anachronism. A fanaticism cannot coexist with intelligence, and constantly tends to burn itself away. It seeks isolation in order to protect itself from its foes and perpetuate its flame. But in this the Mormons were unsuccessful. Their retreat proved to be in the main highway of the continent. The Pacific Railroad has shattered their ecclesiastical supremacy. The discovery of rich mines within two hours ride of Salt Lake City is inundating the Territory with a Gentile population which will soon leave the Mormons in an unpopular minority in their own stronghold. The new colonists carry new fashions, and the Mormon women are no longer content to drudge and dress as in the old days. . . The whole spirit and movement of our Western civilization are against [polygamy's] . . . continuance. . . There is . . . no use in dragging a body already in the death-gasp up to the gallows. The licentiousness and vice and crimes against domestic purity in our great cities hardly justify us in making a national raid against a community which, with all its sins and shortcomings, has abolished the social evil from its borders and provided every woman with at least the semblance of a home.

---

[74] As early as the 1850s the Saints acquired a reputation for turning every objection made against them into "persecution." Alfred Higbie complained, "In every attempt to present their principles in their true light—which they themselves requested—the Mormons cry *"persecution!"* Higbie, *Polygamy vs. Christianity*, 3. And John Thompson told Congress in 1858 that Mormons had a tendency to transform criticism into "Gog and Magog . . . coming up against the Saints!" Thompson, *Mormonism*, 5.

"Babylon Was Polygamic": New Attacks

Pleas for moderation did little to dissipate the gathering anti-Mormon storm. Joseph Smith III (1832–1914), son of the church's first prophet and leader of a rival Mormon faction in the Midwest, vehemently denied that his father taught or practiced polygamy.[75] "Young Joseph," as he was called, claimed special authority for succession to his father's leadership of the church and accused Brigham Young of inventing the doctrine of plural marriage. At a time of growing national concern over the question, Joseph Smith III voiced his claims before a congressional committee:

> . . . all that portion of the church of Jesus Christ of Latter Day Saints, commonly called Mormons, under the leadership of Brigham Young or any one else, who hold to the doctrine of polygamy or plurality of wives and its kindred concomitants, have departed from the principles of the faith delivered to them by my father.[76]

Additional support for such statements, further indicting the Saints' credibility, came from the widow of the prophet, Emma Smith Bidamon. Joseph III and his brother Alexander interviewed their mother in Nauvoo, Illinois in early February 1879. Her words were direct and unequivocal, insisting that her husband, Joseph the prophet, had no revelation approving plural marriage, did not engage in it, and that Brigham Young and others condemned her because she refused to accept "their newfangled notion."[77]

During these same years, Schuyler Colfax, Speaker of the House and later vice president of the United States, traveled to Utah on three separate occasions.[78] During his second visit in 1869, accompanied by eastern journalists,

---

[75] As examples of the RLDS position, see Joseph Smith III, *Polygamy not of God*; [Gurley Sr.], *Polygamic Revelation*; Briggs, *Basis of Brighamite Polygamy*; "Mormonism Arraigned," *Saints Herald* 25:23 (1 Dec. 1878), 353–55. As evidence that the feud still continues, see Price and Price, *Joseph Smith Fought Polygamy*.

[76] "Condition of Utah," *House Report* 96 (39-1), 23 July 1866, Serial 1272, 7. Also see *Memorial to Congress from a Committee of the Reorganized Church of Jesus Christ of Latter Day Saints*; and Joseph Smith [III] to President Ulysses S. Grant, 10 Feb. 1873, in Simon, ed., *Papers of Ulysses S. Grant*, 4:40n.

[77] Joseph Smith III Interview Notes with Emma Smith Bidamon, 1879, Miscellany Collection, fd. 40, CCL-A. Ronald E. Romig, church archivist for the Community of Christ in Independence, Missouri, has carefully prepared a typescript of the exchange, available in CCL-A. Two RLDS organs printed the interview after Mrs. Bidamon's death: "Last Testimony of Sister Emma," *Saints' Herald*, 26:19 (1 Oct. 1879), 289–90; and "Last Testimony of Sister Emma," *Saints' Advocate*, 2:4 (Oct. 1879), 49–52. Utah Mormons, of course, replied with a bale of testimonies from Smith's plural wives and others, contradicting Bidamon's statement. See, for example: "Joseph the Seer's Plural Marriages," *Des. News* [Weekly], 22 Oct. 1879, 28:38, 604/1–5, 605/1.

[78] Accounts of the 1865 visit are in Bowles, *Across the Continent*, 79–130; and Hollister, *Life of Schuyler Colfax*, 258–59.

Joseph Smith III (1832–1914), son of Mormonism's founder, rejected the plurality doctrine and oversaw the emergence of the Reorganized Church of Jesus Christ of Latter Day Saints (now Community of Christ).

Colfax reproached the Saints for not obeying the Morrill Act, engaged in a newspaper debate with Apostle John Taylor, and kept the "Mormon Question" before the public.[79] Edward W. Tullidge, who witnessed these events, said that Colfax's activities marked the real beginning of the nation's anti-polygamy crusade.[80] But a more dramatic event than the Colfax-Taylor exchange occurred when John Philip Newman, chaplain of the U.S. Senate, carried the fight into the heart of Zion by disputing the biblical basis of polygamy before Mormon faithful in their new tabernacle.

The nineteenth century was an age of oratorical spectacle. Wilberforce and Huxley on evolution, Webster's verbal jousting with Hayne and Calhoun over the nature of the Union, and the eighteen-day dispute in 1843 between Alexander Campbell and the Rev. Nathan Lewis Rice concerning baptism were but a few of the better-remembered encounters. The Saints were as given to these tournaments as others of their time. It was in keeping with the tra-

---

[79] H. W. R., "Utah," *New York Times*, 17 Oct. 1869, 19:5637, 3/3–4; Stenhouse, *Rocky Mountain Saints*, 613–14; and Walker, *Wayward Saints*, 212–13, 220–21. The debates between Colfax and Taylor can be read in Colfax, *Mormon Question*.

[80] Tullidge, *History of Salt Lake City*, 358.

As a popular Methodist chaplain to the United States Senate, John Philip Newman (1826–1899) possessed a deep, organ-like voice. Considered one of the greatest orators of the time, he was virtually "court preacher" to President Ulysses S. Grant and was expected to overwhelm Orson Pratt in their 1870 debate on polygamy. Edward Tullidge, believing that Pratt won the contest, called the subsequent phase of the anti-polygamy crusade "Newman's revenge." *Courtesy Library of Congress collections.*

dition of such events, as well as in response to Mormon invitations to disprove their arguments, that the three-day exchange in 1870 between Apostle Orson Pratt and Rev. John Philip Newman occurred. Newman, besides being chaplain to the Senate, was pastor at the Metropolitan Methodist Church in Washington, D.C. His congregation regularly included, among others, President Ulysses S. Grant, Vice President Schuyler Colfax, Chief Justice Salmon P. Chase, and Speaker of the House James G. Blaine. It was to be expected that when he attacked Mormon plurality, particularly contending that the Bible did not support it, the Saints would respond.

Thousands poured into the recently completed tabernacle in Salt Lake City to witness the event. "Never before, in the whole Christian era, had polygamy been so elaborately and ably discussed between two divines, and certainly never was a religious debate so extensively published and read," said Edward Tullidge, with his usual enthusiasm for such occasions.[81] With U.S. Marshal Mathewson T. Patrick acting as umpire, both contestants fanned their Bibles, engaging in what one journalist called "a tournament of quotations."[82] But they also adduced linguistic analysis, sociology, constitution-

---

[81] Tullidge, *Life of Brigham Young,* 405–6.
[82] "Don Quixote in Utah," *New York Times,* 23 Aug. 1870, 19:5903, 4/5.

Orson Pratt (1811–1881) was Mormonism's best-known apologist for the Principle. It was he whom Brigham Young chose to deliver the famous 1852 address announcing and defending plurality. It was also he who, appearing much as he does here, in 1870 debated the practice in the church's new tabernacle with the Rev. John Philip Newman.

al arguments, and mathematical evidence to support their positions. The Saints, of course, were convinced that Pratt won the contest. In the words of Mary Jane Mount Tanner, "Parson Newman came all the way from Washington to argue that point from the Bible but one of our wise men set him to rights."[83] Another observer was probably nearer the truth when he said Pratt and Newman were "equally fatiguing."[84]

The following passages are taken from the last day of the debate and do not contain the full range of topics treated by either speaker. But they illustrate their respective styles of argument.[85]

[83] Tanner, *Fragment*, 168. Without indicating how he measured such opinion, Tullidge said that among those attending the debates, "quite two-thirds of them yielded the palm to the Mormon apostle." *Life of Brigham Young*, 406. For non-Mormons who also gave Pratt the victory, see Whitney, *History of Utah*, 2:483–86. One reporter believed that, piqued by the loss, it was Reverend Newman's influence with President Grant that led to increased pressure on the Saints. See H.V.R., "Washington Letter . . . Our Mormon Elephant," *Cincinnati Commercial*, 7 May 1872, 32:247, 4/3–5. This view was also expressed by Tullidge, *Life of Brigham Young*, 406.

[84] George Alfred Townsend to William H. Hooper, Oct. 1871, in Townsend, *Mormon Trials at Salt Lake City*, 3.

[85] Further correspondence concerning the event, an address by Newman in the Methodist meeting house of Salt Lake City before the contest, and complete transcripts of the first two days of debate were printed in "Mormonism," *New York Herald*, 18 Aug. 1870, 35:230, 4/1–6, 5/1–5; 20 Aug. 1870, 35:232, 5/4–5; 21 Aug. 1870, 35:233, 4/1–6, 5/1; and 23 Aug. 1870, 35:235, 5/1–6. Whitney devoted a long chapter to the encounter in his *History of Utah*, 2:440–86.

"MORMONISM: CONCLUDING ARGUMENT OF PROFESSOR ORSON PRATT,"
NEW YORK HERALD, 3 SEPT. 1870, 35:246, 11/1–6, 12/1.

Professor Pratt then rose and spoke as follows:—

LADIES AND GENTLEMEN—

. . . Yesterday I was challenged by the Reverend Dr. Newman, to bring forth any evidence whatever to prove that there were more than two polygamist families in all Israel during the time of their sojourn in the wilderness. At least this is what I understood the gentleman to say. I shall now proceed to bring forth the proof. . . It was admitted, yesterday afternoon, by Dr. Newman, that there were two and a half millions of Israelites. Now I shall take the position that the females among the Israelites were far more numerous than the males; I mean that portion of them that were over twenty years of age. I assume this for this reason, that from the birth of Moses down until the time that the Israelites were brought out of Egypt some eighty years had elapsed. The destruction of the male children had commenced before the birth of Moses; how many years before I know not. The order of King Pharaoh was to destroy every male child. All the people, subject to this ruler, were commanded to see that they were destroyed and thrown into the river Nile. How long a period this great destruction continued is unknown, but if we suppose that one male child to every two hundred and fifty persons was annually destroyed, it would amount to the number of ten thousand yearly. This would soon begin to tell in the difference between the numbers of males and females. Ten thousand each year would only be one male child to each two hundred and fifty persons. How many would this make from the birth of Moses, or eighty years? It would amount to 800,000 females above that of males. But I do not wish to take advantage in this argument by assuming too high a number. I will diminish it one half, which will still leave 400,000 more females than males. This would be one male destroyed each year out of every five hundred persons. The females, then, over twenty years of age would be 603,550, added to 400,000 surplus women, making in all 1,003,550 women over twenty years of age. The children, then, under twenty years of age, to make up the two and a half millions, would be 892,900, the total population of Israel being laid down at 2,500,000. Now, then, for the number of families constituting this population. The families having first-born males over one month old, (Numbers iii, 43) numbered 22,273. Families having no male children over one month old supposed to be in the ratio of three to one . . . which would make 7,424 additional families. . . Add these to the 22,273 with first-born males, and we have the sum total of 29,697 families in Israel. Now, in order to favor the monogamists' argument, and give them all the advantage possible, we will still add to this number to make it round numbers . . . 303 families more, making thirty thousand families in all. Now we come to another species of calculation founded on this data. Divide 2,500,000 persons by 22,273 first born males, and we find one first-born male to every 112 persons. What a large family for a monogamist! But divide 2,500,000 persons by 30,000 families and the quotient gives eighty-three persons in a family. . . Suppose these families to be monogamic, after deducting husband and wife, we have the very respectable number of eighty-one children to each monogamic wife. And if we assume the number of males and females to be equal, making no allowance for the destruction of the male infants, we shall then have to increase the number of children under twenty years of age so as to keep good the number of 2,500,000. This would still make eighty-one children . . . in each of the 30,000 monogamic families.

Now . . . if we suppose the average number of wives to be seven . . . though there may be men that have no wife at all, and there may be many monogamic families, and there may be many polygamic families having from one up to thirty or forty wives. But we will average them . . . to seven wives apiece. We should then have one husband, to seven wives and seventy-five children, making eighty-three in a family. In the polygamic household this would give an average of over ten children to each of the 210,000 polygamic wives. . . When we take the 30,000 married men from the 603,550 men over twenty years old, we have 573,550 unmarried men in Israel. If we deduct 210,000 married women from 1,003,550 females over twenty years we have 793,550 females. This would be enough to supply all the unmarried men with one wife each, leaving still a balance of 220,000 unmarried females to live old maids or enter into polygamic households. . .

But now then, having brought forth these statistics, let us for a few moments examine the results more closely. . . How can any one assume them to be monogamic and be consistent? . . . I presume that my friend, notwithstanding his great desire and earnestness to overthrow polygamy, I presume that he will not have the conscience to say to this people that one wife can bring forth eighty-one children in a household . . . If they cannot, and we can depend upon these numbers, these biblical statistics, then let Mr. Newman, who assumes that the males and females were equal, show how these great and wonderful households could be produced among Israel if there were only two polygamic families in their midst. It requires something more powerful than that medicinal herb called mandrakes . . . (laughter.) I think there are no mandrakes at the present day that would accomplish such wonders as that. (laughter.) . . .[86]

Having then established that Israel was a polygamic nation, remember that when God gives laws He gives them to a polygamic nation, the monogamic families being the exception. . .

Having discussed the subject so far, I leave it now with all candid persons to judge. Here is the law of God; here is the command of the Most High, general in its nature, not limited, nor can it be proved to be so. There is no law against it, but it stands as immovable as the Rock of Ages, and will stand when all things on the earth and the earth itself shall pass away.—

---

[86] Pratt seemed unable to let go the mathematical argument for ancient Israel's polygamy. See "Discourse by Elder Orson Pratt," 7 October 1874, *Des. News* [Weekly], 6 Jan. 1875, 23:49, 772/1–2.

CONCLUDING ARGUMENT OF DR. NEWMAN.

Dr. Newman then came forward and spoke as follows:—

RESPECTED UMPIRES AND LADIES AND GENTLEMEN—

I had heard, prior to my coming to your city that my distinguished opponent was eminent in mathematics, and certainly his display to-day confirms that reputation. Unfortunately, however, he is incorrect in his statements. First, he assumes that the slaying of the male children of the Hebrews was continued through eighty years. He has failed to produce the proof today. This was his starting point. He assumes it. Where is the proof, either in the Bible or in Josephus? And until he can prove that the destruction of the male children went on for eighty years, then I say that his argument has no more foundation than a vision. Then he makes another blunder. The 603,550 men above twenty years of age mentioned in this case, were men to go to war. They were not the total population of the Jewish nation. And yet my mathematical friend stands here to-day and declares that the whole male population above twenty years of age consisted of 603,550, whereas it is a fact that this number did not include all the males. . .

. . . Now, I propose to follow out the line of argument which I was pursuing yesterday . . . we call your attention to the fact that in the Bible there are only twenty-five or thirty specially recorded cases of polygamy which polygamists of our day claim in support of their position . . . I take up Abraham. It is asserted that he was a polygamist. I deny it. There is no proof that Abraham was guilty of polygamy. What are the facts? When he was called of the Almighty to be the founder of a great nation, then the promise was given to him that he should have a numerous posterity. At that time he was a monogamist; he had but one wife, the noble Sarah. Six years passed and the promise was not fulfilled. Then Sarah, desiring to help the Lord to keep His own promise, brought her Egyptian maid Hagar and offered her as a substitute for herself to Abraham. Mind you, Abraham did not go after Hagar, but Sarah produced her as her substitute. Immediately after the act was performed Sarah discovered her sin, and said, "My wrong be upon thee; I have committed sin, but I did it for thy sake, and therefore the wrong that I have committed be upon thee." And then look at the subsequent facts. By the Divine command this Egyptian girl was sent away from the abode of Abraham, was sent away by mutual consent of the husband and the wife, and by the Divine command. It is said that she was recognized. Never as the wife of Abraham. You cannot prove it from the Bible. . . She was sent away by Divine commandment, and God said unto Abraham—"now walk before me and be thou perfect." These are the facts, my friends. I know that some will refer you to Keturah, but this is the fact in regard to her: Abraham lived thirty-eight years after the death of Sarah. The energy miraculously given to Abraham's body for the generation of Isaac was continued after Sarah's death. To suppose that he took Keturah during Sarah's lifetime is to do violence to his moral character. But it is said that he sent away the sons of Keturah with presents during his lifetime, therefore it must have been during the lifetime of Sarah. But he lived thirty-eight years after the death of Sarah, and he sent these sons away eight years before his death, and they were from twenty-five to thirty years old. Therefore this venerable Patriarch stands forth as a monogamist and not as a polygamist (manifestations of dissent.) . . .

There was another point that I desired to touch upon—that is as to the longevity of nations. We are told here repeatedly and in printed works, that monogamic nations are short-lived, and that polygamic nations are long-lived.[87] I am prepared to go back to the days of Nimrod, and come down to the days of Sardanapalus, and down to the days of Cyrus the Great, and all through those polygamic nations and show that they were short-lived, while on the other hand I am prepared to prove that Greece and Rome outlived the longest-lived polygamic nations of the past. Greece, from the days of Homer down to the first century of our era, and Rome from 750 years before Christ down to the dissolution of that old empire; and that old empire finds a resurrection in the Italians under Victor Emanuel and Garibaldi; and England and Germany and France are all proofs of the longevity of monogamic nations. Babylon is a ruin to-day, and Babylon was polygamic. Egypt, to-day, is a ruin. Her massive piles of ruins bespeak her former glory and her pristine beauty. And the last edition of the polygamic nations—I mean the Turks—that nation is passing away. From the Golden horn and Bosphorus, from the Danube to the Jordan and the Nile, the power of Mahommedanism is passing away before the advance of the monogamic nations of the world. . .[88]

These, my friends, are the arguments in favor of monogamy, and when they can be overthrown, then it is time for us to receive the system of polygamy as it is taught here . . . we cannot give up that grand idea that God's law commands monogamy; that the highest interests of woman, that the highest interests of man, that the dearest interests of the rising generation, that all that binds us to earth and binds us to heaven—all these great interests demand of us the practice of monogamy in marriage—one man with one wife. Then indeed shall be realized the picture portrayed in the Scriptures of the happy family, of the family where the wife is one and the husband one, and the two are equivalents. Then one father and mother centered in one family, shall bring up their children in the nurture and admonition of the Lord—when the husband provides for his family—for, it is said, if a man does not provide for his family he is worse than an infidel. Until all this can be done monogamy shall stand forth as a grand Bible Truth.

---

[87] On such assertions by Mormons, see Chapter Two.

[88] Newman's line of argument here was one taken by many critics of the Mormons. They believed the existence of plural marriage in the Old Testament was irrelevant, for it was an ancient ethos needing replacement by the more egalitarian teachings of the New. See, for example, Ferris, *Utah and the Mormons*, 238; Bowles, *Across the Continent*, 112; and Gov. Stephen S. Harding, in "Message to the Territorial Legislature of Utah," Senate Misc. Doc. 37, 28 Feb. 1863, Serial 1150, 5. Rep. Justin S. Morrill's critique was that Mormon theology denied the possibility of religious progress since the time of the ancients. See *Cong. Globe* (34-3), 23 Feb. 1857, 287.

"Silence and Smoke": Pressures Mount

Anxious to add another pennant to his victories, President Ulysses S. Grant gave special attention to Utah. He named Gen. J. Wilson Shaffer governor and James B. McKean as territorial chief justice, both good Republicans and former military men determined to trample the remaining "twin relic of barbarism." As Leonard Arrington explained, judges played a more crucial role in the struggle than executive officers, making McKean's appointment the more significant of the two.[89] And the new chief justice went directly to work, ignoring territorial laws concerning jury selection, overseeing the indictment of scores of pluralists, including Brigham Young. The recently founded *Salt Lake Tribune* said the contest was now clearly defined: polygamic theocracy versus the authority of the United States.[90] McKean's efforts came to naught, however, when the United States Supreme Court declared his jury-selection procedures improper and he was later retired from the bench.[91]

McKean's frustrations notwithstanding, Grant remained as immovable as he was at Vicksburg and refused to give ground in the fight against Mormon polygamy. There was little surprise that he strongly opposed Utah's fourth request for statehood in 1872. As he would say in 1875:

> In nearly every annual message that I have had the honor of transmitting to Congress I have called attention to the anomalous, not to say scandalous, condition of affairs existing in the Territory of Utah. . . That polygamy should exist in a free, enlightened, and Christian country, without the power to punish so flagrant a crime against decency and morality, seems preposterous.[92]

Ever hopeful, a territorial convention met, wrote a constitution modeled on that of Nevada, and representatives for the new state of "Deseret" were selected. Recognizing that plural marriage was the chief impediment to success, delegates used language in an "Ordinance" accompanying the proposed constitution that said, if Congress prescribed it, Utah would put its pecu-

---

[89] Arrington, "Crusade against Theocracy," 2.

[90] "Braving It Out," *Salt Lake Daily Tribune and Mining Gazette*, 9 Oct. 1871, 1:51 [2/1]. The best overviews of McKean's tenure in Utah remain those of Dwyer, *The Gentile Comes to Utah*, 74–93; Alexander, "Federal Authority Versus Polygamic Theocracy," 85–100; and the long, anecdotal sketch provided in *History of the Bench and Bar of Utah*, 27–47.

[91] *Clinton et al. vs. Englebrecht*, 80 U.S. 434 (1872). For further legal comment, see Firmage and Mangrum, *Zion in the Courts*, 144–46.

[92] Ulysses S. Grant, "Seventh Annual Message," 7 Dec. 1875, *Comp.*, 9:4309. Grant's attitudes may have moderated after visiting Utah Territory in 1875. See Alexander, "Conflict of Perceptions," 38–40.

liar institution to a vote as a condition for admission.[93] Thomas Fitch, a former Republican congressman from Nevada then seeking political office in Utah, was chosen with William Henry Hooper to serve as the state's first senators in Washington. Though not a Mormon, Fitch spoke strongly against the Cullom Bill in 1870, and the Saints considered him a friend.[94] A Washington correspondent for the widely read *Cincinnati Commercial* reported his interview with President Grant.[95]

H. V. R., "THE PRESIDENT AND UTAH,"
CINCINNATI COMMERCIAL, 18 MAY 1872, 32:259, 11/2.

Senator-elect Fitch, from the embryo State of Deseret, called upon the President a few days ago to talk over Utah affairs. He found the President enjoying a cigar.

"Mr. President," said the Colonel, "I want to try and convince you of the advisability of admitting Utah into the sisterhood of States."

"I am unalterably opposed to the admission of Utah," answered the President.

"Yes, but you have been prejudiced against the people out there by unfair advisers," said Fitch.

"I am unalterably opposed to the admission of Utah," was the reply.

"But our population is sufficient; we have made a fair constitution, and it would be a great relief to the people out there to get into the Union."

"I am unalterably opposed to the admission of Utah," again replied the firm man.

"Upon any terms?"

"Yes, upon any terms. At least they should not come in until they learn how to behave themselves."

---

[93] The convention's petition and proposed constitution were submitted to and published by Congress as *Admission of Utah into the Union . . .* , House Misc. Doc. 165 (42-2), 2 April 1872, Serial 1526. The "Ordinance" referred to was similar to pledges required of former southern states when applying for readmission. And, as in those instances, the Utah "Ordinance" affirmed support for the U.S. Constitution, formally rejecting both slavery and involuntary servitude. Additionally, the Utah petition relinquished to the U.S. government all claims to unappropriated lands in the territory, an issue over which conflict had festered. Finally, and peculiar to Utah, it stated: "That such terms, if any, as may be prescribed by Congress as a condition . . . for the admission of the said State into the Union, shall, if ratified by a majority vote of the people thereof, at such time and under such regulations as may be prescribed by this convention, thereupon be embraced within and constitute a part of this ordinance." Ibid., 4–5. Opposition is in *Petition of Residents of Utah Territory*, Senate Misc. Doc. 118 (42-2), 22 Mar. 1872, Serial 1482.

[94] Fitch's remarks during the Cullom Bill debate are in *Cong. Globe* (41-2), 23 Feb. 1870, 1517–19.

[95] This interview was reproduced as "Interview of a Utah Senator with the President: Wasted Argument," *Mil. Star* 34:454 (16 July 1872), 454; then by Roberts, in his *Comprehensive History*, 5:467–68. Both are incorrectly titled, incompletely cited, and contain typographical errors.

"If you refer to polygamy, they will no doubt surrender that for the sake of admission and peace, although it is one of the doctrines of their church."

"And murder is one of the doctrines of the Church, ain't it?"

"No, indeed; there are less murders committed there than in any of the surrounding Territories. As I said before, you have been very much misinformed about the true condition of affairs. You surely don't believe everything you hear against the Mormons?"

"Where there is so much smoke there must be some fire," answered the President.

"Suppose we should say the same about all the lies told about you?"

Silence and smoke.

"By admitting us the troubles out there would be at an end."

Silence and smoke.

"It is of the highest importance to the welfare of her people and development of the rich resources of the Territory that Utah be admitted."

Silence and smoke.

"Is your mind, Mr. President, so firmly made up, that whatever arguments might be adduced would be useless?"

"I am unalterably opposed to the admission of Utah," replied our firm President, and the charming interview ended.

Congress was as stubborn as the president, and Utah waited another quarter-century for its star on the flag. At the same time a crowd of lawmakers began cranking out new bills aimed at crushing Utah's anomalous marriages.[96] When none of the proposals reached the president's desk, Grant hinted at using soldiers to do the job.[97] This proved a sufficient goad, and in mid-1874 Congress passed a bill by Rep. Luke Potter Poland aimed at reforming the court system in Utah. By shifting criminal jurisdiction away from local tribunals, such as probate courts, to district courts dominated by federal appointees, the Poland Act gave greater assurance that Mormon polygamists would be convicted. The law also gave judges in such cases authority to pronounce sentences, rather than juries, and authorized the employment of as many deputy marshals and assistant district attorneys as the territory needed.[98]

---

[96] Brief synopses of efforts by Sens. John A. Logan, Frederick Frelinghuysen, and Reps. William A. Wheeler, James G. Blair, and Samuel Augustus Merritt are in Roberts, *Comprehensive History*, 5:434–39.

[97] "Message from the President of the United States . . . ," Sen. Exec. Doc. 44 (42-3) 14 Feb. 1873, Serial 1545, 3; and Grant, "To the Senate and House of Representatives," 14 Feb. 1873, Simon, ed., *Papers of Ulysses S. Grant*, 24:38.

[98] U.S., *Statutes at Large*, 18:469, pt. 3, 253–56.—*An act in relation to courts and judicial officers in the Territory of Utah*, 23 June 1874. For relevant studies see Allen, "Unusual Jurisdiction of County Probate Courts," 132–41; Powell, "Fairness in Salt Lake County Probate Courts," 256–62; and Gee, "Justice for All or for the 'Elect,'" 129–47.

"A Feature of the Life of Asiatic and of African People": The Supreme Court Speaks

Mormons insisted that the Morrill Law of 1862 was an unconstitutional interference with their religious liberty as guaranteed by the First Amendment to the United States Constitution. Both they and their opponents had long wanted to settle the question by obtaining a pronouncement from the U.S. Supreme Court. George Reynolds (1842–1909), who had recently taken a plural wife, agreed in 1874 to cooperate with prosecutors to test the statute. His indictment and conviction soon followed. Appeals in the case moved up and down territorial tribunals, finally arriving at the steps of the nation's highest court in 1878.[99] During that time, to reinforce its claim that patriarchal marriage was an entirely religious tenet and thereby assist Reynolds's assault on the federal law, church leaders for the first time incorporated the revelation on polygamy in one of the volumes constituting Mormonism's official canon of belief, the *Doctrine and Covenants*. To make it clear that the revelation spoke to more than the notion of eternal family life, what most Mormons chiefly associate with the document today, it was introduced with the words: "Revelation on the Eternity of the Marriage Covenant, including Plurality of Wives."[100] Mormon women, when the case was being heard in the autumn of 1878, gathered by the thousands to add their voices to the cause:

> . . . we solemnly avow our belief in the doctrine of the Patriarchal order of marriage . . . which if lived up to and carried out under the direction of the precepts pertaining to it, and of the highest principles of our nature, would conduce to the long life, strength and glory of the people practicing it; and we therefore endorse it, as one of the most important principles of our holy religion, and claim the right of its practice.[101]

But neither this, nor Reynolds's testimony that living the Principle was required of all who wished to reach the highest level of glory in the hereafter, helped.

In a unanimous decision yet having precedental importance, Chief Justice Waite repeated arguments that polygamy was non-Western, contrary to the nation's traditions, and if permitted could lead to suttee and other forms of barbarous behavior. He also endorsed earlier statements that the First

---

[99] See Gordon, *Mormon Question*, 119–45; Van Orden, "George Reynolds," 53–93; and Firmage and Mangrum, *Zion in the Courts*, 151–59. [100] *D&C* 132 (1876).

[101] "Woman's Mass Meeting," *Des. Eve. News*, 17 Nov. 1878, 11:302 [3/3].

SECTION CXXXII.

Revelation on the Eternity of the Marriage Covenant, including Plurality of Wives. Given through Joseph, the Seer, in Nauvoo, Hancock County, Illinois, July 12th, 1843.

1. Verily, thus saith the Lord unto you, my servant Joseph, that inasmuch as you have inquired of my hand, to know and understand wherein I, the Lord, justified my servants Abraham, Isaac and Jacob; as also Moses, David and Solomon, my servants, as touching the principle and doctrine of their having many wives and concubines:

2. Behold! and lo, I am the Lord thy God, and will answer thee as touching this matter:

3. Therefore, prepare thy heart to receive and obey the instructions which I am about to give unto you; for all those who have this law revealed unto them must obey the same;

4. For behold! I reveal unto you a new and an everlasting covenant; and if ye abide not that covenant, then are ye damned; for no one can reject this covenant, and be permitted to enter into my glory;

5. For all who will have a blessing at my hands, shall abide the law which was appointed for that blessing, and the conditions thereof, as were instituted from before the foundation of the world:

6. And as pertaining to the new and everlasting covenant, it was instituted for the fulness of my glory; and he that receiveth a fulness thereof, must and shall abide the law, or he shall be damned, saith the Lord God.

7. And verily I say unto you, that the conditions of this law are these:—All covenants, contracts, bonds, obligations, oaths, vows, performances, connections, as-

The first official printing of the 1843 revelation approving plural marriage appeared in the 1876 edition of the *Doctrine and Covenants*. An introduction to the document, shown here, made it clear that plural marriage was an integral part of the revelation. This wording was removed from later editions of the work when church leaders sought to diminish attention to polygamy in Mormon society. *From the author's collection.*

Amendment's freedom-of-religion clause sheltered only religious belief, not practice. As Professor Gordon pointed out in her study, not only was the Reynolds decision historically important for the constitutional history of First Amendment freedoms, but it represented an effort to redeem the court's reputation in the wake of *Dred Scott*. It signaled a shift from diminished reform in the South to a "second 'Reconstruction' in the West."[102] As for Reynolds himself, after being convicted and serving less than two years in prison, he returned to the acclaim of his community and was subsequently made a general authority of the church.[103]

REYNOLDS *vs.* UNITED STATES (1879), 98 U.S. 153, 161–68.

MR. CHIEF JUSTICE WAITE delivered the opinion of the court. . .

On the trial, the plaintiff in error, the accused, proved that at the time of his alleged second marriage he was, and for many years before had been, a member of the Church of Jesus Christ of Latter-Day Saints, commonly called the Mormon Church, and a believer in its doctrines; that it was an accepted doctrine of that church "that it was the duty of male members of said church, circumstances permitting, to practise polygamy . . . that this duty was enjoined by different books which the members of said church believed to be of divine origin, and among others the Holy Bible, and also that the members of the church believed that the practice of polygamy was directly enjoined upon the male members thereof by the Almighty God, in a revelation to Joseph Smith, the founder and prophet of said church; that the failing or refusing to practise polygamy by such male members of said church, when circumstances would admit, would be punished, and that the penalty for such failure and refusal would be damnation in the life to come." He also proved "that he had received permission from the recognized authorities in said church to enter into polygamous marriage . . . that Daniel H. Wells, one having authority in said church to perform the marriage ceremony, married the said defendant on or about the time the crime is alleged to have been committed, to some woman by the name of Schofield, and that such marriage ceremony was performed under and pursuant to the doctrines of said church."

. . . the question is raised, whether religious belief can be accepted as a justification of an overt act made criminal by the law of the land. The inquiry is not as to the power of Congress to prescribe criminal laws for the Territories, but as to the guilt of one who knowingly violates a law which has been properly enacted, if he entertains a religious belief that the law is wrong. . .

---

[102] Gordon, *Mormon Question*, 123–24, 130, 144.

[103] Jenson, *Latter-day Saint Biographical Encyclopedia*, 1:206–10; Junius F. Wells, "Living Martyr," *Contributor*, 2:5 (Feb. 1881), 154–57; and Reynolds's own comments gathered in Andrew Jenson, "Prisoners for Conscience Sake," fd. 2, LDS Archives.

Polygamy has always been odious among the northern and western nations of Europe, and, until the establishment of the Mormon Church, was almost exclusively a feature of the life of Asiatic and of African people. At common law, the second marriage was always void . . . and from the earliest history of England polygamy has been treated as an offence against society.

. . . we think it may safely be said there never has been a time in any State of the Union when polygamy has not been an offence against society, cognizable by the civil courts and punishable with more or less severity. In the face of all this evidence, it is impossible to believe that the constitutional guaranty of religious freedom was intended to prohibit legislation in respect to this most important feature of social life. . . Marriage, while from its very nature a sacred obligation, is nevertheless, in most civilized nations, a civil contract, and usually regulated by law. Upon it society may be said to be built, and out of its fruits spring social relations and social obligations and duties, with which government is necessarily required to deal. In fact, according as monogamous or polygamous marriages are allowed, do we find the principles on which the government of the people, to a greater or less extent, rests. Professor Lieber says, polygamy leads to the patriarchal principle, and which, when applied to large communities, fetters the people in stationary despotism, while that principle cannot long exist in connection with monogamy. . .[104]

In our opinion, the statute immediately under consideration is within the legislative power of Congress. It is constitutional and valid as prescribing a rule of action for all those residing in the Territories, and in places over which the United States have exclusive control. . . Laws are made for the government of actions, and while they cannot interfere with mere religious belief and opinions, they may with practices. Suppose that one believed that human sacrifices were a necessary part of religious worship, would it be seriously contended that the civil government under which he lived could not interfere to prevent a sacrifice? Or if a wife religiously believed it was her duty to burn herself upon the funeral pile of her dead husband, would it be beyond the power of the civil government to prevent her carrying her belief into practice?

So here, as a law of the organization of society under the exclusive dominion of the United States, it is provided that plural marriages shall not be allowed. Can a man excuse his practices to the contrary because of his religious belief? To permit this would be to make the professed doctrines of religious belief superior to the law of the land, and in effect to permit every citizen to become a law unto himself. Government could exist only in name under such circumstances. . .

Judgement affirmed.

---

[104] Lieber, *On Civil Liberty and Self-Government*, 82–83. For an essay on Francis Lieber's linkage of polygamy to racial stereotypes, see Cott, *Public Vows*, 115–16.

An "Irrepressible" Conflict

Near the same time, other important developments occurred. Ann Eliza Young, a former plural wife of Brigham Young, toured the nation as a popular lecturer describing what she saw as the oppression and deceit of the Mormon system of marriage.[105] More ominous perhaps than all else was completion of the transcontinental railway in 1869. With the whine of locomotives came the sowing of an enlarged and restive Gentile population among the Saints. "A railway train has done it all," said William Hepworth Dixon, only slightly overstating the importance of this event for the transformation of Mormonism.[106] It was an ancient dilemma that confronted the church's faithful. They were not the first to have the unwashed invade their wilderness Jerusalem. William Bradford feared for the Pilgrims because of the flood of new settlers into their "cuntrie."[107] And the Hebrew psalmist, crowded by the uncircumcised, lamented because Israel had become "a reproach to our neighbours."[108]

Despite such omens, few who believed in the Principle could have predicted what befell them. Wrapped in a providential vision of history and their place in it, Mormons were certain God's protection would continue and they would overcome their enemies. But the social and religious pluralism of early nineteenth-century America was yielding to the intolerance of Victorian morality. To adapt a phrase used by Taylor Stoehr in his account of those opposing free love and easy divorce, "magistrates, clergymen, and vigilantes" were determined to wipe away "every sort of -gamy other than monogamy."[109] Territorial governor Stephen S. Harding, in an 1862 address that so disturbed the Saints they refused to print it and sought to have him removed from office, told a resentful Utah legislature that if Mormons continued on their polygamous course they were destined for not only an "irrepressible" but a losing conflict with the American people.[110] As time proved, his was the clearer eye.

---

[105] Her 1876 book, *Wife No. 19*, was also widely read.

[106] See Vixon, above, in Chapter Five. Samuel Bowles, from whom Dixon acquired some of his ideas, said the same thing in 1865. Regarding Mormon plural marriage, he predicted: "The click of the telegraph and the roll of the overland stages are its death-rattle now; the first whistle of the locomotive will sound its requiem; and the pick ax of the miner will dig its grave." *Across the Continent*, 108.

[107] Bradford, *History of Plymouth Plantation*, 2:151.   [108] Psalms 44:13–14.

[109] Stoehr, *Free Love in America*, 5.

[110] Senate Misc. Doc. 37 (37-2), 1863, Serial 1150, 6; and the Senate Committee on Territories' response, in Report 87 (37-3), 1863, Serial 1151.

Nothing resonated with American readers more than the presumed trauma imposed on first wives and children when a plural wife was brought across the threshold. "Life among the Mormons—The New Wife." *From* Frank Leslie's Illustrated Newspaper, *8 May 1886.*

Chapter 7

"UNLESS WE
DESTROY MORMONISM,
MORMONISM WILL DESTROY US"
The Crusade Full Tilt

Variously referred to by Mormons as the "storm," the "raid," or simply the "active" as opposed to a "passive" phase of national opposition, the 1880s were by all accounts the defining years of the government's long crusade against Mormonism and its marriage system.[1] The Saints recognized the magnitude of the battle confronting them, as illustrated in a stirring 1879 address by Apostle Franklin D. Richards:

> There is no use our laying the flattering unction to our souls that government is not agoing to do this. We have got an example of what they have done to the Southern States, and have no doubt they are just as ready and willing to do that much to abolish polygamy among us *if God will let them*.[2]

Americans were increasingly persuaded that the "now world-noised institution" of Mormon plurality was a serious danger to the nation.[3] "Mormonism in the West, illiteracy in the South, rum in the East," said one writer, "these are the elements of the Devil's Trinity."[4] Another called polygamous

---

[1] For the different appellations, see Roberts, *Life of John Taylor*, 377; Arrington and Quinn, "Latter-Day Saints in the Far West, 1847–1900," 266–67; Ivins, carton 9, fd. 2, Stanley Snow Ivins Collection, Uhi; and Larson, *"Americanization" of Utah*, 61ff. The number of scholarly writings on this phase of the struggle is immense but remains largely the same as those cited in Chapter Six.

[2] "Discourse Delivered By Elder Franklin D. Richards," 6 Oct. 1879, *Des. News* [Weekly], 29 Oct. 1879, 28:39, 610/4.

[3] The language is that of Tullidge, *Women of Mormondom*, 367.

[4] Noble, *Mormon Iniquity*, 3.

Mormonism "the Great Modern Abomination, the most pernicious heresy of this century."[5]

The ferocity of anti-Mormon attacks is astonishing. Rev. George Whitfield Phillips of Massachusetts urged young missionaries to set their sights on Utah because people there needed enlightenment as much as the tribes of darkest Africa.[6] Dilating on the theme of "Oriental" decadence, the sexual practices of Mormon men were cast in the Victorian pornographic mold of Asiatic sensual abandon.[7] Such characterizations dated from the 1850s, but they appeared more widely in the 1880s than at any time before. In her introduction to Jennie Anderson Froiseth's exposé, *Women of Mormonism*, Frances Willard said: "Turkey is in our midst. Modern Mohammedanism has its Mecca at Salt Lake."[8] And former vice president Schuyler Colfax, after a third visit to Salt Lake City in the late 1870s, gave speeches throughout the nation saying, among other things, that "No one can shut his eyes *now* to the insolent defiance our Mormon Turks have flung into the face of the nation." If the country did nothing, Colfax predicted, the Saints would spread, taking their habits with them, and "interior America will be given up to the worst phase of Asiatic barbarism."[9]

Hatred was especially pronounced in the American South where the belief that Mormons seduced proselytes, baptized women naked, and sequestered them in Utah harems was prevalent. Four Mormon missionaries were killed in the region between 1879 and 1890. Others were tarred and feathered, shot at, wounded, and horsewhipped.[10] A Utah deputy marshal shot and killed Edward Meeks Dalton, a fugitive polygamist, in a scrimmage at Parowan.[11]

---

[5] Beers, *Mormon Puzzle and How To Solve It*, 141. Yet another critic called Mormon plurality "the especial curse and disgrace of this country." "The Citadel of Mormonism," *Chicago Evening Journal* 36:243, 6 Feb. 1880 [2/2].

[6] Phillips, *Mormon Menace*, esp. 6–12, 16.

[7] For Victorian pornographic imagery, see Marcus, *Other Victorians*, 197–216.

[8] Froiseth, *Women of Mormonism*, xvi.

[9] As quoted in Coyner, "Letters on Mormonism," 357, 364. Also see Hollister, *Life of Schuyler Colfax*, 472–73.

[10] For accusations of sexual misbehavior, see Wingfield, "Tennessee's Mormon Massacre," 20, 27, 31–32. Accounts of violence against Mormons in the South are extensive: "Missionaries Maltreated," *Des. Eve. News*, 16 July 1887, 20:198 [5/2]; "Persecution and Misrepresentation," ibid., 18 July 1887, 20:199 [2/2–3]; "Elders Wounded," ibid., 14 Jan. 1888, 21:45 [5/4]; Roberts, "Tennessee Massacre," *Contributor* 6:1 (Oct. 1884), 16–23; Nicholson, *Martyrdom of Joseph Standing*; all of Hatch, *There Is No Law*; and Sessions, "Myth, Mormonism, and Murder in the South," 212–25.

[11] Daniel Tyler, "Dalton Murder," *Des. News* [Weekly], 29 Dec. 1886, 35:50, 791/4; and Dix, "Unwilling Martyr: The Death of Young Ed Dalton," 162–77. A U.S. deputy marshal shot Joseph W. McMurrin twice in the bowels in 1885, but McMurrin miraculously survived. See Whitney, *History of Utah*, 3:447–57; and Larson, *"Americanization" of Utah*, 142–45.

And some maliciously circulated rumors that Charles Guiteau, President Garfield's assassin, was a Mormon.[12]

The Reorganized Church of Jesus Christ of Latter Day Saints renewed its attacks, always accompanying its criminations with rehearsals of the claim that there was no evidence demonstrating Mormon approval for polygamy before the 1852 announcement by Brigham Young.[13] Edward W. Tullidge, wearing new denominational colors, suggested that Joseph Smith III be appointed governor of Utah and that, if accompanied by a flood of Reorganized Church missionaries into the territory, destruction of both polygamy and Mormon theocracy would follow.[14] "Next to the Emancipation Proclamation, we need an Anti-Polygamy Proclamation," another petitioner wrote President Hayes. "Is it not in your power to issue such?"[15] And Eli H. Murray, a staunch Republican from Kentucky who was appointed territorial governor in 1880, repeatedly stated that for too long the nation had been lulled by hope that civilization and railroads would overcome the Mormon dream of "polygamic empire." If the issue were not to follow the path of slaveocracy in the Old South and lead the nation into violence, he said, decisive steps must be taken.[16] Using language employed years earlier by Stephen A. Douglas, a former district attorney from the territory declared that the nation had reached the point where it must apply "the knife," as it had with slavery, and carve the "ulcer" of polygamy away.[17]

---

[12] B. H. Roberts said Rev. T. DeWitt Talmage first made the insinuation. Roberts, *Comprehensive History*, 6:26–30.

[13] Joseph Smith III to Pres. Rutherford B. Hayes, 21 Jan. 1879, RG48, N.A. Debate between the cousins over polygamy raged into the next century. Instances of the quarrel are in Littlefield, *Open Letter*; and, *Reply of Pres. Joseph Smith, to L. O. Littlefield*; Musser, *"Race Suicide," Infanticide, Prolicide*; and the ninety-four-page collection of letters between Richard C. Evans, second counselor in the presidency of the Reorganized Church, and Joseph F. Smith Jr., an authority in the Utah church, in *Blood Atonement and the Origin of Plural Marriage*.

[14] Edward W. Tullidge to Pres. Rutherford B. Hayes, 19 Oct. 1879, RG48, N.A.

[15] Rev. John Martin to Pres. Rutherford B. Hayes, 5 Mar. 1879, RG48, N.A.

[16] Again and again Murray referred to the "wretched" and "fanatical" nature of Mormon men who "thrust [first wives] . . . aside for new and fresher companions." Eli Murray, "Report of the Governor of Utah," RSI (1880), 2:522–23. The governor of Idaho spoke similarly, lamenting the number of Saints moving into his territory. Jonathan B. Neil, "Report of the Governor of Idaho," ibid. (1880), 2:553. Both territorial executives predicted that, unless something was done, Mormonism and its "barn-yard system" would spread throughout the western U.S. Murray, "Report," ibid. (1880), 2:522; and, Niel, "Report," ibid., 2:553.

[17] This was Phillip T. Van Zile in an address to the Michigan State Association for Congregational Churches in Detroit, Michigan, on 21 May 1880. It was printed in Froiseth's *Women of Mormonism*, 322.

"The 'Let Alone' Method Has Failed":
Clerics, Women, and Journalists Lead the Assault

Governor Murray's warning to Congress that, so far as polygamy was concerned, *"time will not prove the remedy,"* acquired increasing currency as the 1880s moved along.[18] Utah clergymen were especially active in fomenting objection to Mormon behavior, and their wives and those of Gentile merchants founded the Anti-Polygamy Society in 1878. Soon renamed "The Women's National Anti-Polygamy Society," and with the assistance of a few disaffected Mormon females, chapters were established throughout the United States.[19] Between 1880 and 1883 the organization's publication, the *Anti-Polygamy Standard*, circulated widely outside the territory. Its first number set the tone for subsequent issues with this third-hand, anonymous account of a polygamous home in southern Utah.

"Beauties of Polygamy," *Anti-Polygamy Standard*
1:1 (April 1880), 1.

While traveling in Southern Utah, we came to a small settlement where we were detained for a day or two by inclement weather. We found shelter in the humble, but neat and hospitable home of a monogamist saint, whose family hated polygamy, and through whose influence we were permitted a glance at some of the beastliness that characterizes the peculiar institution. Only a short distance from the dwelling of my friendly entertainers, there stood a miserable adobe hut, I could not conscientiously call it a house, where lived a saint with three wives, all of whom had families. My hostess made some neighborly errand an excuse for paying them a visit and permitted me to accompany her, but before going she made me acquainted with the relationship existing between the three women who were living with and had borne children to the same man. The first and second women were sisters, the latter had been

---

[18] Murray, "Report of the Governor of Utah, *rsi* (1880), 2:523.

[19] "Gentile Ladies Hoist Their Standard," in Dwyer, *Gentile Comes to Utah*, 190–214; and all of Hayward, "Utah's Anti-Polygamy Society." Some also succeeded in obtaining federal support for an "industrial home" where, it was assumed, mistreated plural wives would flee for refuge. Only a handful of women ever took up residence at the facility. See Larson, "Industrial Home for Polygamous Wives," 263–75; and Dwyer, *Gentile Comes to Utah*, 205–14. The federal government's appropriation of $40,000 for the project is found in "Industrial Home in Utah Territory," U.S., *Statutes at Large*, 24:252, 4 Aug. 1886, 902. Some said that the image of degraded, polygamous wives took the place of black slaves as a reform object after the Civil War: Harriet Beecher Stowe's introduction to Mrs. T. B. H. Stenhouse, *Tell It All*," vi; and Casterline, "'In the Toils' Or 'Onward for Zion': Images of the Mormon Woman," 131; and Iversen, "Debate," 592. An insightful exploration of the conflict between toleration for Mormon religion in the name of pluralism and the concern liberals felt for Latter-day Saint women is provided in Baum, "Feminism, Liberalism and Cultural Pluralism," 230–53.

Taken by Andrew J. Russell, this photograph is probably the most famous and often-circulated image used to disparage Mormon plural home life. None in the picture, however, are polygamous. Samuel and Mary Bunting Ashton pose with relatives in front of their cabin in Kaysville, Utah, probably in the 1880s. *From the author's collection.*

a widow with one child when she married her sister's husband. When this child had grown to be about sixteen years old, her step father had also married her, but after a few months she left and was sealed to another man as plural wife by whom she had two children. Then he died, and she returned to her first husband bringing her children with her, the eldest of whom at the time I am speaking of was a girl about fifteen years old, and my informant stated for a fact that the old wretch had thoughts of marrying her too. When we entered the hut the scene that met my eyes totally beggars description. Imagine one low, smoky, filthy room serving as living room, and sleeping apartment for three women and their offspring, some of the latter almost grown up, the majority however being little children. I could never have dreamed of such dirt, rags and squalor existing in a Christian country. I had seen nothing equal to it even among the digger Indians, in fact the latter were quite civilized in comparison. But the worst of my story is yet to come. The young girl of whom my hostess had spoken as a probable bride of her grandfather, was sitting in a corner sobbing and crying. Upon inquiring the cause of her distress, we were told quite frankly that her grandmother had given her a severe castigation for speaking disrespectfully about polygamy and declaring she would never become the wife of her mother's and grandmother's husband. When we left I could not restrain my indignation and I said, "what a loveless religion this is to make such beasts out of human creatures." "It is not religion, but the lack of it that makes them beasts," quietly rejoined my hostess, " and you will find many cases as bad as this one if you travel far in Utah." As I said before, the digger Indians were models of cleanliness and modesty compared with this family, and as my friend had predicted I found more like it as we traveled farther South. But the sequel is still more horrible. About a year afterward we had occasion to pass through that particular settlement again, and for a day were the guests of our former hostess. She told me that the young girl was really sealed to her grandfather, being literally forced into it by her own mother and grandmother under circumstances so revolting that delicacy forbids me from repeating them even to one of my own sex. Even in that polygamic community the excitement was so great that talk was had of lynching the degraded trio, the man and the two elder women, but the feeling soon passed over, and was eventually forgotten or only remembered as an episode of this peculiar religion.

Among Gentile women of Utah few displayed greater devotion to the destruction of polygamy than Jennie Anderson Froiseth (1849–1930). The well-educated wife of an army surveyor at Fort Douglas, she served as vice president of the Anti-Polygamy Society, edited the *Anti-Polygamy Standard*, and was active in temperance and women's suffrage movements.[20] The selection below is an excerpt from Froiseth's book, a volume of reconstituted biographical accounts originally printed in the *Standard*. Froiseth's work was part of the indignation that grew in the 1880s, criticizing patience as a method to erase polygamy from the American landscape.

JENNIE ANDERSON FROISETH, ED.,
WOMEN OF MORMONISM (1882), 284–89.

One of the most specious and dangerous arguments which has been advanced as a reason why Congress should not take measures to arrest the evils of Mormonism, and one that has influenced the opinion of thousands

---

[20] An overview of Froiseth's contributions to the social life of nineteenth-century, non-Mormon Salt Lake City as well as her devoted work in behalf of the Anti-Polygamy Society is in Scott, "Jennie Anderson Froiseth and the Blue Tea," 20–35.

of well-meaning, intelligent, and law-abiding citizens, is the plea that if left alone, Mormonism will execute its own death sentence. Never was there a more fatal and less excusable mistake,—an error that if perpetuated will become a deadly crime. . .

The let-alone theory is a very plausible one, and the let-alone policy a very satisfying one, for those who do not wish to bear the reproaches of conscience for neglect of duty. It is very easy to say, "Mormonism is a crime, and a disgrace to the nation. It ought to be, and shall be, abolished, but there are other methods than congressional interference."

Yes, we answer, there are other methods, and so thought those who were continually opposing the old Anti-Slavery agitation. But those "other methods" terminated in the blood and wreck of a civil war.

It is also very easy to say, "Open the doors of Utah to the outside world, and let civilization, wealth, fashion, luxury, and culture pour in. These will prove more effective than the most stringent legislation."

Even people who have been in the Territory, and think they have studied the subject, will say, "Send bandboxes instead of troops to Utah. Let the milliners and dressmakers have full sway, and they will soon make it impossible for a man to have more than one wife. Then let schools, churches, and civilization (that much abused and misappropriated word) do the rest."

These people will do well to remember that the gates of Utah have now been opened to the world for more than ten years, and that the great transcontinental railroad, which the advocates of the let-alone policy contended would destroy the barbaric institution, has actually given the system the means of indefinite growth, enlargement, and power. Look at the facilities for importing whole cargoes of foreign dupes and slaves, as compared with those of twenty years ago! . . .

And when it is recollected that a large majority of these immigrants are gathered from the most ignorant and credulous classes of Europe, that they are steeped in superstitious fanaticism, and already shorn of manhood and womanhood by being pledged to obey their leaders in all things, temporal as well as spiritual, it may easily be seen how the system is kept up in Utah by these constant reinforcements.[21]

As a Dutch Reformed clergyman and editor of the *Christian Herald*, Thomas DeWitt Talmage (1832–1902) was best known for his sensational addresses as pastor of churches in Brooklyn, New York City, and Washing-

---

[21] The contention that Mormonism sustained itself with infusions of ignorant immigrants was often made. Crossing into Utah, said one observer, was like leaving the United States and entering a foreign country. "They are not Americans," he said. "They come from the lower dregs of monarchy . . . [most are] in a stage of blind belief where they will believe anything; they [*sic*] law of nature is nothing, their own sight is nothing, history is nothing, the light of the sun is nothing compared with that belief." Joseph B. Ros[e]borough, Biographical Sketches, Utah, mid-1880s, CU-B, 25, 36.

ton, D.C. In The Free Tabernacle of Brooklyn, he presided over the largest Protestant congregation on the continent. Talmage spoke on everything from Robert Ingersoll's agnosticism to the wonders of telegraphy. Because of his fame and the thunder of his censure he contributed to growing attention to polygamous Mormonism, what he called, "the seraglio of the republic." After stopping for a short time in Utah during a journey across the continent, he delivered the following address in Brooklyn Tabernacle on 26 September 1880.

[T. DeWitt Talmage], *Brooklyn Tabernacle* (1884), 53–56.

SODOM and Salt Lake City are synonymous. You can hardly think of the one without thinking of the other. . .

I charge Mormonism with being a *great blasphemy*. Brigham Young, in one of his sermons, declared that Christ Himself was a practical polygamist, that Mary and Martha were his plural wives, that Mary Magdalene was another; and he said in the same sermon that the bridal feast in Cana of Galilee, where Christ turned water into wine, was the occasion of one of His own marriages! The whole tendency of the system [is] toward blasphemy. . .

I charge upon Mormonism that it is *an organised filth*, built on polygamy. There is a man in Salt Lake City who has three wives, and they are the *mother, the grandmother, and the grand-daughter*. I observed that there were additions built on the houses, and it was explained to me that when a new wife is taken, then the house is enlarged, forgetting the fact that no house was ever large enough to hold two women married to the same man! Think of a system which applauds a man for such things. Think of a system which teaches that the more wives a man lives with at the same time on earth, the higher his honor in heaven. Think of a system which commends a man for living in marriage at the same time with three sisters. Think of a system which wrecks the happiness of every woman that touches it; for I do not care what they say, God never made a woman who can cheerfully divide her husband's love with another. Every honest woman knows, every honest wife knows she has a right to the entire throne of her husband's affection. They may smile to keep up appearances, but they have an agony of death. . .

I tell you, Mormonism is one great surge of licentiousness; it is

THE SERAGLIO OF THE REPUBLIC;

it is the concentrated corruption of this land; it is the brothel of the nation; it is hell enthroned. This miserable corpse of Mormonism has been rotting in the sun, and rotting and rotting and rotting for forty years, and the United States Government has not had the courage to bury it.

Moreover, it is all the time gaining in influence. Mormonism once meant Utah; now to a certain extent it means Idaho, Arizona, Nevada, Wyoming, New Mexico. Wider and wider and wider, and greater and greater and greater. It is going forth to debauch this nation. . ." Now," you say,

Execute the law against polygamy. . . Mormonism not only antagonizes Christianity, it antagonizes good morals, and the infidel and the Christian stand side by side in denouncing Mormonism as a foe to free institutions. Then, I say away with it! Moral persuasion first, if possible; but moral persuasion, I tell you, will not accomplish it. They have declared over and over again they will let their city go down under the bombshell before they will surrender polygamy; and I tell you that *Mormonism will never be destroyed* until it is destroyed by the guns of the United States Government. . . Why did they not let General Johns[t]on in 1857, with his 2500 troops sent out under the order of President Buchanan, march right on until they did their work? President Buchanan never was charged with excessive courage, and . . . there has not been a president of the United States with enough moral courage since to clean out the national stable.

We all go to look at it. President Grant went to look at it. Schurz, the Secretary, went to look at it. Secretary Thompson went to look at it. President Hayes went to look at it. Everybody goes to look at it. . . If there be any truth in transmigration of souls, I hope that the soul of Andrew Jackson will get into the body of some of our Presidents, and make proclamation that within thirty days all these Mormons must decide upon one wife or go to jail, or quit the country. Arbitration, by all means, but if that will not do, then peaceful proclamation. If that will not do, then howitzer and bombshell and bullets and cannon-ball. . . Come, now, instead of exhuming the wrapped-up and entombed mummy of negro slavery, and tossing it about in these presidential elections, have *one live question*—Mormonism, the white slavery of to-day— and have it decided at the ballot box whether that institution shall go forth with its pestiferous influence, or whether under the law of our civilization and the stroke of the law it shall perish. . .

I have to tell you that unless we destroy Mormonism, Mormonism will destroy us. If God be good and pure and just, He will not let this nation go unwhipped much longer if we allow that iniquity to go unchallenged. Every day as a nation we consent to Mormonism we are defying the hail and the lightning and the tempest, and the drought and the mildew, and the epidemic and the plague, and the hurricane, and the earthquake of an incensed God.

Founded as the *Mormon Tribune* in 1870 by LDS dissenters, the paper passed into less sympathetic hands the next year, and the renamed *Salt Lake Tribune* rapidly became an instrument for attacking everything it considered oppressive in Mormon culture. The journal's vituperation during its first half-century remains legendary. Plurality was an especially fertile subject for *Tribune* editors, who characterized defenses of the practice as "Mormon Dodgeology," spoke of their "polygamic mire," and labeled the Saints' marital ideal as "poly-hog-gamy."[22] *Tribune* journalists used great wells of ink vilifying the practice. Subscribers existed in considerable number outside as well as inside Utah Territory. U.S. Marshal Fred T. Dubois said the paper's circulation in Idaho helped fuel the anti-polygamy movement there.[23] The *Tribune* consistently associated polygamy with the offenses of priestcraft, theocratic tyranny, and Asiatic barbarism.[24]

"What Must Be," *Salt Lake Tribune*,
22 Mar. 1885, 28:135 [2/2].

The poor wretches who, from Tabernacle altar and from editorial sanctums, seek to impress upon the majority here that they are being persecuted, and that their persecutors have none but sordid motives, are, we think, at last wearying their people with their shameless, truthless and senseless iterations. We all know their creed, what they profess, what they aspire to. To two of their rules the American people object; they are objecting louder and louder daily, and these two rules will have to be given up. They will tell you that they advocate nothing which the prophets did not practice as is recorded in the Old Testament. To begin with, we ask the most devout and learned of them to look through the Old Testament, and point out if they can, one picture of true home life, such as we understand by home. It can not be done. Now, let us try to see what a real American home is. It did not have its origin in Asia. There is nothing Asiatic about it. It represents the growth of centuries. It represents the work of 1,800 years. When the wild tribes of Europe were touched with the first sunbeams of civilization, they were but little advanced over any other savage tribes, and, with them, woman was a slave and beast of burden. Gradually they drew together in families; slowly the conviction was pressed upon them that woman was as free and more sacred than man; gradually the one wife and mother became the queen of home, the most sacred figure in the household; her authority was acknowledged and it became a delight to minister to her and to honor her. By this new reverence given to wives and mothers the men themselves became exalted, and women, performing their part, became the mothers of the rulers of the world. The homes thus created became the stay and the glory of the State, and, when tried, the men who were nurtured under the influences of those homes went out from under their humble roofs so brave, so self-poised, and self-contained, that against all foes they were invincible. That home system was transferred to our shores, and, by the

---

[22] See, for example, "Verdict Guilty," *Salt Lake Tribune*, 13 Mar. 1885, 28:127 [4/2–3]; and "Mormon Dodgeology," ibid., 21 Mar. 1885, 28:134 [4/2].

[23] Clements, *Fred T. Dubois's The Making of a State*, 64.

[24] Journalistic hostility between the *Tribune* and Mormon leaders did not end until after World War I, a transition described as moving "From Brimstone to Soothing Syrup." Malmquist, *First 100 Years: A History of The Salt Lake Tribune*, 302.

blending of home-respecting races, and through the trials of redeeming from the wilderness a continent, home took on still further sacredness. When at last independence was achieved, and our form of Government was adopted, it was on the express understanding that it would survive only so long as it rested upon the hallowed homes of the people. The men who advocate polygamy, consciously or unconsciously, are striving to change this anchor on which American hope and security rest, and to substitute the reign which, through four thousand years of history, can not show one picture of pure home life . . . these men in Utah, who claim that they are being persecuted, would tear all this down and substitute the old Asiatic rule which, through the centuries, caused all the shores of the Old World to be strewn with the wrecks of dead nations; . . . For forty years less two this power here in Utah has been swelling. Tens of thousands of the wretched men and women of Utah have been brought here, steeped in hate toward our free government before landing upon our shores, and these and their children have been drilled by falsehood, by perjury and by feeding their lusts into a vast human machine, ready at the beck of a priest to do anything which may be bidden them; but still, now that the attrition of the law begins to bring results, they are sure that they are persecuted. If they will but stop to think they will see that, in any other land on earth, they long ago would have been scattered by the sword, or by banishment, or both. And if they possess the least prescience they can not help but see that unless they lop off from their creed those features which are a menace to liberty and to American homes, their creed itself, and they with it if necessary, will have to go.

"If Any Male Person . . . Cohabits": Acts and Oaths

The decade of the 1880s began deceptively for the Saints when John H. Miles, who married three women on the same day in 1874, had his conviction under the Morrill Act reversed. In this, the only case apart from *Reynolds* tried under the Morrill Law to reach the U.S. Supreme Court, the justices held that Miles's guilt was improperly determined because of evidence his wife Caroline provided, thereby violating common-law guarantees against the practice.[25] Not only did controversy surrounding the case arouse Gentile women in Utah to

---

[25] *Miles vs. United States*, 103 U.S. 304 (1881). An account of the case and other events is in "Decision in the Miles Case," *Des. Eve. News*, 5 April 1881, 14:112 [2/1–2]. The illegal status of polygamous wives complicated the traditional rule of marital silence for evidentiary purposes. For this reason the Miles contest cannot be left without joining to it the ruling in *Bassett vs. United States*, 137 U.S. 496 (1890), and attempts to qualify the uncompelled testimony of a wife in the Edmunds-Tucker Act, section one, below. The best exploration of the issue occurs in Firmage and Mangrum, *Zion in the Courts*, 149–51, 194–98.

As United States senator from Vermont, George Franklin Edmunds (1828–1919) believed that unless Congress acted firmly to eliminate polygamy in Utah, the nation was on the brink of another "irrepressible conflict." *Courtesy of Vermont Historical Society.*

unprecedented levels of protest but, following the lead commenced by Ulysses S. Grant, the nation's presidents regularly reproached the Saints and appealed for action by Congress.[26] In late 1880 President Hayes warned that the longer they delayed, the more difficult the country would find it to eradicate polygamy and restore "sanctity of marriage" to the territory.[27] And President Garfield further expostulated on the topic in 1881.[28]

Chester A. Arthur, taking up where his assassinated predecessor left off, declared that inasmuch as polygamy was the "cornerstone" of their faith and that Mormon settlers were spreading beyond Utah's borders, the government had the "duty of arraying against this barbarous system all the power which under the Constitution and the law they can wield for its destruction."[29] And if Republicans used the "bloody flag" of Civil War memories to curry support for their party, they also reminded the nation in every political plat-

---

[26] For Gentile reactions to the Miles case, see Iversen, *Antipolygamy Controversy*, 107–12.

[27] Rutherford B. Hayes, Fourth Annual Message, 6 Dec. 1880, *Comp.*, 10:4558.

[28] James A. Garfield, Inaugural Address, 4 Mar. 1881, ibid., 10:4601.

[29] Chester A. Arthur, First Annual Message, 6 Dec. 1881, ibid., 10:4644; and Doenecke, *Presidencies of James A. Garfield and Chester A. Arthur*, 84–85.

form they wrote between 1876 and 1888 that the other "relic of barbarism," polygamy, had yet to be expunged.[30] Spurred by so much indignant rhetoric, it did not take the national legislature long to act.

The first session of the Forty-seventh Congress of 1881–1882 witnessed an eruption of proposals for action against the Mormons. No less than twenty-three bills, including proposed amendments to the U.S. Constitution, were offered to deal with the problem.[31] Hundreds of petitions dating from the late 1870s sent by women's organizations, churches, and state legislatures accumulated in mounds on committee tables.[32] The vitriol of these protests was distilled into a law designed to amend the lame, twenty-year-old Morrill Act, and Sen. George Edmunds shepherded it through Congress.[33] President Arthur signed the new legislation in the early spring of 1882.

U.S., *STATUTES AT LARGE*, 22:47, 22 MAR. 1882, 30–32.

Be it enacted by the Senate and House of Representatives of the United States of America in Congress assembled, That section fifty-three hundred and fifty-two of the Revised Statutes of the United States be, and the same is hereby, amended so as to read as follows, namely:

"Every person who has a husband or wife living who, in a Territory or other place over which the United States have exclusive jurisdiction, hereafter marries another, whether married or single, and any man who hereafter simultaneously, or on the same day, marries more than one woman, in a Territory or other place over which the United States have exclusive jurisdiction, is guilty of polygamy, and shall be punished by a fine of not more than five hundred dollars and by imprisonment for a term of not more than five years; . . .

SEC.3. That if any male person, in a Territory or other place over which the United States have exclusive jurisdiction, hereafter cohabits with more than one woman, he shall be deemed guilty of a misdemeanor, and on conviction

---

[30] Johnson and Porter, *National Party Platforms*, 54, 61, 74, and 81.

[31] See "Appendix J," in Poll, "Twin Relic," 393–94. Support for a national marriage law arose from concern not only with Mormon polygamy but from alarm over the extent of divorce in Utah and elsewhere. Cott, *Public Vows*, 110–11.

[32] "Letter from the Secretary of the Interior, Transmitting Certain Petitions for Enforcing the Anti-Polygamy Act of 1862," House Exec. Doc. 58 (45-3), 1 Feb. 1879, Serial 1858; entries under "Polygamy," in index to *Cong. Rec.* (47-1), 5 Dec. 1881–17 Mar. 1882, 328; and the lengthy but incomplete list of petitions sent to Congress in the two years prior to passage of the 1882 Edmunds Law provided in Meservy, "History of Federal Legislation," 69–71.

[33] Senate debate over the bill, especially concerning the long-argued issue of congressional authority in the territories, is in *Cong. Rec.* (47-1) 15–16 Feb. 1882, 13:pt.2, 1152–63, 1195–1217. For accounts of legal and political considerations attending passage of the law, see Poll, "Political Reconstruction of Utah Territory," 111–26; Larson, *"Americanization" of Utah*, 92–97; and Lyman, *Political Deliverance*, 19–40. Edmunds's political views are discussed by Welch, "George Edmunds of Vermont: Republican Half-Breed," 64–73.

thereof shall be punished by a fine of not more than three hundred dollars, or by imprisonment for not more than six months, or by both said punishments, in the discretion of the court.[34]

SEC. 4. That counts for any or all of the offenses named in sections one and three of this act may be joined in the same information or indictment.

SEC. 5. That in any prosecution for bigamy, polygamy, or unlawful cohabitation, under any statute of the United States, it shall be sufficient cause of challenge to any person drawn or summoned as a juryman or talesman, first, that he is or has been living in the practice of bigamy, polygamy, or unlawful cohabitation with more than one woman, or that he is or has been guilty of an offense punishable by either of the foregoing sections . . . or the act of July first, eighteen hundred and sixty-two, entitled "An act to punish and prevent the practice of polygamy in the Territories of the United States and other places, and disapproving and annulling certain acts of the legislative assembly of the Territory of Utah," or, second, that he believes it right for a man to have more than one living and undivorced wife at the same time, or to live in the practice of cohabiting with more than one woman; and any person appearing or offered as a juror or talesman, and challenged on either of the foregoing grounds, may be questioned on his oath as to the existence of any such cause of challenge, and other evidence may be introduced bearing upon the question raised by such challenge; and this question shall be tried by the court. But as to the first ground of challenge before mentioned, the person challenged shall not be bound to answer if he shall say upon his oath that he declines on the ground that his answer may tend to criminate himself; and if he shall answer as to said first ground, his answer shall not be given in evidence in any criminal prosecution against him for any offense named in sections one or three of this act; but if he declines to answer on any ground, he shall be rejected as incompetent.[35]

SEC. 6. That the President is hereby authorized to grant amnesty to such classes of offenders guilty of bigamy, polygamy, or unlawful cohabitation, before the passage of this act, on such conditions and under such limitations as he shall think proper; but no such amnesty shall have effect unless the conditions thereof shall be complied with.

---

[34] "Cohabits" was the term that allowed the government to proceed successfully against pluralists whose marriage ceremonies were secret and without public record. It became, in the words of one scholar, "the principal weapon in the campaign against Mormon polygamists." Davis, "Polygamous Prelude," 10. Justice Blatchford later emphasized the significance of the distinction between formal bigamy and "cohabitation" in *Snow vs. U.S.*, 118 U.S. 351 (1886).

[35] For a Utah Commission chairman's comments made later regarding personal belief as a subject of inquiry when interviewing voters, see Memorandum of A[mbrose] B. Carlton, Chairman of the Utah Commission to Hon. L[ucius] Q. C. Lamar, Sec. of the Interior, 29 Mar. 1889, RG48, N.A. The law's caveat regarding private opinion did not save those taking the oath from jeopardy under the criminal provisions of the law. For discussion of the issue, see the handwritten "Memorial of the Legislative Assembly of the Territory of Utah . . . ," 13 Mar. 1884, RG48, N.A.

SEC. 7. That the issue of bigamous or polygamous marriages, known as Mormon marriages, in cases in which such marriages have been solemnized according to the ceremonies of the Mormon sect, in any Territory of the United States, and such issue shall have been born before the first day of January, anno Domini eighteen hundred and eighty-three, are hereby legitimated.

SEC. 8. That no polygamist, bigamist, or any person cohabiting with more than one woman, and no woman cohabiting with any of the persons described as aforesaid in this section, in any Territory or other place over which the United States have exclusive jurisdiction, shall be entitled to vote at any election held in any such Territory or other place, or be eligible for election or appointment to or be entitled to hold any office or place of public trust, honor, or emolument in, under, or for any such Territory or place, or under the United States.

SEC. 9. That all the registration and election offices of every description in the Territory of Utah are hereby declared vacant, and each and every duty relating to the registration of voters, the conduct of elections, the receiving or rejection of votes, and the canvassing and returning of the same, and the issuing of certificates or other evidence of election in said Territory, shall, until other provision be made by the legislative assembly of said Territory as is hereinafter by this section provided, be performed under the existing laws of the United States and of said Territory by proper persons, who shall be appointed to execute such offices and perform such duties by a board of five persons,[36] to be appointed by the President, by and with the advice and consent of the Senate, not more than three of whom shall be members of one political party; and a majority of whom shall be a quorum. . . The canvass and return of all the votes at elections in said Territory for members of the legislative assembly thereof shall also be returned to said board, which shall canvass all such returns and issue certificates of election to those persons who, being eligible for such election, shall appear to have been lawfully elected, which certificates shall be the only evidence of the right of such persons to sit in such assembly: *Provided*, That said board of five persons shall not exclude any person otherwise eligible to vote from the polls on account of any opinion such person may entertain on the subject of bigamy or polygamy nor shall they refuse to count any such vote on account of the opinion of the person casting it on the subject of bigamy or polygamy; but each house of such assembly, after its organization, shall have power to decide upon the elections and qualifications of its members. . .

Approved, March 22, 1882.

---

[36] This board, or "Utah Commission" as it came to be called, was similar to those employed by Union-imposed governments in former slave states of the South. Utah Commissioners, all of whom in the early years came from outside Utah, exercised extraordinary control especially over electoral matters and were independent from either the legislative or executive authorities of the federal government. Grow, "Study of the Utah Commission," 42–55, 72.

"Hit 'Em Again." *The Judge*, 9 January 1886.
Dressed in Turkish attire, a polygamous "Mormon Bluebeard"
is punished by Sen. George Edmunds, who wields his
anti-Mormon Edmunds Act as a sword.

The first major casualty of the Edmunds Law was territorial delegate George Q. Cannon, who had represented Utah in the nation's capital for a decade. Cannon, one of the most influential men in the territory, was reelected by an overwhelming majority in 1880 but, inasmuch as he had four living wives and the Edmunds Act forbade pluralists to hold public office, the House of Representatives vacated his seat.[37] This was followed by the Utah Commission convening in Salt Lake City, where it undertook its work in the late summer of 1882.[38] Alternately badgered by delegations of accusatory Gentiles and ill-tempered Saints, the commission quickly drew up new voting regulations that required registrants declare under oath that they were not polygamists.[39] It prepared a pamphlet containing procedures to guide election officials, including the oath, and sent it to all precinct registrars. "Rule II" of the pamphlet stated that each "Registration Officer shall . . . require of each person whose name is on . . . [the voter registry] to . . . subscribe" to the oath provided in the pamphlet.[40] The word "shall" made it clear that registrars had no choice in the matter.

When the commission's work was challenged, the U.S. Supreme Court, while upholding the Edmunds Law and empowering the commission to keep polygamists from the polls, said there was no basis in the law for compelling employment of the precise oath given in the commission's instructions.[41] Before the decision came in 1885, however, between ten and twenty thousand Mormons may have been barred from casting ballots in territorial elec-

---

[37] That supporters of the Edmunds Bill were consciously targeting George Q. Cannon, even before passage of the law, is apparent in *To Prevent Persons Living in Bigamy or Polygamy from Holding Any Civil Office of Trust or Profit in Any of the Territories of the United States, and from Being Delegates in Congress*, House Report 386 (47-1) 14 Feb. 1882, Serial 2065. Congressional debate over Cannon's House seat is in *Cong. Rec.* (47-1) 18–19 April 1882, 3001–11, 3045–75. For Cannon's subsequent legal difficulties, including failed efforts to escape capture and his eventual imprisonment, see Cannon, ed., "Prison Diary of a Mormon Apostle," 393–409; and Bitton, *George Q. Cannon*, 248–58.

[38] An account of the commission's early work by one who was a member for seven years and served for a time as its chairman is in Carlton, *Wonderlands*, 47–53.

[39] See A[mbrose] B. Carlton and J[ames] R. Pettigrew of the Utah Commission to Hon. L[ucius] Q. C. Lamar, secretary of the interior, May 1885, marked "Personal," RG48, N.A. Reviewing the history of their efforts in 1893, commission members told how they had been forced to navigate the "Scylla and Charybdis" of pro- and anti-Mormon interests. "So it transpired that the local factions, when not wholly engrossed in fighting each other, turned their attacks alternately or simultaneously against the Utah Commission." "Annual Report of the Utah Commission," RSI (1893), 3:418.

[40] *Rules and Regulations for the Revision of the Registration Lists*, 3–4. For the commission's public justification and explanation of the oath, see "Annual Report of the Utah Commission," RSI (1882), 2:1003–4. Also see "Rules for Registration," *Des. News* [Weekly], 30 Aug. 1882, 31:32, 505/3–5.

[41] *Murphy et al. vs. Ramsey et al.*, 114 U.S. 15 (1885).

tions.[42] The later Edmunds-Tucker Act of 1887 contained more specific language concerning an oath—language that the commission incorporated into a new directive and circulated to registrars.[43] This notwithstanding, beginning in 1885 and continuing thereafter, the commission told election officials that the declaration and other published guidelines were "suggestions" only.[44] Still, registrars seemed invariably to follow the commission's rules, including employment of the oath. Excepting arrest, trial, and imprisonment, the oaths were the most coercive instruments wielded by the federal government during the anti-polygamy crusade.

RULES AND REGULATIONS FOR THE REVISION
OF THE REGISTRATION LISTS, 3–4.

Territory of Utah,
County of Salt Lake } ss.

I _____, being first duly sworn, (or affirmed) depose and say, that I am over twenty-one years of age, and have resided in the Territory of Utah for six months, and in the precinct of _____ one month immediately preceding the date hereof, and (if a male) am a native born or naturalized (as the case may be) citizen of the United States; and a tax-payer in this territory, (or if a female), I am native born, or naturalized, or the wife, widow or daughter, (as the case may be) of a native born or naturalized citizen of the United States; and I do further solemnly swear (or affirm) that I am not a bigamist nor a polygamist; that I have not violated the laws of the United States prohibiting bigamy or polygamy; that I do not live or cohabit with more than one woman in the marriage relation, nor does any relation exist between me and any woman which has been entered into, or continued in violation of the said laws of the United States prohibiting bigamy or polygamy; (and if a woman) that I am not the wife of a polygamist, nor have I entered into any relation with any man in violation of the laws of the United States concerning polygamy and bigamy.

Subscribed and sworn to before me this ___ day of _____, 188_

Registration Officer _____ Precinct.

The Saints were quick to note the commission's inconsistency in ignoring Gentiles who consorted with mistresses and prostitutes while discriminating against Latter-day Saints who treated their companions as spouses "in the

---

[42] Chairman Alexander Ramsey of the Utah Commission said in 1883 that 15,000 Mormons were disqualified. Ramsey to Hon. H[enry]. M. Teller, secretary of the interior, 24 Aug. 1883, RG48, N.A. This number is greater than the figure provided in the commission's published report and in secondary sources since that time.

[43] Carlton, *Circular for the Information of Registration Officers*, 1–2. The relevant part of the Edmunds-Tucker Act is in section 24 of the law, reproduced below.

[44] Ramsey to Sec. of the Interior [Lucius Q. C. Lamar], 24 April 1885; and *Circular for the Information of Registration Officers* (21 April 1885), both in RG48, N.A.

marriage relation."[45] Responding to the allegation, Utah Commission members pointed out that it was not "sexual derelictions" by individuals that the nation sought to punish so much as threats to the monogamous home.

"Report of the Utah Commission,"
28 Oct. 1885, *rsi* (1885), 2:887–88.

The defenders of polygamy in Utah lay much stress upon the fact that the prosecutions under the Edmunds act are directed solely against those who maintain the polygamous relation. They charge that alleged sexual derelictions by persons who do not belong to the Mormon Church are not investigated and punished under the Edmunds law, and that therefore the execution of the law is partial. But this is an error. The law was not directed at individual lascivious practices, but against the assault made by the Mormon Church upon the most cherished institution of our civilization—the monogamous system. The laws for the suppression of polygamy were chiefly inspired by the apprehension that if this practice should be even tolerated anywhere in the United States it might one day become a serious menace to the institution of monogamy, which the world has come to consider the most potential factor for the advancement of civilization everywhere. It is against this danger that the law is aimed, and accordingly the courts have held that the living with two or more undivorced wives at the same time in marital relationship, and holding them out to the world as such, constitutes that kind of cohabitation which is by its very nature an attack upon the monogamic system—the sacred family association which is the chief pride and strength of our social fabric— and to do this is the very offense for which the law provides a punishment.

"That Terrible Persecution": The Judicial Crusade

Near the end of his term in December 1884, Pres. Chester A. Arthur spoke impatiently of Mormon endurance. He urged Congress to continue the existence of the Utah Commission and to extend "absolute" control over the territory. Only that and the "most radical legislation consistent with the restraints of the Constitution," he said, would succeed in suppressing the "abominable practice" of polygamy.[46] The Republican platform of that year, going further than any before, condoned the use of military force to obtain Mormon compliance with the Edmunds Act.[47] Despite a Democratic victory at the polls

---

[45] "Rules for Registration," *Des. Eve. News*, 25 Aug. 1882, 15:233 [2/1–2]; and "'Moral' Anti-'Mormon' Crusade," *Des. News* [Weekly], 23 Dec. 1885, 34:49, 776/1–3.

[46] Chester A. Arthur, Fourth Annual Message, 1 Dec. 1884, *Comp.*, 10:4837.

[47] Johnson and Porter, *National Party Platforms*, 74.

in the autumn of 1884 and the more liberal attitudes of Grover Cleveland, the Saints soon felt the effects of heightened opposition to their way of life. The Utah Commission early ruled that the Edmunds Law denied the right to vote to any who had practiced polygamy since 1862, even if they subsequently became monogamists.[48] And a growing number of legal officers, including long-remembered territorial chief justice Charles S. Zane and U.S. Marshal Edwin A. Ireland, accelerated prosecutions and imprisonments.[49]

The conviction of twice-married Rudger Clawson and the U.S. Supreme Court's ruling upholding the verdict in 1885 affirmed the increasing reach of federal authority. Until that time, most Mormons remained relatively confident that efforts to reform their domestic lives would fail. But following the Clawson case, as Apostle Francis M. Lyman was remembered to say, "The hiding and scattering of polygamists amounted almost to a panic."[50]

Rudger Clawson married Florence Ann Dinwoodey on 1 August 1882. Less than a year later, Lydia Spencer was sealed to him as a plural wife. The Clawson family was prominent in Salt Lake City and Rudger enjoyed celebrity for his courage as a missionary companion to Joseph Standing, the murder victim of a Georgia mob. Indicted in April 1884, Clawson was brought to trial in October of the same year. Numbers of church authorities, including President John Taylor, were called as witnesses. Lydia Spencer could not be found to testify, so the jury was unable to reach a verdict. After being located and subpoenaed, she refused to testify and spent a night in prison for contempt. Rather than see his wife endure further humiliation, Clawson persuaded her to confess to their plural marriage.

Consistent with the Edmunds Act, courts barred from jury service any who believed in plural marriage, whether so married or not.[51] In Rudger Clawson's first trial, numbers were rejected for this reason. The excerpt below, taken from the *Deseret News*'s account of the empanelling process, provides an example.[52]

---

[48] See the ruling in Arthur L. Thomas, Sec. for Utah and Ex-officio Sec. of the Commission, *Order of the Utah Commission, Adopted Friday, September 1, 1882*, RG48, N.A. Punishment for past behavior here was a resurrection of ex post facto devices used during the Civil War and Reconstruction, such as the "Ironclad" loyalty oath. See Hyman, *To Try Men's Souls*, 164, 256–63.

[49] Some of what accounted for aggressiveness by officers was a post–Civil War spirit of resurgent, federal law enforcement throughout the United States, including the payment of marshals' fees based on the number of papers served. See "Federalism Resurgent," in Calhoun, *The Lawmen*, 121–42. There is a discussion of salary and fees paid to the officers, as well as a list of all federal marshals who served in Utah between 1850 and 1896, in Brown, "United States Marshals," 6–7, 213–14 respectively.

[50] As quoted from the apostle's diary by Albert Robison Lyman, Francis Marion Lyman, LDS Archives, 54.

[51] Elimination of Mormons from Utah juries is discussed in Grow, "Utah Commission," 269–71.

"Clawson Case," *Des. Eve. News*, 15 Oct. 1884, 17:276 [3/2].

"David Archibald, on being piled [*sic*] with the questions, turned to the judge and with a marked Scotch accent said: "Your honor, am I here to be tried for my belief?" Sensation, laughter and applause.

Judge Zane (very red in the face, and rapping sharply for order): "Answer the question."

"Well," said the witness, "I believe the ancient patriarchs and prophets"—

"We don't care anything about that," broke in the Judge, "answer the question."

"Well," urged the witness, "I say the ancient patriarchs"—

Again he was interrupted and asked to answer the first question.

"Your honor, I believe it's a revelation of God to the Latter-day Saints, that they are required to obey."

Challenged and excused.

U.S. district attorneys Charles S. Varian and William H. Dickson examined President John Taylor, the most celebrated witness called in the Clawson case. Taylor's answers reveal the diffusion of authority for performing plural marriages that took place in the 1880s. And, as the Utah Commission pointed out in its summary of the trial, Taylor also provided an example of the remarkable opacity that Mormon leaders could display when publicly asked about the Principle.[53]

"Polygamy Trial," *Des. Eve. News*, 18 Oct. 1884, 17:279 [2/2–4].
President John Taylor
was then called, and, being sworn, was asked to take the stand. The court room was now crowded, many coming in with and after the President, and the most intense interest was manifested on all sides.

Q.—Is your hearing good, Mr. Taylor?

A.—Yes, sir.

Q.—You are the President of the Church of Jesus Christ of Latter-day Saints?

---

[52] Transcripts of the trial are not in the Utah Supreme Court Library, Utah State Archives, or the Rudger Clawson Papers at the University of Utah. Papers such as indictments, jury lists, Judge Charles S. Zane's charge to the jury, amounts of fines, terms of imprisonment, and information relating to appeals are in Rudger Clawson, case 117, file number 425, Third District Court of the Territory of Utah, 1884, National Archives and Records Center, Rocky Mountain Region, Denver, Colorado. Many of the same materials are contained in the Rudger Clawson Papers, 1987 Addendum, box 24, fd. 19, Special Collections, UU. Excepting trial transcripts, there are also materials in Jenson, Prisoners for Conscience Sake, fd. 3, LDS Archives. Both the *Deseret News* and *Salt Lake Tribune* followed the case closely, publishing their own transcripts of court proceedings. One easily detects bias in both journals. But the *Tribune*, criticized in court for prejudicial language in its reports, seems to this investigator to have engaged in such flourishes more often than its Mormon counterpart, so *Deseret News* records are the ones used here.

[53] "Report of the Utah Commission," *RSI* (1884), 2:519.

A.—Yes, sir. . .

[After considerable exchange between defending and prosecuting lawyers and the judge over the propriety of that line of questioning, Mr. William H. Dickson asked]: Where are marriages in the Mormon Church—that is, by members of the Mormon faith—celebrated, in the Endowment House or elsewhere?[54]

A.—Sometimes they are, and sometimes elsewhere.

Q.—Where else, if not in the Endowment House?

A.—I do not know that I can say. There is no specific place appointed in which marriages occur. . .

Q.—. . . Are not the plural marriages entered into by the members of the Church, so far as you know, performed in the Endowment House?

A.—No, sir.

Q.—Where are they performed? . . .

A.—I can not say.

Q.—Do you know of any plural marriages entered into by any members of the faith, residents of the Territory of Utah, ever having been performed and entered into outside of any one of the Endowment Houses within the past three years? . . .

A.—I have recollection of many such. . .

Q.—Is there any place called an Endowment House, a temple, or known by any other name, which is set apart as a place for the celebration of marriages. . .

A.—There is no specific place set apart for the celebration of marriages. . .

Q.—When this authority [to perform marriages] is conferred upon any one by you, is it an authority limited to some particular case, or a general authority?

A.—It would be a general authority until rescinded. . .

Q.—Then you do know upon whom you do confer authority?

A.—There are hundreds of people who have authority. . .[55]

Q.—Is there any record of marriages?

A.—I am not acquainted with the records.

Q.—Do you know whether a record of marriages is kept?

A.—It is very probable there is.

Q.—Can you say whether there is or not?

---

[54] Until the completion of a Mormon temple in the 1870s, the Endowment House, constructed in 1855, was commonly but not invariably used to perform plural marriages.

[55] Two days after making these statements, in a sermon given in Ogden, Utah, Taylor spoke further on the issue: "It is the authority of the Priesthood, not the place that validates and sanctifies the ordinance. I was asked if people could be sealed outside. Yes. I could have told them I was sealed outside, and lots of others." John Taylor, 19 Oct. 1884, *Journal of Discourses*, 25:355. The efficacy of sealings performed in locations other than temples, indoors or out, was affirmed again at meetings of the First Presidency and apostles in Abraham H. Cannon Diaries, 14 May 1891, UPB, 14:141.

A.—I think likely there is.

Q.—Did you ever see it?

A.—I do not know that I have.

Q.—If you wanted to see it is there any means of ascertaining where it is?

A.—I could find out by inquiry.

Q.—Will you be good enough to do so?

A.—Well, I am not good enough to do so. . .

Q.—Has any one not authorized the right to celebrate the rites of matrimony?

A.—No, sir. . .

Q.—Who in this city is authorized to celebrate plural marriages?

A.—A great many have been appointed—hundreds. . .

Q.—Are you acquainted with the defendant?

A.—Yes. . .

Q.—Do you know whether he has taken a plural wife or not?

A.—I don't. . .

Q.—Have you any means of knowing whether or not he has entered into plural marriage?

A.—I do not know that I have.

Q.—Do you know that you have no such means?

A.—Yes. . .

President Taylor having exchanged a few words with Judge Zane, left the room, and with him the interest, for a large number went also, for they passed out in swarms after him.

In a second trial based on his plural wife's testimony, the jury convicted Rudger Clawson of polygamy and unlawful cohabitation after only seventeen minutes of deliberation. The Edmunds Act permitted both crimes to be joined in a single indictment. As punishment, Judge Charles S. Zane sentenced Clawson to a total of four years' imprisonment and $800 in fines.[56] Later pardoned by Pres. Grover Cleveland, he left prison in early December 1889. Ordained one of Mormonism's twelve apostles in 1898 and becoming president of that quorum in 1921, Clawson remained devoted to the Principle throughout his life. He was long remembered by the Saints as "one of the first victims of that terrible persecution which began under the Edmunds Law and which made many thousand sufferers for conscience sake."[57]

---

[56] Franklin S. Richards, who subsequently served as defense counsel in case after case for the Mormons, appealed the conviction because of procedures involved when empanelling the grand jury that indicted Clawson. The appeal failed. See *Clawson vs. United States*, 114 U.S. 477 (1885). The most extensive investigation of the Clawson case is the work of Larson, *Prisoner for Polygamy*.

[57] Anderson, "Rudger Clawson," 1:177.

"This Vile System Shall Be Blotted Out": The Crusade Quickens

Territorial and federal courts continued to enforce the Edmunds Act, culling Mormons, polygamous or not, from public office.[58] The U.S. Supreme Court eventually overturned a territorial ruling that nullified the right of polygamous offspring to inherit for the humane reason that it harmed only children, not the pluralists for whom such policies were intended.[59] But until after the Manifesto of 1890, territorial judges successfully refused to naturalize foreign converts to the church on grounds that, because of their doctrine of polygamy, Mormon applicants lacked moral character.[60] Men were found guilty who, only supporting their plural wives, ceased having sexual relations with them. Mere visitation for non-sexual purposes was accepted as proof of illegal cohabitation.[61] And to extend sentences, courts attempted to impose multiple penalties on defendants by segregating their offenses—that is, dividing the duration of their polygamous lives into years, months, or weeks.[62] Unflinching in their devotion to the monogamous home, judicial officers said that it was the appearance or "semblance" of plural marriage, not its conjugal fulfillment, that threatened American society and must be discouraged.[63]

In Idaho, where a sizeable Mormon population resided, the conflict over polygamy raged as fiercely as in Utah. Among those arrested by U.S. Marshal Fred T. Dubois were several polygamists tried in the territorial district court at Blackfoot in the autumn of 1885. Admitting that he was obsessed

---

[58] The attempt at wholesale displacement of Mormons from civil offices in the territory was not entirely successful. See *Wenner vs. Smith*, 4 Utah 238, 9 Pac. 293 (1886); the chapter "The Struggle for Local Offices," in Grow, "Utah Commission," 195–215; and Groberg, "Mormon Disfranchisements," 399–408.

[59] *Cope vs. Cope*, 137 U.S. 682 (1891). A history of inheritance law in Utah, especially as it related to polygamous offspring, is in Linford, "Mormons and the Law," 2:557–79.

[60] Sec. of State William M. Evarts told U.S. diplomats in Europe to discourage the emigration of Mormon converts. "Diplomatic Correspondence, Circular No. 10, Aug. 9, 1879 . . . ," *Papers Relating to the Foreign Relations of the United States, 1879*, 11–12. Plural marriage was made a basis for excluding immigrants in "An Act in Amendment to the Various Acts Relative to Immigration . . . ," U.S., *Statutes at Large*, 26:551, sec. 1, 3 Mar. 1891, 1084. And Mormonism's controversy with the nation is yet visible in immigration law: "Aliens and Nationality," *United States Code Annotated*, Title 8, sec. 1182, sub-sec. 10-A (1999).

[61] *United States vs. Peay*, 5 Utah 263, 14 Pac. 342 (1887); *United States vs. Clark*, 6 Utah 120, 21 Pac. 463 (1889).

[62] *United States vs. Snow*, 4 Utah 280, 9 Pac. 501 (1886); and *Snow vs. United States*, 118 U.S. 346 (1886). For the Supreme Court's subsequent unwillingness to accept segregated offenses in Mormon prosecutions, see *In re Snow* 120 U.S. 274 (1887). Additional commentary is in Firmage and Mangrum, *Zion in the Courts*, 178–85.

[63] See *United States vs. Musser*, 4 Utah 153, 7 Pac. 389 (1885); and *Angus M. Cannon vs. United States*, 116 U.S. 71–74 (1885).

First Presidency member George Quayle Cannon (1827–1901), one of the most influential men in both church and territorial affairs, is here shown in Utah's penitentiary in 1888. Surrounded by other Mormon "co-habs" and two guards, Cannon was one of the few prisoners permitted to keep their beards. *Used by permission, Utah State Historical Society, all rights reserved.*

with stamping out polygamy and armed with the power to empanel juries by open venire, Dubois boasted to a friend that he could constitute juries so dependable they would "convict Jesus Christ."[64]

In their pre-sentencing remarks, Joseph M. Phelps, Alexander Leatham, and Isaac Nash, three Idaho Latter-day Saints convicted of unlawful cohab-

---

[64] This from Dubois's memoir, in Clements, *Fred T. Dubois's The Making of a State*, 110. The setting for the Idaho cases is described in Beal, *History of Southeastern Idaho*, 300–18; and Wells, *Anti-Mormonism in Idaho*, 57–83. For an account of Mormon polygamists imprisoned in Idaho, see Woods and Wells, "Inmates of Honor," 13–22.

itation, illustrate the conflict that religious conviction brought for Mormon polygamists facing criminal prosecution everywhere. Judge Hays gave the first two men the maximum penalty of six months in prison, $300 in fines, and $100 in court costs. Due to his age, Nash's sentence was reduced to three months' incarceration.[65]

"Black Saturday at Blackfoot," *Southern Idaho Independent*,
1:4 (13 Nov. 1885) [2/4–6]; and ibid., 1:5 (20 Nov. 1885) [2/3–6].

———

Stenographically Reported

———

On Saturday, the last day of the District Court at Blackfoot, the United States cases were again called for the purpose of passing upon the defendants.

Judge Hays:—Mr. Joseph M. Phelps,[66] you have been indicted by the grand jury and convicted by a trial jury of unlawful cohabitation. Have you anything to say why the sentence of the court should not now be pronounced upon you?

Mr. Phelps:—I don't know that I have. I am a little sorry that I am arraigned here for a practice that I believe to be Divine doctrine. It is part of my religion and while I am amenable to the laws of the land, I hold there is a higher law. I wish your honor to take this view. I have endeavored all my life to live according to the laws of the land.

I tried a good while to find that Mormonism is wrong. I am convinced that it is divine. I would not give a cent for a religion that does not go further than the bonds of this world. My blood runs as thin as any man's when I see the flag of my country. I love my country and I have always endeavored to instil a patriotic spirit in my children. I do not wish to weary the court, I could say more. . .

Mr. Alex. Leatham[67] have you anything to say why the judgment of the court should not now be pronounced against you? You have been found guilty of illegal cohabitation.

Mr. Leatham:—Please, your honor, I took an oath of allegiance to the government in the year 1863. I have never repented it. I took that oath a dozen times crossing the plains. I was willing to take that oath, and stand by it, a dozen times, every morning before breakfast. Soldiers were there, I guess about

---

[65] For evidence that lighter sentences were also imposed on aged offenders in Utah, see Evans, "Judicial Prosecution," 41–42.

[66] Joseph Morris Phelps (1837–1886) of Montpelier, Idaho, had six wives of record.

[67] Alexander Leatham (1836–1919) seems to have been a resident of Rexburg, Idaho, and was the husband of two wives.

every ten miles, and we had to be corralled and asked if we were willing to take the oath of allegiance. I said "yes." Down South, about San Pete, I did military service three months and was every day in active service from sun up until sun down. I still uphold this government but I must, for conscience sake, preserve that heaven-born right that God has given me.

I have never illegally cohabited with any woman not my wife. I have had two wives. I had them because of my thorough conviction that it is the divine will of the Almighty. It is part of my religion. I hold myself pure and unde-filed. Would to God that all men were just so.

I have a wife now and ten children, nine of them under ten years of age. All I ask is the privilege of taking care of them, of supporting them, of pro-viding for their wants, honorably, and of living my religion a[s] I understand it.

Judge Hays: . . . What have you to say about obedience to the laws of your country in the future?

A:—I have to say this, I have a heaven-born right, that Good [sic] has given me, which I desire not to relinquish either to man or to the government.

Q:—In other words, do you claim the right to marry another woman in the future, if you feel so disposed?

A:—That is part of my religion to have more wives than one. I am fifty years old, and I may never undertake such a thing, but I hold this doctrine to be revealed from God.

Q:—You have no promise, or assurance of future good conduct, or obe-dience to the law of your country?

A:—No man knows what he will do in the future. I have nothing to say about that. . .

Judge Hays: Mr. Isaac Nash, you have been convicted of illegal cohabita-tion, have you anything to say why the sentence of the law should not now be pronounced upon you?[68]

A.—I have been in this country 36 years.

Q.—From what country did you come?

A.—From Wales. As one of the gentlemen said, I have helped to make this country; helped to build bridges, kill snakes and fight the Indians. I brought a wife with me, an invalid. She had no children, and I love children, your honor.

---

[68] Isaac Bartlett Nash (1824–1907) lived in Franklin, Idaho, and was married to two wives. U.S. Attor-ney Fred T. Dubois remembered Nash for his trustworthiness: "I remember the case of a Mr. Nash, a black-smith at Franklin, who after his conviction and his sentence, asked me if he could not go home and arrange his affairs before going to the penitentiary. I told him certainly and that the term of Court would proba-bly last some three weeks longer. If he would turn up in three weeks from that day it would be all right. He was a convicted prisoner and the Marshal was entirely responsible for him as he was not even under bond. On the appointed day Nash turned up. This happened very often." Clements, *Fred T. Dubois's The Mak-ing of a State*, 63.

I loved her and tried to do the best I could to honor the laws of my adopted country. I came here young, and I am now pretty old, 62 years old, although
I don't look that.

In the year 1866 believing that I had knowledge within myself that celestial marriage was a divine law, and one of the ordinances of our church, I
took the opportunity and embraced it. I married another wife. I made a
covenant with her and with my God that I would uphold and cherish her
through time and through all eternity. God has blessed me with children. That
woman is the mother of eight, two I have buried. My first wife had no children through disease; she took to my little children and has acted as a mother to them. I have been a moral man; I hate blasphemy. I have been found
guilty of unlawful cohabitation. That is true if the term means to hold them
out as my wives. They are my wives and I love them.

Q.—Have you anything to say as to what your future conduct will be?

A.—Your honor, I cannot cast away my wife and children. Paralyzed be
my tongue before I shall utter the words, or shall make bastards of my children and my wife an outcast. I ask your honor to look into this and see: I
have not broken the Edmund's [*sic*] law for years and years, unless it be in
holding these women out as my wives. All I ask of you is to be merciful, for
the sake of my children, as your honor will expect to find mercy before the
bar of God. I have no more to say.

Judge Hays: . . . It has been with regret that I have learned since coming
to this territory that a considerable portion of the people propose to stand
out in defiance to the law and bind themselves together for the purpose of
overthrowing and defeating the law of the government. It is with regret that
I have learned this fact, but having learned it I perceive that I have a duty to
perform from which I could not and will not shrink. I say to you in all kindness, but in earnest, that the course which you and your people are pursuing
not only in Idaho but in Utah and in other Territories where they dwell, is
one which must inevitably destroy them as a people. . .

You stand in this temple of justice; you say you claim the right to determine what law you will obey and what law to disobey. You claim the right to
dispute the law of men. Gentlemen you are mistaken. A religion that is built
upon a foundation of crime cannot stand in this age. . .

I am aware that you are hoping that Congress may interfere; that legislation may go backwards. . . The American people are in earnest. They have
determined that polygamy and this vile system shall be blotted out. You are
impressing them by your actions every day.

Your conduct here to-day will impress them still stronger with that belief.
You are arousing a feeling that you know not of. You are starting an avalanche.
It is like an avalanche that gathers on a mountain peak, very little at first, but
it grows stronger and stronger until it sweeps all opposition before it. I say

you know not what you do. You are starting an avalanche that must and will culminate not only in the overthrow of your entire system but will, if necessary, wipe you from existence.

The laws of the country must be obeyed. It is not for you to say which are to be respected and which are to be held for nought. . . I say to you gentlemen, it is a suicidal course. It is not wise. There may be some divine providence that is guiding you on for the purpose of wiping your system from the earth. If so bow in obedience to it and accept the results. . .

Encouraged by billowing anti-Mormon sentiment but frustrated by the Saints' refusal to bend to it, Senator Edmunds repeatedly attempted to stiffen his 1882 enactment by amendment. Only when joined by Rep. John Randolph Tucker of Virginia were his efforts rewarded. Despite Tucker's moderating influence, the finished law incorporated nearly all that the failed Cullom Bill of 1870 had proposed.[69]

Scholarly judgments of the law have not been approving. As some expressed it, the Edmunds-Tucker Act of 1887 "Under even the most generous standards of legislative latitude . . . skirted the boundaries of constitutionality. It was legislation that nakedly attacked a religious institution and imposed civil punishments on an entire group of people solely for their religious beliefs."[70] The new law imposed a more coercive regimen than existed in any state or territory since Reconstruction governments in the South two decades before.

U.S., *STATUTES AT LARGE*, 24:397, 3 MAR. 1887, 635–41.[71]

Be it enacted by the Senate and House of Representatives of the United State of America in Congress assembled, SEC. 1. That in any proceeding or examination before a grand jury, a judge, justice, or a United States commissioner, or a court, in any prosecution for bigamy, polygamy, or unlawful cohabitation, under any statute of the United States, the lawful husband or wife of the person accused shall be a competent witness, and may be called, but shall not be compelled to testify in such proceeding, examination, or prosecution without the consent of the husband or wife, as the case may be; and such witness shall not be permitted to testify as to any statement or communication made by either

---

[69] A list of changes to Edmunds's Senate Bill number 10, most of a moderating nature, is in Tucker's House Judiciary Committee report, *Suppression of Polygamy in Utah . . .* , House Report 2735 (49-1), 10 June 1886, Serial 2443.

[70] Firmage and Mangrum, *Zion in the Courts*, 202.

[71] Provisions not included in this text authorized the U.S. president to appoint probate judges; narrowed ecclesiastical influence over public schools; annulled the Perpetual Emigrating Fund; and nationalized Utah's territorial militia. See Firmage and Mangrum, *Zion in the Courts*, 252–60.

While some alleged that polygamy depleted Mormon health, others believed the Saints possessed extraordinary sexual stamina. Exploiting the latter assumption, F. B. Crouch marketed his "Mormon Elders Damiana Wafers" with the promise that they would cure almost anything. Published in 1887, the cover of this advertising booklet displays an eager suitor confident of his amorous potential owing to the wafers. Inside the cover, Crouch lists maladies for which the magical pills are effective, especially failure of the "vital forces," a Victorian euphemism for sexual disfunction. *From the author's collection.*

husband or wife to each other, during the existence of the marriage relation, deemed confidential at common law.[72]

SEC. 2. That in any prosecution for bigamy, polygamy, or unlawful cohabitation, under any statute of the United States, whether before a United States commissioner, justice, judge, a grand jury, or any court, an attachment for any witness may be issued by the court, judge, or commissioner, without a previous subpoena, compelling the immediate attendance of such witness, when it shall appear by oath or affirmation, to the commissioner, justice, judge, or court, as the case may be, that there is reasonable ground to believe that such witness will unlawfully fail to obey a subpoena issued and served in the usual course in such cases; and in such case the usual witness fee shall be paid to such witness so attached. . .

SEC. 4. That if any person related to another person within and not including the fourth degree of consanguinity computed according to the rules of the civil law, shall marry or cohabit with, or have sexual intercourse with such other so related person, knowing her or him to be within said degree of relationship, the person so offending shall be deemed guilty of incest, and, on conviction thereof, shall be punished by imprisonment in the penitentiary not less than three years and not more than fifteen years.

SEC. 5. That if an unmarried man or woman commit fornication, each of them shall be punished by imprisonment not exceeding six months, or by fine not exceeding one hundred dollars.

SEC. 6. That all laws of the legislative assembly of the Territory of Utah which provided that prosecutions for adultery can only be commenced on the complaint of the husband or wife are hereby disapproved and annulled; and all prosecutions for adultery may hereafter be instituted in the same way that prosecutions for other crimes are. . .

SEC. 9. That every ceremony of marriage, or in the nature of a marriage ceremony, of any kind, in any of the Territories of the United States, whether either or both or more of the parties to such ceremony be lawfully competent to be the subjects of such marriage or ceremony or not, shall be certified by a certificate stating the fact and nature of such ceremony, the full names of each of the parties concerned, and the full name of every officer, priest, and person, by whatever style or designation called or known, in any way taking part in the performance of such ceremony, which certificate shall be drawn up and signed by the parties to such ceremony and by every officer, priest, and person taking part in the performance of such ceremony, and shall be by the officer, priest, or other person solemnizing such marriage or ceremony

---

[72] The original Senate bill provided that the lawful husband or wife of anyone charged with polygamy or polygamous cohabitation could be compelled to testify except in matters of "confidential communications." This was altered to make such testimony voluntary. See *Suppression of Polygamy in Utah*, House Report 2735 (49-1) 1886, Serial 2443, 1.

filed in the office of the probate court, or, if there be none, in the office of court having probate powers in the county or district in which such ceremony shall take place, for record, and shall be immediately recorded, and be at all times subject to inspection as other public records. . .

SEC. 11. That the laws enacted by the legislative assembly of the Territory of Utah which provide for or recognize the capacity of illegitimate children to inherit or to be entitled to any distributive share in the estate of the father of any such illegitimate child are hereby disapproved and annulled; and no illegitimate child shall hereafter be entitled to inherit from his or her father or to receive any distributive share in the estate of his or her father: *Provided*, That this section shall not apply to any illegitimate child born within twelve months after the passage of this act, nor to any child made legitimate by the seventh section of the act entitled "An act to amend section fifty-three hundred and fifty-two of the Revised Statutes of the United States, in reference to bigamy, and for other purposes," approved March twenty-second, eighteen hundred and eighty-two. . .

SEC. 13. That it shall be the duty of the Attorney-General of the United States to institute and prosecute proceedings to forfeit and escheat to the United States the property of corporations obtained or held in violation of section three of the act of Congress approved the first day of July, eighteen hundred and sixty-two . . . and all such property so forfeited and escheated to the United States shall be disposed of by the Secretary of the Interior, and the proceeds thereof applied to the use and benefit of the common schools in the Territory in which such property may be: *Provided*, That no building, or the grounds appurtenant thereto, which is held and occupied exclusively for purposes of the worship of God, or parsonage connected therewith, or burial ground shall be forfeited. . .

SEC. 17. That the acts of the legislative assembly of the Territory of Utah incorporating, continuing, or providing for the corporation known as the Church of Jesus Christ of Latter-Day Saints, and the ordinance of the so called general assembly of the State of Deseret incorporating the Church of Jesus Christ of Latter-Day Saints, so far as the same may now have legal force and validity, are hereby disapproved and annulled, and the said corporation, in so far as it may now have, or pretend to have, any legal existence, is hereby dissolved. That it shall be the duty of the Attorney General of the United States to cause such proceedings to be taken in the supreme court of the Territory of Utah as shall be proper to execute the foregoing provisions of this section and to wind up the affairs of said corporation conformably to law. . .

SEC. 20. That it shall not be lawful for any female to vote at any election hereafter held in the Territory of Utah for any public purpose whatever, and no such vote shall be received or counted or given effect in any manner whatever; and any and every act of the legislative assembly of the Territory of Utah providing for or allowing the registration or voting by females is hereby annulled. . .[73]

SEC. 24. That every male person twenty-one years of age resident in the Territory of Utah shall, as a condition precedent to his right to register or vote at any election in said Territory, take and subscribe an oath or affirmation, before the registration officer of his voting precinct, that he is over twenty-one years of age, and has resided in the Territory of Utah for six months then last passed and in the precinct for one month immediately preceding the date thereof, and that he is a native-born (or naturalized, as the case may be) citizen of the United States, and further state in such oath or affirmation his full name, with his age, place of business, his status, whether single or married, and, if married, the name of his lawful wife, and that he will support the Constitution of the United States and will faithfully obey the laws thereof, and especially will obey the act of Congress approved March twenty-second, eighteen hundred and eighty-two . . . and will also obey this act in respect of the crimes in said act defined and forbidden, and that he will not, directly or indirectly, aid or abet, counsel or advise, any other person to commit any of said crimes. . . As a condition precedent to the right to hold office in or under said Territory, the officer, before entering on the duties of his office, shall take and subscribe an oath or affirmation declaring his full name, with his age, place of business, his status, whether married or single, and, if married, the name of his lawful wife, and that he will support the Constitution of the United States and will faithfully obey the laws thereof, and especially will obey the act of Congress approved March twenty-second, eighteen hundred and eighty-two. . . And will also obey this act in respect of the crimes in said act defined and forbidden, and that he will not, directly or indirectly, aid or abet, counsel or advise, any other person to commit any of said crimes; which oath or affirmation shall be recorded in the proper office and indorsed on the commission or certificate of appointment. All grand and petit jurors in said Territory shall take the same oath or affirmation, to be administered, in writing or orally, in the proper court. No person shall be entitled to vote in any election in said Territory, or be capable of jury service, or hold any office of trust or emolument in said Territory who shall not have taken the oath or affirmation aforesaid. No person who shall have been convicted of any crime under this act, or under the act of Congress aforesaid approved March twenty-second, eighteen hundred and eighty-two, or who shall be a polygamist, or who shall associate or cohabit polygamously with persons of

---

[73] Soon after its arrival in the territory the Utah Commission recommended repealing the right of women to vote in Utah. "Annual Report of the Utah Commission," *RSI* (1882), 2:1007. The Edmunds-Tucker Act incorporated many of the commission's proposals. There is a year-by-year summary of such recommendations in Grow, "Utah Commission," Table 21, 239–43.

the other sex, shall be entitled to vote in any election in said Territory, or be capable of jury service, or to hold any office of trust or emolument in said Territory. . .

SEC. 26. That all religious societies, sects, and congregations shall have the right to have and to hold, through trustees appointed by any court exercising probate powers in a Territory, only on the nomination of the authorities of such society, sect, or congregation, so much real property for the erection or use of houses of worship, and for such parsonages and burial grounds as shall be necessary for the convenience and use of the several congregations of such religious society, sect, or congregation.

Received by the President, February 19, 1887.

[NOTE BY THE DEPARTMENT OF STATE.—The foregoing act having been presented to the President of the United States for his approval, and not having been returned by him to the house of Congress in which it originated within the time prescribed by the Constitution of the United States, has become a law without his approval.][74]

More threatening than all previous measures was the Idaho test oath, a formal attestation required of all voters that denied anyone who was a Mormon—monogamous, plural, or single—the right to participate in elections. Believing the oath could not possibly survive constitutional scrutiny, church authorities carried their challenge of the law to the U.S. Supreme Court where, to their dismay, it was upheld.[75]

The case arose when Samuel D. Davis and other Idaho Mormons resigned their membership in the church in order to vote in an election. After his conviction for criminal conspiracy by the third district court in Idaho, and being remanded to the custody of Oneida sheriff H. G. Beason, Davis appealed to the U.S. Supreme Court. Davis's lawyers, led by Franklin S. Richards, argued that the alleged crimes described in the Idaho law were not in fact criminal and that the statute's voting requirements violated the First Amendment. The Supreme Court's decision, rendered on 3 February 1890, not only left the disfranchising provisions of the Idaho law intact but opened the way for Congress to threaten the imposition of similar penalties on the Territory of Utah. By ruling that Davis could not avoid the restrictions placed on the LDS church

---

[74] Grover Cleveland allowed the ten-day period granted for executive approval of the measure to expire, unlike Lincoln, Grant, and Arthur who had signed earlier laws to suppress polygamy. The bill became law without Cleveland's signature on 3 Mar. 1887 and was upheld by the U.S. Supreme Court in *Late Corporation of the Church of Jesus Christ of Latter-day Saints vs. United States*, 136 U.S. 1 (1890).

[75] Good accounts of anti-Mormon activity in Idaho are in Roberts, *Comprehensive History*, 6:213–14; Wells, "Idaho Anti-Mormon Test Oath," 235–52; and the same author's *Anti-Mormonism in Idaho*, 37–154.

by leaving it, the court's decision represented the most extreme point to which the national crusade against polygamy had arrived.[76] In the words of two legal scholars, the Supreme Court's ruling on the Idaho law made it such that "an individual who was once identified as a Mormon could not escape the law's punishments even by abandoning his religion. To punish an individual for his faith was wrong; to punish him for his former faith was worse."[77]

"Senator Edmunds Has Solemnized More Polygamous Marriages Than Brigham Young": Gentile Dissent

As already noted in Chapter Six, some non-Mormons believed that the government's program of legislative and judicial pressure was ill-conceived. Saying that the reason for polygamy's stubborn survival was the extraordinary influence of church leaders, they urged a shift to political reform as a more important goal. Belief that domination by the church's hierarchy not only accounted for polygamy's persistence but was the greater menace to the nation's republican ways was not new. It was a view expressed by critics from the beginning and one that continued through the 1880s.[78]

By urging elimination of Mormon temporal control, the following newspaper editorial not only illustrates concern with Mormonism's hierarchy but compares the moral attack on polygamy with what it says were errors in approaches taken to the problem of slavery in the South.[79]

---

[76] *Davis vs. Beason*, 133 U.S. 342–48 (1890).

[77] Firmage and Mangrum, *Zion in the Courts*, 234. For more on the context of this case, see Wells, *Anti-Mormonism in Idaho*, 139–43; and Clements, *Fred T. Dubois's The Making of a State*, 160–61, 176–77.

[78] "The Mormon sectarian organization which upholds polygamy has the whole power of making and executing the local legislation of the Territory. . . [Polygamy] can only be suppressed by taking away the political power of the sect which encourages and sustains it," Rutherford B. Hayes argued in his Fourth Annual Message, 6 Dec. 1880, *Comp.*, 10:4558. Also see Hoogenboom, *Rutherford B. Hayes*, 476; and Williams, *Life of Rutherford Birchard Hayes*, 2:225n1, 365. The Utah Commission increasingly spoke of the need to displace Mormonism's civil presence with federal authority. This was a major theme of Grow in his "Utah Commission," 189–92. Fred T. Dubois of Idaho said polygamy, on account of its sensational character, was but a device he and others used to attack the more fundamental Mormon wrong of hierarchical control. Clements, *Fred T. Dubois's The Making of a State*, 48. Perhaps the most articulate exposition of this view was that of Dutton, "Church and State in Utah," 320–30. The essential modern study of this issue is Hansen, *Quest for Empire*, esp. 161–90.

[79] I am indebted to Margaret Humberston, Supervising Librarian at the Connecticut Valley Hist. Museum in Massachusetts, for assistance in examining the *Springfield Daily Union* for this date. The paper has no volume, issue, or whole number.

"THE MORMON CHURCH: NOT POLYGAMY BUT THE
POWER OF THE PRIESTHOOD THE CHIEF DANGER . . . ,"
SPRINGFIELD [MASSACHUSETTS] DAILY UNION, 30 JAN. 1885, 6/3.

When the anti-slavery agitation was at its height popular feeling at the
North was exercised chiefly with the immoral quality of slavery as an institution. Yet the great war of the Rebellion, by which slavery was overthrown,
turned on an altogether different issue, the question, namely, of political sovereignty. . . There were humane men in those days that . . . worked hard . . .
to create a general belief that slavery ought to be dealt with by other agen-
cies than the general government, and the whole North was blinded to the
real purpose of the South.

Popular judgment is to-day repeating the same blunder in the matter of
Mormonism. Attention is fastened upon a single aspect of Mormonism, the
revolting immorality of polygamy, and this conspicuously offensive part is
mistaken for the whole, just as the conspicuous barbarism of slavery was mistaken for the whole of Southern policy. And just as the Northern agitators
exhausted their energies in combating one feature of the Southern policy, without suspecting what was the ambition and purpose lying behind slavery and
upholding it, so are agitators against polygamy wasting their strength in
denouncing a single superficial fact of Mormonism and ignoring the tremendous power back of that fact which is the real menace to American institutions. If they persist in this mistake, the country will one day have another
rude and terrible awakening. It will be discovered all at once that the essential principle of Mormonism is not polygamy at all, but the ambition of an
ecclesiastical hierarchy to wield sovereignty; to rule the souls and lives of its
subjects with absolute authority, unrestrained by any civil power.

Some critics also continued to call for a more patient course in dealing
with the Mormon problem.[80] Those seeking that end, straining at an oar
worked by others for decades, now included Southerners who saw attacks
on Mormonism as a recapitulation of what they considered sectional bully-
ing a generation earlier.[81] There was also Charles Bliss, a sometime Protestant resident in Utah, who stated that the only way to meet Mormonism was
with education and ideas.[82] Policies of coercion, he told President Cleveland,
were counterproductive.

---

[80] The number urging moderation, though unsuccessful, is quite surprising. For a few examples, see:
[Stillman], *Mormon Question*; Curtis, *Letter to the Secretary of the Interior*; and, idem, "A Plea for Religious Liberty . . . ," *Des. Eve. News*, 18 May 1886, 19:149 [1/1–5, 2/2–5]. As in earlier decades, the American public did
not always admire those who called for toleration of the Saints. See, for example, McCormick, "An Anarchist Defends the Mormons,"156–69.

[81] As illustrated by the reproachful speech of U.S. Sen. Joseph Emerson Brown, a former Confederate
governor of Georgia, in *Cong. Rec.* (48-1), 27 May 1884, 4554–56, 4560, 4562. Also see *Defence of the Constitutional and Religious Rights of the People of Utah.*   [82] Bliss, "Weak Point," 783.

CHARLES R. BLISS TO PRESIDENT GROVER CLEVELAND,
PLEASANT VALLEY, UTAH, 20 MAR. 1885, RG48, N.A.

Truly has the blood of the Mormon martyrs been the seed of their
church. . . It matters little how true or false a creed may be it thrives best
when persecution is strongest. . .

Forbidden fruit seems to be the sweetest. . . To keep chickens out of the
garden repeatedly drive them into it. . . If a law was passed compelling every
Mormon to marry and support several wives, feed, clothe and educate their
children there would be few polygamists. . . The fact is that the laws against
polygamy have made more polygamists than anything else. Senator Edmunds
has solemnized more polygamous marriages than Brigham Young.

THE CRUSADE NEARS ITS GOAL

Arguments for an altered strategy converted few of Mormonism's enemies.
Discouraged pluralists increasingly expected that they must sometime submit to "long terms of unlawful imprisonment palmed upon them by [Gen-
tile legal authorities such as] the damdable hounds Dickson and Zane."[83] With
women's suffrage now repealed, alien converts prevented from acquiring citizenship, and well over a thousand "cohabs" forced to watch the struggle
through prison bars, a growing Gentile-dominated Liberal Party won munic-
ipal elections in 1889 and 1890 in the cities of Ogden and Salt Lake City.[84]
The courts upheld sections thirteen and seventeen of the Edmunds-Tucker
Act, imposing disincorporation on the church and seizure of its properties,
leaving only the barest means for maintenance of ecclesiastical functions.[85]

---

[83] Nelson Wheeler Whipple Diaries, vol. 3, 10 Feb. 1887, in possession of Ms. Barbara Gustaveson, Farmington, Utah. The references are to William Howard Dickson, U.S. attorney for Utah, 1884–1887, and Charles
S. Zane, chief justice of Utah's territorial supreme court, 1884–1893.

[84] The church's opponents saw this as signaling the destruction of both polygamy and Mormon theocracy. "Gentile Triumph in Salt Lake City," 139. Further accounts are: "Report of the Governor of Utah,"
RSI (1890), 3:658–60; and "Annual Report of the Utah Commission," ibid., 3:412–13. For the declining ratio
of Mormons to non-Mormons, see Poll et al., Utah's History, 692, Table H; and May, "A Demographic Portrait of the Mormons, 1830–1980," 51. For the number convicted and sent to prison, see "Prosecutions," Des.
Semi-Weekly News, 19 July 1889, 24:50 [3/1]; Jenks, Convictions for Polygamy in Utah and Idaho, House Exec. Doc.
447 (50-1), 13 Sept. 1888, Serial 2561; Exhibits A and B, in Whitney, History of Utah, 3:643–50; and, for Utah
only, A[mos] Milton Musser, "Convictions and Fines of the 'Raid,'" Improvement Era 9:1 (Nov. 1905), 63–66.

[85] While a great deal of judicial maneuvering occurred, the government moved quickly after passage of
the Edmunds-Tucker Act to seize church assets. For the initial skirmishing, see Letter from The Attorney-General, Transmitting, In Response to Senate Resolution of December 10, 1888, a Statement Relative to the Execution of the Law
against Bigamy, Exec. Doc. 21 (50-2), Serial 2610. The Supreme Court upheld repeal of territorial law and
seizure of church properties in Late Corp. of the Church of Jesus Christ of Latter-Day Saints vs. United States, 136 U.S.
1 (1890). Mormon authorities attempted to minimize losses by placing their assets in the hands of trusted
private individuals. Arrington, Great Basin Kingdom, 361–65.

Introduction of the Cullom-Struble Bill in Congress increased the prospect of even greater humiliation. Patterned on the Idaho test oath, it intended to take from every member of the LDS church living in territories of the U.S. the right to vote.[86] Believing, as Utah governor Eli Murray said in 1885, that "it is necessarily true that a good Mormon cannot be a good citizen," polygamy's foes were determined to wipe the practice of plural marriage out of existence.[87] The result was that, as a non-Mormon historian at the time put it, the "long season of prosecution and persecution, of litigations and imprisonments" made the anti-polygamy crusade a program of repression "without parallel in the history of American morals."[88] Impeached by the nation as sexual barbarians and hunted as criminals, the Latter-day Saints experienced the darkest period in their history since the anti-Mormon drivings of Missouri and Illinois.

---

[86] The bill emerged from a joint conference committee in early 1887. All sides expected it would become law, but it was debated for three years and forgotten. A copy of the bill and transcript of the debate surrounding its first presentation in the Senate is in *Cong. Rec.* (49-2), 1887, 1896–1904.

[87] "Report of the Governor of Utah," *RSI* (1885), 2:1016.

[88] This was Hubert Howe Bancroft in his *Literary Industries*, 759. A more recent historian described the government's policies as "unequalled in the annals of federal law enforcement." Linford, "The Polygamy Cases," pt. 2:585. Also see Sears, "Punishing the Saints," 656–58.

Chapter 8

"MEASURING ARMS WITH THE ALMIGHTY"
Mormonism on the Defense

Mormons did all they could to blunt the assault made on their lives and institutions. Wilford Woodruff, who in 1873 said President Grant was like "Phario of Old," was joined by many who compared their circumstances to that of the Israelites in Egypt and to Christians during the early Roman Empire.[1] Eliza R. Snow, successively a plural wife to Joseph Smith and Brigham Young, issued a severe warning: if the Saints were forced to cease practicing polygamy, she said, the American people would shoulder "a heavier responsibility than any nation has ever assumed, with one exception—that of the ancient Jews. . . The controversy is with God—not us."[2] As they viewed it, more than polygamy was imperiled by the government's juggernaut against them. Mormonism itself, the restoration of divine truths, and the tradition of oracular authority were under attack.[3] The eternal family and plurality of wives, they said, were inseparable and must rise and fall together. Both were central features of the Mormon theological edifice.[4] As one Latter-day Saint explained:

---

[1] Kenney, ed., *Wilford Woodruff's Journal*, 18 Feb. 1873, 7:123. As but a few of many examples, see Henry Eyring, "Reminiscences," 27 Jan. 1883, LDS Archives, 63; and Gibson Condie, Reminiscences and Diary, 3 Mar. 1889, LDS Archives. Comparing Mormon difficulties with those of the Israelites in Egypt was considered apt because, as George Q. Cannon pointed out, by forcing them to adopt monogamy with its inclination to birth control and abortion, the federal government, like Pharaoh of old, sought to destroy their children. "Discourse by Prest. Geo. Q. Cannon," *Des. Eve. News*, 13 Dec. 1884, 18:19 [1/1,5].

[2] Snow in "Joseph the Seer's Plural Marriages," *Des. News* [Weekly], 22 Oct. 1879, 28:38, 605/1.

[3] See the insightful article by Elisha, "Sustaining Charisma," 45–63.

[4] Charles W. Penrose in "Plural Marriage," *Mil. Star* 45:29 (16 July 1883), 454; "Discourse by Prest. Geo Q. Cannon," *Des. Eve. News*, 13 Dec. 1884, 18:19 [1/5]; and, "Eternity of the Marriage Covenant," ibid., 20 Feb. 1886, 19:76 [2/1–2].

THE ABANDONMENT OF POLYGAMY, that is considered by some to be so easy of accomplishment, is more untenable even than fighting. However much the people might desire to do this, they could not without yielding every other principle, for it is the very key stone of our faith, and is so closely interwoven into everything that pertains to our religion, that to tear it asunder and cast it away would involve the entire structure.[5]

"WE PREFER TO ROW AGAINST THE CURRENT OF CORRUPTION": CONTINUED DEVOTION TO PLURAL MARRIAGE

Both church members and Gentile friends labeled their accusers as moral hypocrites, driven by political and economic greed.[6] Moreover, by resisting efforts to destroy the Principle, the Saints believed they were securing rights for others as well as themselves, something they had long said Mormons would be called upon to do.[7] Flags in the territory were flown at half-staff; black armbands worn; and leaders cleansed of the nation's wickedness by washing the dust of their enemies from their feet.[8] Intending to fight for their cause in the courts, special funds were created to defend those captured by the marshals.[9]

Along with these actions, the elevating promises associated with the Principle were yet intoned. A plural wife reminded her readers that when it came to patriarchal marriage, "none can disobey it, and be exalted in His presence."[10] And an address prepared by the leaders was read to congregations throughout Utah in 1880 at the conclusion of which members were asked to promise

---

[5] An Old Timer, "Expressions from the People," *Des. Eve. News*, 14 April 1885, 18:120 [4/4]. This is close to George Q. Cannon's statement that if they were to repudiate the Principle, "our Church would cease to be the Church of God, and the ligaments that now bind it together would be severed." Quoted in Bitton, *George Q. Cannon*, 275.

[6] "Polygamy," *Des. News* [Weekly], 16 April 1884, 33:13, 196/1–3; "'Why Don't You Promise to Obey the Law?'" *Des. Eve. News*, 15 Mar. 1887, 20:94 [2/1–2]; and "To Fleece the Mormons," ibid., 30 July 1887, 20:209 [5/2–4]. For examples of non-Mormons who agreed with the Saints, see Codman, *Solution of the Mormon Problem*, 15–16; and Sen. Wilkinson Call of Florida, in *Cong. Rec.* (49-2) 18 Feb. 1887, 1900–4.

[7] It was often said that when the Constitution of the United States hung "by a thread," the Elders of Zion would preserve it. Apostle Erastus Snow narrowed the saving brigade to those who were the "sons and daughters of polygamous Utah." "Discourse by Apostle Erastus Snow," *Des. Eve. News*, 9 Sept. 1882, 15:246 [1/5].

[8] Kenney, ed., *Wilford Woodruff's Journal*, 19 Jan. 1881, 8:6–7; Frederick Kessler Diary 1857–1899, 24 July 1886, Kessler Collection, Special Collections, UU; Rose Berry West, "Pioneer Personal History," WPA Biographical Sketches, box 11, Uhi, 4; Larson and Larson, eds., *Diary of Charles Lowell Walker*, 4 July 1885, 2:653.

[9] "To the Presidents of Stakes and their Counselors, the Bishops and their Counselors, and the Latter-day Saints generally," 26 May 1885, First Presidency Circular Letters, box 1, fd. 1, LDS Archives.

[10] Mary F., "Patriarchal Order of Marriage," *Woman's Exponent* 10:16 (15 Jan. 1882), 121.

they "would stand by the Laws of God and take the consequences rather than obey the laws of man."[11] As often happens with "persecution," polygamous marriages seemed actually to increase.[12] Struck by their defiance, the Utah Commission warned the nation not to expect early success against plurality, for Mormons were a people "wonderfully superstitious and fanatically devoted to their system of religion."[13] A reading of remarks by the Saints at the time demonstrates that the commissioners' apprehensions were justifiably drawn.

Mormons were honored, Helen Mar Whitney wrote in 1884, because the Almighty had chosen them to bear the "cross" of persecution while bringing greater health and happiness to the world. Plural marriage made them the "advanced guard," and Mormons would "yet be looked up to and regarded as the founders of a superior system of Christianity."[14] Speaking in the same vein, Apostle Moses Thatcher (1842–1909) said the Saints would remain apart from the world and refuse to merge with the mainstream of American marital decadence.

"REMARKS BY APOSTLE MOSES THATCHER," 4 APRIL 1884,
DES. NEWS [WEEKLY], 7 MAY 1884, 33:16, 242/1–2.

We hear a great deal about the immorality of this people; but allow me to say, if we permitted ourselves to be led into wickedness; if we would adopt the ways of the Christian age; if we would cast our children into reservoirs and ash pits, on vacant lots and dung heaps, or throw them on to the railroad track; if we would transmit to our sons and daughters disease, and encourage them in ways that lead to death, hell and the grave; we should then have assimilated, as some of our would-be Christianizers have expressed it, with "American institutions;" in other words, then we should be hail fellows well met with the office-seekers, with adventurers, with libertines and other destroyers of other people's peace and happiness. It is because we cannot do this; because we refuse to "assimilate;" because we prefer to row against the current of cor-

---

[11] As told in Larson and Larson, eds., *Diary of Charles Lowell Walker*, 27 Mar. 1880, 2:491–92. Apostle Orson Pratt answered Mormon uncertainty whether to obey the commandment to live polygamy or the laws of their country: "Well, then, what do you say, shall I renounce my religion, because of this law? No. Shall I advise the Latter-day Saints . . . to renounce any part of their doctrines because Congress has denounced it? No. . . . If they wish to renounce them or forsake them, they are at liberty so to do, and be accountable to God, and be disfellowshipped from the Church, because of their disbelief." Pratt, 6 Oct. 1879, *Journal of Discourses*, 20:327.

[12] Sen. George F. Edmunds noted this as early as 1882. See his "Political Aspects of Mormonism," 287. And the Utah Commissioners said in 1884 that "Mormon fanaticism was blown into a flame" and there was "a polygamic revival" among the people. "Annual Report of the Utah Commission," *RSI* (1884), 2:517–18.

[13] "Annual Report of the Utah Commission," *RSI* (1884), 2:520. In an 1882 letter to Senator Edmunds, Schuyler Colfax lamented that even monogamous Mormons were committed to the doctrine in the same way as poor whites in the South were to slavery. Quoted in Hollister, *Life of Schuyler Colfax*, 473.

[14] Whitney, *Why We Practice Plural Marriage*, 53–55, 63–64.

ruption; because the fruits of our labors, political, financial and social are good, and bespeak a higher and better civilization, that we are hated and ostracized, and not because of any immorality that may exist in our midst. We are sensible of the fact that we are not of the world; that if we were, the world would love us as its own. We are sensible of the fact that we have come out from the world, and that, too, for a wise purpose in the wisdom of God. In these mountains we expect to establish the foundation of a civilization that will yet be the admiration of the world. We expect to bequeath to our children the blessings of physical and mental strength such as will enable them to stand the test that will be required of them; and the very principle and tenet of our religion, against which the Christian feeling of the age appears to be so much shocked, will be the chief corner stone in the hands of the builder of rearing the structure that will be different from anything else in the world.

"They Bossed the President": Mormon Women Enter the Fray

Mormon female response to those attacking the Principle, whatever sorrows or criticisms were privately felt, is one of the more interesting features of the conflict. It finds many illustrations and was frequently an object of wonder by Gentile observers.[15] An outsider traveling among them in the 1870s said that Utah women prayed over congressional debates the way other women did over battles of the Civil War.[16] A correspondent to the *Woman's Exponent* expressed their determination:

> We the daughters of Zion are going to step forward, and stand side by side with our brothers, in upholding every doctrine of our Church, Plural Marriage included, and we will say to our sisters "come share with me, my husband and home and we will love each other, and labor for each other's welfare as we do for our own." We will show to the world that we live in that order from choice, not from compulsion, and we will continue to bear testimony that God's special blessings rest upon those who are striving to live that Holy Order in purity before Him.[17]

---

[15] More than one said that Latter-day Saint females were more defiant in defending the Principle than their husbands. It was a phenomenon remarked on by Remy in the 1850s. See his description quoted in Chapter Five. The same was repeated by the Idaho prosecutor, Fred T. Dubois. Clements, *Fred T. Dubois's The Making of a State*, 196; by Lum, *Utah and its People*, 31; and by Coyner, "Letters on Mormonism," 11–12. Similarly, Old Believer women in Russia were known to fight for their religion more fiercely than their men. Billington, *Icon and the Axe*, 137. And Southern ladies could be immovable in behalf of slavery. Like those of Mormon wives, their attitudes were cultivated by societal reinforcement, hierarchical household life, and religious teaching. See Fox-Genovese, *Within the Plantation Household*, 30, 35, 44, 64, 195. I am indebted to Lavina Fielding Anderson for bringing this last parallel to my attention.   [16] Kane, *Twelve Mormon Homes*, 70.

[17] Mary F., "The Patriarchal Order of Marriage," *Woman's Exponent* 10:16 (15 Jan. 1882), 122.

Utah's women in 1870 were the first in the nation to enter polling booths.[18] To what degree giving the elective franchise to Utah females was an attempt by the church's hierarchy to use women's ballots in the quarrel with opponents and to what extent they genuinely believed in political equality for both genders are matters of debate.[19] Mormons contended, as one apostle put it, that "Nowhere in the world are women freer than in Utah."[20] All, they believed, was part of the plan established for the Saints by Providence. As the editor of the *Woman's Exponent* told her readers, so far as the reasons for women acquiring the vote in Utah were concerned, they need only know that "God was in it."[21] Critics, of course, saw the matter differently.[22]

Devoted to the faith, Mormon women embarrassed national suffrage organizations by their support for plurality. The spectacle of wives, the presumed slaves of polygamous bashaws, actively participating in electoral contests seemed a conundrum. And Mormonism's acceptance of greater male sexual drive as a justification for polygamy affronted the advocates of sexual purity in the American home.[23] Gentile spokeswomen who espoused a single standard found the swelling households of Mormon Abrahams morally reprehensible. While the National Woman Suffrage Association under the influence of Susan B. Anthony and Elizabeth Cady Stanton befriended Latter-day Saint women, the more inflexible American Woman Suffrage Association did not. Division over the issue was reflected at the local level, where Anti-Polygamy Society leaders jousted with Mormon churchwomen who used the *Woman's Exponent*

---

[18] "An Act Conferring upon Women the Elective Franchise," 12 Feb. 1870, *Acts, Resolutions, and Memorials* (1870), 8. Wyoming actually passed legislation permitting women to vote a few months earlier than Utah, but ladies in Utah were the first to mark and deposit ballots. For Wyoming's legislation, see Beeton, *Women Vote in the West*, 1–22.

[19] See Alexander, "Experiment in Progressive Legislation," 20–30; Beeton, "Woman Suffrage in Territorial Utah," 100–20; Madsen's introduction to *Battle for the Ballot*, 1–32; and Iversen, "Debate on the American Home," 585–602. An excellent discussion of Mormon women's views of their role and place in society and its modification after the surrender on polygamy is provided in Yorgason, *Transformation*, 31–77.

[20] Moses Thatcher, 28 Aug. 1885, *Journal of Discourses*, 26:314.

[21] Editorial, "Woman's Position in Utah," *Woman's Exponent* 6:9 (1 Oct. 1877), 68. "For Mormon women at this time, the vote and their defense of polygamy were inextricably linked," Iversen observed in *Antipolygamy Controversy*, 23. But see the description of how the female defense of plurality nurtured genuine political aspirations on the part of Mormon women in Van Wagenen, "In Their Own Behalf," 31–43.

[22] Typical was the description by territorial governor George L. Woods: women in Utah, he said, voted "by order of the priesthood . . . it is a common thing, to see a Mormon priest with 6, 8, 10 & sometimes more wives & concubines go to the polls & vote together. It is a common thing for girls 12 years of age & upwards to vote and . . . vote by proxy, vote instead of absent ones, vote in lieu of the dead." George L. Woods, Recollections, cu-b, 58–59.

[23] Chapters Two and Three discuss Mormon belief in the greater sexual need of men compared to women.

as a countering lance to the *Anti-Polygamy Standard.*[24] Recognition that Mormon women were as committed to survival of the Principle as their husbands led to mounting legal hostility including, as Sarah Gordon demonstrates, tactics of purposeful humiliation by indicting plural wives for fornication.[25]

Latter-day Saints of both sexes also opposed suffrage and purity organizations over the proposal for a constitutional amendment that would ban polygamy and regularize monogamy throughout the nation. As the House Judiciary Committee asked in 1886, when answering those who resisted such an amendment, what was to happen when Utah became a state? What was to prevent Mormons, once in possession of statehood, from restoring polygamy and substituting "the Asiatic type" of family for the "European-American type of civilized life"?[26] While it was a campaign that never succeeded, attempts to enshrine opposition to plurality in the nation's highest law continued into the third decade of the twentieth century, making it one of the longer-running efforts to amend the constitution in American history.[27]

The overwhelming majority of Mormon females believed that God led their leaders and that Mormonism's enemies would fail. As one put it: "Mr. Edmunds . . . [is] not fighting a little handful of people in the mountains, but measuring arms with the almighty."[28] Aware of the influence that women had on the nation's image of Mormon family life, church authorities, especially after the *Reynolds* case, recruited female voices to assist them in the struggle. Two articulate veterans of the plural arrangement, Emmeline B. Wells, editor of the *Woman's*

---

[24] Gentile disappointment that enfranchised Mormon women did not eschew polygamy, as well as divisions over the suffrage question in and outside Utah, is treated in Mulvay, "Eliza R. Snow and the Woman Question," 258–64; Beeton, *Women Vote in the West*, 23–81; all the essays in Madsen, *Battle for the Ballot*; and Iversen, *Antipolygamy Controversy*, 53–97, 159–84. As another historian put it: "Who could expect the women of Utah to indirectly admit, by voting against Mormon measures and candidates, that they were whores or concubines, and their children bastards?" Kern, "Love, Labor, and Self-Control," 309.

[25] Gordon, "Mormon Question," 25–27.

[26] *Polygamy*, House Report 2568 (49-1), 24 May 1886, Serial 2442, 7.

[27] Constitutional amendments against polygamy were proposed in the 1870s, but the idea only became epidemic in the 1880s. One scholar counted seventeen congressional proposals for the reform between 1882 and 1889 alone. Ames, *Proposed Amendments to the Constitution*, 272. The plan was an early staple in Utah Commission reports, as in 1887 when two commissioners argued it was necessary "for the protection of monogamy, the bed-rock of American and European civilization, against the inroads of an Asiatic vice." A[mbrose] B. Carlton and John A. McClernand, "Annual Report of the Utah Commission," *RSI* (1887), 2:1354. All the members accepted this view in "Annual Report of the Utah Commission," *RSI* (1893), 3:419. For Mormon opposition, see "Constitutional Amendment Craze," *Des. Eve. News*, 22 Nov. 1883, 17:2 [2/2]; and "Amendments to the Constitution," *Des. News* [Weekly], 7 May 1884, 33:16, 246/1–2. For further commentary, see Iversen, *Antipolygamy Controversy*, 190–91, 197–201, 244.

[28] Zina D. H. Young, "One Who Knows," *Woman's Exponent* 11:21 (1 April 1883), 161.

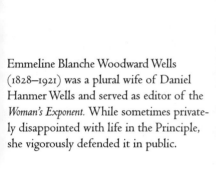

Emmeline Blanche Woodward Wells (1828–1921) was a plural wife of Daniel Hanmer Wells and served as editor of the *Woman's Exponent.* While sometimes private-ly disappointed with life in the Principle, she vigorously defended it in public.

Exponent, and Zina Young Williams, a widowed daughter of Brigham Young, were sent to Washington, D.C., for the purpose of memorializing Congress on behalf of Mormon society, cementing relations with women's suffrage lead-ers, and seeking an audience with President and Mrs. Rutherford B. Hayes.

The ambassadors met with everyone on their agenda and found President and Mrs. Hayes hospitable. As Wells reported in the *Woman's Exponent* account below, the Mormon envoys left President Hayes with no doubt as to their views.[29]

[EMMELINE B. WELLS], "THE MORMON FEMALE,"
WOMAN'S EXPONENT 7:17 (1 FEB. 1879), 187.

Quite interesting it was to see two Mor[mon] wives standing in danger-ous proximity to our most respectable President Hayes pleading for polygamy. This little dramatic scene occurred in the White House last week. And by the same token the Mormon wives took the lead in their argument, and as Orson Pratt floored Hot-scotch Newman in Utah,[30] they bossed the President

[29] For Wells's brief journal account of the episode, see Wells Journals, 13 Jan. 1879, UPB, 5:2.
[30] The Pratt-Newman debate is treated in Chapter Six.

in the debate argumentative at the national capital. Their first direct and inci-
sive question was, "What right has the General Government to ignore territorial laws and tear them away from their husbands, and

TO BASTARDIZE THEIR CHILDREN

And deprive them of all right and inheritance?"

It has no right to do so. In the first place, and most emphatically, the Constitution forbids the passage of ex post facto laws, and so any law interfering
with Mormon marriages previous to its passage would be utterly and absolutely unconstitutional.

Their next point was that these Mormon wives were happy, wanted to live
with their husbands, religiously believed they were right in so doing, and objected not to other women having a share to [their] husband's names and property. Who then would be benefited by tearing them away? How would morality
be served by doing so? Would not only distress, poverty, demoralization result?
There was no good answer to this given. Nor can any very good answer be given.

Congress should see to it that when they do legislate on this Utah question, they should do it like statesmen, and not like fanatics. There are many
and important interests to be considered, and there are not a few of the best
observers who think that the best thing that can be done in the matter is not
to legislate on it at all.

The polygamy of Utah is doing no harm to the United States. The territory as far as the Mormons are concerned, is a type of morality, and we should
be glad to see their representative delegate, [George Q.] Cannon, a gentleman
above reproach, compared, as far as genuine gentlemanliness and purity and
integrity of character is concerned, with any of the high moral Christian statesmen who antagonize the Mormons. But the Christian statesmen would
undoubtedly weaken.[31]

Mrs. Sarah Spencer[32] puts the case in a nutshell when she says that the
differences between the Mormons and the Christian statesmen is that the Mormons marry their mistresses, the congressmen don't.—Capital.

Neither conversation with nor a follow-up letter from the women to President and Mrs. Hayes had any effect.[33] Perhaps Hayes was mindful of another letter sent him at the time, urging continued opposition to polygamy and

---

[31] The ladies, no less than Cannon himself, must have taken pride in the remark of Isabella Beecher
Hooker, suffragette and sister of Henry Ward Beecher, who Cannon remembered saying to him: "I have
told many of my friends that I would rather be your fiftieth wife than be the only wife of hundreds of men
whom I know." As quoted from Cannon's journal, in Cannon, "Mormon Issue in Congress," 143.

[32] Sara J. Spencer, a recording secretary of the National Suffrage Association who had previously cor-
responded with Emmeline B. Wells, and Matilda Joslyn Gage accompanied the Mormon women in their
visit to the White House.

[33] Wells indicated that Hayes asked the women to submit their views to him in writing, which they did.
The letter was more docile than the presentation described in the *Exponent*. Wells and Williams to Pres.
Rutherford B. Hayes, 29 Jan. 1879, RG48, N.A.

warning that "the purpose of the Mormons sending their weman to Washington is to beguild away the hearts of the wise men from doing right concerning our Laws just as they did Solomon."[34] And, as Joan Smyth Iversen
noted, while Mrs. Hayes treated the Mormon women with courtesy, shortly thereafter she became active in Protestant home missionary work that vigorously sought the destruction of polygamy.[35] Later the same year the president in his annual message urged "stringent" enforcement of anti-polygamy
laws, amendments to the Morrill Act, and, if necessary, suspending the rights
of U.S. citizenship for those who violated such laws.[36]

"Officers, Speakers, Singers, and the Martial Band": Protest Meetings

Another Mormon response to the anti-polygamy crusade was to hold mass
meetings protesting government policies. While these commenced years earlier, they became especially common in the 1880s.[37] At the April 1885 general conference of the church, held in Logan, Utah, a committee was established to encourage such gatherings. With Apostle Franklin D. Richards
presiding, Mormon authorities prepared a "Declaration of Grievances and
Protest" and sent it to Pres. Grover Cleveland.[38] Communities throughout
Utah followed with rallies and petitions of their own. A record of one meeting held in Farmington, Utah, is representative of similar events elsewhere.

"Minutes of Davis County Mass Meeting," Des. Eve. News, 6 May 1885, 18:139, 4/4–5.

Pursuant to the call made by the committee appointed at Logan to draft
a series of resolutions and protests to the President and people of the Unit-

---

[34] Margaret Jane Potts to Pres. R. B. Hayes, Philadelphia, 31 Jan. 1879, RG48, N.A. The reference to how Solomon's wives, princesses, and concubines "turned away his heart" is in I Kings, 11:3–4.

[35] Iversen, Antipolygamy Controversy, 28–30.

[36] Hayes, Third Annual Message, 1 Dec. 1879, Comp., 10:4511–12. The high priority that Hayes gave the "Mormon Problem" is discussed in Hoogenboom, Rutherford B. Hayes, 421–23, 447.

[37] See, for example, gatherings in 1863 to protest Governor Harding and the threat to serve Brigham Young with a warrant for violating the 1862 Morrill Act, in History of Brigham Young, 1847–1867, 335–36; that associated with the Cullom Bill of 1870, in "Great Indignation Meeting," Des. Eve. News, 14 Jan. 1870, 3:44 [2/1–5]; and, under same heading, ibid., 15 Jan. 1870, 3:45 [2/1–4]. There was also the mass meeting at the time of the Reynolds case, in "Mormon Ladies on Plural Marriage," ibid., 18 Nov. 1878, 11:303 [2/1–6].

[38] See "Resolution" presented to the conference on 4 April 1885 by Apostle Heber J. Grant following a reading of the "Epistle of the First Presidency," with supporting materials in Clark, ed., Messages, 3:11–13. The handwritten "Declaration of Grievances and Protest" was sent to President Cleveland on 6 April 1885 and is preserved in RG48, N.A.

ed States, in which the wrongs of the people of this Territory were to be set forth, the people of the Davis Stake of Zion assembled *en masse* at Farmington, on Saturday, May 2nd, at 1 P.M., and after listening a short time to music by the Kaysville martial band were called to order by Bishop J. M. Secrist, of Farmington, who nominated Mr. Thomas F. Roueche, of Kaysville, for chairman. Mr. Roueche was unanimously elected. He thanked the assembly for the honor conferred, and asked for the election of a secretary and such other officers as might be deemed necessary. The following were then nominated and unanimously elected to the several offices, respectively:

Joseph Barton, secretary; David Stoker, vice-president; John W. Whitaker and James H. Wilcox, assistant secretaries; Calvin W. Richards, sergeant-at-arms; Geo. Palmer, doorkeeper.

After the organization was completed, Mrs. Dora Robinson, assisted by Mr. Joseph F. Robinson, sang "The Star Spangled Banner," with chorus by the Farmington choir.

The chaplain offered up a prayer and was followed with music by the Kaysville martial band.

The chairman, in plain, concise language, then stated the object of the meeting, and called for the reading of the Declaration of grievances and Protest, prepared by the committee. This was done very ably, in a clear and impressive style by Assistant Secretary J. H. Wilcox. During the reading and at the close, the applause was frequent and hearty.

At the close of the reading, Mrs. E. Brown sang "Land of Washington" assisted in the chorus by the Farmington choir.

Mr. Thomas J. Steed of Farmington moved "that it is the sense of this meeting that we adopt the Declaration of Grievances and Protest as read, and earnestly endorse the sentiments therein contained," and followed with a short, pointed and telling speech in support of his motion.

Speeches were made by Mr. John R. Barnes, of Kaysville, Job Welling, of Farmington, and Joseph Barton, of Kaysville, depicting in a graphic manner the wrongs suffered by the members of the Church of Jesus Christ of Latter-day Saints since the organization of the Church to the present time; the mobbings and drivings in Missouri and other places; the call made for the "Mormon Battalion;" the misrepresentations of Federal officials to the General Government in regard to the "Mormons;" the animosity shown to "Mormons" by officials sent to Utah; the perversion of laws, and partiality in their administration; the high-handed acts of the Utah Commission in arbitrarily and without authority prohibiting the exercise of the elective franchise by members of the Church who were violating no law, but were industrious, virtuous and law abiding citizens of the United States; and who, while so arbitrarily and unjustly keeping this class of citizens from the polls, has carefully guarded and protected the elective franchise of the most depraved and lewd of the non-"Mormon" part of the population. It was also pointed out that the actions of the Federal Judges who are sent here ostensibly to administer the laws impartially, show that they forget the high and important position they occupy, for whenever a "Mormon" is on trial they become vindictive and spiteful, ignoring the written law, and making a law to suit the case in hand—anything to insure a conviction, the end justifying the means. This was illustrated by the words of one of the Federal Judges, who proclaimed: "The mission which God has called upon me to perform in Utah is as much above the duties of other courts and Judges as the heavens are above the earth, and whenever or wherever I may find the local or Federal laws obstructing or interfering, I shall trample them under my feet."[39]

The acts of the Governors of the Territory have not been such as would draw the people towards them, but otherwise.

Allusion was also made to "the one man power" vested in the Governor which has been used to the injury of the Territory. . .

The right of the people to petition for redress and to earnestly protest against the continuance of these abuses were maintained. The speakers were frequently interrupted by applause, and when the vote on the question was called, it showed that all present were of one mind, for the vote was hearty and unanimous.

The Farmington Choir sang an anthem, a vote of thanks was tendered the officers, speakers, singers and the martial band, benediction was pro[nounced] by the Chaplain and the meeting adjourned *sine die*.

The Secretary was instructed to forward a copy of these minutes to the DESERET NEWS and *Salt Lake Herald*.

Joseph Barton
Secretary.

In 1886, a mass meeting of women held in Salt Lake City prepared and sent resolutions to Congress. Additionally, the memorialists objected to what they considered rank illegality and complained of the indelicate manners of legal officers, alleging disregard for their womanhood. Except for their attachment to polygamy, Mormon wives here appear little different in their attitudes than Victorian spokeswomen elsewhere.

"THE LADIES' MASS MEETING," *DES. EVE. NEWS*,
6 MAR. 1886, 19:87 [2/2–8].

MEMORIAL

To the Honorable President, and the Senate and House of Representatives of the United States in Congress Assembled. . .

---

[39] The reference is to Judge James B. McKean, as quoted by Tullidge, *Life of Brigham Young*, 420–21. For doubt as to the credibility of Tullidge's account, see Alexander, "Federal Authority Versus Polygamic Theocracy," 100n46.

On the 22nd of March, 1882, an act of Congress was passed which is now commonly known as the Edmunds law. It was generally understood to have been framed for the purpose of settling what is called the Utah question, by condoning plural marriages up to that date and preventing their occurrence in the future, and also to protect the home, maintain the integrity of the family and shield innocent women and children from the troubles that might arise from its enforcement. But instead of being administered and executed in this spirit, it has been made the means of inflicting upon the women of Utah immeasurable sorrow and unprecedented indignities, of disrupting families, of destroying homes, and of outraging the tenderest and finest feelings of human nature.

The law has been so construed by the courts as to bring its penalties to bear upon the innocent. Men who had honestly arranged with their families so as to keep within the limits of the law, have been punished with the greatest possible severity, and their wives and children have been forced before courts and grand juries, and compelled to disclose the most sacred and private relations which in all civilized countries are held sacred to the parties. The meaning of the law has been changed so many times that no one can say definitely what is its signification. Those who have lived by the law, as interpreted in one case, find, as soon as they are entrapped, that a new rendering is constructed to make it applicable to their own. Under the latest ruling, a man who has contracted plural marriages, no matter at how remote a date, must not only repudiate his families and cease all connection with them, but if he is known to associate with them in the most distant manner, support them and show any regard whatever for their welfare, the offense of unlawful cohabitation is considered to have been fully established, and he is liable to exorbitant fines and imprisonment for an indefinite period, one district judge holding that a separate indictment may be found for each day of such association and recognition. . .

The women who are dependent upon the men whom they regard as their husbands, with whom they have lived, as they have regarded it, in honorable wedlock, must not only be separated from their society and protection, but must be treated as outcasts and be driven forth with their children to shame and distress, for the bare "association" of friendship is counted a crime and punished with all the severity inflicted upon those who have not in any way severed their plural family relations.

In order to fasten the semblance of guilt upon men accused of this offense, women are arrested and forcibly taken before sixteen men and plied with questions that no decent woman can hear without a blush. Little children are examined upon the secret relations of their parents, and wives in regard to their own condition and the doings of their husbands. If they decline to answer they are imprisoned in the penitentiary as though they were criminals. . .

We ask for justice. We appeal to you not to tighten the bonds which are now so tense that we can scarcely endure them. We ask that the laws may be fairly and impartially executed. We see good and noble men dragged to jail to linger among felons, while debauched and polluted men, some of them Federal officers who have been detected in the vilest kind of depravity, protected by the same court and officers that turn all their energies and engines of power toward the ruin of our homes and the destruction of our dearest associations. We see pure women forced to disclose their conjugal relations or go to prison, while the wretched creatures who pander to men's basest passions are left free to ply their horrible trade, and may vote at the polls, while legal wives of men with plural families are disfranchised. We see the law made specially against our people, so shamefully administered that every new case brings a new construction of its meaning, and no home is safe from instant intrusion by ruffians in the name of the law. And now we are threatened with entire deprivation of every right and privilege of citizenship, to gratify a prejudice that is fed on ignorance and vitalized by bigotry.

We respectfully ask for a full investigation of Utah affairs. For many years our husbands, brothers and sons have appealed for this in vain. We have been condemned, almost unheard. Everything reported to our detriment is received; our cries to be heard have been rejected. We plead for suspension of all measures calculated to deprive us of our political rights and privileges, and to harass, annoy and bring our people into bondage and distress, until a commission duly and specially authorized to make full inquiry into the affairs of this Territory, have investigated and reported. And while the blessing of Him who will one day deal out even-handed justice to all, shall rest upon your honorable bodies, your memorialists, as in duty bound, will ever pray, etc.[40]

"No Faithful Soul Dare Disobey": God and Prophets Speak

Some church members began to waver as to whether or not plurality was necessary for exaltation in the life to come.[41] In a poignant letter to President John Taylor, one Mormon wife, describing herself as "a weakly woman and

---

[40] The document, signed by committee members Sarah M. Kimball, M. Isabella Horne, Elmina S. Taylor, Dr. Romania B. Pratt, H. C. Brown, Mary Pitchforth, Ida I. Cook, Ida Coombs, and Mary John, was formally presented to Congress on 6 April 1886. See "Ladies' Memorial," *Des. Eve. News*, 8 April 1886, 19:115 [2/2].

[41] See what sounds like widespread discussion of this question in the communities of American Fork and Provo, Utah, in Niels Nielson to Joseph F. Smith, 22 Jan. 1883, Joseph F. Smith Incoming Correspondence, 1855–1918, box 12, fd. 17, LDS Archives; and L. E. Eggertson to Joseph F. Smith, 27 Aug. 1883, ibid., box 12, fd. 16, LDS Archives, respectively.

As church president during the harshest years of the anti-polygamy campaign, John Taylor (1808–1887) was unyielding in defense of the Principle, expressing himself as unwilling to forfeit plural marriage in exchange for either amnesty or Utah's statehood. *Used by permission, Utah State Historical Society, all rights reserved.*

[her family] . . . in poor circumstances," told Taylor she and her husband had been sealed in the temple and promised in her patriarchal blessing that she would raise her children through the millennium. If she and her husband continued living together monogamously, she asked, "quietly and peaceably and teach thire children the principel of life and salvation and bring them <up> in the fear of the Lord," would they not qualify for exaltation in the celestial kingdom with a "continuation of thire seed forever?" And, if plural marriage is a commandment, she went on, inasmuch as "it would be a sore trial to me for my husband to take an other ~~wfe~~ Wife," would it not serve the same purpose to have dead women sealed to him for, she said, "I could go with him any time and give dead wimen <to him> as many as he wanted[.]" She asked President Taylor to explain the revelation on celestial marriage to her "as you would to one of your own daughters as I am anxious to understand[.]"[42]

Responding within the month, the church's president was unequivocal in stating that the Principle of plural wives was inseparable from the covenant of eternal marriage. The Saints were commanded "to do the works of Abra-

---

[42] Malinda Jane Morrill to President John Taylor, Freemont [*sic*] Piute County, 2 Jan. 1883, John Taylor Presidential Papers, 1877–1887, box 13, fd. 9, LDS Archives, extracted by a church archives employee.

ham," which involved marrying polygamously in this life. "No man or woman has any authority," Taylor said, to prescribe any other path to the highest degree of glory in the hereafter.[43] First Presidency counselor Joseph F. Smith spoke further to the topic at an assembly of priesthood bearers in 1884. He said that the revelation of 1843 was not given to convince church members in Nauvoo of the truth of eternal marriage, for that was already believed. Rather, it was given to persuade doubters that plurality was also a divine principle and one to which they must conform.[44] More of the same was forthcoming from George Q. Cannon, who declared that when he remembered all he had suffered on account of the Principle, he felt "like taking every son of mine & placing his hand on my thigh causing him to swear he will obey it."[45]

Finally, in his journal Thomas Memmott reproduced a letter that Apostle Francis M. Lyman sent to him expressing the same sentiments as Taylor, Smith, and Cannon. Lyman made an additional and important observation, however, one often forgotten in later years. He pointed out that the persecutions the Saints endured could easily be brought to an end if the church would only say that the 1843 revelation spoke only to the eternity of the marriage covenant and did not oblige Mormons to practice polygamy in the present life.[46] These messages were broadcast to the entire church at its semi-annual conference in the autumn of 1885.

AN EPISTLE FROM THE FIRST PRESIDENCY.
TO THE OFFICERS AND MEMBERS OF THE
CHURCH OF JESUS CHRIST OF LATTER-DAY SAINTS (1885),
FIRST PRESIDENCY CIRCULAR LETTERS, 1855–1996,
BOX 1, FD. 1, LDS ARCHIVES.[47]

As all the Saints doubtless understand, there has been no cessation since we last wrote in the work of persecution. It rages, if anything, more fiercely than ever. Under cover of what is called the Edmunds law, the most outra-

---

[43] John Taylor to Malinda Jane Morrill, Salt Lake City, 19 Jan. 1883, as copied into the Journals of Thomas Memmott, Quotation Book Book of Genealogy, reel 3, LDS Archives, 98–100. President Taylor's original letter to Morrill is in his presidential papers but was unavailable for reproduction here. An examination of the document, however, confirmed that it and the copy in Memmott's journal are nearly identical, containing only differences in punctuation.

[44] Thomas Memmott Quotation Book Book of Genealogy, reel 3, LDS Archives, 103. Also see Allen, "'Good Guys' vs. 'Good Guys,'" 167n44.

[45] Thomas Memmott Quotation Book Book of Genealogy, reel 3, LDS Archives.

[46] Francis M. Lyman to Thomas Memmott, 22 Feb. 1888, ibid., reel 3, LDS Archives, 101–3.

[47] Also printed as: "AN EPISTLE from the First Presidency," *Des. Eve. News*, 7 Oct. 1885, 18:267 [2/1–6]; and "AN EPISTLE . . . ," *Woman's Exponent*, 15 Oct. 1885, 14:10, 73–75.

geous acts of oppression are being perpetrated against the Latter-day Saints. The avowal has been openly made that this law was expressly designed for the destruction of a principle of our religion, and in this spirit the prosecutions have been conducted. Thus far no criminal, however guilty, who has not been a "Mormon," has been punished under it. Acts of the most sickening depravity have been committed by non-"Mormons" within easy reach of its arm, but have scarcely had a passing notice. While it is also worthy of note that, up to the present writing, out of all who have been accused and brought before the District Court, only one "Mormon" has been acquitted. The man acquitted, we understand, was charged with being the husband of a woman, on the ground that he had camped in his wagon in a ten acre lot in which her residence stood, and had carried some chickens for her to market! . . .

Well-meaning friends of ours have said that our refusal to renounce the principle of celestial marriage invites destruction. They warn us and implore us to yield. They appeal to every human interest, and adjure us to bow to a law which is admitted on all hands to have been framed expressly for the destruction of the principle which we are called upon to reject. They say it is madness to resist the will of so overwhelming a majority. They say they see the gathering clouds, that they hear the premonitory mutterings of the resistless tempest which is about to break in destructive fury upon our heads, and they call upon us to avert its wrath by timely submission. But they perceive not the hand of that Being who controls all storms, whose voice the tempest obeys, at whose fiat thrones and empires are thrown down—the Almighty God, Lord of heaven and earth, who has made promises to us, and who has never failed to fulfill all His words.

We did not reveal celestial marriage. We cannot withdraw or renounce it. God revealed it, and He has promised to maintain it, and to bless those who obey it. Whatever fate, then, may threaten us, there is but one course for men of God to take, that is, to keep inviolate the holy covenants they have made in the presence of God and angels. . . Upwards of forty years ago the Lord revealed to His Church the principle of celestial marriage. The idea of marrying more wives than one was as naturally abhorrent to the leading men and women of the Church at that day as it could be to any people. They shrank with dread from the bare thought of entering into such relationships. But the command of God was before them in language which no faithful soul dare disobey.

> "For, behold, I reveal unto you a new and an everlasting covenant; and if ye abide not that covenant, then are ye damned; for no one can reject this covenant, and be permitted to enter into my glory.
>
> And as pertaining to the new and everlasting covenant, it was instituted for the fullness of my glory; and he that receiveth a fullness thereof, must and shall abide the law, or he shall be damned, saith the Lord God."[48]

---

[48] The 1843 revelation, in Chapter One.

Damnation was the awful penalty affixed to a refusal to obey this law. It become [sic] an acknowledged doctrine of the Church; it was indissolubly interwoven in the minds of its members with their hopes of eternal salvation and exaltation in the presence of God. For nearly twenty years this continued to be our faith and practice. Then a law was enacted against it. Another twenty years elapsed, and the Edmunds law was passed. Nearly forty years had thus elapsed from the first revelation of this doctrine, during which period thousands had lived and died, firmly believing and solemnly testifying that it was divine. At great sacrifice they had obeyed it, and based their hopes of eternal felicity upon the promises which the revelation contained. They never dreamed that they had not a constitutional right to obey God, especially when in obeying Him they did not interfere with nor encroach upon the rights of any human being, either man or woman. . . What is this "Mormon" problem, so-called, and why should it disturb the people? It is an unpopular religion. But so was that of the ancient Prophets. . .

Have not the Latter-day Saints been taught all the day long that, if they would remain faithful and endure to the end, they must live their religion by keeping every commandment of God? . . . If all who call themselves Latter-day Saints were true and faithful to their God, to His holy covenants and laws, and were living as Saints should, persecution would roll of[f] from us without disturbing us in the least. But it is painful to know that this is not their condition. . . The innocent are thus made to suffer with the guilty; for the Lord has commanded that the inhabitants of Zion must purge themselves from iniquity, folly, covetousness and vanity, and listen to and obey His laws, or they cannot have His protection. He has also said that if His people will obey His laws and keep His commandments, to do them, not in name only, but in reality, He will be their shield and protector and strong tower, and no man will be able to hurt them, for He will be their defense. These trials of our faith and constancy which we are now passing through will be overruled for our good and future prosperity. In days to come we shall be able to look back and perceive with clearness how visibly God's providence is in all that we now witness. . .

Your friends and fellow-laborers in the New and Everlasting Covenant,
John Taylor
George Q. Cannon,
Of the First Presidency of the Church of Jesus Christ of Latter-day Saints.
S.L.C., October 6, 1885.[49]

Severe oppression seems always to turn the eyes of believers skyward, whatever their creed. Owing to hardships confronting them in the 1880s, Mor-

---

[49] Only President John Taylor and First Counselor George Q. Cannon signed the message because Second Counselor Joseph F. Smith was on a mission to Hawaii.

mons raised countless petitions to heaven. And numbers, many said, were answered. More of these communications were received by the church's presidents, so far as is known, than at any time since the fluency in such things by Mormon founder Joseph Smith Jr.[50] Wilford Woodruff (1807–1898), an apostle who became president of the church in 1889, recorded one of the revelations, telling members to remain steadfast in the faith, to adhere to the Principle, and to look for God's certain vengeance on a wicked world.

> "A REVELATION GIVEN TO WILFORD WOODRUFF
> IN THE WILDERNESS OF SAN FRANCISCO MOUNTAIN
> IN ARIZONA ON THE 26 DAY OF JAN 1880," KENNEY, ED.,
> *WILFORD WOODRUFF'S JOURNAL*, 7:617–18, 620.

The Nation is ripened in iniquity and the Cup of the wrath of mine indignation is full, and I will not Stay my hand in Judgment upon this Nation or the Nations of the Earth. I have Decreed wars and Judgments upon the wicked and my wrath and indignation are about to be poured out upon them. And the wicked and rebellious shall know that I am God. As I the Lord have spoken so will I the Lord fullfill. I will spare none who remain in babylon but I will burn them up Saith the Lord of Hosts. As I the Lord have suffered so will I put all Enemies under my feet, for I the Lord utter my word, and it shall be obeyed and the day of wrath and indignation shall Come upon the wicked.

And I say again wo unto that Nation or House or people, who seek to hinder my People from obeying the Patriarchal Law of Abraham which leadeth to a Celestial Glory which has been revealed unto my Saints through the mouth of my servant Joseph for whosoever doeth these things shall be damned Saith the Lord of Hosts and shall be broaken up & washed away from under Heaven by the Judgments which I have sent forth and shall not return unto me void. And thus with the sword and By Blood shed and with famine & Plagues and Earthquakes and the Thunders of heavens and the vivid lightnings shall this Nation and the Nations of the Earth be made to feel the Chastning hand of an Almighty God until they are broaken up and Destroyed, and wasted away from under heaven, and No power Can Stay my hand. Therefore let the wicked tremble. Let them that blaspheme my name hold their lips, for destruction will swiftly over take them.[51]

---

[50] In addition to the revelations cited here, others are at LDS Archives in Salt Lake City, under title of "Revelations Purportedly Given to John Taylor, 1882–1884." These and other sources are gathered, versified, and orthographically corrected in Collier, *Unpublished Revelations*, 118–47.

[51] The Saints, especially Wilford Woodruff, frequently linked the anti-polygamy crusade with the earth's end time. See, for example: Kenney, ed., *Wilford Woodruff's Journal*, 14 Mar. 1882, 8:91; 8:351, 31 Dec. 1885; 8:378, 16 Feb. 1886; 8:420–21, 13 Jan. 1887; and 9:94, 19 May 1890. Also see Wells, "Thoughts on the Times," *Woman's Exponent* 14:7 (1 Sept. 1885), 52; and all of Smith, *Series of Lectures on the Signs of the Times*. The relationship between plural marriage and Mormon millenarianism is most extensively treated in Erickson, *As A Thief in the Night*, 179–211.

All that I the Lord have Spoken through the Mouth of my Prophets and Apostles since the world began concerning the last dispensation and fullness of times, Concerning my Church which has been Called out of the wilderness of darkness and Error, and Concerning the Zion and Kingdom of God and Concerning Babylon the Great, And what I have spoken through the Mouth of My servant Joseph shall all be fulfilled. And though Heaven and Earth pass away my words shall not pass away, but shall all be fulfilled Saith the Lord. . .

Therefore gird up the Loins of your minds and Magnify your Callings in the fear of God and prepare ye for the Coming of the Son of Man which is nigh at the Door. No man knoweth the day nor the hour but the Signs of Both Heaven and Earth indicate his Coming as promised by the Mouth of my deciples. The fig trees are leaving and the hour is nigh.[52]

None were more determined to preserve both the doctrine and practice of plural marriage than President John Taylor (1808–1887).[53] The communication below is titled an "alleged" revelation because, as Richard Van Wagoner says, it is "one of the most controversial revelations in the history of Mormonism."[54] If the location of the original manuscript remains undisclosed, evidence for its existence is nevertheless extensive. Not only have photocopies of the document circulated for years, and not only did contemporaries refer to it, but its content agrees with other statements President Taylor and his colleagues made at the time.[55]

AN ALLEGED REVELATION GIVEN TO PRESIDENT JOHN TAYLOR, 27 SEPT. 1886. PHOTOCOPY IN PRIVATE POSSESSION.

My son John. You have asked me concerning the New & Eve<r>lasting covenant how far it is binding upon my peop[le.]

Thus saith the Lord All commandments that I give <must be obeyed by those, calling themselves by my name> unless they are revoked by my [sic] or by my authority, and how can I revoke an everlasting covenant; For I the Lord

---

[52] This same revelation, written in the hand of George F. Gibbs on 27 May 1895, is in Kenney, ed., *Wilford Woodruff's Journal*, 17 April 1897, 9:463–69. For context, see Alexander, *Things in Heaven and Earth*, 237–39.

[53] As an instance of Taylor's defiant spirit, see the moving account of his last public address in Brief Story of the Life of Joseph Eldridge Robinson, LDS Archives, 11.

[54] Van Wagoner, *Mormon Polygamy*, 128.

[55] See, for example, the statement by President Taylor's son, Apostle John W. Taylor, that he found the revelation among his father's papers and took it into his possession. This as told to the Quorum of Twelve Apostles and recorded in Abraham H. Cannon Diaries, 1 April 1892, UPB, 16:82. Also see references and materials gathered by Quinn, "LDS Authority and New Plural Marriages," 28–29; Collier, *Unpublished Revelations*, 177, 180–206; Allred, *Leaf in Review*, Appendix, sections 1 and 2, 229–238; and the comments of Van Wagoner, *Mormon Polygamy*, 186–87. Cf. Ririe, Statement, 1964, LDS Archives; all of Hales and Anderson, *The Priesthood of Modern Polygamy*; and the 1933 First Presidency statement below, p. 385.

am everlasting my everlasting covenants cannot be abrogated nor done away with; but they stand for ever. Have I not given my word in great plainness on this subject? Yet have not great nembers [*sic*] of my people been negligent in the observance of my law and the keeping of my commandment and yet have I borne with them these many years & this because of their weakness because of the perilous times & furthermore, it is more pleasing to <me> that men should use their free agency in regard to these matters. Nevertheless I the Lord do not change & my word & my covenants & my law do not. & as I have heretofore said by my servant Joseph all those who would enter into my glory must & shall obey my law & have I not commanded men that if they were Abraham's seed and would enter my glory, they must do the works of Abraham. I have not revoked this law nor will I for it is everlasting & those who will enter into my glory must obey the conditions thereof, even so Amen.[56]

"Anything for Statehood": A Divided Road

Despite their prayers, the Saints continued to meet with inclemency and pain. When Mormon law-enforcement officials in Salt Lake City sought to expose the hypocrisy of local enemies, events turned against them. Brigham Y. Hampton, a prominent churchman and member of the police force, along with others, employed prostitutes whom they promised good pay and immunity from arrest if they would tempt important Gentile figures into a lodging where their sexual activities could be reported. When action against those who were seduced by the harlots was brought, however, the prosecution was dismissed and, to his distress, Hampton was convicted and sentenced to prison for establishing a house of ill fame.[57] Consternation in this case can only have been exceeded when, earlier in the decade, the Saints learned of a proposal floated by the *Chicago Evening Journal* urging the nation to solve a double problem by shipping all its Negroes to Utah.[58] Nothing tempered the ferocity of anti-Mormon attacks.

Viewing it as a way to obtain independence from federal control, many leaders became almost obsessed with obtaining statehood. Between the time of Mormon entry into the Valley of the Great Salt Lake in 1847 and the year

---

[56] A versified and orthographically corrected printing of the revelation, as well as an alleged photocopy of the original, is in Collier, *Unpublished Revelations*, 145–46 and 181–83 respectively.

[57] *People vs. Hampton*, 4 Utah 258, 9 Pac. 508 (1886). Also see Baskin, *Reminiscences of Early Utah*, 223–29; and Nichols, *Prostitution, Polygamy, and Power*, 32–36. Nichols further explored the long debate between Utah Mormons and Gentiles over morality, including the Hampton episode, in his "Polygamy and Prostitution," 1–39.

[58] "Why Don't They Move On," *Des. News* [Weekly], 4 Feb. 1880, 29:1, 8/4.

of the Manifesto in 1890, Utah made six formal requests for admission to the Union.[59] All were denied, failing to survive what one scholar called "the burial ground of Utah Constitutions," Congress' House Committee on Territories.[60] As early as the 1860s Brigham Young was remembered to have told Utah territorial delegate William Henry Hooper, "Remember, Brother Hooper, anything for Statehood. Promise anything for Statehood."[61] By the 1880s, a decade that saw them twice refused membership in the family of states, Utah's population was larger than that of any territory until that time in American history.[62] To acquire full parity with other states in the union while remaining faithful to the commandment on plural marriage, Mormon authorities took a divided road.

On one hand, leaders expressed themselves *privately* as unwilling ever to fully forfeit plural marriage in exchange for statehood. Apostle Wilford Woodruff reported in 1882 that in their councils they had "discussed the policy of yielding . . . principal for a State Governmet . . . [but] Presidet Taylor with the rest of us Come to the Conclusion that we Could not swap of the Kingdom of God or any of its Laws or Principals for a State Governmet."[63] When some suggested temporarily suspending plural marriage as a way to win acceptance, that proposal was also rejected.[64] This comported with a remark attributed to Woodruff in 1888 in which he said that divine revocation of polygamy would never occur.[65] George Q. Cannon reassured dispirited Mormon convicts in the territorial prison that, contrary to rumor, their sacrifices were not

---

[59] These were in 1849, 1856, 1862, 1872, 1882, and 1887. For a study of the statehood efforts, see Bernstein, "History of the Constitutional Conventions of the Territory of Utah from 1849 to 1895." Bakken, *Rocky Mountain Constitution Making*, treats the difficulties affecting constitution-writing in the West.

[60] Hickman, "Utah Constitutional Law," 48.

[61] "New Star Cheered," *Chicago Tribune*, 5 Jan. 1896, 55:5, 3/5. Credence for the *Chicago Tribune*'s account arises from the importance with which statehood was frequently urged upon Hooper's predecessor, John M. Bernhisel. See Barrett, "John M. Bernhisel," 150, 166 passim. See also Gov. George Woods's statement to Pres. U. S. Grant, on 13 Nov. 1871, that Mormon leaders wanted statehood on almost any terms. Simon, ed., *Papers of Ulysses S. Grant*, 22:209.

[62] Eli H. Murray, "Report of the Governor of Utah," *RSI* (1880), 2:519. For the failed 1882 attempt at statehood, see all of Admission of Utah as a State in the Union, House Misc. Doc. 43 (47-1) 1882, Serial 2046; "Constitution of the State of Utah, " *Des. Eve. News Supplement*, 27 April 1882, 15:133; and Bernstein, "History of the Constitutional Conventions," 46–50. Utah's unsuccessful effort in 1887 is discussed below.

[63] Kenney, ed., *Wilford Woodruff's Journal*, 27 Nov. 1882, 8:133.

[64] Apostle John Henry Smith suggested to his cousin, Joseph F. Smith, that polygamy be renounced for five years until, statehood attained, it could be restored. John Henry Smith Letterbooks, 3 April 1888, George A. Smith Family Papers, Special Collections, UU. Also see the comments of Godfrey, "Coming of the Manifesto," 18–19; and Wolfinger, "Reexamination of the Woodruff Manifesto," 348–49.

[65] From the Journals of Heber J. Grant, 20 Dec. 1888, Heber J. Grant Collection, LDS Archives. Also see White, "Making of the Convention President," 359.

in vain and church authorities would not betray them by making a "concession" on plural marriage.[66] In response to advice in late 1889 that concessions *must* be made, President Woodruff disclosed that he had been told by revelation that nothing should be promised to the wicked, for God would deal with them in His own way.[67] As late as mid-September 1890, less than ten days before the church president prepared his Manifesto, Apostle John Henry Smith told Saints in southern Utah that "no principle or revelation that God ever gave to his people was to be laid on the shelf as a thing of the past."[68]

At the same time, Mormonism's public response carried a different message. Church authorities publicly conveyed the impression that they were yielding on the question and that reformation was underway. In 1887, for example, a convention was again called to plead Utah's case for statehood. The proposed constitution accompanying the petition included a self-executing section prohibiting "bigamy and polygamy."[69] In 1888 the territorial legislature also enacted Utah's first marriage law. Until then, to assure that plural marriages were immune from attack, Utah's lawmakers purposely avoided the codification of either marriage or anti-polygamy statutes. Seeking a more conciliatory image, the 1888 statute, as elsewhere in the Union, forbade consanguineous and incestuous marriages; unions with idiots, or between white persons and Negroes or Mongolians; and the marriage of girls less than twelve years of age. Authority for licensing and solemnizing marriages was carefully construed. Most importantly, new marriages when "a husband or wife [was yet] living, from whom the person marrying has not been divorced," were prohibited.[70]

The difficulty with such attempts, and one glaring to all who had followed the Mormon controversy over the previous twenty years, was that formal bigamy assumed, as it does in statutory prohibitions today, the solemnization of such unions by a magistrate or other public officer. But Mormon plural marriages

---

[66] Cannon, "Prison Diary," 2 Oct. 1888, 401.

[67] Kenney, ed., *Wilford Woodruff's Journal*, 24 Nov. 1889, 9:67–69; L. John Nuttall Diaries, 23–24 Nov. 1889, UPB, 3:102–3; and Abraham H. Cannon Journals, 19 Dec. 1889, UPB, 2:214.

[68] John Henry Smith, as quoted in Larson and Larson, eds., *Diary of Charles Lowell Walker*, 16 Sept. 1890, 2:718.

[69] Art. 15, sec. 12 of the new constitution prohibited bigamy and polygamy. For copies of the document and repeated urgings for its adoption, see "Step Toward Statehood," *Des. Eve. News*, 17 June 1887, 20:174 [2/1]; "Polygamy Prohibited," ibid., 5 July 1887, 20:188 [3/2]; "Bigamy and Polygamy Provisions," ibid., 6 July 1887, 20:189 [2/1]; and "Constitution," ibid., 8 July 1887, 20:191 [2/1–8]. For the intent to continue polygamy privately once statehood was obtained, see Franklin S. Richards to Joseph F. Smith, 28 June 1887, Franklin S. Richards Correspondence, 1886–1890, Uhi; and Lyman, *Political Deliverance*, 41–68.

[70] "An Act Regulating Marriage," 8 Mar. 1888, *Compiled Laws of Utah . . .* (1888), Ch. 5, secs. 2583–97, 92–94.

were performed *privately* by church rather than state officials. And no announcements or public records of these events were made. Polygamous couples, joined privately in ecclesiastical ceremonies were, so far as the law was concerned, only irregular partners. This is why the Morrill Act of 1862, with its presumption of public, magistrate-performed plural rites, was so ineffective. Not until the Edmunds and Edmunds-Tucker Acts of the 1880s was polygamous "cohabitation" joined with formal bigamy and made criminally punishable. But both the 1887 constitution and the marriage law of 1888 addressed only formal, publicly performed polygamous contractions. As such, church leaders well knew, they were as ineffective as the Morrill Act.[71]

Nevertheless, church agents engaged in vigorous lobbying and political maneuvering to persuade members of Congress and Pres. Grover Cleveland that the proposed 1887 constitution represented a sincere attempt to discontinue polygamy. During congressional hearings on their statehood petition, Mormon representatives testified that those living in polygamy had never amounted to more than 1 or 2 percent of their members and, inasmuch as approval for such marriages was no longer given, even that number was "diminishing with wonderful rapidity." The same witnesses also stated that the revelation on patriarchal marriage had never been binding on the Saints but was "permissive" only. And steps were taken to disassociate the phrase "celestial marriage" from polygamy.[72] While this was a doctrinal mutation not fully completed until after the turn of the century, the 1880s saw statements asserting that "celestial marriage" connoted only marriage for eternity and that this, not polygamy, was what they urged upon their people.

During these same years Mormon leaders established colonies in Mexico and Canada, where the practice would be less visible and those fearing arrest might go to escape imprisonment in the U.S. Mexico proved the better choice for pluralists because of more tolerant attitudes by Mexican officials. While many polygamous families relocated to Canada, they were fewer than those

---

[71] From the beginning of the 1887 statehood movement, President John Taylor was uncomfortable with even the suggestion of compromise. Difficult negotiations involving church authorities, Mormon agents in the nation's capital, and national political leaders at this time are explored in Lyman, *Political Deliverance*, 41–68. Also see John Taylor and George Q. Cannon to William Paxman, 4 Feb. 1887, First Presidency Letter Press Copy Books, LDS Archives, 15:70; and Bitton, *George Q. Cannon*, 282–86.

[72] Franklin S. Richards in *Admission of Utah. Arguments in Favor of the Admission of Utah as a State*, 6–7; evidence given in *Admission of Utah. Argument of Hon. Jeremiah M. Wilson*, 11–12 ; Angus M. Cannon in "Church Suits," *Des. Eve. News*, 29 Feb. 1888, 21:83 [3/3–4]; statements by the same authority in "Annual Report of the Utah Commission," *RSI* (1888), 3:667–69; and the 1887–88 statements described in Alexander, *Things in Heaven and Earth*, 267.

in Mexico, where the number of such men, their wives, and children eventually amounted to thousands, constituting not only the largest but the most prosperous of all foreign colonies in Mexico at the time.[73] These cross-border sanctuaries served both as places of refuge for those already in the Principle and as sites where new plural unions were performed.[74] A policy of dispersing authority for solemnizing polygamous marriages also accompanied colonization. Just as the church's assets were placed in private hands for the purpose of avoiding escheatment under the Edmunds and Edmunds-Tucker Acts, Mormon leaders also delegated permission to solemnize polygamous unions to trusted individuals who were less conspicuous than themselves.[75] According to President John Taylor, ecclesiastical license to marry pluralists was given to hundreds of male priesthood holders in the early and mid-1880s.[76]

The late 1880s also saw a marked decline in the number of publications defending the Principle. While church leaders continued to protest the restrictions and suffering imposed upon them, publicly stated arguments extolling plural marriage nearly disappear after the passage of the Edmunds-Tucker Act in 1887. Wilford Woodruff told associates in 1888 that should anyone begin talking about plural marriage at one of the church's general conferences they should throw their hats at him.[77] And by careful choice of their words, Mormon representatives denied breaking the law and challenged their critics to prove otherwise.[78] Efforts to project the Mormon image as both monogamous and law abiding were especially pronounced in the two years before the Manifesto. President Wilford Woodruff's comments to the press in late 1889 are an example.

---

[73] González Navarro, *Colonización en México*, 63–70. Other accounts of the Mormon experience in Mexico are Romney, *Mormon Colonies in Mexico*; and Tullis, "Early Mormon Exploration and Missionary Activities in Mexico," 289–310. For settlements in Canada, see Brief Account of the Early History of the Canadian Mission, 1887–1895, LDS Archives; Wilcox, "Founding of the Mormon Community in Alberta"; and Erickson, "Alberta Polygamists?" 155–64.

[74] For polygamy in the colonies, see Hardy, *Solemn Covenant*, 167–78; idem, "Mormon Polygamy in Mexico and Canada"; and all of Erickson, "Alberta Polygamists?"

[75] Transfer of church assets to avoid their seizure by government agents is discussed in Arrington, *Great Basin Kingdom*, 362–65.

[76] See the testimony of John Taylor in the Rudger Clawson case in Chapter Seven. Taylor's grandson said the policy of dispersal began in 1882. Taylor, *Kingdom or Nothing*, 301–2, 305n3. Also see the outline of events provided in the same author's *Rocky Mountain Empire*, 20n15.

[77] Woodruff to Franklin S. Richards and Charles W. Penrose, 12 April 1888, Wilford Woodruff Letterpress Copy Book, LDS Archives. Regarding Mormon reticence on polygamy in their conferences at this time, see Carlton, *Wonderlands*, 180.

[78] "We Do Not Believe in 'Polygamy,'" *Des. Eve. News*, 21 Dec. 1881, 15:27 [2/1–2]; "Preaching and Practice of Polygamy," ibid., 13 Dec. 1884, 18:19 [2/1].

"Mormons Abandon Polygamy. President Woodruff
Says The Church Means to Obey The Law.
[By Telegraph To The Herald.],"
New York Herald, 13 Oct. 1889, 54:286, 17/3.

Salt Lake City, Oct. 12, 1889.—I have just had an interesting interview with President Wilford Woodruff, the head of the Mormon Church. He is eighty-two years old, but walked briskly into the reception room of the official residence. He began at once to talk in a cheerful, offhand way.

"We are peculiar people in some respects," he said. "We have been out here by ourselves for a good while. Many wrong impressions have gone out about us. All we ask is for the American people to understand our situation as it really is. I have no fears as to our treatment at the hands of our fellow citizens if we are understood."

It was suggested that the people would like to hear directly from the head of their Church what the attitude is toward . . . the law prohibiting polygamy. Without the slightest hesitation President Woodruff replied with emphasis:—

Mean to Obey the Law.

"We mean to obey it of course. We have no thought of evading or ignoring this or any other law of the United States. We are citizens of this government. We recognize its laws as binding upon us.

"I have refused to give any recommendations for the performance of plural marriages since I have been president. I know that President Taylor, my predecessor, also refused. Since the Edmunds-Tucker law we have refused to recommend plural marriages, and have instructed that they should not be solemnized."

Becoming more and more explicit as he proceeded President Woodruff told of a special case. One of the bishops at the head of a stake, which is a Church designation for a large district, came to him with the petition of a couple to have the plural marriage ceremony performed between them. The stake bishop represented that the parties fully understood the risk they were running. He wanted from the head of the Church a ruling on the course to pursue. "I told the bishop," said President Woodruff, "that it would not do at all. There must be no more plural marriages. I am confident," said the president, "that there have been no more plural marriages since I have been in this position, and yet a case has recently occurred which I will say to you I do not understand at all. It is giving us a good deal of trouble. Perhaps you have heard of it?" The president referred to the Hans Jesperson case.[79] Jesperson is a Dane. He lives in Goshen, at the head of Utah Lake. Recently a neighbor reported to the United States authorities at Provo that he believed Jesperson was sustaining the plural marriage relations with Mrs. Alice Horton. A deputy marshal went out and brought in the Jesperson family and Mrs.

---

[79] For more on the case of Hans Jespersen and the complicity of church authorities in his marriage, see Hardy, *Solemn Covenant*, 129, 139, 142.

Horton. All of them denied knowledge of any improper relationship. At last, Mrs. Horton broke down and testified that she was married to Jesperson on the eighth of last April. She said that part of the ceremony took place in the Temple at Manti, and part of it at the Endowment House in Salt Lake City. This testi[mony] was given before the United States Commissioner. Jesperson was convicted and sentenced to five years in prison for polygamy and three years on another charge. It is the only performance of a plural marriage ceremony this year which the courts have unearthed.

"It seems incredible if it is true," Woodruff said. "It is against all of my instructions. I do not understand it at all. We are looking into it and shall not rest until we get at all the facts. There is no intention on our part to do anything but to obey the law." Resident Gentiles say that the Saints are not worthy of the slightest credence regarding their religion, although they may be upright enough in all other respects.

Woodruff has three wives.

"To show you how I feel," said he, "I will tell you frankly of my own case. I have three wives. I married them before 1860, when there was no law whatever regarding polygamy. I have not visited the houses of my wives for five years. I have kept entirely away because I didn't mean to do anything which might have the appearance of breaking the Edmunds law. But I have fed and clothed these families. I cannot repudiate the obligations I entered into so many years ago.[80]

"It seems to me," he said, "that the law ought to have been made plainer in one respect. It might have marked out the course to be pursued by those who had gone into this thing before the enactment. That would have saved a great deal of trouble. If the provisions had made clear the lines of conduct toward plural wives there would not have been so many cases before the courts."

Few of the church's opponents found Latter-day Saint statements and promises credible. Almost everyone observing the scene knew that plural marriage had simply been taken underground. Referring to church claims that plurality was being discontinued as "the wooden horse of Mormonism," both the Utah Commission and territorial governor successfully recommended against the 1887 request for statehood.[81] In his 1889 report, territorial governor Arthur Thomas expressed astonishment at Mormon dissimulation. Remarking that, in the first place, it spoke poorly of Latter-day Saint conviction to represent themselves as willing to forfeit one of the pillars of their

---

[80] Thomas Alexander described Woodruff as "a spiritual polygamist" but a "practicing monogamist" after 1882. "Odyssey of a Latter-Day Prophet," 178.

[81] "Annual Report of the Utah Commission," *RSI* (1888), 3:669. Comment on Utah's drive for statehood occupied more of Gov. Caleb West's annual report than any other topic. "Report of the Governor of Utah," ibid. (1887), 1:915–25. The petition for statehood finally died without action by Congress in 1889.

faith but, more shameful, he found them employing "evasions, meaningless words, or words of double meaning, hypocritical pretenses, false assertions, and every helpful evasion of word or act."[82] Most importantly, the strategy of posturing surrender while secretly solemnizing polygamous unions established a pattern that continued for years.[83] Consequently we must read the Woodruff Manifesto in the context of such events. By so doing we move the time of Mormon transformation backward from 1890 to the decade of the 1880s when, in response to hardships imposed upon them, church leaders crafted behaviors designed to win public favor.[84]

"Polygamists Got Out of Sight": Mormon Flight from the Law

Gestures of retreat did little to deter deputies and paid "spotters" who swarmed the territory.[85] Church leaders, including Presidents John Taylor and Wilford Woodruff, went on the "underground," hiding in barns, attics, and other obscure locations. By communicating secretly they managed affairs of the church as best they could.[86] A few pluralists, despised as "cowardly Poltroons," "traitors," and "sneaks," abandoned their polygamous wives.[87] As Helen Mar Whitney expressed it when a well-known Mormon bishop renounced the practice to escape prison, it was, she said, "an awful step—[to have] succumbed to *man-made-laws*—renounced his wives & Celestial principle of matrimony, for the sake of the world—Lord have mercy on him—*how sad—how sad*."[88] The majority, however, remained committed and found ways to escape the law.

---

[82] "Report of the Governor of Utah," *RSI* (1889), 3:496; and again in ibid. (1890), 3:660–61.

[83] For plural marriages performed between 1887 and 1890, see Hardy, *Solemn Covenant*, 154n4.

[84] Others have also made this suggestion. Alexander, for example, sees the 1890 Manifesto as but a "way station" situated between events of the 1880s and subsequent changes in the church. "Odyssey of a Latter-Day Prophet," 205. Also see Wolfinger, "Reexamination," 328–49; Lyman, *Political Deliverance*, 43–46, 60; and Shipps, "The Principle Revoked," 69–71. For the influence these policies had on Mormonism's twentieth-century preoccupation with marketing its image, see Hafen, "City of Saints, City of Sinners," 376–77.

[85] On the recruitment of ordinary citizens as informers, paid from a "'spotters' fund," see Evans, "Judicial Prosecution," 24–25.

[86] Relying on the letters of L. John Nuttall and the journal of John M. Whittaker, Larson provides an excellent account of these matters in his *"Americanization" of Utah*, 155–82.

[87] "Not All Disadvantageous," *Des. Eve. News*, 23 Mar. 1885, 18:101 [2/1].

[88] Helen Mar Whitney Diaries, 19 Sept. 1885, Helen Mar Whitney Family Papers, box 3, vol. 8, ULA. "I am sorry to say," wrote Charles Walker, "that some of our brethren have chosen to put away their wives and have promised to live within the Law and advise others to do so, thus forsaking the higher Law of God." Larson and Larson, eds., *Diary of Charles Lowell Walker*, 7 May 1885, 2:646.

There is a large body of folklore connected with Mormon experience flee-ing the marshals during the 1880s. Even when related for amusement, or at their church's expense, if told by and to themselves such stories are nearly always accepted in good humor.[89] Such is the case of Henry Webster Esplin (1854–1943), a bishop in Orderville, Utah, where church members experiment-ed with owning and managing their properties in common. After passage of the Edmunds Law, officers looking for pluralists repeatedly raided homes in the community.

HENRY WEBSTER ESPLIN, AUTOBIOGRAPHICAL SKETCH (1934),
TYPESCRIPT, BOX 3, UHI, 2.

I married two wives on the same day but I never told anyone who was the first wife.[90] Them that was there [in Orderville, Utah] knew, of course. The marshals caught Brother [Thomas] Chamberlain, and Brother [Robert] Cov-ington for polygamy and they went to the "Pen." The people used to be warned when the marshals were coming and I tell you the polygamists got out of sight. Brother Chamberlain lived up above town and he had the road leveled out so he could see what kind of outfit had gone over the road while he had been away or asleep.

Martin Cutler lived at Glendale, Utah and he had two wives, both of them deaf and dumb. [Marshals] Armstrong and McGreary were after the polyg-amists, although Armstrong didn't care much. Armstrong knew these women were deaf and dumb but he didn't tell McGreary who went in and asked the women something. They were smart alright and they knew what he was after so they motioned that they would cut his throat if he didn't get out.

One polygamist, a Mr. [Henry] Lunt from Cedar [City], was blind but the marshals always said that he could see ahead of them because he always left the day before they came.[91]

Mormon bishop Henry Ballard employed another stratagem to avoid the marshals: leaving the country altogether on a church mission. In Ballard's case it was a brief respite, for after returning he was arrested and incarcerated in the territorial prison in 1889.[92]

---

[89] As only two of many such tales, see Austin and Alta Fife, *Saints of Sage and Saddle*, 173, 175; and the examples provided in Brooks, "Cops and Co-Habs," 294–96.

[90] Records in the church's Family History Library in Salt Lake City confirm that Esplin had two wives: Philena Cox (1854–1937) and Keziah Ann Carroll (1857–1942), each of whom bore him twelve children.

[91] Esplin's recollections were first recorded in 1934 and completed by Louise R. Mathews for the Fed-eral Writers' Project, a division of the Works Progress Administration, in 1937.

[92] Henry Ballard (1832–1908) had three wives and presided over a congregation of the Saints in Logan, Utah. See Jenson, "Henry Ballard," *Latter-Day Saint Biographical Encyclopedia*, 1:419.

PRIVATE JOURNAL OF HENRY BALLARD, 1852–1904,
LDS ARCHIVES, 88–89.

1886 The most of this year I had to be away from home

Octr The fore part of this month it became so hot with the Deputies on my tract till I had to come home to Logan in the night and hide up in some of the saints houses, and as soon as I had left my ranch where my Wife Emiley[93] and her familey was living in the summer seasons the Deputies came on the hunt for me, and as they could not find me they arrested her or rather supeaneded [subpoenaed] her to appear before the Grand Jury, and as the Judges had lately begun to try the segregation business upon the Bretheren, that is to make so many cases against a man what they claimed for each offence, so by their infamous acts they could keep a man there in Prison for life, or at least for many years, but some time after this there was a test case made out involving apostle Lorenzo Snow in the case, as he was in the Utah Penitenuary serving out several segragation terms, it was brought before the United States supreme court at Washington and there decided that a man could not be tried for only one offence for the same thing so many of the Brethren was liberated from the Pen upon this Discion of that highest court of the Land[94] But as this was not found out till after I had made up my mind to get away from this unjust perciction and take a Mission to England my native home and visit my relatives and gather geneoligies so I could do more good then spend the rest of my days in Prison I therefore consulted with Apostle F.D. Richards about taking such a mission and his advice was for me to go at once, so I only had 2 days to get ready before starting

Apart from going on foreign missions, hundreds chose to sell their farms at a loss and relocate in Mexico or Canada. Some took refuge in Arizona.[95] Others, believing conditions more threatening in surrounding territories, moved to Utah. Mosiah Lyman Hancock (1834–1907), one of these, transported his wives and children north across the Utah-Arizona line in 1884.[96] His third wife, Martha Maria Cable Mayer (1858–1936) remembered the adventure. Her daughter, Victoria Hancock Jackson (1880–1967), copied the account below from her mother's history.

[93] Emily Reid McNeil (1849–1903), a sister of Ballard's wife, Margaret Reid McNeil (1846–1918), married Henry Ballard as a plural wife on 4 Oct. 1867.

[94] Ballard undoubtedly means to say that in the Snow case the court decided a man could be punished for only one "continuous" commission of unlawful cohabitation with each plural wife. *In re Snow* 120 U.S. 274 (1887).

[95] Arizona officials remarked on the number of pluralists from Utah flooding into the Little Colorado River region as early as 1884. "Report of The Governor of Arizona," *RSI* (1884), 2:530.

[96] With some exceptions, the anti-polygamy movement in Arizona was milder than in either Utah or Idaho. Larson, *"Americanization" of Utah*, 109–10.

VICTORIA H. JACKSON, "SKETCHES OF MOSIAH LYMAN HANCOCK'S
LIFE STORY TAKEN FROM THE HISTORY OF HIS THIRD WIFE,
MARTHA M. HANCOCK," LDS ARCHIVES.

Mosiah stayed in Utah, where the officers were not as bad as they were in Arizona. He stayed until the fall of 1884, then returned to Taylor, [Arizona] and as the officers were after him there, we prepared to leave for Utah. The Government put in cruel Mexicans as officers to arrest the Mormon polygamists. Many of the brethren and wives suffered from this situation. . .

We sold a few things, locked up our house, and left our property for Margaret's [the first wife's] boys to look after. We left Taylor on Christmas Eve, 1884, escaping the officers by traveling ten miles off the road and camping the first nights in the cedars. . .

We traveled till we came to the Little Colorado, which was north of Winslow, I think. As the weather was very cold, there was real thick ice on the water. We had to cut deep to get water for the horses. We were afraid the wagon would break through, so we took the children and goods over and put them on the bank. Esther [another plural wife] drove the team, and Mosiah and I lifted on the wheels, and the wagon went over safely.

After traveling a short distance further, there stood waiting for us . . . [an] officer—a big one. And he had been there watching us while we had crossed the ice. While Esther drove the team, Mosiah and I walked, holding on-to our guns. We took a road leading somewhat away from the officer, then Mosiah walked over to him and asked, "Well, what do you want?"

The officer answered, "Mr. Hancock, I have an order for your arrest."

Mosiah was sorely tried at having to evade the officer so much, and, as he had exerted himself standing in the cold ice and water when we had crossed the river, he was very angry. He jumped up in the air and swung his arms as he usually did when he was angry and excited. He shouted, "Arrest and be damned. Come and get me you son of Hell."

As the officer hesitated to come near, Mosiah jumped into the air again and dared him to come closer. The officer stood as if stunned, and after awhile said, "Go on Mr. Hancock. I don't want you." And he turned and went away. We waited until he was gone, then rode on thankful again to be delivered.

We needed to put up a desperate fight, for it would have been bad for us if he'd taken Mosiah and left Esther and me alone with the children on [sic] that winter wilderness. When we got a watering place (I think it was Jacob's Pools near the Buckskin Mountains), Mosiah took the team, which had traveled all day without water, to a mining place and asked for water. They told him they were U.S. Army officers and would let him have water if he would let them have one of the women with him, for they had no women there. Mosiah knew that he would have not to appear to be opposed to their desires. So he got them to let us have water then by promising that he would see what the girls said about it and then let the officers know the next morning. So

when he told us, I said, "Well, if either of us has to go, I'll go. I'll stand out
where they can see me and you point me out to them."

We did a lot of praying about that also. When Mosiah went with his buck-
et and horses for more water, I saw him pointing me out to them. When they
looked over at me, I waived my gun above my head and yelled out in a very
coarse voice, "Hurrah! Hurrah! For Hell! I'm ready for you!"

Well, they thought I was insane or something else awful; they looked dis-
gusted and said, "Go on, go on, Mr. Hancock. We don't want her."

"Stripes That Run Crosswise": Mormon Polygamists in Prison

As with other hardships brought by the anti-polygamy crusade, imprisonment remains an oft-rehearsed part of Mormon collective memory. With
growing numbers of convictions, territorial prisons filled beyond capacity
and men were ordered to serve their time as far away as South Dakota and
Detroit, Michigan.[97] As many accounts suggest, however, prison life was seldom unbearable. During his incarceration, George Q. Cannon said his fellow inmates in the Utah penitentiary were surprised at the favors granted
them by prison officials. Cannon remarked on how well he felt, saying: "My
cell has seemed a heavenly peace and I feel that angels have been there."[98]
This is not to say Mormon prisoners escaped pain. But their confinements
were generally less onerous than efforts required to elude the law—or as difficult as the lot of wives and children left behind.[99] Moreover, Mormons
jailed for polygamy commonly returned to their communities as living martyrs for the cause.[100]

---

[97] Bashore and Woods, "Consigned to a Distant Prison: Idaho Mormons in the South Dakota Peni-
tentiary," 21–40; Hardy, "'American Siberia': Mormon Prisoners in Detroit," 197–210; Wells, "Law in the
Service of Politics: Anti-Mormonism in Idaho Territory," 40; and Bair and Jensen, "Prosecution of the
Mormons in Arizona," 25–46.

[98] Cannon, "Prison Diary," 7 Oct. 1888, 403; and 26 Sept. 1888, 401, respectively. A balanced account of
life in Utah's prison for Mormons is provided by Bashore, "Life behind Bars," 23–41.

[99] The letters between Jane Jenkins and her husband Andrew Wood Cooley, as reproduced in Hyde and
Cooley, Life of Andrew Wood Cooley, 146–49, provide a moving example of the difficulties experienced by wives
of those sent to prison. Also see the efforts made by a Mormon prisoner to send cheer and encouragement
to wives and children at home in Day, "Eli Azariah Day," 322–41.

[100] See the account of prison life in Sketch of the Experience of William Y[emm] Jeffs in Prison, Jenson, Prisoners for Conscience Sake, fd. 4, LDS Archives, 3, 6–8, 18. On Mormon prisoners being lionized after
their release, see "Annual Report of the Utah Commission," RSI (1889), 3:184. After serving time in the territorial prison at Yuma, Arizona, William Flake took his striped suit with him and proudly wore it in local
parades. Farnsworth, "Polygamist's Prison Diary," 23. Also see Clements, Fred T. Dubois's The Making of a State,
63–64; and the idolizing remarks of Mormon children in Wright, "Mormon Muddle in Utah," 338–39.

Joseph Smith Black (1836–1919) was a bishop in Deseret, Utah, and the husband of three plural wives.[101] Convicted for unlawful cohabitation, Black was sentenced on 10 October 1889 and incarcerated the same day.

JOSEPH SMITH BLACK, AUTOBIOGRAPHY AND DIARY (1889),
L. TOM PERRY SPECIAL COLLECTIONS, UPB, 110, 112–15, 117–18, 121.

At 2 P.M. I appeared before the court [in Provo, Utah] for sentence. This was Oct. 10, 1889. The court asked me about my age.

I answered 52 past.

Court—"When did you marry your Plural Wife?"

I answered, "1860."

He said, "Mr. Black. Have you anything to say to the court?" I answered: Nothing.

Court: you will be sentenced to 75 days in the Penitentiary and costs. The costs amount to $94.50.

I was then put in charge of a Ballif, who conducted me up to an upper room where a few of the brethren who had been sentenced had preceded me. The number continued to increase til there were 12 in the room . . . [Josiah F. Gibbs] had accompanied me from Deseret and was to [have] been sentenced the same afternoon. I kept watch to see him coming, but after a while I was informed that he had unconditionally agreed to obey the law, and abandoned one of his families. . .

We arrived at the Pen about 8 o'clock. We were ordered to leave our things outside. We were then crowded into a space of about 4 feet by 12 between two gates. The outer gate was opened to receive us, and then shut on us before the inner one was opened. Thus we were made to feel near to each other, that being the first process of applying the screw. . . We next ascended a flight of stairs and entered another room of iron, on one side was a long row of books, at the time the thought came into my mind that this may be the place where the acts of men are ~~judged~~ recorded, but I was afterwards informed that it was a library, kept for the accommodation of the prisoners. We <then> ascended another flight of stairs and entered another room, which was similar to that below [but] a little more pleasant . . . a grave looking fellow in stripes sat at the table, and another one of medium size [and] light complexion <and a large mustach> appeared to superintend the business. We were then asked our names, and who we were. . . We were then conducted to an upper room, which they <call the> highest heaven in the institution. An iron gate was opened to us by a guard, and Black and [Joseph L.] Jolley were ushered into cell 55. The bolts were shoved back with an extremely harsh grate on our feel-

---

[101] Black married Cynthia Allred as his first wife in 1856. He married plurals Sarah Barney in 1860, Caroline Thompson in 1861, and Louisa Jane Stocks in 1885.

ings, and for the first time in our life we realized what it was to be prisoners . . . being unacquainted with things and ways here [we] tried to construct a double bed by buckling . . . two pieces of canvas together, on this we made our bed out of our quilts, [and] the space being narrow for two large men, about two feet, I can assure you that the first night of our prison life was spent very uncomfortable, but in spirits we felt well, and before retiring we kneald down together and thanked God that we had been able to endure thus far, conscious that we had commited no willful crime wherefore we should be deprived of our liberty. . .

Those that are able can buy milk at the rate of 3½ cents a pint, which is a great favor. The bread and beef is good and plentiful. Those who have money or friends on the outside can get luxuries sent to them, such as fruit, sweets etc. We are allowed vegetables once a week. This is the prison fare. During the first day we are taken outside, where our heighth, <weight> complecion, nativity and occupation is recorded. My weight was 180 lbs, 6 feet tall. We were then taken into the taylor shop where we were required to leave our citizen clothes and done the stripes that run crosswise. We were then taken into the barber shop and deprived of our beard. When we then looked into the glass we found ourselves changed to other beings, our faces hardly recognizable. Many touching scenes transpire when wives and children sometimes are permitted to come and see ~~them~~ their husbands and fathers. The father being so changed is scarcely recognizable to the wife, and less so to the younger children, who when asked by the father to come to him, get frightened <shrink back>, and cry out, You are not my father, which has caused many a sobe and tear to ~~esea~~ escape from strong men. We try to read, but cannot connect sentences and forget the preceding line. We try to write, and forget how to spell, and finally after making a complete failure lay it all to one side . . . religious services are held on the Sabbath afternoon. In the forenoon the mormons are permitted to hold their Sabbath School, which is appreciated very much. All are compelled to attend divine service in the afternoon, but attendance to Sabbath School is optional . . . [the interior yard] is surrounded by an adobe wall 4 feet thick and 22 feet hight. . . On the west side is the gate and also a stairway leading up to the top of the wall, where ~~our~~ visitors when they get permission go up and view the surroundings, here I have ~~sen~~ seen women stand for hours watching for a chance to see their loved one and gaze upon him when he happend to be in sight. The devotion and heroism of some women are certainly commendable. . . We were allowed to receive all letters written to us, not objectionable, and also allowed to write once a week. . .

December 19, 1889. The time is drawing near when I expect to bid this prison, I hope, a long farewell. My time expires next Monday, the 23d inst. I can say of my cellmate, Joseph L. Jolley of Moroni, Sanpete County, we have spent our time together very agreeably. I can say he is worthy of the name of a Latter-day Saint. I was much grieved with being deprived of his company a few days ago, when for a slight offense he was moved down to the lower tier north among the toughs, and he was also deprived of his mustach in order to humiliate him. I have spent the time as pleasantly with my brethren and associates as the e prison life would admit. I thank God for his Spirit which has been with us to comfort and cheer us in our time of trial, and I pray God to comfort those that have to remain after I go out. I pray to God for the prosperity of Zion and the triumph of Right, in the name of Jesus, Amen.[102]

A Decade of Change

Mormon responses to difficulties thrust upon them by the campaign against plural marriage in the 1880s began a major transformation in Latter-day Saint history. Suffering national vilification, economic loss, and imprisonment, they embraced policies intended to save what some viewed as their most important institution. In the process, Mormons began the reinvention of their identity. The adjustments undertaken were not, however, complete. More enduring alterations followed.

---

[102] An edited account of Black's prison experience is in "Journal of Joseph Smith Black," *Our Pioneer Heritage*, 10:305–10.

Chapter 9

"How Peculiar the Change"
The Manifesto

resident Wilford Woodruff's declaration advising church members to
cease contracting new plural marriages not only bought statehood for
Utah but altered Mormonism itself. Because it spoke to and was officially ratified by church members themselves, Woodruff's 1890 document was
the most significant turn so far made in transformations begun in the 1880s.[1]
Only after a series of interpretive explanations, however, did the original
announcement acquire the authority it enjoys today.

The first nine months of 1890 saw the U.S. Supreme Court sustain the
Edmunds-Tucker Act with its provisions repealing the territory's charter, dis-
incorporating the church, and approving seizure of its properties.[2] Idaho and
its sizeable Latter-day Saint population was granted statehood with a constitution that barred voting rights to immigrant Chinese, Mongolians, American Indians—and Mormons.[3] Canada responded to growing numbers of
Latter-day Saints in Alberta by criminalizing plural marriage there.[4] The Cullom-Struble Bill, with provisions stripping civil rights from anyone living in

---

[1] Annie Clark Tanner, a plural wife and insightful observer, said the Manifesto "was as far reaching in
effect as any other revelation in church history—perhaps even more." *Mormon Mother*, 129. One student remarked:
"with the exception of Joseph Smith's death, it seems that no change within the Church of Jesus Christ of
Latter-day Saints produced as great a reaction as the discontinuance of the practice of plural marriage."
Wight, "Origins and Development," 51. Agreement with these estimates is overwhelming but not unanimous. Grant Underwood, pointing to pre- and post-1890 continuities in Mormonism, suggests that the
"perspective of the pew" must be counted as important as that "from the pulpit," and argues for a recon-
sideration of the significance of the Manifesto. "Re-visioning Mormon History," 403–26.

[2] *Late Corporation of the Church of Jesus Christ of Latter-day Saints vs. United States*, 136 U.S. 1 (1890).

[3] *Constitution of the State of Idaho* (1889), art. 6, sec. 3. Also see "Report of the Governor of Idaho," *RSI*
(1890), 3:427.

[4] The law is found at 53 Victoria, c. 37, sec.11, subsections a–d (1890). It was later encoded into the *Revised
Statutes of Canada* (1892), pt. 5, sec. 278, 104–5.

territories of the United States who believed in Mormon patriarchal marriage, moved closer to passage. Feverish lobbying to delay progress of the law brought no relief.[5] Despondent, Andrew S. Rogers wrote in his diary: "SL. City is now in the hands of the Gentiles and there is a bill in Congress to disfranchise all mormons. What will the end be[?]"[6]

Advised by political friends that no escape remained apart from renunciation of plurality, church authorities were desperate. Joseph Henry Dean reported that President Woodruff told him on 24 September, the day before the Manifesto was issued: "We are like drowning men, catching at any straw that may be floating by that offers any relief! All hell seems to be raging against us and determined upon our destruction!"[7]

"OPEN BELIEVERS IN THE DOCTRINE": THE 1890 UTAH COMMISSION REPORT

Mormon authorities found the 1890 report of the Utah Commission especially alarming. Contrary to what churchmen had told the public, the report alleged that more than forty polygamous sealings had occurred in the previous year. To bring an end to such relationships, the commissioners urged that Congress impose additional punishments, including disfranchisement.[8] A measure of this kind had already been enacted in Idaho and upheld by the U.S. Supreme Court.[9] The commission's findings and comments were sent to Sec. of the Interior John W. Noble on 22 August 1890. Rumor of the report's content circulated before it was publicly released and soon reached the hearing of Mormons themselves.

---

[5] The best scholarly accounts of these events are Larson, *"Americanization" of Utah*, 243–59; Lyman, *Political Deliverance*, 96–135; and idem, "Political Background of the Woodruff Manifesto," 21–39.

[6] Andrew S. Rogers, handwritten autobiographical sketch, Feb. 1890, AZU, 207.

[7] Joseph Henry Dean Diaries, 24 Sept. 1890, LDS Archives. Nels Anderson, in *Desert Saints*, 324–25, may have exaggerated when he said advanced age and fatigue inspired Mormon leaders to write the Manifesto, but there is no question that the national campaign against polygamy affected their health. John W. Young expressed concern in 1887: ". . . the health of some of our leading men, especially Prest. John Taylor & Wilford Woodruff, is very poor, I may say in such a state that either may die at any moment, unless relieved from the strain of persecution." Young to [George A.] Jenks, 14 July 1887, marked "Personal," John Willard Young Letterbooks, 1886–1889, Uhi, 4.

[8] The recommendation was echoed by territorial governor Arthur L. Thomas: "Report of the Governor of Utah," RSI (1890), 3:663–64.

[9] *Davis vs. Beason*, 133 U.S. 342–48 (1890), discussed in Chapter Seven.

"Annual Report of the Utah Commission,"
RSI (1890), 3:414–21.

. . . During the year there have been frequent expressions of the hope that the church would, in some authoritative and explicit manner, declare in favor of the abandonment of polygamy or plural marriage as one of the saving doctrines or teachings of the church; but no such declaration has been made. There is little reason for doubting, so complete is the control of the church over its people, that if such a declaration were made by those in authority it would be accepted and followed by a large majority of the membership of the so-called "Mormon Church," . . .

On the contrary, in all the teachings in the Tabernacle and the church organs every effort of the Government to suppress this crime is still denominated as a persecution, and those charged with ferreting out and prosecuting the guilty are denominated persecutors of the saints.

The church seems to grow more united from day to day under these teachings. At the general conference of the church, held in Salt Lake City in April last, Wilford Woodruff, a disfranchised polygamist, was chosen "as prophet, seer, and revelator, and president of the Church of Jesus Christ of Latter-Day Saints in all the world;" the first time since the death of John Taylor, in 1887, that that office has been filled.

At the same time George Q. Cannon was chosen as first counselor, in the first presidency, and Lorenzo Snow as president of the twelve apostles, all of them being disfranchised polygamists. . .

A large proportion of the twelve apostles and the high dignitaries of the church are polygamists, and all are reputed to be open believers in the doctrine. Indeed, it is believed that no one can be promoted to office in the church unless he professes a belief in it as a fundamental doctrine. . .

The Commission is in receipt of reports from its registration officers, which enumerate forty-one male persons, who, it is believed, have entered into the polygamic relation, in their several precincts, since the June revision of 1889. Crediting them with one plural wife each would give eighty-two persons thus reported as entering into the relation forbidden by law, and said to be forbidden by the church authorities.

When it is remembered that there are a large number of communities and precincts where there are no anti-Mormons to act as registrars, and the commission is compelled to appoint them from the membership of the Mormon Church; that these reports come only from precincts where there are watchful opponents of the crime; that Mormon registrars never report the cases occurring in the precincts in which they serve, and in which plural marriages are probably most frequently entered into, and that the greatest care is observed to keep such marriages secret, so secret that the birth of a child is generally the first cause to suspect the fact of unlawful marriage, it is more than probable that only a small proportion of the polygamous marriages really contracted are reported, and a still smaller proportion where convictions could be . . . had. . .

The Commission in its last report, in view of the fact that the constitutionality of the law known as the Idaho test oath law was then before the Supreme Court, suggested the propriety of enacting a similar law for Utah in case the decision of the court should be in the affirmative. The Supreme Court having so decided, the Commission now recommends such an enactment, believing that it would do more to put an end to the teaching and practice of polygamy than has yet been accomplished by the partial enforcement of existing laws.[10]

"My Advice to the Latter Day Saints": President Woodruff's Proclamation

The Woodruff Manifesto of 1890 stands in juxtaposition to the 1843 revelation on polygamy. One announced divine approval for Mormonism's best-remembered practice, the other the beginning of its demise. On 24 September 1890, Woodruff commented in his journal: "I met with 3 of the Twelve & my Councillors upon an important Subject."[11] The next day there followed a fuller account of what that subject was:

> I have arived at a point in the History of my life as the President of the Church of Jesus Christ of Latter Day Saints whare I am under the necessity of acting for the Temporal Salvation of the Church. The United State Governmet has taken a Stand & passed Laws to destroy the Latter day Saints upon the Subjet of poligamy or Patriarchal order of Marriage. And after Praying to the Lord & feeling inspired by his spirit I have issued the following Proclamation which is sustain by My Councillors and the 12 Apostles: . . .[12]

As the Lord's anointed, Woodruff earnestly believed that divine intent prompted his mind and hand. Although George Q. Cannon, Charles W. Penrose, and others assisted in phrasing the message, the Manifesto appears to be overwhelmingly the work of the church president himself.[13] He alone signed

---

[10] Commission members G. L. Godfrey, A. B. Williams, Alvin Saunders, and R. S. Robertson respectfully submitted and signed the report.

[11] Kenney, ed., *Wilford Woodruff's Journal*, 24 Sept. 1890, 9:112.

[12] Ibid, 25 Sept. 1890, 9:112–14. Also see materials and commentary in Clark, ed., *Messages*, 3:191–95.

[13] Quinn, "New Plural Marriages," 29; Hardy, *Solemn Covenant*, 131; and Bitton, *George Q. Cannon*, 312–13.

First Presidency of the Mormon church at the time of the 1890 Manifesto:
President Wilford Woodruff is standing, with First Counselor George Q.
Cannon on his right, and Second Counselor Joseph F. Smith on his left.
Used by permission, Utah State Historical Society, all rights reserved.

Born in England, Charles William Penrose (1832–1925) served as an apostle and counselor in the First Presidency of the church. He was also an editor of the *Deseret News* and regularly wrote on behalf of plural marriage including its socio-biological advantages.

the finished document and, even before obtaining ratification from the church's general membership, sent it to the press and officials in Washington, D.C.[14]

"OFFICIAL DECLARATION," KENNEY, ED.,
WILFORD WOODRUFF'S JOURNAL, 25 SEPT. 1890, 9:114–16.

To Whom it may Concern

Press dispatches having been sent for Political purposes from Salt Lake City which have been widely published to the Effect that the Utah Commission in their resent report to the secretary of the interior allege that plural marriages are Still being solemnized and that forty or more such marriages have been contracted in Utah since last June or during the past year, also that in public discourses the Leaders of the Church have taught Encourged and urged the Continuance of the practice of Poligamy I therefore as president of the Church of Jesus Christ of Latter Day Saints do hereby in the most solemn manner declare that these charges are fals. We are not teaching poligamy or plural marriage nor permitting any person to Enter into the practice and

---

[14] In his journal, President Woodruff referred to the statement as both a "proclamation" and an "Official Declaration." When printed, the latter was used as its title. Apostle Lorenzo Snow seems to have been the first to call it a "Manifesto," on 6 October 1890 in general conference when he moved that the church formally accept the document. "General Conference," *Des. Eve. News*, 6 Oct. 1890, 23:269 [2/9–3/1]. The same title was employed in a published record of the conference proceedings: *President Woodruff's Manifesto*.

I deny that Either forty or any other number of Plural marriages have during that Period been Solemnized in our temples or in any place in the territory.[15] One Case has been reportd in which the parties alleged that the marriage was performed in the Endowment House in Salt Lake City in the Spring
of 1889, But I have not been able to learn who performed the cerimony. What
Ever was done in the matter was without my knowledge.[16] In consequence of
this alleged occurance the Endowment [House] was taken down by my instruction without Delay.[17]

Inasmuch as laws have been Enacted by congress forbidding plural marriages which laws have been pronounced constitutional by the court of the last
resort, I hereby declare my intention to submit to those laws and to use my
influence with the members of the Church over which I preside to have them
do likewise. There is nothing in my teachings to the Church or those of my
Associates during the time specified which Can reasonably be construed to
inculcate or Encourage poligamy and when any Elder of the Church has used
language which appeared to Convey such teaching he has been promptly
reproved. And I now publicly declair that my advice to the Latter Day Saints
is to refrain from Contracting any Marriage forbidden by the Law of the land.
Wilford Woodruff president of the Church of Jesus Christ of Latter Day Saints.

While church members anticipated presentation of the Manifesto in the
autumn conference of the Saints, it was a telegram from territorial delegate
John T. Caine that prompted leaders to do so.[18] Caine said that Sec. of the
Interior John W. Noble would accept the Manifesto as a contradiction of
Gov. Arthur L. Thomas's and the Utah Commission's claims about continued polygamy only if members of the church endorsed it.[19] Accordingly, on
Monday, 6 October 1890, the day following receipt of the telegram, the Manifesto was read to assembled members attending Mormonism's semi-annual conference in Salt Lake City. When asked to vote for the declaration, a
majority of those present indicated approval although it is likely many refused
to vote for or against the measure, keeping their hands in their laps. It was a

[15] Woodruff's denials were contrary to what he and other church leaders knew. Several such marriages
are documented in Hardy, *Solemn Covenant*, 154n4.

[16] Hans Jespersen's plural marriage to Alice Horton in the spring of 1889 was performed by Franklin
D. Richards, one of the apostles with whom Woodruff consulted before issuing the Manifesto.

[17] The church president's statement that he ordered the Endowment House torn down as evidence of
his determination to end polygamous unions had little relevance for their performance in the future. The
Manti, St. George, and Logan temples were all available for such purposes, and Mormon marriages had
always been solemnized anywhere, indoors and out. See the testimony of John Taylor in Chapter Seven.

[18] Expectation that a vote would be taken on the Manifesto is seen in comments in the Emmeline B.
Wells Journals, 29 Sept. 1890, UPB, 13:109–10; and Juliaetta Bateman Jensen's memory of her father's experience in *Little Gold Pieces*, 129–30.

[19] A. H. Cannon Journals, 5 Oct. 1890, UPB, 13:129.

dramatic moment with numbers fearful of what acceptance of the declaration meant. Women seemed especially shaken. But presiding officers announced the Manifesto as approved and, despite hesitation by some, the document became official Mormon policy.[20]

As with the 1843 revelation approving plurality, the Woodruff Manifesto ending its practice arose from vexed circumstances. And just as the original pronouncement of the Principle grew in implication, so the 1890 Manifesto, conceptually uncertain at first, required years to construe. There was, for example, its presentation and writing style. It was addressed "To Whom it may Concern." Even with the corrections of spelling and grammar made for its publication, it gave the impression of being little more than private opinion publicly expressed. Nowhere was one summoned by the voice of Deity. Nowhere did the work resemble Mormonism's other formal pronouncements from heaven, including those received by Woodruff himself in which the Almighty imparted quite different instructions to His people. And there was the writing's concluding sentence where, with nothing like reproof or command, Woodruff simply *advised* members that, so far as polygamy was concerned they, like he, should obey the law.

There were also the curious comments appended to the proclamation's first printing in an editorial column of the *Deseret News*, probably written by Charles W. Penrose. It described the Manifesto as condensed from an earlier writing and that the finished draft only "poorly" expressed the Mormon president's thoughts.[21] In another piece, the church paper's editor repudiated a Utah commissioner's criticism that said the Manifesto *should* have been issued as a revelation. Revelations were not the products of human whim, Penrose retorted, and when word from on high should come, he stated, it would be soon enough for President Woodruff to say so.[22] The *Woman's Exponent*, more than two months later, not only referred to it as only a "letter" that should discourage law breaking but added, "the fact should not be overlooked that the doctrine or belief of the Church that polygamous marriages are rightful and supported by Divine revelation remains unchanged."[23]

---

[20] "Official Declaration," *Des. Eve. News*, 6 Oct. 1890, 23:269 [2/9]. B. H. Roberts, then a general authority of the church, was one of those who refused to vote for the measure. Sillito, ed., *History's Apprentice*, 226. For an example of the church's continued contention that Woodruff's document was unanimously approved, see *Church History in the Fulness of Times*, 441. A more extensive account of the Manifesto's reception is in Hardy, *Solemn Covenant*, 135–38.

[21] "Official Declaration," *Des. Eve. News*, 25 Sept. 1890, 23:260 [2/1].

[22] "Utah Commissioner's Perversions," ibid., 1 Oct. 1890, 23:265 [2/1–2].

[23] "From The President's Message," *Woman's Exponent* 19:12 (1 Dec. 1890), 93.

"To Hoodwink the Public": Non-Mormon Responses

Most outside the church were suspicious, and some contemptuous, of Woodruff's declaration. The *Salt Lake Tribune* and Utah Commission both belittled President Woodruff and Mormonism's revelatory process.[24] In his annual message for 1890, Pres. Benjamin Harrison noticed that Woodruff's statement contained no rejection of the doctrine of plural marriage, only advice against its practice.

> The recent letter of Wilford Woodruff, president of the Mormon church, in which he advised his people "to refrain from contracting any marriage forbidden by the laws of the land," has attracted wide attention, and it is hoped that its influence will be highly beneficial in restraining infractions of the laws of the United States. But the fact should not be overlooked that the doctrine or belief of the Church that polygamous marriages are rightful and supported by divine revelation remains unchanged. President Woodruff does not renounce the doctrine, but refrains from teaching it, and advises against the practice of it because the law is against it. Now it is quite true that the law should not attempt to deal with the faith or belief of anyone; but it is quite another thing, and the only safe thing, so to deal with the Territory of Utah as that those who believe polygamy to be rightful shall not have the power to make it lawful.[25]

And Josiah Strong (1847–1916), a prominent American clergyman and Christian Socialist, warned that the real threat was not polygamy but priestcraft. He characterized the Manifesto as an exercise in deception.

> JOSIAH STRONG, *Our Country* (1891), 118.
>
> Wilford Woodruff, the President of the Mormon Church has recently issued a proclamation [relating to plural marriage]. . .
>
> If this declaration was made in good faith, it would probably mean that polygamy is to be abandoned, at least for a time. It is, however, the well-nigh universal opinion of Gentiles in Salt Lake City that this manifesto was a mere trick intended for obvious reasons to hoodwink the public. We have seen that

---

[24] "The Pronunciamento," *Salt Lake Tribune*, 8 Oct. 1890, 39:266, 4/2–3; and "Annual Report of the Utah Commission" [1891], *RSI*, 3:424–26, 29.

[25] Harrison, Second Annual Message, 1 Dec. 1890, Richardson, *Comp.*, 12:5553. President Harrison remained cautious regarding Mormonism's surrender. He warned that if Utah gained statehood it could ignore not only its earlier promises but conditions laid down by Congress in enabling legislation as well. Harrison, Third Annual Message, 9 Dec. 1891, *Comp.*, 12:5641. Harrison's concern that statehood would let Utah restore the practice of polygamy rested on sound constitutional grounds. Oklahoma and Arizona later ignored provisions of their enabling acts. Swisher, *American Constitutional Development*, 554–57; and Sears, "Punishing the Saints," 629–31. Without a constitutional amendment, Congress was bound to respect each new state in areas such as marriage, in which the states traditionally exercised independent authority. *Coyle vs. Smith*, 221 U.S. 559 (1911).

polygamy might be destroyed without seriously weakening Mormonism; indeed, its destruction, by allaying suspicion, by creating the impression that the Mormon problem is solved, and by removing the obstacle to Utah's admission as a state, might materially strengthen Mormonism. Any blow to be really effective must be aimed at the priestly despotism. . .

"A CLASS WHO DO NOT RELISH IT": MORMON DOUBTS

Questions concerning the Manifesto's text left Mormons themselves unsure of its provenance.[26] No less than outsiders, church members could not but notice that Woodruff's message differed little from others before it.[27] In addition to the familiar pattern of denial, it seemed a twin to another "Manifesto" issued only eleven months earlier in which authorities spoke to the issues of blood atonement and church involvement in political matters. The 1890 Manifesto, like that of 1889, involved the hand of Charles W. Penrose and was delivered to the public without prior approval from the church's membership.[28] The 1889 Manifesto was not placed in the *Doctrine and Covenants*, and neither was that of 1890, until eighteen years later. Only after the ordeal of the Smoot hearings in Congress would Woodruff's statement be given a place in Mormonism's official compilation of scripture, and then at some distance from the 1843 revelation, so far to the back of the book that it followed both the index and concordance. Unlike sacred dispensations elsewhere in the work titled "revelations," formatted with divided columns and numbered verses, the Manifesto was simply reprinted as it appeared in the *Deseret News* under the title "Official Declaration."[29]

In addition to its writing style and manner of presentation, other aspects of the Manifesto were troubling. It did not, for example, address the matter of continued cohabitation with existing polygamous wives, an issue that evoked

---

[26] For example, see L. John Nuttall Diary, 26 Oct. 1891, UPB, 3:92; remarks made in meetings of the Twelve Apostles as recorded in the A. H. Cannon Journals, 1 April 1892, UPB, 16:79–82; and the instances provided in Hardy, *Solemn Covenant*, 149, 150, 375.

[27] See the acknowledgment made later of pre-Manifesto denials in Cowley, *Wilford Woodruff*, 569.

[28] "Official Declaration," *Des. Weekly*, 21 Dec. 1889, 39:26, 809/1–3, 810/1–2; and Clark, ed., *Messages*, 3:183–87. George Q. Cannon of the First Presidency published both documents in 1891, referring to them as "the two Manifestoes." Cannon, *History of the Mormons*, 17–20. For Penrose's authorship of the 1889 Manifesto, see Godfrey, "Charles W. Penrose," 367–68.

[29] *D&C* (1908), 543–44.

heated discussion among many, including apostles, for years.[30] There was also the question of whether or not the Manifesto was applicable outside the United States. Some believed Woodruff's "advice" that church members desist from entering marriages "forbidden by the Law of the Land" did not, for example, apply to Mexico.[31] Questions of this kind continued to affect the way church members viewed the declaration. Emmeline B. Wells remarked on the uncertainty. With the new policy, she said, "there can be no opportunity for married men to increase their families. All must remain as they are, how peculiar the change after more than 40 years. There is a class who do not relish it all and think the Lord has not been seen in it or had any hand in it."[32] First Presidency member George Q. Cannon spoke to such doubts in a conference address of April 1891, justifying what Woodruff had done.

"Late General Conference," *Des. Eve. News,*
7 April 1891, 24:114, 4/3–6.

President George Q. Cannon

. . . I need hardly refer to that which took place at our last Conference. . . I allude now to the manifesto.

If the Lord were not with this Church, if he were not directing His servants, and the people themselves did not have the testimony of Jesus concerning this work, the issuance of that manifesto would have had a fatal effect upon thousands, perhaps in the Church. I can say for myself that I never shrunk from anything in my life as I did from that. I know it was God who dictated it—that it was issued in accordance with the requirements of the Spirit of God; and I also know that every member of the Church who is living in close communion with the Lord has had a testimony—notwithstanding their natural feelings with reference thereto, notwithstanding the painful consequences which followed its adoption—that it was the right thing to do. . .

There was the law of God on the one hand and the law of the land upon the other, the latter, as we believe, enacted by prejudice and leveled against our religion to destroy us. We considered it necessary, however, that this law [of plural marriage] should be obeyed to the very uttermost. . .

---

[30] A. H. Cannon Journals, 26 Sept. 1890, UPB, 13:112; ibid., 7 Oct. 1890, 13:134; Mariner Wood Merrill Diaries, 7 Oct. 1890, LDS Archives; and, again, A. O. Woodruff Journal, 29–30 Dec. 1899, box 1, fd. 2, Abraham Owen Woodruff Collection, UPB, 168–69. Departing from their advice in the 1880s, the First Presidency and apostles in 1899 told men brought to trial for unlawful cohabitation to rely on their own inspiration in answering judges as to whether they would obey the law. Rudger Clawson Diary, 23 Nov. 1899, box 4, bk. 11, Rudger Clawson Collection, Special Collections, UU, 98.

[31] See those taking this view cited in Hardy, *Solemn Covenant,* 173n27.

[32] Emmeline B. Wells Journals, 9 Oct. 1890, UPB, 13:113–14. Or as James Bywater, a Brigham City pluralist, put it: "There seemed to me to be too much man in it and too little of God." Quoted in Bennion, *Polygamy in Lorenzo Snow's Brigham City,* 29.

We endeavored by our sacrifices to arrest the progress of this crusade against our religious liberty; we honestly believed that we had a right to act as we did. That we have failed, however, in persuading the nation . . . is very clear [at] the present time. We have utterly failed. We have carried this to such an extent that the Lord himself has signified His acceptance of the sacrifices and offerings of the Latter-day Saints. He has said to us, "It is enough now. You having done your duty, this matter must rest with Me;" and we have, in consequence, sustained the issuance of the manifesto . . . and I am not afraid to risk my reputation, if I have one, as a prophet—when [I say] that which we have done will [eventually] be recorded with admiration and praise. . .

I have been compelled to acknowledge my own blindness; I never had such a feeling concerning my own ignorance and inability to comprehend the plans and purposes of God as I have had of late. But I bow to His Supreme wisdom; it is infinite. . .

I have testified, I might say hundreds of times, before public men, that I believed if I had not done in reference to plural marriage I would have been damned utterly. I have said this before leading men; I have said it before the President of the United States. . . I can only speak for myself, but the command came to me. . . I would have been damned if I had not obeyed it. Having this belief embedded in my very nature, what could I do but obey? It was either obedience on the right hand or damnation on the left. Yet, notwithstanding this, I obeyed the law; and hence it is, I say, we need the Spirit of God to be with us, because all these things come in conflict with all our preconceived ideas and that which we have framed in our own minds. . .

I wish to allude to another point. . . Some have said to us they believed that if we had taken the course Daniel did when he was put in the lions' den, and the three Hebrew children when put in the fiery furnace, perhaps it would have been more heroic and more consistent with our profession as Latter-day Saints. . . I have no earthly doubt if President Woodruff had been required to go into the Lions' den or into the fiery furnace . . . he would have done it. . . The three Hebrew children in taking the course they did involved only their own lives; their action did not involve the lives, liberties, and future of a great people. Therefore you can see that the analogy between their case and ours is not a complete one. . .

God guided those men of old to do as they did. God has guided His Church until now; He guided us to do what we have done, and in the history of His dealings with the children of men it will be recorded that we have made as great or greater sacrifices than any people that ever lived. . .

We would never have reached these valleys had not the Lord guided us; and we can look back and see how wonderfully His promises have been fulfilled in our behalf. . . So it will be to the end, and we will be obliged to confess that his wisdom has done it all.[33]

---

[33] For discussion of the same issue by members of the First Presidency and the Twelve Apostles before the conference met, see A. H. Cannon Journals, 3 April 1891, UPB, 14:88–89.

Still, as Apostle Abraham H. Cannon reported, murmuring continued. Visiting at the home of a female Saint in Brigham City, Utah, he said:

> The manifesto was the principal topic of conversation with Sister Snow, and she said that there were over 25 unmarried ladies of her age in Brigham City alone, who would now most likely be left as old maids. There is no doubt but many of the young people sincerely regret the issuance of the manifesto.[34]

"An Uneasy Feeling Among the People": Master-In-Chancery Hearings

Seeking greater credibility both in and outside the church, Mormon leaders decided to use hearings before Master-in-Chancery Charles F. Loofbourow, appointed to deal with expropriated church properties, to better represent themselves.[35] Mormon authorities who expected to testify rehearsed their responses.[36] Their preparations notwithstanding, during the hearings government lawyers pressed President Woodruff so closely that he extended the Manifesto's intent beyond what either he or his colleagues wanted. Woodruff was brought to say his proclamation was inspired by God, something he considered the equivalent of revelation; that it forbade polygamous cohabitation as well as new marriages; and that its prohibitions were binding on Latter-day Saints everywhere in the world.[37] After the chancery proceedings, he responded to criticism from fellow authorities concerning his performance, saying that "he was placed in such a position on the witness stand that he could not answer other than he did."[38] However pleasing Woodruff's statements were to anti-polygamy zealots, his testimony left some inside the church "uneasy." The private record of Charles Walker (1832–1904), a church member living in southern Utah, refers to those affected in this way.

---

[34] A. H. Cannon Journals, 27 April 1891, UPB, 14:121.

[35] Judge Charles Franklin Loofbourow (1842–1904) was born in Ohio and came to Utah in 1889 after studying law in Ohio and Iowa, where he served as a circuit judge. In addition to practicing law in Salt Lake City, he was a member of the city council. The hearings were called to implement the Supreme Court's ruling of 25 May 1891 directing that a master-in-chancery return properties escheated by provisions in the Edmunds-Tucker Act. *Late Corporation . . . vs. U.S.* 140 U.S. 665 (1891). For commentary on the tangled legal issues involved, see Arrington, *Great Basin Kingdom*, 368–69; Linford, "Mormons and the Law," pt. 2:578–80; and Firmage and Mangrum, *Zion in the Courts*, 251–60.

[36] A. H. Cannon Journals, 6 Aug. 1891, 15:26; 20 Aug. 1891, 15:36–38; 26 Aug. 1891, 15:39; Kenney, ed., *Wilford Woodruff's Journal*, 12 Oct. 1891, 9:165.

[37] "Taking of Testimony," *Des. Eve. News*, 20 Oct. 1891, 24:279, 4/5–5/1–2.

[38] Wilford Woodruff, as quoted in A. H. Cannon Journals, 12 Nov. 1891, UPB, 15:121.

LARSON AND LARSON, EDS.,
DIARY OF CHARLES LOWELL WALKER, 2:728.

[St. George, Utah] Oct 20th, 1891 Pres Woodroof, Geo Q Cannon, and Jos F. Smith were before the Lawyers and Master in Chancery, Mr Loafburrow, in the interest of the Church as to the Escheat business. They were interrogated pretty closely by the Lawyers as to the Manifesto and its meaning and genuineness. . . Among other replies Pres Woodroof declared that the doctrine of Plural Marriage was not taught nor entered into and it was his intention to obey the Laws of the U S regarding Polygamy and and he counseled the saints to do so, and if any man entered into Polygamy it would be contrary to his views expressed in the Manifesto and would be liable to be excommunicated from the Church. This announcement by him as Pres of the Church has caused an uneasy feeling among the People, and some think he has gone back on the Revealation on Plural Marriage and its covenants and obligations. Some faint-hearted Men who have entered into Plural Marriage have taken advantage of these sayings in the Lawyers court and have put away their Plural wives that were given them of the Lord and have deserted them to shift for themselves, taking Pres Woodroof's statement as a good excuse for so doing. But the majority of the People say, 'Let us stand still and see the Salvation of God.' And yet some are wavering, and seem to doubt the Power of God to overrule all things for the onward progress of his glorious work, and that He stands at the Helm and will do things according to his own will and his own time and in his own manner.

"STOP MURMURING AND COMPLAINING": PRESIDENT WOODRUFF AFFIRMS THE MANIFESTO WAS GIVEN BY REVELATION

Because questions about the Manifesto continued to arise, President Woodruff spoke on the subject at two stake conferences in northern Utah in the autumn of 1891. Referring to those who doubted divine approval for his action, and reminding his audiences of the disabling burdens brought by anti-Mormon legislation, the president declared that the Manifesto was not only practical but the will of heaven. In his remarks Woodruff built upon comments his counselor, George Q. Cannon, made when the Manifesto was presented in conference more than a year earlier. At that time Cannon said the Manifesto was an inspired answer to prayer and that the costs of continued sufferance by the Saints was too great, an escape for which there was both precedent and revelatory permission.[39] President Woodruff reaffirmed those statements.

"REMARKS MADE BY PRESIDENT WILFORD WOODRUFF AT
CACHE STAKE CONFERENCE, HELD AT LOGAN, SUNDAY AFTERNOON,
NOV. 1ST, 1891," DES. EVE. NEWS, 7 NOV. 1891, 24:295, 4/4–5.

. . . The Latter-day Saints should not get the idea that the Lord has forsaken His people, or that He does not reveal His mind and will; because such an idea is not true. The Lord is with us, and has been with us from the beginning. This Church has never been led a day except by revelation. And who lives or who dies, or who is called to lead this Church, they have got to lead it by the inspiration of Almighty God. . .

I made some remarks last Sunday at Brigham City upon this same principle-revelation. Read the Life of Brigham Young and you can hardly find a revelation that he had wherein he said, "Thus saith the Lord;" but the Holy Ghost was with him; he taught by inspiration and by revelation; but with one exception he did not give those revelations in the form that Joseph did; for they were not written and given as revelations and commandments to the Church in the words and name of the Savior. Joseph said "Thus saith the Lord" almost every day of his life in laying the foundation of this work. But those who followed him have not deemed it always necessary to say "Thus saith the Lord;" yet they have led the people by the power of the Holy Ghost; . . .

I have had some revelations of late, and very important ones to me, and I will tell you what the Lord has said to me. Let me bring your minds to what is termed the manifesto. The Lord has told me by revelation that there are many members of the Church throughout Zion who are sorely tried in their hearts because of that manifesto, and also because of the testimony of the Presidency of this Church and the Apostles before the Master in Chancery. Since I received that revelation I have heard of many who are tried in these things, though I had not heard of any before that particularly. Now, the Lord has commanded me to do one thing, and I fulfilled that commandment at the conference at Brigham City last Sunday, and I will do the same here today. The Lord has told me to ask the Latter-day Saints a question, and He also told me that if they would listen to what I said to them and answer the question put to them, by the spirit and power of God, they would all answer alike, and they would all believe alike with regard to this matter. The question is this: Which is the wisest course for the Latter-day Saints to pursue—to continue to attempt to practice plural marriage, with the laws of the nation against

---

[39] "Remarks by President George Q. Cannon and President Wilford Woodruff . . . ," Des. Eve. News, 11 Oct. 1890, 23:274 [2/3–5]. Divine permission to step aside from a command of heaven in the face of insurmountable opposition is in D&C 124:49, 19 Jan. 1841.

it and the opposition of sixty millions of people, and at the cost of the confiscation and loss of all the Temples, and the stopping of all the ordinances therein, both for the living and the dead, and the imprisonment of the First Presidency and Twelve and the heads of families in the Church and the confiscation of personal property of the people (all of which of themselves would stop the practice), or after doing and suffering what we have through our adherence to this principle to cease the practice and submit to the law, and through doing so leave the Prophets, Apostles and fathers at home, so that they can instruct the people and attend to the duties of the Church, and also leave the Temples in the hands of the Saints, so that they can attend to the ordinances of the Gospel, both for the living and the dead?

The Lord showed me by vision and revelation exactly what would take place if we did not stop this practice. If we had not stopped it . . . all ordinances would be stopped throughout the land of Zion. Confusion would reign throughout Israel and many men would be made prisoners. . .

I know there are a good many men, and probably some leading men, in this Church who have been tried and felt as though President Woodruff had lost the Spirit of God and was about to apostatize. Now, I want you to understand that he has not lost the Spirit, nor is he about to apostatize. The Lord is with him, and with this people. He has told me exactly what to do, and what the result would be if we did not do it. I have been called upon by friends outside of the Church and urged to take some steps with regard to this matter. . . I saw exactly what would come to pass if there was not something done. I have had this spirit upon me for a long time. But I want to say this: I should have let all the temples go out of our hands; I should have gone to prison myself, and let every other man go there, had not the God of heaven commanded me to do what I did do, and when the hour came that I was commanded to do that, it was all clear to me. I went before the Lord, and I wrote what the Lord told me to write. I laid it before my brethren—such strong men as Brother Geo. Q. Cannon, Brother Jos. F. Smith, and the Twelve Apostles. I might as well undertake to turn an army with banners out of its course as to turn them out of a course that they considered to be right. These men agreed with me, and ten thousand Latter-day Saints also agreed with me. Why? Because they were moved upon by the Spirit of God and by the revelations of Jesus Christ to do it. . .

I want the Latter-day Saints to stop murmuring and complaining at the providence of God. Trust in God. Do your duty. Remember your prayers. Get faith in the Lord, and take hold and build up Zion. All will be right. The Lord is going to visit His people, and He is going to cut His work short in righteousness, lest no flesh should be saved. I say to you, watch the signs of the times, and prepare yourselves for that which is to come. God bless you. Amen.[40]

---

[40] In an effort to contradict continuing doubts, recent editions of the *Doctrine and Covenants* have appended parts of this and Woodruff's sermon at Brigham City to the Manifesto. "Excerpts from Three Addresses by President Wilford Woodruff Regarding the Manifesto," *D&C* (1982), 292–93.

"Final End of the Work": The Amnesty Petition

At the same time that Woodruff was affirming divine approval for the Manifesto, another event was in preparation, one of greater importance than anything done so far. This was a formal appeal to the government requesting amnesty for all who yet suffered from penalties imposed by anti-polygamy legislation. This petition, prepared with assistance from sympathetic non-Mormons, ranks with if not above every other official statement made by church leaders, including the Manifesto, in marking abandonment of the plural order. It explicitly linked the term "celestial marriage" with polygamy and admitted that its practice had been taught as a "necessity to man's highest exaltation in the life to come."

It said that President Wilford Woodruff's Manifesto was issued with divine permission and that consequently "the law [the 1843 revelation] commanding polygamy was henceforth suspended." The salience of these statements can hardly be overdrawn. The 1891 petition for amnesty is Mormonism's most conspicuous testament to the social and religious changes underway. Recognizing its significance, the Utah Commission called it "the most important of the documents the church has issued, and contains the most direct and positive statements of its desires and promises for the future which has yet come from that source."[41]

> Amnesty Petition to the President [of the United States]:
> Salt Lake, 19 Dec. 1891. Clark, ed., *Messages*, 3:229–31.
>
> We, the first presidency and apostles of the Church of Jesus Christ of Latter Day Saints, beg respectfully to represent to your excellency the following facts:
>
> We formerly taught our people that polygamy, or celestial marriage, as commanded by God through Joseph Smith, was right; that it was a necessity to man's highest exaltation in the life to come.[42]
>
> The doctrine was publicly promulgated by our president, the late Brigham Young, forty years ago, and was steadily taught and impressed upon the Latter Day Saints up to a short time before September, 1890. Our people are devout and sincere, and they accepted the doctrine, and many embraced and practiced polygamy.

---

[41] "Annual Report of the Utah Commission," *RSI* (1892), 3:465. Also see "Report of the Governor of Utah," *RSI* (1892), 3:428.

[42] Admission that the church had taught the necessity of plural marriage for exaltation was a topic Cannon spoke to when urging support for the Manifesto: "Remarks by President George Q. Cannon and President Wilford Woodruff," *Des. Eve. News*, 11 Oct. 1890, 23:274 [2/3].

When the Government sought to stamp the practice out, our people almost without exception remained firm, for they, while having no desire to oppose the Government in anything, still felt that their lives and their honor as men were pledged to a vindication of their faith, and that their duty towards those whose lives were a part of their own was a paramount one, to fulfill which they had no right to count anything, not even their own lives, as standing in the way. Following this conviction, hundreds endured arrests, trial, fines, and imprisonment, and the immeasurable suffering borne by the faithful people no language can describe. That suffering in abated form still continues. More, the Government added disfranchisement to its other punishment for those who clung to their faith and fulfilled its covenants. According to our faith, the head of our Church receives from time to time revelations for the religious guidance of his people. In September, 1890, the present head of the church, in anguish and prayer cried to God for help for his flock, and received the permission to advise the members of the Church of Jesus Christ of Latter Day Saints that the law commanding polygamy was henceforth suspended.

At the great semi-annual conference, which was held a few days later, this was submitted to the people, numbering many thousands and representing every community of the people in Utah, and was by them in the most solemn manner accepted as the future rule of their lives.

They have been faithful to the covenant made that day.

At the late October conference, after a year had passed by, the matter was once more submitted to the thousands of people gathered together, and they again in the most potential manner ratified the solemn covenant.

This being the true situation and believing that the object of the Government was simply the vindication of its own authority and to compel obedience to its laws, and that it takes no pleasure in persecution, we respectfully pray that full amnesty may be extended to all who are under disabilities because of the operation of the so-called Edmunds and Edmunds-Tucker laws. Our people are scattered; homes are made desolate; many are still in prison; others are banished or in hiding. Our hearts bleed for these. In the past they followed our counsels, and while they are thus afflicted our souls are in sackcloth and ashes. We believe there are nowhere here in the Union a more loyal people than the Latter Day Saints. They know no other country except this. They expect to live and die on this soil. When the men of the South, who were in rebellion against the Government in 1865 threw down their arms and asked for recognition along the old lines of citizenship, the Government hastened to grant their prayer. To be at peace with the Government and in harmony with their fellow citizens who were not of their faith and to share in the confidence of the Government and people, our people have voluntarily put aside something which all their lives they have believed to be a sacred principle.

Have they not the right to ask for such clemency as comes when the claims of both law and justice have been fully liquidated?

As shepherds of a patient and suffering people we ask amnesty for them and pledge our faith and honor for their future.[43]

Territorial governor Arthur L. Thomas and Chief Justice Charles S. Zane both endorsed the petition, and in a personal letter to President Harrison stated:

... were full amnesty granted to date that date would be coupled with your name and in the future the Mormon people would turn to them as does the Colored race to Abraham Lincoln and the day of Jan. 2nd 1863; and if, as we believe the promise made by your petitioners will be fully kept it will associate with your administration the final end of the Work to which the republican party was solemnly pledged by its first national Convention which assembled in Philadelphia in 1856.[44]

By making no reference in the petition to "unlawful cohabitation," church leaders hoped they would be permitted to live out their lives with plural wives married before 1890. And inasmuch as prominent Gentiles in Salt Lake City collaborated in writing the document, local toleration in the matter was inferred.[45] President Harrison's proclamation of amnesty on 4 January 1893, however, pardoned only those who had abstained from *both* new plural marriages and unlawful cohabitation since 1 November 1890. This was undoubtedly what led Wilford Woodruff to lament in his journal: "The Amnesty from President Harrison . . . is of Little benefit to the People."[46]

---

[43] Printed copies of the petition are also found in "Amnesty," *Contributor* 13:4 (Feb. 1892), 196–97; and *Proceedings*, 1:18–19. The petition ended, "And your petitioners will ever pray," and the First Presidency and all twelve apostles signed it.

[44] Arthur L. Thomas and Charles S. Zane to Pres. Benjamin Harrison, 21 Dec. 1891, in White, ed., *Diaries of John Henry Smith*, 266.

[45] Regarding the assistance of prominent local non-Mormons in preparing the petition, see "True History of the Amnesty Petition: An Open Letter from the Tribune to the Mormon People," *Salt Lake Tribune*, 6 Sept. 1899, 59:153, 4/2–6; and White, ed., *Diaries of John Henry Smith*, 19–21 Dec. 1891, 264–66. Political maneuvering accompanying the petition is discussed in Lyman, *Political Deliverance*, 189–90, 205.

[46] Wilford Woodruff, in Kenney, ed., *Wilford Woodruff's Journal*, 5 Jan. 1893, 9:235. A later proclamation by Pres. Grover Cleveland, while affirming that all who qualified under the amnesty were in full possession of their civil rights, also conditioned its pardon on abstention from continued cohabitation with plural wives. "Proclamation No. 14," U.S., *Statutes at Large*, 25 Sept. 1894, 28:1257. Despite these requirements, research by Kenneth Cannon II shows that a strong majority of church leaders continued to live with their plural wives. Cannon II, "Beyond the Manifesto," 24–36.

"Proclamation. No. 42," U.S., *Statutes at Large* 27:1058, 4 Jan. 1893.

By the President of the United States of America.
A Proclamation.

Whereas, Congress, by a statute approved March 22, 1882, and by statutes in furtherance and amendment thereof, defined the crimes of bigamy, polygamy and unlawful cohabitation in the Territories and other places within the exclusive jurisdiction of the United States and prescribed a penalty for such crimes; and

Whereas, on or about the 6th day of October, 1890, the Church of the Latter Day Saints, commonly known as the Mormon Church, through its President, issued a manifesto proclaiming the purpose of said Church no longer to sanction the practice of polygamous marriages, and calling upon all members and adherents of said church to obey the laws of the United States in reference to said subject matter; and

Whereas, it is represented that since the date of said declaration the members and adherents of said Church have generally obeyed said laws and have abstained from plural marriages and polygamous cohabitation; and

Whereas, by a petition dated December 19, 1891, the officials of said Church, pledging the membership thereof to a faithful obedience to the laws against plural marriage and unlawful cohabitation, have applied to me to grant amnesty for past offences against said laws, which request a very large number of influential non-Mormons, residing in the Territories, have also strongly urged; and

Whereas, the Utah Commission, in their report bearing date September 15, 1892, recommend that said petition be granted and said amnesty proclaimed, under proper conditions as to the future observance of the law, with a view to the encouragement of those now disposed to become law-abiding citizens; and

Whereas, during the past two years such amnesty has been granted to individual applicants in a very large number of cases, conditioned upon the faithful observance of the laws of the United States against unlawful cohabitation; and there are now pending many more such applications;

Now, therefore, I, Benjamin Harrison, President of the United States, by virtue of the powers in me vested, do hereby declare and grant a full amnesty and pardon to all persons liable to the penalties of said Act by reason of unlawful cohabitation under the color of polygamous or plural marriage, who have since November 1, 1890, abstained from such unlawful cohabitation; but upon the express condition that they shall in the future faithfully obey the laws of the United States herein before named, and not otherwise. Those who shall fail to avail themselves of the clemency hereby offered will be vigorously prosecuted.

In witness whereof, I have hereunto set my hand and caused the seal of the United States to be affixed.

[SEAL.]

Done at the City of Washington this fourth day of January in the year of our Lord, one thousand eight hundred and ninety-three, and of the Independence of the United States the one hundred and seventeenth.[47]

"The Mormon Is With Us": Gentile Acceptance

With the accumulating promises exacted from the church, a cascade of Gentile approval followed. Among those who early hailed the Manifesto as the long-awaited, ex-cathedra renunciation of plurality was Judge Charles S. Zane, one commonly looked upon by Mormons as among the most intractable of their foes. In 1891 he declared, "the Mormon is with us," and commenced a mounting drum roll of support for accepting the Saints as a changed people.[48] Mormon alignment with Democratic and Republican political organizations and abandonment of the old church-dominated People's Party gave further evidence that the territory was becoming thoroughly American.[49] And Utah's 1892 enactment of a statute patterned on the Edmunds Act, making polygamous cohabitation criminal and punishable by territorial authorities, converted the entire Utah Commission to acceptance of Mormonism's renunciation of polygamous practice.[50]

The momentum of events soon brought other victories. In October 1893, Congress authorized the return of church properties.[51] The ultimate prize followed when the House Committee on Territories recommended granting Utah statehood.

---

[47] The president and Sec. of State John W. Foster signed the document.

[48] Zane, "Death of Polygamy in Utah," 368–75. For a revised, more approving evaluation of Zane generally, see Alexander, "Charles S. Zane . . . Apostle of the New Era," 290–314. Acceptance of Mormon claims by others is illustrated in Arthur L. Thomas, Governor of Utah, to John W. Noble, Sec. of the Interior, Salt Lake City, 6 Nov. 1890, RG48, N.A.; the same official's "Report of the Governor of Utah," RSI (1892), 3:399–401; and comments by Noble himself, in "Annual Report of the Secretary of the Interior," ibid., 1:cxiv.

[49] On the developments mentioned, see A. H. Cannon Journals, 25 May 1891, UPB, 14:151; "Report of the Governor of Utah," RSI (1891), 3:401–12; "Thirteenth Annual Report of the Utah Commission," RSI (1894), 3:481–83; the qualifying remarks of Alexander in his "Utah's Constitution," 267; and all of "The Emergence of the National Parties in Utah," in Lyman, *Political Deliverance*, 150–84.

[50] "An Act to Punish Polygamy and Other Kindred Offenses," 4 Feb. 1892, *Laws of the Territory of Utah* (1892), 30th sess., c.8, sec. 2, 5–7. For the shift in the commissioners' views, see "Annual Report of the Utah Commission," RSI (1893), 3:417–19.

[51] "Joint Resolution. Providing for the disposition of certain property and money. . ." U.S., *Statutes at Large*, 25 Oct. 1893, 28:980. Remaining properties, rents, and monies were returned to the church's First Presidency in another resolution: U.S., *Statutes at Large*, 28 Mar. 1896, 29:758.

Admission of Utah . . . , House Report 162,
2 pts. (53-1) 2 Nov. 1893, Serial 3157, pt.1:20.

[Majority Recommendation of
the House Committee on Territories]

All mouths should be hushed, and all opposition silenced, after the President has amnestied all past offenses; after both political parties in national convention assembled have declared that the time has come for the admission of all the Territories, of which Utah is one; after the Territorial conventions of 1892, wherein both of said great parties declared for statehood, and that the hour is ripe for the admission of Utah; after the legislature of Utah has declared unanimously for statehood; after the governor of the Territory, all of its Territorial officers, and its judiciary, all of whom are Republicans in politics, have declared, that in their opinion polygamy is abolished and at an end; after all the members of the Utah Commission, a commission created expressly to crush and obliterate polygamy have declared their work practically accomplished; after the Mormon Church, through all of its heads and officials, publicly, privately, and in every way possible for mortals to do and proclaim, have with bowed heads, if not in anguish, pledged their faith and honor that nevermore in the future shall polygamy within the Mormon Church be either a doctrine of faith or of practice, there certainly can be but one sentiment, but one opinion among all just-minded legislators in Congress upon the question of duty, and that is to admit Utah as a State into the Federal Union.

Your committee recommend that the bill do pass.

Congress followed by giving its full support to an Enabling Act. Convinced by Mormon pledges that the practice of polygamy was forever at an end, the territory was invited to join the Union with the understanding that the new state must permanently bar plural marriage within its borders.[52] When word of the enactment reached President Woodruff, he was overcome. "Glory to God in the Highest," he declared, "for he fulfills his word to the Sons of Men. What we have been looking for so Long Came to Pass this day."[53]

U.S., *Statutes at Large* 28:138, 16 July 1894, 107–12.

"An Act To enable the people of Utah to form a constitution and State government, and to be admitted into the Union on an equal footing with the original States."

---

[52] For the work of friendly non-Mormons in obtaining Utah's statehood, see Lyman, "Isaac Trumbo," 128–49; and the same author's *Political Deliverance*, 185–254. Members of the Utah Commission had long urged that Utah be admitted as a state only if it incorporated in its constitution a "perpetual prohibition of polygamy," making it "a matter of perpetual public compact." John A. McClernard to Pres. Grover Cleveland, 30 June 1887, Grover Cleveland Papers, ser. 1, film, reel 50, Lib. of Cong.

[53] Kenney, ed., *Wilford Woodruff's Journal*, 13 Dec. 1893, 9:275.

Be it enacted by the Senate and House of Representatives of the United States of America in Congress assembled, That the inhabitants of all that part of the area of the United States now constituting the territory of Utah, as at present described, may become the state of Utah, as hereinafter provided. . .

SEC. 3. That the delegates to the convention thus elected shall meet at the seat of government of said territory on the first Monday in March, eighteen hundred and ninety-five, and, after organization, shall declare on behalf of the people of said proposed state that they adopt the constitution of the United States, whereupon the said convention shall be, and is hereby, authorized to form a constitution and state government for said proposed state.

The constitution shall be republican in form, and make no distinction in civil or political rights on account of race or color, except as to Indians not taxed, and not to be repugnant to the Constitution of the United States and the principles of the Declaration of Independence. And said convention shall provide by ordinance irrevocable without the consent of the United States and the people of said state—

First. That perfect toleration of religious sentiment shall be secured, and that no inhabitant of said state shall ever be molested in person or property on account of his or her mode of religious worship; Provided, That polygamous or plural marriages are forever prohibited. . .

In the spring of 1895 a convention met in Salt Lake City and framed a constitution that included the famous "irrevocable" clause, forever outlawing polygamy in Utah.[54]

CONSTITUTION OF THE STATE OF UTAH (1895) AS CONTAINED IN,
OFFICIAL REPORT OF THE PROCEEDINGS AND DEBATES OF
THE CONVENTION ASSEMBLED AT SALT LAKE CITY ON
THE FOURTH DAY OF MARCH, 1895, 2:1857.

Art. III, sec. 1.
The following ordinance shall be irrevocable without the consent of the United States and the people of this State:

First:—Perfect toleration of religious sentiment is guaranteed. No inhabitant of this State shall ever be molested in person or property on account of his or her mode of religious worship; but polygamous or plural marriages are forever prohibited.

Signed in Washington, D.C., on Saturday morning, 4 January 1896, the proclamation admitted Utah as the nation's forty-fifth state.[55] Rejoicing filled

---

[54] An ably written, illustrated history of the process is available in White, *Charter for Statehood*. On the "irrevocable" clause, see Sears, "Punishing the Saints," 626–31.

[55] Proclamation No. 9, signed by Pres. Grover Cleveland, U.S., *Statutes at Large*, 4 Jan. 1896, 29:876–77.

the streets of Salt Lake City, where the announcement was greeted with "fir-ing of guns, ringing of bells, blowing of whistles, and general jubilation."[56]

The Saints now stood at the door of greater peace and harmony than they had known for a half-century. For other Americans, even before statehood was granted, the Mormon surrender marked, for the second time in their generation, defeat of the remains of "sectionalism."[57] Most importantly, as Gov. Arthur Thomas put it in 1890, the nation could now congratulate itself on "the triumph of the Christian home in Utah."[58]

"Secret But Sacred":
Continued Approval for Polygamous Marriages

Gentile trumpet calls to victory were premature. The granting of statehood to Utah did not bring an end to new plural marriages. One reason Mormon leaders had so eagerly pursued statehood was to assist them in sheltering per-petuation of the Principle. With the prize in hand, Mormon authorities told selected church audiences that plural marriage remained a doctrine of the church, that it better accommodated the familial needs of a healthy society than monogamy, and that only those who lived in plural marriage would become gods.[59] One apostle prophesied that the practice would continue in some form until the Second Coming of Jesus.[60]

---

[56] The event is described in Roberts, *Comprehensive History*, 6:336–37. Also see remarks by John Henry Smith, president of the constitutional convention, in White, ed., *Diaries of John Henry Smith*, 322–39; Lyman, *Political Deliverance*, 255–90; and the section titled, "Utah Achieves Statehood," in Alexander, *Utah the Right Place*, 204–5.

[57] Sen. George Frisbie Hoar, as quoted in "New Revelation," *Salt Lake Tribune*, 9 Oct. 1890, 39:266, 1/6.

[58] Arthur Thomas, "Results of the Action," ibid., 20 Oct. 1890, 39:275, 8/2.

[59] As illustrations, see *Proceedings*, 1:9; B. H. Roberts, "Comment on Dr. Reiner's Letter," *Improvement Era* 1:7 (May 1898), 472, 475, 478, 482; Mrs. John Henry Smith, as quoted in Frank G. Carpenter, "A Chat with President Snow," *Des. Eve. News*, 30 Dec. 1899, 33:35, pt. 2, 16/2–4; comments by Apostle Matthias F. Cow-ley in Rudger Clawson Diaries, 25 Aug. 1900, box 4, bk. 12; and Joseph F. Smith in Rudger Clawson Diaries, 6 Jan. 1901, box 4, bk. 13, both in Rudger Clawson Collection, Special Collections, UU, 184; Joseph W. Muss-er Diaries, 8 July 1901, LDS Archives; and bishopric member Newell K. Young in Pacheco Ward, Mexican Mission, 26 June 1904, LDS Archives.

[60] Apostle Abraham O. Woodruff, a post-1890 polygamist, told a church conference in Mexico in 1900 that "no year will ever pass, whether it be in this country [Mexico], in India, or wherever, from now until the coming of the Saviour, when children will not be born in plural marriage. And I make this prophecy in the name of Jesus Christ." Quoted by conference clerk Joseph Charles Bentley in "Journal and Notes," 18–19 Nov. 1900, LDS Archives, 61. This was almost identical to what Marriner W. Merrill, another apostle, said a year earlier as recorded in Rudger Clawson Diaries, 11 July 1899, box 4, bk. 11, Special Collections, UU, 39.

Commitment to the Principle remained so great that polygamous marriages after 1890 involving common lay members, bishops, stake presidents,
and apostles were approved and solemnized in the hundreds.[61] The leaders
were not insensitive to the risks such activity brought. But rather than allow
the practice to lapse, First Presidency members George Q. Cannon, Lorenzo
Snow, and Wilford Woodruff went so far as to say that until polygamy could
again be openly practiced, worthy men may need to resort to less formal
arrangements, entering secret, privately agreed-upon relationships with
deserving women. Here, as with post-Manifesto polygamy generally, it is not
deceit but intense devotion to the Principle that deserves notice.

ABRAHAM HOAGLAND CANNON JOURNALS,
5 APRIL 1894, UPB, 18:70–71.

Father [George Q. Cannon] now spoke of the unfortunate condition of the
people at present in regard to marriage. A man in Pima [Arizona] married
the widow of a deceased brother. He did not realize till after the Manifesto
was passed his true condition. Now he is raising seed to his dead friend, while
he himself is likely to be left without posterity. Then there are men whose
wives are barren, and are likely to be without representatives in the earth. Young
widows are left with the alternative of marrying Gentiles, or remaining single all their lives. It seems that something will have to be done sooner or later
to remedy these conditions. My son David died without seed, and his brothers cannot do a work for him, in rearing children to bear his name because of
the Manifesto. I believe in concubinage, or some plan whereby men and women
can live together under sacred ordinances and vows until they can be married.
Thus our surplus girls can be cared for, and the law of God to multiply and
replenish the earth be fulfilled. There is the danger of wicked men taking license
from such a condition, and of good people taking offense thereat, but such
a condition would have to be kept secret, untill the laws of our government
change to permit the holy order of wedlock which God has revealed, which
will undoubtedly occur at no distant day, in order to correct the social evil.
I do not say that this plan is the right one, but I appeal to the Lord to reveal
what will be right in the matter to avert threatened evils.—Pres. [Lorenzo]
Snow. "I have no doubt but concubinage will yet be practiced in this Church,
but I had not thought of it in this connection. When the nations are troubled good women will come here for safety and blessing, and men will accept
them as concubines."—Pres. Woodruff: "If men enter into some practice of

---

[61] The most complete listing so far assembled, amounting to 262 new plural marriages between 1890
and 1910, is that contained in Hardy, *Solemn Covenant*, Appendix II, 389–426. Also see Quinn, "LDS Church
Authority and New Plural Marriages," 9–105.

this character to raise a righteous posterity, they will be justified in it. The day is near when there will be no difficulty in the way of good men securing noble wives. There are terrible afflictions at the door of this nation which will take their minds away from this people."

Post-Manifesto plural rites were often performed beyond the nation's borders or at sea. A literal reading of the Manifesto was thought to permit polygamous marriages in nations like Mexico, where it was assumed they were not against the law. Plural ceremonies on water could be accepted as consistent with Woodruff's advice not to marry in violation of the laws of the "land." While such glosses may have satisfied some, these interpretations were without legal foundation. Not only did laws in both Mexico and Canada prohibit polygamous marriage, but locations on territorial waters where such unions are known to have occurred, as between Los Angeles and Catalina Island, were subject to many of the same limitations as those on land.[62]

It is true that Mexican authorities displayed greater lenience toward polygamists than anything the Saints experienced in either the U.S. or Canada. Juarez Stake president Anthony W. Ivins told priesthood members in 1899 that he had authority to seal couples and that such ceremonies could be performed even though no temple existed in Mexico.[63] The large majority of post-Manifesto plural marriages were performed there and participants were advised to remain south of the border.

Anson Bowen Call (1863–1958) provided an example when President Woodruff gave him permission to enter plural marriage after the Manifesto. Call was living in the Mormon settlement of Star Valley, Wyoming, when he and Miss Harriet Cazier became engaged. Call had previously married Mary T. Thompson in 1885. His marriage to Harriet Cazier on 11 December 1890, two months after President Woodruff's declaration, was thus a post-Manifesto union. Subsequently, he married Dora Pratt on 11 March 1898 and Julia Sarah Abegg on 21 January 1903 as plural wives. Call served for forty years as a bishop in the Mexican colonies and was the father of twenty-five children.[64]

---

[62] For legal circumstances affecting Mormon plural marriage in Mexico, Canada, and maritime locations, see Hardy, *Solemn Covenant*, 167–82, 221–22.

[63] Stake quarterly priesthood meeting, 22 July 1899, General Minutes, Colonia Juarez Mexico Stake, bk. E, 1901–1906, LDS Archives, 77. Also see the entirety of the memoir by Ivins's son, Heber Grant Ivins, Polygamy in Mexico, Special Collections, UU.

[64] President Heber J. Grant and J. Reuben Clark Jr. recognized Call's faithfulness in a special letter of commendation on 20 Oct. 1944. Copy in possession of B. Carmon Hardy.

LIFE STORY OF ANSON BOWEN CALL (1954), LDS ARCHIVES, 2.

I was taught all my life, the principles of plural marriage, and accordingly in 1888 I became engaged to Harriet Cazier. I took her to the Logan Temple, where she received her endowments, but they informed us that they could not perform any more plural marriages, as the Temples might be confiscated if they did. . . I talked to Brother Merriner W. Merrill, president of the Temple, who told me that he was awaiting instructions on such matters, and told me that he would write to me and let me know what he learned: but that if I did not hear from him within a month or so, to write and remind him—not to mention it specifically, but just to ask about the matter we were talking about.[65] So in a month I wrote him and he answered and said he had heard nothing, but referred me to President George Q. Cannon, a counselor to the President of the Church. I was still living in Wyoming and hence it was very difficult to get in touch with the authorities in Salt Lake. So after trying several times to contact Brother Cannon, without success, I went to President Wilford Woodruff, President of the Church. He advised me to go into Mexico, and also advised me to sell all my property, because, he said, "If you leave a nest egg, the old hen is pretty apt to come back." Accordingly I sold my property in Wyoming and Utah, and took my wife, and three daughters, and Hattie, my wife-to-be, and started to Mexico, leaving Salt Lake City on November 27, 1890. . .

[After traveling to the international border by rail, then on to the Mormon colony of Colonia Diaz], On December 10, Hattie and I caught a ride . . . into Colonia Juarez. . . We arrived in Juarez on the evening of December 11, and went immediately to the home of Brother A. F. Macdonald, to whom my note of recognition from President Wilford Woodruff was addressed.[66] We found him out cutting kindling for the fire, and when told who we were, he said, "O yes, I've been expecting you." I showed him the note of recognition, but he said he did not need that.[67]

He took us up to his home . . . and without even giving us time to wash, stood up and married and sealed us for time and eternity. Hattie, of course,

---

[65] Apostle Marriner Wood Merrill stated in a meeting of the First Presidency and apostles in 1891 that he did not view the Manifesto as a revelation. Rather, he said, it was "formulated by Prest. Woodruff and endorsed by His Councilors and the Twelve Apostles for expediency to meet the present situation of affairs in the Nation or those against the Church." Marriner Wood Merrill Journals, 20 Aug. 1891, LDS Archives. See reference to this same discussion in A. H. Cannon Journals, 20 Aug. 1891, UPB, 15:37–38.

[66] Alexander Finlay Macdonald (1825–1903) was a Mormon convert from Scotland. As a polygamist he relocated his families to the Mormon colonies in Mexico during the 1880s. There he was appointed to various ecclesiastical offices, including stake patriarch. Except for two or three others, Macdonald seems to have solemnized more post-Manifesto plural marriages than anyone else in the church. See Hardy, *Solemn Covenant*, 168.

[67] Examples of such letters, especially after Anthony W. Ivins became stake president of the colonies in 1896, are George Q. Cannon to Ivins, 27 Dec. 1897, Anthony Woodward Ivins Collection, box 5, fd. 10, Uhi; and George Q. Cannon to Ivins, 1 Feb. 1898, box 107, fd. 13, George A. Smith Family Papers, Special Collections, UU. Victor W. Jorgensen first discovered these letters and brought them to my attention.

was very disappointed, as she, like any other girl, desired to be married in her wedding dress, which she had carried with her from Utah.[68]

Charles Edmund Richardson took a third plural wife in 1904. His daughter recalled how Anthony W. Ivins, stake president in the Mormon colonies of northern Mexico, performed the ceremony.[69]

[GWEN] ELVA RICHARDSON SHUMWAY,
INTERVIEWED BY LEONARD R. GROVER, 25 APRIL 1980,
MESA, ARIZONA, 7–9, OHP.

[Shumway]: Here again, he [Charles Edmund Richardson] received a mission call. It was to have been to England. Then, likely [because] of his mastery of the Spanish language, it was changed. He was called to become a lawyer in order to protect the rights of the Saints in Mexico.

So, he arranged with a Brother [William] Black to run the mill, and moved Mama [Caroline Rebecca Jacobson] back into town. He took Aunt Sade [Sarah Louisa Adams] and her two little girls, Hazel and Alta, and went by train to Mexico City. Here he completed the four year law course in two years and was graduated from the University of Mexico...

Finally, he felt he would have to separate the families, as he needed a home nearer Casas Grandes sixty miles to the south. This is where many of his cases had to be tried if he defended the more southern colonists. So Papa decided to have one of the families move to Juarez. Aunt Sade consented to go. It worked out nicely so that he had this home when he was down there. Here, a year or two later he became interested in Daisie Stout. The Stouts all admired my father a great deal. They were very agreeable to this marriage but time was running out. He didn't have the time to really come back and talk it over with Mama and Aunt Sarah because President Ivins told him that if he was going to marry that he would have to do it now. The Church was stopping polygamy. He [Anthony W. Ivins] still had the sealing power, but it was going to be taken...

G[rover]: This was about 1903?

S[humway]: No, this would have been early 1904. It was probably just weeks or days before the Second Manifesto.[70] They were married on March 12, 1904. David, her oldest son, was born in September of 1906.

G: Did your father then receive permission only from President Ivins?

S: As far as I know that was all he needed. President Ivins had the sealing power and he had been commissioned to perform these marriages. He had

---

[68] Not only is this a further example that Mormon marriage ceremonies at that time could be performed anywhere, but it shows the brevity of the ritual. Brigham H. Roberts once said it took about two minutes. *Proceedings*, 1:743.

[69] Gwen Elva Richardson Shumway was the daughter of Charles Edmund Richardson (1858–1925) and his plural wife, Caroline Rebecca Jacobson (1872–1945). Charles Edmund Richardson's polygamous experience was used in Chapter Four.

[70] President Joseph F. Smith's 1904 declaration, discussed below.

the right and the authority to do so which he had been doing for years. But after the Church clamped down on it, he no longer had the power. It was taken from everyone at this time.

G. Did you ever ask your father how this related, then, with the 1890 Manifesto where the Church said there would be no more polygamist marriages and how it was that they were still marrying down in Mexico?

S: I was a little bit too immature I suppose, to think to ask my father. I wasn't that interested then in it. His first three marriages were performed before 1890. I have been told and, of course, others from down there including President Ivins interpreted it that it applied to where it was against the law of the land. I think up in Canada it was practiced. It wasn't against the law there and down in Mexico it wasn't. They had asked the president of Mexico, Porfirio Diaz, if it was permissible. He said, "to the government of Mexico it doesn't matter whether a man drives his team tandem or single."[71] It was all right for them to have plural wives. So what I've always heard in my youth and all the time is that there were the two manifestos. They speak of the first manifesto and then they speak of the second manifesto when it was completely cut off. Then it was that Apostle [George] Teasdale, and I believe Taylor, were cut off from the Church, whereas Anthony W. Ivins became a member of the first presidency.[72]

G: [Matthias F.] Cowley and [John W.] Taylor.

S: You're right. Cowley and Taylor were disfellowshipped or cut off because they went ahead and assumed the authority and did it anyway. That is my understanding of it. If Anthony W. Ivins had done wrong in performing the plural marriages he did, he would never have been put in the First Presidency afterwards.[73]

Scores of approved post-1890 polygamous sealings also occurred in the U.S., as with George Mousley Cannon, who took two sisters as plural wives in 1901. One of them, Ellen Steffensen Cannon (1877–1963), recalled these events in a 1953 letter to her niece.[74]

---

[71] Both Canada and Mexico made formal, bigamous marriage illegal. Mexican authorities, as explained in Chapter Eight, were more tolerant than Canadian officials toward informal marital arrangements such as those of the Mormons. For further discussion of legal questions in both countries, see Hardy, "Mormon Polygamy in Mexico and Canada," 186–209; and idem, *Solemn Covenant*, 173–82.

[72] President Joseph F. Smith's 1904 proclamation and the Taylor-Cowley resignations from the Quorum of Twelve Apostles are discussed below.

[73] President Joseph F. Smith ordained Anthony Woodward Ivins (1852–1934) an apostle in 1907. He was sustained as a counselor to President Heber J. Grant in 1921.

[74] For an interview with Katherine C. Thomas (1902–1993) in which she confirms the post-Manifesto marriage of her mother and father and tells of efforts to keep it secret, including her use of an alias as an elementary school child, see her oral interview by Leonard Grover, 25 Mar. 1980, Provo, Utah, OHP, 3–4. Katherine Cannon Thomas was born on 9 September 1902 in Apostle Matthias Cowley's home in Preston, Idaho. She was the daughter of Katherine Vaughn Morris (1876–1930), who married George Mousley Cannon (1861–1937) as a plural wife on 7 August 1901.

ELLEN CHRISTINA STEFFENSEN CANNON TO KATHERINE CANNON THOMAS,
28 DEC. 1953, PHOTOCOPY AND TYPESCRIPT,
LEONARD J. ARRINGTON PAPERS, BOX 78, FD. 4, LAHA.

Dear Kathrine [Katherine],

So glad to hear from you and happy that you wish to know about your mother's life. . .

On 17 of June 1900 I was married to George M. Cannon[75] in a room that was dedicated by church apostles for the purpose of plural marriage in constitution Bldg.[76] A short time later your mother was married to him by Apostle Matthew [Matthias] Cowley in same place.

When your mother became pregnant she was sent to Preston, Idaho to home of Mrs. Luella Cowley to be cared for during your birth.[77] A short time later I went up there for same purpose. Your father bot a small house across street from Mrs. Cowley's & she <Kate> & I moved into it. . . The country was worked up over polygame & Debate was on in <U.S.> senate over Reed Smoot. He was accused of polygamy but was not. They tried to keep him out.

The day after Ellen's birth,[78] your mother, you and her mother was sent down to Mexico. Ever so many other women went. Aunt Margeret,[79] most important to us, was there & you folks got an apartment in with her. I stayed in Preston for a year. By then the Church decided it best to stop polygamy. . .

"EXPLICIT AND OFFENSIVE VIOLATION": CRITICISM REVIVES

Rumors of continued plural marriage soon raised a new storm of anti-Mormon protest. Men like Theodore Schroeder and Charles Mostyn Owen clamored for prosecution of those guilty of such relationships, accusing the church

---

[75] George Mousley Cannon married Marian Adelaide Morris as his first wife on Christmas Day, 1884. Regarding Ellen's marriage, one of her brothers later told Stanley Ivins that Ellen had refused to marry Cannon as a plural wife unless Joseph F. Smith performed the marriage. He consented and married the couple in 1900. Alarmed by Smith's denials during the Smoot hearings, Ellen had her brother ask Smith about the validity of her sealing to Cannon. According to Ivins, President Smith said that the marriage was indeed valid but that "he had had to say what he did in Washington to protect the Church." Copy, Stanley Snow Ivins Diary, 29 Nov. [?], cited in Leonard J. Arrington Papers, box 78, fd. 4, LAHA.

[76] The Constitution Building, designed by noted Utah architect Richard Kletting, stood at 34 South Main in Salt Lake City, across the street from ZCMI. Zions Securities, the real-estate arm of the LDS church, razed the building in 1977.

[77] Luella Parkinson Cowley (1870–1962), a plural wife of Apostle Matthias F. Cowley.

[78] Ellen Steffensen Cannon, daughter of George M. and Ellen S. Cannon, was born on 8 December 1902.

[79] Margaret Peart (1869–1944) married John Mousley Cannon as a plural wife on 18 July 1900.

of breaking its promises to the nation.[80] The Brigham H. Roberts case not only baited those like Schroeder and Owen who were eager to publicize Mormon transgression, but cranked the issue into a controversy of national proportions. Roberts, a general authority of the LDS church and a polygamist, apparently took an additional plural wife in 1894.[81] In the autumn of 1898 he was elected to Congress as a representative from Utah. Schroeder, Owen, women's organizations, the Hearst press, and congressmen posturing as moral shields pilloried Roberts as a threat to the American home. The church's new president, Lorenzo Snow, publicly denied reports of a polygamous revival and assured the nation that the Saints were yet faithful to pledges made by Snow's predecessor, Wilford Woodruff.

"MORMON HEAD TO THE WORLD,"
NEW YORK WORLD, 30 DEC. 1898, 39:4, 177/4.

Salt Lake City. Dec. 29.—I declare most solemnly and emphatically that statements that the Mormon Church is encouraging the teaching of polygamy are utterly untrue. Ever since the issuance of the manifesto on this subject by President Wilford Woodruff, my predecessor in office, polygamy or plural marriages have entirely ceased in Utah.

The implied understanding with the nation when Utah entered the Union as a State has been sacredly observed. . .

There have been no polygamous marriages since 1890. There is no movement in the Church for the revival of such unions. . .[82]

LORENZO SNOW

Such statements, replicating denials of the 1880s, persuaded few, and Roberts's accusers succeeded in excluding him from the national legislature, calling his election "an explicit and offensive violation" of the terms under which Utah was admitted as a state.[83]

---

[80] Schroeder, a Gentile lawyer in Salt Lake City, commenced a series of fusillades against the church in 1897 that continued through 1898. These appeared in his periodical, Kinsman. See, for example: "Polygamy and Inspired Lies," Kinsman 1:18 (29 Jan. 1898), 2, et seq. For an overview, see Brudnoy, "Decade in Zion," 241–56; and idem, "Of Sinners and Saints," 261–78. On Owen, see Hardy, Solemn Covenant, 246–47.

[81] Some of what fueled attacks on Roberts came from an article by journalist Eugene Young, a grandson of Brigham Young. In 1899 he identified several post-Manifesto marriages, including that of Brigham H. Roberts. Young, "Revival of the Mormon Problem," 476–89.

[82] Snow made an almost identical declaration one year later, in "Reminiscences of the Prophet Joseph Smith," Des. Eve. News, 23 Dec. 1899, 36:29, 17/3.

[83] "Special Committee on the Case of Brigham H. Roberts, Case of Brigham H. Roberts of Utah," House Report 85, 2 pts. (56-1) 1900, Serial 4021, 1:2–3, 11–12, 40–45. Literature on the Roberts case is extensive. Bunker and Bitton, Mormon Graphic Image, 60–64, review cartoons and other images surrounding the event. Other works are Bitton, "B. H. Roberts Case," 27–46; and White Jr., "The Feminist Campaign for the Exclusion of Brigham Henry Roberts," 44–52. Roberts provided his own account in Comprehensive History, 6:363–74.

Attention to continued performance of Mormon plural marriages in the 1890s was a prelude to conflict over the subject, both in and outside the church, for the next two decades. Calls for a constitutional amendment prohibiting polygamy were revived, and between 1899 and the outbreak of World War I the movement for such a measure acquired widespread support. Rumor that church leaders agreed to secure Mormon votes for Republican candidates in exchange for their opposition to the amendment, whether true or false, failed to diminish enthusiasm for the proposal.[84] References were again made to Mormon resurrection of the "twin relic of barbarism." The Saints, Josiah Strong said, were rapidly spreading beyond the Rocky Mountains and carrying their "oriental barbarism" with them.[85] Democrats, anxious not to be left behind as they were a half-century before, demanded in their 1904 national platform that polygamy be exterminated everywhere in the United States.[86]

Renewed criticism of the church provoked disagreements among First Presidency members and apostles themselves. Differences between Apostle Abraham O. Woodruff, a son of former president Wilford Woodruff, and President Lorenzo Snow illustrate how youthful authorities were sometimes more committed to perpetuation of the Principle than their veteran leaders.

A. O. WOODRUFF JOURNALS, 11 JAN. 1900,
ABRAHAM OWEN WOODRUFF COLLECTION, BOX 1, FD. 2,
L. TOM PERRY SPECIAL COLLECTIONS, UPB, 175–76.

We partook of the bread and wine, emblems of our Master's body and blood. After the Lord's supper Prest. Snow said: so far as I am concerned no plural marriages can be entered into anywhere; in Mexico or elsewhere. John Henry Smith made a speach in absolute discouragement of the practice anywhere. Prest. Cannon moved we accept Prest. Snow's words as the "word of the Lord" it was seconded and again without any chance to express our feelings—and judgment were forced to sustain a motion that some of us were opposed to or be out of harmony with our brethren. I felt forced to sustain this motion and that is why I did it, knowing that if it were not right the responsibility would not rest on me. I absolutely know that a number of the brethren, among them John W. Taylor, Geo. Teasdale and M[atthias] F. Cowley entertained feelings in harmony with my own. I owe my existence to the principle of Polygamy and I have some intense feelings regarding the sustaining of that principle. I am indebted to that principle for my life and any time my Father wants my

---

[84] "Rumor" of such an arrangement is discussed in Arrington and Bitton, *Mormon Experience*, 247.

[85] As quoted in *Amendments to the Constitution Prohibiting Polygamy . . .* , House Doc. 2307 (55-3), 19 Feb. 1899, Serial 3841, 15.

[86] Johnson and Porter, comps., *National Party Platforms*, 133.

life to defend that principle (and those who practice it in righteousness) God being my helper it is at his command. Prest. Brigham Young [Jr.] came to my desk at the close and said, "Bro. Woodruff I want to tell you that the time is not far distant when the question of Polygamy will be changed and practiced again." I said I will hold you responsible for that remark Br. Young. He answered: "You may"![87] Apostle M[arriner] W. Merrill in yesterday's meeting prophesied that "the time will never come in this Church when polygamist children will not be born." I pray God to give me light on this matter as I feel almost sick about it. I want to and intend to be loyal to my Chief.

"They Charge Us With Being Dishonest": Reed Smoot and a Second Manifesto

Controversy erupted again when Apostle Reed Smoot, a monogamist, entered the U.S. Senate in 1903. So much had been said about the revival of polygamy in connection with the Brigham H. Roberts case that Smoot was almost immediately challenged with the expectation that he too could be denied his congressional seat.[88] A long investigation found the church had indeed continued to perform plural marriages after the 1890 Manifesto. While Smoot was found innocent of charges that he was a polygamist, some church leaders refused to give testimony at the hearings, others were caught in their inconsistencies, and several used outright falsehoods. President Joseph F. Smith was one of the latter.[89] Shortly after the church president's testimony, Senator-elect Smoot frankly described to Smith the immense distrust felt by national leaders concerning Mormon honesty. Smoot urged that something be done to reassure the world that the LDS church had indeed discontinued both new polygamous marriages and cohabitation with the wives of older ones.[90] Within weeks

---

[87] Apostle Brigham Young Jr. consistently championed plural marriage and took a post-Manifesto polygamous spouse of his own. Hardy, *Solemn Covenant*, 207–8.

[88] Sears, "Punishing the Saints," 647–50; and Holsinger, "For God and the American Home," 154–60.

[89] As with other church leaders who testified before Congress, Smith attempted to answer the committee as evasively as possible. Still, he stated that he had no knowledge of polygamous marriages performed after 1878 and denied that new plural marriages had occurred anywhere in the world since the Manifesto. He even said that he had not heard anyone advocate or recommend plural marriage since the 1890 Manifesto. *Proceedings*, 1:102, 143, 177, 178, 184, 211, 317–18, 485.

[90] The belief that Mormons were disingenuous concerning polygamy "permeated the whole Senate . . . and I must admit that it is the hardest thing that I have had to meet in life," Smoot told the church president. He had, he said, thought, prayed and "worried . . . [about it] until I can hardly sleep." Smoot to Smith, 23 Mar. 1904, Reed Smoot Collection, box 50, fd. 4, UPB. Other authorities also felt something had to be done to restore Mormon credibility. A. H. Lund Diaries, 2 April 1904, Anthon Hendrik Lund Collection, LDS Archives.

of his embarrassing performance on the witness stand in Washington, D.C., President Smith made an effort to redeem both his and the church's reputation by issuing the following declaration at Mormonism's semi-annual conference on 6 April 1904.

"General Conference of the Church of Jesus Christ of Latter Day Saints . . . Third Day," Seventy-Fourth Annual Conference of the Church . . . , 75–76.[91]

OFFICIAL STATEMENT

Inasmuch as there are numerous reports in circulation that plural marriages have been entered into contrary to the official declaration of President Woodruff, of September 26, 1890, commonly called the Manifesto, which was issued by President Woodruff and adopted by the Church at its general conference, October 6, 1890, which forbade any marriage violative of the law of the land; I, Joseph F. Smith, President of the Church of Jesus Christ of Latter-day Saints, hereby affirm and declare that no such marriages have been solemnized with the sanction, consent or knowledge of the Church of Jesus Christ of Latter-day Saints, and

I hereby announce that all such marriages are prohibited, and if any officer or member of the Church shall assume to solemnize or enter into any such marriage he will be deemed in transgression against the Church and will be liable to be dealt with according to the rules and regulations thereof, and excommunicated therefrom.

Joseph F. Smith,
President of the Church of Jesus Christ of Latter-day Saints. . .

They charge us with being dishonest and untrue to our word. They charge the Church with having violated a "compact," and all this sort of nonsense. I want to see today whether the Latter-day Saints representing the Church in this solemn assembly will not seal these charges as false by their vote. . .

The resolution was then adopted, by unanimous vote of the Conference.

While the 1904 declaration said nothing new, President Smith did take steps that distanced the church further from its polygamous past. He pri-

---

[91] President Smith's 1904 declaration was conspicuously framed in the upper center of the *Des. Eve. News*, 6 April 1904, 1/3–5. The statement, sometimes called the "Second Manifesto," has been interpreted as bringing a stop to unauthorized individuals who entered plural marriages after the Woodruff Manifesto. But authorized plural marriages continued to occur after 1904. See Hardy, *Solemn Covenant*, 311–35. Smith's 1904 declaration has also been described as extending the 1890 Woodruff Manifesto to all the world. Not only had Wilford Woodruff already stated that the 1890 Manifesto applied to church members everywhere, but Smith himself admitted this only weeks before in testimony before Congress. *Proceedings* 1:107–8. Inasmuch as the 1904 address provided no substantive advance over previous statements, it is best seen as an attempt to refurbish the church's image owing to impressions left by Smith and others at the Smoot hearings in Washington, D.C.

vately sent word to apostles and others withdrawing authority for performing new plural marriages, at least for the time being, and directed that no sealings be performed outside the temples.[92] Increasingly, men appointed to the Quorum of Twelve Apostles and other offices of the church were monogamous.[93] Most dramatically, two high leaders, Apostles Matthias F. Cowley and John W. Taylor, were asked to resign from the Quorum because they continued to perform plural marriages and refused to appear as witnesses at the Smoot hearings.[94] None of this, however, lessened criticism of the church. Mormonism's image reached its nadir in 1906 when Pres. Theodore Roosevelt called again for the nation to amend the constitution to criminalize polygamy everywhere.[95] Eventually, Smoot was accepted into the Senate and led the way in reversing the church's long-standing opposition to an anti-polygamy amendment by supporting the measure.[96]

Near this same time, church authorities formalized the already-evolving contention that eternal marriage, not polygamy, was the primary requirement imposed by the 1843 revelation. One of Mormonism's most favored spokesmen, Apostle James Talmage, wrote that plurality was not a "vital tenet" of the church. Neither had it been in the past. It was, he said, but "an incident," never an "essential" of the church's teachings.[97] This was formally communicated to church members in connection with a 1914 circular reiterating the

---

[92] Steps were taken in this direction as early as 1901. But they became more insistent after President Smith's testimony in the Smoot hearings and the subsequent 1904 "Official Statement." For evidence of these changes, see John Henry Smith in John Henry Smith Journals, 1874–1875, 1880–1911, bk. 25, 27 May 1901, George A. Smith Family Papers, Special Collections, UU, 297; John Henry Smith again, in *Proceedings*, 2:295–96; comments of Apostle John W. Taylor, in General Minutes, Colonia Juarez Mexico Stake, bk. E, 1901–1906, 7 Mar. 1903, LDS Archives, 82; Lund Diaries, 18 June 1904, LDS Archives; and Catherine S. Brown, interview, OHP, 12. At the same time, some authorities told church members that curbs on "Celestial marriage" were temporary only. See Apostle George Teasdale, in General Minutes, Historical Record, Juarez Stake, 13 Mar. 1904, LDS Archives, 129.

[93] To assist Senator-elect Smoot, lists were prepared demonstrating the increase in monogamous as opposed to polygamous leaders in the church between 1890 and 1906. George F. Gibbs to Reed Smoot, 7 Jan. 1907, Clark, ed., *Messages*, 4:135–38.

[94] After tendering their resignations from the Quorum in late 1905, Apostles John W. Taylor and Matthias F. Cowley were again called before that body in 1911 for investigation. Taylor was excommunicated and Cowley restricted in use of his priesthood. A transcript of the hearing is in Collier and Knuteson, "Trials of Apostle John W. Taylor and Matthias F. Cowley." Also see Jorgensen and Hardy, "'That Same Old Question of Polygamy and Polygamous Living,'" 436.

[95] See Roosevelt's Sixth Annual Message of 3 Dec. 1906 in, Hagedorn, *Works*, 15:377.

[96] Smoot, "Passing of Polygamy," 117–23. For the pivotal role the Smoot hearings and the abandonment of polygamy played in the transformation of Mormonism, see all of Flake, *Politics of Religious Identity*.

[97] Talmage, *Story of "Mormonism,"* 89. Also see Evans, *One Hundred Years*, 476–77.

church's opposition to new plural marriages.[98] And despite continued, secret approval of plural unions by some leaders, others undertook a formal inquiry into how such marriages still occurred.[99] Together, these events constitute a closing phase in the church's retreat from the Principle. For many Saints, however, it was a time of confusion. Alternating between covert allegiance to polygamy and policies designed to give evidence that they had given it up, Mormonism appeared to some to be going in two directions at once.[100]

Displeasure with church directives discouraging plural marriage is visible in the diary of Ammon M. Tenney, a pluralist in the Mormon colonies of Mexico.[101] Discussing the refuge Mexican soil provided for continued polygamous cohabitation, he believed the new policies, by narrowing the choices young women could make, were driving them into unions with less-worthy suitors. The document also attests to the changed policy requiring that marriage sealings were henceforth to occur only in the church's temples.

AMMON M. TENNEY DIARY, 25 APRIL AND 4 MAY 1905,
BK. 3, FD. 4, AMMON M. TENNEY COLLECTION,
ARIZ. ST. HIST. SOC., TUCSON, ARIZ., 67–68.

25 May [April] 1905

. . . It Must be understood that all this [criticism of continued cohabitation with plural wives since the Manifesto] Pertains only within the lines of the American Government for here in Mexico we are enjoying all the Privileges that Has been established by our Prophets in the Past until recently the Marriage Power has been taken entirely So that no Cealing Can be Solemnized *whatsoever* a Condition to be Much regretted for our young to go So far to reach a Temple and what is Much worse when the extensive range in which Many good opportunities are open

---

[98] In a circular to stake presidents and counselors dated 31 Jan. 1914, the First Presidency stated that: "Celestial marriage—that is, marriage for time and eternity—and polygamous or plural marriage are not synonymous terms. Monogamous marriages for time and eternity, solemnized in our temples in accordance with the word of the Lord and the laws of the Church, are Celestial marriages." Clark, ed., *Messages*, 5:326. Deliberations and decision by apostles on the matter are read in a typewritten extract from a meeting of the twelve apostles, 17 Feb. 1908, Stanley Snow Ivins Collection, box 11, fd. 10, Uhi.

[99] Cloistered efforts to perpetuate plurality while publicly making attempts to end it, including inquisitions by a committee chaired by Apostle Francis M. Lyman, are described and documented in Hardy, *Solemn Covenant*, 290, 310–29.

[100] See remarks of Annie Clark Tanner, *Mormon Mother*, 223; and the memories of Juliaetta Bateman Jensen, in *Little Gold Pieces*, 134–36.

[101] Ammon Meshach Tenney (1844–1925) was a widely respected Mormon frontiersman who spoke Spanish and several Indian languages. He was a missionary to the Indians, a mission president in Mexico, and served time in the Detroit House of Correction for polygamous cohabitation.

May 4th [*sic*]

And it is becoming a daily occurance to witness the Most accomplished young Ladies accept the Hand of young Men Much their inferior & from a Moral & intellectual Stand Point entirely unworthy but too often not having any other opportunity they launch forth upon lifes journey Shrouded with a Spirit of dispondency and only to often to regret at their leasure the step taken while in a State of emotion

"The Mormon Game": The Magazine Crusade

Sensing Mormon equivocation and keen to expose scandal, muckraking journalists flocked to the topic for saleable and salacious stories.[102] Unaware of the tortured nature of the shift occurring inside the church, Burton Hendrick, a journalist studying the scene, called once more for a constitutional amendment as the only way to assure that the Mormon problem would not emerge again.

> Burton J. Hendrick, "Mormon Revival of Polygamy,"
> *McClure's Magazine* 36:4 (Feb. 1911), 449–64.
> What is the official attitude of the Mormon Church toward these evidences that new polygamy exists—that, in hundreds of cases, the Woodruff revelation has been ignored? . . . The church officials now admit that polygamous marriages have taken place, but they deny that such marriages have ecclesiastical sanction. In other words, the Mormon Church is no longer able to control its people. Polygamy is so thoroughly inbred that even a revelation from God can not extirpate it. These new marriages, declare president Smith and his associates, are not performed in the Mormon temples, nor by any regularly authorized Mormon elders. . .
> The anti-Mormon view is that this public repudiation of polygamy is simply a part of the Mormon game. . . The Mormon policy is secretly to promote and encourage polygamy, and outwardly to repudiate it. . .
> . . . there is only one way in which the American people can control the situation. In the old days, when Utah was a Territory, Congress could pass anti-polygamy laws, and the federal government could send its officers into Utah to enforce them. It cannot do this now, because Utah is a State, and the States, under our system of government, have exclusive jurisdiction over the

---

[102] Commencing with "Some New Polygamists," *Salt Lake Tribune*, 13 Nov. 1909, 80:30, 6/3–4, articles appeared in *Everybody's, Cosmopolitan, Collier's,* and elsewhere. While exaggeration occurred, they could also be surprisingly accurate. Attacks on the Mormons flared at the same time in Great Britain. See Thorp, "'Mormon Peril,'" 69–88; and Vousden, "English Editor and the 'Mormon Scare' of 1911," 65–75.

marriage relation. The only way in which the American people can reach polygamy is for them to pass a constitutional amendment giving Congress power to legislate against it. With such an amendment, the federal government could again send its officers into Utah and the other Mormon communities and punish the offenders. If this amendment is adopted, one of two things will happen: either the Mormon Church will abandon polygamy, not only ostensibly, but actually, or it will migrate bodily into some other country—probably Mexico.

THE DECLINE OF MORMON POLYGAMY

Hendrick underestimated not only the growing thirst of Mormon leaders for national approval, but the extent to which compromise had already carried them. By the outbreak of World War I, and certainly with the death of Joseph F. Smith in 1918, officially approved new polygamous marriages virtually ceased and those who had entered such arrangements in earlier years were succumbing to age. Claims of discontinuance made from the 1880s through the time of President Joseph F. Smith's administration gradually congealed into fact. More than one Mormon apostle expressed fear that, step by step, the church was moving toward abandonment of the Principle altogether.[103] It was a process that Utah commissioner John A. McClernand remarked on to Pres. Grover Cleveland: "the more often . . . [they] commit themselves, whether regularly or irregularly, against polygamy, the more they will have increased the obstacles to a retreat from the path of reform."[104]

By the early 1920s, an American writer who had traversed the land of the Saints for the better part of a half-century declared that not only had Mormons verbally abandoned plurality but neither could he find, he said, "the slightest scintilla of evidence" that its practice was anywhere renewed.[105]

---

[103] This was a major theme in Hardy, *Solemn Covenant*, as illustrated by Apostles Heber J. Grant, John W. Taylor, and Abraham O. Woodruff in ibid., 144, 259, 369–70.

[104] McClernand to Cleveland, 30 June 1887, in Grover Cleveland Papers, ser. 1, film, reel 50, Lib. of Cong.

[105] James, *Utah the Land of Blossoming Valleys*, 134.

Chapter 10

"We are Honor Bound"
The Eclipse of
Officially Approved Polygamy

In the course of their development, most great religions find it necessary to cut away some of the doctrinal overgrowth fed by their early enthusiasm.[1] Polygamy was a victim of the pruning Mormonism undertook to secure moral approval for the church and to establish an orthodoxy acceptable to an expanding membership. At the same time, as Latter-day Saint leaders reconfigured their teachings to more closely resemble American society at large, however complete such reformation may have appeared to an outsider, there were individuals who felt betrayed by the new departures.

Rallied by the high importance given the Principle in the old church, as well as memory of approved plural solemnizations after the 1890 Manifesto, a few votaries replicated the pattern of sect formation that has occurred many times in religious history. When mainline Mormonism shed peculiarities offensive to the surrounding community, some inevitably viewed the accommodation as a surrender to the secular world and pledged themselves, like Mormons of the nineteenth century, to restore the gospel "in its fullness."[2] As Wallace Stegner put it, "there will always be the unreconstructed. Faith is a weed with a long taproot."[3]

---

[1] See, for example, the conforming efforts of early Christian fathers described in Van Biema, "Lost Gospels," 55–61; and the winnowing explored in Pagels's *Gnostic Gospels* and Ehrman's *Lost Christianities*.

[2] This pattern, with secularization playing a central role, received its best-known description in the study of medieval Christianity by Troeltsch, *Social Teaching of the Christian Churches*, 1:328–82. For further commentary on secularization and complexities involved with the church/sect typology, see the chapter "Of Churches, Sects, and Cults," in Stark and Bainbridge, *Future of Religion*, 19–37. And for the question of Mormon accommodation to and identity within American culture, the superb bibliographical essay by Klaus J. Hansen is required reading. See his "Mormon History and the Conundrum of Culture," 1–26.

[3] Stegner, *Mormon Country*, 226.

"A SOLEMN COVENANT":
THE RISE OF MORMON FUNDAMENTALISM

Troubled by the church's march to concord, fundamentalists reprised the Saints' early millenarian preoccupation; again advocated a reproductionist sexual ethic; strongly urged patriarchal rule in the home; and asserted "the principle of plural marriage to be the Law of God while monogamy is generally hellish."[4] This reactionary impetus took support from persons who claimed to have been specially set apart during the late 1880s to keep the practice alive. While President John Taylor was in hiding in the autumn of 1886, he studied a declaration that would suspend the practice of plural marriage as a way to mollify government officials. According to some present, after a night of communication with Jesus Christ and the resurrected Joseph Smith, Taylor defiantly rejected the proposal, dictated a revelation on the subject, and commissioned John W. Woolley, his son Lorin, and others to continue plural marriage even if the church officially set it aside.[5]

As Mormonism intensified its commitment to monogamy during the 1920s, private gatherings of individuals devoted to plurality often rehearsed this story. Joseph Lyman Jessop, one of those persuaded that patriarchal marriage was a vital part of Mormonism and must not be abandoned, provides an example.[6]

DIARY OF JOSEPH LYMAN JESSOP, 1: BK. 7,
28 MAR. 1923, 149–50.

We attended a testamony meeting at Brother Dan[iel Rapalyea] Bateman's where we listened to some of the greatest testamonys I ever heard regarding the doctrines of the church which now are seemingly forbidden. Bro. John [Yates] Barlow was talking when we went in the house. A Bro. [Joseph Leslie] Boadbent, a young man who has been traveling all over the central portion of the United States selling the Radio Phones made here at the plant, bore a great testamony of the signs of the times and said that even the missionaries told him that their success was little and that the days of gleaning was mighty poor pick-

---

[4] Diary of Joseph Lyman Jessop, 1: bk. 8, 1 Feb. 1925, 183. For other examples, see Broadbent, *Celestial Marriage?*; Newson, *Is the Manifesto a Revelation?*; and the experiences of Byron Harvey Allred and Joseph White Musser, best told in Bradley, *Kidnapped from that Land*, 18–26.

[5] The September 1886 revelation was reproduced and discussed in Chapter Eight. The circumstances surrounding it have often been retold. See Allred, *Leaf in Review*, esp. 183–93; Collier, "Re-examining the Lorin Woolley Story," esp. 5–15; and the very readable account by President Taylor's grandson, Samuel W. Taylor, in his *Kingdom or Nothing*, 364–68.

[6] I am indebted to Ms. Marianne T. Watson of Salt Lake City for generously making a copy of this, her grandfather's diary, available to me.

ing. Nathan Baldwin Jr.[7] also spoke well. . . Sister [Alice] Belva Barlow spoke of the womens part in this patriarchal order of marriage and said that if the test came that her standing in the church was threatened if she did not give up her advocating this doctrine and stand by her husband, she said, "I'd tell them to take it quick." Israel Barlow carried the thot further. . . Bro. Dan Bateman then told of his experience with Pres. John Taylor in 1886 and 1887. He said on the night of Sept 26, 1886 after Pres. Taylor had been almost driven wild by communications and letters from Presidents of Stakes, Bishops, and High Councilmen and many members of the church asking and pleading and demanding that something be done to stop the practise of plural marriage, the persecution was so great that Pres. Taylor and other leading Brethren were forced to go about from place to place in hiding because their lives were threatened. While at the home of Bro. John [Wickersham] Wooley in Centerville, Pres. Taylor retired to a room and prayed earnestly to the Lord concerning these trials. While thus engaged, he recieved a revelation; and on the following day, (Sept. 27, 1886) in the presence of 13 people he preached the pure gospel for 8 hours, during which time he told them of his revelation and asked them if they were willing to lay down their lives if need be for this principle and they all agreed they would. Then they entered into a solemn covenant and promised that they would see to it that *not a year should pass without plural marriages being performed and children born under the covenant.* During this 8 hours Pres. Taylor stood in mid-air two feet above the floor and in a halo of light, and while speaking (of the manifesto to stop the practise of plural marriage which was already cunningly schemed and planned and then urged his signature) raised his right arm to the square and said, *"Sign that document—Never! I would suffer my right arm to be severed from my body." "Sanction that document—Never! I would rather my tongue to be torn from its roots."* And shortly after that time men in every Stake in the Church from Canada to Mexico were set apart and authorized to perform plural marriages. Four of that little number at Bro. Wolley's are now living. They are Bro. John Wooley (now 90 years old still living in Centerville and the oldest member in the church), Lorin [Calvin] Wooley, A Bro. [George Wright] Earl and Dan Bateman. Bro. Bateman said, "I testify to this in fulfillment of the covenant I made with President Taylor 37 years ago. And this practise *will never cease."*

Bro. Baldwin then bore a faithful testimony and explained from the 28th chapter of Isiah [*sic*] that the Manifesto was "a covenant with death and an Agreement [with] Hell." It was a good meeting.

---

[7] One of the most interesting personalities associated with efforts to renew the Principle, Nathaniel Baldwin (1878–1961) is always placed near the center of incipient Mormon fundamentalism. Best known for his improvements in sound amplification and founding of the Omega Investment Company, it was also said, "If you were interested in polygamy, Baldwin was interested in you." At the height of his company's success in the early 1920s he had hundreds of employees, numbers of whom, like himself, believed in plural marriage. And he, like most of them, was excommunicated from the church. Singer, "Nathaniel Baldwin," 42–53.

In what has been called a "final Manifesto," Mormonism's First Presidency in 1933 denounced the revival of polygamous marriage by fundamentalists. President Heber Jeddy Grant (1856–1945), a former pluralist, is at the top. His first counselor, Anthony Woodward Ivins (1852–1934), while never practicing the Principle, sealed dozens of plural wives to others after the Manifesto and is below, left. Joshua Reuben Clark Jr. (1871–1961), second counselor and below, right, was primary author of the 1933 statement. *Used by permission, Utah State Historical Society, all rights reserved.*

"Born of the Evil One": The lds Church
Condemns Fundamentalist Polygamy

In the late nineteen-twenties and early thirties those objecting to the church's official course grew in number. The dissenters performed new plural marriages and founded *Truth*, a magazine that gave voice to fundamentalist belief, while boldly criticizing the church for its changed ways.[8] Most who agreed with these views quietly conducted meetings in private homes in and around Salt Lake City, but others established colonies in the high deserts of southern Utah and northern Arizona where they could practice plural marriage openly.[9]

At the same time, jealous of their newly won respectability, Mormon authorities drew a clear line between themselves and those insisting on revival of the Principle. The document most visibly marking separation of the official church from its objecting progeny is the 1933 "Official Statement." Prepared by First Presidency member J. Reuben Clark, the message also reflected a consensus by church leaders that a strong rebuttal of fundamentalist claims was needed.[10] More than any other, this "final Manifesto" formally ended not only espousal of, but all effort to restore the Abrahamic, polygamous household as a family ideal in the official lds church.[11]

"An Official Statement from the First Presidency of
The Church of Jesus Christ of Latter-day Saints,"
Des. News, 17 June 1933, Church Section, 1–4.

The First Presidency have recently received letters making inquiry concerning the position of the Church regarding the contracting of polygamous or plural marriages. It is evident from these letters, as well as certain published material . . . that a secret and, according to reputation, an oath-bound organization of misguided individuals is seeking to lead the people to adopt adulterous relations under the guise of a pretended and false polygamous or plural marriage ceremony.

---

[8] Founded and edited by fundamentalist leader Joseph White Musser, *Truth* magazine was published from 1935 to 1956.

[9] There are several good accounts of Mormon fundamentalist development. See Baer, *Recreating Utopia in the Desert*, 31–42; Driggs, "Twentieth-Century Polygamy," 45-58; idem, "'This Will Someday Be the Head,'" 49–80; Bradley, *Kidnapped from that Land*, 6–47; Quinn, "Plural Marriage and Mormon Fundamentalism," 9–23; Van Wagoner, *Mormon Polygamy*, 177–87; and Watson, "Short Creek: 'A Refuge for the Saints.'"

[10] The most thorough examination of Clark's role in the preparation of the 1933 statement, as well as its problems and consequences, is in Quinn, *Elder Statesman*, 237–54.

[11] Driggs used the phrase, "final Manifesto," in his "Twentieth-Century Polygamy," 46. Clark, ed., *Messages*, 5:194, listed nine earlier statements, all saying that the church no longer permitted plural marriage.

While the position of the Church since 1893 has been repeatedly set forth,[12] namely, that polygamous or plural marriages are not and cannot now be performed, yet in order that there may be no excuse for any Church member to be misled by the false representations or the corrupt, adulterous practices of the members of this secret, and (by reputation) oath-bound organization (of which the history of the Nephites and Lamanites show so many counterparts), it is deemed wise again to set out the position of the Church on this matter. . .

Any ceremony pretending to bind man and woman together beyond the period of mortal life, which is not solemnized by one who has been commissioned and authorized by the man who holds the keys of authority to bind upon earth with a covenant which will be binding in heaven, is of no efficacy or force when people are out of the world.

There is but one person on the earth at a time upon whom the keys of this sealing ordinance are conferred. That man is the Presiding High Priest, the President of the Church. He is the bearer of this authority, which he may exercise personally or he may commission others to exercise it under his jurisdiction, for such time, long or short, up to the end of his life, as he may desire.

It was after the revelation of July 1843, which provided that under certain conditions, which are clearly defined, a man may receive more than one woman to be his wife, that plural marriage became a recognized doctrine of the church. . .

While the practice of plural marriage was severely criticized by the ministers of various religious denominations and others, it was not until 1874 that the Congress of the United States took definite steps looking to the suppression of the practice. . .[13]

[After reviewing anti-polygamy legislation and imprisonment of many of the Saints, the statement continues:] September 24th, 1890, President Woodruff promulgated his official declaration to the Church and people of the United States, commonly referred to as The Manifesto. . .

[The statement next describes the Petition of Amnesty, the Enabling Act, Article III of the state's Constitution, and restoration of the church's properties as further evidence of the church's pledge to discontinue polygamy.] . . . Thus our people sacredly covenanted with the Government of the United States that they would obey the civil law. . .

Notwithstanding this covenant, a few misguided members of the Church, some of whom had been signers of the petition praying for amnesty, and beneficiaries of its provisions, secretly associated themselves together for the avowed

---

[12] The choice of 1893 for the date when the church began forbidding plural marriages, or denying that such marriages were occurring, is but one of many curious features in this address. Church statements to this effect, as shown in Chapter Eight, were made even before the Manifesto of 1890.

[13] The government began taking "definite steps" to suppress polygamy with the Morrill Act of 1862, twelve years before the Poland Law of 1874. See Chapter 6.

purpose of perpetuating the practices of polygamous or plural marriage in defiance of the pledge made to the government. . .[14]

[Next follows a summary of statements made by President Joseph F. Smith in 1904, 1910, and 1914 prohibiting plural marriage and threatening excommunication of those found violating the proscription. The First Presidency also repeated the release divinely given to the Saints from the obligation to build a temple in Jackson County, Missouri owing to vigorous opposition by their neighbors at the time.][15]

This principle [of suspending a divine command when opposition makes its implementation exceedingly difficult] applies to plural marriage as it does to all others of his commandments. . .

It is alleged that on September 26–27, 1886, President John Taylor received a revelation from the Lord, the purported text of which is given in publications circulated apparently by or at the instance of this same organization.

As to this pretended revelation it should be said that the archives of the Church contain no such revelation; the archives contain no record of any such revelation, nor any evidence justifying a belief that any such revelation was ever given. . .[16]

The second allegation made by the organization and its members (as reported) is to the effect that President John Taylor ordained and set apart several men to perform marriage ceremonies . . . and gave to those so allegedly authorized the further power to set others apart to do the same thing.

There is nothing in the records of the Church to show that any such ordination or setting apart was ever performed. There is no recollection or report among the officers of the Church to whom such an incident would of necessity be known, that any such action was ever taken.

Furthermore, any such action would have been illegal and void because the Lord has laid down without qualification the principle that "there is never but one on the earth at a time on whom this power and the keys of this priesthood are conferred."[17] The Lord has never changed this rule. . .

No one better knew this principle regarding authority for this sealing power, than President John Taylor and he would not have attempted to violate it. It is a sacrilege to his memory—the memory of a great and true Latter-day Saint, a prophet of the Lord—that those falsehoods should be broadcast by those who professed to be his friends while he lived. . .

We do not wish to pass judgment upon or evaluate the motives of our fellow men—that is for the Lord to do—but we unqualifiedly say, as it is our

---

[14] As Clark certainly knew at the time, from information provided by President Heber J. Grant and fellow-counselor Anthony W. Ivins, more than only a "few" entered plural marriage in the 1890s and after, including bishops, stake presidents, and apostles. Quinn, *Elder Statesman*, 240–44; Hardy, *Solemn Covenant*, 206–43, and all of ibid., Appendix II.   [15] *D&C* 124:49, 19 Jan. 1841.

[16] Discussion of this revelation is provided in both the present chapter and Chapter Eight.

[17] *D&C* 132:7, 12 July 1843, reproduced and discussed in Chapter One.

right and duty to say, that the doctrines these persons preach and the practices they follow, are born of the Evil One and are contrary to the revealed will and word of the Lord. We call upon them to repent and to forsake their false doctrines and evil practices. . .

Celestial marriage—that is, marriage for time and eternity—and polygamous or plural marriage are not synonymous terms. Monogamous marriages for time and eternity, solemnized in our temples in accordance with the word of the Lord and the laws of the Church, are celestial marriages. . .

President Grant is the only man on the earth at this time who possesses these [sealing] keys. He has never authorized any one to perform polygamous or plural marriages; he is not performing such marriages himself; he has not on his part violated nor is he violating the pledge he made to our government at the time of the Manifesto. . .

We reaffirm as true today and as being true ever since it was made in 1904, the statement of President Smith which was endorsed by a General Conference of the Church "that no such marriages have been solemnized with the sanction, consent, or knowledge of the Church of Jesus Christ of Latter-day Saints."

Finally we are in honor bound to the government and people of the United States, upon a consideration we have fully received—Statehood—to discontinue the practice of polygamous or plural marriage, and Latter-day Saints will not violate their plighted faith.

The Church reaffirms its adherence to the declarations of Wilford Woodruff, Lorenzo Snow, and Joseph F. Smith.

It adheres to the pledges made to the government of the United States, and to the Constitutional law of the State of Utah.

We confirm and renew the instructions given to Church officers by President Joseph F. Smith in 1904, in 1910, and in 1914, and direct the officers who administer the affairs of the Church diligently to investigate reported violations of the adopted rule, and . . . to take action against such persons, and finding them guilty, to excommunicate them from the Church. . . We shall hold Church officers responsible for the proper performance of this duty.[18]

Since the 1933 statement, Mormon leaders have attempted to suppress the dissenters by using loyalty oaths, excommunication, and collaboration with government authorities to obtain their arrest.[19] Though fundamentalists raise

---

[18] The entire First Presidency—Heber J. Grant, A. W. Ivins, and J. Reuben Clark Jr.—signed the statement. The "Official Statement" was reprinted as it appeared in the *Deseret News* and circulated as a pamphlet to officers and other church members: "To Presidents of Stakes and Counselors," 17 June 1933, First Presidency Circular Letters, LDS Archives. A copy is also available in Clark, ed., *Messages*, 5:315–30.

[19] Bradley, *Kidnapped from that Land*, 16, 18, 52–63 passim; and Watson, "Fred E. Curtis Papers." As further evidence of Utah's determination to discourage fundamentalist polygamy, the state legislature upgraded the practice from a misdemeanor to a felony in "Unlawful Cohabitation," 21 Mar. 1935, c. 112, sec. 103-51-2, *Laws of the State of Utah* (1935), 220.

the same appeal made by the parent church in the nineteenth-century, calling for respect for their constitutional rights and freedom of religious diversity, church leaders in Salt Lake City display little tolerance for those seeking to revive the plural, domestic habits of their ancestors.[20] The most dramatic
instance of conflict between the two occurred when the state of Arizona
coordinated a military assault on the polygamous community of Short Creek,
Arizona, in 1953. Numbers of men were jailed and scores of women and children relocated in orthodox Mormon homes.[21] The trauma of that experience notwithstanding, polygamous adherents returned to Short Creek
(renamed Colorado City), grew in numbers, and continue the practice of
patriarchal marriage today. Owing partly to public criticism of such tactics,
Mormonism has since confined its attempts at suppressing renewed polygamy
to excommunication.[22]

Nevertheless, Mormon polygamous sects claiming Latter-day Saint lineage now count between twenty and forty thousand followers.[23] Clustered about
different, sometimes rival, religious leaders, they are found in rural and urban
locations throughout western North America.[24] While judicial conflicts have
generally gone against the old modellers, theirs is a powerful movement that,
by its magnitude and theological ties with the early Saints, remains a nettling
presence to the modern church.[25] Whether from memory of its own nineteenth-century experience or the stubborn reminder of contemporary fun-

---

[20] See, for example, "Deseret News and Polygamy," *Truth* 21:10 (Mar. 1956), 289–306.

[21] An account of this episode constitutes the bulk of Bradley's work, *Kidnapped from that Land*. Also see
Van Wagoner, *Mormon Polygamy*, 192–99.

[22] For developments affecting the fundamentalist community and its relationship to the LDS church, see
Van Wagoner's chapter, "Polygamists in the News," in his *Mormon Polygamy*, 200–17; and Quinn, "Plural
Marriage and Mormon Fundamentalism," 58–61.

[23] While estimates vary widely, reports that contemporary fundamentalism may consist of as many as
a hundred thousand followers seem exaggerated to this student. Wright, "Lives of the Saints," 54; and references in Forbes, "'Why Just Have One?'" 1518n4.

[24] For an overview of Mormon fundamentalist groups and estimates of the number of their adherents,
see all of Quinn, "Plural Marriage and Mormon Fundamentalism." A recent account of the major divisions afflicting Mormon polygamous fundamentalism is Driggs, "Imprisonment, Defiance, and Division,"
65–95.

[25] Polygamists lost the only case to reach the U.S. Supreme Court, *Cleveland vs. U.S.*, 329 U.S. 14 (1946).
Numerous other encounters have occurred, sometimes acquiring national attention, but usually ending in
disappointment for pluralists. See Van Wagoner, *Mormon Polygamy*, 200–17; Bradley, *Kidnapped from that Land*,
192–95; and Quinn, "Plural Marriage and Mormon Fundamentalism," 26–29, 58–61. Many scholars, however, expect growing toleration for polygamous marriage in the future. See, for example, references in Hardy,
Solemn Covenant, 346–47; and constitutional arguments in Forbes, "'Why Just Have One?'" For the problem
polygamy creates for Utah's public image, as illustrated by recently convicted pluralist Tom Green, see "Polygamy
Trial Gives World Titillating Look at Utah," *Salt Lake Tribune*, 21 May 2001, 262:37, A-1/2–5, A-10/3–6.

damentalist stalwarts, Mormonism cannot escape its polygamous past.[26] Like Hercules straining to rid himself of the tunic of Nessus, the church has found the shirt of polygamy more easily put on than got off.

In addition to persevering enclaves of devoted fundamentalists, official Mormonism itself bears markings that betray its former attachment to the Principle. Joseph Smith's 1843 revelation approving polygamy, for example, is yet a part of the Mormon canon of scripture. And a Latter-day Saint widower can still be sealed to successive wives with the expectation that all will be his plural companions in the eternities—when the practice will again be honored. But these are faint reminders when compared to the powerful homilies urging the active practice of plurality in church sermons and discourses a century and a half ago. More than this, the church's energetic role in condemning polygamous renewal finds them, ironically, saying many of the same things voiced by nineteenth-century Gentile critics during the anti-polygamy crusade.

Mormonism now exalts monogamy as the preferred household pattern for all in this life, believers and non-Mormons alike. However halting and difficult the struggle, Mormonism's transformation in this regard is succeeding. This, combined with official inattention to its polygamous past, is what most tells the attitude of the modern church on the subject. If filaments of plural wifery yet remain in the garment of Mormon belief, the cut and markings of that dress are increasingly monogamous. A respected LDS authority effectively put the seal of finality on discontinuation of the Principle in this life by saying that, though plurality will recommence in the millennium, monogamy is now "the Lord's law of marriage" and any who practice polygamy are guilty of "gross wickedness."[27]

---

[26] As one of many reminders of early Mormonism's "peculiar institution," a Utah brewery now markets beer carrying the label "Polygamy Porter. Why Have Just One!" Steve Chawkins, "Utah Businesses Have Faith that Ads Shalt Not Offend," *Los Angeles Times*, 16 Feb. 2002, 121:75, A18/1–3. And contemporary efforts to secure the right of marriage for homosexuals lead some to say such largesse will give polygamists the same permission. George F. Will, "Having Judges and Not Lawmakers Create This Right Is a Recipe for Decades of Bitterness," *Orange County Register*, 30 Nov. 2003, Commentary, 6/4–5; and, Naomi Schaefer, "Yes, Polygamy Is Everybody's Business," *Los Angeles Times*, 9 Feb. 2004, Commentary, B-11/1–6.

[27] McConkie, *Mormon Doctrine*, 577–79.

The Legacy of
Mormon Polygamy

A ny fair examination of nineteenth-century Mormon plurality must acknowledge its extraordinary career. Emerging from a milieu overrun with social and religious debate about marital life, the prophet Joseph Smith commanded patriarchal marriage in the name of God. It comported with Mormon claims that they were restoring the truths of earlier prophets and dispensations. More than this, Mormon polygamy boldly reinstated fabled contentions of the ancients, making sexuality a practice of the gods and, going yet further, exhorting its reproductive employment as a high road to divinity for mortals. Secretly practiced at first, and never a way for the majority of Saints, plurality nevertheless became a superscription for the entire faith, especially after its relocation to the Great Basin. Acknowledging that they had embraced the practice, Mormons added to its revelatory validation a battery of arguments promising special reward in this and future worlds alike.

The extent of Mormon pleading for the Principle during these years, both verbal and literary, was enormous. Persuaded that entire universes were to be filled, the Saints believed they waited only, like the prairies of North America, to be seeded by man. This was, they said, the work vouchsafed to father Abraham, whose descendants God promised would be as numerous as sand on the seashore and whose grand works all worthy Latter-day Saints should imitate. But, as Apostle Orson Pratt stated in his famous 1852 address, it was a project that would have taken a very long time if Abraham "had been confined to one wife, like some of those narrow, contracted nations of modern Christianity."[1] Mormons undertook the task with such energy that it may

---

[1] See Pratt's 1852 sermon in Chapter Two.

have constituted the most conspicuous Euro-American departure from formal monogamous marriage in centuries. Instead of emphasizing that fewer
than half of all the Saints ever lived in plural marriage, as some who wish to
diminish its significance in the Mormon past do, given the difficulties brought
by polygamous life it is remarkable that as many obeyed their leaders as did.

Considering that those church members who practiced the "higher law"
were as active as their monogamous fellow believers in transforming the sand
and alkali about them into a fruitful commonwealth, the national anti-
polygamy campaign raised against the church can hardly be justified. The error
of that crusade is found not only in its indictment of the Saints as engraft-
ing a "barbarous" and "Asiatic" form of home life on monogamous America but in the intolerance of its policies. It is a witness to the importance of
the Principle in Mormon thought that the Saints delayed compromise so
long. It seems quite reasonable to assume that, even with the duress of federal law and imprisonment, the practice could have continued indefinitely—
as indeed it has, first as approved, underground, post-Manifesto plural sealings and then as unapproved, underground, fundamentalist unions.

At the same time, the official church's rejection of polygamy in the twentieth century was as adamant as its support for the practice in the nineteenth.
A review of Mormon sermons, public statements, and art over the last hundred years gives the impression that plural marriage had little significance in
the Latter-day Saint past. As if purposely screening their recollections,
approved Mormon speakers and writers rehearse their history nearly blind
to polygamy's conspicuous place in their religious experience, seldom acknowledging that thousands profoundly altered their lives to live it.[2] Official Mormon inattention to the subject is glaring, disregarding documents that shouted its social and biological necessity, ignoring sermons that described it as
important as baptism, and forgetting statements that hailed the Principle as
the "capstone," the "cornerstone" of the latter-day work. Distancing contemporary Mormonism from memory of the Principle, the church's president today says that no more than 2 to 5 percent of members were ever involved
in polygamy and that it is something Mormonism "has had nothing to do

---

[2] Perhaps no better example of the church's official turnabout on plurality can be found than the com-
plete silence on the subject in two officially approved, book-length accounts of the life of Brigham Young.
Appearing sixty years apart, these are Nibley, *Brigham Young* (1937); and *Teachings of the Presidents of the Church:
Brigham Young* (1997).

with . . . for a very long time."[3] Anymore, accounts of Abraham and his importance say nothing of his exemplary role as a practicing pluralist. For Mormons today, "Doing the works of Abraham" carries no obligation in this
life to multiply either wives or children.[4]

Acceptance into the American socio-religious mainstream is so complete
that no Latter-day Saint prophet is soon likely to call his people to restore
the Principle and, like ancient Josiah, rend his clothes for the church's wayward course.[5] Thoroughly assimilated into traditional views, most church members strongly oppose revival of the practice.[6] Moreover, Mormon authorities now promise monogamous couples all the blessings of an eternal career,
including an endless progeny and the presidency of worlds. Temple marriage
ceremonies have been changed to temper the patriarchal tradition that exacted from brides an oath of obedience to their husbands; leaders now signal
greater tolerance for birth control; and departing from earlier policies of
restraint, sexual relations in marriage are permitted for "expressing love and
strengthening emotional and spiritual bonds."[7] The Saints survived martyr-

---

[3] "Pres. Hinckley Speaks Out on Live TV Show," *Church News*, 12 Sept. 1998, 68:37, 4/3–4; comments
on the same interview in Andrea Moore Emmett, "Only for Eternity," 13–15, 17; and president of the church
Gordon B. Hinckley's seeming indifference to the subject in his interview with Wright, "Lives of the Saints,"
40–57. See Chapter Three for estimates enlarging the number of nineteenth-century Mormon polygamists.

[4] See, as only a few examples, Clark, "Abraham," 1:7–9; Rasmussen, "Abrahamic Covenant," 1:9–10; Spencer
W. Kimball, "Example of Abraham," *Ensign* 6:6 (June 1975), 3–7; and Kent P. Jackson, "Abrahamic Covenant:
A Blessing for All People," ibid. 20:2 (Feb. 1990), 50–53.

[5] The story of Josiah's distress upon rediscovering Moses' teachings and the departure of ancient Israel
from them is found in 2 Chronicles 34:14–15, 18–19.

[6] A survey taken in the 1960s found church members overwhelmingly opposed to reviving polygamy,
nearly half saying they would not conform even if church presidents commanded it. Christiansen, "Contemporary Mormons' Attitudes toward Polygynous Practices," 167–70. There are also testaments such as
the painful, condemning memories of Mary Bennion Powell, discussing the polygamous marriages of her
father, Heber Bennion, and other polygamous relatives, in Mary Bennion Powell to Dr. George R. Stewart, CSmH; the reluctance to return to the practice that children of polygamous families expressed in Hardy,
Solemn Covenant, 355n20–22; and one woman's remark that plural marriage in Mormonism's past was one of
the reasons she left the church. Ure, *Leaving the Fold*, 24.

[7] Illustrative of the want of any mention of polygamy as necessary for elevation to the celestial kingdom of heaven is Renato Maldonado, "The Three Degrees of Glory," *Ensign* 35:4 (April 2005), 62–65. Changes
in the marriage covenant for women accompanied other alterations in Mormon temple ceremonies. See
"Comments on Temple Changes Elicit Church Discipline," *Sunstone* 14:3 (June 1990), 59–61. Regarding greater
permissiveness toward both birth control and sexuality within marriage, see "New Church Handbook Says
Birth Control Is Okay," ibid. 22:1 (Mar.–April 1999), 76–77; and the discussion in Proctor, "Bodies, Babies,
and Birth Control," 159–75. The church generally displays a curvilinear adherence to the values of American society at large, as illustrated in its fertility patterns. See Spicer and Gustavus, "Mormon Fertility,"
70–76; and Willis, "Mormon Fertility and the Americanization Hypothesis," 282–84.

dom and persecution, grew impressively in numbers, and made peace with the world in matters of marital sex—while yet holding to the expectation of a compounding hereafter.[8] All that was held out as a reward for living the Principle can now be had without the ordeal of plural wifery. For the majority of believers, polygamy has descended to them as but a curious, sometimes embarrassing doctrinal heirloom.[9]

For those who study it, however, Mormonism's brave adventure with plural marriage, including its modern reversal and flight from the practice, is an instructive subject. As with all historical inquiry, revisiting the topic enlarges humane sensibility and tolerance. It also saves us from what Paul Conkin called the "unpardonable sin" of "historical forgetfulness."[10]

But recollection of the theme does more. It gives the Latter-day Saint polygamous passage, especially those who lived it, a long overdue heraldic place on the tablet of this American Israel's pioneer epoch, a salute to their proud religious audacity, and the determination they displayed by engaging in one of the longest campaigns of civil disobedience in American history. It is a reminiscence abundant with character and sacrifice, forever tempting our gaze.

---

[8] This was the theme of Bernard DeVoto's cynically edged article "The Centennial of Mormonism," 9. For recent essays on the church's impressive growth and the problem of maintaining its identity as a distinct religious movement, see "Mormons: The Church of the West," 25–26; and all of Hansen, "Mormon History and the Conundrum of Culture."

[9] Brodie, "Polygamy Shocks the Mormons," 398–404. Taysom, "Uniform and Common Recollection," 113–44, examines official Mormonism's shifting public memory of the subject. The present author once asked a docent at Mormonism's Museum of Church History and Art why there were no exhibits relating to polygamy. He was told that that part of the church's history was best kept out of sight for the same reason families lock portraits of embarrassing ancestors away in their closets.

[10] Conkin, A Requiem, 180.

BIBLIOGRAPHY

BIBLIOGRAPHIES AND GUIDES CONSULTED

Allen, James B., Ronald W. Walker, and David J. Whittaker. *Studies in Mormon History, 1830–1997 . . . With A Topical Guide to Published Social Science Literature on the Mormons [by] Armand L. Mauss and Dynette Ivie Reynolds.* Urbana and Chicago: Univ. of Illinois Press in Cooperation with the Smith Institute for LDS History, Brigham Young Univ., 2000.

Andrus, Hyrum L., and Richard E. Bennett, comps. and eds. *Mormon Manuscripts to 1846: A Guide to the Holdings of the Harold B. Lee Library.* Provo, Utah: Archives and Manuscripts, Harold B. Lee Library, Brigham Young Univ., 1977.

Bitton, Davis, comp. *Guide to Mormon Diaries and Autobiographies.* Provo, Utah: Brigham Young Univ., 1977.

———. "Mormon Polygamy: A Review Article," *JMH* 4 (1977).

Bringhurst, Newell G., and Lavina Fielding Anderson, eds. *Excavating Mormon Pasts: The New Historiography of the Last Half Century.* S.L.C: Greg Kofford Books, 2004.

Crawley, Peter. *A Descriptive Bibliography of the Mormon Church, Volume One 1830–1847.* Provo, Utah: Religious Studies Center, Brigham Young Univ., 1997.

Ellsworth, George. "Hubert Howe Bancroft and the History of Utah," *UHQ* 22:2 (April 1954).

Fales, Susan L., and Chad J. Flake, comps. *Mormons and Mormonism in U.S. Government Documents: A Bibliography.* S.L.C: Univ. of Utah Press, 1989.

Flake, Chad J., ed. *A Mormon Bibliography 1830–1930 . . .* S.L.C: Univ. of Utah Press, 1978.

———, and Larry W. Draper, comps. *A Mormon Bibliography 1830–1930, Ten Year Supplement.* S.L.C: Univ. of Utah Press, 1989.

Scott, Patricia Lyn. "Mormon Polygamy: A Bibliography, 1977–92," *JMH* 19:1 (Spring 1993).

Wagner, Henry R., and Charles L. Camp. *The Plains and the Rockies: A Critical Bibliography of Exploration, Adventure and Travel in the American West 1800–1865.* Fourth edn. Revised, enlarged and edited by Robert H. Becker. San Francisco: John Howell-Books, 1982.

Whittaker, David J., ed. *Mormon Americana: A Guide to Sources and Collections in the United States.* Provo, Utah: Published by BYU Studies, 1995.

Manuscripts, Oral Interviews, and Other Unpublished Materials

Adams, William. Autobiography of. Typescript. Film. LDS Archives.

Alder, Lorna Call. History of Mary Theresa Thompson Call. Typewritten manuscript. Copy in possession of B. Carmon Hardy, Orange, Calif.

Allen, Andrew Jackson. Record of, 1868–1884. Typescript. MSS A 33, Uhi.

Allred, Mary Eliza Tracy. Typewritten dictation to Emily Black in 1937. Collection of Mormon Biographies. LDS Archives.

Arrington, Leonard J. Papers. MSS 1, Series 9, LAHA.

Badger, Alexander. Collection. Archives. Missouri Hist. Soc., St. Louis, Mo.

Bailey, Charles R[amsden]. Autobiography. Handwritten manuscript. MSS 53, Special Collections, ULA.

Ballard, Henry. Private Journal of, 1852–1904. Typescript. LDS Archives.

Bennion, Lowell C. Patterns of Polygamy Across Mormon Country in 1880. Paper given at Mormon History Association, 11 May 1984, Provo, Utah.

————. Polygamy's Contribution to "Utah's Best Crop" in Cedar City, 1860–1880. Paper given at Western History Association Conference, Fort Worth, Texas, 11 Oct. 2003.

————. What Percentage of Which Population Practiced Polygamy in Springville? Paper given at Mormon History Association, May 1982, Ogden, Utah.

Bentley, Charles. Journal and Notes, Manuscript Record. LDS Archives.

Bergera, Gary. Counting Polygamists: A Review of George D. Smith's Identification of the Earliest Mormon Polygamists. Paper presented at Mormon History Association, 17 May 2002, Tucson, Arizona.

Black, Joseph Smith. Autobiography and Diary, 1889–1890. MS 742, photocopy. L. Tom Perry Special Collections, UPB.

Blood, Jane Wilkie Hooper. Diaries. LDS Archives.

Blood, William. Diaries. LDS Archives.

Brief Account of the Early History of the Canadian Mission, 1887–1895. Alberta Temple Historical Record. Typewritten manuscript. LDS Archives.

Brown, Catherine S. Interviewed by Jessie Embry, 3 May 1976, Provo, Utah, OHP.

Brown, James Stephens. Journals and Account Books. Film. LDS Archives.

Call, Anson Bowen. Life Story of Anson Bowen Call. 1954. Typewritten manuscript. Film. LDS Archives.

Cannon, Abraham Hoagland. Journals. 19 vols., 1879–1895. V MSS 62, L. Tom Perry Special Collections, UPB.

Cannon, Clawson Y., Sr. Interviewed by Jerry D. Lee, 5, 7, 19, 20 Feb. 1974, Provo, Utah, OHP.

Cannon, Ellen, to Katherine C. Thomas, 28 Dec. 1953. Typewritten copy. LAHA.

Christensen, Christian Lyngaa. Reminiscences and Diary. Film. LDS Archives.

Church Historian's Office. History of the Church, 1839–ca.1882. Film. LDS Archives.

Clawson, Rudger. Collection. MS 481, Special Collections, UU.

Clayton, William, to Madison M. Scott, S.L.C., Utah, 11 Nov. 1871. Film. LDS Archives.

Cleveland, Grover. Papers. 9 series. Film. Lib. of Congress.

Condie, Gibson. Reminiscences and Diary. Film. LDS Archives.

Cooke, Sarah A[nn Sutton]. Theatrical and Social Affairs in Utah, S.L.C., 1884. Handwritten manuscript. P-FI9, CU-B.

Cowdery, Oliver. Letterbook. Mormon file. CSmH.

Dalton, Lucinda Lee. Autobiography. Handwritten manuscript addressed to Mrs. Emmeline B. Wells, Circle Valley, Utah, Dec. 1876. P-F20, CU-B.

Dean, Joseph Henry. Diaries. Film. LDS Archives.

Esplin, Henry Webster. Typewritten autobiographical sketch. MSS B 289, Uhi.

Eyring, Henry. Reminiscences. Typescript. LDS Archives.

Fackler, John G. Brief Notes of Travils a cross [sic] the Plains from St. Joseph Mo. to California in 1864. Archives, Mo. Hist. Soc., St. Louis, Mo.

Fielding, Joseph. Diary of, 1837–1859. Film. LDS Archives.

First Presidency Circular Letters. LDS Archives.

First Presidency Letterpress Copy Books. LDS Archives.

Fish, Joseph. Autobiography of, 1840–1926, Revised and Enlarged by Himself from His Journal. Typewritten manuscript, with index, chronology, and notes by his son, Silas L. Fish. MS 257, Ariz. Hist. Soc., Tucson, Ariz..

Forsdick, Stephen. Autobiography. Typescript. LDS Archives.

Gallup, Luke William, to Dear Aunt, 2 July 1869. Film. LDS Archives

———. Reminiscence and Diary, May 1842–Mar. 1891. Film. LDS Archives.

General Minutes, Colonia Juarez Mexico Stake. Film. LDS Archives.

Grant, Heber Jeddy. Journal Books, 1884–1889, Heber J. Grant Collection. LDS Archives.

Green, Caleb. Journal containing A Visit to the Great Salt Lake or Observations during a five month's [sic] Residence in Utah. Caleb Green Collection, 1862. Archives, Mo. Hist. Soc., St. Louis, Mo.

Historian's Office Letterpress Copy Books. Film. LDS Archives.

Holbrook, Joseph. Life of Joseph Holbrook, Written by His Own Hand. Ca. 1871. Film. LDS Archives.

Horne, Mrs. Joseph [Mary Isabella]. Migration and Settlement of the Latter Day Saints, S.L.C., 1884. Handwritten manuscript. P-F 24, CU-B.

Hovey, Joseph Grafton. Reminiscences and Journals, 1845–1856. LDS Archives.

Hyde, Mrs. Mary Ann P[rice]. Autobiography, 20 Aug. 1880, Spring City, Utah Territory. P-F25, CU-B.

Hyer, Merle Gilbert, and Estell Hyer Rire. Interviewed by Tillman S. Boxell, 30 June 1978, Logan Utah. OHP.

Ivins, Anthony Woodward. Collection. B-2, Uhi.

Ivins, Heber Grant. Polygamy in Mexico as Practiced by the Mormon Church, 1895–1905. Typewritten manuscript. Special Collections, UU.

Ivins, Stanley Snow. Collection. MSS B31, Uhi.

Jackson, Victoria H. Sketches of Mosiah Lyman Hancock's Life Story Taken from the History of his Third Wife, Martha M. Hancock. Addendum to Mosiah Lyman Hancock, Autobiography. Typewritten manuscript. Film. LDS Archives.

Jenkins, Archie L. Interviewed by Leonard Grover, 16 Feb. 1980, Newton, Utah. OHP.

Jenson, Andrew. Prisoners for Conscience Sake. Typewritten manuscript. Film. LDS Archives.

Jessop, Joseph Lyman. Diary. 3 vols. Typewritten copy in possession of Marianne T. Watson, S.L.C., Utah.

Johnson, Benjamin Franklin. Papers, 1852–1911. Film. LDS Archives.

Kessler, Frederick. Collection. MS 49, Special Collections, UU.

King, Hannah T[apfield]. Brief Memoir of the Early Mormon Life of. [1880?]. P-F12, CU-B.

Kingsbury, Joseph Corroden. History of, copied from his own handwriting in his little books where he kept his diary by his grand-daughter, Roselia Meservy Watson . . . Typescript. Film. LDS Archives.

Law, William. Letter to Isaac Hill, 20 July 1844. Photocopy. LDS Archives.

Layne, Jonathan Ellis. Life Sketch. Typewritten manuscript. Film. LDS Archives.

LeBaron, Ellice Marie Bentley. Interviewed by Charles Ursenbach, 11 Sept. 1973, Calgary, Canada. LDS Archives.

Lightner, Mary Elizabeth Rollins. Address Delivered at Brigham Young Univ., 14 April 1905. Typescript. Mary Elizabeth Rollins Lightner Papers. V MSS 363, fd. 6, L. Tom Perry Special Collections, UPB.

————. Autobiography. Susa Young Gates Collection, box 14, fd. 4. B-95, Uhi.

Lowe, Glen Doney. Interviewed by Jessie Embry, 28 June 1976, S.L.C., Utah. OHP.

Lund, Anthon Hendrik. Collection. LDS Archives.

Lyman, Albert Robison. Francis Marion Lyman. Typewritten manuscript, 24 Oct. 1941. LDS Archives.

MacKinnon, William P. Statehood for What?: Utah's Shrinking Borders, 1850–1896. Paper presented at Mormon History Association Conference, 18 May 2002, Tucson, Arizona.

Madsen, Peter. Autobiography. Film, LDS Archives.

McConkie, Thora Harvey. Interviewed by Jessie Embry, 8 July 1876, S.L.C., Utah. OHP.

McIntosh, William. Diary of, 1857–1898. Bound, typewritten copy. Box 8670.1 .MI88, L. Tom Perry Special Collections, UPB.

Memmott, Thomas. Journals of, Quotation Book Book of Genealogy. Film. LDS Archives.

Merrill, Marriner Wood. Diaries 1889–1906. LDS Archives.

Miscellaneous Collection. P87, CCL-A.

Miscellany Collection. P19, CCL-A.

Miscellaneous Letters and Papers. P13, CCL-A.

Mormon Papers. Mo. Hist. Soc., St. Louis, Mo.

Mortensen, Winnie Haynie. Interviewed by Leonard R. Grover, 26 Jan. 1980, S.L.C., Utah. OHP.

Musser, Joseph W. Diaries. Film. LDS Archives.

Nauvoo Stake High Council Court Papers, 1839–1844, 4 fds. Film, LDS Archives.

Nuttall, L[eonard] John. Diary, 1876–1904. 4 vols. Typewritten copy. Box 8670.1 .N963, L. Tom Perry Special Collections, UPB.

Pacheco Ward, Mexican Mission. Film. LDS Archives.

Packer, Elizabeth H. Interviewed by Jessie Embry, 1 Sept. 1976, Provo, Utah. OHP.

Parkinson, B[ernice] R[ose]. Life Sketch of Samuel Rose Parkinson. Film. A 225, Uhi.

Penrose, Esther Romania Bunnell. Memoir (1881). LDS Archives.

Powell, Mary Bennion to Dr. George Stewart. 228-page, typewritten letter composed between 26 Jan. and 25 Feb. 1952. Mormon file. Film. CSmH.

Pratt, Belinda Marden. Autobiography (1884). LDS Archives.

Pratt, Mrs. Orson [Sarah Bates]. Workings of Mormonism related by. S.L.C., 1884. Original and typewritten copies. LDS Archives.

Recollections of George L. Woods. Biographical Sketches, Utah. P-F14, CU-B.

Revelations Collection. Film. LDS Archives.

Revelations Purportedly Given to John Taylor, 1882–1884. Film. LDS Archives.

Richards, Mrs. F[ranklin] D[ewey]. Inner Facts of Social Life in Utah by Mrs. F. D. Richards. 1880. Handwritten interview with Mrs. Matilda Coley Griffing Bancroft. III:3 (PF-2) 98–III, CU-B.

Richards, Franklin S. Correspondence, 1886–1890. Typewritten copies. MSS A 132–3, Uhi.

Richards. Joseph H. Diary. George S. Tanner typescript. Mormons and Mormonism in Arizona, 1873–1888 Collection. AZ 276, Special Collections, AZU.

Ririe, Lloyd. Statement concerning the purported ordination of John W. Woolley, 1964. Typewritten MS, LDS Archives.

Robinson, Ebenezer. Collection. LDS Archives.

Robinson. Joseph Eldridge. Brief Story of the Life of. Partly handwritten, partly typewritten manuscript. LDS Archives.

Robinson, Joseph Lee. History of (18 Feb. 1811–1 Jan. 1893). Typewritten manuscript and journal. Film. LDS Archives.

Rogers, Andrew S. Handwritten, autobiographical sketch, 1882–1897. Bound copy. Mormons and Mormonism in Arizona, 1873–1888 Collection. AZ 276, fd. 12, Special Collections, AZU.

Romney, Hannah Hood Hill. Autobiography. Filmed typescript. MS 146, CSmH.

Ros[e]borough, Joseph B. Typewritten manuscript. Biographical Sketches, Utah, mid-1880s. P-F 15, CU-B.

Shumway, [Gwen] Elva. Interviewed by Leonard R. Grover, 25 April 1980, Mesa, Arizona. OHP.

Smith, Charles. Journals, Record Book and Papers. MSS SC 5543, L. Tom Perry Special Collections, UPB.

Smith, George A. Papers of the Family of, 1731–1969. MS 36, Special Collections, UU.

Smith, George D. Mormon Plural Marriage: An Historical Perspective. Paper presented at Sunstone Symposium, 7 Mar. 1992, Burbank, California.

Smith, Joseph, [Jr.]. History of the Church. Film, LDS Archives.

Smith, Joseph F. Affidavits [on celestial marriage], 1869–1915. 4 fds. LDS Archives.

———. Incoming Correspondence, 1855–1918. LDS Archives.

Smoot, Reed. Collection. MSS 1187, L. Tom Perry Special Collections, UPB.

Solomon, William Henry. Diary 1873–1874. Henry S. Tanner typescript. Mormons and Mormonism in Arizona, 1873–1888 Collection. Az 276, fd. 13, Special Collections, AZU.

Stout, Abraham L. Interviewed by Tillman S. Boxell, 5 Sept. 1978, S.L.C. OHP.

Stout, Hosea. Reminiscences and Journals, 1845–1869. Film. LDS Archives.

Stucki, Ezra Spori. Address in Paris, Idaho. Aug. 1954. Typewritten manuscript. LDS Archives.

Subject Folder Collection. P22, CCL-A.

Tanner, Mary J[ane] to Mr. [Hubert Howe] Bancroft, Provo City, Utah, 29 Oct. 1880. P-F12, CU-B.

Taylor, John. Family Papers. Raymond Taylor typewritten copies. MS 50, Special Collections, UU.

————. Presidential Papers, 1877–1887. LDS Archives.

————. An alleged revelation given to, 27 Sept. 1886. Photocopy in private possession.

Tenney, Ammon M[eshack]. Collection. MS 785, Ariz. St. Hist. Soc., Tucson, Ariz.

Walser, Asenath Skousen. Interviewed by Jessie Embry, 26 May 1976, Lindon, Utah. OHP.

Watson, Marianne T. Fred E. Curtis Papers: L.D.S. Church Surveillance of Fundamentalist Mormons 1937 to 1954. Paper presented at Sunstone Symposium, S.L.C., Utah, 10 Aug. 2001.

Wells, Emmeline B[lanche Woodward]. Journals, 1844–1891. 14 vols., typescript. MSS 1407, L. Tom Perry Special Collections, UPB.

West, Rose Berry. Pioneer Personal History. Typescript. Box 11, WPA Biographical Sketches. MSS B 289, Uhi.

Whipple, Nelson Wheeler. Autobiography and Journal, 1859–1887. LDS Archives.

————. Diaries. 3 vols. In possession of Ms. Barbara Gustaveson, Farmington, Utah.

Whitney, Helen Mar Kimball. Autobiography, 30 Mar., 1881. Film. LDS Archives.

————. Family Papers. MSS 179, ULA.

Wilson, Melissa Stevens. Looking Backward from 1962 to 1902. Typewritten manuscript. Copy in possession of B. Carmon Hardy, Orange, Calif.

Woodruff, Abraham Owen. Collection. V MSS 777, L. Tom Perry Special Collections, UPB.

Woodruff, Phebe W[hittemore] Carter. Autobiographical Sketch. 9 Dec. 1880. Biographical Sketches, Utah. PF-13, CU-B.

Woodruff, Wilford. Letterpress Copy Book. Film. LDS Archives.

Woods, George L. Recollections. Biographical Sketches, Utah. P-F14, CU-B.

Wyatt, William L. Interviewed by Jessie Embry, 19 June 1976, Logan, Utah. OHP.

Young, Brigham. Collection. Film. LDS Archives.

————. Collection. Film. MS 566, UU.

————. Letterbook 1851–1855. Film. LDS Archives.

Young, Brigham., Jr. Journals, 1862–1900. Film. LDS Archives.

Young, John Willard. Letterbooks, 1886–1889. Dale L. Morgan typescript and summaries. MSS A 1341, Uhi.

Published and Unpublished Government Documents

Acts and Resolutions Passed at the Third Annual Session of the Legislative Assembly of the Territory of Utah . . . (1854).

Acts, Resolutions and Memorials, Passed by the First Annual, and Special Sessions, of the Legislative Assembly, of the Territory of Utah . . . 1851 (1852).

Acts, Resolutions, and Memorials, Passed and Adopted during the Nineteenth Annual Session of the Legislative Assembly of the Territory of Utah (1870).

Admission of Utah as a State in the Union. Memorial of Citizens of the Territory of Utah Asking for the Admission of Utah as a State in the Union, 27 April 1882. House Misc. Doc. 43 (47-1) 1882, Serial 2046.

Admission Of Utah Into The Union. Memorial of the Convention to Frame a Constitution for Admission of Utah into the Union as a State . . . 1872. House Misc. Doc. 165 (42-2) 2 April 1872, Serial 1526.

Admission of Utah. Argument of Hon. Jeremiah M. Wilson, Made before the House Committee on Territories, January 19–22, 1889 . . . Wash., D.C: GPO, 1889.

Admission of Utah. Arguments in Favor of the Admission of Utah as a State . . . Made before the Committee on Territories of the United States Senate, First Session Fiftieth Congress, Saturday, February 18, 1888. Wash., D.C: GPO, 1888.

Admission of Utah . . . House Report 162, in 2 pts. (53-1) 2 Nov. 1893, Serial 3157.

Amendments to the Constitution Prohibiting Polygamy . . . House Doc. 2307 (55-3) 19 Feb. 1899, Serial 3841.

Annals of Congress, 1789–1824.

Annual Reports of Territorial Governors. *RSI.*

Annual Reports of the Utah Commission, 1882–1896. *RSI.*

Bartholow, Roberts, Assistant Surgeon. "Sanitary Report—Utah Territory," *Statistical Report on the Sickness and Mortality in the Army of the United States Compiled from the Records of the Surgeon General's Office Embracing a Period of Five Years, from January, 1855 to January, 1860.* Edited by Thomas Lawson. Senate, Executive Doc. 52 (36-1) 1860, Serial 1035.

Carlton, A[mbrose] B. *Circular for the Information of Registration Officers.* N.p., 19 Mar. 1887.

————, Chairman of the Utah Commission. Memorandum of, to Hon. L[ucius] Q. C. Lamar, Secretary of the Interior. S.L.C., Utah, 29 Mar. 1889. RG48, N.A.

———— and J. R. Pettigrew of the Utah Commission to Hon. L[ucius] Q. C. Lamar, Secretary of the Interior, S.L.C., Utah, May 1885. Marked Personal. RG48, N.A.

Case of Brigham H. Roberts of Utah . . . Report [to accompany H. Res. 107] January 20, 1900. House Report 85, 2 pts. (56-1) 1900, Serial 4021.

Circular for the Information of Registration Officers, ([S.L.C.] 21 April 1885). RG48, N.A.

Clawson, Rudger. Case 117, file 425, Third District Court of the Territory of Utah, 1884, National Archives and Records Center, Rocky Mountain Region, Denver, Colorado.

"Condition of Utah." House Report 96 (39-1) 23 July 1866, Serial 1272.

Congressional Debates, 1824–1837.

Congressional Globe, 1833–1873.

Congressional Record, 1873–

Constitution of the State of Idaho (1889).

Constitution of the State of Utah (1895).

"Declaration of Grievances and Protest," to President [Grover] Cleveland. S.L.C., Utah, 6 April 1885. RG48, N.A.

Evarts, William M., Secretary of State. "Diplomatic Correspondence, Circular No. 10, Aug. 9, 1879, Sent to Diplomatic and Consular Officers of the United States, 1879." *Papers Relating to the Foreign Relations of the United States.* Wash., D.C: GPO, 1879.

"Governor's Message to the Territorial Legislature of Utah." Senate Misc. Doc. 37 (37-2) 1863, Serial 1150.

Hearings before the Committee on Territories in Regard to the Admission of Utah as a State. Wash., D.C: GPO, 1889.

Hughey, William Proctor, to President Grover Cleveland, St. Louis, Missouri, 5 April 1885. RG48, N.A.

Jenks, George A. *Convictions for Polygamy in Utah and Idaho: Letter from the Acting Attorney-General, in Reply to the Resolution of the House in Relation to Convictions for Polygamy in Utah and Idaho.* House Exec. Doc. 447 (50-1) 13 Sept. 1888, Serial 2561.

Laws of the State of Utah. Passed at the Regular Session of the Twenty-First Legislature . . . 1935.

Laws of the Territory of Utah (1892).

Letter from The Attorney-General, Transmitting, In Response to Senate Resolution of December 10, 1888, a Statement Relative to the Execution of the Law against Bigamy. Exec. Doc. 21 (50-2) 12 Dec. 1888, Serial 2610.

"Letter from the Secretary of the Interior, Transmitting Certain Petitions for Enforcing the Anti-Polygamy Act of 1862." House Exec. Doc. 58 (45-3) 1 Feb. 1879, Serial 1858.

"Memorial of the Legislative Assembly of the Territory of Utah to the President and Senate and House of Representatives of the United States, in Congress assembled," 13 Mar. 1884. RG48, N.A.

"Memorial." Senate Misc. Doc. 112 (41-2) 12 Apr. 1870, Serial 1408.

"Message from the President of the United States, in Relation to the Condition of Affairs in the Territory of Utah." Sen. Exec. Doc. 44 (42-3) 14 Feb. 1873, Serial 1545.

"Message to the Territorial Legislature of Utah." Senate Misc. Doc. 37 (37) 28 Feb. 1863, Serial 1150.

Official Report of the Proceedings and Debates of the Convention Assembled at Salt Lake City on the Fourth Day of Mar., 1895, to Adopt a Constitution for the State of Utah. 2 vols. S.L.C: Star, 1898.

Pacific Reporter, 1883–1931.

"Petition of 22,626 Women of Utah Asking for The Repeal of Certain Laws, the Enactment of Others, and the Admission of the Territory of Utah as a State." House Misc. Doc. 42 (44-1) 13 Jan. 1876, Serial 1698.

Petition of Residents of Utah Territory, Praying That the Protection of the General Government May Not Be Withdrawn from Them by the Admission of that Territory as a State. Senate Misc. Doc. 118 (42-2) 22 Mar. 1872, Serial 1482.

Polygamy. House Report 2568 (49-1) 24 May 1886, Serial 2442.

Potts, Margaret Jane to Pres. R[utherford] B. Hayes, 31 Jan. 1879. RG48, N.A.

Ramsay, Alexander, Chairman of the Utah Commission, to Hon. Henry M. Teller, Secretary of the Interior, 24 Aug. 1883. RG48, N.A.

———, Chairman of the Utah Commission to Secretary of the Interior [Lucius Q. C. Lamar], S.L.C., 24 April 1885. RG48, N.A.

. . . Reorganized Church of Jesus Christ of Latter Day Saints, Complainant vs. The Church of Christ at Independence, Missouri . . . Complainant's Abstract of Pleading and Evidence. Lamoni, Iowa: Herald Publishing House and Bindery, 1893.

Revised Statutes of Canada (1892).

Revised Statutes of the State of Utah, In Force Jan.1, 1898.

Rules and Regulations for the Revision of the Registration Lists, and the Conduct of the Election, 7 Nov. 1882. S.L.C: Tribune Printing and Publishing Co., 1882.

Special Committee on the Case of Brigham H. Roberts. "Case of Brigham H. Roberts of Utah . . . Report [to accompany H.Res. 107] January 20, 1900." (56-1) 1900, Serial 4021.

"Speech of Hon. J[ustin] S. Morrill, of Vermont, In the House of Representatives, February 23, 1857." *Cong. Globe* (34-3), appendix, 280–88.

Suppression of Polygamy in Utah . . . House Report 2735 (49-1) 1886, Serial 2443.

Supreme Court of the United States, October Term, 1889. No. 1261. Samuel D. Davis, Appellant, vs. H. G. Beason, Sheriff of Oneida County, Idaho Territory. Brief for Appellant. Franklin S. Richards, Jeremiah M. Wilson, Samuel Shellabarger, For Appellant. Wash., D.C: Gibson Bros., Printers and Bookbinders, 1889.

Thomas, Arthur L., Governor of the Territory of Utah, to John W. Noble, Secretary of the Interior, S.L.C., Utah, 6 Nov. 1890. RG48, N.A.

———, Secretary for Utah and Ex-officio Secretary of the [Utah] Commission. *Order of the Utah Commission, Adopted Friday, September 1, 1882.* RG48, N.A.

To Prevent Persons Living in Bigamy or Polygamy from Holding Any Civil Office of Trust or Profit in Any of the Territories of the United States, and from Being Delegates in Congress. House Report 386 (47-1) 14 Feb. 1882, Serial 2065.

United Kingdom. *Statutes of the Realm*, 1235–1948.

United States Code Annotated.

United States Statutes at Large. 1789–.

United States Supreme Court Reports.

Utah Expedition, The. Message from the President of the United States, Transmitting Reports from the Secretaries of State, of War, of the Interior, and of the Attorney General, relative to the military expedition ordered into the Territory of Utah. House Exec. Doc. 71 (35-1) 26 Feb. 1858, Serial 955.

Utah Reports of Cases Determined in the Supreme Court of the Territory of Utah. San Francisco: Bancroft and Co., 1876–96.

War of the Rebellion: A Compilation of the Official Records of the Union and Confederate Armies. Series 1, Vol. 50—In Two Pts: Operations on the Pacific Coast, 1 Jan. 1861–30 June 1865. House Doc. 59 (55-1) 1897, Serial 3584.

Wells, Emmeline B. and Zina Young Williams to President Rutherford B. Hayes, 29 Jan. 1879. RG 48, N.A.

Theses and Dissertations

Alexander, Thomas G. "Utah Federal Courts and the Areas of Conflict, 1850–1896." M.A. thesis, Utah St. Univ., 1961.

Bachman, Danel W. "A Study of the Mormon Practice of Plural Marriage before the Death of Joseph Smith." M.A. thesis, Purdue Univ., 1975.

Barrett, Gwynn William. "John M. Bernhisel: Mormon Elder in Congress." Ph.D. diss., BYU, 1968.

Bennett, Richard Edmond. "Mormons at the Missouri: A History of the Latter-day Saints at Winter Quarters and at Kanesville, 1846–52—A Study in American Overland Trail Migration." 2 vols. Ph.D. diss., Wayne St. Univ., 1984.

Bernstein, Jerome. "A History of the Constitutional Conventions of the Territory of Utah from 1849 to 1895." M.S. thesis, Utah St. Univ., 1961.

Bishop, Michael Guy. "The Celestial Family: Early Mormon Thought on Life and Death, 1830–1846." Ph.D. diss., Southern Ill. Univ., 1981.

Brekus, Catherine A. "Let Your Women Keep Silence in the Churches": Female Preaching and Evangelical Religion in America, 1740–1845." 2 vols. Ph.D. diss., Yale Univ., 1993.

Brown, Vernal A. "United States Marshals in Utah Territory to 1896." M.S. thesis, Utah St. Univ., 1970.

Burgess-Olson, Vicky. "Family Structure and Dynamics in Early Utah Mormon Families—1847–1885." Ph.D. diss., Northwestern Univ., 1975.

Cannon, Mark Wilcox. "The Mormon Issue in Congress 1872–1882 Drawing on the Experience of Territorial Delegate George Q. Cannon." Ph.D. diss., Harvard Univ., 1960.

Casterline, Gail Farr. "'In the Toils' Or 'Onward for Zion': Images of the Mormon Woman, 1852–1890." M.A. thesis, Utah St. Univ., 1974.

Ehat, Andrew F. "Joseph Smith's Introduction of Temple Ordinances and the 1844 Mormon Succession Question." M.A. thesis, BYU, 1981.

Ellsworth, Samuel George. "A History of Mormon Missions in the United States and Canada, 1830–1860." Ph.D. diss., Univ. of Calif., Berkeley, 1951.

Evans, Rosa Mae McClellan. "Judicial Prosecution of Prisoners for LDS Plural Marriages: Prison Sentences, 1884–1895." M.A. thesis, BYU, 1986.

Godfrey, Kenneth W. "Causes of Mormon Non-Mormon Conflict in Hancock County, Illinois, 1839–1846." Ph.D. diss., BYU, 1967.

Grover-Swank, E. Victoria. "Sex, Sickness and Statehood: The Influence of Victorian Medical Opinion on Self-Government in Utah." M.A. thesis, BYU, 1980.

Grow, Stewart Lofgren. "A Study of the Utah Commission 1882–1896." Ph.D. diss., Univ. of Utah, 1954.

Hayward, Barbara. "Utah's Anti-Polygamy Society 1878–1884." M.A. thesis, BYU, 1980.

Hickman, Martin Berkeley. "Utah Constitutional Law." Ph.D. diss., Univ. of Utah, 1954.

Katz, Suzanne Adel. "Sisters in Salvation: Patterns of Emotional Loneliness among Nineteenth Century Non-Elite Mormon Polygamous Women." M.A. thesis, Calif. St. Univ., Fullerton, 1987.

Kern, Louis John. "Love, Labor, and Self-Control: Sex Roles and Sexuality in Three Nineteenth-Century American Utopian Communities." Ph.D. diss., Rutgers Univ., 1977.

Law, Wesley R. "Mormon Indian Missions—1855." M.A. thesis, BYU, 1954.

Madsen, Carol Cornwall. "A Mormon Woman in Victorian America." Ph.D. diss., Univ. of Utah, 1985.

Meservy, Joseph Robert. "A History of Federal Legislation against Mormon Polygamy and Certain United States Supreme Court Decisions Supporting Such Legislation." M.S. thesis, BYU, 1947.

Mouritsen, Dale C. "A Symbol of New Directions: George Franklin Richards and the Mormon Church, 1861–1950." Ph.D. diss., BYU, 1982.

Neff, Karen Preece. "Attitudes toward Women's Rights and Roles in Utah Territory, 1847–1887." M.S. thesis, Utah St. Univ., 1982.

Parkin, Max H. "The Nature and Cause of Internal and External Conflict of the Mormons in Ohio between 1830 and 1838." M.A. thesis, BYU, 1966.

Poll, Richard D. "The Mormon Question, 1850–1865: A Study in Politics and Public Opinion." Ph.D. diss., Univ. of Calif., Berkeley, 1948.

———. "The Twin Relic: A Study of Mormon Polygamy and the Campaign by the Government of the United States for Its Abolition, 1852–1890." M.A. thesis, Texas Christian Univ., 1939.

Pollock, Gordon. "In Search of Security: The Mormons and the Kingdom of God on Earth, 1830–1844." Ph.D. diss., Queen's Univ., 1977.

Shipps, Jo Ann Barnett. "The Mormons in Politics: The First Hundred Years." Ph.D. diss., Univ. of Colorado, 1965.

Tappan, Paul Wilbur. "Mormon-Gentile Conflict: A Study of the Influence of Public Opinion on In-Group Versus Out-Group Interaction with Special Reference to Polygamy." Ph.D. diss., Univ. of Wisc., 1939.

Turner, Charles Millard. "Joseph Smith III and the Mormons of Utah." Ph.D. diss., Graduate Theological Union, Berkeley, Calif., 1985.

Van Orden, Bruce Arthur. "George Reynolds: Secretary, Sacrificial Lamb, and Seventy." Ph.D. diss., BYU, 1986.

Van Wagenen, Lola. "Sister-Wives and Suffragists: Polygamy and the Politics of Woman Suffrage 1870–1896." Ph.D. diss., N.Y. Univ., 1994.

Whittaker, David J. "Early Mormon Pamphleteering." Ph.D. diss., BYU, 1982.

Wight, Lyle O. "Origins and Development of the Church of the Firstborn of the Fullness of Times." M.A. thesis, BYU, 1963.

Wilcox, Archie G. "Founding of the Mormon Community in Alberta." M.A. thesis, Univ. of Alberta, 1950.

Woodford, Robert J. "The Historical Development of the *Doctrine and Covenants*." 3 vols. Ph.D. diss., BYU, 1974.

Books

Abu-Lughod, Lila. *Veiled Sentiments: Honor and Poetry in a Bedouin Society*. Berkeley, Los Angeles, and London: Univ. of Calif. Press, 1986.

Alexander, Thomas G. *Mormonism in Transition: A History of the Latter-Day Saints, 1890–1930*. Urbana and Chicago: Univ. of Ill. Press, 1986.

———. *Things in Heaven and Earth: the Life and Times of Wilford Woodruff, a Mormon Prophet*. S.L.C: Signature Books, 1991.

———. *Utah the Right Place: The Official Centennial History*. S.L.C: Gibbs-Smith Publisher, 1995.

Ali, Maulana Muhammad. *The Holy Qur'an: Arabic Text, English Translation and Commentary*, 2nd rev. edn. Columbus, Ohio: Ahmadiyyah Anjuman Isha'at Islam, Lahore, Inc. USA, 1995.

Allen, David O. *India, Ancient and Modern. Geographical, Historical, Political, Social and Religious; with a Particular Account of the State and Prospects of Christianity*. Boston: John P. Jewett & Co., 1856.

Allen, James B., and Glen M. Leonard. *Story of the Latter-day Saints*. S.L.C: Deseret Book Co., 1976.

———, and Richard O. Cowan. *Mormonism in the Twentieth Century*. Provo, Utah: BYU Press, 1969. Rev. edn.

————. *Trials of Discipleship: The Story of William Clayton, a Mormon.* Urbana and Chicago: Univ. of Ill. Press, 1987.

Allred, B. Harvey. *A Leaf in Review of the Words and Acts of God and Men Relative to the Fullness of the Gospel.* Draper, Utah: Review and Preview Publishers, 1980. 2nd edn. rev. by Rhea Allred Kunz et al.

Alter, J. Cecil. *Utah, The Storied Domain: A Documentary History of Utah's Eventful Career . . .* 3 vols. Chicago and N. Y: American Hist. Soc., Inc., 1932.

Altman, Irwin, and Joseph Ginat. *Polygamous Families in Contemporary Society.* N.Y.C: Cambridge Univ. Press, 1996.

Ames, Herman. *Proposed Amendments to the Constitution of the United States during the First Century of its History.* 1896; Lenox Hill Publishing reprint, 1970.

Anderson, Devery S. and Gary James Bergera, eds. *Joseph Smith's Quorum of the Anointed: A Documentary History.* S.L.C: Signature Books, 2005.

Anderson, Nels. *Desert Saints: The Mormon Frontier in Utah.* Chicago and London: Univ. of Chicago Press, 1942.

Arndt, Karl J. R. *George Rapp's Harmony Society 1785–1847.* Philadelphia: Univ. of Pa. Press, 1965.

Arrington, Leonard J., and Davis Bitton. *The Mormon Experience: A History of the Latter-day Saints.* N.Y.C: Alfred A. Knopf, 1979.

————. *Brigham Young: American Moses.* N.Y.C: Alfred A. Knopf, 1985.

————. *Great Basin Kingdom: An Economic History of the Latter-day Saints, 1830–1900.* Cambridge, Mass: Harvard Univ. Press, 1958.

————. *Kate Field and J. H. Beadle: Manipulators of the Mormon Past.* American West Lecture. S.L.C: n.p., 1971.

Athearn, Robert G. *Westward the Briton.* Lincoln: Univ. of Nebr. Press, 1953.

Augustine, Saint. *The City of God.*

Baer, Hans A. *Recreating Utopia in the Desert: A Sectarian Challenge to Modern Mormonism.* Albany: St. Univ. of N.Y. Press, 1988.

Bagley, Will, ed. *The Pioneer Camp of the Saints: The 1846 and 1847 Mormon Trail Journals of Thomas Bullock.* Vol. 1: *Kingdom in the West, The Mormons and the American Frontier.* Spokane, Wash: The Arthur H. Clark Co., 1997.

————, ed. *Scoundrel's Tale: The Samuel Brannan Papers.* Vol. 3: *Kingdom in the West: The Mormons and the American Frontier.* Spokane, Wash: The Arthur H. Clark Co., 1999.

Bakken, Gordon Morris. *Rocky Mountain Constitution Making, 1850–1912.* Westport, Conn: Greenwood Press, 1987.

————. *Development of Law on the Rocky Mountain Frontier: Civil Law and Society, 1850–1912.* Westport, Conn., and London: Greenwood Press, 1983.

Bancroft, Hubert Howe. *History of Utah, 1540–1886.* Vol. 26: *The Works of Hubert Howe Bancroft.* San Francisco: The History Company, Publishers, 1889.

————. *Literary Industries. A Memoir.* Vol. 39: *The Works of Hubert Howe Bancroft.* San Francisco: The History Company, Publishers, 1890.

Baskin, Robert Newton. *Reminiscences of Early Utah.* [S.L.C: Tribune-reporter Printer Co.], 1914.

Bates, Catherine. *A Year in the Great Republic.* 2 vols. London: Ward and Downey, 1887.

Beadle, J[ohn] H[anson]. *Life in Utah; or, the Mysteries and Crimes of Mormonism. Being an Exposé of the Secret Rites and Ceremonies of the Latter-Day Saints, with a Full and Authentic History of Polygamy and the Mormon Sect from its Origin to the Present Time.* Philadelphia, Chicago, Cincinnati: National Publishing Co., 1870.

Beal, M[errill] D. *History of Southeastern Idaho: An Intimate Narrative of Peaceful Conquest by Empire Builders . . .* Caldwell, Idaho: The Caxton Printers, 1942.

Beecher, Jonathan, and Richard Bienvenu, eds. and trans. *The Utopian Vision of Charles Fourier: Selected Texts on Work, Love, and Passionate Attraction.* Boston: Beacon Press, 1971.

Beers, Robert W. *The Mormon Puzzle and How To Solve It.* N.Y.C: Funk and Wagnalls, 1887.

Beeton, Beverly. *Women Vote in the West: The Woman Suffrage Movement 1869–1896.* N.Y.C. and London: Garland Publishing, Inc., 1986.

Belisle, Orvilla S. *The Prophets; or, Mormonism Unveiled . . .* Philadelphia: W.W. Smith; London: Trubner & Co., 1855.

Bennett, John C. *The History Of The Saints; or, An Exposé of Joe Smith and Mormonism.* Boston: Leland & Whiting; N.Y: Bradbury, Soden, & Co.; Cincinnati: E.S. Norris & Co., 1842.

Bennion, Janet. *Women of Principle: Female Networking in Contemporary Mormon Polygyny.* N.Y.C. and Oxford: Oxford Univ. Press, 1998.

Bennion, Lowell C., Alan L. Morrell, and Thomas Carter. *Polygamy in Lorenzo Snow's Brigham City: An Architectural Tour.* S.L.C: College of Architecture & Planning, Univ. of Utah, 2005.

Bertrand, L[ouis] A[lphonse]. *Mémoires d'un Mormon.* Paris: E. Jung-Treuttel, [1862].

Beveridge, Albert J[eremiah]. *Abraham Lincoln, 1809–1858.* 4 vols. Boston and N.Y.C: Houghton Mifflin Co., 1928.

The Bible & Polygamy. Does the Bible Sanction Polygamy? A Discussion between Professor Orson Pratt, One of the Twelve Apostles of the Church of Jesus Christ of Latter-day Saints, and Rev. Doctor J. P. Newman, Chaplain of the United States Senate, in the New Tabernacle, Salt Lake City, August 12, 13, and 14, 1870 . . . S.L.C: Published at the Deseret News Steam Printing Establishment, 1877.

Bigler, David L. *Forgotten Kingdom: The Mormon Theocracy in the American West, 1847–1896.* Vol. 2: *Kingdom in the West: The Mormons and the American Frontier.* Will Bagley, ed. Spokane, Wash: The Arthur H. Clark Co., 1998.

———. *Fort Limhi: The Mormon Adventure in Oregon Territory 1855–1858.* Vol. 6: *Kingdom in the West: The Mormons and the American Frontier.* Will Bagley, ed. Spokane, Wash: The Arthur H. Clark Co., 2003.

Billington, Ray Allen. *Land of Savagery, Land of Promise: the European Image of the American Frontier in the Nineteenth Century.* N.Y.C. and London: W.W. Norton & Co., 1981.

Billington, James H. *The Icon and the Axe: An Interpretive History of Russian Culture.* N.Y.C: Alfred A. Knopf, 1966.

Binet, Jacques. *Marriage en Afrique noire.* Paris: Les Éditions du Cerf, 1959.

Birge, Julius C. *The Awakening of the Desert.* Boston: Richard G. Badger, 1912.

Bitton, Davis. *George Q. Cannon: A Biography.* S.L.C: Deseret Book Co., 1999.

Bloom, Harold. *American Religion: The Emergence of a Post-Christian Nation.* N.Y.C: Simon & Schuster, 1992.

Bowles, Samuel. *Across the Continent: A Summer's Journey to the Rocky Mountains, the Mormons, and the Pacific States, with Speaker Colfax. By Samuel Bowles, Editor of the Springfield (Mass.) Republican.* Springfield, Mass: Samuel Bowles & Co; N.Y.C: Hurd & Houghton, 1866.

————. *Our New West. Records of Travel between The Mississippi River and the Pacific Ocean . . .* Hartford, Conn: Hartford Publishing Co., 1869.

Bradford, William. *A History of Plymouth Plantation 1620–1647.* 2 vols. N.Y.C: Mass. Hist. Soc. edn., 1912; reissued by Russell & Russell, 1968.

Bradley, Martha Sonntag. *Kidnapped from that Land: The Government Raids on the Short Creek Polygamists.* S.L.C: Univ. of Utah Press, 1993.

————, and Mary Brown Firmage Woodward. *4 Zinas: A Story of Mothers and Daughters on the Mormon Frontier.* S.L.C: Signature Books, 2000.

Briggs, Jason W. *The Basis of Brighamite Polygamy: A Criticism upon the (so called) Revelation of July 12th, 1843 . . .* Lamoni, Iowa: Reorganized Church of Christ, [1875].

Brimhall, George Washington. *The Workers of Utah.* Provo City, Utah: Printed by the Enquirer Co., 1889.

Broadbent, Joseph Leslie, comp. *Celestial Marriage?* [S.L.C: n.p., 1927].

Brocchus, Perry E., Judge. *Letter of Judge Brocchus, of Alabama, to the Public, upon the Difficulties in the Territory of Utah.* Wash., D.C: Henry Polkinhorn, 1859.

Brodie, Fawn M[cKay]. *No Man Knows My History: The Life of Joseph Smith, the Mormon Prophet.* N.Y.C: Alfred A. Knopf, 1971. 2nd rev. edn.

Brooks, Juanita, ed. *Not by Bread Alone: The Journal of Martha Spence Heywood, 1850–56.* S.L.C: Utah St. Hist. Soc., 1978.

————, ed. *On the Mormon Frontier: The Diary of Hosea Stout, 1844–1861.* 2 vols. S.L.C: Univ. of Utah Press, 1964.

Brown, James Stephens. *Life of a Pioneer. Being the Autobiography of James S. Brown.* S.L.C: George Q. Cannon & Sons, Co., 1900.

Brown, William. *A History of Missions, or, of the Propagation of Christianity among the heathen, since the Reformation.* 2 vols. Philadelphia: B. Coles, 1816.

Browne, Thomas. *Religio Medici.* London: Andrew Crooke, 1642.

Brundage, James A. *Law, Sex, and Christian Society in Medieval Europe.* Chicago and London: Univ. of Chicago Press, 1987.

Buerger, David John. *The Mysteries of Godliness: A History of Mormon Temple Worship.* San Francisco: Smith Research Associates, 1994.

Bunker, Gary L., and Davis Bitton. *The Mormon Graphic Image, 1834–1914: Cartoons, Caricatures, and Illustrations.* S.L.C: Univ. of Utah Press, 1983.

Burton, Richard F[rancis]. *The City of the Saints, and Across the Rocky Mountains to California.* London: Longman, Green, Longman, and Roberts, 1861.

Bush, Lester E., Jr. *Health and Medicine among the Latter-day Saints: Science, Sense, and Scripture.* N.Y.C: Crossroad Publishing Co., 1993.

Bushman, Claudia L. *Mormon Sisters: Women in Early Utah.* Cambridge, Mass: Emmeline Press Limited, 1976.

Cairncross, John. *After Polygamy Was Made a Sin: The Social History of Christian Polygamy.* London: Routledge & Kegan Paul, 1974.

Calhoun, Arthur W. *A Social History of the American Family from Colonial Times to the Present.* 3 vols. Cleveland, Ohio: The Arthur H. Clark Co., 1917–19.

Calhoun, Frederick S. *The Lawmen: United States Marshals and their Deputies, 1789–1989.* Wash., D.C., and London: Smithsonian Institution Press, 1989.

Cannon, Donald Q., and Lyndon W. Cook, eds. *Far West Record: Minutes of the Church of Jesus Christ of Latter-day Saints, 1830–1844.* S.L.C: Deseret Book Co., 1983.

Cannon, George Q[uayle]. *The History of the Mormons, Their Persecutions and Travels, by President George Q. Cannon. Also the Two Manifestoes of the Presidency of the Church of Jesus Christ of Latter-day Saints and Members of the Council of the Apostles.* S.L.C: George Q. Cannon & Sons, 1891.

Carlton, Ambrose B. *The Wonderlands of the Wild West, with Sketches of the Mormons.* N.p., 1891.

Catlin, George. *Letters and Notes on the Manners, Customs, and Condition of the North American Indians . . .* 2 vols. London: David Bogue, 1844.

Chandless, William. *A Visit to Salt Lake; being a Journey across the Plains and a Residence in the Mormon Settlements at Utah.* London: Smith, Elder and Co., 1857.

Chronicles of Courage. 8 vols. S.L.C: Daughters of Utah Pioneers, 1990–97.

Church History in the Fulness of Times. The History of the Church of Jesus Christ of Latter-day Saints. Prepared by the Church Educational System. Rev. ed. S.L.C: The Church of Jesus Christ of Latter-day Saints, 1993.

Clayton, William. *The Latter-day Saints' Emigrants' Guide . . .* St. Louis: Republican Steam Power Press, 1848.

Cleland, Robert Glass, and Juanita Brooks, eds. *A Mormon Chronicle: The Diaries of John D. Lee, 1884–1876.* 2 vols. San Marino, Calif: The Huntington Library, 1955.

Clements, Louis J., ed. *Fred T. Dubois's The Making of a State.* Rexburg, Idaho: Eastern Idaho Publishing Co., 1971.

Clignet, Remi. *Many Wives, Many Powers: Authority and Power in Polygynous Families.* Evanston, Ill: Northwestern Univ. Press, 1970.

Codman, John. *A Solution of the Mormon Problem.* N.Y.C: G.P. Putnam's Sons, 1885.

Colenso, John William. *A Letter to an American Missionary from the Bishop of Natal.* Pietermaritzburg: James Archbell, 1856.

Colfax, Schuyler. *The Mormon Question. Being a Speech of Vice-President Schuyler Colfax, at Salt Lake City. A Reply thereto by Elder John Taylor; and a Letter of Vice-President Colfax Published in the "New York Independent," with Elder Taylor's Reply.* S.L.C: Deseret News Office, 1870.

Collier, Fred C. "Re-examining the Lorin Woolley Story," *Doctrine of the Priesthood* 1:2 (Feb. 1981).

——, and Knut Knuteson, eds. "Trials of Apostle John W. Taylor and Matthias F. Cowley." *Doctrine of the Priesthood* 4:1 (Jan. 1987).

——, comp. and ed. *Unpublished Revelations of the Prophets and Presidents of The Church of Jesus Christ of Latter Day Saints.* Vol. 1. S.L.C: Collier's Publishing Co., 1981. 2nd edn. rev.

Compton, Todd. *In Sacred Loneliness: The Plural Wives of Joseph Smith.* S.L.C: Signature Books, 1997.

Conkin, Paul K. *American Originals. Homemade Varieties of Christianity.* Chapel Hill and London: Univ. of North Carolina Press, 1997.

——. *A Requiem for the American Village.* Lanham, Boulder, N.Y.C., and Oxford: Rowman & Littlefield, 2000.

Cook, Lyndon W., and Milton V. Backman Jr., eds. *Kirtland Elders' Quorum Record, 1836–1841.* Provo, Utah: Grandin Book Co., 1985.

——. *Nauvoo Marriages Proxy Sealings: 1843–1846.* Provo, Utah: Grandin Book Co., 2004.

Cooper, Rex Eugene. *Promises Made to the Fathers: Mormon Covenant Organization*, Publications in Mormon Studies, vol. 5. S.L.C: Univ. of Utah Press, 1990.

Cooper, Thomas. *Strictures Addressed To James Madison On The Celebrated Report Of William H. Crawford, Recommending The Intermarriage Of Americans With The Indian Tribes. Ascribed To Judge Cooper, And Originally Published By John Binnes, In The Democratic Press.* Philadelphia: J. Harding, 1824.

Cott, Nancy F. *Public Vows: A History of Marriage and the Nation.* Cambridge, Mass., and London: Harvard Univ. Press, 2000.

Cowley, Matthias F. *Wilford Woodruff, Fourth President of the Church of Jesus Christ of Latter-day Saints* . . . S.L.C: Deseret News, 1909.

Craig, Samuel G. *Perfectionism.* Philadelphia: Presbyterian and Reformed Publishing Co., 1967.

Crocheron, Augusta Joyce. *Representative Women of Deseret, A Book of Biographical Sketches* . . . S.L.C: J.C. Graham & Co., 1884.

Cross, Whitney R. *The Burned-over District: The Social and Intellectual History of Enthusiastic Religion in Western New York, 1800–1850.* Ithaca: Cornell Univ. Press, 1950.

Cullom, Shelby M. *Personal Recollections of Shelby M. Cullom Senior United States Senator from Illinois.* Chicago: A.C. McClurg & Co., 1911.

Curtis, George Ticknor. *Letter to the Secretary of the Interior on the Affairs of Utah, Polygamy, "Cohabitation," &c.* Wash. D.C: Gibson Bros., 1886.

Daly, Martin, and Margo Wilson. *Sex Evolution and Behavior: Adaptations for Reproduction.* North Scituate, Mass: Duxbury Press, 1978.

Daniel, Norman. *Islam and the West: the Making of an Image.* Oxford: Oneworld Publications, Ltd., 1993. Rev. edn.

Daynes, Kathryn M. *More Wives than One: Transformation of the Mormon Marriage System, 1840–1910.* Urbana and Chicago: Univ. of Ill. Press, 2001.

De Rupert, A. E. D. *Californians and Mormons.* N.Y.C: John Wurtele Lovell, 1881.

Defence of the Constitutional and Religious Rights of the People of Utah. Speeches of Senators [George V.] *Vest,* [John T.] *Morgan,* [Wilkinson] *Call,* [Joseph E.] *Brown,* [George H.] *Pendleton and* [Lucius Q. C.] *Lamar.* S.L.C: n.p., 1882.

Defense of Plural Marriage by the Women of Utah County. Provo, Utah: Enquirer Office, 1878.

Degler, Carl N. *At Odds: Women and the Family in America from the Revolution to the Present.* N.Y.C: Oxford Univ. Press, 1980.

[Delany, Patrick]. *Reflections upon Polygamy, and the Encouragement Given to that Practise* . . . London: J. Roberts, 1737.

Deseret News, Extra, containing A Revelation on Celestial Marriage, A Remarkable Vision, Two Discourses, Delivered By President Brigham Young, One Discourse by Elder Orson Pratt; Remarks By Elders H.C. Kimball, John Taylor, and others . . . Great S.L.C., U.T., 14 Sept. 1852.

Dixon, William Hepworth. *New America.* Philadelphia: J.B. Lippincott & Co., 1867.

———. *Spiritual Wives,* 2 vols. London: Hurst & Blackett, 1868.

———. *White Conquest,* 2 vols. London: Chatto and Windus, 1876.

Doctrine and Covenants of The Church of The Latter Day Saints: Carefully Selected from the Revelations of God, and Compiled by Joseph Smith Junior, Oliver Cowdery, Sidney Rigdon, Frederick G. Williams, [Presiding Elders of said Church.] *Proprietors.* Kirtland, Ohio: Printed by F.G. Williams & Co. for the Proprietors, 1835.

Doctrine and Covenants, of the Church of Jesus Christ of Latter-day Saints, Containing the Revelations given to Joseph Smith, Jun., The Prophet, for the Building up of the Kingdom of God in the Last Days. S.L.C., Utah Territory: Deseret News Office, 1876.

Doctrine and Covenants, of the Church of Jesus Christ of Latter-day Saints, Containing the Revelations given to Joseph Smith, Jun., the Prophet, for the Building up of the Kingdom of God in the Last Days. S.L.C: Deseret News, Printers and Publisher, 1908.

Doctrine and Covenants of the Church of Jesus Christ of Latter-Day Saints. S.L.C: Church of Jesus Christ of Latter-day Saints, 1982.

Doenecke, Justus D. *The Presidencies of James A. Garfield and Chester A. Arthur.* Lawrence: The Regents Press of Kans., 1981.

Dwight, Sereno Edwards. *The Hebrew Wife or the Law of Marriage Examined in Relation to the Lawfulness of Polygamy and to the Extent of the Law of Incest.* N.Y.C: Leavitt, Lord & Co., 1836.

Dwyer, Robert J. *The Gentile Comes to Utah: A Study in Religious and Social Conflict (1862–1890).* S.L.C: Western Epics, 1971. rev. ed.

Ehrman, Bart B. *Lost Christianities: The Battles for Scripture and the Faiths We Never Knew.* Oxford and N.Y.C: Oxford Univ. Press, 2003.

Ekins, Roger Robin, ed. *Defending Zion: George Q. Cannon and the California Mormon Newspaper Wars of 1856–1857.* Vol. 5: *Kingdom in the West: The Mormons and the American Frontier.* Will Bagley, ed. Spokane, Wash: The Arthur H. Clark Co., 2002.

Ellsworth, George S., ed. *Dear Ellen: Two Mormon Women and Their Letters.* S.L.C: Tanner Trust Fund, Univ. of Utah, 1974.

Embry, Jessie L. *Mormon Polygamous Families: Life in the Principle.* S.L.C: Univ. of Utah Press, 1987.

Emmons, S. Bulfinch. *Philosophy of Popular Superstitions and the Effects of Credulity and Imagination upon the Moral, Social, and Intellectual Condition of the Human Race.* Boston: L. P. Crown, 1853.

An Enduring Legacy. 12 vols. S.L.C: Daughters of Utah Pioneers, 1978–89.

Erickson, Dan. *"As A Thief in the Night": The Mormon Quest for Millennial Deliverance.* S.L.C: Signature Books, 1998.

Erle, Manfred. *Ehe im Naturrecht des 17. Jahrhunderts: Ein Beitrag zu den geistesgeschichtlichken Grundlagen des modernen Eherechts.* Göttingen: n.p., 1952.

Esmein, A[dhémar]. *Marriage en droit canonique, par A. Esmein.* 2 vols. Paris: L. Larose et Forcel, 1891.

Esquivel Obrégon, Toribio. *Apuntes para la historia del derecho en Mexico . . .* 4 vols. Mexico, D.F: Editorial Polis, 1937–48.

Essays of Arthur Schopenhauer. Thomas Bailey Saunders, trans. N.Y.C: A. L. Burt [1892].

Evans, Beatrice Cannon, and Janath Russell Cannon, eds. *A Cannon Family Historical Treasury.* N.p: George Cannon Family Association, 1967.

Evans, John Henry. *One Hundred Years of Mormonism. A History of the Church of Jesus Christ of Latter-day Saints from 1805 to 1905.* 3rd edn. S.L.C: Deseret Sunday School Union, 1909.

Faragher, John Mack. *Women and Men on the Overland Trail.* New Haven and London: Yale Univ. Press, 1979.

Ferris, Benjamin G. *Utah and the Mormons: The History, Government, Doctrines, Customs, and Prospects of The Latter-Day Saints . . .* N.Y.C: Harper & Brothers, Publishers, 1854.

Ferris, Mrs. Benjamin G. *The Mormons at Home; With Some Incidents of Travel from Missouri to California, 1852–3. In A Series of Letters.* N.Y.C: Dix & Edwards; London: Sampson, Low & Son & Co., 1856.

Fielding, Robert Kent. *The Unsolicited Chronicler: An Account of the Gunnison Massacre, Its Causes and Consequences Utah Territory, 1847–1859.* Brookline, Mass: Paradigm Publications, 1993.

Fife, Austin and Alta. *Saints of Sage and Saddle: Folklore among the Mormons.* Bloomington: Ind. Univ. Press, 1956.

Fifer, J. Valerie. *American Progress: The Growth of the Transport, Tourist and Information Industries in the Nineteenth-Century West seen through The Life and Times of George A. Crofutt Pioneer and Publicist of the Transcontinental Age.* Chester, Conn: Globe Pequot Press, 1988.

Firmage, Edwin Brown, and Richard Collin Mangrum. *Zion in the Courts: A Legal History of the Church of Jesus Christ of Latter-day Saints, 1830–1900.* Urbana and Chicago: Univ. of Ill. Press, 1988.

Fiske, John. *American Political Ideas.* N.Y.C: Harper & Brothers, 1901.

Flake, Kathleen. *The Politics of American Religious Identity: The Seating of Senator Reed Smoot, Mormon Apostle.* Chapel Hill and London: Univ. of North Carolina Press, 2004.

Flanders, Robert Bruce. *Nauvoo: Kingdom on the Mississippi.* Urbana: Univ. of Illinois Press, 1965.

Flew, R. Newton. *The Idea of Perfection in Christian Theology: An Historical Study of the Christian Ideal for the Present Life.* Oxford: Clarendon Press, 1934.

Flint, Timothy. *The History and Geography of the Mississippi Valley . . .* 2 vols. Cincinnati: E.H. Flint; Boston: Carter, Hendee, and Co., 1833. Third edn.

Ford, Thomas. *A History of Illinois, from its Commencement as a State in 1818 to 1847 . . .* Chicago: S.C. Griggs & Co.; N.Y.C: Ivison & Phinney, 1854.

Foster, Craig L. *Penny Tracts and Polemics: A Critical Analysis of Anti-Mormon Pamphleteering in Great Britain, 1837–1860.* S.L.C: Greg Kofford Books, 2002.

Foster, Lawrence. *Religion and Sexuality: Three American Communal Experiments of the Nineteenth Century.* N.Y.C: Oxford Univ. Press, 1981.

Fowler, Orson S. *Sexual Science; Including Manhood, Womanhood, and their Mutual Interrelations . . .* Cincinnati, Memphis and Atlanta: National Publishing Co., 1870.

Fowler, Lorenzo Niles. *Marriage: Its History and Ceremonies, with a Phrenological and Physiological Exposition of the Functions and Qualifications for Happy Marriages.* N.Y.C: Fowler & Wells, 1847.

Fox-Genovese, Elizabeth. *Within the Plantation Household: Black and White Women of the Old South.* Chapel Hill: Univ. of N.C. Press, 1988.

Froiseth, Jennie Anderson, ed. *The Women of Mormonism; or The Story of Polygamy as Told by the Victims Themselves.* Detroit: C.G.G. Paine, 1882.

[Fulton, Gilbert A., Jr., and Rulon Allred]. *The Most Holy Principle.* 4 vols. Murray, Utah: Gems Publishing Co., 1970–75.

———. *That Manifesto.* Kearns, Utah: Deseret Publishing Co., 1974.

Furness, Clifton Joseph, ed. *The Genteel Female: An Anthology.* N.Y.C: Alfred A. Knopf, 1931.

Furniss, Norman F. *The Mormon Conflict, 1850–1859.* New Haven and London: Yale Univ. Press, 1960.

Gallichan, Walter M. *Women under Polygamy.* London: Holden and Hardingham, 1914.

Gates, Paul Wallace. *A History of Public Land Law Development.* Wash., D.C: U.S. Govt. Printing Office, 1968.

Gay, Peter. *Education of the Senses.* Vol. 1: *The Bourgeois Experience, Victoria to Freud.* N.Y.C. and Oxford: Oxford Univ. Press, 1984.

Givens, Terryl L. *The Viper on the Hearth: Mormons, Myths, and the Construction of Heresy.* N.Y.C. and Oxford: Oxford Univ. Press, 1997.

Godbe, William S. *Polygamy: Its Solution in Utah—A Question of the Hour. An Address Delivered in Liberal Institute, Sunday, July 30, 1871* . . . S.L.C: Office of the Salt Lake Tribune, 1871.

Goetzmann, William H., and William N. Goetzmann. *The West of the Imagination.* N.Y.C. and London: W. W. Norton & Co., 1986.

González Navarro, Moisés. *La Colonización en México 1877–1910.* México: Talleres de impresión de estampillas y valores, 1960.

[Goodwin, Charles Carroll]. *History of the Bench and Bar of Utah.* S.L.C: Interstate Press Association, 1913.

Gordon, Sarah Barringer. *The Mormon Question: Polygamy and Constitutional Conflict in Nineteenth-Century America.* Chapel Hill and London: Univ. of N.C. Press, 2002.

Graffam, Merle H., ed. *Salt Lake School of the Prophets Minute Book 1883.* Palm Desert, Calif: ULC Press, 1981.

Greeley, Horace. *An Overland Journey from New York to San Francisco in the Summer of 1859.* N.Y.C: C.M. Saxton, Barker & Co.; San Francisco: H.H. Bancroft & Co., 1860.

Grégoire, M. *L'Influence du christianisme sur la condition des femmes.* Paris: Boudouin Frères, 1821.

Grimké, Sarah M. *Letters on the Equality of the Sexes, and the Condition of Woman* . . . Boston: Isaac Knapp, 1838.

Grindle, Wesley. *New Medical Revelations, Being a Popular Work on the Reproductive System, Its Debility and Diseases.* Philadelphia: n.p., 1857.

Grossberg, Michael. *Governing the Hearth: Law and the Family in Nineteenth-Century America.* Chapel Hill and London: Univ. of North Carolina Press, 1985.

Gunnison, J[ohn] W[illiams]. *The Mormons, or, Latter-Day Saints, in the Valley of the Great Salt Lake: A History of their Rise and Progress, Peculiar Doctrines, Present Condition, and Prospects, Derived from Personal Observation, during a Residence among Them.* Philadelphia: Lippincott, Grambo & Co., 1852.

[Gurley, Zenos Hovey, Sr.]. *Polygamic Revelation: Fraud! Fraud! Fraud!* . . . Lamoni, Iowa: True Latter Day Saints' Herald Office, n.d.

Hafen, Mary Ann. *Recollections of a Handcart Pioneer of 1860: A Woman's Life on the Mormon Frontier.* Lincoln and London: Univ. of Nebr. Press, 1983; reprint from original 1938 edn., excluding appendix B, Family Record.

Hagedorn, Hermann, ed. *The Works of Theodore Roosevelt.* 19 vols. N.Y.C: Charles Scribner's Sons, 1926.

Hale, Van. *Defining the Mormon Doctrine of Deity.* Sandy, Utah: Mormon Miscellaneous, 1985.

Hales, Brian C., and J. Max Anderson. *The Priesthood of Modern Polygamy: An LDS Perspective.* S.L.C: Northwest Publishing Co., 1992.

Haller, Mark H. *Eugenics: Hereditarian Attitudes in American Thought.* New Brunswick, N.J: Rutgers Univ. Press, 1963.

Hamilton, Thomas. *Men and Manners in America.* 2 vols. Edinburgh: William Blackwood; London: T. Cadell, Strand, 1833.

Hansen, Klaus J. *Mormonism and the American Experience.* Chicago and London: Univ. of Chicago Press, 1981.

————. *Quest for Empire: The Political Kingdom of God and the Council of Fifty in Mormon History*. East Lansing, Mich: Mich. St. Univ. Press, 1967.

Hardy, B. Carmon. *Solemn Covenant: The Mormon Polygamous Passage*. Urbana and Chicago: Univ. of Ill. Press, 1992.

Hardy, Lady [Mary Anne McDowell] Duffus. *Through Cities and Prairie Lands. Sketches of an American Tour*. N.Y.C: R. Worthington, 1881.

Hart-Davis, Rupert, ed. *Letters of Oscar Wilde*. N.Y.C: Harcourt, Brace & World, Inc., 1962.

Hartog, Hendrik. *Man and Wife in America: A History*. Cambridge, Mass: Harvard Univ. Press, 2000.

Hatch, Charles M., and Todd M. Compton, eds. *A Widow's Tale: The 1884–1896 Diary of Helen Mar Kimball Whitney*. Logan, Utah: Utah St. Univ. Press, 2003.

Hatch, Nathan O. *The Democratization of American Christianity*. New Haven: Yale Univ. Press, 1989.

Hatch, Nelle Spilsbury. *Mother Jane's Story*. Wasco, Calif: Shafer Publishing Co., 1964.

————, and B. Carmon Hardy, comps. and eds. *Stalwarts South of the Border*. Anaheim, Calif: n.p., 1985.

Hatch, William Whitridge. *There Is No Law . . . A History of Mormon Civil Relations in the Southern States, 1865–1905*. N.Y.C., Washington, and Hollywood: Vantage Press, 1968.

Haven, Jesse. *Celestial Marriage, and the Plurality of Wives! . . .* Cape Town, South Africa: W. Foelscher, 1854.

Hawthornthwaithe, Samuel. *Mr. Hawthornthwaithe's Adventures among the Mormons, as an Elder during Eight Years*. Manchester, Eng: Pub'd by the author, 1857.

Heart Throbs of the West. Kate B. Carter, comp. 12 vols. S.L.C: Daughters of Utah Pioneers, 1939–51.

Heywood, Ezra Harvey. *Cupid's Yokes: or, The Binding Forces of Conjugal Life. An Essay . . . Wherein is Asserted the Natural Right and Necessity of Sexual Self-Government; . . .* Princeton, Mass: Cooperative Publishing Co., 1877.

Higbie, Rev. Alfred. *Polygamy vs. Christianity; A Discourse Against Polygamy, and Baptism for the Dead. Delivered at Watsonville, June 14th, 1857*. San Francisco: Printed by B.F. Street, 1857.

Hill, Donna. *Joseph Smith: The First Mormon*. Garden City, N.Y: Doubleday & Co., Inc., 1977.

Hill, Ivy Hooper Blood, ed. *Jane Wilkie Hooper Blood: Autobiography and Abridged Diary*. Logan, Utah: J.P. Smith Printing, Inc., 1966.

Hill, Marvin S. *Quest for Refuge: The Mormon Flight from American Pluralism*. S.L.C: Signature Books, 1989.

Hillman, Eugene. *Polygamy Reconsidered: African Plural Marriage and the Christian Churches*. Maryknoll, N.Y: Orbis Books, 1975.

Hingston, E. P., ed. *Artemus Ward (His Travels) Among the Mormons . . .* London: John Camden Hotten, 1865.

History of Brigham Young, 1847–1867. Berkeley, Calif: MassCal Associates, 1964.

Holbrook, Joseph. *History of Joseph Holbrook 1806–1885 Written by His Own Hand*. Typed and edited by Mabel F. Holbrook and Ward C. Holbrook. N.p., n.d.

Hollister, O[vanda] J[ames]. *Life of Schuyler Colfax*. N.Y.C. and London: Funk & Wagnalls, 1886.

Holzapfel, Richard Neitzel, and Jeni Broberg Holzapfel, eds. *A Woman's View: Helen Mar Whitney's Reminiscences of Early Church History*. Provo, Utah: Religious Studies Center, BYU, 1997.

Hoogenboom, Ari. *Rutherford B. Hayes: Warrior and President.* Lawrence: Univ. Press of Kans., 1995.

Hooker, Thomas. *The Christians Two Chief Lessons, viz. Selfe-Denial, and Selfe-Tryall . . .* London: T. Badger, 1640.

Howard, John J. *A Plea for Polygamy: Being an Attempt at a Solution of the Woman-Question.* Boston: John J. Howard, 1875.

Hyde, John, Jun. *Mormonism: Its Leaders and Designs.* N.Y.C: W.P. Fetridge & Co., 1857.

Hyde, Myrtle Stevens, and Everett L. Cooley. *Life of Andrew Wood Cooley: A Story of Conviction.* Provo, Utah: Andrew Wood Cooley Family Association, 1991.

Hyman, Harold M. *To Try Men's Souls: Loyalty Tests in American History.* Berkeley and Los Angeles: Univ. of Calif. Press, 1960.

Iversen, Joan Smyth. *The Antipolygamy Controversy in U.S. Women's Movements, 1880–1925: A Debate on the American Home.* N.Y.C: Garland Publishing Co., 1997.

Jackson, Joseph H. *A Narrative of the Adventures and Experience of Joseph H. Jackson in Nauvoo . . .* Warsaw, Ill: n.p., 1844.

Jacob, Udney Hay. *Extract, From A Manuscript Entitled The Peace Maker, Or The Doctrines Of The Millennium: Being A Treatise On Religion And Jurisprudence, Or A New System Of Religion And Politics. For God, My Country, And My Rights. By Udney Hay Jacob, An Israelite, And A Shepherd of Israel.* Nauvoo, Ill: J. Smith, Printer, 1842.

James, George Wharton. *Utah the Land of Blossoming Valleys.* Boston: The Page Co., 1922.

James, William. *Varieties of Religious Experience: A Study in Human Nature Being the Gifford Lectures on Natural Religion Delivered at Edinburgh in 1901–1902.* N.Y.C., London, and Bombay: Longmans, Green, and Co., 1902.

[Jencks, E. N.] *History and Philosophy of Marriage; or, Polygamy and Monogamy Compared. By a Christian Philanthropist.* Boston: James Campbell, 1869.

Jensen, Juliaetta Bateman. *Little Gold Pieces: The Story of My Mormon Mother's Life.* S.L.C: Stanway, 1948.

Jenson, Andrew. *Latter-day Saint Biographical Encyclopedia. A Compilation of Biographical Sketches of Prominent Men and Women in the Church of Jesus Christ of Latter-day Saints.* 4 vols. S.L.C: A. Jenson History Co. and the Deseret News, 1901–36.

Jessee, Dean C., ed. and comp. *The Personal Writings of Joseph Smith.* S.L.C: Deseret Book, 1984.

Johannson, Robert W. *Stephen A. Douglas.* Urbana and Chicago: Univ. of Illinois Press, 1997, Illini Books edn. of 1973 Oxford Univ. Press original.

Johnson, Allen. *Stephen A. Douglas: A Study in American Politics.* N.Y.C: The Macmillan Co., 1908.

Johnson, Annie Richardson, Elva Richardson Shumway, and Enola Johnson Mangelson. *Charles Edmund Richardson: Man of Destiny.* Mesa, Ariz: The Annie R. Johnson Irrevocable Present Interest Trust, 1982.

Johnson, Benjamin F[ranklin]. *Why the "Latter Day Saints" Marry A Plurality of Wives. A Glance at Scripture and Reason, in Answer to an Attack through the Polynesian, upon the Saints for Polygamy.* San Francisco: Excelsior, 1854.

———. *My Life's Review by Benjamin F. Johnson.* Independence, Mo: Zion's Printing & Publishing Co., 1947.

Johnson, Donald Bruce, and Kirk H. Porter, comps. *National Party Platforms, 1840–1972.* Urbana, Chicago, and London: Univ. of Ill. Press, 1973.

Johnson, Paul E., and Sean Wilentz. *The Kingdom of Matthias*. N.Y.C. and Oxford: Oxford Univ. Press, 1994.

Kane, Elizabeth Wood. *Twelve Mormon Homes Visited in Succession on a Journey through Utah to Arizona*. S.L.C: Tanner Trust Fund and Univ. of Utah Library, 1974.

Kane, Thomas. *Three Letters to the New York Herald from J. M. Grant, of Utah*. [N.Y.C., 1852].

Kanter, Rosabeth Moss. *Commitment and Community: Communes and Utopias in Sociological Perspective*. Cambridge, Mass: Harvard Univ. Press, 1972.

Kelly, Charles, ed. *Journals of John D. Lee, 1846–47 and 1859*. S.L.C: Univ. of Utah Press, 1984.

Kenney, Scott G., ed. *Wilford Woodruff's Journal, 1833–1898 Typescript*. 9 vols. Midvale, Utah: Signature Books, 1983–85.

Kern, Louis J. *An Ordered Love: Sex Roles and Sexuality in Victorian Utopias—the Shakers, the Mormons, and the Oneida Community*. Chapel Hill: Univ. of N.C. Press, 1981.

Kimball, Stanley B. *Heber C. Kimball: Mormon Patriarch and Pioneer*. Urbana, Chicago, and London: Univ. of Ill. Press, 1981.

———, ed. *On the Potter's Wheel: The Diaries of Heber C. Kimball*. S.L.C: Signature Books in association with Smith Research Associates, 1987.

Kraditor, Aileen S. *Up from the Pedestal*. Chicago: Quadrangle Books, 1968.

Lamar, Howard R. *The Far Southwest, 1846–1912: A Territorial History*. New Haven: Yale Univ. Press, 1966.

Larson, A. Karl and Katharine Miles Larson, eds. *Diary of Charles Lowell Walker*. 2 vols. Logan, Utah: Utah St. Univ. Press, 1980.

Larson, Gustive O. *The "Americanization" of Utah for Statehood*. San Marino, Calif: The Huntington Library, 1971.

Larson, Stan, ed. *Prisoner for Polygamy: The Memoirs and Letters of Rudger Clawson at the Utah Territorial Penitentiary, 1884–87*. Urbana and Chicago: Univ. of Illinois Press, 1993.

Launius, Roger D. *Joseph Smith III: Pragmatic Prophet*. Urbana: Univ. of Ill., 1988.

Lawson, John. *History of Carolina; Containing the Exact Description and Natural History of that Country: . . .* London: W. Taylor and J. Baker, 1714.

[Lea, Henry Charles]. *Bible View of Polygamy by Mizpah*. Philadelphia: n.p., n.d.

Lecky, William Edward Hartpole. *History of European Morals from Augustus to Charlemagne*. 2 vols. London: Longman's, Green & Co., 1869.

Lee, John D. *Mormonism Unveiled; Or The Life and Confessions of the Late Mormon Bishop, John D. Lee; . . .* St. Louis: Bryan, Brand & Co.; N.Y.C: W.H. Stelle & Co., 1877.

Leonard, Glen M. *Nauvoo: A Place of Peace, A People of Promise*. S.L.C. and Provo, Utah: Deseret Book Co. and BYU Press, 2002.

Lieber, Constance L., and John Sillito, eds. *Letters from Exile: The Correspondence of Martha Hughes Cannon and Angus M. Cannon, 1886–1888*. S.L.C: Signature Books in association with Smith Research Associates, 1989.

Lieber, Francis. *On Civil Liberty and Self-Government*. London: Richard Bentley, 1853.

Linn, William Alexander. *The Story of the Mormons, from the Date of their Origin to the Year 1901*. N.Y.C: The Macmillan Co.; London: Macmillan & Co., Ltd., 1902.

Littlefield, Lyman Omer. *An Open Letter, Addressed to President Joseph Smith, Jr., of the Re-Organized Church of Jesus Christ of Latter Day Saints, and Others Conspicuous at Conference Recently Held in the Temple at Kirtland, O.* Logan, Utah: n.p., 1883.

——. *Reminiscences of Latter-Day Saints, Giving an Account of Much Individual Suffering Endured for Religious Conscience.* Logan, Utah: Utah Journal Co., Printers, 1888.

Logue, Larry M. *A Sermon in the Desert: Belief and Behavior in Early St. George, Utah.* Urbana and Chicago: Univ. of Ill. Press, 1988.

Long, E. B. *The Saints and the Union: Utah Territory during the Civil War.* Urbana, Chicago, and London: Univ. of Ill. Press, 1981.

Long, Jay L., and Betsy W. Long. *Charles Ramsden Bailey: His Life and Families.* Midvale, Utah: Eden Hill, 1983.

Ludlow, Daniel H., ed. *Encyclopedia of Mormonism.* 4 vols. N.Y.C: Macmillan Publishing Co., 1992.

Lum, D[yer] D[aniel]. *Utah and its People. Facts and Statistics Bearing on the "Mormon Problem" . . . By a Gentile . . .* N.Y.C: R. O. Ferrier & Co., 1882.

Lyman, Edward Leo. *Political Deliverance: The Mormon Quest for Utah Statehood.* Urbana and Chicago: Univ. of Ill. Press, 1986.

Macfarlane, L. W. *Yours Sincerely, John M. Macfarlane.* S.L.C: Published by L. W. Macfarlane, 1980.

Mackay, Charles [Mayhew Henry, pseud.]. *Religious, Social, and Political History of the Mormons, or Latter-Day Saints, from their Origin to the Present Time . . . Edited, with Important Additions, by Samuel M. Smucker . . .* N.Y.C. and Auburn [New York]: Miller, Orton & Milligan, 1856.

[Madan, Martin]. *Thelypthora; or A Treatise on Female Ruin . . . ,* 3 vols. London: J. Dodsley, 1780. Second edn. rev., 1781.

Madsen, Brigham D. *Glory Hunter. A Biography of Patrick Edward Hunter.* S.L.C: Univ. of Utah Press, 1990.

——. *Gold Rush Sojourners in Great Salt Lake City 1849 and 1850.* S.L.C: Univ. of Utah Press, 1983.

Madsen, Carol Cornwall, ed. *Battle for the Ballot: Essays on Woman Suffrage in Utah, 1870–1896.* Logan: Utah St. Univ. Press, 1997.

Malmquist, O[rvin] N[ebeker]. *The First 100 Years: A History of The Salt Lake Tribune 1871–1971.* S.L.C: Utah St. Hist. Soc., 1971.

Marcus, Steven. *The Other Victorians: A Study of Sexuality and Pornography in Mid-Nineteenth-Century England.* N.Y.C: Basic Books, Inc., 1964.

Marquardt, H. Michael. *The Joseph Smith Revelations: Text & Commentary.* S.L.C: Signature Books, 1999.

——. *The Strange Marriages of Sarah Ann Whitney to Joseph Smith the Mormon Prophet, Joseph C. Kingsbury and Heber C. Kimball.* S.L.C: Utah Lighthouse Ministry, 1982. Rev. edn.

Mauss, Armand L. *All Abraham's Children: Changing Mormon Conceptions of Race and Lineage.* Urbana and Chicago: Univ. of Illinois Press, 2003.

McClintock, James H. *Mormon Settlement in Arizona: A Record of Peaceful Conquest of the Desert.* Phoenix, Ariz: n.p., 1921.

McConkie, Bruce R. *Mormon Doctrine.* S.L.C: Bookcraft, 1966. Rev. edn.

McCulloch, J. H., Jr., *Researches, Philosophical and Antiquarian, Concerning the Aboriginal History of America.* Baltimore: Fielding Lucas, Jr., 1829.

McDannell, Colleen, and Bernhard Lang, *Heaven: A History.* New Haven: Yale Univ. Press, 1988.

Memorial to Congress from a Committee of the Reorganized Church of Jesus Christ of Latter Day Saints, on the Claims and Faith of the Church. Plano, Ill: Printed at the True Latter Day Saints' Herald Steam Book Office, [1870].

Mernissi, Fatima. *Beyond the Veil: Male-Female Dynamics in Modern Muslim Society.* Bloomington: Indiana Univ. Press, 1987.

Miner, John. *Dr. Miner's Defense; being a concise relation of the church's process against him, for professing the doctrine of polygamy* [with] *his several pleas in vindication.* Hartford, Conn: Hudson & Goodwin, 1781.

Mintz, Steven, and Susan Kellogg. *Domestic Revolutions: A Social History of American Family Life.* N.Y.C. and London: Free Press, 1988.

Montesquieu, Charles-Louis de Secondat, Baron de la Bréde et de. *Spirit of Laws,* 1748. Trans. by Thomas Nugent. London: J. Nourse and P. Vaillant, 1750.

Morgan, Dale L. *The State of Deseret.* S.L.C: Utah St. Hist. Soc., 1940.

Morgan, Lewis Henry. *Ancient Society; or Researches in the Lines of Human Progress from Savagery through Barbarism to Civilization.* London: Macmillan and Co., 1877.

Mormoniad. Boston: A. Williams & Co., 1858.

Morris, Celia. *Fanny Wright: Rebel in America.* Urbana and Chicago: Univ. of Ill. Press, 1992.

Moss, Carolyn J. *Kate Field: Selected Letters.* Carbondale and Edwardsville: Southern Ill. Univ. Press, 1996.

Mulder, William, and A. Russell Mortensen, eds. *Among the Mormons: Historic Accounts by Contemporary Observers.* N.Y.C: Alfred A. Knopf, 1958.

Muncy, Raymond Lee. *Sex and Marriage in Utopian Communities: 19th Century America.* Bloomington and London: Ind. Univ. Press, 1973.

Murdock, George Peter. *Social Structure.* N.Y.C: Macmillan Co., 1960.

Murphy, John Mortimer. *Rambles in North-Western America from the Pacific Ocean to the Rocky Mountains . . .* London: Chapman and Hall, 1879.

Musser, A[mos] Milton. *"Race Suicide," Infanticide, Prolicide, Leprocide vs. Children: Letters to Messrs. Joseph Smith and Wm. H. Kelley Aggressively Defensive . . .* [S.L.C.]: n.p., 1904.

Musser, Ellis Shipp, ed. *The Early Autobiography and Diary of Ellis Reynolds Shipp, M.D.* S.L.C: Deseret News Press, 1962.

Myers, Sandra L. *Westering Women and the Frontier Experience, 1800–1915.* Albuquerque: Univ. of N.M. Press, 1982.

Napheys, George H. *The Physical Life of Woman: Advice to the Maiden, Wife, and Mother . . .* Philadelphia: H.C. Watts & Co.; Boston: G. M. Smith & Co., 1876.

Newson, Robert. *Is the Manifesto a Revelation? . . .* S.L.C: n.p., n.d.

Nibley, Preston. *Brigham Young: The Man and His Work.* S.L.C: Deseret News Press, 1937.

Nichols, Jeffrey. *Prostitution, Polygamy, and Power: Salt Lake City, 1847–1918.* Urbana and Chicago: Univ. of Ill. Press, 2002.

Nicholson, John. *The Martyrdom of Joseph Standing; or, the Murder of a "Mormon" Missionary. A True Story . . .* S.L.C: Deseret News Co., Printers, 1886.

Noble, Frederick Alphonso. *The Mormon Iniquity, a Discourse Delivered before the New West Educational Commission in the First Congregational Church, Sunday Evening, Nov.2, 1884 . . .* Chicago: Jameson & Morse, Printers, 1884.

O'Dea, Thomas F. *The Mormons.* Chicago and London: Univ. of Chicago Press, 1957.

Oaks, Dallin H., and Marvin S. Hill. *Carthage Conspiracy: The Trial of the Accused Assassins of Joseph Smith.* Urbana, Chicago, and London: Univ. of Ill. Press, 1976.

Opinions Concerning the Bible Law of Marriage by One of the People. Philadelphia: Claxton, Remson, & Haffelfinger, 1871.

Our Pioneer Heritage. Kate B. Carter, comp. 20 vols. S.L.C: Daughters of Utah Pioneers, 1958–77.

Paddock, A. G. [Cornelia]. *Fate of Madame LaTour: A Story of Great Salt Lake.* N.Y.C: Fords, Howard, & Hulbert, 1881.

Pagels, Elaine. *Adam, Eve, and the Serpent.* N.Y.C: Random House, 1988.

———. *Beyond Belief: The Secret Gospel of Thomas.* N.Y.C: Random House, 2003.

———. *The Gnostic Gospels.* N.Y.C: Random House, 1979.

Paley, William. *Principles of Moral and Political Philosophy,* 2 vols. London: R. Faulder, 1785. Ninth edn. rev., 1793.

Parker, William Belmont. *The Life and Public Services of Justin Smith Morrill.* Boston and N.Y.C: Houghton Mifflin Co., 1924.

Partridge, Scott H., ed. *Eliza Maria Partridge Journal.* Provo, Utah: Grandin Book Co., 2003.

Perrot, Michelle. *From the Fires of Revolution to the Great War,* vol. 4: *A History of Private Life,* Philippe Ariès and Georges Duby, eds.; Arthur Goldhammer, trans. Cambridge, Mass., and London: Harvard Univ. Press, 1990.

Peters, Francis E. *The Monotheists: Jews, Christians, and Muslims in Conflict and Competition.* Vol. 1: *The Peoples of God.* Princeton and Oxford: Princeton Univ. Press, 2003.

Phillips, George Whitfield. *The Mormon Menace: A Discourse before the New West Education Commission on its Fifth Anniversary at Chicago November 15, 1885.* Worcester, Mass: n.p., 1886.

Pioneer Pathways. 4 vols. S.L.C: Daughters of Utah Pioneers, 1998–.

Poll, Richard D., *et al. Utah's History.* Provo, Utah: BYU Press, 1978.

Pomeroy, Earl. *The Pacific Slope: A History of California, Oregon, Washington, Idaho, Utah, and Nevada.* N.Y.C: Alfred A. Knopf, 1965.

Porter, Larry C. *A Study of the Origins of The Church of Jesus Christ of Latter-day Saints in the States of New York and Pennsylvania, 1816–1831.* Provo, Utah: Joseph Fielding Institute for Latter-day Saint History and BYU St., 2000.

[Pratt, Belinda Marden]. *Defence of Polygamy, by a Lady of Utah, in a Letter To Her Sister in New Hampshire.* Great S.L.C: n.p., 1854.

Pratt, Parley P[arker]. *An Appeal to the Inhabitants of the State of New York, Letter to Queen Victoria . . . The Fountain of Knowledge, Immortality of the Body, and Intelligence and Affection . . .* Nauvoo, Ill: John Taylor Printer, [1844].

———. *"Mormonism!" "Plurality of Wives!" An Especial Chapter, for the Especial Edification of Certain Inquisitive News Editors, Etc. San Francisco, July 13th, 1852.* San Francisco, n.p., 1852.

———. *Scriptural Evidences in Support of Polygamy.* San Francisco: George Q. Cannon, 1856.

———. *Marriage and Morals in Utah. An Address by P.P. Pratt Read in Joint Session of the Legislature in the Representatives' Hall, Fillmore City, Dec. 31, 1855, by Mr. Thomas Bullock, Chief Clerk of the House.* Liverpool: Orson Pratt; London: L.D.S. Book & Star Depot, 1856.

Pratt, Parley P., Jr., ed. *Autobiography of Parley Parker Pratt, One of the Twelve Apostles of the Church of Jesus Christ of Latter-day Saints . . .* N.Y.C: Russell Brothers, 1874.

Prémontval, André Pierre le Guay de. *Monogamie; ou l'unité dans le marriage . . .* 3 vols. The Hague: P. van Cleef, 1751–52.

President Woodruff's Manifesto: Proceedings at the Semi-Annual General Conference of the Church of Jesus Christ of Latter-day Saints, Monday Forenoon, October 6, 1890. [S.L.C: n.p., 1890].

Price, Richard and Pamela. *Joseph Smith Fought Polygamy. How Men Nearest the Prophet Attached Polygamy to His Name in Order to Justify Their Own Polygamous Crimes.* Vol. 1. Independence, Mo: Price Publishing Co., 2000.

Pufendorf, Samuel von Freiherr. *Of the Law of Nature and Nations . . . , 1672.* Basil Kennett, trans. London: J. Walthoe, R. Wilkin, 1729. 4th edn. rev.

Quinn, D. Michael. *The Mormon Hierarchy.* Vol. 1: *Origins of Power.* S.L.C: Signature Books in association with Smith Research Associates, 1994.

————. *The Mormon Hierarchy.* Vol. 2: *Extensions of Power.* S.L.C: Signature Books in association with Smith Research Associates, 1997.

————. *Elder Statesman: A Biography of J. Reuben Clark.* S.L.C: Signature Books, 2002.

Rae, William Fraser. *Westward by Rail: the New Route to the East.* N.Y.C: D. Appleton & Co., 1871.

Rapson, Richard L. *Britons View America: Travel Commentary, 1860–1935.* Seattle and London: Univ. of Washington Press, 1971.

Remy, Jules. *Voyage au Pays des Mormons. Relation, géographie, histoire naturelle, histoire, théologie, moeurs et coutumes . . .* 2 vols. Paris: E. Dentu, 1860.

————. *Journey to Great-Salt-Lake City . . .* 2 vols. London: W. Jeffs, 1861.

Reply of Pres. Joseph Smith, to L. O. Littlefield, in Refutation of the Doctrine of Plural Marriage. Lamoni, Iowa: Published by the Reorganized Church of Jesus Christ of Latter Day Saints, 1885.

Richards, Franklin D., and James A. Little, comps. *Compendium of the Doctrines of the Gospel.* S.L.C: Deseret News Co., Printers, 1884. 2nd edn.

Ridlon, G[ideon] T[ibbetts], Sr. *Saco Valley Settlements and Families . . .* Portland, Me: Published by the Author, 1895.

Riley, Glenda. *Building and Breaking Families in the American West.* Albuquerque: Univ. of N.M. Press, 1996.

————. *Women on the American Frontier.* St. Louis, Mo: Forum Press, 1977.

Roberts, Brigham H[enry]. *The Life of John Taylor, Third President of the Church of Jesus Christ of Latter-day Saints.* S.L.C: George Q. Cannon and Sons Co., 1892.

————. *Outlines of Ecclesiastical History.* S.L.C: George Q. Cannon & Sons Co., 1895.

Rockwell, William Walker. *Doppelehe Des Landgraffen Philipp Von Hessen.* Marburg: N.G. Elwert'sche Verlagsbuchhandlung, 1904.

Romney, Thomas Cottam. *The Mormon Colonies in Mexico.* S.L.C: Deseret Book, 1938.

Rosen, Christine. *Preaching Eugenics: Religious Leaders and the American Eugenics Movement.* Oxford: Oxford Univ. Press, 2004.

Rosenberg, Charles E. *The Trial of the Assassin Guiteau: Psychiatry and Law in the Gilded Age.* Chicago and London: Univ. of Chicago Press, 1968.

Ross, Frederick A., and John William Colenso. *Dr. Ross and Bishop Colenso; or, The Truth Restored in Regard to Polygamy and Slavery . . .* Philadelphia: Henry B. Ashmead, 1857.

Ruxton, George Frederick. *Life in the Far West.* Edinburgh and London: William Blackwood and Sons, 1849.

Ryan, Michael. *The Philosophy of Marriage . . .* London: H. Bailliere, 1839. 3rd edn.

Said, Edward W. *Orientalism.* N.Y.C: Pantheon Books, 1978.

Sanford, Mrs. John. *Woman in her Social and Domestic Character.* Boston: Leonard C. Bowles, 1833.

Schroeder, H. J. *Canons and Decrees of the Council of Trent: Original Text with English Translation.* St. Louis and London: B. Herder Book Co., 1941.

Sears, Hal. *The Sex Radicals*. Lawrence: The Regents Press of Kans., 1977.

Sessions, Gene A. *Mormon Thunder: A Documentary History of Jedediah Morgan Grant*. Urbana, Chicago, and London: Univ. of Ill. Press, 1982.

Seventy-Fourth Annual Conference of the Church of Jesus Christ of Latter-day Saints Held in the Tabernacle, Salt Lake City, April 3rd, 4th and 6th, 1904, with a full Report of the Discourses . . . S.L.C: Deseret News, 1904.

Shelford, Leonard. *A Practical Treatise of the Law of Marriage and Divorce . . .* Philadelphia: John S. Littell, 1841.

Shook, Charles A. *The True Origins of Mormon Polygamy*. Cincinnati: Standard Publishing Co., 1914.

Short, Dennis R., comp. *Questions on Plural Marriage with a Selected Bibliography and 1600 References*. N.p., 1974.

Sillito, John, ed. *History's Apprentice: The Diaries of B. H. Roberts, 1880–1898*. S.L.C: Signature Books in association with Smith Research Associates, 2004.

Simon, John Y., ed. *The Papers of Ulysses S. Grant*. 24 vols. Carbondale and Edwardsville: Southern Illinois Univ. Press, 1967.

Sinclair, Keith, ed. *A Soldier's View of Empire: The Reminiscences of James Bodell, 1831–92*. London, Sydney, Toronto: The Bodley Head, 1982.

Smith, Andrew F. *The Saintly Scoundrel: The Life and Times of Dr. John Cook Bennett*. Urbana and Chicago: Univ. of Ill. Press, 1997.

Smith, Eliza R[oxcy] Snow. *The Biography and Family Record of Lorenzo Snow . . .* S.L.C: Deseret News, 1884.

Smith, George A. *The Rise, Progress and Travels of the Church . . .* S.L.C: Deseret News, 1872. 2nd edn. rev.

Smith, George D., ed. *An Intimate Chronicle: The Journals of William Clayton*. S.L.C: Signature Books in association with Smith Research Associates, 1991.

Smith, Joseph III. *Polygamy not of God. Joseph Smith's Fourth Letter to L. O. Littlefield*. [Lamoni, Iowa: True Latter Day Saints' Herald Office, 1883].

[Smith, Joseph F.] *Blood Atonement and the Origin of Plural Marriage: A Discussion . . .* S.L.C: Deseret News Press, 1905.

Smith, Robert. *A Series of Lectures on the Signs of the Times . . . and the Last Judgment*. Payson, Utah: Juvenile Instructor Office, 1887.

Spencer, Orson. *Patriarchal Order, Or Plurality of Wives!* Liverpool: S.W. Richards, 1853.

Stansbury, Howard. *An Expedition to the Valley of the Great Salt Lake of Utah: . . .* London: Sampson Low, Son and Co.; Philadelphia: Lippincott, Grambo, and Co., 1852.

Stark, Rodney, and William Sims Bainbridge. *The Future of Religion: Secularization, Revival and Cult Formation*. Berkeley, Los Angeles, and London: Univ. of Calif. Press, 1985.

Stein, Stephen J. *The Shaker Experience in America: A History of the United Society of Believers*. New Haven and London: Yale Univ. Press, 1992.

Stegner, Wallace. *Mormon Country*. N.Y.C: Duell, Slaon & Pearce, 1942.

Stenhouse, [Fanny] Mrs. T. B. H. *"Tell It All": The Story of a Life's Experience in Mormonism. An Autobiography . . .* Hartford, Conn: A.D. Worthington and Co., 1874.

Stenhouse, Thomas B. H. *The Rocky Mountain Saints: . . .* N.Y.C: D. Appleton and Company, 1873.

[Stillman, James W.]. *The Mormon Question. An Address . . .* Boston: J.P. Mendum, 1884.

Stoehr, Taylor. *Free Love in America: A Documentary History.* N.Y.C: AMS Press, Inc., 1979.

Strong, Josiah. *Our Country: Its Possible Future and Its Present Crisis.* N.Y.C: The Baker and Taylor Co., 1891. Rev. edn.

Sumner, Charles. *Charles Sumner: His Complete Works.* 20 vols. Boston: Lee and Shepherd, 1900.

Swetnam, Susan Hendricks. *Lives of the Saints in Southeast Idaho: An Introduction to Mormon Pioneer Life Story Writing.* Moscow: Univ. of Idaho Press; Boise: Idaho St. Hist. Soc., 1991.

Swisher, Carl Brent. *American Constitutional Development.* N.Y.C: Houghton Mifflin Co., 1954.

Talmage, James E[dward]. *The Story of "Mormonism" and the Philosophy of "Mormonism."* S.L.C: Deseret News, 1914.

[Talmage, Thomas DeWitt]. *Brooklyn Tabernacle. A Collection of 104 Sermons Preached by T. DeWitt Talmage, D.D.* N.Y.C. and London: Funk & Wagnalls Co., 1884.

Tanner, Annie Clark. *A Mormon Mother: An Autobiography.* S.L.C: Tanner Trust Fund and Univ. of Utah Library, 1973. Rev. edn.

Tanner, Mary Jane. *A Fragment: The Autobiography of Mary Jane Mount Tanner.* Margery W. Ward and George S. Tanner, eds. S.L.C: Published by Tanner Trust Fund, Univ. of Utah Library, 1980.

Taylor, John. *Three Nights' Public Discussion between Revds. C.W. Cleeve, James Robertson, and Philip Cater and Elder John Taylor, of the Church of Jesus Christ of Latter-day Saints, at Boulogne-sur-Mer, France . . .* Liverpool: John Taylor, 1850.

Taylor, Samuel W. *Rocky Mountain Empire: The Latter-day Saints Today.* N.Y.C: Macmillan Co., 1978.

————. *The Kingdom or Nothing: The Life of John Taylor, Militant Mormon.* N.Y.C: Macmillan Publishing Co.; London: Collier Macmillan Publishers, 1976.

Teachings of the Presidents of the Church: Brigham Young. S.L.C: Published by the Church of Jesus Christ of Latter-day Saints, 1997.

Thatcher, Moses. *La poligamia mormona y la monogamia cristiana comparadas.* [Cuidad] Mexico: E.D. Orozco y co., 1881.

The Mormon Problem. A Letter to the Massachusetts Members of Congress on Plural Marriage . . . By a Citizen of Massachusetts. Boston: James Campbell, 1882.

Thompson, John. *Mormonism—Increase of the Army. Speech of Hon. John Thompson, of New York. Delivered in the House of Representatives, January 27, 1858.* Washington, D.C: Buell & Blanchard, 1858.

Three Letters to the New York Herald, from J.M. Grant, of Utah [N.Y.C: n.p., 1852].

Tocqueville, Alexis De. *Democracy in America.* Henry Reeve text as revised by Francis Bowen. 2 vols. 1835, 1840; N.Y.C: Alfred A. Knopf, 1945.

Towers, John. *Polygamy Unscriptural: or Two Dialogues . . .* London: Alex Hogg and J. Trapp, 1781.

Townsend, George Alfred. *The Mormon Trials at Salt Lake City.* N.Y.C: American News Company, 1871.

Treasures of Pioneer History. Kate B. Carter, comp. 6 vols. S.L.C: Daughters of Utah Pioneers, 1952–57.

Troeltsch, Ernst. *The Social Teaching of the Christian Churches.* Olive Wyon, trans. 2 vols. London: George Allen & Unwin Ltd.; N.Y.C: The Macmillan Co., 1931.

Tucker, Pomeroy. *Origin, Rise and Progress of Mormonism. Biography of its Founders and History of its Church . . .* N.Y.C: D. Appleton and Co., 1867.

Tullidge, Edward W[heelock]. *Life of Brigham Young; or, Utah and Her Founders.* N.Y.C: Tullidge & Crandall, 1876.

———. *The History of Salt Lake City and Its Founders* . . . S.L.C: Edward W. Tullidge, [1886].

———. *The Women of Mormondom*. N.Y.C: [Tullidge and Crandall], 1877.

Twain, Mark [Samuel Langhorne Clemens]. *Roughing It.* Hartford, Conn: American Publishing Co., 1872. Republished with an intro. by Harriet Elinor Smith. Berkeley: Univ. of Calif. Press, 1993.

Tyler, Alice Felt. *Freedom's Ferment: Phases of American Social History from the Colonial Period to the Outbreak of the Civil War*. Minneapolis: Univ. of Minn. Press, 1944.

Underwood, Grant. *The Millenarian World of Early Mormonism*. Urbana: Univ. of Ill. Press, 1993.

Unruh, John D., Jr. *The Plains Across: The Overland Emigrants and the Trans-Mississippi West, 1840–1860*. Urbana, Chicago, and London: Univ. of Ill. Press, 1979.

Ure, James W. *Leaving the Fold: Candid Conversations with Inactive Mormons*. S.L.C: Signature Books, 1999.

Utah and its People. Facts and Statistics Bearing on the "Mormon Problem." By a Gentile. N.Y.C: R.O. Ferrier & Co., 1882.

Utah Bill, A Plea for Religious Liberty. Speech of Hon. W.H. Hooper, of Utah, Delivered in the House of Representatives, March 23, 1870, together with the Remonstrance of the Citizens of Salt Lake City, in Mass Meeting, held March 31, 1870, to the Senate of the United States. Wash., D.C: Gibson Bros., Printers, 1870.

Van Wagoner, Richard S. *Mormon Polygamy: A History*. S.L.C: Signature Books, 1989. 2nd edn. rev.

———. *Sidney Rigdon: A Portrait of Religious Excess*. S.L.C: Signature Books, 1994.

Vogel, Dan. *Early Mormon Documents*. 5 vols. S.L.C: Signature Books, 1996.

———. *Indian Origins and the Book of Mormon: Religious Solutions from Columbus to Joseph Smith*. S.L.C: Signature Books, 1986.

———. *Joseph Smith: The Making of a Prophet*. S.L.C: Signature Books, 2004.

Walker, Ronald W. *Wayward Saints: The Godbeites and Brigham Young*. Urbana and Chicago: Univ.of Ill. Press, 1998.

Walters, Ronald G. *American Reformers, 1815–1860*. N.Y.C: Hill & Wang, 1978.

Ward, Artemus [Charles Farrar Browne]. *The Complete Works of Artemus Ward* . . . N.Y.C: G.W. Dillingham Co., Publishers, 1898. Rev. edn.

Ward, Austin N. [pseud.]. *Male Life among the Mormons; or, the Husband in Utah* . . . Maria Ward, ed. Philadelphia: John E. Potter & Co., [1863].

Ward, Maria N. [pseud.]. *Female Life among the Mormons. A Narrative of Many Years Experience* . . . London: C.H. Clarke, [1855].

Ward, Maurine Carr, ed. *Winter Quarters: The 1846–1848 Life Writings of Mary Haskin Parker Richards*. Logan: Utah St. Univ. Press, 1996.

Warfield, Benjamin Breckinridge. *Perfectionism*. 2 vols. N.Y.C: Oxford Univ. Press, 1931.

Warren, Samuel M. *A Compendium of the Theological Writings of Emanuel Swedenborg*. N.Y.C: Swedenborg Foundation, Inc., 1974.

Webster, Noah. *American Dictionary of the English Language* . . . 2 vols. N.Y.C: S. Converse, 1828.

Wells, Merle W. *Anti-Mormonism in Idaho, 1872–92*. Vol. 4: *Studies in Mormon History*. James B. Allen, ed. Provo, Utah: BYU Press, 1978.

Werner, Morris Robert. *Brigham Young*. N.Y.C: Harcourt, Brace and Company, 1925.

West, Franklin L. *Life of Franklin D. Richards: President of the Council of the Twelve Apostles Church of Jesus Christ of Latter-Day Saints*. S.L.C: Deseret News Press, 1924.

Westermarck, Edward. *The History of Human Marriage.* 3 vols. N.Y.C: The Allerton Book Company, 1922. 5th rev. edn.

White, Jean Bickmore, ed. *Church, State, and Politics: The Diaries of John Henry Smith.* S.L.C: Signature Books in association with Smith Research Associates, 1990.

———. *Charter for Statehood: The Story of Utah's State Constitution.* S.L.C: Univ. of Utah Press, 1996.

Whiting, Lilian. *Kate Field: A Record.* Boston: Little, Brown and Co., 1899.

Whitley, Colleen, ed. *Worth their Salt: Notable but often Unnoted Women of Utah.* Logan: Utah St. Univ. Press, 1996.

Whitney, Helen Mar. *Plural Marriage as Taught by the Prophet Joseph. A Reply to Joseph Smith, Editor of the Lamoni (Iowa) "Herald."* S.L.C: Juvenile Instructor Office, 1882.

———. *Why We Practice Plural Marriage. By a "Mormon" Wife and Mother . . .* S.L.C: Juvenile Instructor Office, 1884.

Whitney, Orson Ferguson. *History of Utah . . .* 4 vols. S.L.C: G.Q. Cannon and Sons Co., 1892–1904.

———. *Through Memory's Halls: the Life Story of Orson F. Whitney as Told by Himself.* Independence, Mo: Zion's Printing and Publishing Co., 1930.

Widmer, Kurt. *Mormonism and the Nature of God: A Theological Evolution, 1830–1915.* Jefferson, N.C., and London: McFarland & Co., Inc., 2000.

Widtsoe, John A. *Evidences and Reconciliations.* 3 vols. S.L.C: Bookcraft, 1960.

Williams, Charles R. *Life of Rutherford Birchard Hayes: Nineteenth President of the United States.* 2 vols. Boston and N.Y.C: Houghton Mifflin Co., 1914.

Willis, Henry Parker. *Stephen A. Douglas.* Philadelphia: George W. Jacobs & Co., 1910.

Wright, Henry C. *Marriage and Parentage . . .* Boston: Bela Marsh, 1855. 2nd edn.

Württemberg, Paul Wilhelm, Duke of. *Travels in North America 1822–1824.* W. Robert Nitske, trans.; Savoie Lottinville, ed. 1835. Norman: Univ. of Okla. Press, 1973.

Wyl, W. [Wilhelm Ritter von Wymetal]. *Joseph Smith, The Prophet, his Family and his Friends; a Study Based on Facts and Documents with Fourteen Illustrations.* S.L.C: Tribune Printing and Publishing Co., 1886.

Yelverton, Thérèse (Viscountess Avonmore) [pseud.]. *Teresina in America,* 2 vols. London: Richard Bentley and Son, 1875.

Yorgason, Ethan R. *Transformation of the Mormon Culture Region.* Urbana and Chicago: Univ. of Ill. Press, 2003.

Young, Ann Eliza. *Wife No. 19, or the Story of A Life in Bondage, Being a Complete Exposé of Mormonism . . .* Chicago, Ill.; Cincinnati, Ohio: Dustin Gilman & Co., 1876.

Young, Kimball. *Isn't One Wife Enough?* N.Y.C: Henry Holt and Co., 1954.

Articles and Book Chapters

Alexander, Thomas G. "A Conflict of Perceptions: Ulysses S. Grant and the Mormons," *Ulysses S. Grant Assoc. Newsletter* 8:4 (July 1971).

———. "An Experiment in Progressive Legislation: The Granting of Woman Suffrage in Utah in 1870," *UHQ* 38:1 (Winter 1970).

———. "Charles S. Zane . . . Apostle of the New Era," *UHQ* 34:1 (Fall 1966).

————. "Federal Authority Versus Polygamic Theocracy: James B. McKean and the Mormons 1870–1875," *Dialogue* 1:3 (Autumn 1966).

————. "The Odyssey of a Latter-Day Prophet: Wilford Woodruff and the Manifesto of 1890," *JMH* 17 (1991).

————. "Wilford Woodruff and the Changing Nature of Mormon Religious Experience," *Church History* 45:1 (Mar. 1976).

Allen, James B. "The Unusual Jurisdiction of County Probate Courts in the Territory of Utah," *UHQ* 36:2 (Spring 1968).

————. "'Good Guys' vs. 'Good Guys': Rudger Clawson, John Sharp, and Civil Disobedience in Nineteenth-century Utah," *UHQ* 48:2 (Spring 1980).

Aman, Peter. "Prophet in Zion: The Saga of George J. Adams," *New England Qtly.* 37:4 (Mar.–Dec. 1964).

Anderson, Lavina Fielding. "Lucinda L. Dalton," in *Sister Saints.* Vicky Burgess-Olson, ed. [Provo, Utah: BYU Press, 1978].

Anderson, Nephi. "Rudger Clawson," in *Latter-Day Saint Biographical Encyclopedia. A Compilation of Biographical Sketches of Prominent Men and Women in the Church of Jesus Christ of Latter-day Saints; . . .* Andrew Jenson, ed. and comp. 4 vols. S.L.C: Andrew Jenson History Company, 1901–36.

Arrington, Leonard, and D. Michael Quinn. "The Latter-Day Saints in the Far West, 1847–1900," in *The Restoration Movement: Essays in Mormon History.* F. Mark McKiernan, Alma R. Blair, and Paul M. Edwards, eds. Lawrence, Kans: Coronado Press, 1973.

————, and Jon Haupt. "Intolerable Zion: The Image of Mormonism in Nineteenth Century American Literature," *Western Humanities Rev.* 22:3 (Summer 1969).

————, ed. "Crusade against Theocracy: the Reminiscences of Judge Jacob Smith Boreman of Utah, 1872–1877." *The Huntington Library Qtly.* 24:1 (Nov. 1960).

Bachman, Danel W. "New Light on an Old Hypothesis: The Ohio Origins of the Revelation on Eternal Marriage," *JMH* 5 (1978).

————. "Authorship of the Manuscript of Doctrine and Covenants Section 132," in *Sidney B. Sperry Symposium, January 26, 1980: A Sesquicentennial Look at Church History.* Provo, Utah: BYU Department of Religious Instruction and Church Educational System, 1980.

————, and Ronald K. Esplin. "Plural Marriage," in *Encyclopedia of Mormonism.* Daniel H. Ludlow, ed. 4 vols. N.Y.C: Macmillan Publishing Co., 1992.

Bair, JoAnn Woodruff, and Richard L. Jensen. "Prosecution of the Mormons in Arizona Territory in the 1880s," *Arizona and the West* 191 (Spring 1977).

Bartholow, Roberts. "Physiological Aspects of Mormonism, and the Climatology, and Diseases of Utah and New Mexico. A Discourse Delivered by Request before the Academy of Medicine, and Published by Order of that Body," *Cincinnati Lancet and Observer* 10:4 (April 1867).

Bashore, Melvin L., and Fred E. Woods. "Consigned to a Distant Prison: Idaho Mormons in the South Dakota Penitentiary," *South Dakota History* 27:1–2 (Spring/Summer 1997).

————. "Life behind Bars: Mormon Cohabs of the 1880s," *UHQ* 47:1 (Winter 1979).

Baum, Bruce. "Feminism, Liberalism and Cultural Pluralism: J. S. Mill on Mormon Polygyny," *Journal of Political Philosophy* 5:3 (1997).

Bean, L. L., and G. P. Mineau. "The Polygyny-Fertility Hypothesis: A Re-evaluation," *Population Studies* 40:1 (Mar. 1986).

Bedwell, Jessica. "Polygamy and the Assimilation of Scandinavian Immigrants in Richfield, Utah, 1880," *Genealogical Journal* 27: 3–4 (1999).

Beecher, Maureen Ursenbach. "Women in Winter Quarters," *Sunstone* 8:4 (July–Aug. 1983).

———, Carol Cornwall Madsen, and Lavina Fielding Anderson. "Widowhood among the Mormons: the Personal Accounts," in *On Their Own: Widows and Widowhood in the American Southwest 1848–1939*. Arlene Scadron, ed. Urbana and Chicago: Univ. of Ill. Press, 1988.

———, ed. "The Iowa Journal of Lorenzo Snow," *BYU St.* 24:3 (Summer 1984).

———. "Women's Work on the Mormon Frontier," *UHQ* 49:3 (Summer 1981).

Beeton, Beverly. "Woman Suffrage in Territorial Utah," *UHQ* 46:2 (Spring 1978).

Bennion, John. "Mary Bennion Powell: Polygamy and Silence," *JMH* 24:2 (Fall 1998).

Bennion, Lowell "Ben." "The Incidence of Mormon Polygamy in 1880: 'Dixie versus Davis Stake,'" *JMH* 11 (1984).

———. "Mormon Country a Century Ago: A Geographer's View," in *The Mormon People*. Thomas G. Alexander, ed. Provo, Utah: BYU Press, 1980.

Benoit, Pierre. "Révélation et Inspiration," *Études Bibliques* 70 (1963).

Bergera, Gary James. "The Church and Plural Marriage," *7th East Press* 2:2 (12 Oct. 1982).

———."Secretary to the Senator: Carl A. Badger and the Smoot Hearings," *Sunstone* 8:1–2 (Jan.–April 1983).

———. "'Illicit Intercourse,' Plural Marriage, and the Nauvoo Stake High Council, 1840–1844," *John Whitmer Hist. Assoc. Journal* 23 (2003).

———. "Earliest Eternal Sealings for Civilly Married Couples Living and Dead," *Dialogue* 35:3 (Fall 2003).

———. "Buckeye's Laments: Two Early Insider Exposés of Mormon Polygamy and Their Authorship," *Journal of the Ill. St. Hist. Soc.* 96:4 (Winter 2003).

———. "Identifying the Earliest Mormon Polygamists, 1841–44," *Dialogue* 38:3 (Fall 2005).

Bishop, M. Guy. "Eternal Marriage in Early Mormon Marital Beliefs," *Historian* 53:1 (Nov. 1990).

Bitton, Davis. "The B. H. Roberts Case of 1898–1900," *UHQ* 25:1 (Winter 1957).

———. "George Francis Train and Brigham Young," *BYU St.* 18:3 (Spring 1978).

———. "Mormon Polygamy: A Review Article," *JMH* 4 (1977).

Blair, Alma R. "RLDS Views of Polygamy: Some Historiographical Notes," *John Whitmer Hist. Assoc. Journal* 5 (1985).

Bliss, Charles R. "The Weak Point of Mormonism," *Century Magazine* 23:5 (Mar. 1882).

Booth, Wayne. "Rhetoric of Hypocrisy, Virtuous and Vicious," *Dialogue* 33:1 (Spring 2000).

[Bowles, Samuel]. "Interesting Sketch . . . The Mormons . . . ," *Portland [Maine] Transcript: An Independent Family Journal of Literature, Science, News, &c* 29:25 (16 Sept. 1865).

Bradley, Martha Sonntag. "Out of the Closet and into the Fire: The New Mormon Historians Take on Polygamy," in *Excavating Mormon Pasts: The New Historiography of the Last Half Century*. Newell G. Bringhurst and Lavina Fielding Anderson, eds. S.L.C: Greg Kofford Books, 2004.

———, and Mary Brown Firmage Woodward. "Plurality, Patriarchy, and the Priestess: Zina D. H. Young's Nauvoo Mariages," *JMH* 20:1 (Spring 1994).

Bradshaw, M. Scott. "Joseph Smith's Performance of Marriages in Ohio," *BYU St.* 39:4 (2000).

Brodie, Fawn M. "Polygamy Shocks the Mormons," *American Mercury* 62:268 (April 1946).

Brooks, Juanita. "A Close-Up of Polygamy," *Harper's* 168 (Feb. 1934).

———. "Cops and Co-Habs," *UHQ* 29:3 (Summer 1961).

———. "From the Journal of John Pulsipher," *Western Humanities Review* 2:4 (Oct. 1948).

———. "A Hint to Young Men in Search of Wives," *UHQ* 29:3 (July 1961).

———. "Indian Relations on the Mormon Frontier," *UHQ* 12:1–2 (Jan.–April 1944).

Brown, Barbara Barrett. "William Derby Johnson, Jr.," in *Stalwarts South of the Border*. Nelle Spilsbury Hatch and B. Carmon Hardy, eds. and comps. [Anaheim, Calif: n.p., 1985].

Brown, Roger Lee. "The Rise and Fall of the Fleet Marriages," in *Marriage and Society: Studies in the Social History of Marriage*. R. B. Outhwaite, ed. N.Y.C: St. Martin's Press, 1981.

Brudnoy, David. "A Decade in Zion: Theodore Schroeder's Initial Assault on the Mormons," *Historian* 37:2 (Feb. 1975).

———. "Of Sinners and Saints: Theodore Schroeder, Brigham Roberts, and Reed Smoot," *Journal of Church and State* 14:2 (Spring 1972).

"Buckeye's First Epistle to Jo," *Warsaw Signal*, 25 April 1844, New Series—1: 11, whole no. 128.

Buerger, David John. "'The Fulness of the Priesthood': The Second Anointing in Latter-day Saint Theology and Practice," *Dialogue* 16:1 (Spring 1983).

———. "The Adam-God Doctrine," *Dialogue* 15:1 (Spring 1982).

Bunker, Gary L., and Davis Bitton. "Illustrated Periodical Images of Mormons 1850–1860," *Dialogue* 10:3 (Spring 1977).

Burgoyne, Robert H., and Rodney W. Burgoyne. "Belief Systems and Unhappiness: The Mormon Woman Example," *Dialogue* 11:3 (Autumn 1978).

Bush, Lester E., Jr. "A Peculiar People: The Physiological Aspects of Mormonism 1850–1975," *Dialogue* 12:3 (Autumn 1979).

Bushman, Claudia. "Edward Tullidge and the Women of Mormonism," *Dialogue* 33:4 (Winter 2000).

Campbell, Bruce L., and Eugene E. Campbell. "The Mormon Family," in *Ethnic Families in America: Patterns and Variations*. Charles H. Mindel and Robert W. Habenstein, eds. N.Y.C., Oxford and Amsterdam: Elsevier, 1976.

Campbell, Eugene E., and Bruce L. Campbell. "Divorce among Mormon Polygamists: Extent and Explanations," *UHQ* 46:1 (Winter 1978).

Cannon, Charles A. "The Awesome Power of Sex: The Polemical Campaign against Mormon Polygamy," *Pacific Hist. Rev.* 43:1 (Feb. 1974).

Cannon, Connie Duncan. "Jane Snyder Richards: The Blue-White Diamond," in *Sister Saints*. Vicky Burgess-Olson, ed. [Provo, Utah: BYU Press, 1978].

Cannon, Donald Q., ed. "Leopold Bierwirth's Impressions of Brigham Young and the Mormons, 1872." *BYU St.* 40:2 (2001).

Cannon, George Q. "The Improvement of Our Species," *Western Standard* 2:22 (7 Aug. 1857).

Cannon, Kenneth L. II. "A Strange Encounter: The English Courts and Mormon Polygamy," *BYU St.* 22:1 (Winter 1982).

———. "'Rocky Mountain Common Law': The Extra legal Punishment of Seducers in Early Utah," *UHQ* 51:4 (Fall 1983).

———. "Beyond the Manifesto: Polygamous Cohabitation among LDS General Authorities after 1890," *UHQ* 46:1 (Winter 1978).

Cannon, M. Hamlin, ed. "The Prison Diary of a Mormon Apostle," *Pacific Hist. Rev.* 16:4 (Nov. 1947).

Casterline, Gail Farr. "Ellis R. Shipp," in *Sister Saints.* Vicky Burgess-Olson, ed. [Provo, Utah: BYU Press, 1978].

Chamie, J. "Polygyny among Arabs," *Population Studies* 40:1 (Mar. 1986).

Charles, Melodie Moench. "Precedents for Mormon Women from Scriptures," in *Sisters in Spirit: Mormon Women in Historical and Cultural Perspective.* Maureen Ursenbach Beecher and Lavina Fielding Anderson, eds. Urbana and Chicago: Univ. of Ill. Press, 1987.

Christiansen, John R. "Contemporary Mormons' Attitudes toward Polygynous Practices," *Journal of Marriage and the Family* 25:2 (May 1963).

Clark, E. Douglas. "Abraham," in *Encyclopedia of Mormonism.* Daniel H. Ludlow, ed. 4 vols. N.Y.C: Macmillan Publishing Co., 1992.

Clayton, William. "William Clayton's Testimony," in Andrew Jenson, ed. *Hist. Record* 6:3–5 (May 1887).

Clignet, Remi, and Joyce A. Sween. "For a Revisionist Theory of Human Polygyny," *Signs: Journal of Women in Culture and Society* 6:3 (Spring 1981).

Coates, Lawrence G. "Mormons and Social Change among the Shoshoni, 1853–1900," *Idaho Yesterdays* 15:4 (Winter 1972).

Cobb, James T. "Mrs. Stearns and Mormonism," *Tullidge's Qtly. Magazine* 1:3 (April 1881).

Cohen, Charles L. "No Man Knows My Psychology: Fawn Brodie, Joseph Smith, and Psychoanalysis," *BYU St.* 44:1 (2005).

Cohen, Shaye. "Menstruants and the Sacred in Judaism and Christianity," in *Women's History and Ancient History.* Sarah B. Pomeroy, ed. Chapel Hill and London: Univ. of N.C. Press, 1991.

"Comments on Temple Changes Elicit Church Discipline," *Sunstone* 14:3 (June 1990).

Compton, Todd. "Fanny Alger Smith Custer: Mormonism's First Plural Wife?" *JMH* 22:1 (Spring 1996).

————. "Fawn Brodie on Joseph Smith's Plural Wives and Polygamy: A Critical View," in *Reconsidering No Man Knows My History: Fawn Brodie and Joseph Smith in Retrospect.* Newell G. Bringhurst, ed. Logan, Utah: Utah State Univ. Press, 1996.

————. "A Trajectory of Plurality: An Overview of Joseph Smith's Thirty-three Plural Wives," *Dialogue* 29:2 (Summer 1996).

Comstock, Sarah. "The Mormon Woman: Polygamy as it Works Out in the Daily Routine of the Family," *Collier's* 44 (6 Nov. 1909).

Cook, Lyndon W. "William Law, Nauvoo Dissenter," *BYU St.* 22:1 (Winter 1982).

Cott, Nancy F. "Passionlessness: An Interpretation of Victorian Sexual Ideology, 1790–1850," in *A Heritage of Her Own: Toward a New Social History of American Women.* Nancy F. Cott and Elizabeth H. Pleck, eds. N.Y.C: Simon and Schuster, 1979.

Cowley, Luella Parkinson. "Parkinson Romance," in "Pioneer Courtships," *Daughters of Utah Pioneers Historical Pamphlet.* Kate B. Carter, comp. May 1940.

Coyner, John M. "Letters on Mormonism," in *Hand-book on Mormonism . . .* S.L.C., Chicago, and Cincinnati: Hand-book Publishing Co., 1882.

Cracroft, Richard H. "Distorting Polygamy for Fun and Profit: Artemus Ward and Mark Twain Among the Mormons," *BYU St.* 14:2 (Winter 1974).

————. "'Ten Wives Is All You Need': Artemus Twain and the Mormons—Again," *Western Humanities Rev.* 38:3 (Autumn 1984).

————. "Gentle Blasphemer: Mark Twain, Holy Scripture, and the Book of Mormon," *BYU St.* 11:2 (Winter 1971).

Davis, Ray Jay. "Polygamous Prelude," *American Journal of Legal History* 6:1 (Jan. 1962).

Day, Robert B. "Eli Azariah Day: Pioneer Schoolteacher and 'Prisoner for Conscience Sake,'" *UHQ* 35:4 (Fall 1967).

Daynes, Kathryn M. "Family Ties: Belief and Practice in Nauvoo," *John Whitmer Hist. Assoc. Journal* 8 (1988).

De Pillis, Mario. "The Quest for Religious Authority and the Rise of Mormonism," *Dialogue* 1 (Spring 1966).

DeVoto, Bernard. "The Centennial of Mormonism," *American Mercury* 19:73 (Jan. 1930).

Dix, Fae Decker. "Unwilling Martyr: The Death of Young Ed Dalton," *UHQ* 41:2 (Spring 1973).

Dorius, Guy L. "Marriage and Family: 'Ordained of God,'" in *The Doctrine and Covenants: A Book of Answers* . . . Leon R. Hartshorn, Dennis A. Wright, and Craig J. Ostler, eds. S.L.C: Deseret Book Co., 1996.

Driggs, Ken[neth David]. "'This Will Someday Be the Head and Not the Tail of the Church': A History of the Mormon Fundamentalists at Short Creek," *Journal of Church and State* 43:1 (Winter 2001).

————. "After the Manifesto: Modern Polygamy and Fundamentalist Mormons," *Journal of Church and State* 32:2 (Spring 1990).

————. "Imprisonment, Defiance, and Division: A History of Mormon Fundamentalism in the 1940s and 1950s," *Dialogue* 38:1 (Spring 2005).

————. "The Prosecutions Begin: Defining Cohabitation in 1885," *Dialogue* 21:1 (Spring 1988).

————. "Twentieth-Century Polygamy and Fundamentalist Mormons in Southern Utah," *Dialogue* 24:4 (Winter 1991).

Dunfey, Julie. "'Living the Principle' of Plural Marriage: Mormon Women, Utopia, and Female Sexuality in the Nineteenth Century," *Feminist Studies* 10:3 (Fall 1984).

Dushku, Judith Rasmussen and Patricia Rasmussen Eaton-Gadsby. "Augusta J. Crocheron," in *Sister Saints.* Vicky Burgess-Olson, ed. [Provo, Utah: BYU Press, 1978].

Dutton, C. E. "Church and State in Utah," *Forum* 5 (May 1888).

Eaton-Gadsby, Patricia Rasmussen and Judith Rasmussen Dushku, "Emmeline B. Wells," in *Sister Saints.* Vicky Burgess-Olson, ed. [Provo, Utah: BYU Press, 1978].

[Edmunds, George F.]. "Political Aspects of Mormonism," *Harper's* 64:380 (Jan. 1882).

Elisha, Omri. "Sustaining Charisma: Mormon Sectarian Culture and the Struggle for Plural Marriage, 1852–1890," *Nova Religio* 6:1 (2002).

Eliason, Eric A. "Curious Gentiles and Representational Authority in the City of the Saints," *Religion and American Culture: A Journal of Interpretation* 11:2 (Summer 2001).

Embry, Jessie L. "Ultimate Taboos: Incest and Mormon Polygamy," *JMH* 18:1 (Spring 1992).

Emmett, Andrea Moore. "Only for Eternity," *Salt Lake City Weekly*, 28 Jan. 1999.

Erickson, Dan. "Alberta Polygamists? The Canadian Climate and Response to Mormonism's 'Peculiar Institution,'" *Pacific Northwest Qtly.* 86:4 (Fall 1995).

"Erunt Tres Aut Quattuor In Carne Una: Aspekte der neuzeithen Polygamiediskusion," in *Zur Geschichte des Familien—und Erbrechts: Politische Implikationen und Perspektiven.* Frankfurt am Main: Vittorio Klosermann, 1987.

Farnsworth, Janet Webb. "Polygamist's Prison Diary," *Arizona Highways* 77:11 (Nov. 2001).

Forbes, Stephanie. "'Why Just Have One?' An Evaluation of the Anti-Polygamy Laws under the Establishment Clause," *Houston Law Rev.* 39:5 (Spring 2003).

Forshey, C. G., and Samuel A. Cartwright. "Hereditary Descent; or, Depravity of the Off-spring of Polygamy among the Mormons," *DeBow's Rev.* 30 (1861).

Foster, Lawrence. "A Little-known Defense of Polygamy from the Mormon Press in 1842," *Dialogue* 9:4 (Winter 1974).

———. "Polygamy and the Frontier: Mormon Women in Early Utah," *UHQ* 50:3 (Summer 1982).

———. "The Psychology of Religious Genius: Joseph Smith and the Origins of New Religious Movements," *Dialogue* 26:4 (Winter 1993).

Fryer, Judith. "American Eves in American Edens," *American Scholar* 44:1 (Winter 1974–75).

Gates, Susa Young. "Family Life Among the Mormons," *North American Rev.* 150: 400 (Mar. 1890).

Gayler, George R. "The Expositor Affair: Prelude to the Downfall of Joseph Smith," *Northwest Missouri State College Studies* 25:1 (Feb. 1961).

Gee, Elizabeth D. "Justice for All or for the 'Elect'? Utah County Probate Courts, 1855–1872," *UHQ* 48:2 (Spring 1980).

"Gentile Triumph in Salt Lake City," *Harper's* 34:1731 (22 Feb. 1890).

Godfrey, Kenneth W. "A New Look at the Alleged Little Known Discourse by Joseph Smith," *BYU St.* 9:1 (Autumn 1968).

———. "Charles W. Penrose and His Contributions to Utah Statehood," *UHQ* 64:4 (Fall 1996).

———. "The Coming of the Manifesto," *Dialogue* 5: 3 (Autumn 1970).

———. "Plural Marriage," in *Encyclopedia of Latter-day Saint History*, Arnold K. Garr, Donald Q. Cannon, and Richard O. Cowan, eds. S.L.C: Deseret Book Co., 2000.

Goodson, Stephanie Smith. "Plural Wives," in *Mormon Sisters: Women in Early Utah*. Claudia L. Bushman, ed. Cambridge, Mass: Emmeline Press, Limited, 1976.

Gordon, Sarah Barringer. "'Our National Hearthstone': Anti-Polygamy Fiction and the Sentimental Campaign Against Moral Diversity in Antebellum America," *Yale Journal of Law and the Humanities* 8:2 (Summer 1996).

———. "The Mormon Question: Polygamy and Constitutional Conflict in Nineteenth-Century America," *Journal of Supreme Court History* 28:1 (2003).

———. "A War of Words: Revelation and Story Telling in the Campaign against Mormon Polygamy," *Chicago-Kent Law Rev.* 78:2 (2003).

Groberg, Joseph H. "The Mormon Disfranchisements of 1882–1892," *BYU St.* 16:3 (Spring 1976).

Hafen, Thomas K. "City of Saints, City of Sinners: The Development of Salt Lake City as a Tourist Attraction 1869–1900," *Western Hist. Qtly.* 28:3 (Autumn 1997).

Hansen, Klaus. "Mormon Sexuality and American Culture," *Dialogue* 10:2 (Autumn 1976).

———. "Mormon History and the Conundrum of Culture: American and Beyond," in *Excavating Mormon Pasts: The New Historiography of the Last Half Century*. Newell G. Bringhurst and Lavina Fielding Anderson, eds. S.L.C: Greg Kofford Books, 2004.

Hardy, B. Carmon and Dan Erickson. "'Regeneration—Now and Evermore!': Mormon Polygamy and the Physical Rehabilitation of Humankind," *Journal of the History of Sexuality* 10:1 (Jan. 2001).

————. "Lords of Creation: Polygamy, the Abrahamic Household, and Mormon Patriarchy," *JMH* 20:1 (Spring 1994).

————. "'American Siberia': Mormon Prisoners in Detroit in the 1880s," *Michigan History* 50:3 (Sept. 1966).

————. "Early Mormon Polygamy in Mexico and Canada: A Legal and Historiographical Review," in *The Mormon Presence in Canada*. Brigham H. Card *et al.*, eds. Edmonton: Univ. of Alberta Press, 1990.

Hare, E. H. "Masturbatory Insanity: The History of an Idea," *The Journal of Mental Science* 108:452 (Jan. 1962).

Hart, Edward L. "John Hyde, Jr: An Earlier View," *BYU St.* 16:2 (Winter 1976).

Hatch, Cora May, and Sarah Olive Johnson. "Charles William Merrell," in *Stalwarts South of the Border*. Nelle Spilsbury Hatch and B. Carmon Hardy, eds. and comps. [Anaheim, Calif: n.p., 1985].

Haven, Charlotte. "A Girl's Letters from Nauvoo," *Overland Monthly*, new series, 16:96 (Dec. 1890).

Hendrick, Burton J. "The Mormon Revival of Polygamy," *McClure's Magazine* 36:4 (Feb. 1911).

Holbrook, Thelma, ed. "The Life of Joseph Holbrook, Written by His Own Hand," *An Enduring Legacy*. Vol. 1. S.L.C: Daughters of Utah Pioneers, 1978.

Holsinger, M. Paul. "For God and the American Home: The Attempt to Unseat Senator Reed Smoot, 1903–1907," *Pacific Northwest Qtly.* 60:3 (July 1969).

————. "Henry M. Teller and the Edmunds-Tucker Act," *Colorado Magazine* 48:1 (Jan. 1971).

————. "J. C. Burrows and the Fight against Mormonism: 1903–1907," *Michigan History* 52:3 (Fall 1968).

————. "Philander C. Knox and the Crusade against Mormonism, 1904–1907," *Western Pennsylvania Hist. Magazine* 52:1 (Jan. 1969).

Holzapfel, Richard Neitzel. "The Flight of the Doves from Utah Mormonism to California Morrisitism: The Saga of James and George Dove," in *Differing Visions: Dissenters in Mormon History*. Roger D. Launius and Linda Thatcher eds. Urbana and Chicago: Univ. of Ill. Press, 1994.

Homer, Michael W. "The Judiciary and the Common Law in Utah Territory, 1850–61," *Dialogue* 21:1 (Spring 1988).

Horowitz, Maryanne C. "Aristotle and Woman," *Journal of the History of Biology* 9:2 (Fall 1976).

Howard, Richard P. "The Nauvoo Heritage of the Reorganized Church," *JMH*, 16 (1990).

Hulett, James Edward, Jr. "The Social Role of The Mormon Polygamous Male," *American Sociological Rev.* 8:3 (June 1943).

————. "Social Role and Personal Security in Mormon Polygamy," *American Journal of Sociology* 45:4 (Jan. 1940).

Hulmston, John K. "Mormon Immigration in the 1860s: The Story of the Church Trains," *UHQ* 58:1 (Winter 1990).

"In Her Own Words: A Feminist [Vicky Burgess-Olson] Studies Mormon Polygamy and Remarkably Finds That It Liberated Their Wives," *People Weekly* 10:2 (10 July 1978).

Irving, Gordon. "The Law of Adoption: One Phase of the Development of the Mormon Concept of Salvation, 1830–1900," *BYU St.* 14:3 (Spring 1974).

Iversen, Joan Smyth. "A Debate on the American Home: The Antipolygamy Controversy, 1880–1890," *Journal of the History of Sexuality* 1:4 (April 1991).

————. "Feminist Implications of Mormon Polygamy," *Feminist Studies* 10:3 (Fall 1984).

Ivins, Stanley S. "Notes on Mormon Polygamy," *Western Humanities Rev.* 10:3 (Summer 1956).

James, Kimberly Jensen. "'Between Two Fires': Women on the 'Underground' of Mormon Polygamy," *JMH* 8 (1981).

Jennings, Warren A. "The First Mormon Mission to the Indians," *Kansas Hist. Qtly.* 37:3 (Autumn 1971).

Jenson, Andrew. "Henry Ballard," in *Latter-Day Saint Biographical Encyclopedia: A Compilation of Biographical Sketches of Prominent Men and Women in the Church of Jesus Christ of Latter-day Saints.* 4 vols. S.L.C: The Andrew Jenson History Company, 1901.

————. "Plural Marriage," *Hist. Record*, 6:3–5 (May 1887).

————. "The Twelve Apostles," *Hist. Record* 6:3–5 (May 1887).

Jessee, Dean C. "The Writings of Brigham Young," *Western Hist. Qtly.* 4:3 (July 1973).

Johnson, Benjamin Franklin. "Benjamin F. Johnson's Testimony," in Andrew Jenson, ed. *Hist. Record* 6:3–5 (May 1887).

Johnson, Jeffrey Ogden. "Determining and Defining 'Wife': The Brigham Young Households," *Dialogue* 20:3 (Fall 1987).

Jones, Arnita Ament. "Free Love and Communal Households: Robert Dale Owen and Fanny Wright on Women's Rights," *Indiana Academy of the Social Sciences Proceedings, 1974,* Third Series (Oct. 1974).

Jones, Sondra. "Saints or Sinners? The Evolving Perceptions of Mormon-Indian Relations in Utah Historiography," *UHQ* 72:1 (Winter 2004).

Jorgensen, Victor W. and B. Carmon Hardy. "'That Same Old Question of Polygamy and Polygamous Living': The Taylor-Cowley Affair and the Watershed of Mormon History," *UHQ* 48:1 (Winter 1980).

Juster, Susan. "The Spirit and the Flesh: Gender, Language, and Sexuality in American Protestantism," in *New Directions in American Religious History.* Harry S. Stout and D. G. Hart, eds. N.Y.C. and Oxford: Oxford Univ. Press, 1997.

Kincaid, John. "Extinguishing the Twin Relics of Barbaric Multiculturalism—Slavery and Polygamy—From American Federalism," *Publius: Journal of Federalism* 33:1 (Winter 2003).

Kingsbury, Joseph C. "Joseph C. Kingsbury's Testimony," in Andrew Jenson, ed. *Hist. Record* 6:3–5 (May 1887).

Kunz, Phillip R. "One Wife or Several? A Comparative Study of Late Nineteenth-Century Marriage in Utah," in *The Mormon People: Their Character and Traditions.* Thomas G. Alexander, ed. Charles Redd Monographs in Western History, No. 10. Provo, Utah: BYU Press, 1980.

————, and James E. Smith. "Polygyny and Fertility: Establishing a Focus," in *Selected Papers in Genealogical Research.* Phillip R. Kunz, ed. Provo, Utah: Institute of Genealogist Studies, 1973.

————, and Stan L. Albrecht. "Religion, Marital Happiness, and Divorce," *International Journal of Sociology of the Family* 7 (Dec. 1977).

Lamar, Howard R. "Statehood for Utah: A Different Path," *UHQ* 39:4 (Fall 1971).

Lambert, Neal. "Saints, Sinners and Scribes: A Look at the Mormons in Fiction," *UHQ* 36:1 (Winter 1968).

Larson, Gustive O. "The Mormon Reformation," *UHQ* 27:1 (Winter 1958).

————. "The Land Contest in Early Utah," *UHQ* 29:4 (Oct.1961).

————. "An Industrial Home for Polygamous Wives," *UHQ* 38:3 (Summer 1970).

LeBaron, E. Dale. "Benjamin Franklin Johnson in Nauvoo: Friend, Confidant, and Defender of the Prophet," *BYU St.* 32:1–2 (1992).

Linford, Orma. "Mormons and the Law: The Polygamy Cases," pt. 1. *Utah Law Rev.* 9:2 (Winter 1964).

————. "Mormons and the Law: The Polygamy Cases," pt. 2. *Utah Law Rev.* 9:3 (Summer 1965).

————. "Mormons, the Law, and the Territory of Utah," *American Journal of Legal History* 23:3 (July 1979).

Logue, Larry. "A Time of Marriage: Monogamy and Polygamy in a Utah Town," *JMH* 11 (1984).

————. "Tabernacles for Waiting Spirits: Monogamous and Polygamous Fertility in a Mormon Town," *Journal of Family History* 10:1 (Spring 1985).

[Ludlow, Fitz-Hugh]. "Among the Mormons," *Atlantic Monthly* 13:78 (April 1864).

Lyman, Edward Leo. "Isaac Trumbo and the Politics of Utah Statehood," *UHQ* 41:2 (Spring 1973).

————. "The Political Background of the Woodruff Manifesto," *Dialogue* 24:3 (Fall 1991).

Lynn, Karen. "Sensational Virtue: Nineteenth-Century Mormon Fiction and American Popular Taste," *Dialogue* 14:3 (Autumn 1981).

————. "Courtship and Romance in Utah Territory: Doing Away with 'The Gentile Custom of Sparkification,'" in *Sidney B. Sperry Symposium, January 26, 1980: A Sesquicentennial Look at Church History*. Provo, Utah: BYU Department of Religious Instruction and the Church Educational System, 1980.

Lyon, T. Edgar. "Religious Activities and Development in Utah, 1847–1910," *UHQ* 35:4 (Fall 1967).

MacKinnon, William P. "Epilogue to the Utah War: Impact and Legacy," *JMH* 29:2 (Fall 2003).

————. "'Like Splitting a Man Up His Backbone': The Territorial Dismemberment of Utah, 1850–1896," *UHQ* 71:2 (Spring 2003).

Madsen, Carol Cornwall. "'At Their Peril': Utah Law and the Case of Plural Wives, 1850–1900," *Western Hist. Qtly.* 21:4 (Nov. 1990).

————. "Emmeline B. Wells: 'Am I Not a Woman and a Sister?'" *BYU St.* 22:2 (Spring 1982).

"Mahomet of the West," *Overland Monthly* 7:3 (Sept. 1871).

Marquardt, H. Michael. "John Whitmer and the Revelations of Joseph Smith," *John Whitmer Hist. Assoc. Journal* 21 (2001).

May, Dean L. "Mormons," in *Harvard Encyclopedia of American Ethnic Groups.* Stephan Thernstrom, ed. Cambridge, Mass. and London, England: The Belknap Press of Harvard Univ. Press, 1980.

————. "A Demographic Portrait of the Mormons, 1830–1980," in *After 150 Years: The Latter-day Saints in Sesquicentennial Perspective*. Thomas G. Alexander and Jessie L. Embry, eds. Charles Redd Monographs in Western History, No. 13. Provo, Utah: Charles Redd Center for Western Studies, 1983.

————. "People on the Mormon Frontier: Kanab's Families of 1874," *Journal of Family History* 1 (1976).

————. "The Making of Saints: The Mormon Town as a Setting for the Study of Cultural Change," *UHQ* 45:1 (Winter 1977).

McCormick, John S. "An Anarchist Defends the Mormons: The Case of Dyer D. Lum," *UHQ* 44:2 (Spring 1976).

McKay, Douglas. "The Puissant Procreator: Contemporary Humorists Made Much of the Mormon Prophet's Nuberical Wifery," *Sunstone* 7:6 (Nov.–Dec. 1982).

Mineau, Geraldine P. "Utah Widowhood: A Demographic Profile," in *On Their Own: Widows and Widowhood in the American Southwest 1848–1939 Journal of Family History.* Arlene Scadron, ed. Urbana and Chicago: Univ. of Ill. Press, 1988.

Morin, Karen M. and Jeanne Kay Guelke. "Strategies of Representation, Relationship, and Resistance: British Women Travelers and Mormon Plural Wives, ca. 1870–1890," *Annals of the Assoc. of American Geographers* 88:3 (Sept. 1998).

"Mormons," *Harper's* 1:17 (25 April 1857).

"Mormons: The Church of the West," *Economist* 362: 8259 (9 Feb. 2002).

Muhsam, H. V. "Fertility of Polygamous Marriages," *Population Studies* 10:1 (July 1956).

Mulvay, Jill C. "Eliza R. Snow and The Woman Question," *BYU St.* 16:2 (Winter 1976).

Murdock, George Peter. "World Ethnographic Sample," *American Anthropologist* 59:4 (Aug. 1957).

Nash, John D. "Salmon River Mission of 1855," *Idaho Yesterdays* 11:1 (Spring 1967).

Neuman, Robert. "Priests of the Body and Masturbatory Insanity in the Late Nineteenth Century," *Psychohistory Rev.* 6:3 (Spring 1978).

"New Church Handbook Says Birth Control Is Okay," *Sunstone* 22:1 (Mar.–April 1999).

Newell, Linda King. "Emma Hale Smith and the Polygamy Question," *John Whitmer Hist. Assoc. Journal* 4 (1984).

Nichols, Jeffrey D. "Polygamy and Prostitution: Comparative Morality in Salt Lake City, 1847–1911," *JMH* 27:2 (Fall 2001).

Norman, Keith E. "How Long O Lord? The Delay of the Parousia in Mormonism," *Sunstone* 8:1–2 (Jan.–April 1983).

Oaks, Dallin H. "The Suppression of the Nauvoo Expositor," *Utah Law Rev.* 9:4 (Fall 1965).

Ostler, Blake T. "The Mormon Concept of God," *Dialogue* 17:2 (Summer 1984).

Pace, D. Gene. "Wives of Nineteenth-Century Mormon Bishops: A Quantitative Analysis," *Journal of the West* 21:2 (April 1982).

Perrot, Michelle. "Roles and Characters," in *From the Fires of Revolution to the Great War*, vol. 4: *A History of Private Life.* Philippe Ariès and Georges Duby, eds. 5 vols. Cambridge, Mass., and London: The Belknap Press of Harvard Univ. Press, 1990.

Peterson, Paul H. "The Mormon Reformation of 1856–1857: The Rhetoric and the Reality," *JMH* 15 (1989).

Poll, Richard D. "The Legislative Anti-Polygamy Campaign," *BYU St.* 26:4 (Fall 1986).

———. "The Mormon Question Enters National Politics, 1850–1856," *UHQ* 25:2 (Spring 1957).

Powell, Jay E. "Fairness in Salt Lake County Probate Courts," *UHQ* 38:3 (Summer 1970).

Potter, J. "The Growth of Population in America, 1700–1860," in *Population in History: Essays in Historical Demography.* D. V. Glass and D. E. C. Eversley, eds. London: Edward Arnold Publishers, Ltd., 1965.

Pratt, Steven. "Eleanor McLean and the Murder of Parley P. Pratt," *BYU St.* 15:2 (Winter 1975).

Proctor, Milissa. "Bodies, Babies, and Birth Control," *Dialogue* 36:3 (Fall 2003).

Quinn, D. Michael. "Latter-day Saint Prayer Circles," *BYU St.* 19:1 (Fall 1978).

————. "LDS Authority and New Plural Marriages, 1890–1904," *Dialogue* 18:1 (Spring 1985).

————. "Plural Marriage and Mormon Fundamentalism," *Dialogue* 31:2 (Summer 1998).

Rasmussen, Ellis T. "Abrahamic Covenant," in *Encyclopedia of Mormonism*. Daniel H. Ludlow, ed. 4 vols. N.Y.C: Macmillan Publishing Co., 1992.

Richards, Mary Stovall. "'And He Shall Rule Over Thee': Patriarchy in Two Nineteenth-Century American Subcultures," *Journal of Mississippi History* 63:4 (2001).

Rockwood, Jolene Edmunds. "The Redemption of Eve," in *Sisters in Spirit: Mormon Women in Historical and Cultural Perspective*. Maureen Ursenbach Beecher and Lavina Fielding Anderson, eds. Urbana and Chicago: Univ. of Ill. Press, 1987.

Rosenberg, Charles. "Bitter Fruit: Heredity, Disease, and Social Thought in Nineteenth-Century America," in *Perspectives in American History*. Donald Fleming and Bernard Bailyn, eds. Cambridge, Mass: Charles Warren Center for Studies in American History, 1974.

————. "Sexuality, Class and Role in 19th Century America," *American Qtly.* 25:2 (May 1973).

"Scenes in an American Harem," *Harper's* 1:41 (10 Oct. 1857).

Scott, Patricia Lyn. "Jennie Anderson Froiseth and the Blue Tea," *UHQ* 71:1 (Winter 2003).

————. "Sarah Ann Sutton Cooke: 'The Respected Mrs. Cooke,'" in *Worth Their Salt Too: More Notable but Often Unnoted Women of Utah*. Colleen Whitley, ed. Logan: Utah St. Univ. Press, 2000.

————. "The Widow and the Lion of the Lord: Sarah Ann Cooke vs. Brigham Young," *JMH* 30:1 (Spring 2004).

Sears, L. Rex. "Punishing the Saints for Their 'Peculiar Institution': Congress on the Constitutional Dilemmas," *Utah Law Rev.* 2001:3 (2001).

Sellers, Charles S. "Last Witness." *Improvement Era* 14:6 (April 1911), 544–47.

Sessions, Gene A. "Myth, Mormonism, and Murder in the South," *South Atlantic Qtly.* 75:2 (Spring 1976).

Sevey, Ketura F. B. "Alfred Baker," in *Stalwarts South of the Border*. Nelle Spilsbury Hatch and B. Carmon Hardy, eds. and comps. [Anaheim, Calif: n.p., 1985].

[Sharp, Thomas]. "Why Oppose The Mormons?" *Warsaw Signal and Agricultural, Literary and Commercial Register*, 25 April 1844, New Series, 1:11, whole no. 128.

Sherer, Mark A. "Answering Questions No Longer Asked: Nauvoo, Its Meaning and Interpretation in the RLDS Church/Community of Christ," *Sunstone* 123 (July 2002).

Shipps, Jan. "The Principle Revoked: A Closer Look at the Demise of Plural Marriage," *JMH* 11 (1984).

————. "The Prophet Puzzle: Suggestions Leading Toward a More Comprehensive Interpretation of Joseph Smith," *JMH* 1 (1974).

Singer, Merrill. "Nathaniel Baldwin, Utah Inventor and Patron of the Fundamentalist Movement," *UHQ* 47:1 (Winter 1979).

Smith, George D. "Nauvoo Roots of Mormon Polygamy, 1841–46: A Preliminary Demographic Report," *Dialogue* 27:1 (Spring 1994).

————. "Strange Bedfellows: Mormon Polygamy and Baptist History," *Free Inquiry* 16:2 (Spring 1996).

Smith, James E., and Phillip R. Kunz. "Polygyny and Fertility in Nineteenth-Century America," *Population Studies* 30:3 (Nov. 1976).

Smith-Rosenberg, Carroll, and Charles Rosenberg. "Female Animal: Medical and Biological Views of Woman and Her Role in Nineteenth-Century America," *Journal of American History* 60:2 (Sept. 1973).

Smoot, Reed. "Passing of Polygamy," *North American Rev.* 187:626 (Jan. 1908).

Snow, Edwina Jo. "William Chandless: British Overlander, Mormon Observer, Amazon Explorer," *UHQ* 54:2 (Spring 1986).

Snow, Eliza Roxcy. "Sketch of My Life," in *The Personal Writings of Eliza Roxcy Snow.* Maureen Ursenbach Beecher, ed. Logan, Utah: Utah St. Univ. Press, 2000.

Spencer, Geoffrey F. "Anxious Saints: The Early Mormons, Social Reform, and Status Anxiety," *John Whitmer Hist. Assoc. Journal* 1 (1981).

Spicer, Judith C., and Susan O. Gustavus. "Mormon Fertility through Half a Century: Another Test of the Americanization Hypothesis," *Social Biology* 21:1 (Spring 1974).

Stolberg, Michael. "Self-pollution, Moral Reform, and the Venereal Trade: Notes on the Sources and Historical Context of ONANIA (1716)," *Journal of the History of Sexuality* 9:1–2 (Jan.–Apr. 2000).

Tanner, John S. "Making a Mormon of Milton," *BYU St.* 24:2 (Spring 1984).

Taysom, Stephen C. "Uniform and Common Recollection: Joseph Smith's Legacy, Polygamy, and the Creation of Mormon Public Memory, 1852–2002," *Dialogue* 35:3 (Fall 2002).

Thorp, Malcolm R. "'Mormon Peril': The Crusade against the Saints in Britain, 1910–1914," *JMH* 2 (1975).

Trautmann, Frederic, ed and trans. "Salt Lake City through a German's Eyes: A Visit by Theodore Kirchhoff in 1867," *UHQ* 51:1 (Winter 1983).

Tullis, F. LaMond. "Early Mormon Exploration and Missionary Activities in Mexico," *BYU St.* 22:3 (Summer 1982).

Underwood, Grant. "Re-visioning Mormon History," *Pacific Hist. Rev.* 55:3 (Aug. 1986).

Van Biema, David. "Lost Gospels," *Time* 162:25 (22 Dec. 2002).

Van Orden, Bruce A., ed. "Writing to Zion: The William W. Phelps Letters (1835–1836)," *BYU St.* 33:3 (1993).

Van Wagenen, Lola. "In Their Own Behalf: the Politicization of Mormon Women and the 1870 Franchise," *Dialogue* 24:4 (Winter 1991).

Van Wagoner, Richard S. "Sarah M. Pratt: The Shaping of an Apostate," *Dialogue* 19:2 (Summer 1986).

———. "Mormon Polyandry in Nauvoo," *Dialogue* 18:3 (Fall 1985).

Vogel, Ursula. "Political Philosophers and the Trouble with Polygamy: Patriarchal Reasoning in Modern Natural Law," *History of Political Thought* 12:2 (Summer 1991).

Vousden, Peter J. "English Editor and the 'Mormon Scare' of 1911," *BYU St.* 41:1 (2002).

Wahlquist, Wayne L. "A Review of Mormon Settlement Literature," *UHQ* 45:1 (Winter 1977).

Walker, Ronald W. "'Seeking the Remnant': The Native American During the Joseph Smith Period," *JMH* 19:1 (Spring 1993).

Waters, Christine Croft. "Romania P. Penrose," in *Sister Saints.* Vicky Burgess-Olson, ed. [Provo, Utah: BYU Press, 1978].

Watson, Marianne T. "Short Creek: 'A Refuge for the Saints,'" *Dialogue* 36:1 (Spring 2003).

Welch, Richard E., Jr., "George Edmunds of Vermont: Republican Half-Breed," *Vermont History* 36:1 (Spring 1968).

Wells, Merle W. "Law in the Service of Politics: Anti-Mormonism in Idaho Territory," *Idaho Yesterdays* 25:1 (Spring 1981).

————. "The Idaho Anti-Mormon Test Oath, 1884–1892," *Pacific Hist. Rev.* 24:3 (Aug. 1955).

Welter, Barbara. "The Cult of True Womanhood, 1820–1860," in *The American Family: A Social-Historical Perspective.* Michael Gordon, ed. N.Y.C: St. Martin's Press, 1973.

White, Jean Bickmore. "Martha H. Cannon," in *Sister Saints.* Vicky Burgess-Olson, ed. [Provo, Utah: BYU Press, 1978].

————. "The Making of the Convention President: The Political Education of John Henry Smith," *UHQ* 39:4 (Fall 1971).

White, O. Kendall, Jr. "Ideology of the Family in Nineteenth-Century Mormonism," *Sociological Spectrum* 6:3 (Autumn 1986).

White, William Griffin, Jr. "Feminist Campaign for the Exclusion of Brigham Henry Roberts from the Fifty-Sixth Congress," *Journal of the West* 17:1 (Jan. 1978).

Whittaker, David J. "The Bone in the Throat: Orson Pratt and the Public Announcement of Plural Marriage," *Western Hist. Qtly* 18:3 (July 1987).

————. "Early Mormon Polygamy Defences," *JMH* 2 (1984).

————. "Mormons and Native Americans: A Historical and Bibliographical Introduction," *Dialogue* 18:4 (Winter 1985).

"William H. Hooper, the Utah Delegate and Female Suffrage Advocate," *Phrenological Journal and Life Illustrated* 51:5 (Nov. 1870).

Willis, John. "Mormon Fertility and the Americanization Hypothesis: Some Further Comments," *Social Biology* 22:3 (Fall 1975).

Wills, John A. "'Twin Relics of Barbarism,'" *Publications of the Hist. Soc. of Southern California* 1: pt.5 (1890).

Wingfield, Marshall. "Tennessee's Mormon Massacre," *Tennessee Hist. Qtly.* 17:1 (Mar. 1953).

Wolfinger, Henry J. "Reexamination of the Woodruff Manifesto in the Light of Utah Constitutional History," *UHQ* 39:4 (Fall 1971).

Wood, Gordon S. "Evangelical America and Early Mormonism," *New York History* 61:4 (Oct. 1980).

Woods, Fred, and Merle W. Wells. "Inmates of Honor: Mormon Cohabs in the Idaho Penitentiary, 1885–1890," *Idaho Yesterdays* 40:3 (Fall 1996).

Woolley, S[amuel] A[mos]. "Bishop S. A. Woolley's Testimony," in Andrew Jenson, ed., *Hist. Record* 6:3–5 (May 1887).

Wright, G. Frederick. "Mormon Muddle in Utah," *Nation* 51:1322 (30 Oct. 1890).

Wright, Lawrence. "Lives of the Saints: At a Time when Mormonism Is Booming, the Church Is Struggling with a Troubled Legacy," *New Yorker,* 21 Jan. 2002.

Young, Eugene. "Revival of the Mormon Problem," *North American Rev.* 168:509 (April 1899).

Young, Kimball. "Variations in Personality Manifestations in Mormon Polygynous Families," in *Studies in Personality Contributed in Honor of Lewis M. Terman.* N.Y.C. and London: McGraw-Hill Book Co., Inc., 1942.

"Z." "Review," *Cincinnati Literary Gazette* 3:25 (18 June 1825).

Zane, Charles S. "Death of Polygamy in Utah," *Forum* 12:1 (Sept. 1891).

"Zur Genese Theologisch-Juristischer Kontroversen (de polygamia)," in *Recht, Religion und Ehe: Orientierungswandel und gelehrte Kontroversen im Übergang vom 17. zum 18. Jahrhundert.* Stephan Bucholz, ed. Frankfurt am Main: Vittorio Klosterman, 1988.

INDEX

Abdülmecid I: 232

Abel (son of Adam and Eve): 217

Abolitionists: with Republicans opposed to Mormon pl. mar., 234–235

Abraham: 84, 117, 324; polygamous household of as model for the Saints, 61, 63–66, 100–102, 103–105, 137, 198, 200, 216–217, 248, 320–321, 326, 389; family of, 78, 82, 97, 122, 198, 258–259; doing polygamous works of, no longer stressed by modern church, 391

Adam (first man): 130–131, 200

Adams, Jerome: 175

Adultery: distinguished from pl. mar., 65; punishable by death, 83; grounds of complaint for prosecution of, 299

Agriculture and industry, Mormon: impressive appearance of, 206–208, 249–250, 251

Alger, Fanny: 42, 43, 44

Allen, "Nellie" Lowe: 153

Allen, Andrew Jackson: 244–245

Allen, Betsy Lowe: 153

Allen, Clarence: 153

Allen, Florence: 153

Allen, James Carson: 153

Allred, Alta Matilda Rolph: 173

Allred, Byron Harvey Sr: 172–173

Allred, Mary Eliza Tracy: 172–174

Allred, Phoebe Irene Cook: 173

American Woman Suffrage Association: 311

Amnesty: 357–359, 359–361

Anabaptists: 27

Angel with drawn sword: confronting Joseph Smith, 71–72

Animal sacrifice: 52–53

Anthony, Susan B: 311

Anti-polygamy crusade: 269; Mormon reaction to, 199, 290, 308, 322, 330, 333; successor to anti-slavery movement, 203, 272; arguments of, 204–208, 245–246, 287, 303–304; described Mormons as thoughtlessly submissive to their leaders, 215, 217; chronological phases of, 223; Mormon resistance to, 245, 246, 308, 315–319; alleged commencement of, 253; and judicial reform, 260–262; violent nature of in American South, 270; and Republican congressmen and presidents in 1880s, 279–283; historic nature of, 306; looked upon as an attack on essentials of Mormonism, 307–308; arguments now used by official church against fundamentalists, 388; unjustified, 390

Anti-Polygamy Society: 311–312

Anti-Polygamy Standard (newspaper): 312; founding of, 272. See also Woman's Exponent

Apaches: as polygamists, 185–186

Apostasy among Christians: loss of pl. mar. as one cause of, 86–88, 90, 105–106

Arizona: 174, 276, 335, 336, 349, 383, 387

Arthur, Chester A: 280, 281, 287, 302

Ashley, James M: 244

Asiatics, depraved: Mormon polygamy so described, 220–221, 231–233, 237, 270; reference to in Reynolds case, 266; Mormon culture described as, 278–279; revived reference to, 372; error of characterization of, 390

Assimilation: Mormon opposition to, with American marital practices, 309–310

Athearn, Robert: 186

Badger, Alexander: 206–207

Bailey, Charles Ramsden: 157–160

Bailey, Hannah Jones: 160

Bailey, Johannah Adamson: 159, 160

Bailey, Susannah Hawkins: 159, 160

Baldwin, Nathaniel: 381

Ballantyne, Richard: 81

Ballard, Emily Reid McNeil: 335

Ballard, Henry: 334–335

Ballard, Margaret Reid McNeil: 335

Bancroft, Hubert Howe: 91

Bancroft, Matilda Coley Griffing: 145, 146

Baptists: 38

Barlow, Alice Belva: 381

THE EDITOR

B. Carmon Hardy was born in Vernal, Utah, of Mormon pioneer stock. He spent most of his youth in the state of Washington, where he attended high school while working on farms and ranches. He graduated from Washington State University with a degree in history in 1957 and completed an M.A. degree in history at Brigham Young University in 1959, working with R. Kent Fielding and Hugh Nibley. At Wayne State University he studied with Alfred Kelly in American Constitutional History, Finley Hooper in Greece and Rome, and Norman Guice in Latin American History. He was awarded his Ph.D. in 1963.

From 1961 to 1966 Dr. Hardy served as an assistant professor at Brigham Young University, teaching the history and the philosophy of education. In the autumn of 1966 he commenced a long career (forty years thus far) at California State University, Fullerton. In addition to survey courses in American History and World Civilization, he taught American Constitutional History, American Intellectual History, and graduate courses in History and Theory. He has published studies of early Christianity and education, the Third and Fourth Amendments to the U.S. Constitution, and the history of Mormonism. He is best known for *Solemn Covenant: The Mormon Polygamous Passage*, in which he examined church-approved post-Manifesto polygamous marriages between 1890 and 1910. This work won the Mormon History Association's best book award in 1992. Though officially retired, he continues to teach and lecture and hopes to continue researching and writing for many years.

Dr. Hardy lives in Orange, California, with his wife, Kamillia M. Hardy. They share five children, seven grandchildren, and a growing number of great-grandchildren.

KINGDOM IN THE WEST SERIES

T he role of the Church of Jesus Christ of Latter-day Saints in the settlement of the American West has been a subject of controversy and fascination for 150 years. KINGDOM IN THE WEST: *The Mormons and the American Frontier*, a series from The Arthur H. Clark Company, explores the story of the Mormon people and their part in the wider history of the American West. Using primary source documents, most of them never before published, the projected set of twenty volumes examines the Mormons' religious vision and political ambitions, revealing how they saw themselves and how they appeared to others.

The series' first volume, *The Pioneer Camp of the Saints*, brought the Latter-day Saint people to the Great Basin via the Mormon Trail journals of Thomas Bullock. In *Forgotten Kingdom: The Mormon Theocracy in the American West, 1847–1896*, David L. Bigler provided a narrative overview of the Latter-day Saint movement in the American West. *Scoundrel's Tale: The Samuel Brannan Papers* told the audacious story of the most colorful Mormon in California's history. *Army of Israel: Mormon Battalion Narratives*, used source documents to tell the story of one of the West's most amazing adventures, the march of the Mormon Battalion. In Volume 5, *Defending Zion: George Q. Cannon and the California Mormon Newspaper Wars of 1856–1857*, Roger Robin Ekins collected writings from the *Western Standard* and the opposition press, painting a vivid picture of the debate over Mormonism that led to the Utah War. In *Fort Limhi*, David Bigler returned to tell the story of the Mormon adventure in Oregon Territory from 1855 to 1858 and its surprising impact on the resolution of the Utah War. With Ken Owens's *Gold Rush Saints*, the series returned to look at California Mormons during the great rush for riches. Carmon Hardy's volume, *Doing the Works of Abraham*, outlines the theory and practice of Mormon polygamy and its central role in the faith's political struggles of the late nineteenth century. Subsequent volumes will focus on the Utah War and the Mountain Meadows Massacre, Mormon-Indian relations, and dissenters in the Mormon West.

Series subscriptions are welcomed. Manuscript proposals of a documentary nature may also be submitted. Address inquiries to the publisher:

THE ARTHUR H. CLARK COMPANY
7800 Venture Drive
Norman, Okla. 73069-8218
(405) 325-5609